The Musician's Guide to Fundamentals

The Musician's Guide to Fundamentals

Jane Piper Clendinning
Florida State University College of Music

Elizabeth West Marvin
Eastman School of Music

Joel Phillips
Westminster Choir College of Rider University

W. W. NORTON & COMPANY · NEW YORK · LONDON

W. W. Norton & Company has been independent since its founding in 1923, when William Warder Norton and Margaret D. Herter Norton first published lectures delivered at the People's Institute, the adult education division of New York City's Cooper Union. The firm soon expanded its program beyond the Institute, publishing books by celebrated academics from America and abroad. By mid-century, the two major pillars of Norton's publishing program—trade books and college texts—were firmly established. In the 1950s, the Norton family transferred control of the company to its employees, and today—with a staff of 400 and a comparable number of trade, college, and professional titles published each year—W. W. Norton & Company stands as the largest and oldest publishing house owned wholly by its employees.

Editor: Maribeth Payne
Assistant editor: Ariella Foss
Emedia editor: Steve Hoge
Emedia editorial assistant: Nicole Sawa
Managing editor, College: Marian Johnson
Project editor: Justin Hoffman
Developmental editor: Susan Gaustad
Proofreaders: Barbara Necol, Debra Nichols
Senior production manager, College: Ben Reynolds
Design director: Rubina Yeh
Designer: Lisa Buckley
College permissions manager: Megan Jackson
Photo editor: Junenoire Mitchell
Composition by Jouve North America
Music engraving by Philip Thomas
Additional music engraving by David Botwinik
Manufacturing by Courier—Westford, MA

Library of Congress Cataloging-in-Publication Data

Clendinning, Jane Piper.
    The musician's guide to fundamentals / Jane Piper Clendinning, Elizabeth West Marvin, Joel Phillips.—1st ed.
       p. cm.
    Includes index.
    ISBN 978-0-393-92874-7 (pbk.)
    1. Music theory.   I. Marvin, Elizabeth West, 1955–   II. Phillips, Joel, 1958–   III. Title.
    MT6.C5677 2012
    781—dc23
                          2011035210

W. W. Norton & Company, Inc., 500 Fifth Avenue, New York, NY 10110
wwnorton.com

W. W. Norton & Company Ltd., Castle House, 75/76 Wells Street, London W1T 3QT

2 3 4 5 6 7 8 9 0

To our teachers, colleagues, and students—
with whom we have shared the joy of music, and from
whom we continue to learn—and, with thanks,
to our families for their patience and support

Brief Contents

CHAPTER 1 Pitch Notation and the Grand Staff   1

CHAPTER 2 Accidentals and Half and Whole Steps   25

CHAPTER 3 Simple Meters   45

CHAPTER 4 Beat Subdivisions and Syncopation   69

CHAPTER 5 Compound and Other Meters   91

CHAPTER 6 Major Scales and Keys   119

CHAPTER 7 Minor Scales and Keys   147

CHAPTER 8 Intervals   177

CHAPTER 9 Triads and the Dominant Seventh Chord   213

CHAPTER 10 Melody Harmonization and Cadences   245

CHAPTER 11 Form in Folk and Popular Songs   277

CHAPTER 12 Blues and Other Popular Styles   303

Anthology   333

Appendix 1   Try It Answers   A-1

Appendix 2   Reading Review Answers   A-15

Appendix 3   Glossary   A-17

Appendix 4   The Overtone Series   A-25

Appendix 5   The Diatonic Modes   A-27

Appendix 6   The C-Clefs   A-31

Appendix 7   Basic Guitar Chords   A-33

Appendix 8   Piano Fingerings for Selected Scales   A-37

Appendix 9   Connecting Chords   A-41

CHAPTER 7 Minor Scales and Keys 147

Parallel Keys 147

Natural Minor 148

Harmonic Minor 149

Melodic Minor 151

Comparing Scale Types 153

Relative Keys 154

Minor Key Signatures and the Circle of Fifths 156

Identifying the Key from a Score 158

Did You Know? 159 ▪ Terms You Should Know 159
▪ Questions for Review 159 ▪ Reading Review 160 ▪
Class Activities 161 ▪ Workbook 167 ▪ Aural Skills 173

CHAPTER 8 Intervals 177

Intervals 177

Interval Quality 179

Inverting Intervals 181

Spelling Intervals 182

Augmented and Diminished Intervals 188

Compound Intervals 191

Consonance and Dissonance 192

Did You Know? 193 ▪ Terms You Should Know 193
▪ Questions for Review 193 ▪ Reading Review 194 ▪
Class Activities 195 ▪ Workbook 201 ▪ Aural Skills 209

CHAPTER 9 Triads and the Dominant
Seventh Chord 213

Triads 213

Triad Inversion 214

Triad Qualities in Major Keys 215

Triad Qualities in Minor Keys 216

Spelling Triads 218

The Dominant Seventh Chord 222

Seventh Chord Inversion 223

Spelling the Dominant Seventh Chord 224

Did You Know? 225 ▪ Terms You Should Know 225
▪ Questions for Review 225 ▪ Reading Review 226 ▪
Class Activities 227 ▪ Workbook 233 ▪ Aural Skills 241

CHAPTER 10 Melody Harmonization
and Cadences 245

Triads on $\hat{1}$, $\hat{4}$, and $\hat{5}$
and the Seventh Chord on $\hat{5}$ 245

Harmonizing Major Melodies with
the Basic Phrase Model 249

Cadence Types 250

The Subdominant in the Basic Phrase 253

Melodic Embellishments 255

Harmonizing Minor-Key Melodies 256

Did You Know? 258 ▪ Terms You Should Know 258
▪ Questions for Review 259 ▪ Reading Review 259 ▪
Class Activities 260 ▪ Workbook 265 ▪ Aural Skills 273

CHAPTER 11 Form in Folk
and Popular Songs 277

Melody and Paired Phrases 277

Quaternary Song Form 278

32-Bar Song Form 279

Writing Melodies 281

Writing Keyboard Accompaniments 284

Form in Later Popular Music 288

Did You Know? 290 ▪ Terms You Should Know 290
▪ Questions for Review 290 ▪ Reading Review 291 ▪
Class Activities 292 ▪ Workbook 295 ▪ Aural Skills 301

CHAPTER 12 Blues and Other
Popular Styles 303

Pentatonic Scales 303

The Blues Scale and the 12-Bar Blues 306

Seventh Chords 309

Chord Extensions and Sus Chords 312

Did You Know? 314 ▪ Terms You Should Know 314
▪ Questions for Review 314 ▪ Reading Review 315 ▪
Class Activities 316 ▪ Workbook 323 ▪ Aural Skills 331

Anthology   333

Johann Sebastian Bach, Invention in D Minor   334

Béla Bartók, "Bulgarian Rhythm" (No. 115), from *Mikrokosmos*   336

Count Basie and Neil Hefti, "Splanky"   338

Ludwig van Beethoven, Piano Sonata in C Minor, Op. 13 (*Pathétique*), second movement, excerpt   339

John Barnes Chance, *Variations on a Korean Folk Song*, excerpt   341

Jeremiah Clarke, *Trumpet Voluntary (Prince of Denmark's March)*, excerpt   345

Stephen Foster, "Oh! Susanna"   350

George and Ira Gershwin, "'S Wonderful!" from *Funny Face*   351

Patrick S. Gilmore, "When Johnny Comes Marching Home"   356

"Greensleeves"   357

Don Henley, Glenn Frey, and Randy Meisner, "Take It to the Limit"   358

"Home on the Range"   363

James Horner, Barry Mann, and Cynthia Weil, "Somewhere Out There," from *An American Tail*   364

Scott Joplin, "Solace"   368

Jonathan Larson, "Seasons of Love," from *Rent*, excerpt   372

Wolfgang Amadeus Mozart, String Quartet in D Minor, K. 421, third movement   377

Mozart, *Variations on "Ah, vous dirai-je Maman,"* excerpts   379

"My Country, 'Tis of Thee" (America)   381

John Newton, "Amazing Grace"   382

Joel Phillips, "Blues for Norton"   383

William "Smokey" Robinson, Jr., "You've Really Got a Hold on Me"   387

Richard Rogers and Lorenz Hart, "My Funny Valentine," from *Babes in Arms*   392

Franz Schubert, Waltz in B Minor, Op. 18, No. 6   396

"Simple Gifts"   397

Meredith Willson, "Till There Was You," from *The Music Man*   398

Appendix 1   Try It Answers   A-1

Appendix 2   Reading Review Answers   A-15

Appendix 3   Glossary   A-17

Appendix 4   The Overtone Series   A-25

Appendix 5   The Diatonic Modes   A-27

Appendix 6   The C-Clefs   A-31

Appendix 7   Basic Guitar Chords   A-33

Appendix 8   Piano Fingerings for Selected Scales   A-37

Appendix 9   Connecting Chords   A-41

Music Credits   A-43

Photo Credits   A-45

Index of Musical Examples   A-47

Index of Terms and Concepts   A-51

- **Try It** exercises are scattered throughout chapters to provide opportunities to practice new concepts. They give you immediate feedback on your understanding and prepare you for the assignments at the end of the chapter. When you see one of these exercises, try it, then check your answer in Appendix 1. Only then will you know that you understand the concept and can apply it in your music-making.

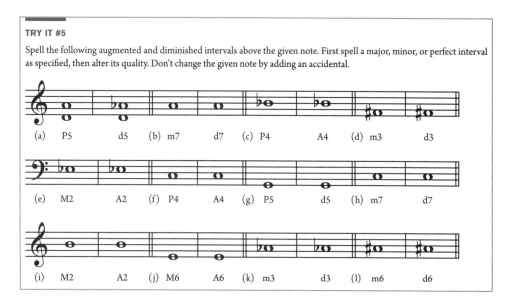

TRY IT #5

Spell the following augmented and diminished intervals above the given note. First spell a major, minor, or perfect interval as specified, then alter its quality. Don't change the given note by adding an accidental.

(a) P5   d5   (b) m7   d7   (c) P4   A4   (d) m3   d3

(e) M2   A2   (f) P4   A4   (g) P5   d5   (h) m7   d7

(i) M2   A2   (j) M6   A6   (k) m3   d3   (l) m6   d6

- Since many concepts can be learned in more than one way, **Another Way** boxes offer alternative explanations. Use the method that works best for you.

ANOTHER WAY You can identify triads apart from their scale context by considering their intervals. Triads with each quality built above F are shown below for comparison.

P5 [ ]m3]M3   P5 [ ]M3]m3   d5 [ ]m3]m3

F major   F minor   F diminished

- Every chapter ends with a list of **Terms You Should Know**, **Questions for Review**, and a **Reading Review**. The **Questions for Review** are open-ended questions about chapter content; formulate answers to them in your own words. **Reading Reviews** are short matching quizzes; answers are provided in Appendix 2. These tools will help you test your mastery of the material covered before you move on to the next chapter.
- A **Did You Know?** box also appears at the end of each chapter to explain historical background for featured composers and pieces.

Did You Know?

Stephen Foster (1826–1864) is considered the first great American songwriter. His melodies, many written as parlor ballads or for minstrel shows, are so much a part of American culture that we often think of them as traditional folk songs rather than published, attributed compositions. "Oh! Susanna" was premiered in Andrews's Eagle Ice Cream Saloon in Pittsburgh on September 11, 1847. This song, with its nonsensical lyrics, became the unofficial theme song of the California gold rush, which began in January of the following year.

End-of-chapter activities and assignments invite you to practice what you've learned:

- **Class Activities** emphasize the skills you need to understand and recall musical patterns. Activities include singing and rhythm reading, keyboard practice, listening and writing activities, and more.
- Three or four double-sided, tear-out-and-turn-in **Workbook Assignments** give you the opportunity to master the concepts presented in each chapter. These assignments, which include abundant drill and practice, reinforce concepts in the order that they appear; headings within the chapter indicate when you are ready to complete each assignment.
- One or two **Aural Skills Assignments** round out each chapter. These assignments often guide you through the process of notating music on the recordings disc.

In the back of the book, along with the answers to Try It and Reading Review exercises, you will find the **Glossary** and several **Appendixes** that provide additional information on topics such as guitar chords, the overtone series, the diatonic modes, and C-clefs. In addition, there are two **Indexes**: one for composers and pieces studied and another for terms and concepts.

Using the Anthology

As part of this text, we have included a short **Anthology** with musical scores for 25 pieces. Our spiral-learning approach revisits the anthology's core repertoire from chapter to chapter as you learn new concepts—a single piece might illustrate pitch identification, meter, scales, and triads. By the second or third time you "visit" a particular work, it will seem like an old friend. We hope that you will listen to the music until you know each work well enough to hear it in your head, the same way you can hear familiar songs from the radio, TV, or movies just by thinking about them.

We have chosen music for study that we like and that our students have enjoyed. Some of the works should be familiar to you, and other pieces may be new. The anthology includes pieces for varied performing ensembles in contrasting musical styles—from American popular songs to classical sonatas, from a piano rag to a piano waltz, from a guitar solo to a choral hymn. Complete recordings of nearly all the anthology pieces are available on the recordings disc that accompanies this text. Links to purchase and download additional recordings are available on StudySpace.

Electronic Resources

The *Musician's Guide to Fundamentals* is accompanied by a student website—StudySpace (wwnorton.com/studyspace) that includes selected recordings from the text, links to purchase additional recordings, chapter-by-chapter flash cards of new terms, quizzes, an interactive virtual keyboard and guitar, and the Norton MusicMixer, which allows you to experiment with a variety of rhythms and chord progressions.

To the Instructor

The *Musician's Guide to Fundamentals* is a comprehensive teaching and learning package for undergraduate music fundamentals classes that integrates technological resources with a textbook and audio recordings. In addition, we have designed the package with numerous support mechanisms to help you efficiently prepare for class.

- The **Answer Key** includes answers to all exercises in the same format and pagination as the text and instructions and resources for class activities.

- The **Instructor's Manual** by Peter Martens (Texas Tech University), available for download from the Norton Resource Library, offers a wealth of materials, including chapter overviews, teaching strategies, class activities, supplemental repertoire, additional exercises, and test questions.
- **Coursepacks**, including chapter-based quizzes, are available for all widely used course-management systems.
- You will no longer need to plan for a trip to the library before class to find a recording of the work you will be studying; this package includes **recordings** of nearly all the core repertoire, as well as all dictation exercises, in high-quality professional performances. In addition, "bonus tracks" (Bach, Newton, and Joplin) demonstrate alternative performances.

We hope that all users of this textbook—student and teacher alike—will get to know the repertoire, find the class activities and aural assignments challenging and enjoyable, and emerge from this class with some new skills that will contribute to their lifelong engagement with music listening and performance.

Our Thanks to . . .

A work of this size and scope is helped along the way by many people. We are especially grateful for the support of our families. Our work together as coauthors has been incredibly rewarding, and we are thankful for that collaboration and friendship. While working on the project, we received encouragement and useful ideas from music fundamentals teachers across the country. We thank these teachers for their willingness to share their years of experience with us.

For subvention of the recordings that accompany the text, and for his continued support of strong music theory pedagogy, we thank Douglas Lowry (Dean of the Eastman School of Music). For performance of many of the short examples in the text, we thank Richard Masters, whose sight-reading abilities, flexibility, and good grace are all appreciated. We also thank Don Gibson (Dean of Florida State University's College of Music) for his enthusiasm and unfailing support. For pedagogical discussions over the years, we are grateful to our colleagues at Florida State University, the Eastman School of Music, Westminster Choir College, and to the College Board's AP Music Theory Test Development Committee members and AP readers. Special thanks to Peter Martens for his thorough and meticulous checking of workbook exercises and for his work on the Instructor's Manual. Thanks also to Elizabeth A. Clendinning for writing the StudySpace quizzes.

We are indebted to the thorough and detailed work of our prepublication reviewers, whose careful reading of the manuscript inspired many improvements large and small: Lyn Ellen Burkett (University of North Carolina at Asheville), Robert Carl (Hartt School, University of Hartford), Don Fader (University of Alabama), Taylor Greer (Pennsylvania State University), Judy Cervetto Hedberg (Portland Community College), Rebecca Jemian (Ithaca College), Joan F. Jensen (Tulane University), Laura L. Kelly (The University of Texas at San Antonio), Laila R. Kteily-O'Sullivan (University of North Texas), Linda Apple Monson (George Mason University), Kathy Murray (Missouri State University), Shaugn O'Donnell (The City College of New York), Malia Roberson (California Lutheran University), Peter J. Schoenbach (Curtis Institute of Music), Paul Sheehan (Nassau Community College), Jason Roland Smith (Ohio University School of Music), Jennifer Snodgrass (Appalachian State University), and Stephen Zolper (Towson University). We also acknowledge that the foundation of this book rests on writings of the great music theorists of the past and present, from the sixteenth to the twenty-first century, from whom we have learned the "tools of the trade" and whose pedagogical works have inspired ours.

For the production of the recordings, our thanks go to recording engineers Mike Farrington and John Ebert, who worked tirelessly with Elizabeth Marvin at Eastman on recording and editing sessions, as well as to Helen Smith, who oversees Eastman's Office of Technology and Media

Production. We also acknowledge the strong contributions of David Peter Coppen, archivist of the Eastman Audio Archive at the Sibley Music Library, for his work researching archived performances and contacting faculty and alumni for permission to include their performances among our recordings. We finally thank the faculty and students of the Eastman School who gave so generously of their time to make these recordings. The joy of their music-making contributed mightily to this project.

We are indebted to the W. W. Norton staff for their commitment to *The Musician's Guide to Fundamentals* and their painstaking care in producing this volume. Most notable among these are Susan Gaustad, whose knowledge of music and detailed, thoughtful questions made her a joy to work with, and music editor Maribeth Payne, whose vision has helped launch this book with great enthusiasm. We are grateful for Norton's forward-thinking technology editor Steve Hoge, who helped refine our ideas for the book's website and made them a reality. Justin Hoffman project edited the text, seeing the book through to completion and keeping track of many details; he oversaw coordination of the text with recordings and capably edited the Instructor's Manual. Lisa Buckley created the design, Barbara Necol and Debra Nichols provided expert proofreading, Megan Jackson pursued copyright permissions, Nicole Albas developed marketing strategies, Kate Maroney handled final editing of the recordings with a great eye and ear for detail, and Ben Reynolds oversaw the production of this text through to completion. Our gratitude to one and all.

Jane Piper Clendinning

Elizabeth West Marvin

Joel Phillips

The Musician's Guide
to Fundamentals

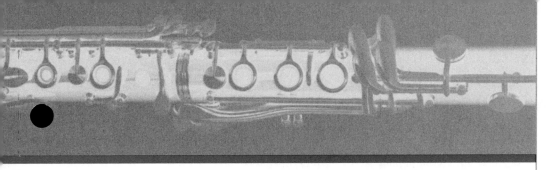

TOPICS

- musical contour
- introduction to pitch notation: letter names
- the piano keyboard: naming white keys
- staff notation
- treble and bass clefs
- naming pitches with octave numbers
- ledger lines
- the grand staff
- writing music in a score

MUSIC

- John Barnes Chance, *Variations on a Korean Folk Song*
- Aaron Copland, "Simple Gifts," from *Appalachian Spring*
- James Horner, Barry Mann, and Cynthia Weil, "Somewhere Out There," from *An American Tail*
- Elton John and Tim Rice, "Circle of Life," from *The Lion King*
- Scott Joplin, "Solace"
- Joel Phillips, "Blues for Norton"
- Lalo Schifrin, theme from *Mission: Impossible*

CHAPTER 1

Pitch Notation and the Grand Staff

Musical Contour

Listen to the lyrical clarinet solo drawn from Copland's ballet *Appalachian Spring*, shown in music notation in Example 1.1. Follow the shape of the musical line as you listen.

EXAMPLE 1.1   Copland, "Simple Gifts," from *Appalachian Spring*, mm. 1–3a 🔊

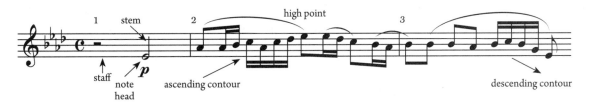

© Copyright 1950 by The Aaron Copland Fund for Music. Copyright renewed. Boosey & Hawkes Inc., sole licensee. Reprinted by permission of Boosey & Hawkes Inc.

The musical notation above—the **score**—shows various symbols that represent musical sounds. The most basic symbol is the **note**. Each note, written as a small oval (either black or hollow) attached to a **stem** going either up or down, represents a single musical sound, or **pitch**. Notes are written higher or lower on the five horizontal lines of a musical **staff**; this shows graphically the "shape," or **contour**, of a melody. Pitches 1 to 5 of "Simple Gifts" represent an **ascending contour**, and the notation on the staff likewise moves upward from left to right, each note higher than the previous one. The final four pitches move downward in a **descending contour**. Most music—like Copland's melody—moves both up and down, with melodic contours forming arches and waves, often with a single high point, as marked in the middle of this tune.

Introduction to Pitch Notation: Letter Names

Drawing a melody's contour may give a general idea of its shape, but you need more precise information to play the tune correctly.

> **KEY CONCEPT** In a musical score, each note has a **letter name**—A, B, C, D, E, F, or G—which is determined by its position on the staff.

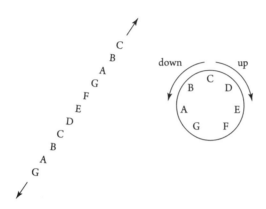

To count up beyond G, start over with A; to count down below A, start over again with G. You can also think of the seven letter names around a circle, like a clock. Think of the movement as upward when you count forward or clockwise, and downward when you count backward or counterclockwise. For example, five notes above E is B: E–F–G–A–B. Six notes below E is G: E–D–C–B–A–G. When counting, be sure to include the first and last letter names of the series: three above F is A (count F–G–A, not G–A–B).

In this seven-name system, each letter name reappears every eighth position (eight above or below D is another D).

> **KEY CONCEPT** Pitches separated by eight letter names are an **octave** apart. ("Oct-" means "eight," as in "octopus.") The repetition of letter names reflects the way we hear: pitches an octave apart sound similar. This principle is called **octave equivalence**.

TRY IT #1

Find the letter name requested.

(a) 7 above D: <u> C </u>   (f) 5 above F: _____   (k) 2 above G: _____

(b) 5 above A: _____   (g) 3 above C: _____   (l) 4 above B: _____

(c) 3 below B: _____   (h) 8 below D: _____   (m) 6 below D: _____

(d) 6 below C: _____   (i) 4 below E: _____   (n) 5 below F: _____

(e) 2 below E: _____   (j) 6 above G: _____   (o) 7 above E: _____

The Piano Keyboard: Naming White Keys

Look at the diagram in Figure 1.1 to identify pitch locations on the keyboard. (Or use the model keyboard in your text, or on the book's website.) The white key immediately to the left of any group of two black keys is a C, and the white key immediately to the left of any three black keys is an F; each is indicated by an arrow. Write in the remaining letter names for the white keys in the figure, using the black-key groupings to find your place.

> **KEY CONCEPT** **Middle C** is the C closest to the middle of the keyboard. No black key appears between E and F or between B and C.

FIGURE 1.1   Piano keyboard

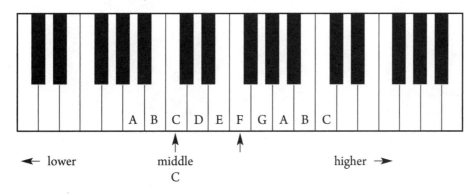

Staff Notation

As shown in Example 1.1, the staff (plural is staves) consists of five lines and four spaces, which are generally read from bottom to top, with the bottom line called the first and the top line the fifth (see Example 1.2). As a first step in writing pitches, ovals called notes or **note heads** are drawn on the lines or in the spaces of the staff (most notes will also require stems, as we'll see later). Black note heads are played for a shorter duration than hollow ones. Higher pitches are notated toward the top of the staff, lower pitches toward the bottom, as marked.

EXAMPLE 1.2   Note heads on a staff

Treble and Bass Clefs

The letter names of the notes in Example 1.2 can't be identified without a **clef**, the symbol that appears on the far left of every staff. The clef shows which line or space represents which pitch (and in which octave). In Example 1.3, notes are written on the **treble clef**, sometimes called the G-clef. Its shape somewhat resembles a cursive capital G, and the end of its curving line (in the center) rests on the staff line for G. All the other pitches can be read from G by counting up or down in the **musical alphabet**. The note above the highest staff line (F) is G. The note below the lowest staff line (E) is D, and the note below that, with the little line through it, is middle C. The treble clef represents the higher notes on a keyboard.

As soon as possible, memorize the note names for each line and space. Learn the "line notes" together and the "space notes" together, as in Example 1.4. To remember note names of the lines (E G B D F), you might make up a sentence whose words begin with these letters, like "Every Good Bird Does Fly." The spaces simply spell the word F A C E.

EXAMPLE 1.3   Treble clef (G-clef)

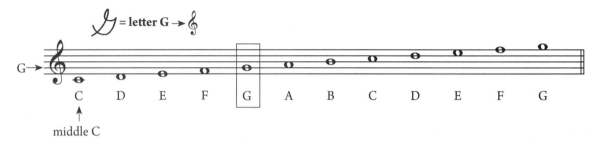

middle C

EXAMPLE 1.4   Treble-clef lines and spaces

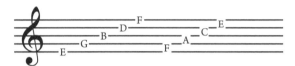

TRY IT #2

(a) Write the letter name of each pitch in the blanks below.

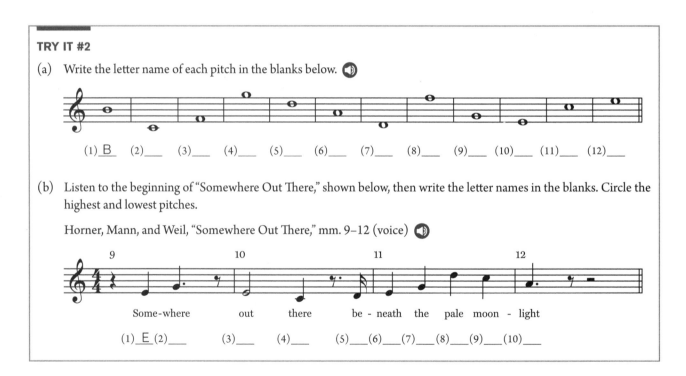

(1) B   (2)___   (3)___   (4)___   (5)___   (6)___   (7)___   (8)___   (9)___   (10)___   (11)___   (12)___

(b) Listen to the beginning of "Somewhere Out There," shown below, then write the letter names in the blanks. Circle the highest and lowest pitches.

Horner, Mann, and Weil, "Somewhere Out There," mm. 9–12 (voice)

Some-where   out   there   be - neath   the   pale   moon - light

(1) E (2)___   (3)___   (4)___   (5)___(6)___(7)___(8)___(9)___(10)___

Now listen to Example 1.5, the beginning of Chance's *Variations on a Korean Folk Song*, while looking at the music shown in the example. This lower-sounding melody is written in the **bass clef**.

EXAMPLE 1.5   Chance, *Variations on a Korean Folk Song*, mm. 1–4a 🔊

The bass clef, representing the lower notes on a keyboard, is also known as the F-clef: it somewhat resembles a cursive capital F, and its two dots surround the line that represents F. Other pitches may be counted from F, or memorized according to their positions on the staff, shown in Example 1.6. Example 1.7 shows the lines and spaces labeled with their letter names. Two ways to remember the bass-clef spaces (A C E G) are "All Cows Eat Grass" and "All Cars Eat Gas." The bass-clef lines (G B D F A) might be "Great Big Doves Fly Away."

EXAMPLE 1.6   Bass clef (F-clef) 🔊

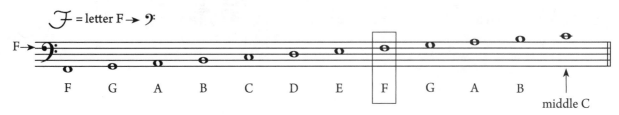

EXAMPLE 1.7   Bass-clef lines and spaces

TRY IT #3

(a)   Identify the pitches on the bass staff below with letter names. 🔊

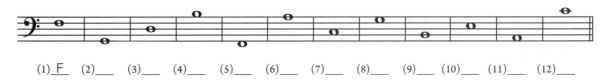

(1) _F_   (2) ___   (3) ___   (4) ___   (5) ___   (6) ___   (7) ___   (8) ___   (9) ___   (10) ___   (11) ___   (12) ___

(b)   Listen to the beginning of "Blues for Norton." The lowest part is shown below. Then write the letter names for the pitches that have blanks beneath them. Circle the highest and lowest pitches.

Phillips, "Blues for Norton" (bass line), mm. 2–3 🔊

(1) _F_   (2) ___   (3) ___   (4) ___   (5) ___   (6) ___   (7) ___   (8) ___

ASSIGNMENT 1.1

Naming Pitches with Octave Numbers

In the bass and treble clefs, letter names reappear in different octaves, as seen in the previous examples. To specify exactly in which octave a pitch appears, use octave numbers.

> **KEY CONCEPT**   As Figure 2.1 shows, the lowest C on a standard piano keyboard is designated C1, and the highest is C8; middle C is C4. The number for a particular octave includes all the pitches from C up to the following B.

The B above C4, for example, is B4; the B below C4 is B3. The white notes below C1 on the piano are A0 and B0. This pitch labeling system is standard for today's musicians, acousticians, and engineers.

FIGURE 1.2   Piano keyboard with octave numbers

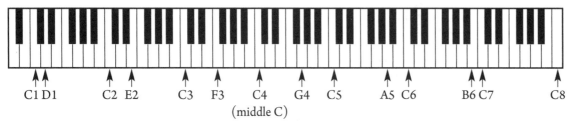

C1 D1   C2 E2   C3 F3   C4   G4 C5   A5 C6   B6 C7   C8
(middle C)

Ledger Lines

Some of the pitches on the piano keyboard, including middle C, cannot be notated on the five lines and four spaces of the treble or bass staff.

> **KEY CONCEPT**   When music extends above or below the staff, extra lines—called **ledger lines**—are drawn to accommodate these notes (Example 1.8). Read ledger lines (and the spaces between them) just like other staff lines and spaces: by counting forward or backward in the musical alphabet.

EXAMPLE 1.8   Ledger lines above and below the staff

(a) Treble clef 🔊

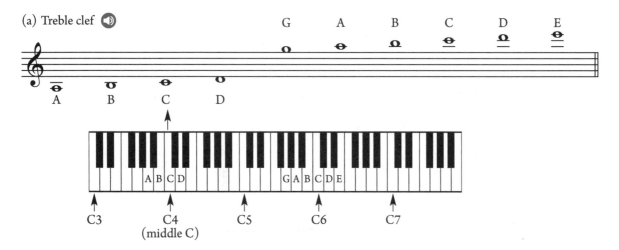

(b) Bass clef 🔊

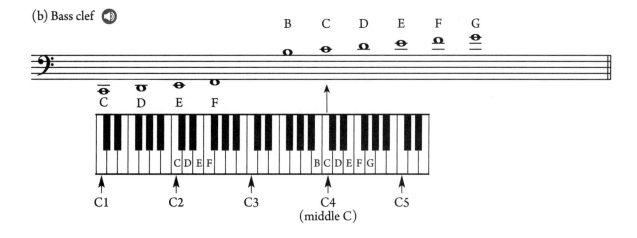

(c) Octaves from C2 to C6 🔊

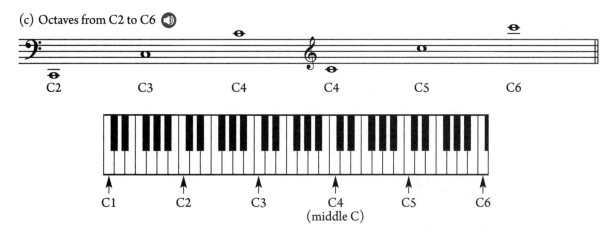

> **KEY CONCEPT** The highness or lowness of a pitch (in other words, the octave in which it lies) is called its **register**. Whether an instrument is playing in its higher or lower register can determine its **timbre**, or sound quality.

Singing voices also have different registers, which can be used to create certain moods and effects. In Example 1.9, from "Circle of Life," the low range of the melody is important to setting the mood. Some pitches are marked with their octave numbers; try identifying others.

EXAMPLE 1.9   John and Rice, "Circle of Life," from *The Lion King*, mm. 1–8 🔊

It takes a little practice to identify notes written with ledger lines. Example 1.10 provides a few landmarks for each clef.

> **KEY CONCEPT** The ledger-line notes below the treble staff are F A C; those above the staff are A C E. The ledger-line notes below the bass staff are A C E; those above the staff are C E G.

EXAMPLE 1.10 Ledger-line landmarks

(a) Treble clef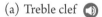

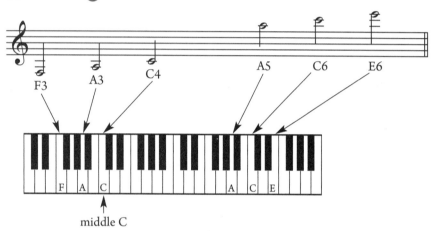

(b) Bass clef

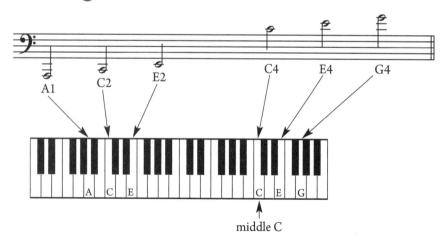

Write the letter name and octave number for each pitch given below.

(a) 🔊

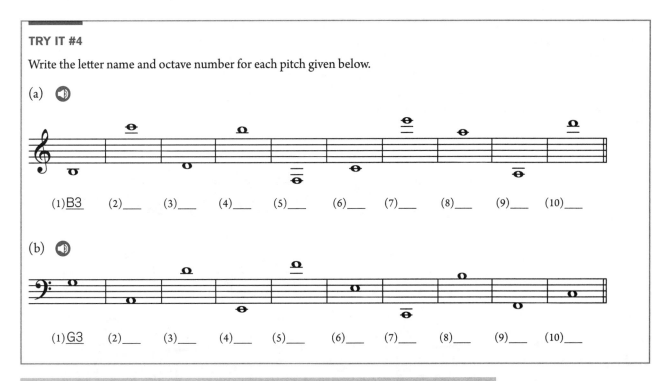

(1) <u>B3</u>   (2) ___   (3) ___   (4) ___   (5) ___   (6) ___   (7) ___   (8) ___   (9) ___   (10) ___

(b) 🔊

(1) <u>G3</u>   (2) ___   (3) ___   (4) ___   (5) ___   (6) ___   (7) ___   (8) ___   (9) ___   (10) ___

The Grand Staff

Keyboards, and other instruments that play very high and low notes, read music on the grand staff like the one in Example 1.11.

> **KEY CONCEPT**   A treble staff and a bass staff connected by a curly brace make a **grand staff**.

Ledger lines may extend above and below the grand staff. Notes that fill in the middle, between the two staves, may be written in either clef. In the example, the notes in parentheses are alternate notations for those without parentheses.

EXAMPLE 1.11   **The grand staff with pitches in its middle register** 🔊

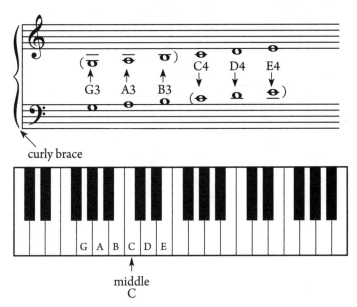

curly brace

middle
C

Listen to the opening of Joplin's "Solace," while following the score in Example 1.12. This passage shows ledger lines between the staves. The octave designation of the bass-clef F, written with ledger lines at the beginning of the example, is F4. This note could also have been written in the treble clef on the bottom space. In piano music with ledger lines written between the staves, the ranges of the two hands overlap; the clef shows which hand is supposed to play a particular note. Treble clef generally indicates the right hand, bass clef the left hand.

EXAMPLE 1.12   Joplin, "Solace," mm. 5–12

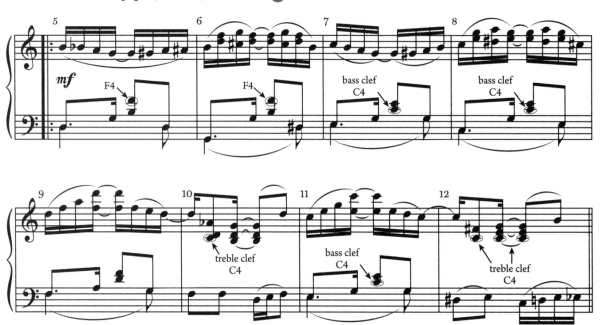

TRY IT #5

The example on the grand staff below includes many notes written with ledger lines. For each note with a blank beneath it, write the letter name and octave number. Then locate these pitches on a keyboard.

Schifrin, theme from *Mission: Impossible*, mm. 1–2

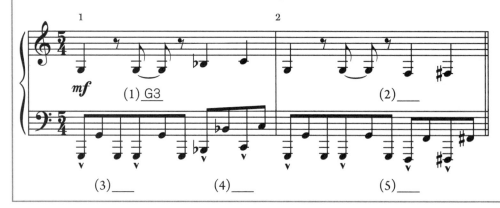

Writing Music in a Score

Writing music correctly (and neatly) helps those performing your music to read fluently and without errors. You can draw a treble clef in a single continuous curved line, or in two strokes as shown in Example 1.13: (1) first draw a wavy line from top to bottom, like an elongated S; then (2) draw a second line that starts at the top and curves around it (ending on the G line). The bass clef is drawn in two steps as well: (1) draw an arc that looks a bit like a backward C, then (2) add two dots that surround the F line.

EXAMPLE 1.13   Drawing clefs

When you draw note heads on the staff, make them oval-shaped rather than round, and they should not be so large that it's hard to tell whether they sit on a line or in a space (Example 1.14a).

> **KEY CONCEPT**   Most notes have thin vertical lines, called stems, that extend above or below the note head. If a note lies below the middle line of the staff, its stem usually goes up, on the right side of the note head; if a note lies on or above the middle line, its stem goes down, on the left side (part b).

The stem of a note on the middle line can, however, go up if the notes around it have stems up (both stem directions are shown in part b). The length of the stem from bottom to top spans about an octave.

EXAMPLE 1.14   Notation guidelines

(a)

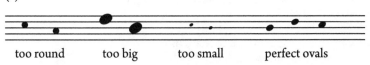

too round   too big   too small   perfect ovals

(b)

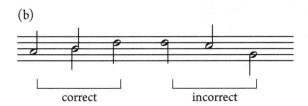

correct   incorrect

Example 1.15 shows ledger lines drawn correctly and incorrectly. When you write notes above the staff, draw ledger lines through the note heads or beneath them, but never above them. Note heads below the staff have ledger lines through them or above them, but never beneath. Draw ledger lines the same distance apart as staff lines.

EXAMPLE 1.15   Ledger-line pitches

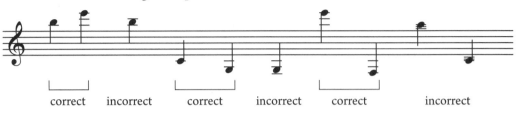

correct   incorrect   correct   incorrect   correct   incorrect

SUMMARY

When notating music, write neatly so that others can read your score easily and accurately.

- Draw a clef at the beginning of each staff.
- To indicate a grand staff, draw a long line and curly brace to connect the treble and bass staves on the left side.
- Draw both black and hollow note heads as neat ovals on or between staff lines.
- For ledger-line notes, draw ledger lines parallel to staff lines, the same distance apart, and between the note head and the top or bottom staff line.
- Draw straight, thin stems that span about an octave and follow the guidelines for stem direction.

You will learn more notational guidelines for rhythm and other topics in later chapters.

ASSIGNMENT 1.3, AURAL SKILLS 1.1

Did You Know?

Sir Elton John was born Reginald Kenneth Dwight in 1947. The child of a musician, he began studying piano at age four and won a scholarship to the Royal Academy of Music at age eleven. By the 1970s, John had become a pop superstar with a Top 40 single every year from 1970 to 1996. Among his most famous songs are "Your Song," "Goodbye Yellow Brick Road," songs from *The Lion King* (including "Circle of Life," Example 1.9), and "Candle in the Wind." This last song, originally a tribute to Marilyn Monroe, John rerecorded as a tribute to Princess Diana after her untimely death in 1997. "Candle in the Wind" became his biggest hit ever, selling over three million copies in the United States in its first week. John contributed royalties from this recording to Princess Diana's favorite charities.

Terms You Should Know

clef	letter name	octave equivalence
treble	ledger line	pitch
bass	middle C (C4)	register
contour	musical alphabet	score
ascending	note	staff (staves)
descending	note head	stem
grand staff	octave	timbre

Questions for Review

1. Which alphabet letters represent pitches?
2. Why are clefs necessary?
3. Why is a treble clef also called a G-clef? Why is a bass clef also called an F-clef?
4. What are the letter names for the lines on the treble staff? on the bass staff?
5. What are the letter names for the spaces on the treble staff? on the bass staff?
6. How many letter names apart are notes that span an octave?
7. What is the purpose of ledger lines?
8. When is a grand staff used? What does it consist of?
9. To which side of the note head do ascending stems connect? To which side do descending stems connect?
10. How do you decide whether stems should go up or down?

Reading Review

Match the terms on the left with the best answer on the right.

_____ (1) E–G–B–D–F   (a) 𝄞

_____ (2) score   (b) five lines and four spaces on which music is notated

_____ (3) ledger lines   (c) notation of a piece of music

_____ (4) octave equivalence   (d) letter names for treble-clef spaces

_____ (5) clef   (e) attached to note heads above the middle line

_____ (6) musical contour   (f) similarity in sound of notes with the same letter name

_____ (7) F–A–C–E   (g) the shape of a musical line

_____ (8) treble-clef symbol   (h) letter names for treble-clef lines

_____ (9) G–B–D–F–A   (i) used to notate pitches above or below the staff lines

_____ (10) A–C–E–G   (j) ovals written on a staff to represent pitches

_____ (11) bass-clef symbol   (k) attached to note heads below the middle line

_____ (12) notes   (l) specifies the octave register of a pitch

_____ (13) octave number   (m) middle C

_____ (14) grand staff   (n) treble- and bass-clef staves joined with a curly brace

_____ (15) stems down   (o) letter names for bass-clef lines

_____ (16) C4   (p) letter names for bass-clef spaces

_____ (17) stems up   (q) symbol that gives notes on a staff their letter names

_____ (18) staff   (r) 𝄢

Ⓢ Additional review and practice available at wwnorton.com/studyspace

Class Activities

Because singing and playing piano can help you understand and remember musical concepts, these performing activities will make up a significant part of your study. Most of these activities can be completed in class: sing as a group, or arrange to use the piano in groups. Others can be practiced on your own, if you have access to a keyboard.

When singing:
- Don't be shy; sing out with enthusiasm!
- Don't worry about the quality of your voice. For our purposes, you only want to sing accurate pitches and rhythm.
- Sing every chance you get. Everything improves with practice.
- Sing a warm-up pattern first (like the one below) to orient your voice and ear to the music.

When playing:
- Keep your fingers curved.
- Don't depress any pedals for now.
- Typically, play different notes with different fingers. When it matters, specific fingering will be suggested.

A. Singing

For each warm-up pattern below, sing on the syllables given, in order to achieve an open and free sound. Also practice on the "lyrics" shown, *do-re-mi-fa-sol*, or numbers $\hat{1}$ to $\hat{5}$. You will learn more about these lyrics in Chapter 6.

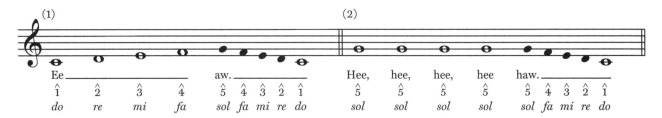

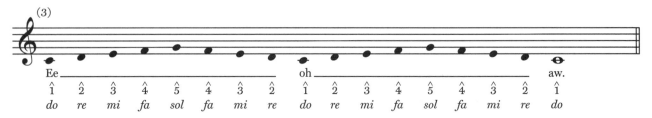

Refer to this page when warming up by yourself. Sing these melodies often until your voice becomes stronger and your range wider. To begin, play a pitch on the keyboard that you can sing comfortably; sing a pattern starting on this pitch. Then play the next-higher note and sing the pattern again. Continue, each time one note higher, until the melody gets too high; then stop. Choose a new pattern and repeat the process.

B. At the keyboard

1. Play the following notes on the keyboard in two or more different octaves.

Solo: Play additional random white-key notes, then say their letter names. *Duet*: One person plays a pitch and the other person names it, then switch roles. *Variation*: Sing each note as you play.

(a) C	(f) D	(k) G	(p) C
(b) A	(g) B	(l) F	(q) E
(c) E	(h) A	(m) D	(r) D
(d) G	(i) C	(n) A	(s) B
(e) F	(j) E	(o) B	(t) G

2. Play the following notes on the keyboard in the octave specified.

(a) B5	(f) F5	(k) E5	(p) D6
(b) F3	(g) D4	(l) F4	(q) G4
(c) E2	(h) G6	(m) A3	(r) A5
(d) A4	(i) B3	(n) C1	(s) E3
(e) C6	(j) A2	(o) B4	(t) F6

C. Listening and writing

After establishing a home pitch, your teacher will create a melody by pointing to a series of items—pitches, letter names, or piano keys—like those shown below.

1. When the teacher points to an item, immediately sing it with its letter name.
2. Once the melody is complete, sing it until you have memorized it.
3. Write the melody with letter names, or notate it on a treble or bass staff with pitches.
4. Make your own point-and-sing exercises. *Solo*: Point to an item, sing it, then check your pitch by playing it at the keyboard.
   Duet: Point to the chart while a partner sings, then switch roles.

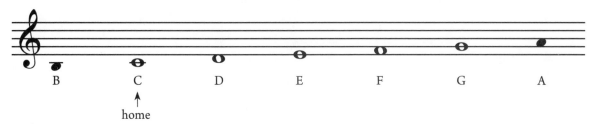

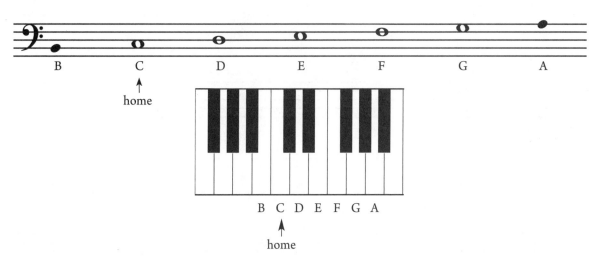

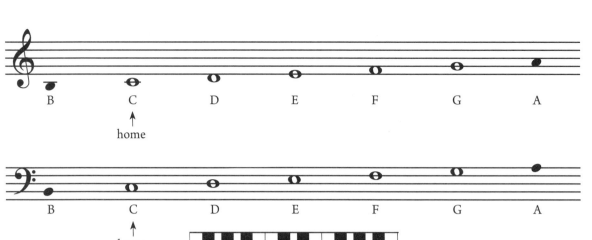

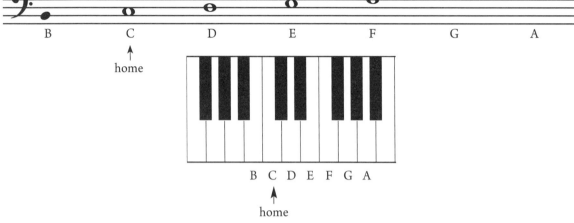

Workbook ASSIGNMENT 1.1

1. Letter names

a. Fill in the letter name requested. Remember to count the letter you begin with.

(1) 6 above C: __A__

(2) 3 above G: _____

(3) 2 below F: _____

(4) 7 below A: _____

(5) 4 above D: _____

(6) 2 above E: _____

(7) 4 below D: _____

(8) 5 below E: _____

(9) 7 above C: _____

(10) 5 below B: _____

(11) 7 above G: _____

(12) 3 below A: _____

b. On the keyboards below, write each letter name on its corresponding key.

(1) C, D, G, B

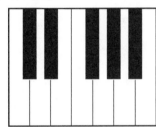

(2) E, F, A, B

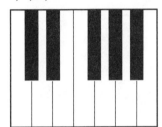

c. On the keyboards below, write each letter name on *every* key with that name (in three octaves).

(1) C, E, A

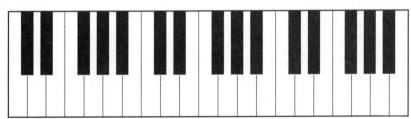

(2) G, B, D

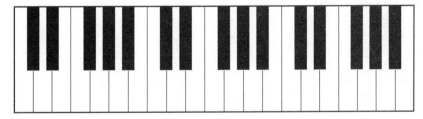

2. Drawing clefs

a. Trace the treble clefs given in dotted lines; then draw additional clefs.

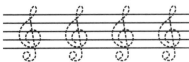

b. Trace the bass clefs given in dotted lines; then draw additional clefs.

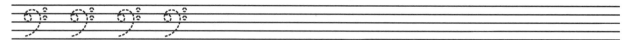

3. Reading notes in treble and bass clefs

a. Write the letter name of each pitch in the blank provided.

(1) __C__ (2) ____ (3) ____ (4) ____ (5) ____ (6) ____ (7) ____ (8) ____

(9) __B__ (10) ____ (11) ____ (12) ____ (13) ____ (14) ____ (15) ____ (16) ____

b. In each blank, write the letter name of the note above.

(1) Stevie Wonder, "You Are the Sunshine of My Life," mm. 5–11

You are   the sun - shine...
__C__

(2) Horner, Mann, and Weil, "Somewhere Out There," mm. 13–16

Some - one's think-in' of   me   and lov - ing me   to - night.
__A__

Workbook ASSIGNMENT 1.2

1. Identifying pitches with ledger lines and octave numbers

a. For each pitch notated on the staff, write its number on the correct key of the keyboard. Write the letter name and octave number on the blank beneath, as shown.

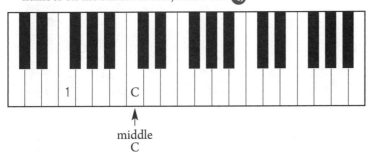

(1) _F3_ (2) ____ (3) ____ (4) ____ (5) ____ (6) ____ (7) ____

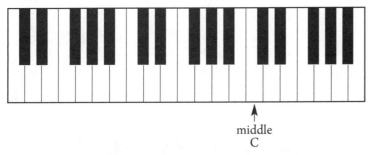

(8) _C2_ (9) ____ (10) ____ (11) ____ (12) ____ (13) ____ (14) ____

b. Beneath each pitch, write its letter name and octave number.

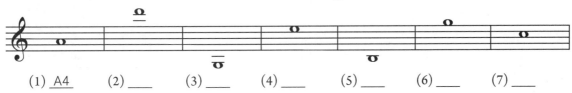

(1) _A4_ (2) ____ (3) ____ (4) ____ (5) ____ (6) ____ (7) ____

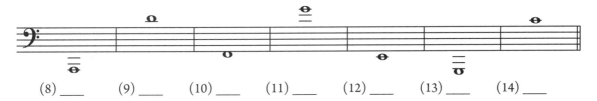

(8) ____ (9) ____ (10) ____ (11) ____ (12) ____ (13) ____ (14) ____

c. In the passages below, write the letter name and octave number for any ledger-line note marked with an arrow.

(1) Mozart, *Variations on "Ah, vous dirai-je Maman,"* mm. 1–8

C4 ___ ___ ___ ___ ___

(2) Mozart, *Variations*, Var. VII, mm. 187–192

___ ___ ___ ___

(3) Horner, Mann, and Weil, "Somewhere Out There," mm. 16b–20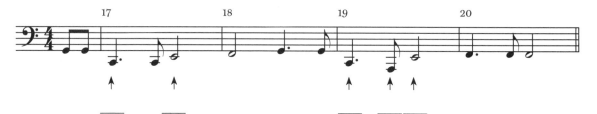

___ ___ ___ ___ ___

2. Writing pitches with ledger lines and octave numbers

For each number on the keyboard, write the corresponding hollow note head on the staff below it. Write the letter name and octave number in the blank provided.

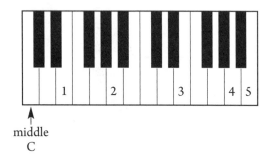

middle
C

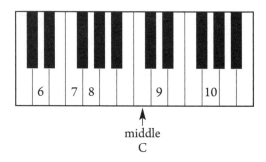

middle
C

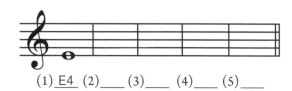

(1) E4 (2) ___ (3) ___ (4) ___ (5) ___

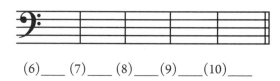

(6) ___ (7) ___ (8) ___ (9) ___ (10) ___

Workbook   ASSIGNMENT 1.3

1. Writing pitches with ledger lines, stems, and octave numbers

a. For each note requested, neatly write a hollow note head on the correct line or space of the staff, then add a stem that extends in the correct direction.

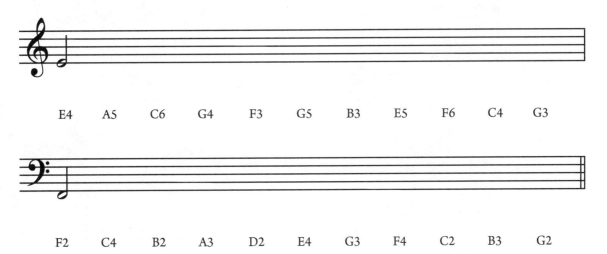

| E4 | A5 | C6 | G4 | F3 | G5 | B3 | E5 | F6 | C4 | G3 |

| F2 | C4 | B2 | A3 | D2 | E4 | G3 | F4 | C2 | B3 | G2 |

b. In the first row of blanks below the staff, label each pitch with letter name and octave number. Then, above or below the given note, rewrite the note in the new octave as specified. In the second row of blanks, write the letter name with its new octave number.

(1) Rewrite exactly two octaves lower.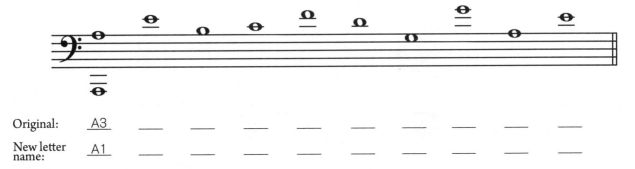

Original: A3 ___ ___ ___ ___ ___ ___ ___ ___ ___ ___

New letter name: A1 ___ ___ ___ ___ ___ ___ ___ ___ ___ ___

(2) Rewrite exactly two octaves higher.

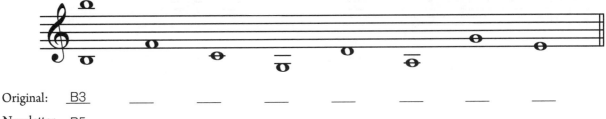

Original: B3 ___ ___ ___ ___ ___ ___ ___ ___

New letter name: B5 ___ ___ ___ ___ ___ ___ ___ ___

2. Arranging: Changing clef and octave

Rewrite the pitches of each melody down one or two octaves as specified, on the staff provided. Copy the original notation, but change stem direction as needed.

a. Elton John and Tim Rice, "Circle of Life," from *The Lion King*, mm. 1–3. Write the music down one octave.

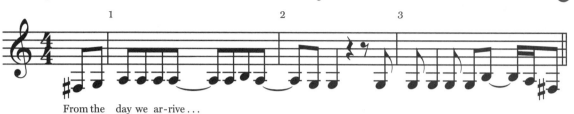

b. Billy Joel, "Piano Man," mm. 71b–78. Write the music down two octaves.

c. Rewrite the beginning of "Amazing Grace" up one octave, as though scored for violin or flute. You'll need to use ledger lines.

Workbook   AURAL SKILLS 1.1

Listen to an excerpt from a familiar melody. The excerpt consists of four segments. Segments 1 and 2 each include four pitches. Segments 3 and 4 each have three pitches.

1. Focus on segment 1, the first four pitches. Which of the following best diagrams the segment's contour?

a. /   b. \   c. /\   d. \/

2. Focus on the ending. Which of the following best diagrams segment 4's contour?

a. /   b. \   c. /\   d. \/

3. Which of the following best describes how the segments are organized?

Segment 1	Segment 2	Segment 3	Segment 4
a. idea 1	idea 1 repeated	idea 2	idea 1 returns
b. idea 1	idea 1 repeated	idea 2	idea 2 repeated
c. idea 1	idea 2	idea 3	idea 4
d. idea 1	idea 2	idea 1 returns	idea 2 returns

4. On the staff below, notate segment 1 with the pitches C, D, and E.

a. Draw a treble-clef sign.

b. Begin on middle C. First, draw its ledger line below the staff, then draw its oval note head on this ledger line. (Don't worry about stems or rhythm for now.)

c. Notate the rest of segment 1's pitches. Make sure your note heads stay only on the appropriate line or in the appropriate space.

5. On the staff below, notate segment 4 with the pitches E, F, and G.

a. Draw a treble clef.

b. Begin on E4, the first (lowest) staff line. Draw its oval note head on this line. (Again, don't worry about stems or rhythm.)

c. Notate segment 4's remaining pitches. Make sure your note heads stay only on the appropriate line or in the appropriate space. Hint: Think of the segment's contour (the answer to question 2).

6. On the staff below, notate the pitches of the *entire* melody.

a. Draw a treble clef.

b. Begin with segment 1, your answer to question 4.

c. To continue with segments 2 and 3, consult your answer to question 3.

d. Conclude with segment 4, your answer to question 5.

Play your answer at the keyboard. Sing with the letter names C, D, E, F, and G. Tune your singing to the sound of the keyboard.

7. On the staff below, notate the pitches of the entire melody in the bass clef, down one octave.

a. Draw a bass clef.

b. Consult your answers to question 6.

Again, play your answer at the keyboard.

8. On the staff below, notate the entire melody in bass clef, beginning on middle C and using ledger lines. It should sound in the same octave as your answer for question 6.

TOPICS

- sharps, flats, and naturals
- double sharps and flats
- writing pitches with accidentals
- half steps and whole steps
- hearing half and whole steps

MUSIC

- John Barry and Tim Rice, "All Time High"
- Scott Joplin, "Solace"
- Mel Leven, "Cruella de Vil," from *101 Dalmations*
- Willie Nelson, "On the Road Again"

CHAPTER 2

Accidentals and Half and Whole Steps

Sharps, Flats, and Naturals

Listen to the melody from Joplin's "Solace" while looking at Example 2.1. The first four notes in each line are marked on the keyboard below.

EXAMPLE 2.1   Joplin, "Solace," mm. 1–8a (right hand only)

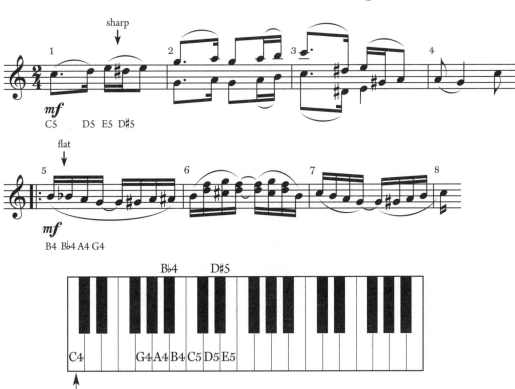

The fourth note of this melody is D♯5 (D-sharp 5), which is played on the black key between D5 and E5. On the second line, the second note is B♭4 (B-flat 4), played on the black key between B4 and A4.

The black keys are named in relation to the white keys next to them as Figure 2.1 shows. The black key immediately *above* (to the right of) any white key gets the white note's name plus a **sharp** (♯). The two black keys grouped together are C♯ (C-sharp) and D♯, and the three black keys grouped together are F♯, G♯, and A♯.

FIGURE 2.1   Names for white and black keys

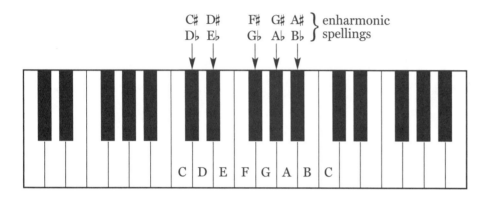

The black key immediately *below* (to the left of) any white key gets the white note's name plus a **flat** (♭). The group of two black keys may also be called D♭ (D-flat) and E♭, and the three black keys may also be called G♭, A♭, and B♭. Every black key has two possible names: one with a sharp and one with a flat.

> **KEY CONCEPT**   When pitches have different names but make the same sound and are played with the same key on the keyboard (D♭ = C♯), their spellings are called **enharmonic** (see Figure 2.2). Enharmonic notes sound the same but are spelled differently—like the words "too" and "two."

A sharp sign (♯) raises any note to the next (often a black key, but sometimes a white key). A flat sign (♭) lowers any note to the next (often black, but sometimes white). This span—from a note to its closest neighbor—is called a half step (p. 30). Look again at Figure 2.1 to see C and C♯, or E and E♭: both pairs are half steps and include a white then a black key.

Sharp and flat symbols are called **accidentals**, though there is nothing "accidental" about their use or placement. A third common accidental, called a **natural** (♮), is shown in Example 2.2, from later in Joplin's piano rag. A natural returns a pitch to its "natural" state. In measure 18 of Example 2.2, in the left hand (bass clef) you would first play F♯ followed by F♮, and in the right hand (treble clef) D♯ followed by D♮—in both cases, a black key followed by a white one.

EXAMPLE 2.2   Joplin, "Solace," mm. 17–20 🔊

There is no black key immediately to the right of E; the next note up is F. E♯ is therefore played on a white key and is enharmonic with F. B♯ is also a white key, and is enharmonic with C. On the flat side, C♭ is enharmonic with B, and F♭ is enharmonic with E. These enharmonic spellings for white keys are shown in Figure 2.2.

FIGURE 2.2   Enharmonic spellings for white keys 🔊

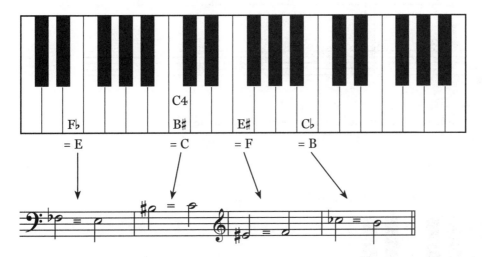

To see how composers use enharmonic notes in pieces of music, look back at the beginning of the second line of Example 2.1. Joplin has considered the musical context in which pitches appear, and written a B♭ as the musical line travels down, but an A♯ as the line moves up.

Double Sharps and Flats

Examples 2.3 and 2.4 show two other accidentals: the **double sharp** (𝄪) and **double flat** (♭♭). A double sharp (𝄪) raises a pitch two half steps (a **whole step**; see p. 30) above its letter name. A double flat (♭♭) lowers a pitch two half steps (whole step) below its letter name. The double sharp (F𝄪4) appears on the first note of Willie Nelson's melody and in the second line. A double flat (B♭♭3) appears as marked in the bass-clef piano part of "All Time High" (from one of the James Bond films).

EXAMPLE 2.3   Nelson, "On the Road Again," mm. 7b–14

Just   can't   wait to   get . . .

EXAMPLE 2.4   Barry and Rice, "All Time High," mm. 33b–37a

So hold   on   tight . . .

Double sharped or flatted notes are often played on the white keys of the piano. For example, the F✕4 in the Nelson song is enharmonic with G, and the B♭♭ in "All Time High" is enharmonic with A. Figure 2.3 shows other examples.

FIGURE 2.3   Enharmonic pitches with double sharps and flats

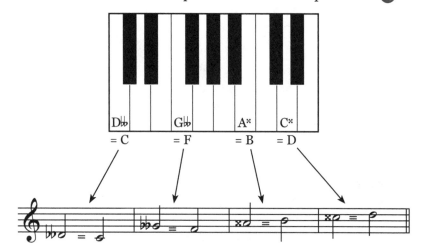

Accidentals:

♯ (sharp):	raises the pitch a half step
♭ (flat):	lowers the pitch a half step
× (double sharp):	raises the pitch a whole step
♭♭ (double flat):	lowers the pitch a whole step
♮ (natural):	cancels a sharp, double sharp, flat, or double flat

Enharmonic notes: sound the same but are spelled differently

Writing Pitches with Accidentals

As you can see in Example 2.5, the beginning of "Cruella de Vil," in a musical score an accidental is positioned before (to the left of) the note head.

EXAMPLE 2.5   Leven, "Cruella de Vil," mm. 1–2a 🔊

When you write or say note names, however, the accidental goes after (to the right of) the note name; for example, C♯ (C-sharp). For an accidental on a space (see the A♭ and F♯ above), the middle of the accidental is centered within the space, not on the line above or below. For an accidental on a line (see the B♭ and D♭), the line passes through its middle. Always be careful to notate an accidental exactly on the line or space you intend, not floating above or below the note, and to place the accidental before the note.

TRY IT #1

(a)   Name the enharmonic equivalent.

(1)   G♭ is enharmonic with <u>F♯</u>

(2)   B♯ is enharmonic with ____

(3)   A♯ is enharmonic with ____

(4)   E♯ is enharmonic with ____

(5)   D♭ is enharmonic with ____

(6)   B is enharmonic with ____

(7)   A♭ is enharmonic with ____

(8)   E♭ is enharmonic with ____

(b) For each note below, write its letter name in the space beneath. Then write the enharmonically equivalent note in the blank measure to the right, and that note's name beneath.

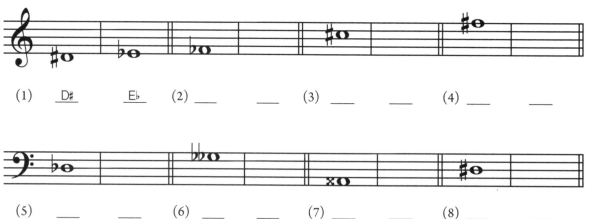

(1) __D#__ __Eb__ (2) ___ ___ (3) ___ ___ (4) ___ ___

(5) ___ ___ (6) ___ ___ (7) ___ ___ (8) ___ ___

Half Steps and Whole Steps

The distance between any two notes is called an **interval**. The first two intervals in "Solace," shown in Example 2.6—B4 to Bb4 and Bb4 to A4—are half steps; the third, A4 to G4, is a whole step. Half and whole steps are basic building blocks in music.

EXAMPLE 2.6   Joplin, "Solace," mm. 5–8a (right hand only) 🔊

> **KEY CONCEPT**   A **half step** (or **semitone**) is the interval between any pitch and the next closest pitch on the keyboard in either direction. The combination of two half steps forms a **whole step** (or **whole tone**). A whole step always has one note in between.

Example 2.7 shows half and whole steps on the keyboard. Usually a half step (part a) spans a white key to a black key (like B to A#) or black to white (like Gb to G). The only exceptions are B to C and E to F, which naturally span a half step. Whole steps (part b) usually span two keys of the same color: white to white (like C to D) or black to black (like Bb to Ab). Again, those spelled with E, F, B, or C are exceptions.

EXAMPLE 2.7   Half and Whole Steps

(a) Half steps

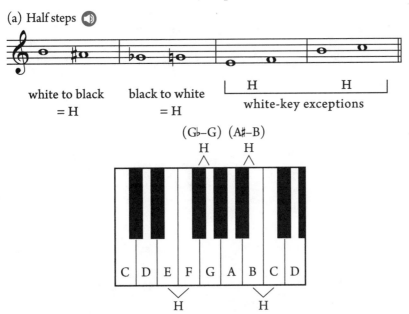

white to black
= H

black to white
= H

H   H
white-key exceptions

(Gb–G) (A#–B)
H   H

C D E F G A B C D

H   H

(b) Whole steps

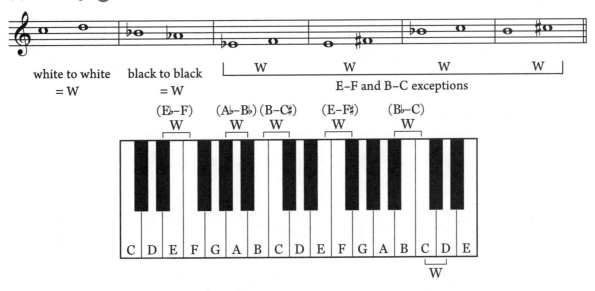

white to white
= W

black to black
= W

W   W   W   W
E–F and B–C exceptions

(Eb–F) (Ab–Bb) (B–C#)   (E–F#)   (Bb–C)
W   W   W   W   W

C D E F G A B C D E F G A B C D E

W

Half steps that are spelled with two different letter names (G–Ab) are called **diatonic half steps**. Half steps that are spelled with the same letter name (G–G#) are called **chromatic half steps**. Both spellings are correct; they are enharmonic equivalents. Both types of half steps are found in Example 2.7: B–A#, E–F, and B–C are diatonic half steps; Gb–G is a chromatic half step.

> **SUMMARY**
>
> Half and whole steps:
> 1. (a) Half steps usually span keys of different colors: white to black or black to white (Example 2.7a).
>   (b) The exceptions are E–F and B–C, the white-key half steps (Example 2.7a).
> 2. (a) Whole steps usually span keys the same color: white to white or black to black (Example 2.7b).
>   (b) The exceptions are Eb–F, E–F#, Bb–C, and B–C# (Example 2.7b).
> 3. Double-check the spelling of any half or whole step that includes E, F, B, or C.

(a) Name the pitch requested, then for the half steps, identify an enharmonically equivalent pitch.

A half step:

(1) above G: <u>G♯</u> or <u>A♭</u>

(2) below C♯: ____ or ____

(3) below B: ____ or ____

(4) above E: ____ or ____

(5) above D: ____ or ____

A whole step:

(6) above F♯: ____

(7) below C: ____

(8) above D: ____

(9) above C♯: ____

(10) below B♭: ____

(b) Identify whether each pair of pitches below spans a whole step (W), half step (H), or neither (N).

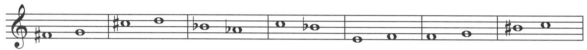

(1) <u>H</u>   (2) ____   (3) ____   (4) ____   (5) ____   (6) ____   (7) ____

(8) ____   (9) ____   (10) ____   (11) ____   (12) ____   (13) ____   (14) ____

(c) Identify each pair of bracketed pitches as a whole step (W), half step (H), or neither (N).

Leven, "Cruella de Vil," mm. 1–2

Hearing Half and Whole Steps

Listen now to Example 2.8 to hear the difference in sound between half and whole steps. When you hear a whole step (C–D), you can imagine a note between them on the keyboard (C♯). When you hear a half step, you can't. Practice playing whole and half steps at the keyboard. For each whole step, insert the note between to hear how it divides the whole step in half.

EXAMPLE 2.8   Whole steps divided in half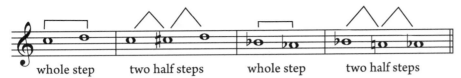

whole step two half steps whole step two half steps

ASSIGNMENT 2.2, 2.3, AURAL SKILLS 2.1

Did You Know?

Scott Joplin's father was a former slave. One of Joplin's most famous compositions, "The Maple Leaf Rag" (published in 1899), earned him one penny for every sheet-music copy sold. His opera *Treemonisha* (composed in 1911) won an award for being the "most American opera" ever written, yet Joplin never saw it fully staged. Joplin's music was played in bars, dance halls, and other popular gathering places from the 1890s to the 1910s. It became popular once again in the 1970s after it was featured in the movie *The Sting* (1973), with Paul Newman and Robert Redford. Joplin's rags have remained among the best-known American music of the early twentieth century.

Terms You Should Know

accidentals	enharmonic
flat (♭)	interval
sharp (♯)	half step (semitone)
natural (♮)	chromatic half step
double flat (♭♭)	diatonic half step
double sharp (×)	whole step (whole tone)

Questions for Review

1. What is the effect of adding a sharp to a note? adding a flat? adding a natural?
2. What is an example of an enharmonic spelling?
3. What is the effect of adding a double sharp to a note? a double flat?
4. Does an accidental precede or follow a note's letter name when spoken or written? Does an accidental precede or follow the note head in a musical score?
5. Which white-key pairs on the keyboard don't have a black key between them?
6. Which pairs of white keys span a half step? Which span a whole step?
7. Are there any half steps that span a black key to a black key?
8. How can you distinguish whole and half steps by ear?

Reading Review

Match the terms on the left with the best answer on the right.

_____ (1) half step

_____ (2) interval

_____ (3) enharmonic spelling

_____ (4) ♯

_____ (5) ♭

_____ (6) whole step

_____ (7) ♭♭

_____ (8) ×

_____ (9) accidentals

_____ (10) chromatic half step

_____ (11) natural

_____ (12) diatonic half step

(a) symbol that raises a pitch a whole step

(b) the distance between two pitches

(c) symbol that raises a pitch a half step

(d) half step with a different letter name for each note

(e) interval between any key on the keyboard and the next closest key

(f) symbol that lowers a pitch a whole step

(g) interval spanning two half steps

(h) notes written with different letter names that sound the same

(i) half step with the same letter name for both notes

(j) symbols that indicate how much to raise or lower a pitch

(k) symbol that cancels a sharp or flat

(l) symbol that lowers a pitch a half step

Ⓢ Additional review and practice available at wwnorton.com/studyspace

Class Activities

A. At the keyboard

1. Play the following pitches on a piano, or touch them on your model keyboard. Then name an enharmonic spelling. (Middle C is C4.)

(a) C♯4   (f) D♯3   (k) G♭4   (p) C♭5

(b) A♭3   (g) B♭5   (l) F♯2   (q) E♭2

(c) E♭5   (h) A♭4   (m) D♭5   (r) D♯4

(d) G♯2   (i) C♮2   (n) A♯2   (s) B♭4

(e) F♯4   (j) E♯3   (o) B♯3   (t) G♭3

2. Start with the given pitch, then move your finger on the piano (or along your model keyboard), following the pattern of whole and half steps indicated. Write the name of the pitch at the end of the sequence.

(a) Begin on C: down W, down H, down W, up H, up H = _____A_____

(b) Begin on E: up W, up H, up W, down H, up W, up W = _____

(c) Begin on F♯: down W, down W, up H, down W, down H, up W = _____

(d) Begin on A♭: up W, up W, up W, down H, up W, up W = _____

(e) Begin on C♯: down W, up H, up W, up W, up H, up H = _____

(f) Begin on B: up H, up H, down W, down H, down W, down W = _____

(g) Begin on D: up H, down W, down W, down H, down H, up W = _____

(h) Begin on E♭: down W, down W, down H, down W, up H, up H = _____

B. Listening and writing

1. Hearing accidentals 🔊

Listen to the following pairs of notes (played in class or on your recording). First a pitch will be played, then raised or lowered one half step. Its original accidental is given. Circle the arrow that shows the pitch's change of direction, then circle its new accidental.

(a) sharp	↑	(↓)	♭	(♮)	♯
(b) natural	↑	↓	♭	♮	♯
(c) flat	↑	↓	♭	♮	♯
(d) sharp	↑	↓	♭	♮	♯
(e) natural	↑	↓	♭	♮	♯
(f) natural	↑	↓	♭	♮	♯

2. Hearing half and whole steps

Listen to the following pairs of notes (played in class or on your recording). Each pair will be repeated. The pitches make either a half step (H) or whole step (W). Write H or W in the blank, and ↑ for ascending or ↓ for descending.

(a) ____W↑____   (f) _____   (k) _____   (p) _____

(b) _____   (g) _____   (l) _____   (q) _____

(c) _____   (h) _____   (m) _____   (r) _____

(d) _____   (i) _____   (n) _____   (s) _____

(e) _____   (j) _____   (o) _____   (t) _____

C. Singing

Mark the half steps with brackets, as shown in Melody 1. Then perform the melodies below in the following ways.

- Echo melodies after your teacher.
- Sing the hollow notes so they last twice as long as filled notes.
- Sing on a neutral syllable (like "la") or with letter names.
- Play the melodies at the keyboard.
- Play at the keyboard and sing with a neutral syllable or letter names.
- Play the melodies on another instrument if you can.

Melody 1

Melody 2

Melody 3

Melody 4

Melody 5

Melody 6

Workbook ASSIGNMENT 2.1

1. Identifying pitches with accidentals

a. On the keyboard diagram below, middle C is labeled for you. Below the diagram, write one letter name for each white key marked with an arrow; above, write two possible enharmonic names for each black key marked with an arrow.

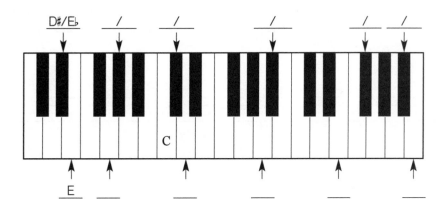

b. Write the name of each pitch, together with its octave number, in the blank beneath the staff.

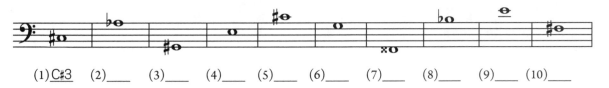

(1) C#3   (2) ___   (3) ___   (4) ___   (5) ___   (6) ___   (7) ___   (8) ___   (9) ___   (10) ___

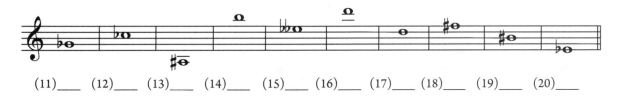

(11) ___   (12) ___   (13) ___   (14) ___   (15) ___   (16) ___   (17) ___   (18) ___   (19) ___   (20) ___

2. Writing pitches with accidentals

a. Use the staves below to practice writing accidentals.

(1) Write flat signs before each pitch.   (2) Write natural signs.

(3) Write sharp signs before each pitch.   (4) Write natural signs.

b. Notate each numbered keyboard pitch with a hollow note head on the staff, above the corresponding number. Write the letter name and octave number in the blank. (Choose either enharmonic spelling for black keys.)

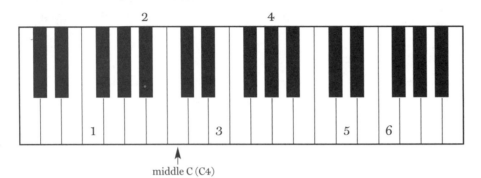

middle C (C4)

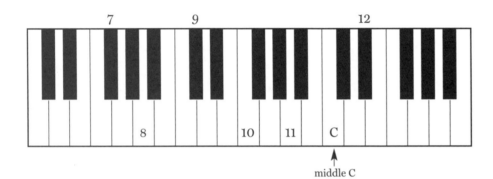

(1) F3   (2) ___   (3) ___   (4) ___   (5) ___   (6) ___

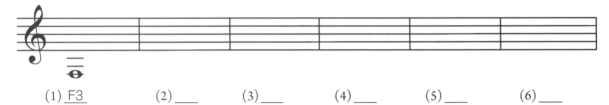

middle C

(7) ___   (8) ___   (9) ___   (10) ___   (11) ___   (12) ___

c. Write the specified pitches using hollow note heads.

(1)   (2)   (3)   (4)   (5)   (6)   (7)

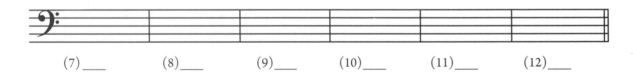

C♯5   B♭3   F4   D♭5   G♯5   E4   C4

(8)   (9)   (10)   (11)   (12)   (13)   (14)

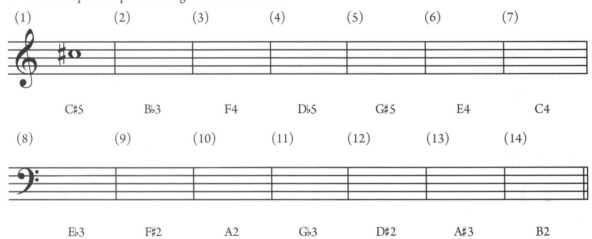

E♭3   F♯2   A2   G♭3   D♯2   A♯3   B2

Workbook ASSIGNMENT 2.2

1. Reading and writing enharmonic pitches

a. In the first row of blanks below the staff, write the letter name for each pitch. In the second row, give the letter name of one possible enharmonic equivalent.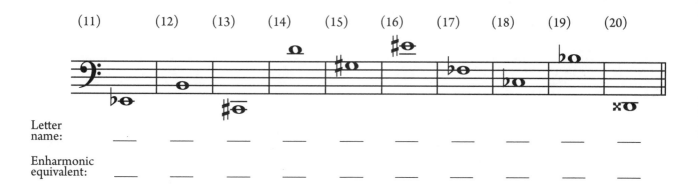

Letter name: Gb ___ ___ ___ ___ ___ ___ ___ ___ ___

Enharmonic equivalent: F# ___ ___ ___ ___ ___ ___ ___ ___ ___

Letter name: ___ ___ ___ ___ ___ ___ ___ ___ ___ ___

Enharmonic equivalent: ___ ___ ___ ___ ___ ___ ___ ___ ___ ___

b. Notate an enharmonic equivalent for each pitch below.

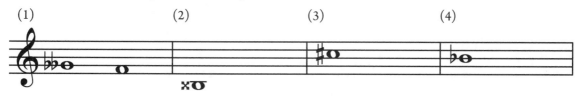

2. Identifying and writing half and whole steps

a. For each pair of pitches, write W (whole step), H (half step), or N (neither) in the blank.

(1) G♯–A __H__

(2) E♭–F♯ ____

(3) A♭–B♭ ____

(4) B–C ____

(5) F♯–G♯ ____

(6) D♯–C♯ ____

(7) A–G♯ ____

(8) C–B♭ ____

(9) E♯–F ____

b. Write a whole step above the given note. Use adjacent letter names (not the same letter name).

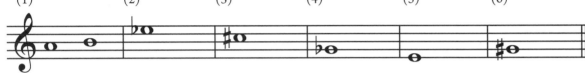

c. Write a whole step below the given note. Use adjacent letter names.

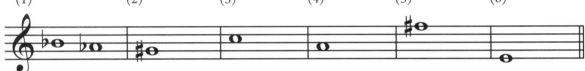

d. Write a half step above the given note. When you write black-key pitches, choose either enharmonic spelling; remember to write a natural sign, if needed, to cancel a sharp or flat.

e. Write a half step below the given note. For black-key pitches, use either enharmonic spelling.

Workbook ASSIGNMENT 2.3

1. Identifying and writing whole and half steps

a. Label each pair below as a whole step (W), half step (H), or neither (N).

(1) __W__   (2) ___   (3) ___   (4) ___   (5) ___   (6) ___

(7) ___   (8) ___   (9) ___   (10) ___   (11) ___   (12) ___

(13) ___   (14) ___   (15) ___   (16) ___   (17) ___   (18) ___

(19) ___   (20) ___   (21) ___   (22) ___   (23) ___   (24) ___

b. Write the specified whole or half step above the given note. For half steps, write the chromatic spelling (same letter names).

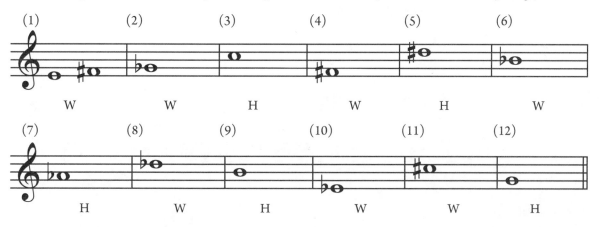

(1) W   (2) W   (3) H   (4) W   (5) H   (6) W

(7) H   (8) W   (9) H   (10) W   (11) W   (12) H

c. Write the specified whole or half step below the given note. For half steps, write the diatonic spelling (different letter names).

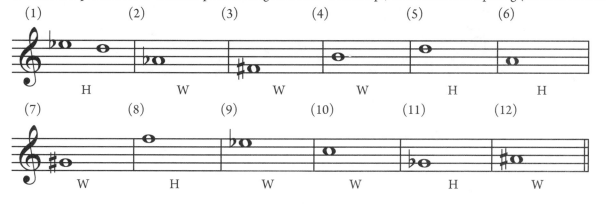

(1) H   (2) W   (3) W   (4) W   (5) H   (6) H

(7) W   (8) H   (9) W   (10) W   (11) H   (12) W

2. Identifying whole and half steps in musical literature

Each melody below features whole and half steps. Beneath each bracketed interval, write W or H in the blank. The first melody has been started for you. Listen to the recorded examples to hear how the whole and half steps sound or play the pitches at the piano.

a. Sousa, "The Stars and Stripes Forever," mm. 1–4a

b. "Greensleeves," mm. 1–4a

c. Chance, *Variations on a Korean Folk Song*, mm. 12–15a

© Copyright 1967 by Boosey & Hawkes Inc., renewed. Reprinted by permission.

d. John Williams, "Imperial March," from *The Empire Strikes Back*, mm. 5–8

e. Bruce Miller, theme from *Frasier*, mm. 2–5

NAME _____

Workbook   AURAL SKILLS 2.1

1. Playing and hearing half and whole steps

a. Play each of these half (H) and whole (W) steps at the keyboard in any octave. Name the second pitch you play with an adjacent (different) letter name and write it in the blank. The first one is completed for you.

(1) H above A __B♭__   (6) H below C ____   (11) W above E ____

(2) W below A♭ ____   (7) W above E♭ ____   (12) W below A ____

(3) H above F♯ ____   (8) H below F♯ ____   (13) W above D♭ ____

(4) W below D♯ ____   (9) W above A♯ ____   (14) W below D♭ ____

(5) H above E ____   (10) H below E♭ ____   (15) H above D♯ ____

b. Beginning with the given pitch, a two-pitch pattern will be played on the recording, then repeated. In the blank beneath each exercise, write the interval between the two pitches, W or H. Notate the second pitch with an adjacent note name and with its accidental—♭, ♮, or ♯.

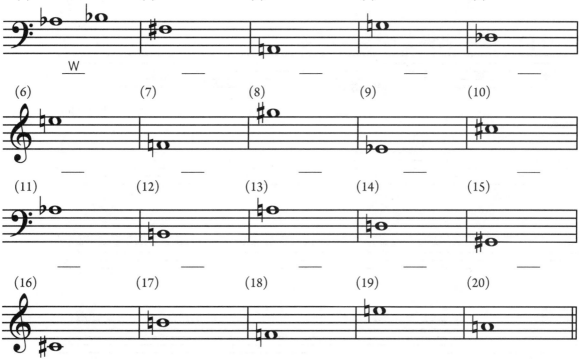

2. Performing a melody at the keyboard

- Listen to the recording of either "Amazing Grace" or "Home on the Range" enough times that you can sing it from memory in an octave that is comfortable for you.
- Find the song's music in your anthology. Say the letter name for each pitch, and play it on the keyboard. Play every F as F♯ (we will learn why in Chapter 6).
- Compare what you play with what you remember from singing the melody, and correct any mistakes. When you can play the pitches well, play them with the correct rhythm too, if possible. Be ready to sing and play the melody in class.

3. Composing with whole and half steps

a. Compose four short melodies—two in the treble clef and two in the bass clef. Follow the steps below.

- Choose a different "home" pitch for each melody. Start and end each melody on this pitch.
- Include 10–12 pitches in each melody. Make a pleasing contour.
- Compose in a register you or a partner can sing comfortably. (Keep most pitches on the staff, with few ledger lines.)
- Use only adjacent letter names (e.g., B–C, F–G–A–G).
- Notate all accidentals, even naturals (on white keys).
- Write two or three times as many whole steps as half steps.
- Notate with note heads only. Mix hollow and filled note heads, playing or singing hollow ones twice as long as filled ones.

b. Prepare to perform your melodies in the following ways.

- Sing on a neutral syllable (such as "la") or with letter names.
- Play the melodies at the keyboard.
- Play at the keyboard and sing with a neutral syllable or letter names.
- Play melodies on another instrument.

Sample melody 1

C = home

Sample melody 2

B♭ = home

Your melodies

TOPICS

- duple, triple, and quadruple meters
- tempo markings and conducting patterns
- rhythmic notation
- meter signatures
- counting rhythms in simple meters
- rests

MUSIC

- John Barnes Chance, *Variations on a Korean Folk Song*
- Jeremiah Clarke, *Trumpet Voluntary*
- George and Ira Gershwin, "'S Wonderful!" from *Funny Face*
- James Horner, Barry Mann, and Cynthia Weil, "Somewhere Out There," from *An American Tail*
- Jonathan Larson, "Seasons of Love," from *Rent*
- Wolfgang Amadeus Mozart, *Variations on "Ah, vous dirai-je Maman"*
- "My Country, 'Tis of Thee"
- John Newton, "Amazing Grace"
- Joel Phillips, "Blues for Norton"
- Richard Rodgers and Lorenz Hart, "My Funny Valentine," from *Babes in Arms*
- John Philip Sousa, "The Stars and Stripes Forever"
- Meredith Willson, "'Till There Was You," from *The Music Man*

CHAPTER 3

Simple Meters

Duple, Triple, and Quadruple Meters

Listen to the beginning of "'S Wonderful!" a Broadway show tune by George and Ira Gershwin, and tap your foot in time to the music. This tap represents the work's primary pulse, or **beat**. Now listen for a secondary pulse moving faster than your foot tap. Tap the secondary pulse in one hand, while your foot continues with the beat. This secondary pulse is the **beat division**.

Beats typically divide into two or three parts. When you tap the beat division in your hand, you'll notice that there are two hand taps to one foot beat: the beat divides into two.

> **KEY CONCEPT**   Pieces with beats that divide into two are in **simple meter**.

Now listen to "My Country, 'Tis of Thee," sung by a choir. Tap the primary beat and division as shown below. Again, the beat divides into twos—the song is in simple meter.

Counts:	1		2		3		1		2		3	
Beat:	tap		tap		tap		tap		tap		tap	
Lyrics:	My		coun-		try,		'tis ———————				of	thee
Division:	tap	tap	tap	tap	tap	tap	tap	tap	tap	tap	tap	tap

Besides dividing, primary beats also *group* into twos, threes, or fours. As you listen to each piece, try saying "1-2, 1-2" aloud (one number per primary beat); if the piece doesn't seem to fit that pattern, try "1-2-3, 1-2-3." "'S Wonderful!" groups in twos, and "My Country" groups in threes. Listen again while following the diagrams.

Counts:	1		2		1		2		1		2		1		2	
Beat:	tap		tap		tap		tap		tap		tap		tap		tap	
Lyrics:	Life has	just be-	gun ———————		Jack has	found his	Jill ———————										
Division:	tap	tap	tap	tap	tap	tap	tap	tap	tap	tap	tap	tap	tap	tap	tap	tap

> **KEY CONCEPT**   A work's **meter** tells (1) how its beats are divided, and (2) how they are grouped. When beats group into units of two, the meter is called **duple**. When they group into threes, the meter is **triple**. When they group into fours, the meter is **quadruple**.

To determine the meter of a composition by ear: (1) listen for the beat and tap it with your foot, (2) listen for the beat division (simple meters will divide beats in two parts), and (3) listen for the groupings of the beat. Try conducting (see the patterns below) or counting to determine whether the meter is duple, triple, or quadruple.

The chart below summarizes the meters of the pieces discussed so far.

Piece	Meter type
"My Country, 'Tis of Thee"	simple triple
"'S Wonderful!"	simple duple

Tempo Markings and Conducting Patterns

When only a few musicians are playing together, one may "count off" "1-2, 1-2," "1-2-3," or "1-2-3-4" to help everyone start together at the same time and at the same speed, or **tempo** (plural is either "tempos" or "tempi"). Selecting the correct tempo for a performance is important to conveying the character or mood of a piece. The most common tempo indications (in Italian) are the following:

> Slower tempos: *grave, largo, larghetto, adagio*
>
> Medium tempos: *andantino, andante, moderato, allegretto*
>
> Faster tempos: *allegro, vivace, presto, prestissimo*
>
> Increasing in tempo (gradually faster): *accelerando* (abbreviated *accel.*)
>
> Decreasing in tempo (gradually slower): *ritardando* (abbreviated *rit.*)

With larger groups, such as a wind ensemble or choir, a conductor sets the tempo and helps keep the musicians playing to the same beat. Conductors outline specific patterns for each duple, triple, or quadruple meter, as shown in Figure 3.1. Conduct the duple pattern with the recording of "'S Wonderful!"; for "My Country," use the triple pattern. For a quadruple pattern, listen to Clarke's *Trumpet Voluntary*.

FIGURE 3.1   Conducting patterns

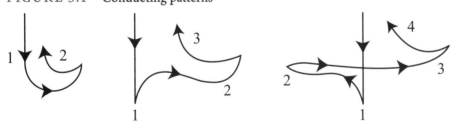

As you practice the **conducting patterns**, you may feel a physical weight on the **downbeat**—the downward motion of the hand on beat 1. You may also feel anticipation on the **upbeat**—the upward lift of the hand for the final beat of each pattern. The "weight" of the downbeat and the "lift" of the upbeat reflect the strong and weak beats of each measure.

> **KEY CONCEPT**   In duple meters, the first beat is **strong** and the second is **weak**, making an alternating pattern of strong-weak. In triple meters, the pattern is strong-weaker-weakest, and in quadruple meters, strong-weak-strong-weak, with the first beat stronger than the third. Strong beats in a meter are heard as **metrical accents**.

An **accent** adds weight, emphasis, or loudness to a musical element. Notated accents (>) instruct the performer to play with a sudden burst of loudness. Metrical accents are not necessarily louder; their emphasis comes from their metrical position on a strong beat.

In addition to showing the beat, a conductor's gestures and expressions may also convey the mood of the music, coordinate breaths, and indicate the volume, or **dynamic level**. As with tempo markings, dynamic markings are often in Italian, and are typically abbreviated.

	pp	*p*	*mp*	*mf*	*f*	*ff*
	pianissimo	*piano*	*mezzo piano*	*mezzo forte*	*forte*	*fortissimo*
dynamic level:	softest		medium			loudest

crescendo (grow louder) →   ← *diminuendo* (grow softer)

Rhythmic Notation

When listening to the music at the beginning of the chapter, you probably noticed that some pitches lasted longer and others were shorter. The patterns of longer and shorter durations in music are called the **rhythm**. Rhythm and meter are two different, but related, aspects of musical time. Meter defines beat groupings and divisions, while rhythm consists of durations of pitches and silences heard in relation to the underlying meter.

Look at Example 3.1, the beginning of "Amazing Grace." For now, focus on the labeled parts of the notation. The short vertical lines (**bar lines**) divide the staff into **measures**, or **bars**; numbers above the staff are measure numbers, to help you find a location in a piece.

EXAMPLE 3.1   Newton, "Amazing Grace," mm. 1–4a 🔊

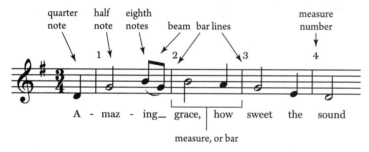

The example features three of the most common note values in music: **quarter**, **half**, and **eighth notes**. The half note lasts twice as long as the quarter; the quarter note lasts twice as long as the eighth. Eighth notes can be written two ways: **beamed** together as in the example, or with a **flag** attached to the right of the stem, as in Figure 3.2. Write flags on the right side of the stem, whether the stem goes up or down. If eighth notes are beamed together, take the stem direction of the second note, as in the first measure above. For more than two beamed notes, choose the stem direction based on the majority of the pitches; don't change direction within the beamed group.

FIGURE 3.2   Parts of a note

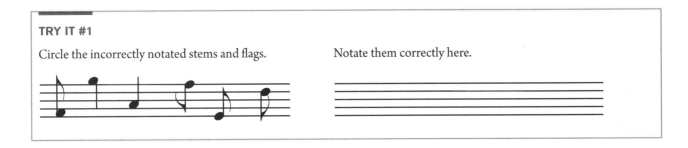
Now consider Example 3.2, the last few measures of the vocal melody from "Seasons of Love," to learn two additional note values.

EXAMPLE 3.2   Larson, "Seasons of Love," from *Rent*, mm. 59b–61 ◆ 2:37–2:52

The notes with two beams are **sixteenth notes**. They may be written with either two beams or two flags, and they last half as long as eighth notes. The last measure contains a **whole note**—a hollow note head with no stem. A whole note lasts four times as long as a quarter note and twice as long as a half note.

The chart in Figure 3.3 sums up the basic note durations in simple meter and how these notes relate to each other: a whole note divides into two half notes, a half note divides into two quarters, and so on. You can create even smaller note values by adding beams or flags to the stem; a thirty-second note, for example, has three flags or beams and a sixty-fourth note has four.

FIGURE 3.3   Chart of rhythmic durations

Meter Signatures

Listen to the melody of "Amazing Grace," shown in Example 3.3, and tap or conduct along with the music. The meter type is simple triple; this is indicated on the staff by the symbol $\frac{3}{4}$—called the **meter signature**. The 3 means that there are three beats in a measure, and the 4 indicates that the quarter note gets one beat—it is the **beat unit**. The quarter note before the first bar line is an **anacrusis** (or upbeat or **pickup**)—a weak beat that precedes the first strong one.

EXAMPLE 3.3   Newton, "Amazing Grace," mm. 1–4a 🔊

A - maz - ing— grace, how sweet the sound

> **KEY CONCEPT**   In simple meters: the top number of the meter signature is 2, 3, or 4 to show the number of beats in a measure (duple, triple, or quadruple); the lower number represents the type of note that gets one beat (2 = half note, 4 = quarter note, 8 = eighth note, 16 = sixteenth note). In sum, the meter signature shows "how many" (top number) of "what" (bottom number) constitutes a measure.

Examples 3.4 and 3.5 show simple duple and simple quadruple meters. In Example 3.4, a familiar melody ("Twinkle, Twinkle, Little Star") used by Mozart for a set of keyboard variations, both hands play the beat unit—the quarter note. In Example 3.5, the bottom staff clearly shows the quarter-note beats, while the upper parts have different rhythmic patterns within the $\frac{4}{4}$ meter. On the grand staff or on multiple staves, the meter signature appears on each staff.

EXAMPLE 3.4   Mozart, *Variations on "Ah, vous dirai-je Maman,"* mm. 1–8

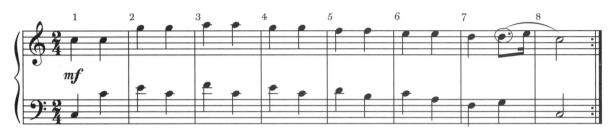

EXAMPLE 3.5   Clarke, *Trumpet Voluntary*, mm. 1–4

Both examples share another rhythmic device: a dot.

KEY CONCEPT   A **dot** beside a note adds to that note half of its own value.

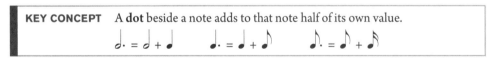

In Example 3.5, the dotted-quarter notes (circled) in the trumpet melody last a beat and a half; the dotted-half notes in the organ last three beats. In Example 3.4, the dotted-eighth in measure 7 lasts three-quarters of a beat.

You will often see meter signatures that consist of symbols other than numerals. For example, the symbol ℂ, called "common time," is sometimes written instead of $\frac{4}{4}$, as in Example 3.6.

EXAMPLE 3.6   Willson, "'Till There Was You," mm. 1–4a

The quarter note is the most common beat unit, but it's not the only possibility. For example, "The Stars and Stripes Forever," shown in Example 3.7, is a march in a quick tempo with half notes felt as the beat unit and pairs of quarter notes as the beat division (see m. 3). The meter signature could be written as $\frac{2}{2}$—two beats to the measure, with a half note receiving the beat—but more often we find $\frac{2}{2}$ written as ¢, called *alla breve* or "cut time."

EXAMPLE 3.7   Sousa, "The Stars and Stripes Forever," mm. 1–4a

There are various reasons why composers choose a particular beat unit. Sometimes it's to remind the performer of a particular compositional type—such as *alla breve* for marches. A piece may be notated with a longer beat unit for ease of reading, to avoid notating quick-moving rhythms with sixteenth or thirty-second notes. The meter may also suggest a tempo: an eighth-note beat unit might indicate a faster tempo and a lively motion.

SUMMARY

Meter signatures you are likely to see in simple meters include the following.

Simple duple:	$\frac{2}{2}$	¢	$\frac{2}{4}$
Simple triple:	$\frac{3}{2}$	$\frac{3}{4}$	$\frac{3}{8}$
Simple quadruple:	$\frac{4}{2}$	$\frac{4}{4}$	c	$\frac{4}{8}$

Counting Rhythms in Simple Meters

To count rhythms in a simple-meter piece, you first need to look at the meter signature and identify the beat unit and beat division. For example, if the beat unit is a quarter note, the beat division is two eighths; if the beat unit is a half note, the beat division is two quarters. Figure 3.4 shows how to interpret various simple meter signatures; the first three are the most common.

FIGURE 3.4   Beat and division in simple meters

Meter signature	Beats per measure	Beat unit	Beat division
$\frac{2}{4}$	2	♩	♫
$\frac{3}{4}$	3	♩	♫
$\frac{4}{4}$	4	♩	♫
$\frac{3}{2}$	3	♩ (half)	♩ ♩
$\frac{3}{8}$	3	♪	♫
$\frac{4}{8}$	4	♪	♫

The **quarter rest** (𝄽) lasts as long as a quarter note, and the **eighth rest** (𝄾) lasts as long as an eighth note. These symbols in the example tell the instrumentalists how long to count before beginning to play. Counts are shown below the temple-block part.

Figure 3.5 shows each type of rest with its corresponding note value in simple meter. A **whole rest** may represent four quarter-note beats or two half-note beats; it can also last a whole measure, regardless of how many beats are in that measure. Whole rests are usually centered between the bar lines, but smaller rests are positioned to reflect where the beats occur, as shown in Example 3.10. To write shorter rests, like the thirty-second (𝄿), just add additional flags to the sixteenth. Like other rhythmic values, rests may be dotted.

FIGURE 3.5   Note values and rests

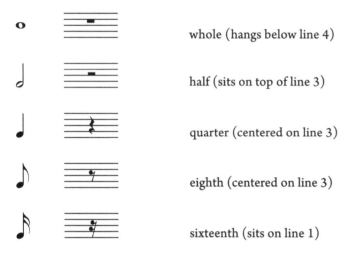

whole (hangs below line 4)

half (sits on top of line 3)

quarter (centered on line 3)

eighth (centered on line 3)

sixteenth (sits on line 1)

ASSIGNMENT 3.2, 3.3

Counts for rests are written in parentheses to show that these durations don't actually sound. Listen to Example 3.11 and practice counting the rhythms along with the bass line. We will consider the rhythms of the upper lines in Chapter 4.

EXAMPLE 3.11   Phillips, "Blues for Norton," mm. 1–4 (piano and bass) 🔊

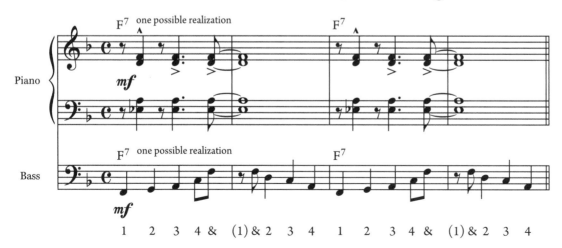

TRY IT #5

Write the counts for each rhythm. Then rewrite in the meter indicated.

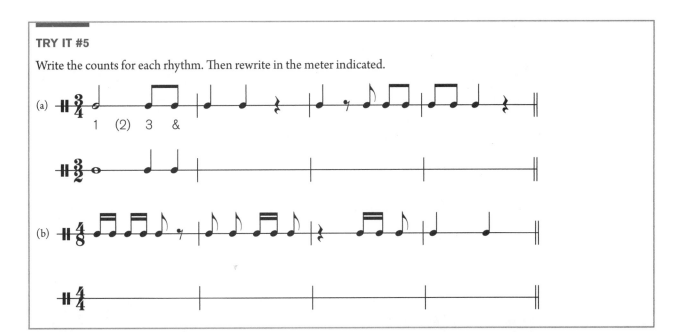

(a) $\frac{3}{4}$ 1   (2)   3   &

$\frac{3}{2}$

(b) $\frac{4}{8}$

$\frac{4}{4}$

AURAL SKILLS 3.1

Did You Know?

Much of the time when we think about music, we focus more on the sounds and don't pay much attention to the silences. Twentieth-century composer John Cage (1912–1992) forced us to do just the opposite when he composed his famous *4′33″* (1952)—a three-movement work where each movement has a duration selected by the performer, but is marked "Tacet" (a term usually telling certain instrumentalists not to play in one movement of a multimovement work). The title, *4′33″*, refers to the duration of the whole piece. The performers indicate the start and end of each movement in some way—by lifting their instruments up and down or by opening and closing the piano keyboard cover—but make no sounds. The piece is not completely silent, however; normally people in the audience make some sound by moving, coughing, shuffling program pages, etc. Through this work and his writings, including *Silence* (1961), Cage inspired musicians and listeners to think about what happens between the sounds—in the silences.

Terms You Should Know

accent	flag	eighth
anacrusis	measure	sixteenth
bar	meter	pickup
bar line	simple	rest
beam	duple	whole
beat	triple	half
strong	quadruple	quarter
weak	meter signature	eighth
beat division	metrical accent	sixteenth
beat unit	note	rhythm
conducting patterns	whole	rhythm clef
dot	half	tempo
downbeat	quarter	upbeat
dynamic level		

Questions for Review

1. How do you decide if a piece is in duple, triple, or quadruple meter?
2. How do you decide which conducting pattern to use?
3. Where do the stronger metrical accents fall in simple triple meter? in simple duple meter? in simple quadruple meter?
4. Explain the difference between rhythm and meter.
5. Draw the parts of an eighth note. Draw one above the middle staff line and another below it.
6. On which side of a note are stems drawn? On which side of the stem are flags drawn?
7. What are the most common simple meter signatures?
8. What do the upper and lower parts of a meter signature represent in simple meters?
9. Which numbers may appear in the upper and lower positions of the meter signature in simple meters?
10. What is the beat unit in 𝄴? in 𝄵?

Reading Review

Match the terms on the left with the best answer on the right.

_____ (1) meter	(a) meter type with beats that divide into two
_____ (2) quarter note	(b) equal in duration to two quarter rests
_____ (3) beat unit	(c) the type of note that gets one beat
_____ (4) rhythm	(d) filled note with two flags or beams
_____ (5) whole note	(e) the sequence of pitches and silences in music
_____ (6) 𝄴	(f) indicates how loud or soft the music should be
_____ (7) simple meter	(g) term that includes both beat division and grouping
_____ (8) duple meter	(h) examples are $\frac{3}{2}$, $\frac{3}{4}$, and $\frac{3}{8}$
_____ (9) dot	(i) filled note with a stem
_____ (10) meter signature	(j) counted the same as $\frac{4}{4}$
_____ (11) triple meter	(k) examples are $\frac{2}{2}$ and $\frac{2}{4}$
_____ (12) $\frac{3}{4}$	(l) the speed of the beats
_____ (13) sixteenth note	(m) notation symbol that shows the beat unit and the number of beats in a bar
_____ (14) dynamic marking	(n) has three quarter-note beats per measure
_____ (15) rhythm clef	(o) *alla breve*, or cut time
_____ (16) anacrusis	(p) upbeat
_____ (17) 𝄵	(q) adds to a note or rest half its value
_____ (18) half rest	(r) used to notate unpitched percussion parts
_____ (19) tempo	(s) duration equal to two half notes

Ⓖ Additional review and practice available at wwnorton.com/studyspace

Class Activities

A. Listening for meter

Listen to the beginning of each of the following pieces. Focus on the grouping of the beats to decide whether the meter is simple duple, triple, or quadruple. Conduct along as you listen.

Henley, Frey, and Meisner, "Take It to the Limit"   (1) _____

"Michael Finnigin"   (2) _____

Horner, Mann, and Weil, "Somewhere Out There"   (3) _____

Larson, "Seasons of Love"   (4) _____

Mozart, String Quartet in D Minor, K. 421, third movement   (5) _____

B. Reading rhythms

Perform the following rhythms as musically as possible, following dynamic markings. As you perform, tap or conduct the beats. Speak with rhythm syllables or counts (if instructed to do so) or a neutral syllable such as "ta," and give a slight emphasis to each downbeat.

Rhythm 1

Rhythm 2

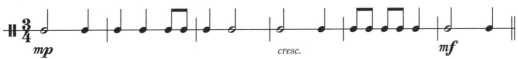

Rhythm 3

Rhythm 4

Rhythm 5

Rhythm 6

Rhythm 7

C. Composing a simple-meter rhythm

Your teacher will ask teams of three or four students to compose an eight-measure rhythmic duet that features only the rhythmic patterns below. Each person notates one measure, then passes the marker (or chalk) to the next person. Repeat until the composition is complete. Add dynamic and tempo markings. Perform and critique these compositions in class.

Write in simple quadruple, simple triple, or simple duple meter. For simple triple, add one ♩ to any pattern.

Patterns

D. Singing at sight

- First review the vocal warm-ups in the Chapter 1 Class Activities.
- Study the rhythm in each of the following melodies. Perform it on "ta," or on rhythm syllables, while tapping a steady beat (or conducting). Begin with a slow tempo; repeat at a faster tempo.
- Once you are confident with the rhythm, play the first note on the piano or another instrument, and begin learning the pitches, singing on the numbers or syllables marked. Practice without rhythm; play the pitches at a keyboard or sing

together in class. Then sing the entire melody, checking the pitches at the keyboard *after* you sing. Finally put pitches and rhythm together at a slow tempo; repeat at a faster tempo.

Melody 1

Melody 2

Melody 3 Mozart, *Variations on "Lison dormait,"* mm. 1–8 (adapted)

E. Listening and writing

1. Your teacher will display a chart of four different rhythmic patterns like those numbered below. As soon as the teacher points to a pattern, tap or speak its syllables until he or she points to another. Later, your teacher will perform the same patterns without the visual display: identify them by ear and notate them on the following staves.

Patterns

2. Error detection in simple meters

In the rhythms below, the quarter note lasts one beat. Identify one measure in each example that has an **incorrect** number of beats for the meter specified. Circle the incorrect measure.

a. simple triple

b. simple duple

c. simple quadruple

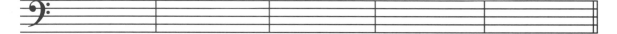

d. simple triple

e. simple quadruple

3. Notating quarter, half, and eighth notes with correct stem direction

Write the notes requested below, placing them on a variety of lines and spaces. Choose notes so that roughly half require stems up and half stems down. Be sure that your stem direction, flags, and beaming follow correct notation guidelines.

a. In each measure, write two beamed eighth notes and a quarter note.

b. In each measure, write a quarter note, then two eighth notes with flags.

c. In each measure, write a half note, then two quarter notes.

d. In each measure, write a quarter note, two beamed eighth notes, four beamed sixteenth notes, and a quarter note.

Workbook ASSIGNMENT 3.2

1. Reading meters with quarter-note beats

a. For each rhythm below, write the appropriate meter signature at the beginning of the line. Assume a quarter-note beat unit.

(1) 🔊 **3/4**

(2) 🔊

(3) 🔊

(4) 🔊

b. At each position marked by an arrow, add one note to complete the measure in the meter indicated.

(1) **4/4**

(2) **3/4**

(3) **2/4**

(4) **4/4**

c. For each rhythm below, provide the missing bar lines that correspond with the meter signature given.

(1) 🔊 **2/4**

(2) 🔊 **3/4**

(3) 🔊 **4/4**

(4) 🔊 **3/4**

(5) 🔊 **4/4**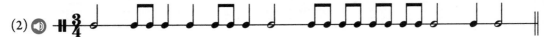

2. Understanding dots

Finish the chart below to show the equivalent durations.

𝅗𝅥·	=	𝅗𝅥	+	♩
♩·	=	♩	+	
	=	♪	+	♬
𝅝·	=	𝅝	+	
𝅗𝅥·	=		+	♩
♩·	=		+	♪

3. Writing rests

a. On the staff below, write four whole rests and four half rests.

Whole: Half:

b. On the staff below, write four quarter rests and four eighth rests.

Quarter: Eighth:

c. Following each note, write a corresponding rest of the same duration.

Workbook ASSIGNMENT 3.3

1. Counting rhythms with quarter-note beats and rests

Write the counts (1 & 2 &) beneath each rhythm and melody below. Put the counts that occur during sustained notes or rests in parentheses.

a.

1 (2) 3   1 & 2 & 3

b.

c.

d. Elvis Presley, "Love Me Tender," mm. 5–8

Love me ten - der, love me sweet, nev - er let me go.

e. Lionel Richie, "Three Times a Lady," mm. 11–14

Now that we've come to the end of our rain - bow

f. Bono and U2, "Miracle Drug," mm. 29–32a (the last measure is incomplete)

Free - dom has a scent like the top of a new - born ba - by's head.

2. Counting rhythms with half- and eighth-note beats

a. For each rhythm, provide the missing bar lines that correspond with the meter signature given. Then add the counts below.

(1)

1 (2) 3   4

(2)

(3)

(4)

(5)

b. Rewrite each of the following rhythms on the line below it, in the new meter specified. The resulting rhythm should sound the same as the original. Add the proper counts beneath the rhythm you have written.

(1)

(2)

(3)

(4)

Workbook AURAL SKILLS 3.1

1. Hearing simple meters

Listen to the beginning of each of the following pieces. Focus on the grouping of the beats to decide whether the meter is simple duple, triple, or quadruple. Try conducting along as you listen. Write the meter type in the blank.

🔊 Bach, "O Haupt voll Blut und Wunden" (a) _____

🔊 Joplin, "Solace" (b) _____

🔊 Schubert, Waltz in B minor (c) _____

🔊 Beethoven, *Pathétique* Sonata, second movement (d) _____

2. Listening to and writing a simple meter rhythm

Listen to an excerpt from a song from a musical by American composer Lionel Bart, and complete the following exercises. 🔊

a. Focus on the rhythm of this melody.

(1) Tap the beat with your foot. Then sing the melody from memory on "la." Keep a steady tempo, even if it is slower than the recording.

(2) Tap the beat with your foot and its divisions with your left hand. Then sing the melody from memory while tapping.

(3) Conduct the beats. When comfortable conducting, sing the melody from memory. As you sing, imagine the beat divisions to keep your rhythm precise.

b. On the staff below, choose one line or space and notate only the rhythm, with the correct note values.

c. On the staff below, notate the rhythm again, this time in a different simple quadruple meter, with an eighth-note beat unit.

3. Writing a rhythmic composition

Write a four-measure rhythmic duet in which the top part speaks the word "yes" and the bottom part says "no." Use the sample composition below as a model. Write durations and rests so that the two words always begin on a different beat or part of the beat, never together. Be ready to perform with a partner, or have the entire class read your composition as a musical argument. In performance, slowly *crescendo* to the final measure.

Sample 🔊

Space to work out your ideas

Final composition

TOPICS
- beat subdivisions
- ties and slurs
- syncopation
- triplets
- rhythmic variations in performance

MUSIC
- Ludwig van Beethoven, Piano Sonata in C Minor, Op. 13 (*Pathétique*), second movement
- Don Henley, Glenn Frey, and Randy Meisner, "Take It to the Limit"
- James Horner, Barry Mann, and Cynthia Weil, "Somewhere Out There," from *An American Tail*
- Scott Joplin, "Pine Apple Rag"
- Joplin, "Solace"
- Don McLean, "American Pie"
- John Newton, "Amazing Grace"
- Richard Rodgers, "My Funny Valentine," from *Babes in Arms*
- Franz Schubert, Waltz in B minor, Op. 18, No. 6

CHAPTER 4

Beat Subdivisions and Syncopation

Beat Subdivisions

Listen to the lyrical opening of the second movement of Beethoven's *Pathétique* Sonata, following the score in Example 4.1. The right-hand melody (in the treble clef) and the bass line (lowest part in the bass clef), which move primarily in quarter and eighth notes, show the beat and beat divisions of this simple duple meter. The sixteenth notes between those parts represent the **beat subdivision**— counted 1 e & a, as labeled in the example.

EXAMPLE 4.1   Beethoven, *Pathétique* Sonata, second movement, mm. 1–4a 🔊

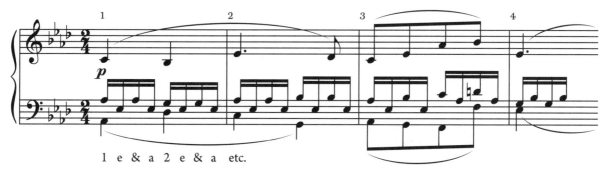

> **KEY CONCEPT**   In simple meters, the beat divides into twos and subdivides into fours. A ♩ beat, for example, divides into ♫ and subdivides into 𝅘𝅥𝅰𝅘𝅥𝅰𝅘𝅥𝅰𝅘𝅥𝅰 (or a combination, such as ♪𝅘𝅥𝅰𝅘𝅥𝅰♪).

There are only seven basic rhythmic patterns made from divisions and subdivisions of a quarter-note beat; all are shown in Figure 4.1 with the counts written underneath. These patterns can be combined and recombined in many ways to create interesting and varied rhythms. Patterns 6 and 7 include dotted-eighth notes: since these last as long as three sixteenth notes, they are paired with a sixteenth note to complete the beat. A rest may be substituted for any duration in the following patterns; some examples are given in Figure 4.2.

FIGURE 4.1   Rhythmic patterns for one quarter-note beat

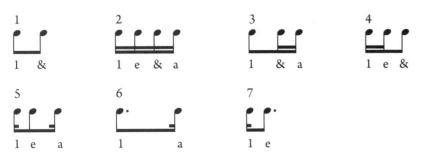

FIGURE 4.2   Quarter-note beat patterns with rests

Listen to the beginning of "Solace" while following the music in Example 4.2. Three of the seven patterns from Figure 4.1 appear in these measures. Locate the patterns, and write the counts underneath each one. In the last measure, which does not feature any of the seven patterns, the counts are written in for you.

EXAMPLE 4.2   Joplin, "Solace," mm. 1–4

Example 4.3 shows incorrect beaming, and illustrates how correcting the notation clarifies the beat units.

EXAMPLE 4.3   Beaming to reflect the quarter-note and half-note beat unit

(a) Incorrect

(b) Correct

1   2   3   &   4 e & a   1 e &   2   &   3 e & a   4

(a) Incorrect

(b) Correct

1   (2)   &   3   &   1 e & a 2   3   &   1   & a 2 e & a 3

Ties and Slurs

Another passage from "Solace," shown in Example 4.4, illustrates an element of rhythmic notation we have not yet considered: the **tie**. Ties are small arcs connecting the note heads of two *identical* pitches, which may have the same or different durations. A tie makes the first note sound as long as the two notes' durations added together; the second note is not played separately. In the right-hand part of measure 5, Joplin ties the final sixteenth note G4 of beat 1 to the first G4 of beat 2; similar ties are found in measures 6 and 7. When ties extend across a beat, as here, write the "silent" count in parentheses to remember where the beat comes, even if no new note sounds on it. Do the same for dots that extend across a beat, as in measure 3 of Example 4.5.

EXAMPLE 4.4   Joplin, "Solace," mm. 5–8a

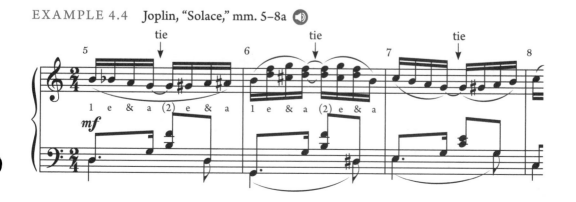

EXAMPLE 4.5   Schubert, Waltz in B Minor, mm. 1–4

Every measure of Example 4.5 also includes arcs that connect two or more *different* pitches. These lines are called **slurs**. They affect **articulation** by showing how to bow a stringed instrument or tongue a wind or brass instrument, for example, but they don't change the duration of the pitches. In piano music, they tell the performer to play the slurred notes smoothly (or legato); in vocal music, the slurred notes are sung on one syllable or in one breath.

TRY IT #1

Beneath each rhythm, write the appropriate counts (with dotted and tied counts in parentheses).

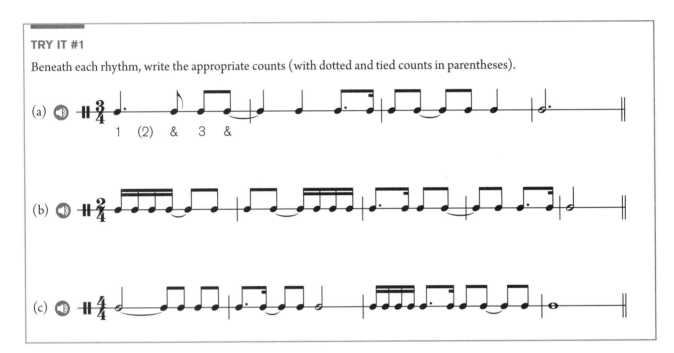

(a)

1 (2) & 3 &

(b)

(c)

ASSIGNMENT 4.1

Syncopation

Look at Example 4.6, in cut time (¢), and tap the rhythm, using the counts underneath (think 1 e & a, 2 e & a). This rhythm, one of the *clave* patterns from Afro-Cuban music, has been incorporated into many other popular styles. After the first note, all the notes are off the beat until the last one, which falls on beat 2.

EXAMPLE 4.6   *Clave* pattern

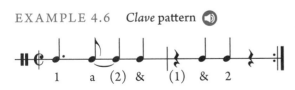

1   a (2) &   (1) & 2

Syncopations are created when an expected accent is displaced—moved to another beat or part of a beat by dots, ties, rests, dynamic markings, or accent marks. We've already seen two syncopated rhythm patterns (5 and 7) in Figure 4.1 (both reproduced in Figure 4.3). In each, the longest duration of the rhythm is on the "e" of 1 e & a instead of the stronger (expected) 1 or &. Other types of syncopation are shown by the arrows in Example 4.7.

FIGURE 4.3   Syncopated patterns within a quarter-note beat 🔊

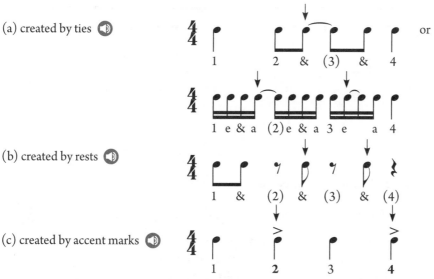

EXAMPLE 4.7   Types of syncopated rhythms

(a) created by ties 🔊

(b) created by rests 🔊

(c) created by accent marks 🔊

In Example 4.8, the arrows mark syncopations within the beat in measures 1 and 3 and across the beat in measures 2 and 4. Syncopations across the beat are usually notated with ties, like those in measures 2 and 4; here, the expected accent on beat 2 comes earlier, on the first of the tied notes.

EXAMPLE 4.8   Joplin, "Pine Apple Rag," mm. 1–4 🔊

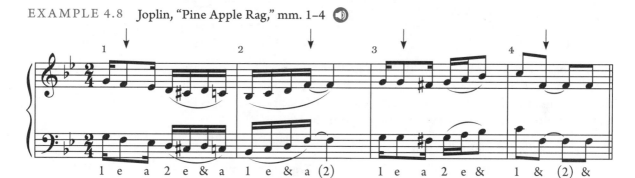

In Example 4.9, from "American Pie," the syncopations span two beats in $\frac{4}{4}$ meter. The ♪♩♪ rhythm, counted "1 & (2) &" in measure 31, is a rhythmic augmentation (with durations lasting twice as long) of the ♫♪ pattern, counted "1 e a," in measure 1 of the Joplin rag. The last syncopation in measure 31 is created by the entrance of the word "love" on the offbeat.

EXAMPLE 4.9   McLean, "American Pie," mm. 30–31a 🔊

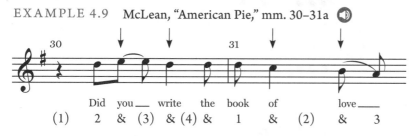

Syncopations require a strong sense of the underlying beat for the displaced accents to play against. When you read music with syncopations, look first for the common patterns, and use the counting syllables to count any unfamiliar ones. When performing, tap the steady beat to feel the metrical displacement of the syncopation.

TRY IT #2

The rhythm below is drawn from measures 9–12 of Joplin's "Solace." Write the counts beneath, and mark each syncopation with an arrow. All arrows should line up with "e" or "a" of the 1 e & a pattern. Perform the rhythm aloud. 🔊

1 e & a

Triplets

In simple meters, it is possible to divide a beat into three parts instead of the usual two.

> **KEY CONCEPT**   A **triplet** is a three-part division of the beat in a simple-meter piece.

Example 4.10 shows a passage from "Take It to the Limit." The piece is in $\frac{3}{4}$ meter, but in measure 54, three eighths are beamed together with a small 3 above the beam. This indicates that three eighth notes make up the beat instead of two. We count the triplet "1 la li" to emphasize the even division into three parts, and to avoid confusing it with the counts for division in two or four parts.

EXAMPLE 4.10   Henley, Frey, and Meisner, "Take It to the Limit," mm. 51–54 🔊

1 la (2) 3 &   1 la (2 3)   1 la (2) 3 &   1 la (2) 3 la li

In measures 51–53, there are other triplets consisting of an eighth and a quarter ($\overset{3}{\sqcap}$). The quarter substitutes for two eighths and is counted "1 la." The reverse ($\overset{3}{\sqcap}$) is counted "1 li." While triplet divisions are most common at the beat unit, it's possible to divide two beats or entire measures into three parts as well. Figure 4.4 summarizes the possibilities.

FIGURE 4.4   Notation of triplet divisions

Duration	Normal division	Triplet notation		
♪	(two sixteenths)	(triplet sixteenths)	(triplet)	(triplet)
♩	(two eighths)	(triplet eighths)	(eighth-quarter)	(quarter-eighth)
♩ (half)	(two quarters)	(triplet quarters)	(quarter-half)	(half-quarter)
𝅝	(two halves)	(triplet halves)	(half-whole)	(whole-half)
1	1 &	1 la li	1 li	1 la

Rhythmic Variations in Performance

Blues, gospel, jazz, Broadway show tunes, and many other forms of popular music gain much of their character through their distinctive rhythm. A jazz improviser, for example, might take a simple but memorable melody and "jazz it up" by adding embellishments in rhythm and pitch. "My Funny Valentine" (p. 392 in your anthology) has been treated in a variety of ways by performers ranging from Miles Davis to Barbra Streisand to the Grateful Dead. The rhythms are uncomplicated, and the melody includes mostly half and whole steps. This simplicity makes the song an excellent framework for rhythmic and melodic variation. If you like, download a few different versions (some are suggested on StudySpace) to compare.

Gospel performance may also feature improvisation, and the pitches and rhythms you see on the score may differ substantially from what you hear. Listen to two versions of "Amazing Grace," while following the melody in your anthology (p. 382). In one performance, a verse sung by unaccompanied voice is followed by two verses with guitar. This arrangement is folk-like in its simplicity, and the singer (a soprano) performs the melody as shown in the score. In contrast, the other performance, by a lower, contralto voice and piano, is highly embellished. The singer freely improvises on the tune with additional pitches, variations in the rhythm, and repeated text to create a performance that is uniquely her own, while the pianist improvises an accompaniment to match.

In another common rhythmic variation, known as "**swung eighths**," the score shows pairs of eighth notes in a simple meter, but the performer plays or sings them unevenly, holding on to the first eighth a little too long and bringing in the second one after the &—as if they were notated as triplets: (♪♪). Compare the Eagles' recording of "Take It to the Limit" with the recording of Example 4.10. In the version by the Eagles, the eighth notes on the last beat of measures 51 and 53 are swung.

In popular music styles, where the score is sometimes a **transcription** (notated from a recorded performance), you find many more syncopations than in classical music. Sometimes syncopated melodies may imply a simpler underlying tune. Compare, for example, two versions of a passage from "Somewhere Out There," shown in Example 4.11. The first (a) is the melody as it appears in published form (anthology, p. 364); the second (b) is a plainer version. Listen to (b), then compare it with (a) to hear how much livelier the melody is with the syncopations and embellishments as published. In performance, the singer may add even more variants.

EXAMPLE 4.11   Horner, Mann, and Weil, "Somewhere Out There," mm. 17–24a

(a) Original

(b) Simple version

Some - where   out   there   some - one's say-ing a   prayer   that

we'll   find   one a - noth - er   in that big some - where out   there.

TRY IT #3

Circle each syncopation in Example 4.11a that is created by tying a note to the beginning of a beat, by placing a rest at the beginning of a beat, or by accenting a weak part of the beat. Such strategies are effective ways of creating a syncopated melody from a simpler one.

When you compose songs of your own, you might first create a simple melodic line with a basic rhythm, and then vary it—for example, delay a pitch or pull it ahead of the beat to make syncopations, or use triplets. When you analyze rhythmically elaborate music, be alert for the underlying simpler framework, and consider how the composer took something basic and made it memorable.

AURAL SKILLS 4.1

Did You Know?

The Beethoven sonata movement in this chapter is marked *Adagio cantabile* ("Slow, with a songlike character"). By the late eighteenth century, it had become customary to add a tempo marking ("moderately fast") or an expression marking ("lively") to designate the tempo and character of the music. With the invention of the **metronome**—a mechanical device that produces evenly spaced clicks at different speeds—composers began to indicate the tempo precisely in beats per minute (for example, "♩ = 120" means 120 quarter notes per minute). Beethoven was one of the first prominent composers to use the metronome and to promote its use by adding metronome settings to many of his pieces. Unfortunately, early metronomes were not as precise as modern ones; as a result, we don't know for certain the tempi that Beethoven intended from his markings. In this century, many editions include metronome markings to assist performers in choosing a tempo.

Terms You Should Know

articulation	slur	tie
beat subdivision	swung eighths	transcription
metronome	syncopation	triplet

Questions for Review

1. What is the difference between a beat division and a beat subdivision?
2. Write seven rhythmic patterns that fill one quarter-note beat unit in simple meter.
3. If the beat unit is a half note, what note values represent the beat division and subdivision?
4. In simple meter, what note value is generally paired with a dotted quarter to fill out the beat? What note value is generally paired with a dotted eighth?
5. What guidelines are used to determine which notes to beam together?
6. What types of rhythmic patterns make syncopations?
7. How is a tie different from a slur?
8. How do you represent a three-part division of a beat in simple meters?
9. What note values represent a triplet division of a quarter-note beat unit? of a half-note beat unit?

Reading Review

Match the terms on the left with the best answer on the right.

_____ (1) four sixteenth notes	(a) arc connecting the note heads of two identical pitches; means to hold for their combined duration
_____ (2) tie	(b) arc connecting two or more different pitches
_____ (3) slur	(c) subdivision of a quarter-note beat
_____ (4) 1 e & a	(d) counting syllables for a common syncopation pattern
_____ (5) syncopation	(e) division of a quarter-note beat
_____ (6) two eighth notes	(f) counting syllables for a subdivided beat
_____ (7) triplet	(g) counting syllables for a triplet
_____ (8) 1 e a	(h) rhythmic displacement of accents
_____ (9) 1 la li	(i) beat division into three parts in simple meter

Ⓢ Additional review and practice available at wwnorton.com/studyspace

Class Activities

A. Reading rhythms

Perform the rhythms below on "ta" or counting syllables, as directed. Keep a steady beat by tapping the pulse or conducting, and follow the dynamic markings. Your teacher may ask you to write the counts below the rhythms.

Rhythm 1

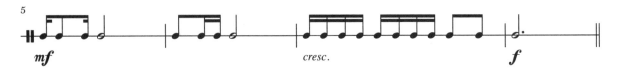

Rhythm 2

Rhythm 3

Rhythm 4

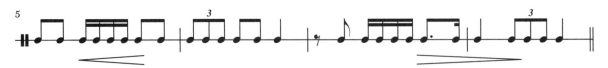

B. Rhythmic duets

Perform the rhythms below in two groups or with two different sounds (men vs. women, taps vs. claps, no vs. yes, etc.) so that the interplay between lines can be heard. Observe all dynamic markings.

Duet 1

Duet 2

C. At the keyboard: Playing and singing melodies with triplets

For each melody:

- Practice the warm-up on the piano with your right hand. Begin with the thumb on the first note and use each finger. Play 1–2–3–4–5 ascending and descending, and sing along on "la."
- Practice just the rhythm of the melody on "ta" while tapping the beat (or conducting). Then practice just the pitches on the keyboard (don't worry about fingering for now).
- Play the rhythm and pitches together at a slow tempo, then a faster tempo. Sing the melody on the numbers given underneath at a slow tempo, then a faster tempo. (We'll learn what the numbers represent in Chapter 6.)

Warm-up

Melody 1

Warm-up

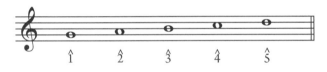

Melody 2

Warm-up 🔊

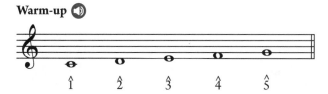

Melody 3 Alan Jay Lerner and Frederick Loewe, "Wand'rin' Star," from *Paint Your Wagon* (adapted), mm. 1–8

Warm-up 🔊

Melody 4 Clara Edwards, "Into the Night," mm. 3–6a

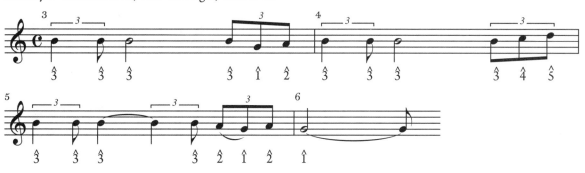

Warm-up 🔊

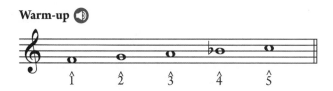

Melody 5 George David Weiss, Hugo Peretti, and Luigi Creatore, "Can't Help Falling in Love," from *Blue Hawaii*, mm. 5–12

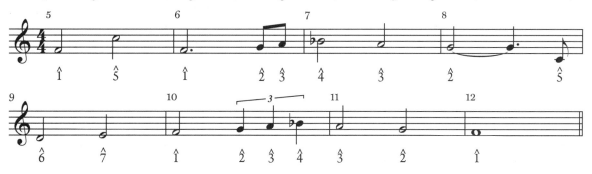

D. Listening and writing

1. Your teacher will display simple-meter rhythm patterns like those below. As soon as the teacher points to a pattern, play, sing, or tap it until he or she points to another. Later, your teacher will hide the patterns and perform them. This time, identify the rhythm pattern(s) by ear, and notate your answers on your own staff paper or in the space below. Either write with a counting system as specified by your teacher; notate the pattern(s); or write the pattern number(s).

2. Make your own point-and-sing exercises with the chart above. *Solo*: Point to an item, then sing it. *Duet*: Point to the chart while a partner sings, then switch roles.

3. Your teacher will combine rhythmic patterns with pitches in the octave from C to C. Identify the patterns by ear; notate the pitches and rhythmic patterns together on your own staff paper or in the space below.

Workbook ASSIGNMENT 4.1

1. Dots and ties

a. For each rhythm below, provide the missing bar lines that correspond with the meter signature given.

b. Rewrite the following rhythms with dots in place of tied notes. Be careful to beam your answers correctly. Write the correct counts beneath the rewritten rhythm, then perform it.

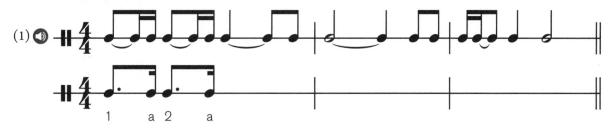

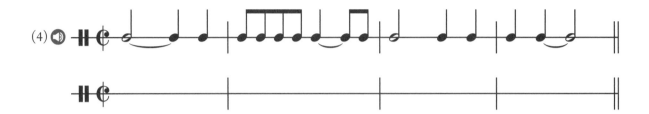

2. Beaming

Rewrite each of the following rhythms with correct beams to reflect the quarter-note beat unit. Add the proper counts beneath the rhythm, and read the rhythm out loud on "ta" or with counting syllables.

1 & a 2 e &

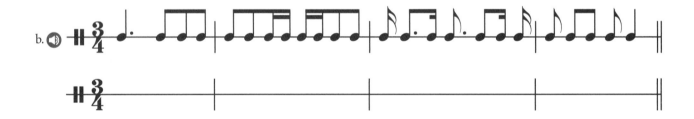

Workbook   ASSIGNMENT 4.2

1. Rhythms with divisions, subdivisions, dots, and rests

a. For each rhythm below, provide the missing bar lines that correspond with the meter signature given.

b. At each arrow, add one note to complete the measure in the meter indicated. For now, don't worry about beaming guidelines.

2. Counting rhythms with dots, ties, and syncopations

In the melodies below, write the appropriate counts beneath the notes. (Note: The final measure of a melody may be incomplete.) Place an arrow above each syncopation.

a. Joplin, "Solace," mm. 9–10

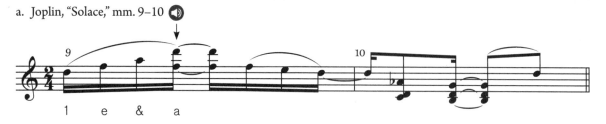

1   e   &   a

b. Carole King, "You've Got a Friend," mm. 4b–8a

When you're down . . .

c. Larson, "Seasons of Love," mm. 40b–44a 1:47–1:59

In   truth   that   she   learned . . .

d. Horner, Mann, and Weil, "Somewhere Out There," mm. 26b–28a

it   helps   to   think ___   we   might ___   be   wish - in'   on   the   same ___   bright   star.

Workbook   ASSIGNMENT 4.3

1. Syncopation

In each of the following examples, write an arrow above each syncopated rhythm. Then write in the appropriate counts below each rhythm.

a. Joplin, "Solace," mm. 29–33 🔊

1 e a 2 e & a

b. Joplin, "Solace," mm. 53–56 🔊

c. John Philip Sousa, "The Stars and Stripes Forever," mm. 1–4 🔊

d. Larson, "Seasons of Love," mm. 1–4 🔽 0:00–0:11

2. Triplets

a. For each of the following rhythms, supply the missing bar lines corresponding to the meter shown.

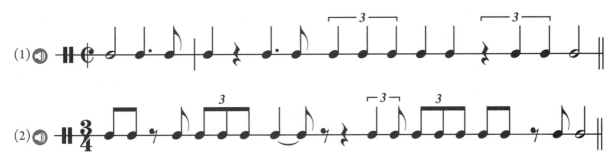

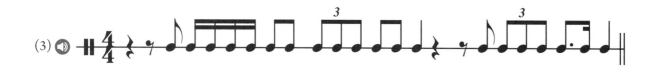

(3)

b. At each arrow, add one note to complete any measure with too few beats. Write the counts beneath your answer, then perform the rhythm you have written.

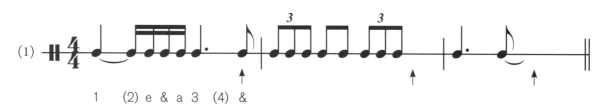

1   (2) e & a 3 (4) &

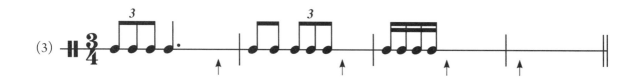

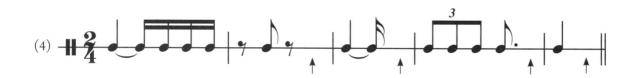

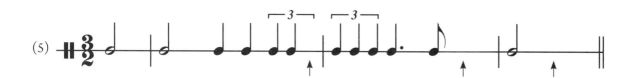

3. Composition with dots, ties, and syncopations

Write a four-measure rhythm in $\frac{4}{4}$ that contains two syncopations (one using a tie), two dotted rhythms, and two rests.

Workbook   AURAL SKILLS 4.1

1. Listening to and writing a melody with beat divisions

Listen to an excerpt from a piano sonata by Joseph Haydn, and complete the exercises below.

a. Focus on the rhythm of the higher part.

(1) Tap the beat with your foot. Then sing the melody on a neutral syllable, such as "la." Keep a steady tempo, even if it is slower than the recorded performance.

(2) Tap the beat with your foot and its divisions with your left hand. Sing the melody from memory on a neutral syllable as you tap.

(3) Conduct the beats in duple meter. When comfortable conducting, sing the melody from memory. As you sing, imagine the beat divisions and subdivisions to keep your rhythm precise. Now conduct the beats in quadruple meter and sing as before.

b. Notate the rhythm in quadruple meter.

(1) On *each* staff below, draw a meter signature for common time.

(2) On the treble staff, write a quarter-note anacrusis, then notate the rest of the melody's rhythm on any line or space. For divided or subdivided beats, beam notes to reflect the beat.

(3) After the anacrusis, and then after every four beats, draw a bar line. On a grand staff, bar lines extend from the top line of the treble staff to the bottom line of the bass staff.

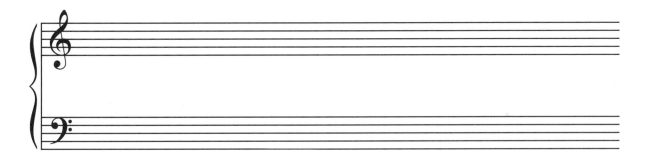

c. Now listen to the excerpt again, focusing on the rhythm of the lower part. On the bass staff, notate the rhythm of the lower part on any line or space. Vertically align notes in the bass and melody that sound at the same time. The bar lines will also help you to align the two parts.

d. Read your rhythmic notation. Tap the rhythm of the melody in one hand and the rhythm of the lower part in the other. Does your performance sound like the rhythm of the recording? Listen again to correct any errors.

e. If you had notated the rhythm in $\frac{2}{4}$ instead of in common time (𝄴), how would your answers to b and c be different?

2. Writing a rhythmic composition with beat subdivisions

Compose a rhythmic duet for two performers, using only the rhythmic patterns listed below.

- Write eight measures, in either $\frac{3}{4}$ or $\frac{4}{4}$ meter.
- Use no ties.
- Include eighth, quarter, and half rests only.
- Vary the complexity: both voices should sound together at times. At other times, when one voice is rhythmically active, the other voice may have rests or longer notes.
- Include dynamic markings to add musical interest.
- If you like, write a text to be recited with your rhythm.

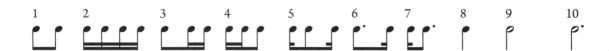

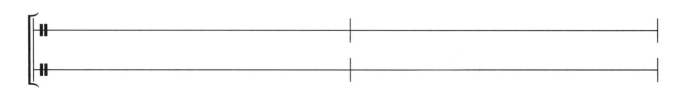

TOPICS

- compound meters
- meter signatures
- subdivisions
- other compound meters
- syncopation and duplets
- asymmetrical meters and changing meter

MUSIC

- Béla Bartók, "Bulgarian Rhythm"
- Bartók, "Syncopation"
- Dave Brubeck, "Blue Rondo à la Turk"
- Christopher Cerf and Norman Stiles, "Dance Myself to Sleep," from *Sesame Street*
- Patrick S. Gilmore, "When Johnny Comes Marching Home"
- Fanny Mendelssohn Hensel, "Nachtwanderer"
- "Home on the Range"
- John Lennon and Paul McCartney, "Norwegian Wood"
- Smokey Robinson, "You've Really Got a Hold on Me"
- Lalo Schifrin, theme from *Mission: Impossible*

CHAPTER 5

Compound and Other Meters

Compound Meters

Listen to two contrasting folk songs, "Greensleeves" and "When Johnny Comes Marching Home." Tap the primary beat in each with your foot. In both songs, the primary beats are grouped in twos, therefore the meter is duple. Now listen for the divisions of the beat, and tap them with your hand. In both songs, the division of the beat is into threes. Unlike triplets in simple meter—which only occur occasionally—there is a three-part division of the beat all the way through these songs. The meter for each song is **compound duple**.

> **KEY CONCEPT** In **compound meters**, each beat divides into three parts. Like simple meters, the beats may group into twos (duple), threes (triple), or fours (quadruple); the conducting patterns for duple, triple, and quadruple compound meters are the same as for simple meters.

When counting in compound meters, use the same syllables as for triplets: 1 la li, 2 la li, and so on. Listen to the beginning of "When Johnny Comes Marching Home" again, this time following the music shown in Example 5.1. Sing along using the counting syllables. This passage features two of the most common rhythmic patterns in compound meter: ♪ ♪ ♪ (counted 1 la li) and ♩ ♪ (1 li). The tied notes in measure 3 work the same as in simple meters: the note sounds as long as the two durations connected by the tie, and the count for the tied beat is written in parentheses.

EXAMPLE 5.1   Gilmore, "When Johnny Comes Marching Home," mm. 1–3a

Other Compound Meters

The compound meters we have considered—$\frac{6}{8}$, $\frac{9}{8}$, and $\frac{12}{8}$—are by far the most common, but others are also possible. Figure 5.4 lists the various possibilities and shows typical patterns for each beat unit. The dotted-half and dotted-eighth beat units were more prevalent in music written before the nineteenth century than they are today.

FIGURE 5.4   Compound meter signatures and typical patterns

(a) Meter signatures

	Meter signature (Beat unit)		
compound duple:	$\frac{6}{4}$ ($\downarrow$.)	$\frac{6}{8}$ ($\downarrow$.)	$\frac{6}{16}$ ($\downarrow$.)
compound triple:	$\frac{9}{4}$ ($\downarrow$.)	$\frac{9}{8}$ ($\downarrow$.)	$\frac{9}{16}$ ($\downarrow$.)
compound quadruple:	$\frac{12}{4}$ ($\downarrow$.)	$\frac{12}{8}$ ($\downarrow$.)	$\frac{12}{16}$ ($\downarrow$.)

(b) Typical patterns for each beat unit

Example 5.6 shows how the folk song "Home on the Range" would look if notated with three different beat units. The first version (a) is the familiar one, in $\frac{6}{8}$; parts (b) and (c) feature dotted-eighth and dotted-half beat units. All three versions are counted the same, and if performed at the same tempo they would sound the same, though they look quite different.

EXAMPLE 5.6 "Home on the Range" with dotted-eighth and dotted-half beat units

(a) Original version, $\frac{6}{8}$ ($\downarrow$· beat unit)

Oh, give me a home, where the buf - fa - lo roam, Where the deer and the an - te - lope play; ___

li 1 la li 2 li ta 1 ta li 2 li ta 1 li ta 2 ta li 1 (2)

(b) Written in $\frac{6}{16}$ ($\downarrow$· beat unit)

li 1 la li 2 li ta 1 ta li 2 li ta 1 li ta 2 ta li 1 (2)

(c) Written in $\frac{6}{4}$ ($\downarrow$· beat unit)

li 1 la li 2 li ta 1 ta li 2 li ta 1 li ta 2 ta li 1 (2)

TRY IT #2

For each rhythm below, provide the missing bar lines that correspond with the meter specified. Where possible, use the beamings to help you decide.

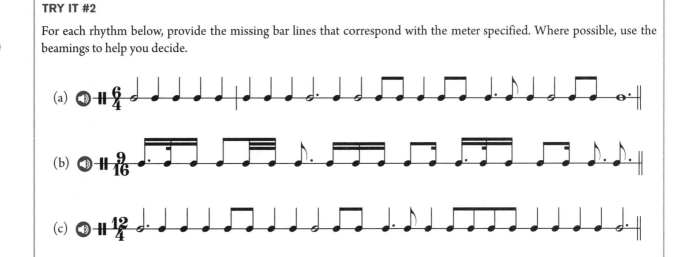

AURAL SKILLS 5.1

Syncopation and Duplets

Just as in simple meters, ties and rests in compound meters can create offbeat accents, or syncopation. Three methods for making syncopations in compound meters are shown in Figure 5.5.

FIGURE 5.5 Types of syncopation in compound meters

(a) Ties from a weak part of a beat across a stronger beat

1 la li (2) la   or   1 ta ta ta

(b) An accent mark on a weak beat or the weak part of a beat

1 **la** li 2 la **li**

(c) A rest on the strong part of a beat that causes a weaker part to sound accented

(1) la (2) ta li

Example 5.7 shows syncopations (marked with arrows) in the melody of "You've Really Got a Hold on Me." In measure 15, on "hold," the weaker third eighth note is tied across to beat 2, delaying the word "on." This creates an offbeat emphasis on the division of both beats 1 and 2. In measure 16, the singer has an accented offbeat entrance (on "Baby") an eighth note ahead of the beat.

EXAMPLE 5.7   Robinson, "You've Really Got a Hold on Me," mm. 14–16 ⊘ 0:39–0:47

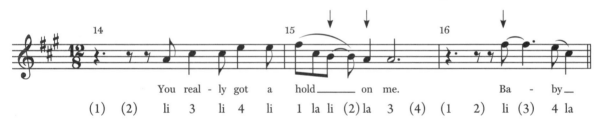

You real - ly got   a   hold_____ on me.   Ba - by__

(1) (2)   li   3   li   4   li   1 la li (2)la   3   (4)   (1)   2)   li (3)   4 la

Typical syncopations within the beat are shown in Figure 5.6, where the dotted-quarter note is the beat unit. As the figure shows, ties are often renotated so that an eighth note substitutes for two sixteenths tied together.

FIGURE 5.6   Typical syncopations within the beat in compound meters

1 ta ta li   1 la ta ta   1 ta ta ta

While in simple meters you sometimes encounter triplets, which divide the beat into three parts instead of the usual two, the reverse is true in compound meters: you occasionally see a beat divide into two parts instead of the usual three. This two-part division is called a **duplet**. Look at Example 5.8, from "You've Really Got a Hold on Me." The melody is in $\frac{12}{8}$, with an overall counting pattern of 1 la li, 2 la li, 3 la li, 4 la li, but in measure 13, the second beat is replaced with a duplet ("on me"), marked with a 2 above the beam. This beat is counted 2 &, just as two eighths would be in simple meter with a quarter-note beat. Here, the second half of the duplet is tied over to make a syncopation.

EXAMPLE 5.8   Robinson, "You've Really Got a Hold on Me," mm. 12–13   0:31–0:37

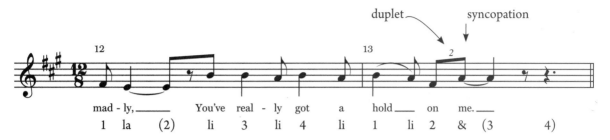

Figure 5.7 shows how duplets are notated with other beat units.

FIGURE 5.7   Notation of duplets

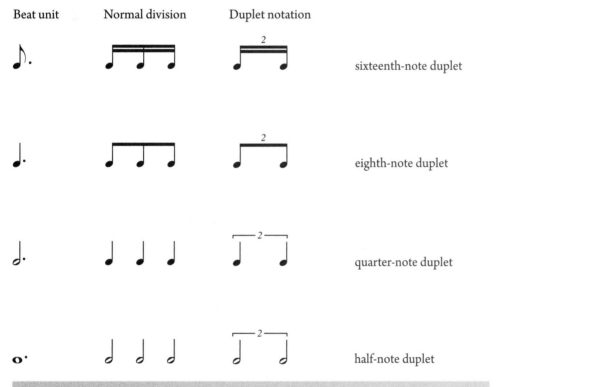

Asymmetrical Meters and Changing Meter

All the simple and compound meters we have studied so far are considered **symmetrical**, with the primary beats in each measure equally spaced. Now listen to the beginning of Bartók's "Bulgarian Rhythm," shown in Example 5.9. The meter signature is $\frac{5}{8}$—an **asymmetrical meter**—with primary beats of unequal duration (♩. ♩). Each measure lasts for five eighth notes and divides into two unequal "halves": in part (a), the first half divides into three eighths, the second half into two. You can see the unequal beat units in the left hand, which shifts between dotted-quarter and quarter notes. We count such rhythms by shifting between the syllables for compound and simple meters. For the right-hand rhythm, count 1 la li, 2 &, making sure to keep the eighth-note duration consistent. Later in the piece, the division reverses, as in part (b): to 2 + 3. There, count 1 &, 2 la li. When reading such rhythms, keep the ♪ duration steady.

EXAMPLE 5.9   Bartók, "Bulgarian Rhythm"

(a) Mm. 1–4

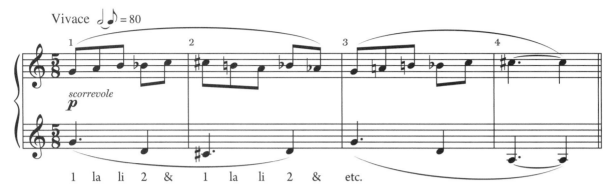

(b) Mm. 9–12

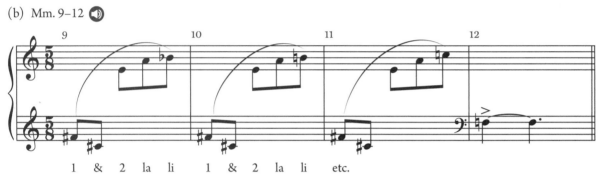

For another example of an asymmetrical meter, look at the *Mission: Impossible* theme shown in Example 5.10. This tune, with a meter signature of $\frac{5}{4}$, implies five quarter-note beats per measure. The beaming and accent marks in the left hand's ten eighth notes indicate the grouping 3 + 3 + 2 + 2. Rather than counting this passage as five quarter-note beats, we hear four unequal beats (♩. ♩. ♩ ♩) in a driving, syncopated rhythm.

EXAMPLE 5.10   Schifrin, theme from *Mission: Impossible*, mm. 1–2

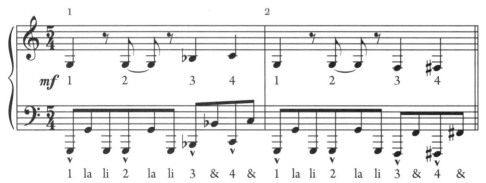

Other asymmetrical meter signatures you might encounter are $\frac{5}{16}$, $\frac{7}{8}$, and $\frac{7}{16}$; meters with 5 as the top number are usually conducted in two uneven beats, those with 7 on top are generally conducted in three. Even symmetrical meters may be divided asymmetrically. For example, $\frac{9}{8}$ may be divided into 2 + 2 + 2 + 3 eighth notes, as in Example 5.11, a piano work by Dave Brubeck. This example has four beats per measure, with the fourth slightly longer than the others.

EXAMPLE 5.11   Brubeck, "Blue Rondo à la Turk," mm. 1–4 🔊

Finally, you might find more than one meter in a single piece. Take a look at Example 5.12, another composition by Bartók, where each measure has a different meter signature, as marked by arrows. This technique is called **changing meter**.

EXAMPLE 5.12   Bartók, "Syncopation," mm. 1–3 🔊

Changing meter is typically found in twentieth-century and contemporary pieces, which often also feature asymmetrical meters and shifting accents. Example 5.13, from "You've Really Got a Hold on Me," shows one instance. Most of this song is in compound quadruple meter ($\frac{12}{8}$), but measure 22 is in compound triple ($\frac{9}{8}$), following the duplet syncopation in measure 21. Changing meters are marked with arrows.

EXAMPLE 5.13   Robinson, "You've Really Got a Hold on Me," mm. 20–24a 🔽 1:25–1:41

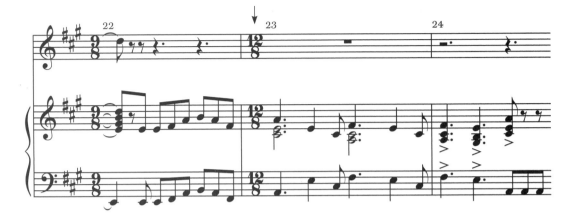

ASSIGNMENT 5.4

Did You Know?

William "Smokey" Robinson was inducted into the Rock and Roll Hall of Fame in 1987, in honor of his extended career as singer-songwriter with the Miracles and his role as talent scout and record producer. During his long association with Detroit-based Motown Records—once the largest black-owned company in the United States—and its founder, Berry Gordy, Robinson worked as songwriter and producer with the Miracles, the Temptations, and Marvin Gaye. Gordy took Robinson under his wing when the young artist was still a teenager, and he released the Miracles' first single when Robinson was eighteen. The group became a hit during the 1960s and early 70s, with such songs as "You've Really Got a Hold on Me," "I Second That Emotion," and "The Tears of a Clown." With Ronnie White of the Miracles, Robinson wrote "My Girl," which became a #1 hit for the Temptations. After splitting from the Miracles in 1972, Robinson enjoyed a strong solo career. In 1999, he received a Lifetime Achievement Award at the Grammy ceremony.

Terms You Should Know

asymmetrical meter	compound meter	duplet
changing meter	compound duple	symmetrical meter
	compound triple	
	compound quadruple	

Questions for Review

1. Explain the difference between simple meter and compound meter.
2. How do you decide if a piece is in simple or compound meter?
3. How do you know whether a compound meter is duple, triple, or quadruple?
4. What do the upper and lower parts of a meter signature represent in compound meters?
5. Which numbers may appear in the upper and lower positions of compound meter signatures?
6. What are the most common compound meter signatures?
7. In $\frac{6}{8}$ meter, how many beats does a dotted-half last? a dotted-quarter?
8. If the beat unit is a dotted-quarter note, what note values represent the beat division and subdivision? if the beat unit is a dotted-half note?

9. What do you need to remember when notating rests in compound meters?
10. Where do the metrical accents fall in compound meters?
11. What guidelines do you follow to decide which notes to beam together in compound meter?
12. Write four common rhythmic patterns that fill one dotted-quarter beat in compound meter.
13. Write four additional patterns of your choice, including beat subdivisions, to fill one dotted-quarter beat unit in compound meter.
14. How is syncopation created in compound meters?
15. How do you decide if a meter is symmetrical or asymmetrical?
16. How do asymmetrical meters sound different from symmetrical ones? Give an example of each.

Reading Review

Match the terms on the left with the best answer on the right.

_____	(1) 1 ta li	(a)	meter type with equally spaced beats of the same length
_____	(2) changing meter	(b)	notation must reflect the beat unit
_____	(3) symmetrical meter	(c)	type of note that gets one beat in compound meters
_____	(4) $\frac{9}{16}$	(d)	meter type where each beat divides in threes
_____	(5) beat subdivision in $\frac{6}{8}$	(e)	counting syllables for ♩ ♪ ♪ in $\frac{6}{8}$
_____	(6) duplet	(f)	counting syllables for ♩. ♪ ♪ in $\frac{6}{8}$
_____	(7) asymmetrical meter	(g)	compound meter with four beats per measure
_____	(8) $\frac{6}{4}$	(h)	a grouping of eighths in $\frac{5}{8}$
_____	(9) 2 + 2 + 3	(i)	compound meter with three beats per measure
_____	(10) 1 la li	(j)	adjacent measures with different meters
_____	(11) compound meter	(k)	division of the beat in two parts in compound meter
_____	(12) $\frac{12}{8}$	(l)	six sixteenth notes
_____	(13) 3 + 2	(m)	meter type with unequally spaced beats of different lengths
_____	(14) 1 ta la ta li	(n)	compound meter with two beats per measure
_____	(15) beaming guideline	(o)	counting syllables for ♪♪♪♪♪♪ in $\frac{6}{8}$
_____	(16) dotted note	(p)	a grouping of eighths in $\frac{7}{8}$

Ⓢ Additional review and practice available at wwnorton.com/studyspace

Class Activities

A. Hearing simple and compound meters

Listen to the following examples to determine whether they are in simple or compound meter, then circle your choice. Tap the beats with your foot and the beat divisions with your hand. Remember that simple-meter beats divide into twos and fours, while compound-meter beats divide into threes.

1. 🔊   simple   compound

2. 🔊   simple   compound

3. 🔊   simple   compound

4. 🔊   simple   compound

5. 🔊   simple   compound

B. Reading and writing rhythmic patterns in compound meters

1. Performing compound-meter beat patterns

Look at the example below, which features the most common compound-meter beat patterns. First tap all the beats with your foot and beat divisions with your hand; then chant each beat pattern on a neutral syllable such as "ta" or the syllables written beneath the example. 🔊

Memorize the look and sound of each pattern.

2. Team composition

In teams of three to four people, compose a sixteen-measure rhythmic composition in ⁶₈ meter. Choosing only from the beat patterns shown below, take turns notating one measure. After your turn, pass the marker (or chalk) to the next team member. Keep passing the marker until the composition is complete. Each team should make sure that all rhythms are notated correctly. Perform and critique these compositions in class.

C. Reading rhythms

Perform the following rhythms on "ta" or counting syllables, as directed. Keep a steady beat by tapping the pulse or conducting, and follow the dynamic markings. (Optional: Write the counts below each rhythm.)

Rhythm 1

Rhythm 2

Rhythm 3

Rhythm 4

Rhythm 5

Rhythm 6   Perform as a duet.

D. At the keyboard: Playing and singing melodies in compound meter

The following melodies feature the $\hat{1}-\hat{2}-\hat{3}-\hat{4}-\hat{5}$ pattern we sang in previous chapters, plus a few additional notes above and below. We provide the $\hat{1}-\hat{2}-\hat{3}-\hat{4}-\hat{5}$ pattern as a warm-up for each, beginning on the same note as the melody.

- Practice the warm-up on the piano with your right hand. Begin with the thumb on the first note and use each finger. Play $\hat{1}-\hat{2}-\hat{3}-\hat{4}-\hat{5}$ ascending and descending, sing along with it.
- Practice just the rhythm of the melody on "ta" or counting the syllables while tapping the beat (or conducting). Then practice just the pitches on the keyboard (don't worry about fingering for now).
- Play the rhythm and pitches together at a slow tempo, and then a faster tempo. Sing the melody on the numbers or syllables given, first at a slow tempo, and then a faster tempo.

Warm-up 🔊

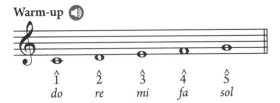

Melody 1   "Whoopee Ti-Yi-Yo" (abridged), mm. 1–8

Melody 2   Harold Arlen and E. Y. Harburg, "We're Off to See the Wizard," from *The Wizard of Oz*, mm. 1–8

Use the previous warm-up melody.

Fol - low   the   Yel - low   Brick   Road.   Fol - low   the   Yel - low   Brick   Road.
$\hat{1}$ $\hat{2}$ $\hat{3}$ $\hat{4}$ $\hat{3}$ $\hat{2}$ $\hat{1}$ $\hat{1}$ $\hat{2}$ $\hat{3}$ $\hat{4}$ $\hat{3}$ $\hat{2}$ $\hat{1}$
do   re   mi   fa   mi   re   do   do   re   mi   fa   mi   re   do

Fol - low, fol - ow,   fol - low, fol - low,   fol - low   the   Yel - low   Brick   Road.
$\hat{1}$ $\hat{1}$ $\hat{1}$ $\hat{1}$ $\hat{6}$ $\hat{6}$ $\hat{7}$ $\hat{7}$ $\hat{1}$ $\hat{1}$ $\hat{1}$ $\hat{1}$ $\hat{7}$ $\hat{6}$ $\hat{5}$
do   do   do   do   la   la   ti   ti   do   do   do   do   ti   la   sol

Warm-up

$\hat{1}$ $\hat{2}$ $\hat{3}$ $\hat{4}$ $\hat{5}$
do   re   mi   fa   sol

Melody 3   Philip P. Bliss, "Wonderful Words of Life," mm. 1–8

Sing   them   o - ver   a - gain   to   me,   won - der - ful words   of   life;
$\hat{3}$ $\hat{3}$ $\hat{3}$ $\hat{4}$ $\hat{3}$ $\hat{3}$ $\hat{2}$ $\hat{2}$ $\hat{5}$ $\hat{2}$ $\hat{2}$ $\hat{3}$ $\hat{2}$ $\hat{1}$ $\hat{5}$
mi   mi   mi   fa   mi   mi   re   re   sol   re   re   mi   re   do   sol

let   me   more   of   their   beau - ty   see,   won - der - ful words   of   life;
$\hat{3}$ $\hat{3}$ $\hat{3}$ $\hat{4}$ $\hat{3}$ $\hat{3}$ $\hat{2}$ $\hat{2}$ $\hat{5}$ $\hat{2}$ $\hat{2}$ $\hat{3}$ $\hat{2}$ $\hat{1}$
mi   mi   mi   fa   mi   mi   re   re   sol   re   re   mi   re   do

E. Listening and writing

1. Performing and notating beat patterns

Point and sing: Your teacher will display beat patterns like those shown below. Perform each pattern as soon as he or she points to it, then repeat it (sing on syllables or a neutral syllable "ta"). Change when the teacher points to another pattern.

Identify and notate:

Identify the pattern(s) your teacher performs. Then notate your answers.

Options for writing what you hear:

- Write with a counting system of words or syllables as specified by your teacher.
- Notate the pattern(s) in music notation on the staff paper provided.
- Write the pattern number(s).

Make your own point-and-sing exercises with the chart on p. 107.

Solo: Point to an item then sing it.

Duet: Point to the chart while a partner sings. Switch roles and perform again.

2. Melodies

Your teacher will perform a number of melodies (calls), then ask you to perform or write what you heard. Try to memorize the call as quickly as possible. These exercises will help you learn the fundamental patterns of compound meters. The pitches in these calls extend from C to C (C–D–E–F–G–A–B–C).

Workbook ASSIGNMENT 5.1

1. Simple and compound meters

For each meter in the chart below, provide the meter type (e.g., simple triple), the beat unit, and the number of beats per measure.

Meter	Meter type	Beat unit	Beats per measure
$\frac{9}{8}$	compound triple	♩.	3
¢	_____	_____	_____
$\frac{12}{8}$	_____	_____	_____
$\frac{3}{4}$	_____	_____	_____
$\frac{2}{4}$	_____	_____	_____
$\frac{6}{8}$	_____	_____	_____

2. Understanding beats and divisions

a. For each rhythm or melody below, write the appropriate meter signature at the beginning of the line.

(1)

(2)

(3)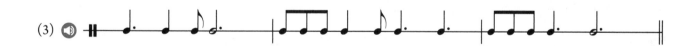

(4) Leigh Harline and Ned Washington, "Hi-Diddle-Dee-Dee," from *Pinocchio*, mm. 17–20a

Hi – did - dle - dee - dee_____ An act – or's life for me_____

b. At each position marked by an arrow, add one note value to complete the measure in the meter indicated.

c. For each rhythm or melody, provide the missing bar lines that correspond with the meter signature given. Then add counting syllables beneath the rhythms, and practice counting aloud.

(4) Joe Darion and Mitch Leigh, "The Impossible Dream," from *Man of La Mancha*, mm. 1–4

To   dream . . .

Workbook   ASSIGNMENT 5.2

1. Divisions and subdivisions in compound meter

For each rhythm or melody, provide the missing bar lines that correspond with the meter signature given.

a.

b.

c.

d. "The Butterfly"

e. Fanny Mendelssohn Hensel, "Schwanenlied" (adapted)

f. Ludwig van Beethoven, String Quartet in F Major, Op. 18, No. 1, second movement (cello part, adapted)

2. Understanding rests

a. Write the appropriate counting syllables for the melodies below in the meter given. If the beginning of a beat coincides with a rest, write the count in parentheses.

(1) Wolfgang Amadeus Mozart, "Sull' aria," from *The Marriage of Figaro*, mm. 2–6 🔊

Translation: On the breeze, what a gentle zephyr [will whisper].

(2) Handel, "Rejoice greatly," from *Messiah* (alternate version), mm. 9–14 🔊

b. At each position marked with an arrow, add one rest to complete the measure in the meter indicated. Then add counting syllables beneath the rhythms, and practice counting aloud. If a beat begins with a rest, write the count in parentheses.

Workbook ASSIGNMENT 5.3

1. Divisions and subdivisions in compound meter

a. Write the appropriate meter signature at the beginning of each rhythm below, then speak or tap each rhythm.

(1)

(2)

(3)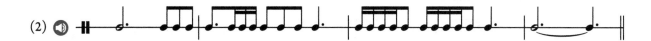

(4)

b. At each position marked by an arrow, add one note value to complete the measure in the meter indicated.

(1)

(2)

(3)

(4)

2. Beaming to reflect the meter

a. Rewrite the following rhythms with correct beaming to reflect the beat. Practice the rhythms on "ta" or counting syllables, and be prepared to perform them in class.

b. Vocal music, especially in older editions, is often written with beaming that corresponds to the syllables of the sung text. Rebeam the vocal line (using beams instead of flags) to reflect the meter and beat unit instead. Omit the text from your answer.

Robert Schumann, "Ich hab' im Traum geweinet," from *Dichterliebe*, mm. 10–11a

Translation: [Tears] flowed down my cheeks.

Workbook ASSIGNMENT 5.4

1. Asymmetrical meters

a. Write the appropriate meter signature at the beginning of each rhythm below.

b. The following excerpts are drawn from *Mikrokosmos*, a collection of piano pieces by Béla Bartók. Write the meter signature for each in the blank provided.

(1) "In the Style of a Folk Song," (No. 100), mm. 1–2

(2) "Bulgarian Rhythm," (No. 115), mm. 1–2

(3) "Fifth Chords," (No. 120), mm. 1–2

2. Changing meters

The following melodies, also from *Mikrokosmos*, feature changing meters. Write the correct signature in each position marked by an arrow.

a. "Unison" (No. 137), mm. 1–5

b. "From the Diary of a Fly" (No. 142), mm. 1–4

c. "Change of Time" (No. 126), mm. 1–6

d. "Two-Part Study" (No. 121), mm. 1–3

e. "Two-Part Study" (No. 121), mm. 13–15

Workbook   AURAL SKILLS 5.1

1. Listening to and writing rhythms in compound meter

Listen to a portion of two traditional melodies in $\frac{6}{8}$ meter and write their rhythms. Each melody consists of four segments; each segment is four beats (two measures) long. Notate only the rhythm. Begin with an eighth-note anacrusis (upbeat), and notate the rhythms with the patterns given in Class Activity B2 (p. 104).

a. 🔊

Hint: Segments 1–3 have the same rhythm; segment 4 has a different rhythm.

Segment 1

Segment 2

Segment 3

Segment 4

b. 🔊

Hint: Segments 1 and 3 have the same rhythm; segments 2 and 4 have different rhythms.

Segment 1

Segment 2

Segment 3

Segment 4

2. Writing a rhythmic composition with beat subdivisions in compound meter

Compose a rhythmic duet for two performers, using only the rhythmic patterns below.

- Write eight measures in $\frac{6}{8}$ meter.
- Don't include ties. Use eighth, quarter, and dotted-quarter rests only.
- Vary the complexity: Both voices should sound together at times. At other times, when one voice is rhythmically active, the other voice may have rests or longer notes.
- Include dynamic markings to add musical interest.
- If you would like, write a text to be recited with your rhythm.

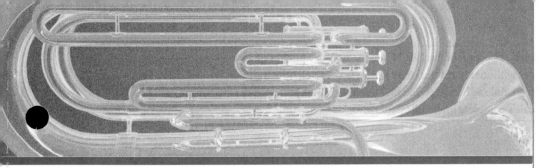

TOPICS

- scales
- scale types: chromatic, whole-tone, and major
- scale degrees
- writing major scales
- major key signatures
- the circle of fifths

MUSIC

- Smokey Robinson, "You've Really Got a Hold on Me"
- "Simple Gifts"
- John Philip Sousa, "The Stars and Stripes Forever"
- "Twinkle, Twinkle, Little Star"
- Meredith Willson, "Till There Was You," from *The Music Man*

CHAPTER 6

Major Scales and Keys

Scales

Listen to and compare the beginning of two melodies: Sousa's "The Stars and Stripes Forever" (Example 6.1) and Willson's "Till There Was You" (Example 6.2). Each melody is based on a specific group of pitches, which sound very different because the pitches are drawn from different scale types. The collection of pitches in each melody, listed starting on E♭, appears below for comparison.

EXAMPLE 6.1   Sousa, "The Stars and Stripes Forever," mm. 1–4

(a) Melody

(b) Pitches of the melody

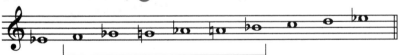

EXAMPLE 6.2   Willson, "Till There Was You," mm. 1–5a

(a) Melody

(b) Pitches of the melody

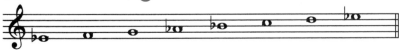

numbers as you sing or play them, you can then translate them into staff notation. For instance, Example 6.7 gives each scale step in C major, and Example 6.8 shows how these numbers can help you write the beginning of "Twinkle, Twinkle, Little Star." To write this melody in another key (E♭, for example)—known as **transposing** the melody—use the same degrees in that scale: E♭ (= 1̂), E♭, B♭ (= 5̂), B♭, C (= 6̂), C, B♭, and so on.

EXAMPLE 6.7   C major scale with scale-degree numbers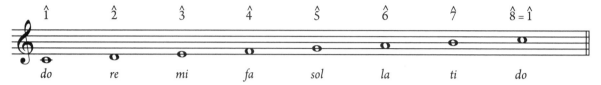

EXAMPLE 6.8   "Twinkle, Twinkle, Little Star," mm. 1–4

(a) In C major

(b) In E♭ major

Another method for sight-singing, **movable-*do* solfège**, or **solfège** for short, assigns each scale degree a syllable—*do, re, mi, fa, sol, la, ti, do*—as shown beneath the scale in Example 6.7. In the movable-*do* system, 1̂ is always *do*, 2̂ is always *re*, 3̂ is always *mi*, and so on—no matter which scale is used, as Example 6.8 shows.

AURAL SKILLS 6.1

> **ANOTHER WAY** A third method for sight-singing, called **fixed-*do* solfège**, always associates *do* with C, *re* with D, *mi* with E, *fa* with F, and so forth, regardless of the scale. Fixed-*do* solfège is analogous to singing letter names, while movable-*do* solfège is comparable to singing scale-degree numbers.

In addition to scale-degree numbers or solfège, musicians often refer to scale degrees by name, given in Example 6.9. Scale degree 1̂ is called the **tonic**—it is the "tone" on which the scale is built—while 5̂ is the **dominant**: its musical function "dominates" tonal music, as will be clear in future chapters. Scale degree $\hat{3}$ is the **mediant**, since it falls in the "medial" position midway between $\hat{1}$ and $\hat{5}$. Scale degree $\hat{2}$ is called the **supertonic**—"super-" means "above" (as in "superhuman" or "superior")—to fix its position immediately above $\hat{1}$. As Example 6.9b shows, this relationship of $\hat{2}$ above $\hat{1}$ is mirrored by $\hat{7}$ below $\hat{1}$; $\hat{7}$, the **leading tone**, gets its name from its tendency to lead upward toward the tonic. (In fact, $\hat{7}$ is sometimes called a **tendency tone** because of this strong tendency to pull up to $\hat{1}$.) Scale degree $\hat{4}$ is the **subdominant**; "sub-" means "below" (as in "submarine" or "subordinate"). This label originates from the idea that $\hat{4}$ lies the same distance below the tonic as the dominant lies above. Similarly, the **submediant**, $\hat{6}$, lies three scale steps below the tonic (just as the mediant lies three scale steps above).

EXAMPLE 6.9   Scale-degree names

(a) Arranged $\hat{1}$ to $\hat{1}$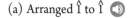

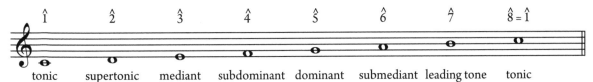

(b) Arranged with $\hat{1}$ in the middle

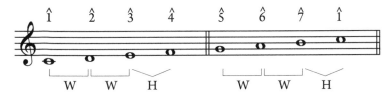

Writing Major Scales

All major scales share the same pattern of whole and half steps between adjacent notes: W–W–H–W–W–W–H. An easy way to remember this pattern is to think of the position of half steps in a C major scale, which is made of the white keys from one C to the next. Another easy way is to divide the scale into two four-note groups (or **tetrachords**) with a whole step between them, as shown in Example 6.10. These groups, each making the pattern W–W–H, are called **major tetrachords** because of their role in the major scale.

EXAMPLE 6.10   Major scale from two major tetrachords

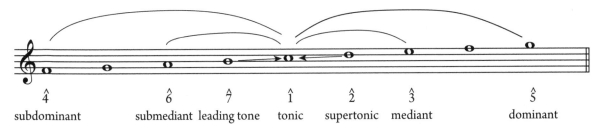

accidental different from those in the key signature. Such accidentals apply to all repetitions of the pitch (in that octave) for the rest of the measure; the next bar line cancels the accidental.

In Figure 6.1, all the major key signatures are notated in treble and bass clefs. You should memorize them, since many skills covered in future chapters build on this knowledge. In a key signature, the order of the sharps is F♯–C♯–G♯–D♯–A♯–E♯–B♯. The order of the flats is the same, only backward: B♭–E♭–A♭–D♭–G♭–C♭–F♭. Sharps and flats must be written in this order and centered on the lines and spaces shown in Figure 6.1. In a music score, the key signature is always written between the clef sign and meter signature (in alphabetical order: clef, key, meter). If the key is C major, there are no sharps or flats and thus no key signature.

FIGURE 6.1   Major key signatures

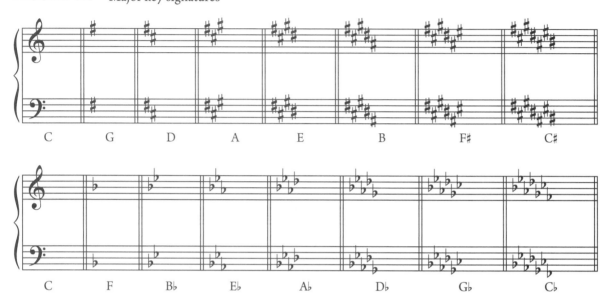

ANOTHER WAY A common mnemonic (memory) device to help you remember the first four flats is the word "bead." One handy sentence to remember for the order of both sharps and flats is "Father Charles Goes Down And Ends Battle." When you read it forward, the first letter of each word gives the order of sharps; when you read it backward ("Battle Ends And Down Goes Charles's Father"), you get the order of flats.

TRY IT #3

Write the key signature for the major keys specified below, in both treble and bass clefs.

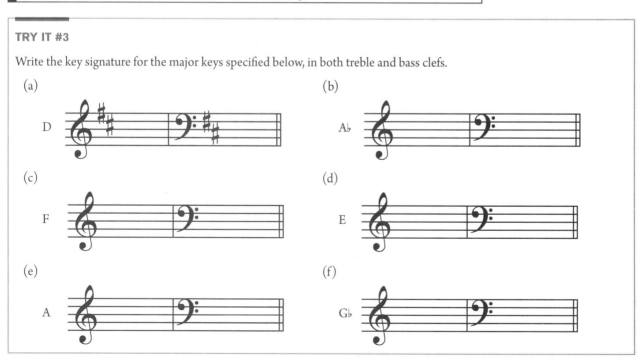

Although you should memorize which key signature goes with which key, you can also determine the key from the signature. For sharp keys, the last sharp of the signature is $\hat{7}$ of the key. To find the tonic, go up a diatonic half step. For example, in the key signature with four sharps (shown in Figure 6.2a), if D♯ is $\hat{7}$, then E is $\hat{1}$, and the key is E major. For flat keys, the last flat of the signature is $\hat{4}$ of the key. Beginning with that note, count down four scale steps (as in part b) to find the name of the key. As a shortcut (part c), take the next-to-last flat of the signature (for example, for B♭–E♭–A♭, the key is E♭): that will be the name of the key. For F major, however, since there is only one flat (B♭), you have to count down four steps (part d)—or better yet, memorize the signature.

FIGURE 6.2   Determining the major key from key signatures

(a) Sharp keys:

Count up a half step.

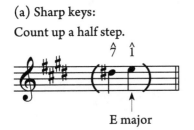

E major

(b) Flat keys:

Count down four scale steps.

E♭ major

(c) Flat-key shortcut:

Next-to-last flat.

E♭ major

(d) F major:

Count down four scale steps.

F major

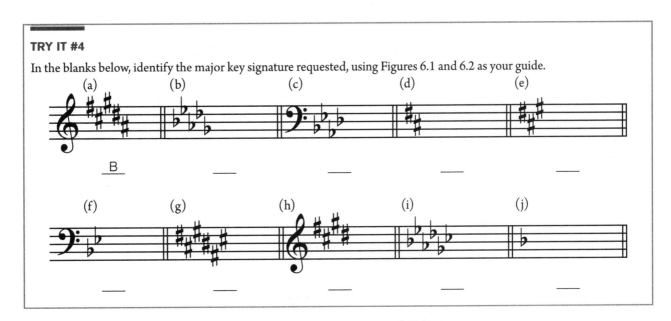

TRY IT #4

In the blanks below, identify the major key signature requested, using Figures 6.1 and 6.2 as your guide.

(a) B   (b) ___   (c) ___   (d) ___   (e) ___

(f) ___   (g) ___   (h) ___   (i) ___   (j) ___

ASSIGNMENT 6.2

If a piece has three sharps in its key signature, you might assume the piece is in A major, but the key signature alone is not enough to identify the key. (Three sharps can also indicate F♯ minor, as we will see in Chapter 7.) To tell the key of a piece, always check the beginning and end of the melody or bass line for scale-degree patterns like $\hat{3}$–$\hat{2}$–$\hat{1}$ or $\hat{5}$–$\hat{1}$. Look back at Example 6.13, the beginning of "You've Really Got a Hold on Me," and at Example 6.14, the end of the song. The melody in 6.13 starts with an A, $\hat{1}$ in A major, and the first two measures emphasize $\hat{3}$, $\hat{2}$, and $\hat{1}$. The end of the melody (in m. 32 of Example 6.14) is $\hat{3}$–$\hat{2}$–$\hat{1}$. The final two bass notes (mm. 33–34 in the bass clef) are $\hat{5}$–$\hat{1}$. All are signs that the song is truly in A major.

EXAMPLE 6.14   Robinson, "You've Really Got a Hold on Me," mm. 30b–34 ⬇ 1:12–1:25

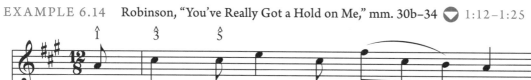

TRY IT #5

In what key is "Simple Gifts"? How do you know? 🔊

- Key signature suggests what key? _____

- First six scale degrees? _____

- Last six scale degrees? _____ Key of piece: _____

"Simple Gifts"

The Circle of Fifths

You may have noticed in Figure 6.1 that each time a new sharp is added, the new key is five scale steps higher than the last; and each time a new flat is added, the new key is five scale steps lower than the last. That is, C major has no sharps or flats, G major (five steps higher) has one sharp, D major (five steps higher than G) has two sharps, and so on. This relationship between keys is sometimes represented around a circle, like the one in Figure 6.3, called the **circle of fifths**. The keys that require sharps appear around the right side, with each key (proceeding clockwise from C) a fifth higher. The keys that require flats appear around the left side of the circle, with each key (going counterclockwise from C) a fifth lower. After F (one flat), each key on the left side of the circle has a flatted note as the tonic (Bb, Eb, Ab, etc.). You may find the circle of fifths a helpful aid as you memorize the key signatures.

FIGURE 6.3   Circle of fifths

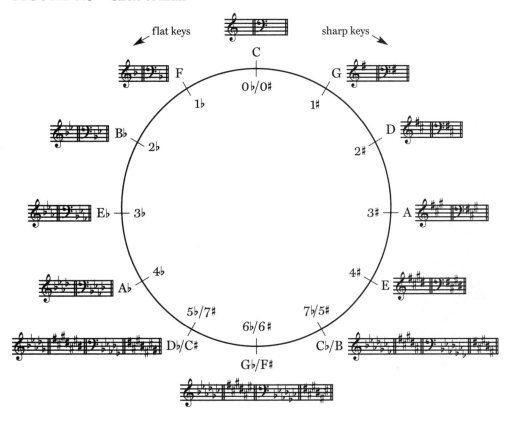

Did You Know?

Where does the term "diatonic" come from? This and many other music terms derive from the music theory of the ancient Greeks. Looking to the Greek roots of these words can help you remember their meaning. "Diatonic" begins with the prefix "dia-," meaning "through" or "across" (like "diagonal"). If you think "across" the piano's white keys, you've got a diatonic collection. "Tonic" comes from the same root as "tone." "Chromatic" derives from the Greek chroma, meaning "color." Chromatic collections use all twelve possible pitch colors.

Terms You Should Know

circle of fifths
half step
  chromatic
  diatonic
key signature
major key
major tetrachord
scale
  chromatic

diatonic
major
whole-tone
scale degree
tonic
supertonic
mediant
subdominant
dominant

submediant
leading tone
scale step
solfège
  movable *do*
  fixed *do*
tendency tone
transpose

Questions for Review

1. How do you decide which accidentals to use in a chromatic scale?
2. How are chromatic and whole-tone scales similar? How do they differ from major scales?
3. What is the half- and whole-step pattern for an ascending major scale?
4. What syllable systems can be used to label scale steps in a major scale? What are the characteristics of each?
5. What steps do you follow to write a major scale?
6. What is the difference between a chromatic half step and a diatonic half step?
7. Why do we use specific spellings of pitches to notate a major scale? For example, why would an E♭ major scale include an A♭ and not a G♯?
8. List the order of sharps in the key signature for F♯ major.
9. List the order of flats in the key signature for C♭ major.
10. What major key has three sharps? two flats? five flats?
11. What do you need to consider besides the key signature to identify the key of a piece?
12. How is the circle of fifths organized, and what does it show?

Reading Review

Match the terms on the left with the best answer on the right.

_____ (1) key signature

_____ (2) circle of fifths

_____ (3) D major

_____ (4) F major

_____ (5) whole-tone scale

_____ (6) B–E–A–D–G–C–F

_____ (7) fixed *do*

_____ (8) chromatic scale

_____ (9) major scale

_____ (10) major tetrachord

_____ (11) solfège syllables

_____ (12) E♭ major

_____ (13) clef, key, meter

_____ (14) F–C–G–D–A–E–B

_____ (15) movable *do*

(a) has three flats in its key signature

(b) order of sharps in a key signature

(c) scale built of all half steps

(d) sharps or flats at the beginning of the staff (after the clef) that help determine the key

(e) the order of flats in a key signature

(f) diatonic scale with the pattern W–W–H–W–W–W–H

(g) arrangement of key signatures by number of sharps or flats

(h) has one flat in its key signature

(i) has two sharps in its key signature

(j) order of symbols at the beginning of the staff

(k) system where scale degree $\hat{1}$ is *do*; like reading scale-degree numbers

(l) scale built of all whole steps

(m) *do–re–mi–fa–sol–la–ti*

(n) pattern of W–W–H in a major scale

(o) system where the note C is *do*; like reading letter names

Ⓢ Additional review and practice available at wwnorton.com/studyspace

Class Activities

A. At the keyboard

1. Play the first five notes of a C major scale (with the intervals W–W–H–W), one note per finger, as shown in the diagram. Your thumbs are numbered 1, index fingers are 2, middle fingers are 3, and so on. In your left hand, begin with your fifth finger on $\hat{1}$ and end with your thumb on $\hat{5}$. In your right hand, begin with your thumb on $\hat{1}$ and end with your fifth finger on $\hat{5}$.

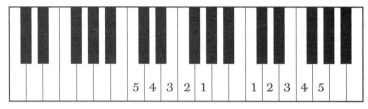

Fingering: L.H.   R.H.

Beginning on each pitch below, play the five-finger pattern in both hands at the same time, in separate octaves. While playing, sing with letter names, solfège syllables, or scale-degree numbers.

(a) A (A–B–C♯–D–E)   (e) B   (i) A♭
(b) F   (f) F♯   (j) B♭
(c) G   (g) E   (k) G♯
(d) E♭   (h) C♯   (l) G♭

2. Now play an entire ascending major scale with the fingering below: four notes in each hand (W–W–H), separated by a whole step.

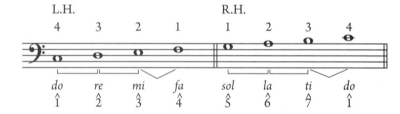

Fingering: L.H.   R.H.   middle C

Playing all the following scales with this same fingering will help you remember the whole- and half-step "feel" of the pattern. (These fingerings are only for memory recall of the pattern; they don't replace traditional scale fingerings used by keyboard performers.)

Beginning on each pitch below, play the major scale and sing each letter name. (Recall that each pitch must have a different letter name.) Play again and sing with solfège syllables or scale-degree numbers.

(a) D
(b) F
(c) Ab
(d) *B/Cb

(e) Eb
(f) *F♯/Gb
(g) A
(h) C

(i) E
(j) G
(k) Bb
(l) *Db/C♯

*Consider each of these pitches as the tonic pitch as you sing the letter names.

B. Reading rhythms

Perform the following rhythms on "ta" or counting syllables, as directed. Keep a steady beat by tapping the pulse or conducting, and follow the dynamic markings.

Rhythm 1

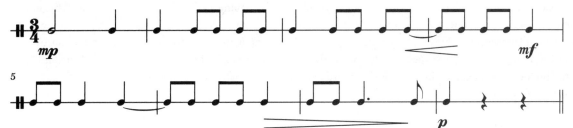

Rhythm 2

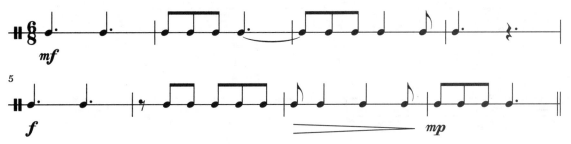

Rhythm 3

Rhythm 4

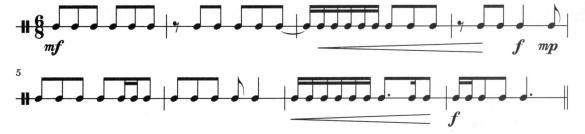

Rhythm 5

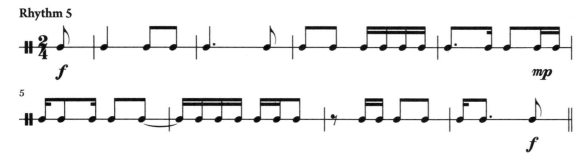

C. Singing at sight

1. The following melodies may be sung as a group activity in class or assigned as homework. First determine the key, and play the major scale at the keyboard (using the fingering you learned in A2). Play the first pitch of the melody (if not $\hat{1}$), and sing down to the tonic pitch to orient yourself. Sing the scale on scale-degree numbers or solfège syllables as you play.

2. Then study the rhythm. Perform it on "ta" or on counting syllables, while tapping a steady beat (or conducting). Begin with a slow tempo; repeat at a faster one.

3. Once you are confident with the rhythm, begin learning the pitches. Sing in an octave that's comfortable for you. Sing on numbers, solfège, or la, as your teacher specifies. Practice without rhythm; play the pitches at a keyboard if it is helpful. Then sing the entire melody, checking the pitches at the keyboard *after* you sing. Finally put pitches and rhythm together at a slow tempo; repeat at a faster one.

Melody 1 Kurt Weill and Maxwell Anderson, "September Song," mm. 1–8

Melody 2 Bach, Musette, BWV Anh. 126, mm. 1–8 (adapted)
This melody begins on *sol* ($\hat{5}$).

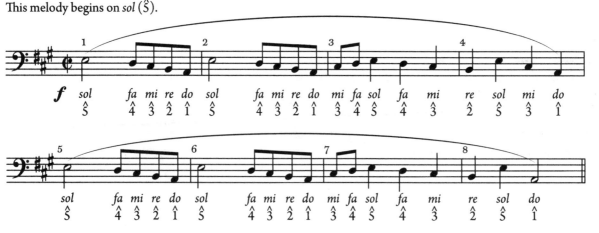

Melody 3 Beethoven, Sonatina in G, Romanze (adapted), mm. 1–8a
This melody begins on *mi* ($\hat{3}$). Write in solfège syllables or numbers as needed.

Melody 4 Harvey Worthington Loomis, "The Frog in the Bog"
The next two melodies are rounds. In a round, the numbers above the staff indicate when each part enters. To sing this round, divide into three groups. When the first group reaches 2, the second group sings from the beginning. When the first group reaches 3, the third group sings from the beginning.

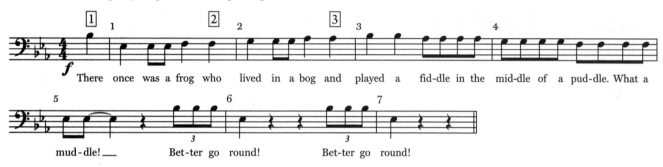

Melody 5 "Come, Follow Me"
This melody has a wide vocal range—sing it in a lower key if this one is too high. Once you have learned the melody, sing it with your class as a round.

D. Listening and writing

1. Call and response. Your teacher will perform short patterns made from $\hat{1}$ to $\hat{5}$ of the major scale, then ask you to respond by performing or writing what you have heard. Try to memorize the call as quickly as possible. When performing your response, maintain the call's pitch, rhythm, and tempo. When writing, include scale-degree numbers or solfège syllables along with the rhythm of the call. If a key is announced, write the pitches and rhythm together on staff paper of your own.

2. Point and sing. After establishing a tonic pitch, your teacher will create a melody by pointing to a series of items—pitches, letter names, solfège syllables, or scale-degree numbers—like those shown in the following charts. When the teacher points to an item, immediately sing it. Perform the melody until you have memorized it. Then use the pitches, letter names, syllables, or numbers to write the melody on the staff. Make your own point-and-sing exercises with a partner to practice.

Singing scale patterns from *sol* to *sol* ($\hat{5}$–$\hat{5}$)

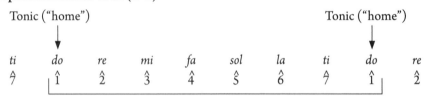

Singing scale patterns from *do* to *do* ($\hat{1}$–$\hat{1}$)

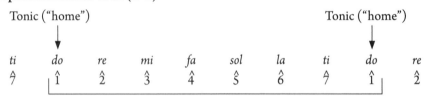

Workbook ASSIGNMENT 6.1

1. Writing chromatic scales

Write one-octave chromatic scales as requested below, both ascending (with sharps) and descending (with flats). For scales that begin with a flat, write flats and naturals ascending.

a. C chromatic scale

b. A chromatic scale

c. F chromatic scale

d. B♭ chromatic scale

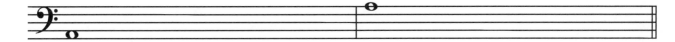

2. Writing major scales

Beginning on the pitch given, build a major scale by adding flats or sharps in front of the remaining pitches as needed. Be sure to follow the correct pattern of whole and half steps: W–W–H–W–W–W–H. Label the whole and half steps as shown in a.

a.   b.

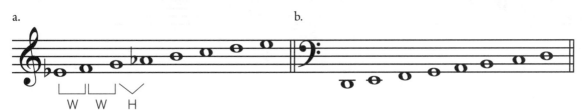

c.   d.

3. Writing major scales with scale-degree numbers

Beginning on the pitch given, write an ascending and descending major scale, following the correct pattern of whole and half steps. Start by writing in the note heads, label whole and half steps, then add flats or sharps as needed. Write the scale-degree number above each note.

a. F♯ Major

b. A Major

c. C♯ Major

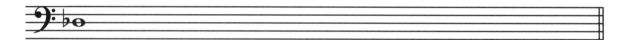

d. D♭ Major

4. Writing whole-tone scales

For each set of pitches below, add accidentals to create a whole-tone scale. Label each whole step.

a.   b.

c.   d.

Workbook ASSIGNMENT 6.2

1. Key signature warm-up

On the staves below, copy the seven sharps and seven flats in order in each clef. As you write each sharp or flat, say the name of the major key that goes with the number of sharps or flats that you've written so far.

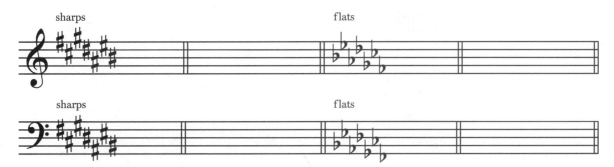

2. Writing key signatures

a. Write the key signature for each sharp key below. Remember: Think down one diatonic half step from the name of the key; this note will be the last sharp.

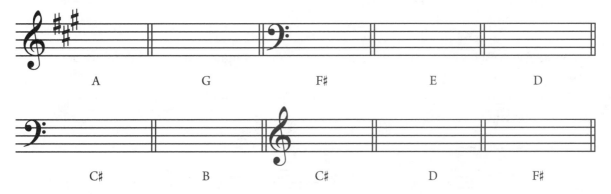

A   G   F♯   E   D

C♯   B   C♯   D   F♯

b. Write the key signature for each flat key below. Remember: Write one flat beyond the name of the key.

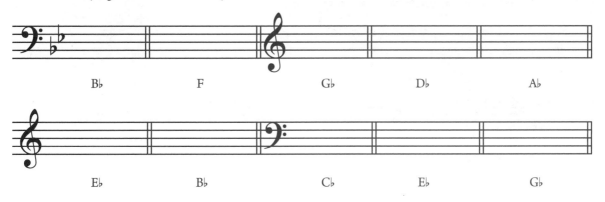

B♭   F   G♭   D♭   A♭

E♭   B♭   C♭   E♭   G♭

c. Write the key signature for each major key indicated. Remember that the sharps and flats must appear in the correct order and octave.

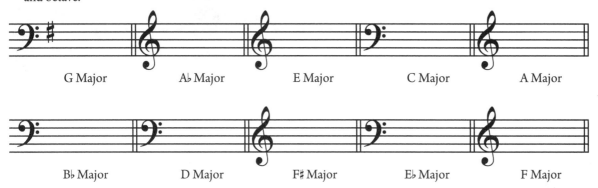

G Major	Ab Major	E Major	C Major	A Major

Bb Major	D Major	F# Major	Eb Major	F Major

3. Identifying keys from key signatures

a. Identify the name of each sharp key given below. Circle the last sharp (the leading tone of the key), then go up a half step to name the key.

D ___   ___   ___   ___   ___

___   ___   ___   ___   ___

b. Identify the name of each flat key below. Circle the next-to-last flat to get the name of the key (*or* go down four scale steps from the last flat).

Eb ___   ___   ___   ___

___   ___   ___   ___

c. Identify the name of the major key associated with each key signature below.

Bb ___   ___   ___   ___   ___   ___   ___

___   ___   ___   ___   ___   ___   ___

Workbook ASSIGNMENT 6.3

1. Writing major scales from scale degrees

Given the scale degree notated on the left, write the appropriate ascending major scale. Begin by writing whole notes on each line and space of the scale, then fill in the necessary accidentals. Write the scale-degree numbers to check your answer.

2. Identifying the key from a melody

Look at the key signature and melodic cues from the beginning and end of each song excerpt below to determine the key. Write the name of the major key or "not major" in the blank. If major, label the scale degrees of the notes to confirm that they fit well in the key you have chosen.

a. "Drink to Me Only," mm. 1–4

Key: ___F major___

b. Elvis Presley, "Love Me Tender," mm. 5–8

Key: _____

c. "Shalom, Chaverim," mm. 4b–8

Translation: Peace until we meet again

Key: _____

d. Franz Schubert, "Der Lindenbaum," from *Winterreise*, mm. 8b–12a

Translation: By the fountain in front of the gate, there stands a linden tree.

Key: _____

e. "Masters in This Hall," mm. 5–8

Key: _____

Workbook   AURAL SKILLS 6.1

1. Hearing half and whole steps (review)

a. Listen to the recording. Beginning with the given pitch, a three-pitch melody will be played. In the blanks beneath each exercise, write W or H between pitches 1 and 2 and between pitches 2 and 3. Then notate pitches 2 and 3 with adjacent note names and the appropriate accidental. 🔊

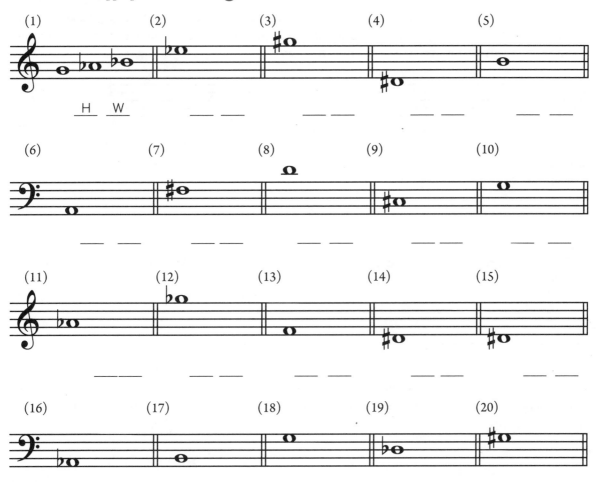

b. Listen to an excerpt from a melody by American composer Cole Porter, then identify the melody's whole and half steps. Write W or H in the blanks beneath the staff. Then use this information to write the appropriate accidental before *each* of the other notes. 🔊

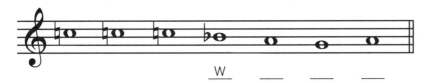

2. Listening to and writing a major-key melody

Listen to an excerpt from a familiar melody, and complete the following exercises. 🔊

a. The excerpt consists of two five-note segments. Notate segment 1's five-pitch melody in scale-degree numbers and solfège syllables, beginning on $\hat{1}$, or *do*.

scale degrees: $\quad\hat{1}$ ___ ___ ___ ___

solfège syllables: $\quad do$ ___ ___ ___ ___

b. On the staff below, notate segment 1's pitches, beginning on C3, with open note heads. Don't worry yet about rhythm. Between pitches, write W for whole step or H for half step (except for repeated notes). Play your solution at a keyboard and compare with the recorded performance; correct any errors you hear.

c. Now notate segment 2's five-pitch melody in numbers and syllables, beginning on $\hat{3}$, or *mi*.

scale degrees: $\quad\hat{3}$ ___ ___ ___ ___

solfège syllables: $\quad mi$ ___ ___ ___ ___

d. On the staff below, notate segment 2's pitches, beginning on E3, with open note heads. Between pitches, write W for whole step or H for half step. Check your solution at a keyboard and correct any errors.

e. On the rhythm staff below, sketch in the rhythm of the entire melody (segments 1 and 2) in common time (𝄴). Use correct notation, beaming, and bar lines. Then write the entire melody (pitches and rhythms) on the staff below in C major.

Workbook   AURAL SKILLS 6.2

We return to a song by Lionel Bart that we listened to in Chapter 3, this time focusing on the pitches of the melody. The excerpt consists of two segments, each seven pitches long. 🔊

1. Notate segment 1, the first seven pitches, in each of the following ways.

(a) Beginning on *do*, write segment 1 with solfège syllables.

<u>do</u>   ___   ___   ___   ___   ___   ___

(b) Beginning on $\hat{1}$, write segment 1 with scale-degree numbers.

<u>$\hat{1}$</u>   ___   ___   ___   ___   ___   ___

(c) Beginning on C, write segment 1 with letter names.

<u>C</u>   ___   ___   ___   ___   ___   ___

(d) On the staff below, notate the pitches of segment 1 with open note heads. Begin with C3. For now, don't worry about the rhythm.

2. Notate segment 2, the melody's last seven pitches, in each of the following ways.

(a) Beginning on *mi*, write segment 2 with solfège syllables.

<u>mi</u>   ___   ___   ___   ___   ___   ___

(b) Beginning on $\hat{3}$, write segment 2 with scale-degree numbers.

<u>$\hat{3}$</u>   ___   ___   ___   ___   ___   ___

(c) Beginning on E, write segment 2 with letter names.

<u>E</u>   ___   ___   ___   ___   ___   ___

(d) On the staff below, notate the pitches of segment 2. Begin with E3. Again, don't worry about the rhythm.

3. On the rhythm staff below, notate the rhythm of the melody, beginning with four eighth notes.

4. On the staff below, notate both pitches and rhythm of the melody.

5. Use scale-degree numbers or solfège syllables to help you write the melody in D major, beginning on D3. Write the correct key signature. Check your answer at a keyboard, and correct any errors.

Now write the melody in A♭ major, beginning on A♭4. Write the correct key signature. Check your answer at a keyboard, and correct any errors.

TOPICS

- parallel keys
- natural minor
- harmonic minor
- melodic minor
- comparing scale types
- relative keys
- minor key signatures and the circle of fifths
- identifying the key from a score

MUSIC

- Johann Sebastian Bach, Invention in D minor
- Jim Croce, "Time in a Bottle"
- Patrick S. Gilmore, "When Johnny Comes Marching Home"
- Wolfgang Amadeus Mozart, *Variations on "Ah, vous dirai-je Maman"*
- Mozart, String Quartet, K. 421, third movement
- Richard Rodgers and Lorenz Hart, "My Funny Valentine"
- Franz Schubert, Waltz in B minor, Op. 18, No. 6

CHAPTER 7

Minor Scales and Keys

Parallel Keys

Listen to the beginning of the theme and a variation on "Ah, vous dirai-je Maman" (otherwise known as "Twinkle, Twinkle, Little Star"), and compare the right-hand parts shown in Examples 7.1 and 7.2.

EXAMPLE 7.1   Mozart, *Variations on "Ah, vous dirai-je Maman,"* mm. 1–8 (right hand)

(a) Melody

(b) Pitches of the melody

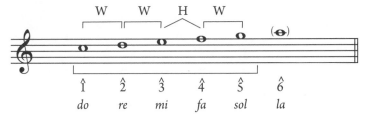

EXAMPLE 7.2   Mozart, *Variations*, Var. VIII, mm. 193–200 (right hand)

(a) Melody

(b) Pitches of the melody

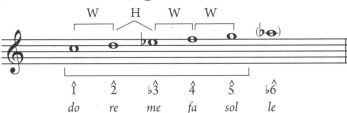

The beginning of Example 7.2 immediately signals the shift to the **minor mode** by its first three notes: C–D–E♭. The first five notes of each example, given in part (b)—C–D–E–F–G in Example 7.1 and C–D–E♭–F–G in Example 7.2—differ by only one note: $\hat{3}$ is lowered from E to E♭. (Write the third scale degree in minor as ♭$\hat{3}$ to show that it has been lowered when compared with major, even if the note itself does not have a flat.) These scale segments differ in their arrangement of whole and half steps: W–W–H–W in major becomes W–H–W–W in minor, as marked. Major and minor scales that share the same tonic always share their first five notes, except that $\hat{3}$ becomes ♭$\hat{3}$. (In the Mozart example, $\hat{6}$ also becomes ♭$\hat{6}$. This is usually the case in minor keys, but it may vary with scale type, as we will see shortly.)

> **KEY CONCEPT** These melodies are written in **parallel keys**: C major and C minor. **Parallel major** and **minor** keys share the same tonic but have different key signatures and a different arrangement of whole and half steps.

The shared tonic between parallel keys is a powerful relationship. It is easy to move between them by changing the accidentals or key signature, as in the Mozart example. This shift is known as a **change in mode**.

Now look at the solfège syllables provided in Examples 7.1 and 7.2. Because $\hat{1}$, $\hat{2}$, $\hat{4}$, and $\hat{5}$ are identical, sing them with the same syllables: *do, re, fa,* and *sol*; because the third scale degree differs, shift the syllable from *mi* in major to *me* in minor. (This system, called *do*-based minor, is only one of several for singing in minor keys. Your teacher may specify another.)

Natural Minor

One way to spell a **minor scale** is by taking the parallel major scale (Example 7.3a) and lowering $\hat{3}$, $\hat{6}$, and $\hat{7}$ one chromatic half step, to ♭$\hat{3}$, ♭$\hat{6}$, and ♭$\hat{7}$ (Example 7.3b). The result is known as the **natural minor** scale, with a W–H–W–W–H–W–W pattern of whole and half steps. We refer to $\hat{3}$, $\hat{6}$, and $\hat{7}$ (with black note heads in the example) as the **modal scale degrees** because they help distinguish between major and minor modes. Their solfège syllables reflect the change: *mi* becomes *me*, *la* becomes *le*, and *ti* becomes *te*.

EXAMPLE 7.3   Major scale and parallel natural minor

(a) C major

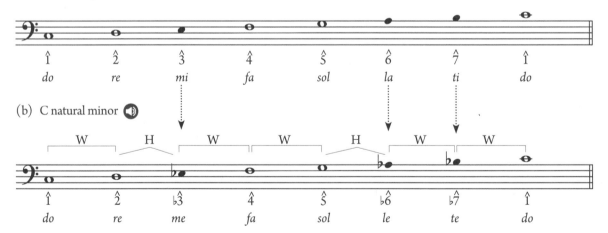

In major keys, there is a special "pull" from $\hat{7}$ up to $\hat{1}$, from the half-step tension of the leading tone wanting to move up to the tonic (*ti* to *do*). In natural minor, there is no half-step pull between ♭$\hat{7}$ and $\hat{1}$ (*te* to *do*): these scale degrees are a whole step apart, a defining characteristic of the natural minor sound. Listen to Example 7.4a, in E minor, to hear the whole step D to E in measures 15–16. The E natural minor scale is written as part (b). Here, ♭$\hat{7}$ (D) sounds relatively stable, and has none of the pull that a leading tone (D♯) would have to E.

EXAMPLE 7.4   Gilmore, "When Johnny Comes Marching Home"

(a) Measures 12b–16

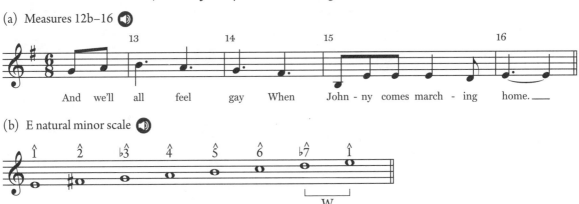

And we'll all feel gay When John - ny comes march - ing home. ___

(b) E natural minor scale

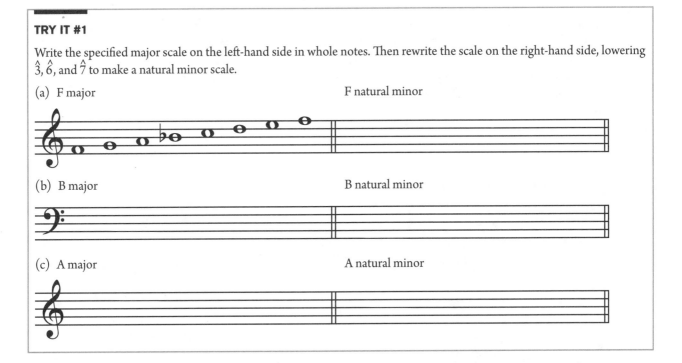

TRY IT #1

Write the specified major scale on the left-hand side in whole notes. Then rewrite the scale on the right-hand side, lowering $\hat{3}$, $\hat{6}$, and $\hat{7}$ to make a natural minor scale.

(a) F major   F natural minor

(b) B major   B natural minor

(c) A major   A natural minor

Harmonic Minor

Now listen to the first eight measures of a minor-key waltz for piano by Franz Schubert, shown in Example 7.5. In measure 1, the upper voice outlines $\hat{1}$, $\flat\hat{3}$, and $\hat{5}$ of the minor scale beginning on B. Every A in Schubert's waltz (left hand, mm. 2, 4, 6, and 7), however, has a sharp, which converts $\flat\hat{7}$ to $\hat{7}$, the leading tone to B. Here, there is the upward pull of leading tone to tonic, just as in major keys.

EXAMPLE 7.5   Schubert, Waltz in B minor, mm. 1–8a

Example 7.6 shows the scale that corresponds with the waltz. This scale, known as **harmonic minor**, features a half-step relation between $\hat{7}$ and $\hat{1}$ that was missing in natural minor. Because $\hat{7}$ now functions as a leading tone, we sing it on *ti* (not *te*), as in major.

EXAMPLE 7.6   B harmonic minor scale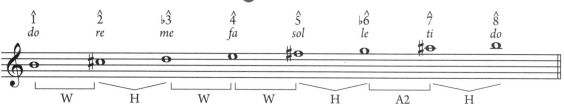

In this scale, the interval between $\flat\hat{6}$ and $\hat{7}$ (*le* and *ti*)—G to A♯ in Example 7.6—is larger than a whole step. It is an **augmented second** (**A2**), equivalent to a step and a half. Because of the unusual sound of the A2, harmonic minor is not typically heard in pieces *as a scale*. Instead, the leading tone will generally appear as part of the harmony (the underlying chords, see Chapter 9), as in the Schubert waltz—hence the name, harmonic minor.

Listen to the opening of Bach's Invention in D minor (Example 7.7a), where the $\flat\hat{6}$ and leading tone combination appears melodically. Here Bach places $\hat{7}$ (C♯) below $\flat\hat{6}$ (B♭), in measures 1–2 and 5–6, to avoid the melodic A2. Part (b) of the example shows how these scale degrees are typically handled: write $\hat{7}$ (*ti*) so that it moves up to $\hat{1}$ (*do*); write $\flat\hat{6}$ (*le*) so that it moves down to $\hat{5}$ (*sol*).

EXAMPLE 7.7   Bach, Invention in D minor, mm. 1–7a (right hand)

(a) Bach's melody

(b) Melodic separation of $\hat{7}$ from $\flat\hat{6}$ (*ti* from *le*)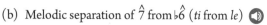

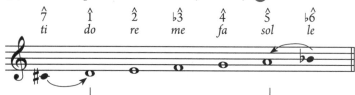

> **KEY CONCEPT**   To write a harmonic minor scale, begin with natural minor and raise $\flat\hat{7}$ a chromatic half step to make the leading tone (*ti*). If you begin with a major scale, lower $\hat{3}$ to $\flat\hat{3}$ and $\hat{6}$ to $\flat\hat{6}$.

These alterations sometimes result in odd-looking combinations of accidentals, as in Example 7.8. Part (a) shows a scale with flats and a sharp, the result of raising $\flat\hat{7}$ (F) to create a leading tone. The harmonic minor scale in part (b) begins on a sharped note; such scales typically need a double sharp for the leading tone.

EXAMPLE 7.8   Spelling of harmonic minor scales

(a) G harmonic minor 🔊

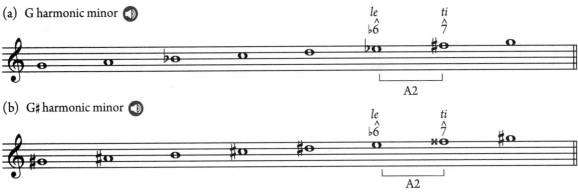

(b) G♯ harmonic minor 🔊

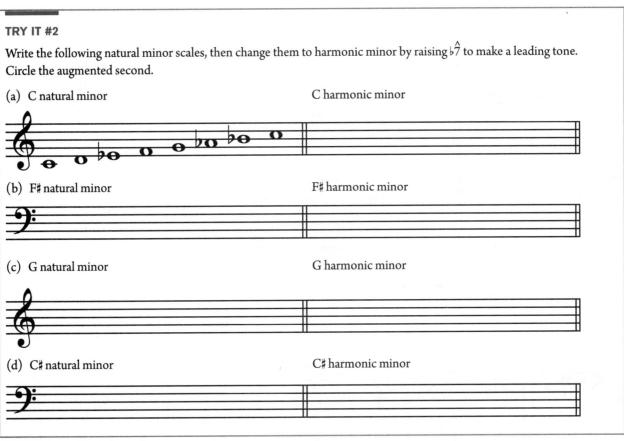

TRY IT #2

Write the following natural minor scales, then change them to harmonic minor by raising ♭$\hat{7}$ to make a leading tone. Circle the augmented second.

(a) C natural minor   C harmonic minor

(b) F♯ natural minor   F♯ harmonic minor

(c) G natural minor   G harmonic minor

(d) C♯ natural minor   C♯ harmonic minor

Melodic Minor

Yet another variant of the minor scale is **melodic minor**, which differs in its ascending and descending forms.

> **KEY CONCEPT**   Melodic minor is written with $\hat{6}$ and $\hat{7}$ when the scale ascends, reaching upward toward the tonic. In its descending form, it's written with ♭$\hat{7}$ and ♭$\hat{6}$ (like natural minor), pulling downward toward $\hat{5}$.

The left-hand part of the Mozart variation shown in Example 7.9, in C minor, illustrates how this scale is applied in music. Listen to the lowest part. In measure 197, Mozart raises ♭$\hat{7}$ to the leading tone (B♭ to B♮), but he also raises ♭$\hat{6}$ to $\hat{6}$ (A♭ to A♮) to avoid the potential augmented second (A♭ to B♮). In measure 198, ♭$\hat{6}$ (A♭) returns because the overall direction of the line here is downward.

EXAMPLE 7.9   Mozart, *Variations on "Ah, vous dirai-je Maman,"* Var. VIII, mm. 197–200
(left-hand part) 🔊

Example 7.10 shows the C melodic minor scale in its ascending and descending forms. Variability in the sixth and seventh scale degrees is typical in minor-key pieces. In C minor, the sixth may appear as A♭ or A♮, while the seventh may appear as B♭ or B♮ depending upon the context and the direction of the melodic line. Solfège syllables for the ascending form of melodic minor match those for major (*la–ti–do*), while syllables for the descending form match those for natural minor (*do–te–le*).

EXAMPLE 7.10   C melodic minor scale 🔊

Follow the bass line of Example 7.11, a song in D minor, to see the variability of the sixth and seventh scale degrees in a different musical context. The bass descends chromatically from the tonic D in measure 9 to ♭6̂ (B♭) in measure 13. The line then ascends back to D in measure 16, through the ascending melodic minor (5̂–6̂–7̂, A–B♮–C♯) in measure 15.

EXAMPLE 7.11   Croce, "Time in a Bottle," mm. 9–16a 🔊

chromatic scale segment

melodic minor segment (♭6̂ descending, 6̂ and 7̂ ascending)

Comparing Scale Types

In Example 7.12, C major is aligned with all three forms of the C minor scale. Play each scale. To tell them apart by ear, listen first for the quality of the third ($\hat{3}$ or $\flat\hat{3}$; *mi* or *me*). Then listen for the leading tone: there is no leading tone in natural minor (but $\flat\hat{7}$ instead). In harmonic minor, there *is* a leading tone, and you will hear it approached by the A2 ($\flat\hat{6}$–$\hat{7}$, or *le–ti*). Finally, you hear $\hat{6}$ (*la*) only in major or ascending melodic minor.

EXAMPLE 7.12 Four scales beginning on C
(a) Major

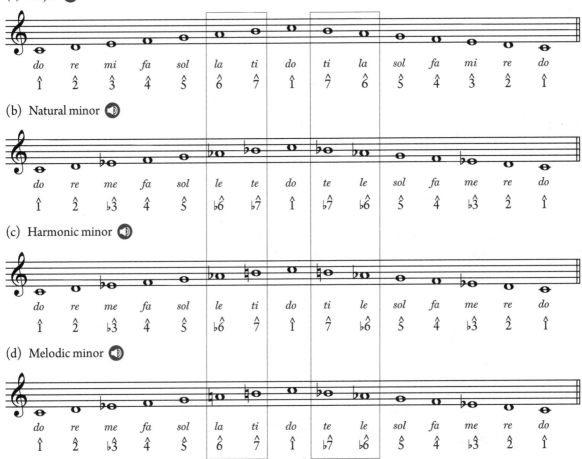

Scale-degree names in minor are identical to those in major (tonic, subdominant, etc.) with only a couple of exceptions. The $\flat\hat{7}$ in natural minor is called the **subtonic** because of its placement a whole step below the tonic, and the raised $\hat{6}$ in melodic minor is simply known as the **raised submediant**.

SUMMARY

- To write a natural minor scale:
    (a) write a major scale, then add accidentals to lower $\hat{3}$, $\hat{6}$, and $\hat{7}$ a chromatic half step; or
    (b) write whole and half steps above the tonic in the pattern W–H–W–W–H–W–W (use each letter name once).
- To write a harmonic minor scale, begin with a natural minor scale and then raise $\flat\hat{7}$ to $\hat{7}$, ascending and descending.
- To write a melodic minor scale, begin with a natural minor scale and then raise $\flat\hat{6}$ and $\flat\hat{7}$ to $\hat{6}$ and $\hat{7}$ ascending only. The ascending form is like major, with $\flat\hat{3}$. The descending form is identical to natural minor.

TRY IT #3

Write the following melodic minor scales, ascending and descending.

(a) B melodic minor

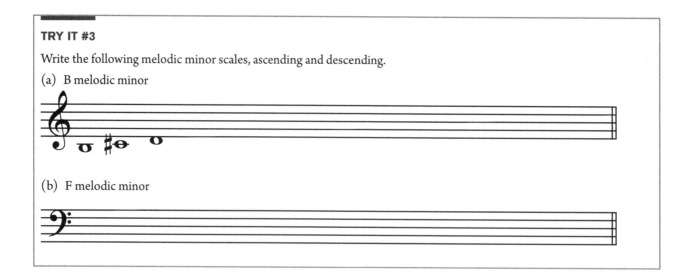

(b) F melodic minor

ASSIGNMENT 7.2

Relative Keys

Example 7.13 shows the first and last phrases of the jazz standard "My Funny Valentine." Listen to a performance of the complete song. Then listen to just the measures in the example—the first four and last four—to determine the key of each passage. Decide by ear what the tonic pitch is for (a) and (b); sing it, then listen for $\hat{3}$ or $\flat\hat{3}$ to decide whether the key is major or minor.

EXAMPLE 7.13   Rodgers and Hart, "My Funny Valentine"

(a) Measures 1–4 ◆ 0:00–0:14

(b) Measures 33–36 ◆ 1:53–2:11

For part (a), you probably sang C, the first note of the vocal line and the lowest note of the piano accompaniment. This passage is in C minor: the singer's line begins $\hat{1}$–$\hat{2}$–$\flat\hat{3}$ (*do–re–me*), and the piano plays C3 throughout. Compare this with the end of the song in (b): here the singer ends on E♭, and the lowest note of the piano is also E♭. If E♭ is the tonic, then the vocal line of this phrase begins $\hat{1}$–$\hat{2}$–$\hat{3}$ (*do–re–mi*). Part (b) is in E♭ major. Though most of the music we have studied in this book stays in one key throughout, many pieces (like this one) change keys; a process called **modulation**. In this song, the change requires no new accidentals or key signature because C minor and E♭ major share the same key signature: three flats.

> **KEY CONCEPT** Keys that share the same key signature (but different tonics) are called **relative keys**.

Example 7.14 aligns the scales of E♭ major and C natural minor to show how they are related: they share all the same notes.

EXAMPLE 7.14 E♭ major and C natural minor scales 🔊

E♭ major

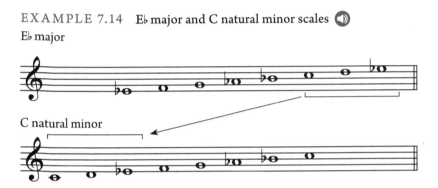

C natural minor

Every major scale has its **relative minor** scale, and every minor scale has its **relative major**. To find the relative minor of any major scale or key, identify $\hat{6}$ of the major scale: that pitch is the tonic of the relative minor. As Example 7.15 shows, the relative minor scale of G major is E minor.

EXAMPLE 7.15 Finding the relative (natural) minor 🔊

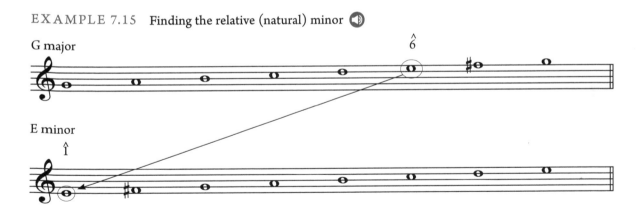

G major

E minor

A shortcut for finding the relative minor key is to count *down* three half steps from the major-key tonic. Be sure to choose the correct spelling: it should conform to the key signature of the major key and span three different letter names. To find the relative minor of A major:

(1) Count down three letter names: A G F.
(2) Count down three half steps: A to A♭, A♭ to G, G to G♭.
(3) Change the spelling if it disagrees with step 1. We must respell G♭ as F♯, giving the answer of F♯ minor.

Reading Review

Match the terms on the left with the best answer on the right.

_____ (1) $\hat{3}$, $\hat{6}$, and $\hat{7}$

_____ (2) half step

_____ (3) natural minor scale

_____ (4) whole step

_____ (5) relative keys

_____ (6) raised submediant

_____ (7) harmonic minor scale

_____ (8) subtonic

_____ (9) parallel keys

_____ (10) descending melodic minor

(a) distance from $\hat{2}$ to $\flat\hat{3}$ in natural minor

(b) differs from major by three modal scale degrees

(c) D major and B minor

(d) D major and D minor

(e) $\flat\hat{7}$ in a natural minor scale

(f) differs from natural minor by the raised leading tone

(g) modal scale degrees

(h) $\hat{6}$ in an ascending melodic minor scale

(i) pitches are the same as in natural minor

(j) distance from $\flat\hat{7}$ to $\hat{1}$ in natural minor

Ⓢ Additional review and practice available at wwnorton.com/studyspace

Class Activities

A. At the keyboard

1. Five-finger patterns

(a) All three forms of the minor scale share $\hat{1}$ to $\hat{5}$. The parallel major scale shares these scale degrees as well, except that the third is $\hat{3}$ in major and $\flat\hat{3}$ in minor.

Play each pattern below in both hands (separately, then together), one octave apart, fingerings 5–4–3–2–1 (left hand) and 1–2–3–4–5 (right hand). Sing on scale-degree numbers or solfège syllables as you play.

	W	W	H	W		W	H	W	W	

	do	re	mi	fa	sol	do	re	me	fa	sol
Solfège:										
Scale degree:	$\hat{1}$	$\hat{2}$	$\hat{3}$	$\hat{4}$	$\hat{5}$	$\hat{1}$	$\hat{2}$	$\flat\hat{3}$	$\hat{4}$	$\hat{5}$
Left-hand fingers:	5	4	3	2	1	5	4	3	2	1

(b) Follow the same model for each tonic note below. First play a major pattern ($\hat{1}$ to $\hat{5}$) with each hand in a separate octave (hands alone and then together). Then lower its third note by a half step and play a minor pattern. While playing, sing on letter names, scale-degree numbers, or solfège syllables.

(1) A	(4) E♭	(7) E	(10) B♭
(2) F	(5) B	(8) C♯	(11) G♯
(3) G	(6) F♯	(9) A♭	(12) D

2. Three types of minor scales

(a) Play each of the following C minor scales while singing along on numbers or syllables, using the fingerings marked in the example. Listen for the changes in sound (always in the right hand) as you move from natural to harmonic and then to melodic minor.

Natural minor

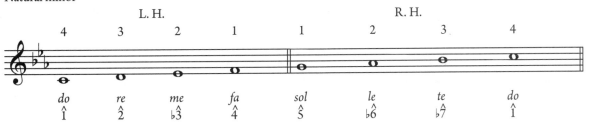

Harmonic minor

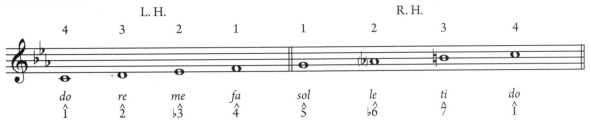

Melodic minor

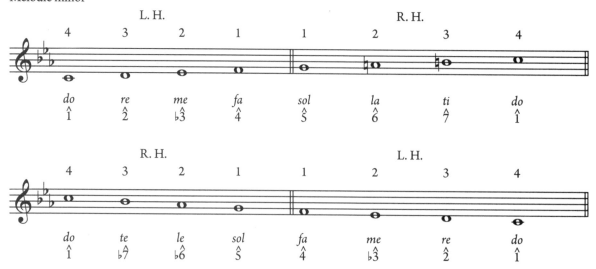

(b) From each of the following tonic notes, perform the three types of minor scale—natural, harmonic, and ascending and descending melodic. As you play, sing each letter name, scale-degree number, or solfège syllable.

(1) D   (4) B   (7) A   (10) G

(2) F   (5) E♭   (8) C   (11) B♭

(3) G♯   (6) F♯   (9) E   (12) C♯

B. Reading rhythms

Perform the following rhythms on "ta" or counting syllables, as directed. Keep a steady beat by tapping the pulse or conducting.

Rhythm 1

Rhythm 2

Rhythm 3

Rhythm 4 (Duet: Perform with two people or groups.)

C. Listening for major and minor keys

Listen to the beginning of each excerpt to determine whether it is in a major or minor key, then circle your choice.

1. Franz Schubert, "Allegretto," D. 915 🔊   major   minor

2. Fanny Mendelssohn Hensel, "Waldeinsam" 🔊   major   minor

3. Franz Schubert, "Wanderer Fantasy," Op. 15, Adagio 🔊   major   minor

4. Ludwig van Beethoven, Sonata for Violin and Piano, Op. 30, No. 2, first movement 🔊   major   minor

5. Joseph Haydn, Piano Sonata No. 9, Scherzo 🔊   major   minor

D. Singing at sight

All of the following melodies are in minor keys. Before singing, determine each melody's key, and play that natural minor scale at the keyboard, using any fingering that is comfortable. Then identify scale segments, if present, that suggest harmonic or melodic minor (look for accidentals). When singing harmonic and melodic minor, concentrate especially on singing the whole and half steps in tune.

Work on the rhythm and pitches separately, using scale-degree numbers or solfège syllables to help you, before putting them together. Check at the piano to correct any errors.

Melody 1

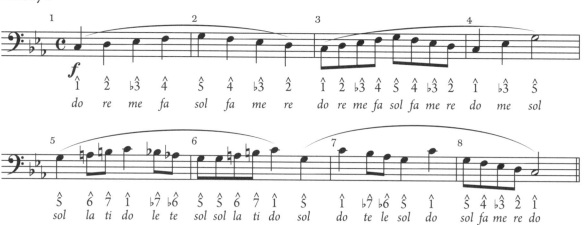

Melody 2

Melody 3 "Once More My Soul" (American folk hymn)

This melody begins with an anacrusis on *sol* ($\hat{5}$)

Melody 4

E. Listening and writing

1. Call and Response. Your teacher will perform short patterns made from minor scales, then ask you to respond by performing or writing what you have heard. Try to memorize the call as quickly as possible. When performing your response, maintain its pitch, rhythm, and tempo. When writing your response, write scale-degree numbers or solfège syllables along with the rhythm of the call. If a key is announced, write the pitches and rhythm together on staff paper of your own.

2. Point and Sing. After establishing a tonic pitch, your teacher will create a melody by pointing to a series of items—pitches, letter names, solfège syllables, or scale-degree numbers—like those shown in the following chart. When the teacher points to an item, immediately sing it. Perform the melody until you have memorized it. Then use the pitches, letter names, syllables, or numbers of the melody to write it on the staff. Make your own point-and-sing exercises with a partner to practice.

Tonic ("home")

ti	*do*	*re*	*me*	*fa*	*sol*	*le*
$\hat{7}$	$\hat{1}$	$\hat{2}$	$\flat\hat{3}$	$\hat{4}$	$\hat{5}$	$\flat\hat{6}$

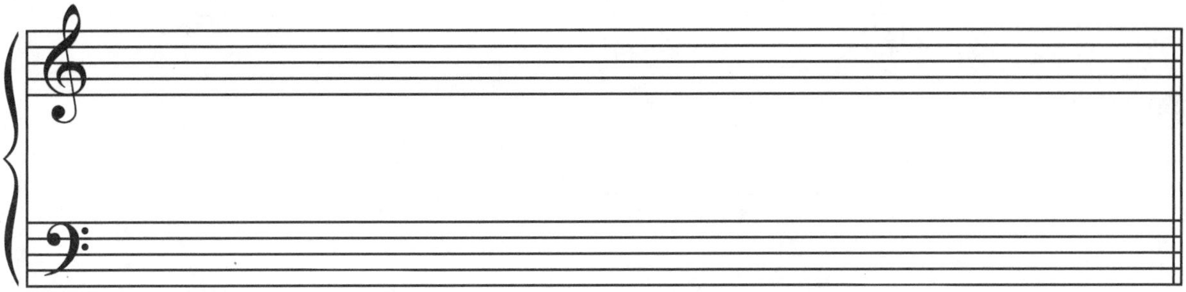

Letters: ___ ___ ___ ___ ___ ___ ___

Workbook ASSIGNMENT 7.1

1. Parallel major and natural minor

a. The first five notes of a major or minor scale are given below. In the blank provided, identify the scale as "major" or "minor."

(1) 🔊

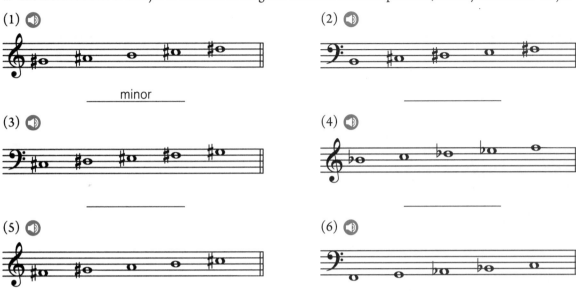

<u>   minor   </u>

(2) 🔊

_____

(3) 🔊

_____

(4) 🔊

_____

(5) 🔊

_____

(6) 🔊

_____

b. Write each specified major scale, placing sharps or flats as needed before each note. Next to each major scale, write its parallel natural minor scale (change $\hat{3}$, $\hat{6}$, and $\hat{7}$ to $\flat\hat{3}$, $\flat\hat{6}$, and $\flat\hat{7}$). Write either scale-degree numbers or solfège syllables beneath the minor scale.

(1) D major   D natural minor

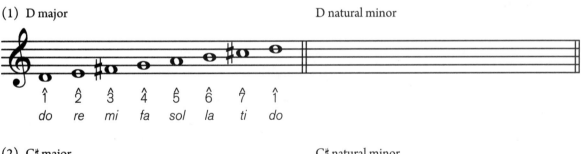

$\hat{1}$ $\hat{2}$ $\hat{3}$ $\hat{4}$ $\hat{5}$ $\hat{6}$ $\hat{7}$ $\hat{1}$

do   re   mi   fa   sol   la   ti   do

(2) C♯ major   C♯ natural minor

(3) E major   E natural minor

(4) F♯ major   F♯ natural minor

(5) B♭ major   B♭ natural minor

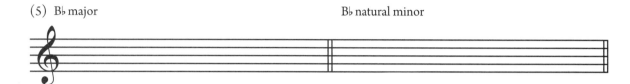

2. Writing natural minor scales

- Write the specified tonic pitch (which may have an accidental).
- Write the basic scale pitches above it (without accidentals).
- EITHER

(1) Label the spaces between pitches with W–H–W–W–H–W–W.
(2) Add the necessary accidentals to conform with the whole- and half-step pattern.

OR

(1) Imagine the parallel major key signature.
(2) Lower scale degrees $\hat{3}$, $\hat{6}$, and $\hat{7}$.

a. C natural minor   b. B natural minor

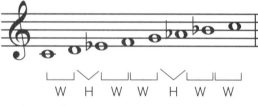

c. G natural minor   d. D natural minor

e. C♯ natural minor   f. F natural minor

g. E♭ natural minor   h. F♯ natural minor

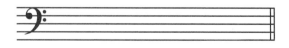

Workbook ASSIGNMENT 7.2

1. Writing harmonic minor

a. Write the natural minor scales specified below, adding the necessary accidentals. To the right, write a harmonic minor scale beginning on the same note. Circle the augmented second.

(1) D natural minor

D harmonic minor

(2) F natural minor

F harmonic minor

(3) E natural minor

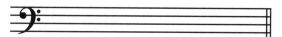

E harmonic minor

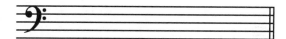

(4) B natural minor

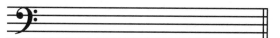

B harmonic minor

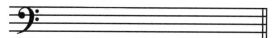

b. Notate the melodies given below in scale-degree numbers and solfège syllables (no rhythm required). If you know the name of the tune, write it in the blank.

(1) Write this melody in B minor.

$\hat{5}$ $\hat{4}$ $\flat\hat{3}$ $\hat{1}$ $\hat{2}$ $\flat\hat{3}$ $\hat{2}$ $\hat{1}$ $\hat{5}$ $\hat{4}$ $\flat\hat{3}$ $\hat{1}$ $\hat{2}$ $\flat\hat{3}$ $\hat{2}$ $\hat{1}$
sol fa me do re me re do sol fa me do re me re do

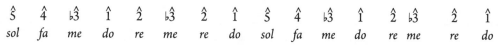

Name of melody: _____

(2) Write this melody in D minor.

$\hat{5}$ $\hat{1}$ $\hat{1}$ $\hat{2}$ $\flat\hat{3}$ $\hat{1}$ $\flat\hat{3}$ $\flat\hat{3}$ $\hat{4}$ $\hat{5}$ $\hat{5}$ $\hat{1}$ $\flat\hat{7}$ $\hat{5}$
sol do do re me do me me fa sol sol do te sol

Name of melody: _____

2. Writing melodic minor

Write each natural minor scale specified. Then below it, rewrite as an ascending and descending melodic minor scale, adding accidentals as necessary. Finally, label each pitch of the melodic minor scale with the appropriate scale-degree number or solfège syllable.

a. A natural minor

A melodic minor

b. F♯ natural minor

F♯ melodic minor

c. G natural minor

G melodic minor

Workbook   ASSIGNMENT 7.3

1. Writing relative major and minor scales

- In each exercise below, first write the specified major scale, adding accidentals as needed. Circle $\hat{6}$ and write the letter name beneath.
- On the second staff, write the relative natural minor beginning with the circled $\hat{6}$.
- Copy the natural minor scales on the next two staves, altering as necessary to write the harmonic and melodic minor scale ascending.

a. F major

b. A♭ major

c. G major

d. B major

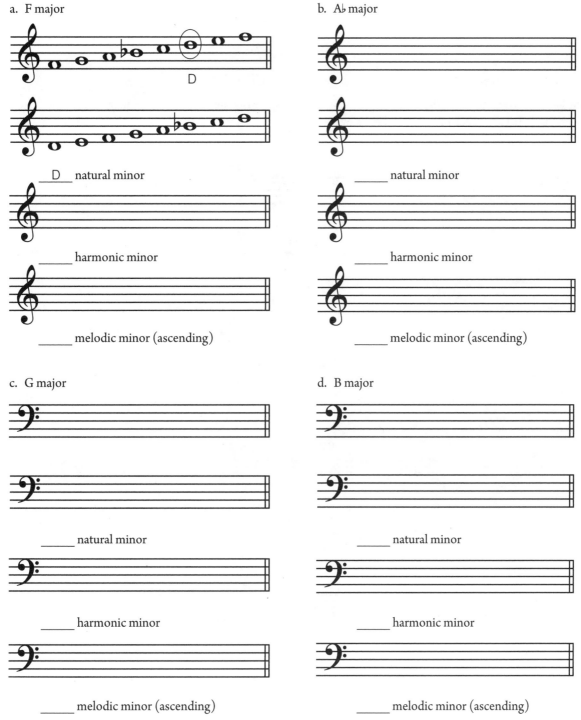

_____ natural minor

_____ harmonic minor

_____ melodic minor (ascending)

2. Reading and writing minor key signatures

Write the name of the key represented by each signature. Write the major key (uppercase letter) in the top row, and minor key (lowercase letter) in the bottom row.

major: __B♭__ ____ ____ ____ ____ ____ ____

minor: __g__ ____ ____ ____ ____ ____ ____

major: ____ ____ ____ ____ ____ ____ ____

minor: ____ ____ ____ ____ ____ ____ ____

3. Analyzing keys from melodies

Determine the key of each melody from the key signature and scale degrees. Write the name of the key in the blank. Then circle the correct relationship between each pair of melodies below.

a. Clarke, *Trumpet Voluntary*, mm. 5–8

Key: _____

b. Tomás Luis de Victoria, "O magnum mysterium," mm. 4b–9

Key: _____

Translation: [O great mystery] and wondrous sacrament

c. George and Ira Gershwin, "'S Wonderful!" mm. 29–36

Key: _____

d. Henry Purcell, "Ah, Belinda, I am prest," from *Dido and Aeneas*, mm. 68–72

Key: _____

| Clarke and Victoria | parallel keys | relative keys |
| The Gershwins and Purcell | parallel keys | relative keys |

Workbook   AURAL SKILLS 7.1

Listen to part of a traditional work song, and complete the following exercises. 🔊

Exercises 1–4 focus on the singer's melody.

1. Beginning with a quarter-note anacrusis, notate the rhythm in $\frac{4}{4}$ meter on the rhythm staff provided. Write the meter signature and bar lines. Beam notes to show the correct beat unit.

2. Beginning on $\hat{5}$ (*sol*), write the melody with solfège syllables or scale-degree numbers.

3. On the staves below, notate the pitches of the melody with hollow note heads in the key of G minor. Begin with D3, and write an appropriate clef and key signature.

4. Now notate both pitches *and* rhythm of the melody on the staves below. Remember to write an appropriate clef, key signature, and meter signature. For help, consult your answers to questions 1–3.

Exercises 5–7 focus on the bass line, the lowest part in the piano.

5. Beginning on $\hat{1}$ (*do*), write the first four pitches of the bass line with solfège syllables or scale-degree numbers.

6. On the staff below, notate the first four pitches of the bass line in the key of G minor. Begin with G3, and write the appropriate clef and key signature.

7. The bass line's first four pitches belong to which minor scale form? Circle the correct answer.

(a) natural (descending melodic) $(\hat{1}{-}\flat\hat{7}{-}\flat\hat{6}{-}\hat{5}$; *do–te–le–sol*)

(b) harmonic $(\hat{1}{-}\hat{7}{-}\flat\hat{6}{-}\hat{5}$; *do–ti–le–sol*)

(c) ascending melodic $(\hat{1}{-}\hat{7}{-}\hat{6}{-}\hat{5}$; *do–ti–la–sol*)

8. Transpose the melody (the answer to question 4) to the key of E minor. Notate your response in the treble clef, beginning on B3. For help, recall the syllables or numbers in question 2.

Workbook AURAL SKILLS 7.2

1. Follow the instructions below to compose two minor-key melodies.

- Write one melody in treble clef and one in bass clef, each one should be eight measures long.
- For one melody, choose a simple meter signature; for the other, a compound meter signature. Include beat patterns from those below.

simple-meter beat patterns

compound-meter beat patterns

- Choose a different tonic pitch for each melody, in a key that you can sing comfortably. Begin and end each melody on the tonic pitch.
- Write the minor key signature that goes with the tonic pitch.
- Create an interesting contour.
- End measure 4 inconclusively (e.g., on $\hat{2}$; *re*); end measure 8 conclusively (e.g., on $\hat{1}$; *do*)
- When ascending from $\hat{5}$ (*sol*), choose pitches from the ascending melodic scale: $\hat{5}$–$\hat{6}$–$\hat{7}$–$\hat{1}$ (*sol–la–ti–do*).
- When descending from $\hat{1}$ (*do*), choose pitches from the natural (descending melodic) scale: $\hat{1}$–♭$\hat{7}$–♭$\hat{6}$–$\hat{5}$ (*do–te–le–sol*).

2. Prepare to perform your melodies in the following ways.

- Sing with solfège syllables, scale-degree numbers, or letter names.
- Play them at the keyboard.
- Play at the keyboard and sing with syllables, numbers, or letter names.
- Play them on another instrument.

Now listen to "Greensleeves," the first eight measures of which are shown in Example 8.2. The first interval of the melody, A4 to C5, is a third (A B C). The melody in measure 1 (notated with stems up) features only seconds. These intervals and those in the Clarke example, measured between successive pitches, are called **melodic intervals**.

EXAMPLE 8.2   "Greensleeves," mm. 1–8

Listen again, now paying attention to the intervals formed between the dotted-quarter notes (stems down) and the melody. Intervals between pitches heard at the same time are **harmonic intervals**. Name them the same way as melodic intervals—by counting the letter names or lines and spaces encompassed by the interval. In Example 8.2, the harmonic interval circled in measure 3, between C4 and A4, is a sixth (C D E F G A); the interval circled in measure 8 is an **octave**. Octaves are abbreviated "8ve." You may also encounter the abbreviation "8va" from the Italian "ottava," appearing with a bracket above or below a group of notes. This means to play the notes transposed up or down an octave.

If two parts play the exact same pitch, this "interval," which spans no actual space, is called a **unison** and abbreviated U. In choral singing, when all women or all men sing a melody together, they are singing "in unison." (When women and men sing the same melody, they typically sing in octaves.)

Example 8.3 illustrates all the types of harmonic and melodic interval sizes up to an octave.

EXAMPLE 8.3   Interval sizes

(a) Melodic intervals

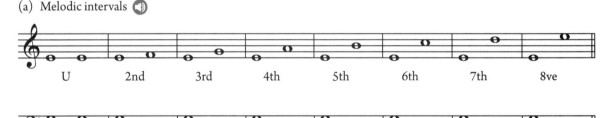

(b) Harmonic intervals

| U | 2nd | 3rd | 4th | 5th | 6th | 7th | 8ve |

(c) Unisons and seconds with stems

U   U 2nd   2nd   2nd 2nd

> **KEY CONCEPT**   Learn these landmarks on the staff to identify interval size quickly:
> 1. Thirds, fifths, and sevenths are always written with both pitches on lines or both on spaces.
>   - For thirds, the lines or spaces are adjacent.
>   - For fifths, skip one line or space.
>   - For sevenths, skip two lines or spaces.
> 2. Seconds, fourths, sixths, and octaves always have one pitch on a line and one on a space.

The two note heads in harmonic intervals should be aligned one above the other, except for unisons and seconds, whose note heads are side by side (Example 8.3b and c). A unison may be written as a single note head with two stems, one up and one down (part c). The lower note of a second is written to the left, unless each note gets a separate stem.

TRY IT #1

As quickly as possible, write the correct interval size beneath each example below. Identify intervals 3, 5, 7 by their line-line or space-space placement, and intervals 2, 4, 6, 8 by their line-space or space-line placement.

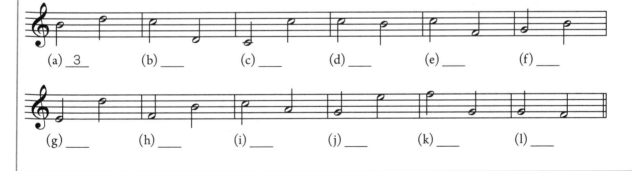

(a) __3__   (b) ____   (c) ____   (d) ____   (e) ____   (f) ____

(g) ____   (h) ____   (i) ____   (j) ____   (k) ____   (l) ____

Interval Quality

Listen to George and Ira Gershwin's "'S Wonderful!" while following the melody line in Example 8.4. All the thirds from the melody are isolated in part (b). If you play these thirds on a keyboard and count the half steps they span (remember to check the key signature!), you'll find that some span three half steps (the thirds in mm. 5–6 and 7–8) and some span four half steps (the thirds in mm. 9–10 and 11–12).

Intervals related by **inversion** share the same notes in reversed order (one of the two pitches is displaced by an octave). Intervals related by inversion are the unison and octave, second and seventh, third and sixth, and fourth and fifth; in each case, the sum of the two intervals is 9.

As Example 8.8 shows, a perfect interval inverts to another perfect interval. A major interval inverts to a minor interval (and vice versa): for example, a M3 inverts to a m6 (part b) and a M2 inverts to a m7 (part c).

SUMMARY

When inverting an interval:
(1) Keep one pitch stable and move the other one up or down an octave.
  - Perfect intervals remain perfect.
  - Major intervals invert to minor.
  - Minor intervals invert to major.
(2) The two interval sizes always sum to 9.
  - 1 inverts to 8.   - 8 inverts to 1.
  - 2 inverts to 7.   - 7 inverts to 2.
  - 3 inverts to 6.   - 6 inverts to 3.
  - 4 inverts to 5.   - 5 inverts to 4.

Spelling Intervals

In this chapter, you will learn three ways to identify and spell intervals: (1) by key signatures and scales, (2) by interval patterns in the C major scale, and (3) by inversion. Find the method that allows you to spell intervals most quickly and accurately, then use a second one to check your work.

Method 1:
In this method, you imagine the bottom note of an interval as the tonic of a major or minor key. The upper note lies somewhere in the scale and is spelled with accidentals belonging to that key. See Example 8.9 to follow these steps (shown in order vertically).

Step 1: Write the note heads of the interval on the lines or spaces.
Step 2: Think of the key signature of the bottom note.
Step 3: Add accidentals if necessary.
  - If perfect (U, 4, 5, 8) or major (2, 3, 6, 7), add an accidental to the upper note if needed to match the *major* key signature of the bottom note (parts a and c).
  - If minor (3, 6, 7), add an accidental to the upper note if needed to match the *minor* key signature of the bottom note (b and d).
  - If you want a m2, follow step 1, then add an accidental to the upper note if needed to make a diatonic half step.

EXAMPLE 8.9 Spelling intervals from major and minor scales

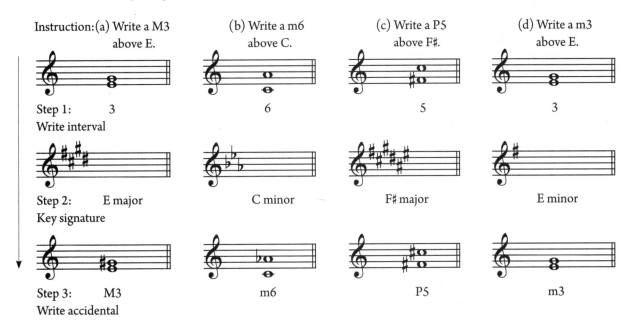

Instruction: (a) Write a M3 above E. (b) Write a m6 above C. (c) Write a P5 above F♯. (d) Write a m3 above E.

Step 1: 3   6   5   3
Write interval

Step 2: E major   C minor   F♯ major   E minor
Key signature

Step 3: M3   m6   P5   m3
Write accidental

Since a minor interval is a half step smaller than a major interval, you can also use a major key signature (if you know it better) to spell a minor interval:

(1) Write the corresponding major interval based on the major key signature of the bottom note.

(2) Lower the top note by a chromatic half step (but don't change the letter name).

EXAMPLE 8.10 Spelling minor intervals from major key signatures

To spell a m7 above D: (1) Spell a M7.   (2) Lower the top note.

To spell a m3 above G: (1) Spell a M3.   (2) Lower the top note.

TRY IT #2

(a) Identify the size and quality of each melodic interval in the following keys. 🔊

A♭ major

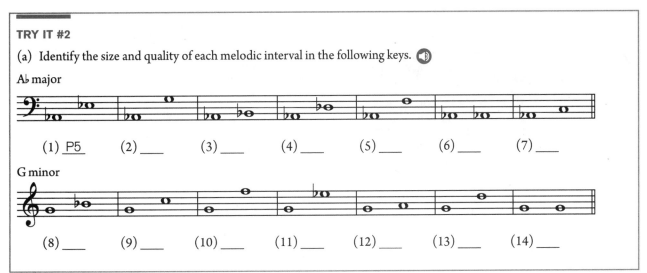

(1) P5   (2) ___   (3) ___   (4) ___   (5) ___   (6) ___   (7) ___

G minor

(8) ___   (9) ___   (10) ___   (11) ___   (12) ___   (13) ___   (14) ___

(b) Notate each melodic interval specified below.

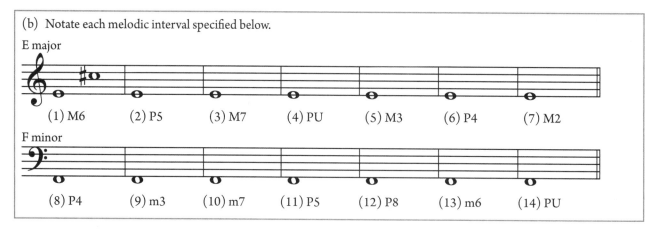

E major

(1) M6   (2) P5   (3) M7   (4) PU   (5) M3   (6) P4   (7) M2

F minor

(8) P4   (9) m3   (10) m7   (11) P5   (12) P8   (13) m6   (14) PU

Method 2:

Some musicians find it quick and easy to memorize the intervals found in the C major scale—by visualizing them on the keyboard (the white-note keys), on another instrument, or on the lines and spaces of a staff with no accidentals. Example 8.11 shows seconds, for instance, marked on the keyboard from C4 to C5 (a) and arranged on the staff (b). All seconds within the C major scale are M2, except for E–F and B–C, which are m2. As part (c) shows, the interval quality is unchanged if you add the same accidental to both notes.

EXAMPLE 8.11   Seconds within the C major scale

(a) On the keyboard

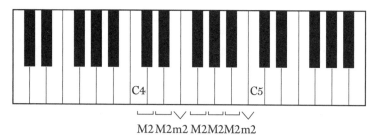

M2 M2 m2 M2 M2 M2 m2

(b) On the staff

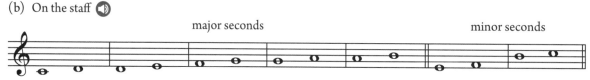

major seconds   minor seconds

(c) On the staff with matching accidentals added

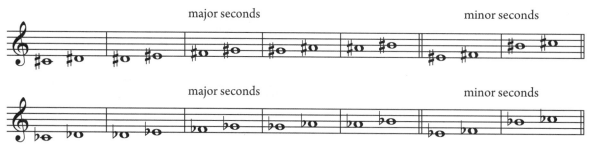

major seconds   minor seconds

major seconds   minor seconds

Memorize the qualities of the white-key thirds and fourths (Examples 8.12 and 8.13) as well and play them at the keyboard. As with seconds, if a third or fourth has matching accidentals, it retains the size and quality of the white-key interval. For instance, all white-key fourths are perfect except F–B, and they remain perfect if matching accidentals are added to both pitches.

EXAMPLE 8.12   Thirds within the C major scale

(a) On the keyboard

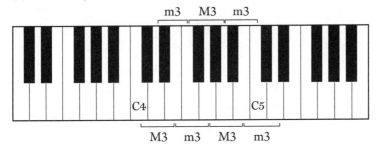

(b) On the staff

EXAMPLE 8.13   Fourths

(a) Within the C major scale

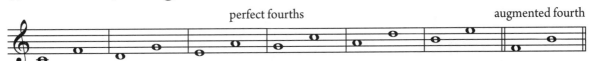

(b) With accidentals

TRY IT #3

Identify each second, third, and fourth below. Intervals with matching accidentals on both notes will have the same quality as their white-key counterparts.

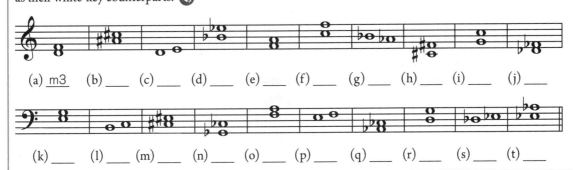

(a) _m3_   (b) ____   (c) ____   (d) ____   (e) ____   (f) ____   (g) ____   (h) ____   (i) ____   (j) ____

(k) ____   (l) ____   (m) ____   (n) ____   (o) ____   (p) ____   (q) ____   (r) ____   (s) ____   (t) ____

To spell intervals with the "white-key" (C major) method, remember:

(1) The quality of an interval remains unchanged when the same accidental is added to *both* notes. For example, F–G is a M2 as are Fb–Gb and F#–G#.

(2) Minor intervals are a chromatic half step smaller than major. You can make a major interval into a minor one by lowering the top note (F–G becomes F–Gb) or raising the bottom note (F–G becomes F#–G), in which case the accidentals no longer match.

To write any interval by the white-key method:

- If the given note is a white key, write the white-key interval first, and identify its quality (based on the memorized patterns in C major). Then adjust its size by adding a flat or sharp to the other note (Example 8.14a).
  (1) To make a major interval minor, lower the top note or raise the bottom note.
  (2) To make a minor interval major, raise the top note or lower the bottom note.
- If the given note has an accidental, write the proper note head for the interval size and add a matching accidental, then follow the same procedure (part b).
- If you are asked to write an interval up or down from a given note, do not change the given note; make any adjustments for quality on the other note.

EXAMPLE 8.14 Spelling intervals by C major patterns

(a) Start with a white-key interval and alter the top note.

1. Spell a m3 above C: 2. Spell a M3 above D:

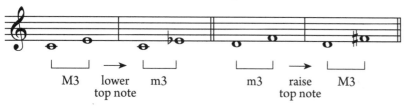

(b) Start with matching accidentals and alter the top note.

1. Spell a m3 above C#: 2. Spell a M3 above Db:

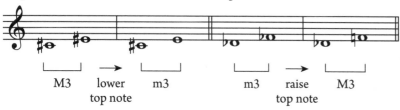

ASSIGNMENT 8.1

Method 3:

Inversions provide a quick shortcut for spelling wide intervals, such as fifths, sixths, and sevenths. As Example 8.15a shows, you can identify the seventh D–C by thinking of its inversion, the second C–D. You know that C–D is a M2; therefore its inversion is a m7. This process works with or without accidentals: since C# up to D# is a M2, D# up to C# is a m7. Part (b) shows how to identify two other sevenths. Follow parts (c) and (d) for fifths and sixths.

EXAMPLE 8.15 Identifying larger intervals from their inversions

(a) Identifying sevenths by the quality of seconds

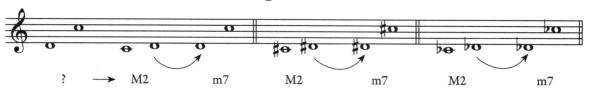

(b) Identifying sevenths by the quality of seconds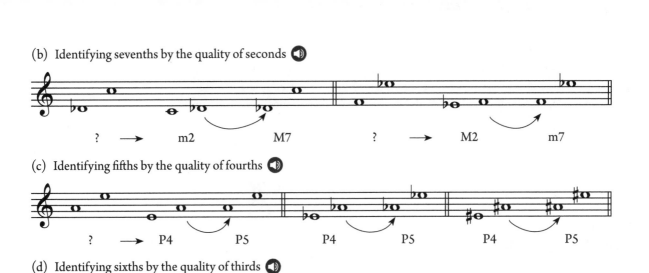

? → m2　　　M7　　　　　? → M2　　　m7

(c) Identifying fifths by the quality of fourths

? → P4　　　P5　　　P4　　　P5　　　P4　　　P5

(d) Identifying sixths by the quality of thirds

? → m3　　　M6　　　　　? → M3　　　m6

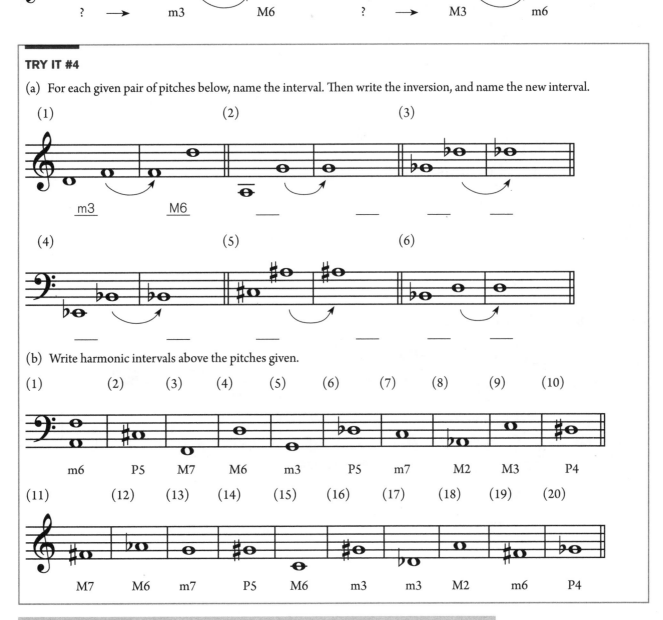

TRY IT #4

(a) For each given pair of pitches below, name the interval. Then write the inversion, and name the new interval.

(1)　　　　　　　(2)　　　　　　　(3)

m3　　　M6　　　___　___　　　___　___

(4)　　　　　　　(5)　　　　　　　(6)

___　___　　　___　___　　　___　___

(b) Write harmonic intervals above the pitches given.

(1)　(2)　(3)　(4)　(5)　(6)　(7)　(8)　(9)　(10)

m6　P5　M7　M6　m3　P5　m7　M2　M3　P4

(11)　(12)　(13)　(14)　(15)　(16)　(17)　(18)　(19)　(20)

M7　M6　m7　P5　M6　m3　m3　M2　m6　P4

ASSIGNMENT 8.2

Finally, you can check the quality of any interval by counting its half steps. The table below summarizes the information you need to know. Be careful to write the note heads for the interval's size (spanning the correct number of letter names) first, before counting half steps. Otherwise, you may confuse enharmonic intervals like the A4 and d5 (tritones), which we consider next.

Interval name	Abbreviation	Interval type	Number of half steps
unison	U	1	0
minor second	m2	2	1
major second	M2	2	2
minor third	m3	3	3
major third	M3	3	4
perfect fourth	P4	4	5
tritone	A4 or d5	4 or 5	6
perfect fifth	P5	5	7
minor sixth	m6	6	8
major sixth	M6	6	9
minor seventh	m7	7	10
major seventh	M7	7	11
octave	P8	8	12

Augmented and Diminished Intervals

Bach's Invention in D minor (Example 8.16) provides examples of two additional interval types: **augmented** and **diminished**. Listen to the beginning, and focus on the bracketed intervals—the dramatic leap from B♭4 down to C♯4 and back up in measures 1–2, and the right-hand G4 to C♯5 in measure 4.

EXAMPLE 8.16   Bach, Invention in D Minor, mm. 1–5

If the B♭ in measure 1 dropped down to a C4 instead of C♯4, the interval would be a m7. The interval here is a half step smaller than a m7: a diminished seventh (d7). Now look at measure 4. If this interval were the white-key notes G4–C5, it would be a perfect fourth (P4); G4–C♯4 is a half step larger, making an augmented fourth (A4). These diminished and augmented intervals are produced by the variants of $\hat6$ and $\hat7$ that are available in harmonic and melodic minor scales.

> **KEY CONCEPT** When a major or perfect interval is made a chromatic half step larger, call it augmented (C up to A♯ is an A6). When a minor or perfect interval is made a chromatic half step smaller, call it diminished (C up to G♭ is a d5).

As previously mentioned, all the fifths and fourths made between pairs of white-key pitches are perfect except one: the interval between F and B (see Example 8.17). This interval may be spelled as a diminished fifth (d5) or an augmented fourth (A4), depending on where it is positioned within the major scale (Example 8.18). When $\hat4$ is lower than $\hat7$, it's an augmented fourth (F–B in C major); $\hat7$ lower than $\hat4$ makes a diminished fifth (B–F). Since the interval spans exactly three whole steps, it is called the **tritone** ("tri" means "three"). The A4 and d5 are the only inversionally related intervals that are exactly the same size: they each encompass six semitones.

EXAMPLE 8.17 Fourths made with white-key pitches 🔊

EXAMPLE 8.18 The A4 and d5 in a C major scale 🔊

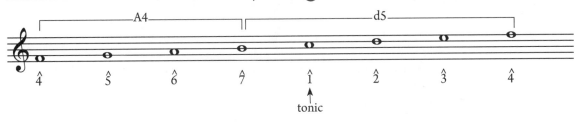

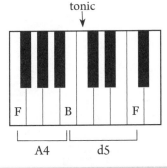

AURAL SKILLS 8.1

The A4 and d5 are the only diminished and augmented intervals that fall within the major and natural minor scales. Others can be made by raising or lowering diatonic scale degrees by a half step, but only a few—including the A2, A6, and d7—are often found in pieces of music. To spell an augmented or diminished interval, first spell a major, perfect, or minor interval, then use accidentals to adjust its size, as shown in Example 8.19. Don't change the letter name of either pitch.

EXAMPLE 8.19   Spelling augmented and diminished intervals

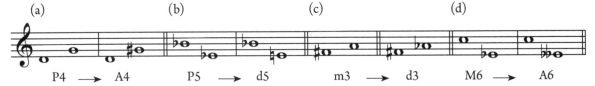

The charts below show the interval size produced when you make an interval one chromatic half step smaller (left arrow) or larger (right arrow):

d3 ← m3 → M3   d4 ← P4 → A4   d6 ← m6 → M6   d7 ← m7 → M7
m3 ← M3 → A3   d5 ← P5 → A5   m6 ← M6 → A6   m7 ← M7 → A7

For a	start with	add an accidental to move one pitch
diminished 3, 6, 7	minor 3, 6, 7	inward a half step
diminished 4, 5, 8	perfect 4, 5, 8	inward a half step
augmented 2, 6	major 2, 6	outward a half step
augmented 4, 5, 8	perfect 4, 5, 8	outward a half step

> **KEY CONCEPT**   Diminished and augmented intervals can usually be respelled as major or minor intervals. These spellings are **enharmonically equivalent**: for example, A2 and m3 (C–D♯ and C–E♭), d4 and M3 (C–F♭ and C–E), A5 and m6 (C–G♯ and C–A♭), and so on.

It is also possible to make doubly augmented or doubly diminished intervals, though they are rare. They are sometimes spelled with double sharps or double flats or with one note sharped and the other flatted (Example 8.20). To write them, follow the directions above (without changing any letter names), but move one pitch inward or outward a *whole* step, rather than a half.

EXAMPLE 8.20   Doubly augmented (dA) and diminished (dd) intervals

(a) Fourths

(b) Thirds

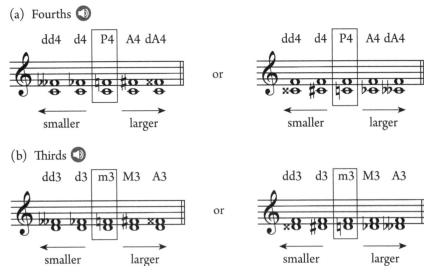

Spell the following augmented and diminished intervals above the given note. First spell a major, minor, or perfect interval as specified, then alter its quality. Don't change the given note by adding an accidental.

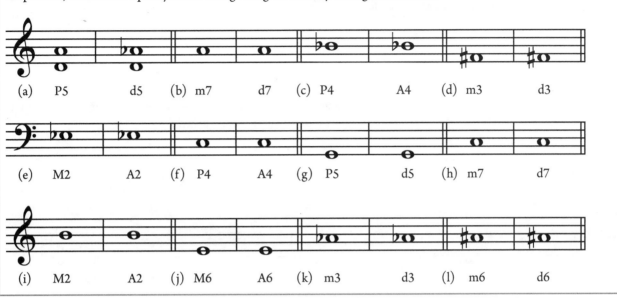

Compound Intervals

If you look back at the score of "Greensleeves" in Example 8.2 (reproduced in Try it #6), you will see that in measure 1 the first harmonic interval actually spans more than an octave: it is an octave plus a third, A3 to C5. This interval is sometimes called a tenth, since it spans ten letter names (counting both the first and last). Intervals larger than an octave are **compound intervals**. **Simple intervals** are an octave or smaller in size. The most common compound intervals are ninths, tenths, elevenths, and twelfths—which correspond to an octave plus a second, third, fourth, and fifth, as shown in Example 8.21. To name a compound interval, add 7 to the simple interval. (Add 7 rather than 8 because we began numbering the unison with 1 rather than 0.) For example, a second plus an octave equals a ninth, and a fourth plus an octave equals an eleventh.

EXAMPLE 8.21   Compound intervals

(a) Calculation

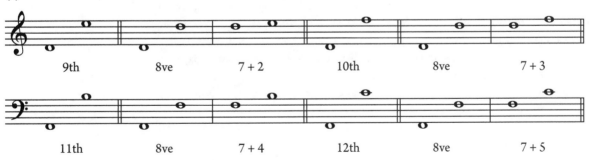

(b) Conversion chart

9th = 2nd   12th = 5th
10th = 3rd   13th = 6th
11th = 4th   14th = 7th

There are times when you need to label the span of an interval as a ninth, tenth, or twelfth because the exact musical space spanned by an interval is important to the way it sounds. However, you can usually label compound intervals as simple ones, without regard for the "extra" octaves between pitches, writing 4 instead of 11, or 5 instead of 12. Guidelines for determining the quality of compound intervals are the same as for simple ones.

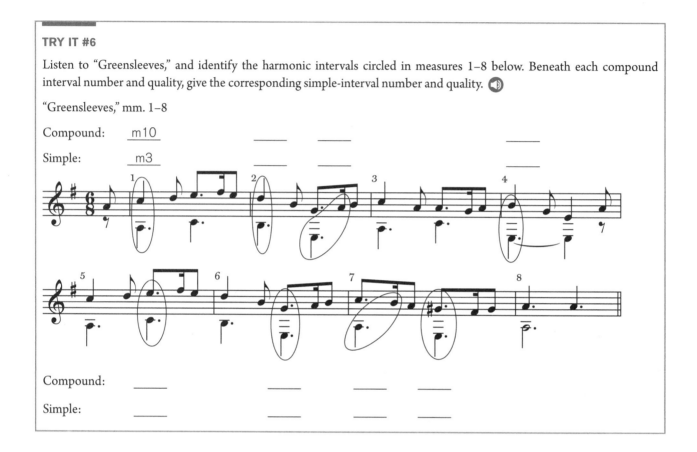

TRY IT #6

Listen to "Greensleeves," and identify the harmonic intervals circled in measures 1–8 below. Beneath each compound interval number and quality, give the corresponding simple-interval number and quality.

"Greensleeves," mm. 1–8

Compound: _m10_ _____ _____ _____

Simple: _m3_ _____ _____ _____

Compound: _____ _____ _____ _____

Simple: _____ _____ _____ _____

Consonance and Dissonance

Over the course of music history, intervals have been characterized as **consonant** if they sound pleasing to the ear or tonally stable, and **dissonant** if they sound jarring, clashing, or as if they need to move somewhere else to find a resting point. Consonance and dissonance are relative terms based on acoustics and compositional practice: what sounds consonant to us today may have sounded dissonant to musicians a century ago.

As a rule of thumb, consider perfect unisons, fifths, and octaves and major and minor thirds and sixths to be consonant. Consider seconds and sevenths to be dissonant, as well as any augmented or diminished intervals such as A4 and d5. The fourth as a melodic interval is consonant, but as a harmonic interval it may be treated as a dissonance.

Adding octaves doesn't change consonance or dissonance: tenths are consonances, as are thirds; ninths are dissonances, as are seconds. The concepts of consonance and dissonance will be useful when you write music of your own, since dissonant intervals tend to move toward consonant ones in pieces. This motion toward consonance is called **resolution**: dissonant intervals create the "need" to resolve, typically to the closest consonant interval, as illustrated in Example 8.22.

EXAMPLE 8.22   Resolutions of dissonances to consonances

A4 ⟶ 6th   d5 ⟶ 3rd

The common harmonic dissonances have standard resolutions: for example, the upper note of a minor seventh tends to resolve down. Resolutions of A4 and d5 are shown in the example above. As inversionally related intervals, they resolve in complementary ways: the A4 resolves out (to a sixth) and the d5 resolves in (to a third). For either, the underlying motion is the same, if viewed in relation to the scale: $\hat{7}$ resolves up to $\hat{1}$, while $\hat{4}$ resolves down to $\hat{3}$.

SUMMARY

- Consonant intervals: PU, P5, P8, m3, M3, m6, M6, melodic P4
- Dissonant intervals: m2, M2, m7, M7, any augmented or diminished interval, harmonic P4

ASSIGNMENT 8.3, 8.4

Did You Know?

In New York City over a hundred years ago, music publishers were concentrated in an area of Manhattan known as Tin Pan Alley, so named because the dozens of pianos being played in publishers' offices sounded like people banging on tin pans. One of these pianists was George Gershwin, who left school in 1913 at the age of fifteen to become Tin Pan Alley's youngest song salesman for $15 a week. At the same time, he decided to try his own hand at composition. Gershwin became widely known in 1919, when singer and showman Al Jolson incorporated the song "Swanee" into his act. Among Gershwin's most famous large-scale works are *Rhapsody in Blue* (1924), *An American in Paris* (1928), and *Porgy and Bess* (1935). The last of these, an opera featuring an all African American cast, includes one of his most well-loved songs, "Summertime."

Terms You Should Know

consonant	interval inversion	octave
dissonant	interval quality	resolution
interval	augmented	tritone
compound	diminished	unison
enharmonically equivalent	major	
harmonic	minor	
melodic	perfect	
simple		

Questions for Review

1. What is meant by interval size? by interval quality?
2. Which interval sizes may be major or minor? perfect? diminished or augmented?
3. How do you invert intervals?

4. Describe at least three methods for spelling intervals.
5. Describe how to label (or spell) larger intervals by inverting them.
6. How do you identify the name of compound intervals?
7. Which intervals are considered consonant? dissonant?
8. What should you alter to turn a P4 into a d5? a M6 into an A6? a m3 into an A3?
9. What interval is enharmonically equivalent to a d3? an A4? a m7?
10. Respell D–A♭ enharmonically, then provide the interval name for each spelling.

Reading Review

Match the terms on the left with the best answer on the right.

_____ (1) interval quality	(a) the distance between pitches measured by counting letter names only
_____ (2) interval	(b) interval that spans two half steps
_____ (3) interval size	(c) interval that spans three half steps
_____ (4) melodic interval	(d) spans more than an octave
_____ (5) harmonic interval	(e) major, minor, perfect, augmented, or diminished
_____ (6) F–B	(f) distance to ♭$\hat{3}$, ♭$\hat{6}$, or ♭$\hat{7}$ above a minor-key tonic
_____ (7) minor interval	(g) U, 4, 5, 8
_____ (8) augmented interval	(h) the interval from $\hat{1}$ up to $\hat{5}$
_____ (9) perfect fifth	(i) the distance in pitch between any two notes
_____ (10) major third	(j) the distance in pitch between two successive notes in a melody
_____ (11) minor third	(k) interval that spans four half steps
_____ (12) unison	(l) distance to $\hat{2}$, $\hat{3}$, $\hat{6}$, or $\hat{7}$ above a major-key tonic
_____ (13) P4	(m) "distance" between a note and itself
_____ (14) major second	(n) interval that spans one half step
_____ (15) enharmonic intervals	(o) the distance between two notes played simultaneously
_____ (16) perfect interval	(p) the distance between notes eight letter names apart
_____ (17) m6	(q) inversionally related intervals
_____ (18) E–F, B–C	(r) inversion of M3
_____ (19) major interval	(s) the only white-key seconds that are not major
_____ (20) m3	(t) inversion of P5
_____ (21) diminished interval	(u) inversion of M6
_____ (22) octave	(v) the only white-key fourth that is not perfect
_____ (23) sum to 9	(w) half step larger than major or perfect interval
_____ (24) minor second	(x) half step smaller than minor or perfect interval
_____ (25) compound interval	(y) sound the same but are spelled differently

---

@ Additional review and practice available at wwnorton.com/studyspace

Class Activities

A. Singing and playing major-scale intervals at the keyboard

1. Perform the C major scale with the fingering shown. In a comfortable octave, sing up and down with scale-degree numbers, note names, or solfège syllables.

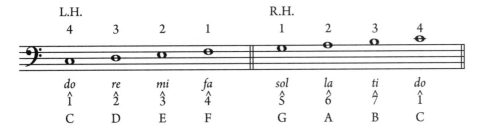

2. Use the examples in (a) and (b) below as models for playing and singing intervals above and below the tonic in a major scale. Try to associate particular intervals with particular fingerings and syllables. Begin as shown, and continue the pattern until you sing "perfect octave." While one student or group plays the keyboard, the rest of the class should sing along. Refer to the interval summaries in (c) and (d) for help.

(a)

(b)

(c) An ascending major scale produces all major and perfect intervals above its tonic pitch.

(d) A major scale produces all minor and perfect intervals below its tonic pitch.

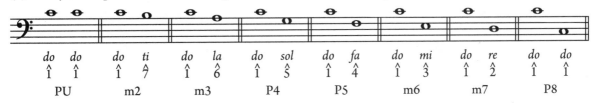

3. Now transpose these patterns to other keys. For each interval requested below, imagine the given pitch as the tonic of a major scale. Play the scale (with the fingerings given in #1), then find the interval. Sing along on numbers or solfège.

Intervals above:

(a) M6 above D

(b) M2 above A♭

(c) M3 above F♯

(d) M7 above D♭

(e) P5 above B♭

(f) P4 above B

(g) M7 above E♭

(h) M6 above C♯

(i) M3 above G♭

(j) P8 above G

(k) M3 above A

(l) P5 above A♭

(m) M2 above D♭

(n) P4 above F

(o) M6 above E

Intervals below:

(a) m2 below A

(b) m6 below C♯

(c) P8 below A♯

(d) m7 below E♭

(e) m2 below D♭

(f) P4 below A♭

(g) m7 below B

(h) m3 below F♯

(i) m6 below E

(j) m3 below F

(k) m3 below A♭

(l) P5 below F

(m) m3 below C♯

(n) P4 below B♭

(o) P5 below A

B. Singing and playing minor-scale intervals at the keyboard

1. Play the altered version of the minor scale shown below, while singing the scale-degree numbers, solfège, or note names. Play also the C natural-minor scale (with D♮ rather than D♭) to compare.

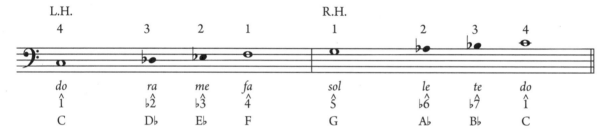

2. Use the examples in (a) and (b) below as models for playing and singing intervals above and below the tonic in a minor scale with the ♭2̂ variant. Begin as shown, and continue the pattern until you sing "perfect octave." Refer to the interval summaries in (c) and (d) for help.

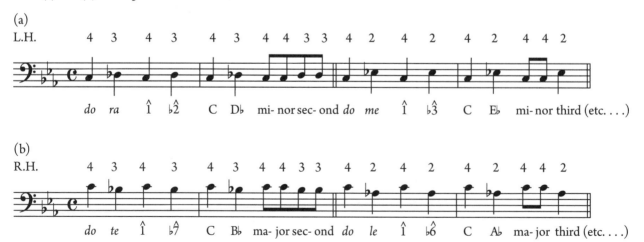

(c) An ascending minor scale (altered with ♭2̂) produces all minor and perfect intervals above its tonic pitch.

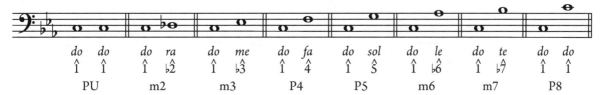

do	do	do	ra	do	me	do	fa	do	sol	do	le	do	te	do	do
1̂	1̂	1̂	♭2̂	1̂	♭3̂	1̂	4̂	1̂	5̂	1̂	♭6̂	1̂	♭7̂	1̂	1̂
PU		m2		m3		P4		P5		m6		m7		P8	

(d) A descending minor scale (altered with ♭2̂) produces all major and perfect intervals below its tonic pitch.

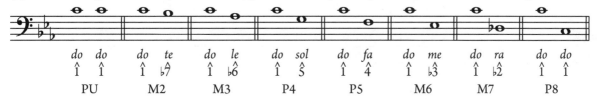

do	do	do	te	do	le	do	sol	do	fa	do	me	do	ra	do	do
1̂	1̂	1̂	♭7̂	1̂	♭6̂	1̂	5̂	1̂	4̂	1̂	♭3̂	1̂	♭2̂	1̂	1̂
PU		M2		M3		P4		P5		M6		M7		P8	

3. Now transpose this pattern to other keys. For each interval requested below, imagine the given pitch as the tonic of an altered minor scale. Play the scale, then find the interval requested. Sing along on numbers or solfège.

Intervals above:

(a) m7 above G

(b) m6 above B

(c) m3 above E

(d) m7 above E♭

(e) P4 above G♭

(f) P5 above A

(g) m7 above D

(h) m3 above D

(i) m6 above E

(j) m3 above A

(k) P8 above F♯

(l) P5 above F

(m) m6 above C♯

(n) P4 above A♭

(o) m3 above F♯

Intervals below:

(a) M2 below D

(b) M6 below E♭

(c) M3 below B♭

(d) M2 below F♯

(e) M2 below D♭

(f) P4 below G

(g) M6 below B

(h) M7 below F♯

(i) M6 below E

(j) M3 below F

(k) M3 below A♭

(l) M7 below C

(m) M3 below C♯

(n) M6 below B♭

(o) M2 below A

C. Listening and writing: Interval identification

Each of the following exercises consists of a set of ten intervals that will be played for you in class. (The intervals are also recorded for practice at home.) Each interval begins with the given pitch. In the blank beneath the staff, write the interval's quality and size (M3, m6, P5, etc.). Then write the second pitch in the staff, including any necessary accidental. Don't alter the given pitch.

As a class activity, your teacher may wish to divide this into stages:

- On the first hearing, sing the interval back, then write the size only (6, 3, 2, 5, etc.). You may sing up or down the scale to count scale degrees.
- On the second hearing, sing back, and add the interval quality (M6, m3, m2, P5, etc.).
- On the third hearing, discuss these answers and add notation on the staff.

1. Ascending major and perfect intervals 🔊

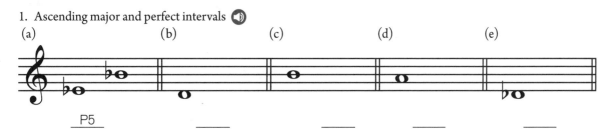

(a)   (b)   (c)   (d)   (e)

P5

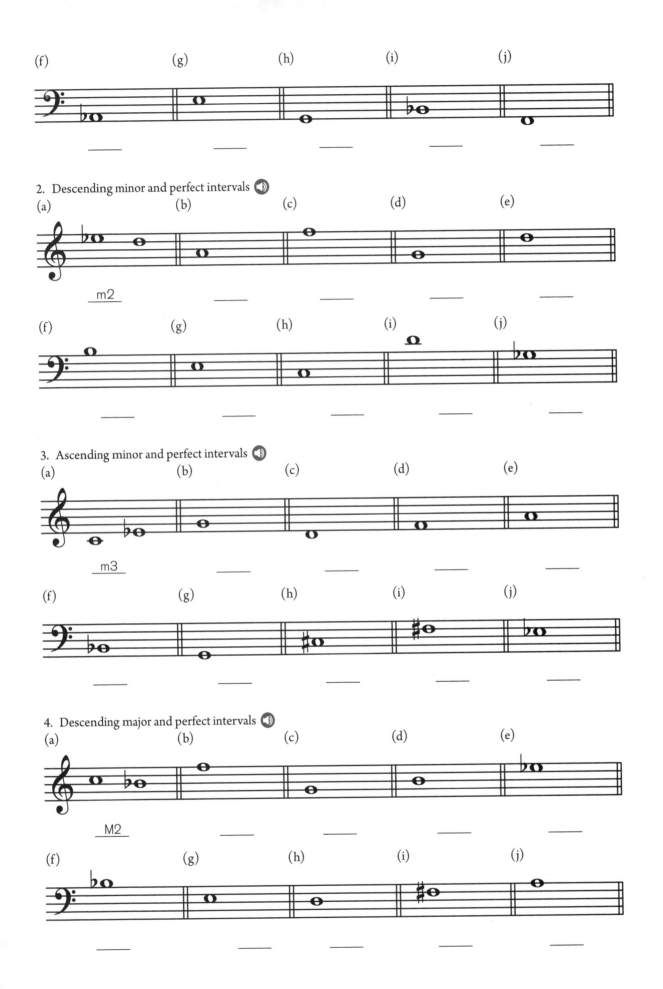

2. Descending minor and perfect intervals

(a) m2 (b) (c) (d) (e)

(f) (g) (h) (i) (j)

3. Ascending minor and perfect intervals

(a) m3 (b) (c) (d) (e)

(f) (g) (h) (i) (j)

4. Descending major and perfect intervals

(a) M2 (b) (c) (d) (e)

(f) (g) (h) (i) (j)

D. Singing at sight

For each of the following melodies, first determine the key and play that major scale at the keyboard; sing along on scale-degree numbers or solfège syllables. Play the first pitch of the melody (if not $\hat{1}$) and sing up or down to the tonic pitch to orient yourself.

These melodies are ordered by type of interval featured. Before working on the melody, identify examples of the interval. Play and sing the interval; find its position in the scale you just played. Then practice rhythm and pitches separately before putting them together.

Melodies featuring seconds and thirds

Melody 1 "Banana Boat Song," mm. 1–10

Melody 2 "Shenandoah" (American folk tune)
Begins on *sol* ($\hat{5}$).

Melodies featuring fourths and fifths

Melody 3 Wolfgang Amadeus Mozart, "Alleluia," mm. 1–4
This melody may be sung as a round.

Melody 4 Robert Lowry, "How Can I Keep from Singing," mm. 1–8a
Begins on *sol* ($\hat{5}$).

My life flows on in end-less praise a-bove earth's lam-en-ta-tion. I hear the sweet though far off hymn that hails a new cre-a-tion.

Melody 5 Victor Young, "When I Fall in Love" (adapted), mm. 1–8
Begins on *sol* ($\hat{5}$).

When I fall in love it will be for-ev-er, or I'll nev-er fall in love.____

Melodies featuring sixths and sevenths

Melody 6 George F. Root, "There's Music in the Air," mm. 1–8a
Begins on *sol* ($\hat{5}$).

There's mu-sic in the air,____ when the ear-ly morn is nigh, And faint its blush is seen____ On the bright and laugh-ing sky.

Melody 7 "Music Alone Shall Live"
This melody may be performed as a round.
Begins on *mi* ($\hat{3}$).

All things shall per-ish from un-der the sky. Mu-sic a-lone shall live, mu-sic a-lone shall live, mu-sic a-lone shall live, ne-ver to die.

Workbook   ASSIGNMENT 8.1

1. Writing melodic intervals

Write a whole note on the correct line or space to make each interval specified below. Don't add sharps or flats. Check your answers by counting the letter names from the given note to the one you have written, remembering to include the given note.

a. Write the specified melodic interval above the given note.

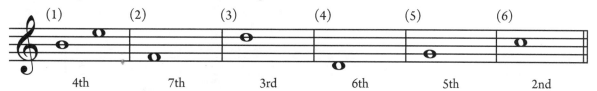

   (1)   (2)   (3)   (4)   (5)   (6)

   4th   7th   3rd   6th   5th   2nd

b. Write the specified melodic interval below the given note.

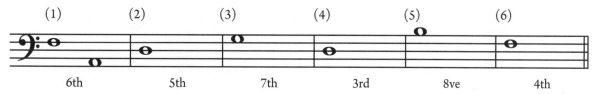

   (1)   (2)   (3)   (4)   (5)   (6)

   6th   5th   7th   3rd   8ve   4th

2. Identifying interval size in context

For each circled interval, write the correct interval size in the blank provided.

a. Mozart, Piano Sonata in C Major, K. 545, first movement, mm. 1–4

b. Bach, "Aus meines Herzens Grunde," mm. 1–4

Translation: From my heart's foundation

3. Writing major and perfect intervals

First write a note head to make the correct interval size, then add a flat or sharp if necessary to make the correct quality. Don't change the given pitch.

a. Write the specified melodic interval above the given note.

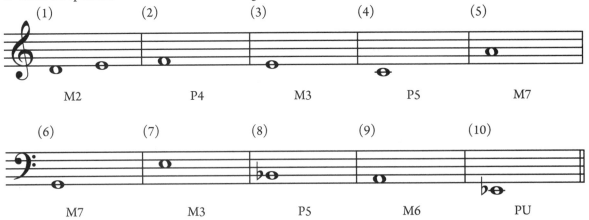

b. Write the specified harmonic interval above the given note.

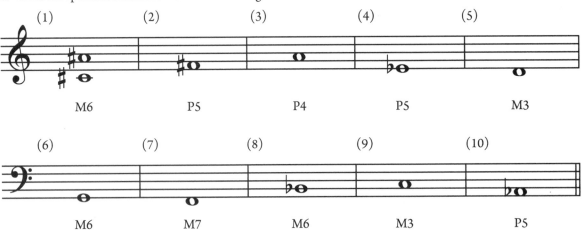

4. Identifying intervals

Label each interval with its size and quality (e.g., m6). 🔊

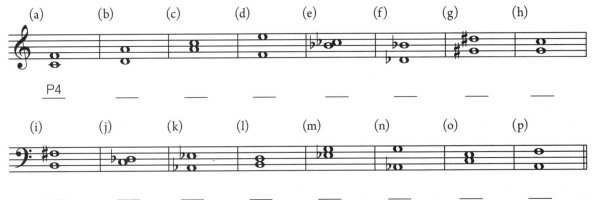

Workbook ASSIGNMENT 8.2

1. Writing intervals

a. Write each specified harmonic interval above the given note. Don't change the given pitch.

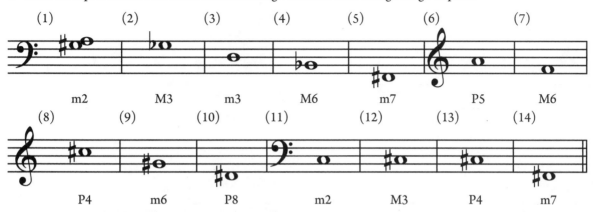

b. Write each specified harmonic interval below the given note.

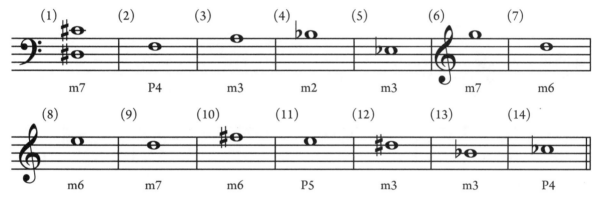

c. Write the specified melodic interval below the given note.

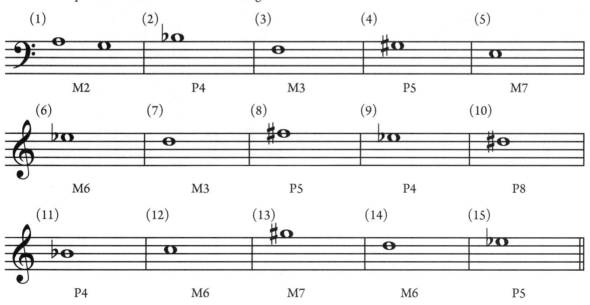

2. Inverting intervals

a. Identify each interval shown below, then invert the interval by rewriting the second note, followed by the first note transposed up an octave. Identify the new interval you have written.

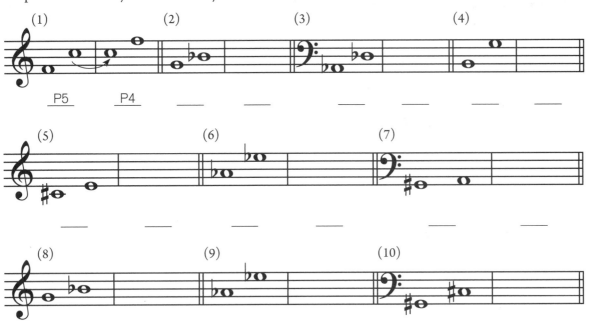

b. Identify each interval shown below, then invert the interval by rewriting the second note, followed by the first note transposed down an octave. Identify the new interval you have written.

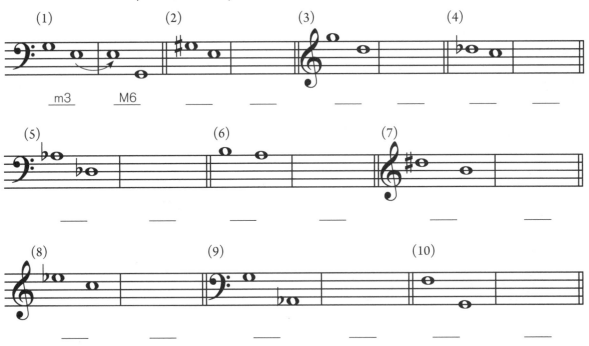

Workbook ASSIGNMENT 8.3

1. Identifying diminished and augmented intervals

Write the name (e.g., A4) under each interval. 🔊

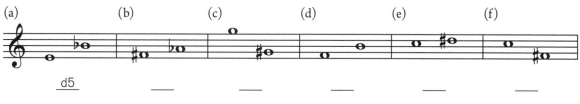

(a)   (b)   (c)   (d)   (e)   (f)

d5   ___   ___   ___   ___   ___

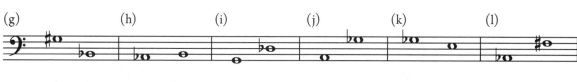

(g)   (h)   (i)   (j)   (k)   (l)

___   ___   ___   ___   ___   ___

(m)   (n)   (o)   (p)   (q)   (r)

___   ___   ___   ___   ___   ___

2. Writing diminished and augmented intervals

a. Write each specified melodic interval below the given note.

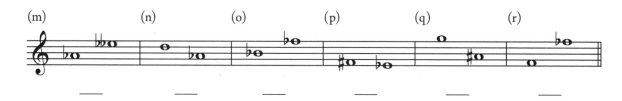

(1)   (2)   (3)   (4)   (5)   (6)   (7)

d4   A2   A6   d5   A8   d4   d3

b. Write each specified melodic interval above the given note.

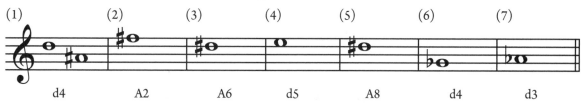

(1)   (2)   (3)   (4)   (5)   (6)   (7)

A6   A2   d5   d8   d7   d3   A4

3. Writing melodic compound intervals

Write the specified compound interval above or below the given note. (Hint: Subtract 7 to find the simple-interval equivalent.)

a. Write the compound interval above the given note.

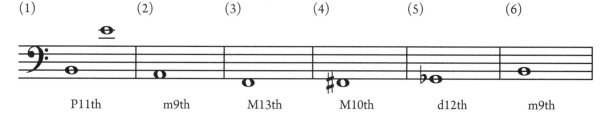

(1)   (2)   (3)   (4)   (5)   (6)

P11th   m9th   M13th   M10th   d12th   m9th

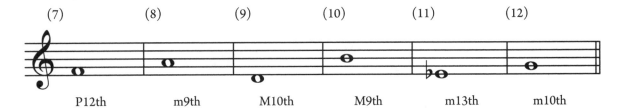

P12th   m9th   M10th   M9th   m13th   m10th

b. Write the compound interval below the given note.

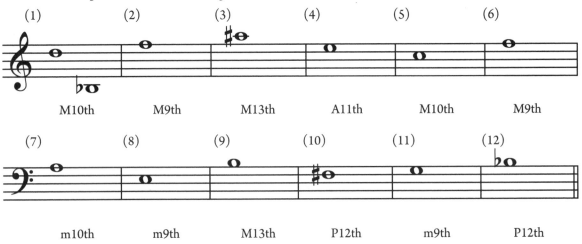

M10th   M9th   M13th   A11th   M10th   M9th

m10th   m9th   M13th   P12th   m9th   P12th

4. Intervals in context

Listen to the excerpt before analyzing it. Write the names of the circled pitches in the blank above the staff, incorporating accidentals from the key signature, then label the intervals with both quality and size (e.g., M7) in the blank below the staff.

Willson, "Till There Was You," mm. 16b–24a 🔊

Workbook ASSIGNMENT 8.4

1. Identifying intervals

Label each interval with its size and quality (e.g., m6).

2. Writing melodic intervals

Write a whole note on the correct line or space to make each interval specified below. Don't add sharps or flats to the given note. Check your answers by counting the letter names from the given note to the one you have written, remembering to include the given note.

a. Write the specified melodic interval above the given note.

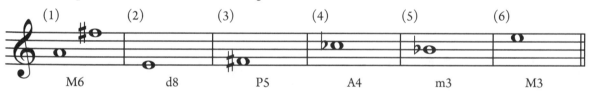

b. Write the specified melodic interval below the given note.

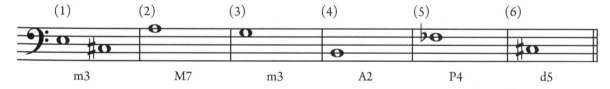

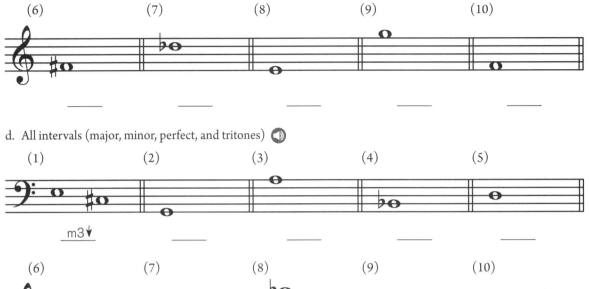

d. All intervals (major, minor, perfect, and tritones)

2. Intervals from familiar music

Sometimes the easiest way to remember the sound of an interval is to associate it with a familiar melody. Play each interval below, then write the name of a piece or song that begins with or features the interval, either ascending or descending. Be prepared to sing your examples in class.

m2 _____

M2 _____

m3 _____

M3 _____

P4 _____

P5 _____

m6 _____

M6 _____

m7 _____

M7 _____

P8 _____

Workbook   AURAL SKILLS 8.2

Listen to a work for piano by Béla Bartók before completing the following exercises.

1. Focus your attention on the right-hand melody. Which is the first melodic interval?

(a) m3   (b) M3   (c) P4   (d) P5

2. Notate the rhythm of the melody in simple duple meter with the quarter note as the beat unit. Include the meter signature and bar lines.

3. Write the melody with scale-degree numbers or solfège syllables. Your answer should begin with $\hat{1}$–$\hat{5}$–$\hat{5}$ or *do–sol–sol*.

4. Beginning on A4, notate the pitches of the melody on the staves below. Provide the appropriate clef and key signature (or accidentals).

5. Now focus your attention on the left-hand accompaniment. Which of the following best represents the rhythm of the accompaniment?

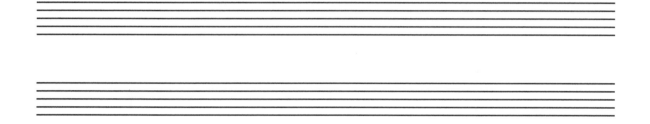

6. The left-hand part consists of two harmonic intervals. Which is the first harmonic interval?

(a) m3   (b) M3   (c) P4   (d) P5

7. Which is the second harmonic interval of the left-hand part?

(a) m3   (b) M3   (c) P4   (d) P5

TOPICS

- triads
- triad inversion
- triad qualities in major keys
- triad qualities in minor keys
- spelling triads
- the dominant seventh chord
- seventh chord inversion
- spelling the dominant seventh chord

MUSIC

- "My Country, 'Tis of Thee"

CHAPTER 9

Triads and the Dominant Seventh Chord

Triads

In most musical settings, melodic and harmonic intervals sound together: the horizontal and vertical components join to form a musical fabric, called a musical **texture**. A familiar musical style that illustrates this principle is hymn style, also called **SATB**. In hymn-style settings, there are usually four parts—two sung by women (labeled S for **sopranos** and A for **altos**) and two sung by men (T for **tenors** and B for **basses**). The top part (the soprano line) usually sings the melody, the lowest part (the bass line) provides a foundation, and the other voices fill in intervals between them. When the voices sing together, they form **chords**.

> **KEY CONCEPT** When all voices in a musical texture move together with nearly identical rhythm, as in hymn or SATB style, the texture is **homophonic**.

Listen to the familiar patriotic song "My Country, 'Tis of Thee," shown in Example 9.1, to hear several different types of chords. As with scales, you can examine chord types by collecting the pitches used (leaving out repeated notes) and writing them in order within an octave. The pitches in each chord of the first measure of the example are shown below the staff; each of these chords is a triad, as shown in Example 9.1.

EXAMPLE 9.1   "My Country, 'Tis of Thee," mm. 1–6 🔊

Triads are three-note chords; in their most basic position, they are built from stacking two thirds, one on top of the other, as shown in Example 9.2. The lowest note in this position is the **root** of the chord. The middle note (a third above the root) is the **third**, and the top note (a fifth above the root) is the **fifth**. The **major triad** has a M3 between its root and third and a m3 between its third and fifth; the **minor triad** has the opposite—a m3 between root and third and a M3 on the top. The difference between triad types is known as **quality**. Triads are named by the letter name of their root combined with their quality (e.g., G major or B minor): the first chord in "My Country" is an F major triad, the second is a D minor triad, and the third is a G minor triad, as shown. To make a four-note chord like those in Example 9.1, one of the members of the triad (usually the root) will be **doubled**—that is, the same chord member will appear in two places, one or more octaves apart.

EXAMPLE 9.2   Intervals in major and minor triads 🔊

Triad Inversion

Sometimes you will see triads arranged so that they are not stacked in thirds above their root. For an example, look at the third chord of "My Country" in Example 9.1. It is a G–B♭–D triad, but the third of the chord (B♭) is in the bass and also is doubled.

> **KEY CONCEPT**   When the root of the chord is in the bass, the chord is in **root position**. If a chord member other than a root is in the bass, the chord is said to be **inverted**: when the third is in the bass, the chord is in **first inversion**; when the fifth is in the bass, the chord is in **second inversion**.

When triads are inverted, they sound different from root position because there are different intervals between the lowest and upper parts. Inverted chords retain their basic harmonic identity, however, and are named by their root even when the root is not in the bass.

With root-position chords, you hear the intervals P5 and either M3 or m3 above the bass, but inversions bring out other intervals that can be made with the chord's tones, as shown in Example 9.3a: m6, M6, and P4. It is customary to label a triad and its inversions with numbers that represent their intervals, which are called **figures** from their use in an eighteenth-century compositional style called figured bass. First inversion is labeled ⁶₃ (there's a sixth and a third above the bass) or simply 6, second inversion is ⁶₄, and root position is ⁵₃, though root position is often not labeled at all. Part (b) shows these chords voiced in four parts, with a typical doubling. In Example 9.3, compound intervals are reduced to simple ones; 6 and 3 (not 13 and 10) for first inversion.

EXAMPLE 9.3   C major triad and its inversions

(a) Inversion labels 🔊

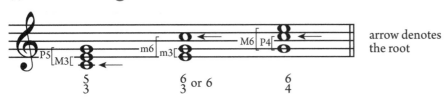

arrow denotes the root

(b) Typical doubling

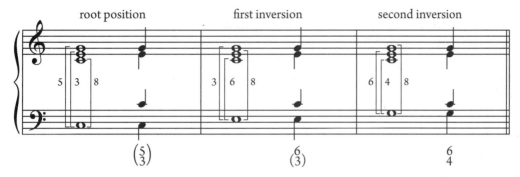

Sometimes you find a triad's root position followed by both inversions in turn, as in Example 9.4. Here, consider the F major chord to extend for all of measure 7, even though no F sounds on beats 2 and 3. If you were accompanying this with guitar, you would keep strumming the F major chord for both measures 7 and 8.

EXAMPLE 9.4   "My Country, 'Tis of Thee," mm. 7–10 🔊

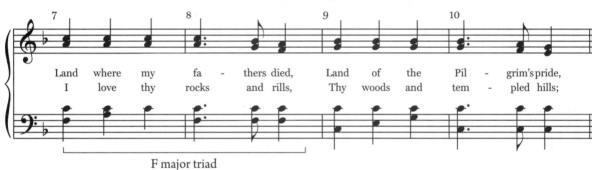

F major triad

Triad Qualities in Major Keys

Example 9.5 gives the quality for each triad built on scale degrees of the F major scale.

EXAMPLE 9.5   Triads built above the F major scale and their qualities 🔊

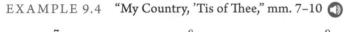

Scale degree:	$\hat{1}$	$\hat{2}$	$\hat{3}$	$\hat{4}$	$\hat{5}$	$\hat{6}$	$\hat{7}$
Quality:	M	m	m	M	M	m	d

In major keys, the triads built on $\hat{1}$, $\hat{4}$, and $\hat{5}$ are major, and the triads built on $\hat{2}$, $\hat{3}$, and $\hat{6}$ are minor. The triad built on $\hat{7}$, with a diminished fifth between its root and fifth and both of its thirds minor, is called a **diminished triad**.

ANOTHER WAY You can identify triads apart from their scale context by considering their intervals. Triads with each quality built above F are shown below for comparison.

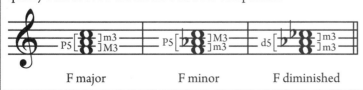

F major   F minor   F diminished

There are several ways to label chords. You can refer to triads in a key by the scale degree on which they are built (for example, "a triad on $\hat{2}$") or by the scale-degree name: tonic, subdominant, dominant, and so on refer both to the scale degrees and to the triads built on them. Musicians often label chords with **Roman numerals**, as shown in Example 9.6. The Roman numerals are a handy way of labeling both a chord's scale-degree position (I to vii°) and also its quality: a capital numeral indicates a major triad (I, IV, V), and a lowercase numeral a minor triad (ii, iii, vi). For diminished triads, add a small raised (superscript) circle to the lowercase numeral (vii°).

EXAMPLE 9.6   Triad labels in F major

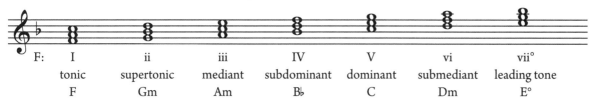

F:	I	ii	iii	IV	V	vi	vii°
	tonic	supertonic	mediant	subdominant	dominant	submediant	leading tone
	F	Gm	Am	Bb	C	Dm	E°

You can also indicate if a chord is inverted by adding its figure as a superscript (V^6, ii^6). When these Arabic numerals are combined with Roman numerals, they identify the chord's scale degree, quality, and inversion—providing a lot of information in one space-saving label.

In popular music, chords are labeled by their root and quality, without a specific reference to their place in the key (without a Roman numeral). In this book, we will identify major and minor triads as follows:

G major triad	G
G minor triad	Gm or Gmin
G diminished triad	G° or Gdim
G augmented triad	G^+ (see p. 217)

Your teacher may prefer another system, such as an uppercase letter for major and a lowercase letter for minor. There are many variants on these labels.

Example 9.7 illustrates how to label the chords from the opening measures of "My Country, 'Tis of Thee." The key of the piece, F, is given to the left, before the Roman numerals.

EXAMPLE 9.7   "My Country, 'Tis of Thee," m. 1

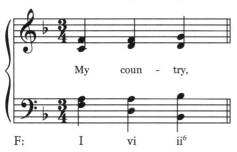

Triad Qualities in Minor Keys

Example 9.8a shows the triads that can be built above the scale degrees of a natural minor scale. The triads on $\hat{1}$, $\hat{4}$, and $\hat{5}$ are minor; those on $\hat{3}$, $\hat{6}$, and $\hat{7}$ are major; and the triad on $\hat{2}$ is diminished.

EXAMPLE 9.8   Triads built above the G minor scale 🔊

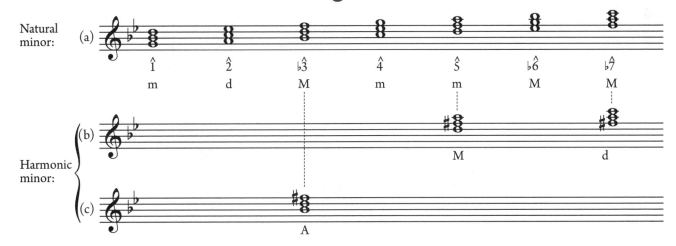

As we learned earlier, ♭$\hat{7}$ in minor is often raised to make a leading tone. In that case, the triads on $\hat{5}$ and $\hat{7}$ become major and diminished, respectively (part b). Part (c) illustrates what happens to the triad on ♭$\hat{3}$ (B♭–D–F♯) with the raised leading tone: there are now major thirds between both root and third and third and fifth. Since the interval between the root and fifth is an augmented fifth, this type of chord is called an **augmented triad** (labeled A). Unlike the other triads in the example, this one is not usually found in minor-key pieces.

The Roman numerals for each triad in G minor are shown in Example 9.9, along with the scale-degree names and chord symbols.

EXAMPLE 9.9   Triad labels in G minor 🔊

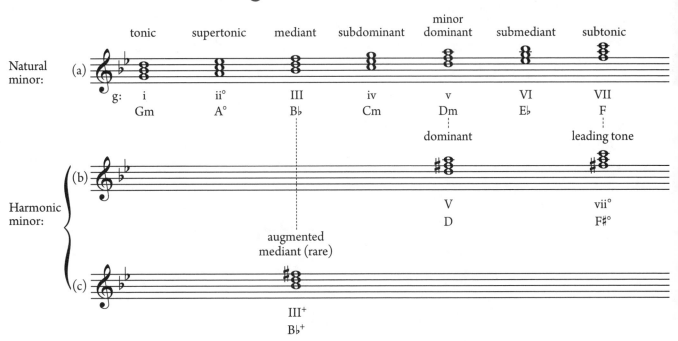

To label an augmented chord (Example 9.9c), add a superscript plus sign to an uppercase Roman numeral (III⁺). When analyzing music with Roman numerals, always indicate the key at the beginning of your analysis (an uppercase letter for major keys, lowercase for minor keys).

> **KEY CONCEPT** Triads that appear often in minor keys are i, ii°, iv, V, VI, and vii°. The major triad on $\hat{5}$ (V) and the diminished triad on the leading tone (vii°) are more typical than the minor v and major VII, because of their strong leading-tone-to-tonic motion. When you write V and vii° in minor keys, remember to raise $\flat\hat{7}$ to $\hat{7}$ to make the leading tone.

Spelling Triads

Triads are essential building blocks for music in many styles. Here, we learn three ways to identify and spell triads: (1) by key signatures, (2) by triads in the C major scale, and (3) by intervals. Find the method that allows you to spell triads most quickly and accurately, then use a second one to check your work.

Method 1:

This method draws on your knowledge of key signatures and scales. Always begin by writing the note heads stacked in thirds above the root, without accidentals: either line-line-line or space-space-space. Imagine a major triad in a major key, where the root is the tonic and the upper notes are $\hat{3}$ and $\hat{5}$. Then think about which notes need accidentals in the major key signature of the root. Example 9.10 illustrates the procedure for an A major triad. First write notes on three consecutive spaces starting from A, then think of the A major key signature: sharps on F, C, and G. C needs to be sharped: A–C♯–E. Part (b) follows the same procedure to spell an E♭ major triad.

EXAMPLE 9.10   Building a major triad from a major key signature

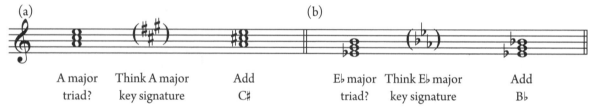

| | A major triad? | Think A major key signature | Add C♯ | | E♭ major triad? | Think E♭ major key signature | Add B♭ |

> **TRY IT #1**
>
> Use the key-signature method to spell major triads above the roots given.
>
>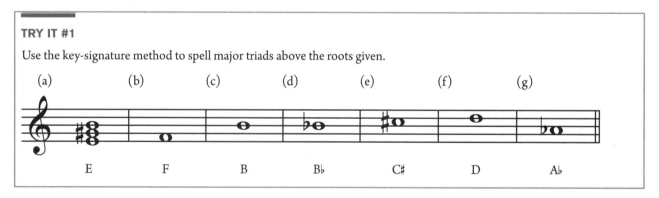
>
> (a) E (b) F (c) B (d) B♭ (e) C♯ (f) D (g) A♭

For minor triads, you can use the same method but imagine the minor key signature, as shown in Example 9.11; or you can write a major triad and lower the third by a chromatic half step (without changing the letter name).

EXAMPLE 9.11   Building a minor triad from a minor key signature
(a) Step 1: Write the root, third, and fifth (line-line-line or space-space-space)

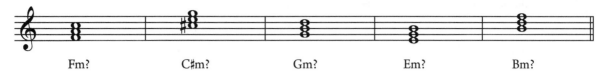

(b) Step 2: Imagine the minor key signature for the root

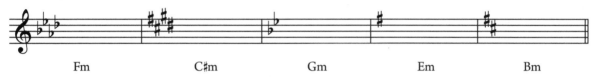

(c) Step 3: Write accidentals corresponding to $\hat{1}$–$\flat\hat{3}$–$\hat{5}$ of the minor key

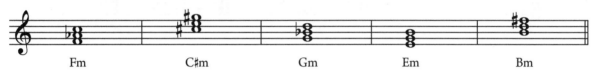

TRY IT #2

(a) Write the minor key signature for each root.

(b) Now write the triad corresponding to $\hat{1}$–$\flat\hat{3}$–$\hat{5}$ of the minor key above.

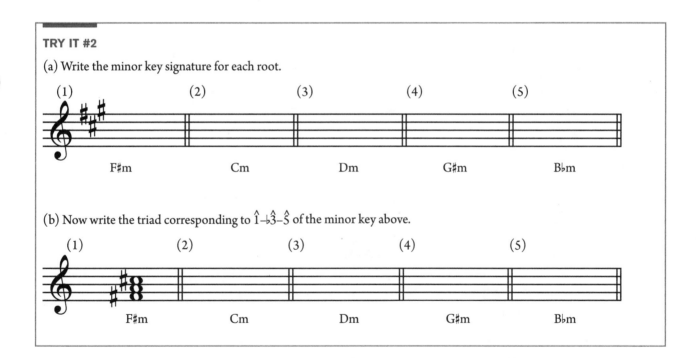

ASSIGNMENT 9.1, AURAL SKILLS 9.1, 9.2

Method 2:

If you like to visualize triads on the keyboard or staff, first learn the qualities of each scale-degree triad in C major (Example 9.12) from the piano white keys or note heads on the staff.

EXAMPLE 9.12   Spelling triads from C major

(a) White-key triads

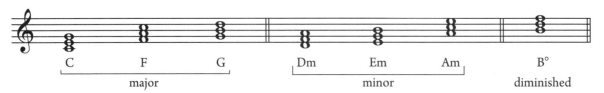

(b) For triads on C, F, and G

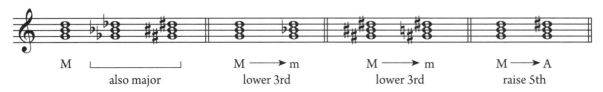

(c) For triads on D, E, and A

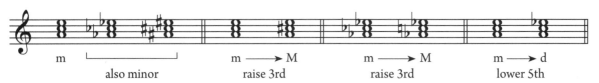

(d) For triads on B

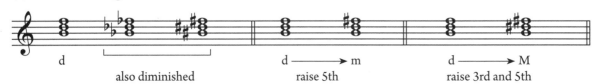

Now use this information to build the other types of triads.

- Triads on C, F, and G remain major if all the accidentals match (part b). To make a minor triad, lower the third a half step. To make an augmented triad, raise the fifth a half step.
- Triads on D, E, and A remain minor if all the accidentals match (part c). To make a major triad, raise the third a half step. To make a diminished triad, lower the fifth a half step.
- Triads on B remain diminished if all the accidentals match (part d). To make a minor triad, raise the fifth a half step. To make a major triad, raise both the third and fifth a half step.

Method 3:

Finally, you can spell triads by dividing them into their component intervals, following the steps below (Example 9.13).

1. Write the root of the triad.
2. Add the fifth:
   (a) For a major or minor triad, write a P5 above the root.
   (b) For an augmented triad, make it an A5.
   (c) For a diminished triad, make it a d5.
3. Add the third:
   (a) For a major or augmented triad, add a M3 above the root.
   (b) For a minor or diminished triad, add a m3 above the root.

EXAMPLE 9.13   Spelling triads by intervals

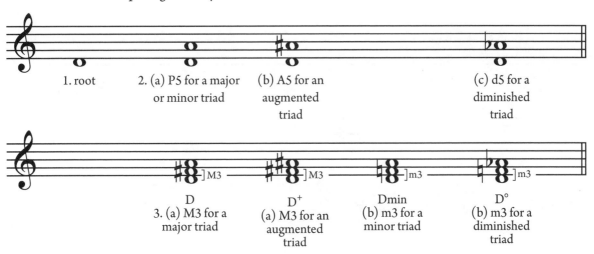

You can also spell root-position triads by stacked thirds (Example 9.14) or write a major triad (from its key signature) and spell the others by adding accidentals to raise or lower the third and fifth (Example 9.15).

EXAMPLE 9.14   Spelling triads in stacked thirds

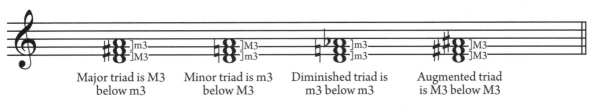

EXAMPLE 9.15   Spelling triads as alterations of major

TRY IT #3

Write the following major and minor triads, then alter each major triad to make it augmented and each minor triad to make it diminished.

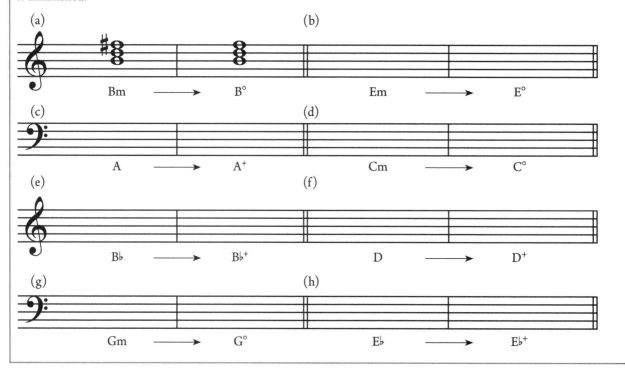

ASSIGNMENT 9.2, 9.3

The Dominant Seventh Chord

Some four-note chords have four *different* pitches (with no doubling), as shown in Example 9.16, the end of "My Country, 'Tis of Thee." The chord on the last beat of measure 13, shown below the staff, has four notes stacked in thirds above $\hat{5}$ (C): the C major triad (C–E–G) plus another third (B♭). This type of chord, with a **third**, **fifth**, and **seventh** above the **root**, is called a **seventh chord**. The most frequently encountered seventh chord, built on the fifth scale degree, is called the **dominant seventh chord**. The dominant seventh chord is normally written V^7 ("five-seven") or indicated by the letter name of its root plus a 7 (for example, A7 for a dominant seventh chord built on the root A).

EXAMPLE 9.16 "My Country, 'Tis of Thee," mm. 13–14

Seventh Chord Inversion

Seventh chords may also be inverted, as shown in measures 9–10 of Example 9.17. The chord here is a dominant seventh (in the key of F), C–E–G–B♭, appearing successively with the root, third, and fifth in the bass. Since they include four chord members, seventh chords have three inversions in addition to root position.

EXAMPLE 9.17   "My Country, 'Tis of Thee," mm. 7–10

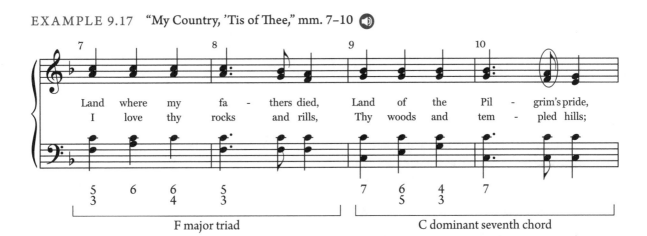

Example 9.18a shows a G dominant seventh chord (in the key of C) in root position, then first, second, and third inversion. The first set of numbers beneath each indicates all the intervals formed above the bottom note—for example, the root position has 7, 5, and 3 above the bass, while the first inversion has 6, 5, and 3. These figures are usually simplified: 7 for root position, $\frac{6}{5}$ for first inversion, $\frac{4}{3}$ for second inversion, and $\frac{4}{2}$ or 2 for third inversion.

EXAMPLE 9.18   G dominant seventh chord and its inversions

(a) On a treble staff

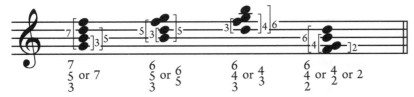

(b) In SATB voicing

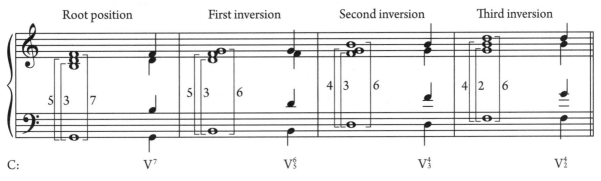

Part (b) shows the same chord in SATB voicing. Inverted seventh chords are usually complete in four parts—nothing is doubled—but you may encounter the root-position dominant seventh chord with two roots ($\hat{5}$), a third ($\hat{7}$), and a seventh ($\hat{4}$), but no fifth ($\hat{2}$).

The inversion of a triad or seventh chord is determined by the bass, the lowest-sounding pitch.

- If the root is lowest (in the bass), it is **root position**.
- If the third is lowest, it is in **first inversion**.
- If the fifth is lowest, it is in **second inversion**.
- If the seventh of a seventh chord is lowest, it is in **third inversion**.

Spelling the Dominant Seventh Chord

To spell a dominant seventh chord, use one of the methods below.

Method 1:

First write a major triad, then add a minor third above the triad's fifth, as shown in Example 9.19. Check that the interval between the root and seventh is a minor seventh.

EXAMPLE 9.19   Spelling a dominant seventh chord

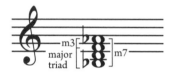

Method 2:

Write the note head for the seventh chord's root, then stack three thirds above it (line-line-line-line or space-space-space-space). In which key is this note $\hat{5}$? Complete the spelling of the seventh chord using accidentals from that key signature. Check the intervals above the bass using method 1 above.

TRY IT #4

Spell a dominant seventh chord above each of the roots provided.

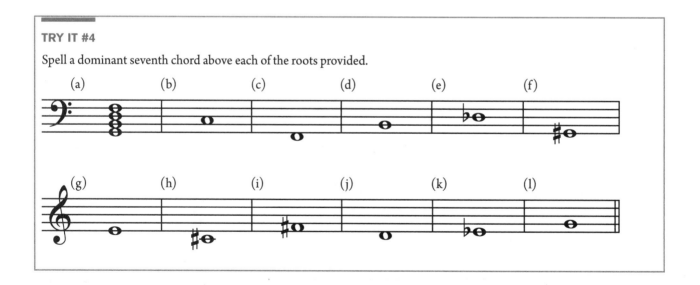

Did You Know?

The melody that we know as "My Country, 'Tis of Thee," or "America," is even more well-known in England as "God Save the King" (or "God Save the Queen," depending on the current monarch). The origin of the melody remains a mystery. It was first published in England in 1744, and became popular after a version with words by Thomas Arne was performed in London's Drury Lane and Covent Garden theaters in September 1745. Arne's lyrics rallied support for King George II and decried the Scots, led by "Bonnie Prince Charlie," his Stuart rival for the throne. Later, both Beethoven and Haydn incorporated this melody into their own compositions.

In the 1790s, the melody became the Danish national anthem, and, with the "God Save the King" text, it has also remained a national song for former British colonies besides the United States, including Canada and Australia. The text beginning "My country, 'tis of thee," written by Samuel Francis Smith, was first performed on July 4, 1831. Over a century later, on August 28, 1963, Martin Luther King quoted Smith's lyrics in his "I have a dream" speech from the steps of the Lincoln Memorial, as he called on the nation to "let freedom ring."

Terms You Should Know

chord	alto	triad qualities
chord members	tenor	augmented
root	bass	diminished
third	seventh chord	major
fifth	texture	minor
seventh	triad	triad and seventh chord
dominant seventh chord	triad names	positions
doubling	tonic	root position
figures	supertonic	first inversion
homophony	mediant	second inversion
inverted chords	subdominant	third inversion
Roman numerals	dominant	
SATB	submediant	
soprano	leading tone	

Questions for Review

1. What is the difference between a major and minor triad? a minor and diminished triad? a major and augmented triad?
2. What are the intervals in a major triad? in a minor triad?
3. Which Arabic numerals are used to show each triad position (root position, first inversion, second inversion)?
4. What are several methods for spelling triads?
5. On which scale degrees are major triads found in major keys? in minor keys?
6. On which scale degrees are minor triads found in major keys? in minor keys?
7. On which scale degrees are diminished and augmented triads found in major keys? in minor keys?
8. What information does a Roman numeral provide?
9. What are two methods for spelling a dominant seventh chord?

Reading Review

Match the terms on the left with the best answer on the right.

_____ (1) Roman numerals

_____ (2) ^{6}

_____ (3) ^{7}

_____ (4) D–F–A

_____ (5) first inversion

_____ (6) third inversion

_____ (7) root

_____ (8) doubling

_____ (9) D–F♯–A♯

_____ (10) triad

_____ (11) third

_____ (12) root position

_____ (13) second inversion

_____ (14) fifth

_____ (15) $^5_3$

_____ (16) $^6_4$

_____ (17) D–F–A♭

_____ (18) $^6_5$

_____ (19) D–F♯–A

_____ (20) dominant seventh chord

_____ (21) $^4_3$

_____ (22) $^4_2$

(a) major triad

(b) chord position with the third of a triad or seventh chord in the bass

(c) triad member that is a M3 or m3 above the root

(d) minor triad

(e) triad member that is a P5, d5, or A5 above the root

(f) diminished triad

(g) figure for a first-inversion triad

(h) chord position with the root of a triad or seventh chord in the bass

(i) figure for a root-position seventh chord

(j) the seventh chord built on $\hat{5}$

(k) augmented triad

(l) used to represent the scale degree of the root and the quality of triads and seventh chord

(m) figure for a first-inversion seventh chord

(n) figure for a second-inversion triad

(o) chord position with the seventh of a seventh chord in the bass

(p) chord position with the fifth of a triad or seventh chord in the bass

(q) figure for a root position triad

(r) the lowest note of a triad or seventh chord stacked in thirds

(s) figure for a second-inversion seventh chord

(t) placing one of the three elements of a triad in two voices to get four parts

(u) figure for a third-inversion seventh chord

(v) chord that may be represented as two stacked thirds

Additional review and practice available at wwnorton.com/studyspace

Class Activities

A. At the keyboard

Major and minor triads

1. Play $\hat{1}$ to $\hat{5}$ of a major scale: think of the key signature or the pattern of whole and half steps (W–W–H–W). Now perform a major triad: $\hat{1}$, $\hat{3}$, and $\hat{5}$ of the scale segment you just played. Play with both hands an octave apart, and sing along with letter names, solfège syllables, or scale-degree numbers. (In class, one student may play while the others sing.)

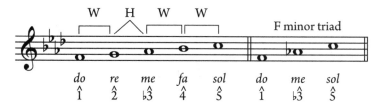

2. Play $\hat{1}$ to $\hat{5}$ of a minor scale: think of the key signature or the pattern of whole and half steps (W–H–W–W). Perform a minor triad: $\hat{1}$, $\flat\hat{3}$, and $\hat{5}$. Play with both hands an octave apart, and sing with letter names, solfège syllables, or scale-degree numbers.

3. For each pitch given below, follow instructions 1 and 2 above.

   When you have mastered the scale segment and triad at the keyboard, play *only* the tonic pitch and then sing the triad alone on syllables or numbers. Pay careful attention to the tuning of the third! When moving from major to minor, lower $\hat{3}$ to $\flat\hat{3}$.

(a) D	(f) B	(k) G♭
(b) G	(g) E♭	(l) A♭
(c) A	(h) C	(m) B♭
(d) E	(i) C♯	(n) F♯
(e) F	(j) D♭	(o) C♭

4. Augmented and diminished triads get both their name and their distinctive sound from the quality of their fifth. To make an augmented triad, perform a major triad, then raise its fifth a half step; the intervals from the root are a M3 and an A5. To make a diminished triad, perform a minor triad, then lower its fifth by a half step; the intervals are a m3 and a d5.

■ Consider each given pitch to be the root of a chord. First perform a major triad, then raise the fifth a half step to create an augmented triad. While you play, sing the pitches with letter names. Each time you alter the fifth, keep the same letter, but change its accidental (for example, A becomes A♯, not B♭).

(a) C	(e) E	(i) F♯
(b) A	(f) B	(j) B♭
(c) G	(g) A♭	(k) C♯
(d) F	(h) E♭	(l) G♯

■ Now from each of the given roots above, perform a minor triad, then lower the fifth a half step to create a diminished triad.

B. Reading rhythms

These rhythms provide a review of duplets and triplets (Chapter 5). Read on "ta" or counting syllables while tapping a steady beat or conducting. Remember to perform all dynamic indications and accents.

Rhythm 1

Rhythm 2

Rhythm 3

C. Singing at sight

First determine the key of the melody, and play that major or minor scale at the keyboard; sing along on scale-degree numbers or solfège syllables. Most of these melodies feature the tonic triad; sing a warm-up on $\hat{1}$–$\hat{3}$–$\hat{5}$–$\hat{3}$–$\hat{1}$–$\hat{7}$–$\hat{1}$ before beginning the melody. (You may write the syllables or numbers above or below the notes before singing.)

Practice singing rhythm and pitches separately before putting them together. Check yourself at the keyboard *after* you sing the melody.

Melody 1 "I Had a Little Nut Tree," mm. 1–4a

I had a lit-tle nut tree; noth-ing would it bear, But a sil-ver nut-meg and a gold-en pear.

Melody 2 Joseph Haydn, Seven German Dances, No. 6, mm. 1–8 (adapted)

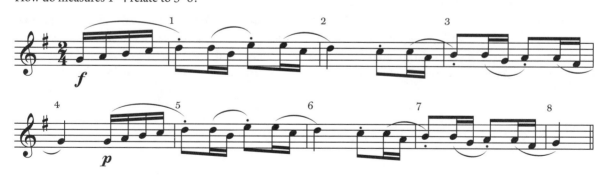

Melody 3 Leopold Mozart, Burleske, mm. 1–8a
How do measures 1–4 relate to 5–8?

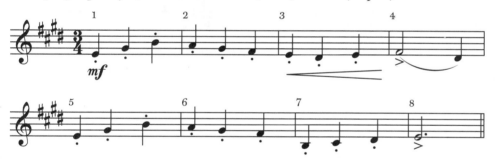

Melody 4 "St. James Infirmary"
What is the quality of the triad outlined in this melody?

Melody 5 "Down in the Valley," mm. 1–8
This melody begins on *sol–do* ($\hat{5}$–$\hat{1}$).

Down in the val - ley, the val - ley so low, _____ Hang your head

o - ver, hear the wind blow. _____ Hear the wind blow, dear, hear the wind

blow, _____ Hang your head o - ver, hear the wind blow. _____

D. Listening and writing

1. Call and response. Your teacher will perform short patterns made from a major or minor scale, then ask you to respond by performing or writing what you have heard. Try to memorize the call as quickly as possible; listen for major or minor triads in the patterns. When performing your response, maintain its pitch, rhythm, and tempo. When writing your response, write scale-degree numbers or solfège syllables along with the rhythm of the call. If a key is announced, write the pitches and rhythm together on staff paper of your own.

2. Point and sing. After establishing a tonic pitch, your teacher will create a melody by pointing to a series of items—pitches, letter names, solfège syllables, or scale-degree numbers—like those shown in the following charts. When the teacher points to an item, immediately sing it. Listen for major or minor triads. Perform the melody until you have memorized it. Then use the pitches, letter names, syllables, or numbers of the melody to write it on the staff. Make your own point-and-sing exercises with a partner to practice.

Singing scale patterns from *sol* to *sol* ($\hat{5}$–$\hat{5}$)

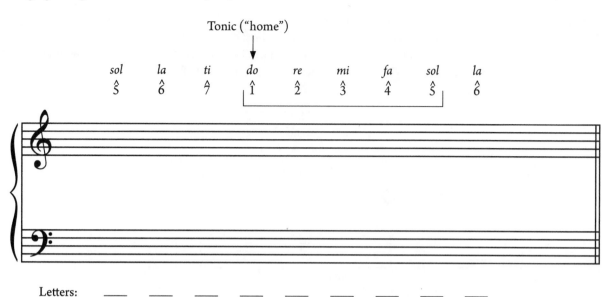

Tonic ("home")

sol	la	ti	do	re	mi	fa	sol	la
$\hat{5}$	$\hat{6}$	$\hat{7}$	$\hat{1}$	$\hat{2}$	$\hat{3}$	$\hat{4}$	$\hat{5}$	$\hat{6}$

Letters: ___ ___ ___ ___ ___ ___ ___ ___ ___

Singing scale patterns from *do* to *do* ($\hat{1}$–$\hat{1}$)

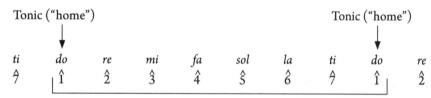

Tonic ("home")   Tonic ("home")

ti	do	re	mi	fa	sol	la	ti	do	re
$\hat{7}$	$\hat{1}$	$\hat{2}$	$\hat{3}$	$\hat{4}$	$\hat{5}$	$\hat{6}$	$\hat{7}$	$\hat{1}$	$\hat{2}$

Letters: ___ ___ ___ ___ ___ ___ ___ ___ ___ ___

E. Hearing triad qualities

Each exercise below consists of ten recorded root-position triads. These may be used for class discussion of strategies for hearing and writing, or for individual practice. The root of each triad is notated on the staff; don't change the given pitch. In the blank, write the triad's quality (M, m, A, or d). Then notate the third and fifth, including any necessary accidentals. For example, if you hear a minor triad whose root is B♭. Write "m" in the blank. Then notate the third and fifth.

1. Major and minor triads (played as a melody)

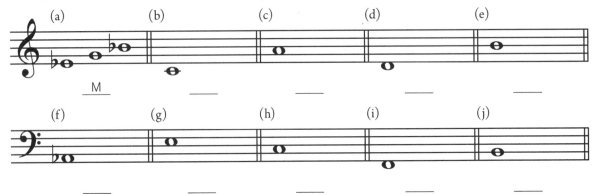

2. Major and minor triads (played as a chord)

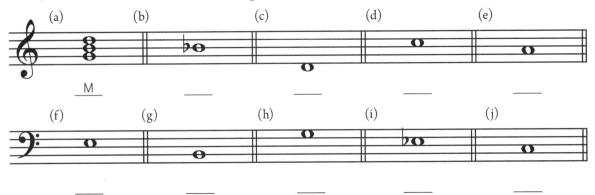

3. Diminished and augmented triads (played as a melody)

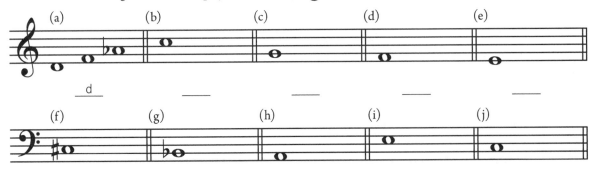

Workbook   ASSIGNMENT 9.1

1. Building triads above major scales

Write the requested ascending major scale in whole notes. Above each scale degree, write the third and fifth to make a triad, adding accidentals as needed for that key. Write M (major), m (minor), or d (diminished) under each triad to show the quality, then provide the Roman numeral.

a.

Triad
quality: M   m   m   ___   ___   ___   ___

Roman
numeral: F: I   ii   iii   ___   ___   ___   ___

b.

Triad
quality: ___   ___   ___   ___   ___   ___   ___

Roman
numeral: A: ___   ___   ___   ___   ___   ___   ___

c.

Triad
quality: ___   ___   ___   ___   ___   ___   ___

Roman
numeral: E: ___   ___   ___   ___   ___   ___   ___

d.

Triad
quality: ___   ___   ___   ___   ___   ___   ___

Roman
numeral: D♭: ___   ___   ___   ___   ___   ___   ___

2. Identifying triad roots, quality, and inversion

For each of the triads below, write the triad type in the first row of blanks, using a capital letter and, if other than major, the abbreviation for quality. In the second row of blanks, indicate the position as root or inversion ($\frac{5}{3}$, $\frac{6}{3}$, or $\frac{6}{4}$). 🔊

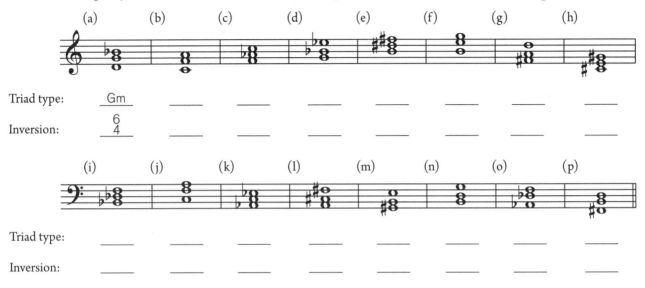

Triad type: Gm   ___   ___   ___   ___   ___   ___   ___

Inversion: $\frac{6}{4}$ ___   ___   ___   ___   ___   ___   ___

Triad type: ___   ___   ___   ___   ___   ___   ___   ___

Inversion: ___   ___   ___   ___   ___   ___   ___   ___

3. Identifying major and minor triads in musical contexts

In the following excerpt, identify each chord by writing the triad (stacked in thirds) on the staff. Then in the blanks below, write M (for major) or m (minor) to indicate the chord quality. Remember to apply accidentals from the key signature. Finally, write a Roman numeral for each chord in the key specified.

"Old Hundredth," mm. 1–6a 🔊

Triad
quality: M   M   M   ___   ___   ___   ___   ___   ___   ___   ___

Roman
numeral: G: I   I   V   ___   ___   ___   ___   ___   ___   ___

Workbook ASSIGNMENT 9.2

1. Building triads above minor scales

Write the requested ascending harmonic minor scale in whole notes. Above each scale degree, write the third and fifth to make a triad, adding accidentals as needed for that key. Use the leading tone (raised) for triads build on $\hat{5}$ and $\hat{7}$. Write M (major), m (minor), or d (diminished) under each triad to show the quality, then provide the Roman numeral.

a.

Triad
quality: m   d   M   ___   ___   ___   ___

Roman
numeral: Bm: i   ii°   III   ___   ___   ___   ___

b.

Triad
quality: ___   ___   ___   ___   ___   ___   ___

Roman
numeral: Cm: ___   ___   ___   ___   ___   ___   ___

c.

Triad
quality: ___   ___   ___   ___   ___   ___   ___

Roman
numeral: F♯m: ___   ___   ___   ___   ___   ___   ___

d.

Triad
quality: ___   ___   ___   ___   ___   ___   ___

Roman
numeral: Dm: ___   ___   ___   ___   ___   ___   ___

2. Identifying major and minor triads

Identify the root and quality of each triad below (e.g., B♭m). 🔊

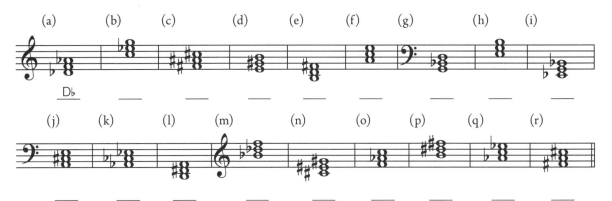

3. Identifying major and minor triads in musical contexts

In the following excerpt, identify each chord by writing the triad (stacked in thirds) on the staff. Then in the blanks below, write M (for major) or m (minor) to indicate the chord quality. Remember to apply accidentals from the key signature. Finally, write a Roman numeral for each chord in the key specified. (For now, ignore circled notes.)

"Nun danket," mm. 1–4 🔊

Triad
quality: ___ M ___ M ___ M ___ ___ ___ ___ ___ ___ ___ ___

Roman
numeral: E♭: ___ I ___ I ___ I ___ ___ ___ ___ ___ ___ ___ ___

Workbook ASSIGNMENT 9.3

1. Writing major triads

a. Write the major key signature requested, then write the tonic triad (built from scale degrees $\hat{1}$, $\hat{3}$, and $\hat{5}$), using accidentals from the key signature to spell it.

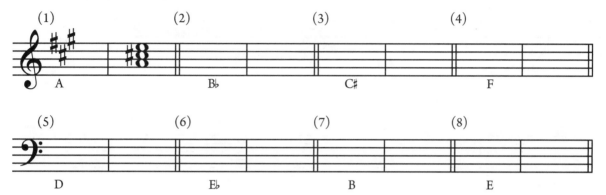

b. Write major triads above each note below. First draw the note heads (line-line-line or space-space-space), then think of the major key signature of the bottom note to help you spell the chord.

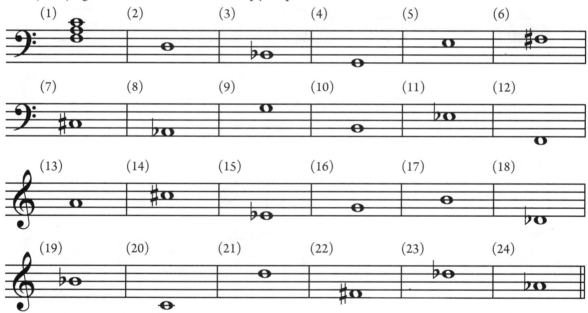

2. Writing minor triads

a. Rewrite each major triad below, lowering its third to make a minor triad.

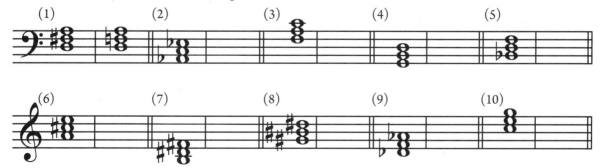

b. Consider each pitch below as the root of a minor triad, then complete the triad.

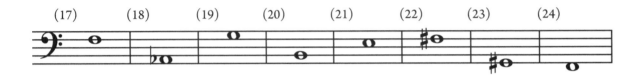

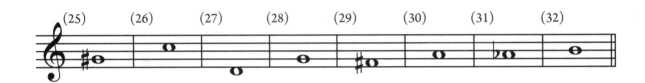

3. Identifying major and minor triads in musical contexts

In the following excerpt, identify each chord by writing the triad (stacked in thirds) on the staff. Then in the blanks below, write M (for major) or m (minor) to indicate the chord quality. Remember to apply accidentals from the key signature. Finally, write a Roman numeral for each chord in the key specified.

Johann Pachelbel, Canon for Three Violins and Keyboard in D Major, mm. 1–2

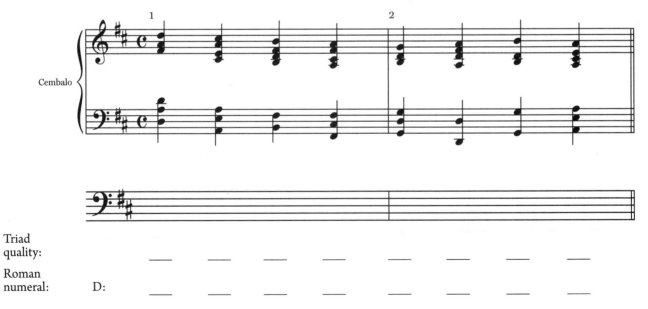

Triad
quality: ___   ___   ___   ___   ___   ___   ___   ___

Roman
numeral: D: ___   ___   ___   ___   ___   ___   ___   ___

Workbook ASSIGNMENT 9.4

1. Writing major and minor triads

Write each triad specified below.

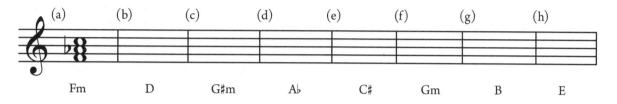

Fm   D   G♯m   A♭   C♯   Gm   B   E

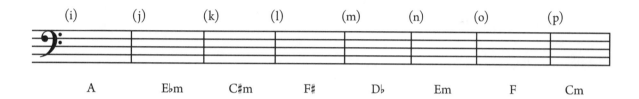

A   E♭m   C♯m   F♯   D♭   Em   F   Cm

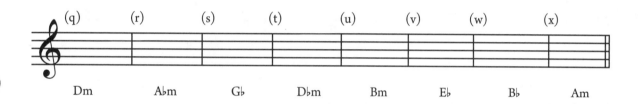

Dm   A♭m   G♭   D♭m   Bm   E♭   B♭   Am

2. Writing dominant seventh chords

Write a dominant seventh chord above each given root, following one of the methods described in the chapter. Don't change the given pitch.

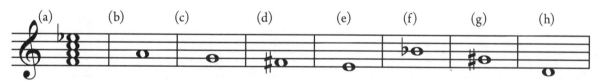

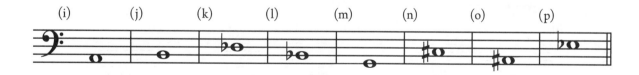

3. Writing triads

Write the requested triads below stacked in thirds, following one of the methods described in the chapter. Don't change the given pitch. An example is shown for each, with the starting note indicated by an arrow.

a. Each pitch below is the root of a triad.

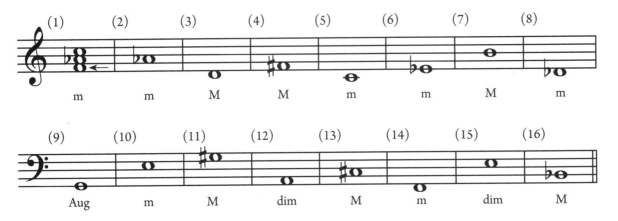

b. Each pitch below is the third of a triad.

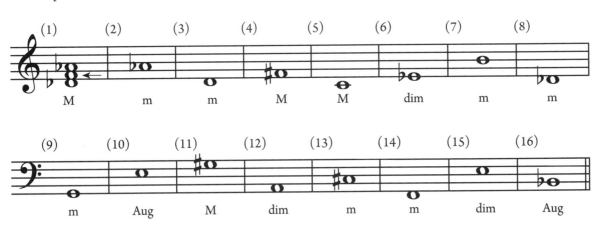

c. Each pitch below is the fifth of a triad.

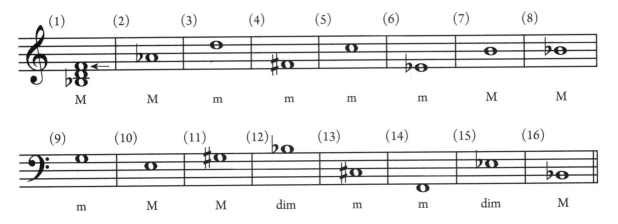

Workbook AURAL SKILLS 9.1

Listen to the beginning of a piano work by Franz Schubert, and complete the following exercises. 🔊

1. Throughout the excerpt, the melody is doubled at which interval?

(a) m3   (b) P5   (c) M6   (d) P8

2. Beginning with an eighth-note anacrusis, notate the rhythm of the excerpt in compound duple meter. Write bar lines and beam notes to show correct beat groups.

3. Beginning with $\hat{1}$–$\hat{1}$–♭$\hat{3}$–$\hat{5}$ (*do–do–me–sol*), write the melody with solfège syllables or scale-degree numbers.

4. Beginning with C4, notate the pitches of the melody on the staff below.

5. On which scale is this melody based?

(a) major   (c) ascending melodic minor
(b) natural (descending melodic) minor

6. Referring to your answers to questions 2–4, notate both pitches and rhythm of the melody on the staff below.

Musical challenges!

7. Rewrite the melody in the key of D minor. For help, recall the syllables or numbers in question 3.

8. On the staff below, transcribe the answer to question 7 to its parallel major key. (Remember: Parallel major has the same tonic pitch, but a different key signature.)

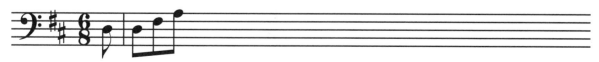

9. On the staff below, transcribe the answer to question 7 to its relative major key. Write an key signature. (Remember: Relative major has the same key signature, but a different tonic pitch.)

Workbook AURAL SKILLS 9.2

Composing and performing melodies

1. Compose two melodies that incorporate melodic thirds within the tonic triad.

- Choose a different tonic pitch for each melody, one in a major key and one in a minor key. Write one in treble clef and one in bass clef.
- Write the correct key signature. Choose a key that you can sing comfortably.
- Include at least 10–12 pitches in each melody, starting on the tonic pitch. Create interesting rhythms and contours.
- If you write $\hat{7}$, be sure that it moves up to $\hat{1}$. If you write $\flat\hat{7}$, it should move down to $\flat\hat{6}$.
- Add tempo and dynamic markings, and make the score appear as musical as possible.

2. Prepare to perform your melodies in the following ways.

- Sing on letter names, solfège syllables, or scale-degree numbers.
- Play at the keyboard or other instrument.
- Play on an instrument while you sing along.

Melody 1

Melody 2

TOPICS

- triads on $\hat{1}$, $\hat{4}$, and $\hat{5}$ and the seventh chord on $\hat{5}$
- harmonizing major melodies with the basic phrase model
- cadence types
- the subdominant in the basic phrase
- melodic embellishments
- harmonizing minor-key melodies

MUSIC

- Johann Sebastian Bach, "Wachet auf" (Chorale No. 179)
- Chartres
- Stephen Foster, "Oh! Susanna"
- "Go Down, Moses"
- Don Henley, Glenn Frey, and Randy Meisner, "Take It to the Limit"
- "Home on the Range"
- "Michael Finnigin"
- "My Country, 'Tis of Thee"
- Joel Phillips, "Blues for Norton"
- St. George's Windsor
- Franz Schubert, Waltz in B Minor
- "Wayfaring Stranger"

CHAPTER 10

Melody Harmonization and Cadences

Triads on $\hat{1}$, $\hat{4}$, and $\hat{5}$ and the Seventh Chord on $\hat{5}$

Three triads often encountered in major- and minor-key pieces are those built on $\hat{1}$, $\hat{4}$, and $\hat{5}$—the tonic, subdominant, and dominant triads. They may appear as chords in an accompaniment or may form the framework for a melody. Listen to the opening of "Take It to the Limit" (through measure 17) while following the score in your anthology, then refer to the excerpts in Example 10.1. The melody begins (part a) with the pitches of the tonic triad in the key of C major: C–E–G ($\hat{1}$–$\hat{3}$–$\hat{5}$). It is accompanied by a C major triad. Part (b) shows the end of the excerpt; the last note (D) is harmonized with notes from the dominant triad in C major: G–B–D ($\hat{5}$–$\hat{7}$–$\hat{2}$).

EXAMPLE 10.1 Henley, Frey, and Meisner, "Take It to the Limit"

(a) Mm. 4b–6a 🔻 0:14–0:19

All a - lone   at the end

C–E–G = tonic triad
($\hat{1}$–$\hat{3}$–$\hat{5}$)

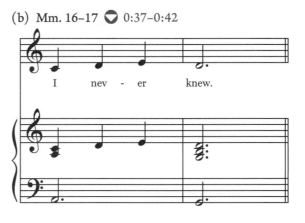

(b) Mm. 16–17 🔻 0:37–0:42

I   nev - er   knew.

G–B–D = dominant triad
($\hat{5}$–$\hat{7}$–$\hat{2}$)

The tonic triad—formed from $\hat{1}$, $\hat{3}$ (or $\flat\hat{3}$) and $\hat{5}$—is the most essential element in creating a sense of the key. A good way to locate the tonic triad at the keyboard is to play the five-finger pattern from $\hat{1}$ to $\hat{5}$ as in Example 10.2, then press your thumb, middle, and little fingers down as shown to make the chord.

EXAMPLE 10.2   The tonic triad in major keys

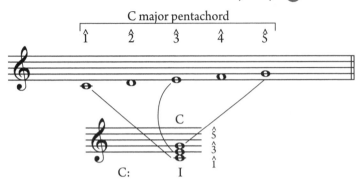

The next most essential chord for establishing a key is the dominant triad, $\hat{5}$–$\hat{7}$–$\hat{2}$ (Example 10.3). Sometimes this triad is extended by another third to make $\hat{5}$–$\hat{7}$–$\hat{2}$–$\hat{4}$, the dominant seventh chord, a chord so familiar that you probably will recognize its sound instantly.

EXAMPLE 10.3   The dominant triad and dominant seventh chord in C major

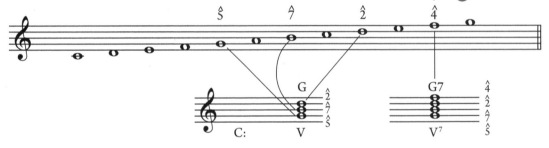

The chord built on $\hat{4}$, the subdominant triad, is $\hat{4}$–$\hat{6}$–$\hat{1}$ (Example 10.4). Since the tonic, subdominant, and dominant triads in a major key are all major, they help give pieces a "major" sound.

EXAMPLE 10.4   The subdominant triad in C major

On the staves below, write the scale for each major key listed, adding the appropriate accidentals. Label each pitch with a scale-degree number. Then write the tonic, subdominant, and dominant triads for each key, and label them with chord symbols above and Roman numerals below, as shown. The root of each triad is provided.

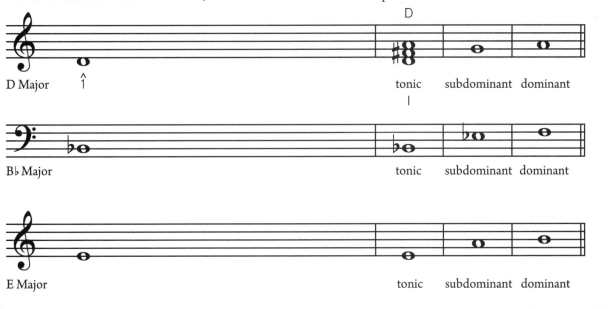

D Major $\hat{1}$ — tonic   subdominant   dominant

B♭ Major — tonic   subdominant   dominant

E Major — tonic   subdominant   dominant

The most common triads in minor-key pieces are also the tonic, subdominant, and dominant. If you spell these triads with the accidentals from a minor key signature, each has a minor quality. As we have seen, it is standard practice for composers to raise ♭$\hat{7}$ to make a leading tone, yielding the harmonic minor scale and a major dominant triad (Example 10.5).

EXAMPLE 10.5   Triads on $\hat{1}$, $\hat{4}$, and $\hat{5}$ (and V⁷) in B harmonic minor 🔊

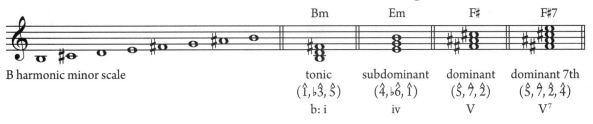

B harmonic minor scale

tonic	subdominant	dominant	dominant 7th
($\hat{1}$, ♭$\hat{3}$, $\hat{5}$)	($\hat{4}$, ♭$\hat{6}$, $\hat{1}$)	($\hat{5}$, $\hat{7}$, $\hat{2}$)	($\hat{5}$, $\hat{7}$, $\hat{2}$, $\hat{4}$)
b: i	iv	V	V⁷

Listen to a minor-key melody accompanied by the tonic triad and dominant seventh: the opening measures of Schubert's Waltz in B Minor (Example 10.6). Focus first on the melody in the right-hand part (treble clef), then write scale-degree numbers over the melody notes for measures 1–4.

EXAMPLE 10.6   Schubert, Waltz in B Minor, mm. 1–8a 🔊

In measure 1, the scale degrees in both hands are exactly the same—$\hat{1}$, ♭$\hat{3}$, and $\hat{5}$ (*do–me–sol*), the tonic triad in B minor—but in different octaves and arrangements. The melody in this measure outlines the tonic triad, and is harmonized with that chord. In measure 2, the melody has $\hat{2}$, $\hat{4}$, and $\hat{5}$—pitches of the V⁷ chord, which are accompanied by $\hat{5}$, $\hat{7}$, and $\hat{4}$. Both hands together make the complete V⁷ (F♯–A♯–C♯–E).

> **KEY CONCEPT**   When harmonizing melodies in minor keys, raise ♭$\hat{7}$ in the dominant harmony to make a leading tone (see Chapter 9), unless the melody features ♭$\hat{7}$ from the natural minor scale.

The arrangement of musical lines in Example 10.6—with melody in one hand and chords in the other—is called **melody and accompaniment**, one of the most common musical textures.

TRY IT #2

Write the scale requested, then the corresponding triads on $\hat{1}$, $\hat{4}$, and $\hat{5}$. Label the triads with chord symbols and Roman numerals as shown. For the harmonic minor scales, make the dominant a major triad (write $\hat{7}$ rather than ♭$\hat{7}$) and add a dominant seventh chord.

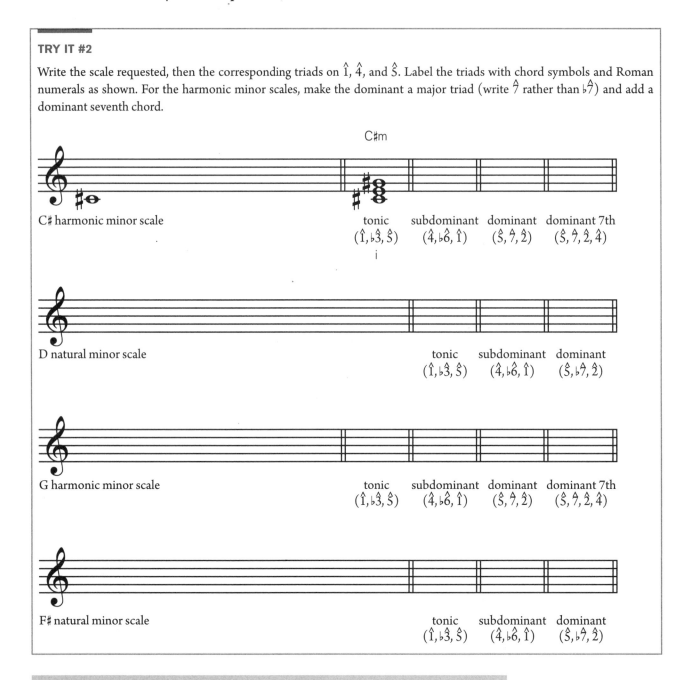

C♯ harmonic minor scale

tonic ($\hat{1}$,♭$\hat{3}$,$\hat{5}$) subdominant ($\hat{4}$,♭$\hat{6}$,$\hat{1}$) dominant ($\hat{5}$,$\hat{7}$,$\hat{2}$) dominant 7th ($\hat{5}$,$\hat{7}$,$\hat{2}$,$\hat{4}$)

D natural minor scale

tonic ($\hat{1}$,♭$\hat{3}$,$\hat{5}$) subdominant ($\hat{4}$,♭$\hat{6}$,$\hat{1}$) dominant ($\hat{5}$,♭$\hat{7}$,$\hat{2}$)

G harmonic minor scale

tonic ($\hat{1}$,♭$\hat{3}$,$\hat{5}$) subdominant ($\hat{4}$,♭$\hat{6}$,$\hat{1}$) dominant ($\hat{5}$,$\hat{7}$,$\hat{2}$) dominant 7th ($\hat{5}$,$\hat{7}$,$\hat{2}$,$\hat{4}$)

F♯ natural minor scale

tonic ($\hat{1}$,♭$\hat{3}$,$\hat{5}$) subdominant ($\hat{4}$,♭$\hat{6}$,$\hat{1}$) dominant ($\hat{5}$,♭$\hat{7}$,$\hat{2}$)

ASSIGNMENT 10.1

Look again at the opening to Schubert's waltz, shown in Example 10.7, focusing this time on the chords in the left-hand part. The Roman numerals below the staff indicate where Schubert uses tonic and dominant harmonies. The two harmonies alternate, one per measure, until measures 7–8. There, the pace of harmonic change speeds up, with two chords in measure 7 leading to a resting point in measure 8. This measure concludes a musical phrase.

> **KEY CONCEPT** A **phrase** is a basic unit of musical thought, similar to a sentence in language. The typical phrase—like most sentences—has a beginning, a middle, and an end. The end is marked by a **cadence**: the harmonic, melodic, and rhythmic features that make the phrase sound like a complete thought. Phrases are typically 4 or 8 measures in length.

EXAMPLE 10.7   Schubert, Waltz in B Minor, mm. 1–8a 🔊

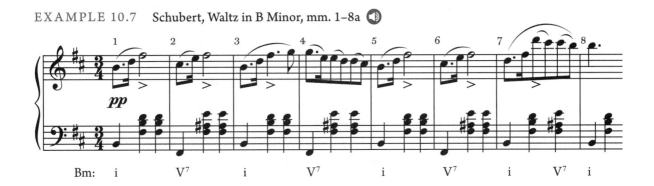

The rate at which chords change, called the **harmonic rhythm**, is one of the ways you can distinguish one style from another: a harmonic rhythm of one or two chords per measure is typical of waltzes; in hymns, every beat may have a new chord type; and in folk styles, the same chord may last for two or three measures. In all of these styles, the harmonic rhythm tends to speed up at the cadence to articulate the phrase ending.

Harmonizing Major Melodies with the Basic Phrase Model

Listen to "Oh! Susanna" while following the score in your anthology (p. 350). At the second verse, where the guitar accompaniment begins, listen to how the chords change. Example 10.8 shows the second verse harmonized with two chords: D (the tonic) and A7 (the dominant seventh). The melody helps the accompanist decide which chords to use. For example, measures 1–3 feature Ds, F♯s, and As, while measure 4 begins with an E that would clash with a D chord but works well with an A7. (The circled notes, labeled P and N, are not part of the chord; these will be discussed on p. 255.)

Also shown above the staff as part of the chord symbols are fretboad diagrams, illustrating guitar fingerings. The vertical lines represent guitar strings, the horizontal lines show the frets, and the black dots indicate where to place your fingers. (See Appendix 7 for more on guitar chords.)

EXAMPLE 10.8   Foster, "Oh! Susanna" mm. 1–8a (verse 2) 🔊

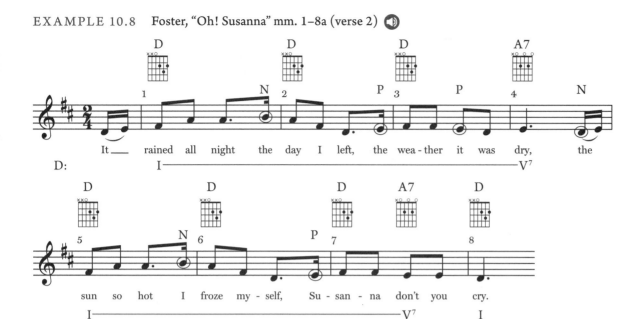

Chords that harmonize a melody usually appear in a specific order, called a **chord progression**. A simple folk song may require only two chords: tonic and dominant. The tonic chord usually comes first to establish the key, followed by a dominant triad or seventh chord. After the chords progress from tonic to dominant, they almost always return "home" to tonic in a progression known as the **basic phrase**: I–V–I. Use the basic phrase progression to guide you in melody harmonization; as we add more chords we will show their typical positions within the basic phrase.

Cadence Types

Every phrase ends with a cadence. Cadences are typically marked by a longer melody note (as in mm. 4 and 8 of Example 10.8) or by rests that break up the flow of the tune. Importantly, they are also marked by specific melodic–harmonic patterns known as the half, authentic, plagal, and deceptive cadence types. Of these, the half and authentic types are by far the most common.

Phrases may end on a dominant chord for an inconclusive sound. Listen again to Example 10.8, focusing on the end of the first phrase, at the words "it was dry" (m. 4). This type of ending is called a **half cadence** (abbreviated **HC**). The word "half" signals that the musical idea has not come to an end but must continue to another phrase before it can sound complete. Half cadences end on a dominant harmony accompanying a melody that ends on $\hat{2}$ (or less commonly on $\hat{5}$ or $\hat{7}$).

Often, as in "Oh! Susanna," a phrase ending on a half cadence is paired with another phrase that begins the same way but returns to tonic. This basic phrase progression sounds more complete, and the music can end here. Measures 5–8 of Example 10.8 follow this pattern. The cadence in measure 8, called an **authentic cadence** (**AC**), is formed when a dominant harmony moves to a tonic harmony to make a conclusive phrase ending. For the strongest type of ending, called a **perfect authentic cadence** (**PAC**), use the progression V or V^7 to I with both chords in root position (root of the chord in the bass) and the melody ending with $\hat{2}$–$\hat{1}$ or $\hat{7}$–$\hat{1}$. For a somewhat less conclusive authentic cadence—an **imperfect authentic cadence** (**IAC**)—end the melody on $\hat{3}$ or $\hat{5}$ or write the dominant harmony in an inversion.

You may encounter two additional types of inconclusive cadences in music: the deceptive cadence and the plagal cadence. To see a deceptive cadence, look at Example 10.9, a German chorale by J. S. Bach. The melody in measures 19 and 20 descends $\hat{3}$–$\hat{2}$–$\hat{1}$ to the tonic (E♭), and the V⁷ seems prepared to resolve to I, but instead it moves to vi—a chord that shares two of its three pitches with I (E♭ and G), but has a minor quality. This bait-and-switch strategy gives the cadence its name: a **deceptive cadence** (**DC**) moves from V or V⁷ to vi, instead of I. In this chorale, Bach places the deceptive cadence here because he is setting two phrases with different text but the same melody—after the DC, the repetition of the phrase (mm. 21–24) ends with a PAC.

EXAMPLE 10.9   Bach, "Wachet auf," mm. 17–24 🔊

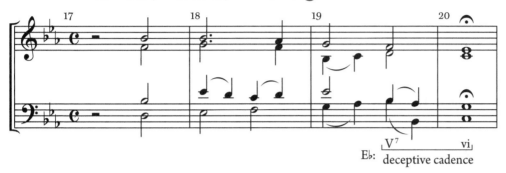

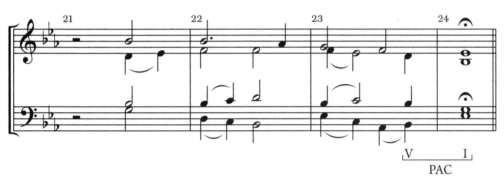

Not all V–vi motion creates a deceptive cadence; you may instead find a deceptive resolution of the dominant harmony in the middle of a phrase that cadences a few beats, or even a few measures, later. For an example, listen to the opening of "My Country, 'Tis of Thee," shown in Example 10.10.

EXAMPLE 10.10   My Country, 'Tis of Thee," mm. 1–6 🔊

Although phrases are typically organized in four-bar units, this one consists of four bars plus two additional measures that end with a PAC. The first four bars end with a **deceptive resolution** of V⁷ to vi; here, the deception is not really a "cadence," since the music moves on immediately to the PAC. This type of V–vi deceptive resolution is more common than a phrase ending with a true DC.

In the first two measures, most of the notes are $\hat{1}$, $\hat{3}$, and $\hat{5}$, members of the tonic triad in G major. These are harmonized with a tonic triad (G), indicated by the chord symbol G above the staff and Roman numeral I below. Measures 3 and 4 feature mostly $\hat{5}$, $\hat{7}$, and $\hat{2}$, which belong to the dominant triad, D major. These four measures make a phrase with a tonic-to-dominant progression, ending with a HC in measure 4. Measures 5–6 are the same as measures 1–2 and may be harmonized the same. To create contrast between measure 5 and measure 1, you could insert a subdominant chord (C) between two tonic chords, I–IV–I, to harmonize the repeated Gs: "wind" (I), "blew them" (IV), "off" (I). Scale degrees $\hat{2}$ and $\hat{5}$ in measure 7 should be set with a V^7 (D7), leading to the final I chord (G) and making an AC in measure 8. Measures 5–8 make a complete basic phrase.

Harmonizing Minor-Key Melodies

You can harmonize minor melodies with triads on $\hat{1}$, $\hat{4}$, and $\hat{5}$ in much the same way as major-key melodies. The only difference is in the treatment of the seventh scale degree—whether to add an accidental to make a leading tone or to use the minor dominant (v). Compare the first eight measures of two melodies, "Go Down, Moses" and "Wayfaring Stranger," shown in Examples 10.16 and 10.17.

EXAMPLE 10.16   "Go Down, Moses," mm. 1–8

EXAMPLE 10.17   "Wayfaring Stranger," mm. 1–8

Before beginning any harmonization, sing through the melody on numbers or syllables or play it on an instrument to hear how it sounds. Then use the numbers or syllables to help choose appropriate chords. "Go Down, Moses" is based on the G harmonic minor scale, with two flats in the key signature and an F♯ leading tone (making $\hat{7}$–$\hat{1}$). In contrast, "Wayfaring Stranger" shows no leading tone (C♯) and ends ♭$\hat{7}$–$\hat{1}$ (C♮–D); its pitches are drawn from the natural minor scale. Each melody ends with dominant-to-tonic motion, but "Go Down, Moses" calls for a major dominant triad in measure 7, and "Wayfaring Stranger" takes a minor dominant. To harmonize these melodies, use the chords in G harmonic minor and D natural minor, respectively.

In Example 10.18, the beginning of "Go Down, Moses," scale degrees appear beneath the staff and chord symbols above. Each chord choice corresponds with the melody, and the progression of chords follows the i–V–i basic phrase model. The dominant seventh at the cadence makes a harmonically strong ending.

EXAMPLE 10.18   "Go Down, Moses," mm. 1–4a

In Example 10.19, the end of "Wayfaring Stranger," the subdominant (Gm) in measure 7 extends the tonic sound. The circled G in measure 5 is a passing tone, moving between the chord tones F and A. If you have access to a guitar or keyboard, sing the melody with these chords. Then harmonize the rest of these two melodies yourself (Examples 10.16 and 10.17), following the guidelines below.

EXAMPLE 10.19   "Wayfaring Stranger," mm. 4b–8

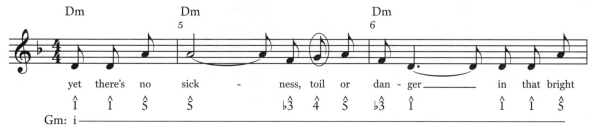

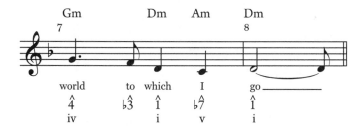

To harmonize a melody with triads on $\hat{1}$, $\hat{4}$, and $\hat{5}$:

- First play or sing it with scale-degree numbers or solfège syllables.
- Let the scale-degree function of the melody notes (tonic, dominant, etc.) help you choose appropriate chords:

If the melody features	use
$\hat{1}$ or $\hat{3}$ ($\flat\hat{3}$ in minor)	tonic harmony (I or i).
$\hat{2}$ or $\hat{7}$	dominant harmony (V or V^7).
$\hat{4}$ or $\hat{6}$ ($\flat\hat{6}$ in minor)	subdominant harmony (IV or iv).
$\flat\hat{7}$ in minor	minor dominant (v).
$\hat{5}$	either tonic or dominant harmony; let your ear be your guide.

- Plan phrase beginnings and endings first, then fill in the remaining chords.
- Listen for the end of each phrase. If the melody ends on $\hat{2}$, $\hat{5}$, or $\hat{7}$, use dominant harmony. If it ends on $\hat{1}$ or $\hat{3}$, use tonic harmony.
- If a portion of the melody includes several members of a triad, harmonize it with that triad.
- Where possible, follow the I–V–I or I–IV–V–I progression of the basic phrase; you may also use IV between two tonic triads.
- Aim for a fairly uniform harmonic rhythm. In folk or popular styles, the chord may change just once or twice per measure.

ASSIGNMENT 10.3, 10.4

Did You Know?

Stephen Foster (1826–1864) is considered the first great American songwriter. His melodies, many written as parlor ballads or for minstrel shows, are so much a part of American culture that we often think of them as traditional folk songs rather than published, attributed compositions. "Oh! Susanna" was premiered in Andrews' Eagle Ice Cream Saloon in Pittsburgh on September 11, 1847. This song, with its nonsensical lyrics, became the unofficial theme song of the California gold rush, which began in January of the following year.

Terms You Should Know

basic phrase	plagal (PC)	passing tone
cadence	half (HC)	harmonic rhythm
authentic (AC)	chord progression	melody and accompaniment
deceptive (DC)	deceptive resolution	phrase
imperfect authentic (IAC)	embellishing tone	
perfect authentic (PAC)	neighbor tone	

Questions for Review

1. Which scale degrees make up the dominant seventh chord?
2. How do you know when a phrase ends?
3. What are the chords in a basic phrase progression?
4. For each cadence type, what harmonies end a phrase?
5. What are two typical ways for a IV chord to be used in a phrase?
6. How do you know whether a note in a melody is a chord member or an embellishing tone?
7. What are the steps in harmonizing a major-key melody?
8. What quality (major or minor) are the chords above $\hat{1}$, $\hat{4}$, and $\hat{5}$ of a major scale? of a natural minor scale? of a harmonic minor scale?
9. Which scale degree is typically raised in minor? In what chords is it usually raised?
10. How is harmonizing a minor-key melody different from harmonizing a major-key melody?

Reading Review

Match the terms on the left with the best answer on the right.

_____ (1) tonic triad

_____ (2) harmonic rhythm

_____ (3) authentic cadence

_____ (4) dominant triad

_____ (5) chord progression

_____ (6) deceptive cadence

_____ (7) subdominant triad

_____ (8) cadence

_____ (9) phrase

_____ (10) plagal cadence

_____ (11) embellishing tones

_____ (12) passing tone

_____ (13) neighbor tone

_____ (14) half cadence

(a) an embellishing tone approached and left by step in the same direction

(b) phrase ending on the dominant (V or V^7), with $\hat{2}$ or $\hat{5}$ in the melody

(c) triad built on $\hat{5}$

(d) the rate at which chords change

(e) triad built on $\hat{1}$

(f) the harmonic, melodic, and rhythmic features that end a musical phrase

(g) phrase ending with IV–I

(h) an embellishing tone that moves by step away from a chord tone, then returns

(i) the order of chords harmonizing a melody

(j) a basic unit of musical thought, similar to a sentence in language

(k) dominant-to-tonic phrase ending, with $\hat{1}$ or $\hat{3}$ in the melody

(l) notes in a melody that are not a part of the harmony

(m) triad built on $\hat{4}$

(n) substitutes vi for I at the phrase ending

Ⓖ Additional review and practice available at wwnorton.com/studyspace

Class Activities

A. At the keyboard

1. Play the following major scales (using any fingering), then for each, play major triads built on $\hat{1}$, $\hat{4}$, and $\hat{5}$ and the dominant seventh chord built on $\hat{5}$.

Example: D major

(a) D major	(d) B♭ major	(g) E major
(b) G major	(e) C major	(h) E♭ major
(c) F major	(f) A major	(i) A♭ major

2. Play the following natural minor scales (using any fingering), then for each, play minor triads built on $\hat{1}$, $\hat{4}$, and $\hat{5}$. Play the harmonic minor scale, then play the major triad and dominant seventh chord built on $\hat{5}$.

Example: D minor

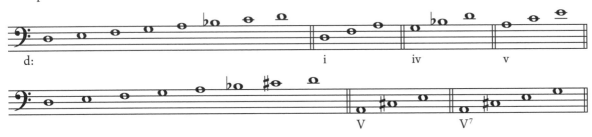

(a) D minor	(d) B minor	(g) E minor
(b) G minor	(e) C minor	(h) F♯ minor
(c) F minor	(f) A minor	(i) C♯ minor

B. Ensemble singing at sight

Each of the following sight-singing examples draws on your study of triads. Sing on scale-degree numbers or solfège syllables while tapping a steady pulse or conducting.

Melody 1 Stephen Foster, "Better Times Are Coming"

This melody is harmonized with I, IV, and V chords. Identify the chord in each measure, as well as any passing or neighboring tones. Sing in class along with the piano accompaniment.

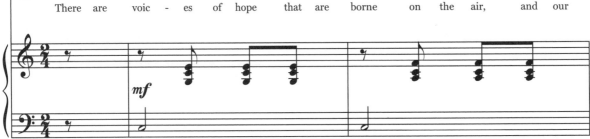

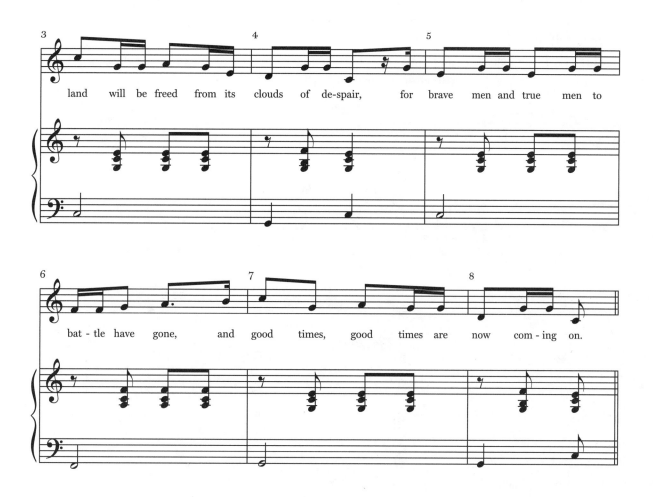

land will be freed from its clouds of de-spair, for brave men and true men to bat-tle have gone, and good times, good times are now com-ing on.

Melody 2 J. S. Bach, "Jesu, Priceless Treasure" (adapted), mm. 1–2

This tune sets the triads in four parts. Practice singing each line in a comfortable register, then sing the four parts together with piano accompaniment. Which part is the most challenging?

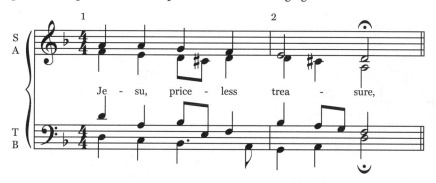

Je - su, price - less trea - sure,

Melody 3 "Dona nobis pacem"

This melody begins with notes drawn from the tonic triad and dominant seventh chord. Practice it as a class, then sing as a round. A new group of voices begins when the previous group reaches the ②.

Translation: Grant us peace

Melody 4 William Boyce, "Alleluia"

This melody begins with a descending major scale. At the position marked with a ② the melody features notes drawn from the tonic and dominant triads. Practice it as a class, then sing as a round. The melody ends on 3̂.

C. Group improvisation

Improvise a melody to go with the harmonic accompaniment given below. Make this a class project, with the teacher at the piano and members of the class improvising melodies with their voices or another instrument they play. If a member of the class plays guitar, add guitar accompaniment; read the guitar tabs above the piano music. If any class members play a bass instrument (or have a bass voice), they can play the bass line to create a small ensemble.

The music, in G major, is organized in four two-measure units, which may be repeated as many times as you like, with different class members supplying an improvised melody each time. Each unit consists of three major triads: I, IV, and V. The final measure, a tonic triad, is to be added at the conclusion of the performance.

Getting oriented: Your teacher will play the tonic pitch, G, at the keyboard and then play and sing the G major scale up and down to orient you to the key. While your teacher or a class member plays the bass line, sing the bass-clef melody by itself. Then play and sing each of the treble-clef melodies. Now you are ready to begin improvising your own melody.

Pitches: For the pitches of your melody, choose chord members (G, B, or D in m. 1), but also experiment with passing tones or neighbor tones between chord members (for example, you might use G–A–B in measure 1). Create an interesting contour. Let your ear guide you to create music similar to what you have already heard; some repetition of melodic and rhythmic patterns is characteristic of good improvisations.

Rhythm: For the rhythm of your melody, choose from the eight rhythmic patterns shown. You will use two patterns in each measure. Feel free to repeat patterns from measure to measure: for example, you could use four eighth notes and a half note (patterns 2 and 8) in each measure.

For a simpler exercise: Improvise only in the odd-numbered measures (over the whole-note chord), then sing the given melody pitches on half notes in the even-numbered measures.

Throughout your improvisation, treat the melody given in each two-measure unit as an outline for your improvisation. Feel free to include these notes in your melody. Above all, have a good time! Don't worry if your improvisation is less than perfect. Trying is how you learn and improve.

Sample melody (improvised in odd-numbered measures)

Work space to try out your ideas

D. Listening and writing

Your teacher will perform short patterns that include triads from major and minor scales, then ask you to respond by performing or writing what you have heard. Try to memorize the call as quickly as possible. When performing your response, maintain its pitch, rhythm, and tempo. When writing your response, write scale-degree numbers or solfège syllables along with the rhythm of the call. If a key is announced, write the pitches and rhythm below.

Workbook ASSIGNMENT 10.1

1. Writing triads on $\hat{1}$, $\hat{4}$, and $\hat{5}$ in major keys

Write each major scale below (adding accidentals), then to the right, write the specified triads in that key.

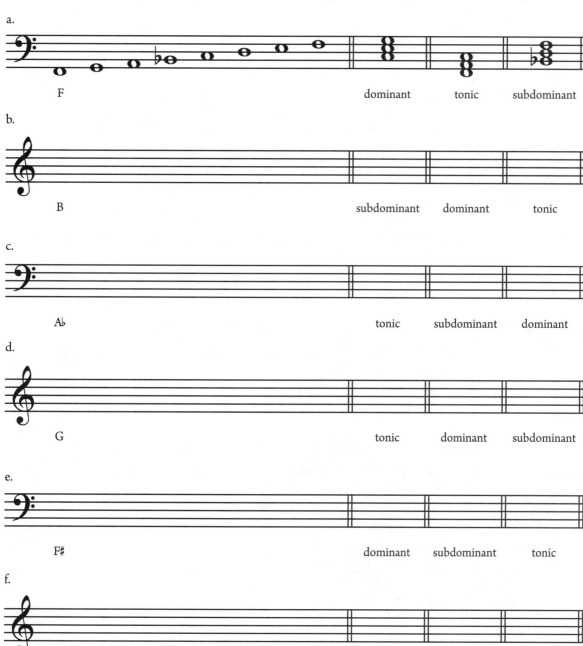

a.

F

dominant   tonic   subdominant

b.

B

subdominant   dominant   tonic

c.

A♭

tonic   subdominant   dominant

d.

G

tonic   dominant   subdominant

e.

F♯

dominant   subdominant   tonic

f.

B♭

tonic   dominant   subdominant

2. Writing triads on $\hat{1}$, $\hat{4}$, and $\hat{5}$ in minor keys

For each key below, write the key signature and the requested triads in that key, then label them with letter name and quality (for example, Am, D7):

Workbook ASSIGNMENT 10.2

1. Cadence Types

Identify the key of each excerpt below. Then label the cadence at the end as a half cadence (HC) or an authentic cadence (AC). Refer to the chord symbols to identify the chords at the cadence.

a. Robert Lowry, "How Can I Keep from Singing?," mm. 4b–8a

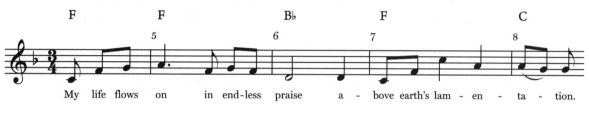

My life flows on in end-less praise a - bove earth's lam - en - ta - tion.

Key: _____F_____   Cadence: _____HC_____

b. Rodgers and Hart, "My Funny Valentine," mm. 33–36 1:54–2:11

Each day is Val - en - tine's day. _____

Key: _____   Cadence: _____

c. Rodgers and Hammerstein, "Edelweiss," from *The Sound of Music*, mm. 5–12

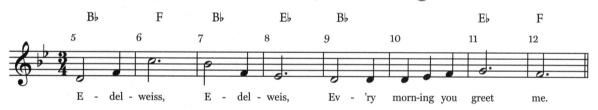

E - del - weiss, E - del - weis, Ev - 'ry morn-ing you greet me.

Key: _____   Cadence: _____

d. Horner, Mann, and Weil, "Somewhere Out There," mm. 39b–42

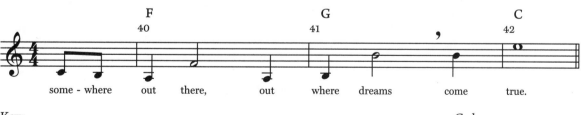

some - where out there, out where dreams come true.

Key: _____   Cadence: _____

e. If the chord symbol for measure 42 of "Somewhere Out There" were Am, the cadence type would be: _____

2. Interpreting Chord Symbols

On the staves below, write each chord specified by the chord symbols above the melody. Write all necessary accidentals, including those in the key signature.

a. Bono and U2, "All Because of You," mm. 5–8

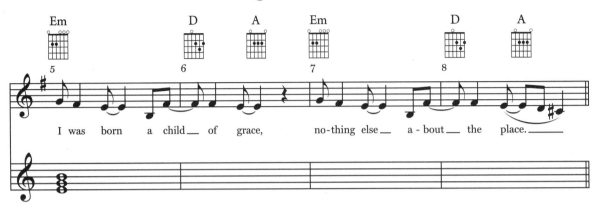

b. Bono and U2, "One Step Closer," mm. 25–28a

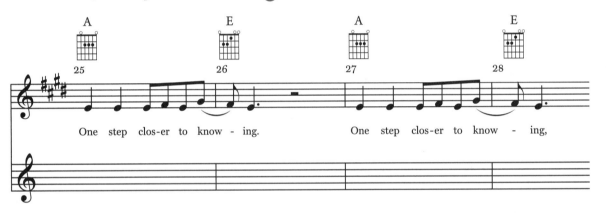

3. Matching

Match the pitches in the first column with the harmonies in the second.

__e__	(1) E–G♯–B	(a)	tonic in B♭ minor
_____	(2) B–D–F♯	(b)	subdominant in C minor
_____	(3) A–C–E	(c)	tonic in F♯ minor
_____	(4) G–B♭–D	(d)	subdominant in E minor
_____	(5) F–A♭–C	(e)	dominant in A harmonic minor
_____	(6) C♯–E–G♯	(f)	dominant in B♭ harmonic minor
_____	(7) B♭–D♭–F	(g)	subdominant in G minor
_____	(8) F–A–C	(h)	dominant in E natural minor
_____	(9) F♯–A–C♯	(i)	tonic in C♯ minor
_____	(10) C–E♭–G	(j)	subdominant in D minor

Workbook ASSIGNMENT 10.3

1. Harmonizing major-key melodies

For each children's song or folk tune, play or sing the melody to determine the key, write in the scale degrees, then select chords. Write the appropriate chord symbols in the blanks above the staff to represent the tonic, subdominant, and dominant seventh harmonies and the Roman numerals below, after the key indication. Use the subdominant between two tonic harmonies or before the dominant. Write one or two chords per measure. After you finish, sing the melody while playing the chords on a keyboard or guitar.

a. "Little Brown Jug"

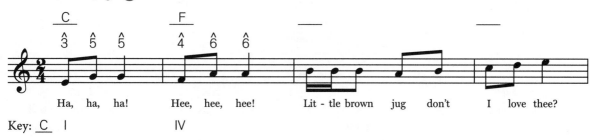

Key: C I   IV

b. "Clementine" 🔊

Key: ____

c. "Yankee Doodle"

Yan - kee Doo - dle   went   to   town   a - ri - ding   on   a   po - ny,

Key: _____

Stuck   a   fea - ther   in   his   cap   and   called   it   ma - ca - ro - ni!

2. Analysis

The progression in this familiar passage is based on chords studied in this chapter. Skips between chord tones and embellishments add interest to the melody. Listen to this excerpt, then look at the bass-clef part to identify the chord for each measure. Write the chord in the blank below the staff, and circle and label any passing or neighbor tones in the treble-clef melody.

Sousa, "The Stars and Stripes Forever," mm. 37–52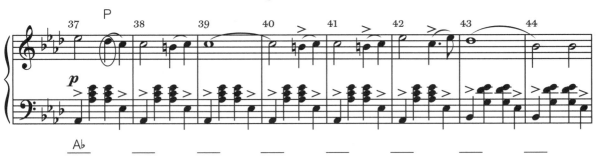

Workbook   ASSIGNMENT 10.4

1. Harmonizing minor-key melodies

Play or sing each melody to determine the key; write the scale degrees above the pitches. In the blanks above each staff, write chord symbols to harmonize the melodies, and write the Roman numerals below. Sing the melody while playing the chords on a keyboard or guitar.

a. "Wade in the Water"
(This natural minor tune is altered at the cadence with a leading tone. Choose an appropriate harmony there.)

Key: Dm   i

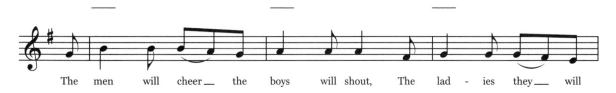

b. Gilmore, "When Johnny Comes Marching Home," mm 8b–16

Key: ____

3. Major, minor, diminished, and augmented triads (played as a chord)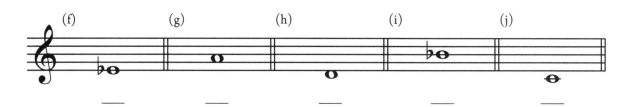

(a)　　　(b)　　　(c)　　　(d)　　　(e)

(f)　　　(g)　　　(h)　　　(i)　　　(j)

TOPICS

- melody and paired phrases
- quaternary song form
- 32-bar song form
- writing melodies
- writing keyboard accompaniments
- form in later popular music

MUSIC

- The Black Eyed Peas, "I Gotta Feeling"
- Stephen Foster, "Oh! Susanna"
- George and Ira Gershwin, "'S Wonderful!" from *Funny Face*
- "Greensleeves"
- John Lennon and Paul McCartney, "Ticket to Ride"
- "Merrily We Roll Along"
- "Simple Gifts"
- Taylor Swift, "Love Story"
- Meredith Willson, "Till There Was You," from *The Music Man*

CHAPTER 11

Form in Folk and Popular Songs

Melody and Paired Phrases

Listen to the folk song "Greensleeves," arranged here for guitar, and consider the patterns of musical repetition and contrast formed by its phrases. When you consider a piece's division into sections, its patterns of repetition and contrast, and its harmonic structure (including changes of key), you are considering its **form**. Example 11.1 shows the first two phrases of the song.

EXAMPLE 11.1   "Greensleeves," mm. 1–8

Phrase 1

G: (HC)

Phrase 2

(PAC)

EXAMPLE 11.3   Willson, "Till There Was You," mm. 1–16a (melody)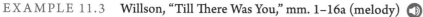

FIGURE 11.2   Phrase structure for measures 1–16a of "Till There Was You"

```
                    a              a'
                    8              8
              ⌒‾‾‾‾‾‾‾‾⌒   ⌒‾‾‾‾‾‾‾‾⌒
              mm. 1–8a       mm. 8b–16a
        E♭:       HC             PAC
```

Now look at measures 16b–24a of "Till There Was You" in your anthology. These measures, coming after the initial parallel period, form a contrasting phrase that features a sweeping ascending contour and higher register, with a musical climax on "wonderful roses," ending on a half cadence. The opening melody then returns in measure 24b, nearly identical to the second phrase (mm. 9–15). We can now diagram the entire form of "Till There Was You" as **a a' b a'**, shown in Figure 11.3.

FIGURE 11.3   32-bar song form in "Till There Was You"

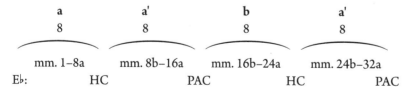

```
          a            a'            b            a'
          8            8            8            8
    ⌒‾‾‾‾‾‾⌒  ⌒‾‾‾‾‾‾⌒  ⌒‾‾‾‾‾‾⌒  ⌒‾‾‾‾‾‾⌒
    mm. 1–8a    mm. 8b–16a   mm. 16b–24a   mm. 24b–32a
  E♭:     HC          PAC          HC           PAC
```

> **KEY CONCEPT**   In 32-bar song form, the contrasting third phrase (here **b**) is known as the **bridge** or "the middle eight." The bridge may change keys or may end inconclusively (on a HC or no cadence) to prepare for the return of the opening phrase **a**.

Listen to the Gershwins' "'S Wonderful!" (anthology, p. 351); its form is shown in Figure 11.4. In this type of song, a 32-bar song form is preceded by a musical section that provides the setting and context for the song. The opening section is known as the **verse**, and the 32-bar song form is called the **refrain**. In performance, the refrain is typically repeated to make the song longer, but the verse is usually heard only once at the beginning (if at all—it is sometimes omitted). **Verse–refrain** form is typical for classic Broadway show tunes from the Tin Pan Alley era and some jazz standards.

FIGURE 11.4   Form of "'S Wonderful!"

Introduction	Verse	Refrain (32-bar song form)
mm. 1–4	mm. 5–28	mm. 29–60

TRY IT #2

Using your anthology score and recording, draw a phrase chart for the refrain of "'S Wonderful!" showing which measures constitute each phrase. Include phrase arcs, measure numbers, letters for phrases, and cadence types.

a

mm. 29–36

AURAL SKILLS 11.1

Writing Melodies

Because there are so many types of melodies, no list of instructions can cover all the possibilities. Before beginning, you should have a style of melody in mind and should immerse yourself in examples of that style. This chapter will focus on writing periods and quaternary song forms in a folk style similar to "Greensleeves," and "Oh! Susanna."

Most melodies move primarily by step (**conjunct motion**), with just a few well-placed larger intervals (**disjunct motion**). In their disjunct portions, melodies might move through the notes of a triad, with small **skips** of a third or fourth; wider jumps with larger intervals, called **leaps,** are employed less often. As you begin to write your own tunes, build melodic shapes that are fairly simple, with stepwise motion and small skips, and with clear harmonic goals at each cadence. As a very general principle, melodies often begin in a middle register, ascend to a high point, then descend to the tonic, making an arch shape. The end of each phrase is marked by one or more notes of longer duration. When phrases are paired, the first phrase will often take an arch shape but descend only to $\hat{2}$; the second phrase will then fall to the tonic to make a period.

To write a period (each phrase four measures long):

1. Map out eight blank measures on staff paper—four on the top staff and four aligned beneath them on the bottom staff.
2. Sketch the end of each phrase first: the first ending on $\hat{3}$–$\hat{2}$ (HC) in measure 4, and the second ending on $\hat{2}$–$\hat{1}$ or $\hat{7}$–$\hat{1}$ (PAC) in measure 8.

3. Begin the melody in measure 1 on a member of the tonic triad ($\hat{1}$, $\hat{3}$, or $\hat{5}$). If you want to include an anacrusis, write one that suggests a dominant harmony (perhaps with $\hat{5}$ or $\hat{7}$), moving to $\hat{1}$ on the downbeat of measure 1. Include notes from the tonic triad in the first measure to imply a tonic chord, and embellish them with passing or neighbor tones if you wish.

4. Even though you are only writing a melody, think about a logical progression of chords that the tune implies. You started with a tonic harmony and have planned a HC in measure 4. As you plan the rest of the melody, remember the phrase model: incomplete (I–V or I–IV–V) or complete (I–V–I or I–IV–V–I). Select melodic pitches from these harmonies to fit the model. Imply a harmonic rhythm of one or two chords per measure. (Melodies often begin with a slower harmonic rhythm that speeds up near the cadence.)

5. Sketch a melodic outline with tones from the chords you selected; continue to add passing and neighboring embellishments. If you include a leap, follow it by stepwise motion in the opposite direction. Create at least two memorable ideas, or **motives**, that you use more than once. They may be melodic or rhythmic motives.

6. Copy one or two measures of the beginning of phrase 1 into the beginning of phrase 2. Then write a continuation of phrase 2 that connects to the PAC. Where possible, use motives from the beginning of the phrase.

7. Melodies often have one high point, or **climax**. Build yours so that its highest note is stated only once or twice. (Not all songs have a single climax, but it is a good idea to keep this in mind as a goal to shape your melody.) Avoid a static melodic line: do not hover around a single pitch.

If you wish to write a quaternary song form:

1. To write a song with **a a' b a'** structure, begin with the parallel period you have already written. It makes up the first two phrases of the form.

2. Add two more empty staves, then write on phrase 4 first by copying phrase 2. Phrase 4 can be identical to phrase 2, or you may embellish it slightly or (in a texted song) change the lyrics.

3. Now return to phrase 3, the contrasting **b** phrase, or bridge. Consider allowing this phrase to rise to the highest register of the song, making the musical climax. Create a contrasting rhythmic pattern, such as one using longer durations, to contrast with rhythmic motives of the **a** phrases. End the bridge with a harmonically inconclusive cadence to prepare for the return of **a**.

All these principles are at work in "Oh! Susanna" The melody begins with an antecedent–consequent pair (Example 11.4): the first phrase comes to rest on $\hat{2}$ over a half cadence (m. 4), and the second concludes with $\hat{2}$–$\hat{1}$ over a PAC (m. 8). Though their endings are different, the two phrases begin identically (**a a'**), forming a parallel period. The tune also illustrates several other melody-writing principles. It features a memorable ♪♪ ♪.♪ rhythmic motive that recurs throughout, and it outlines the underlying harmonic progression (shown with chord symbols) with chord tones decorated by passing and neighbor tones.

EXAMPLE 11.4 Foster, "Oh! Susanna" mm. 1–8

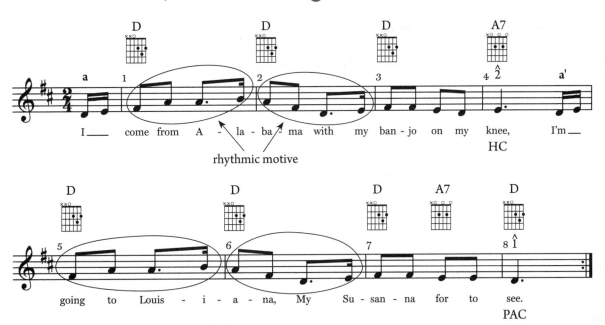

rhythmic motive

I___ come from A - la - ba - ma with my ban - jo on my knee, I'm___

going to Louis - i - a - na, My Su - san - na for to see.

Example 11.5 shows the contrasting **b** phrase and return of the opening **a** material to complete the form. The **b** phrase contrasts with the rest of the song with its longer-duration quarter notes, and with the absence of an anacrusis and the ♩♩ ♩. ♩ motive. The highest pitch in the melody, B4, heard briefly in the **a** phrases as an embellishing sixteenth-note neighbor tone, sounds for a full measure (m. 10); in its new rhythmic and harmonic context in the **b** phrase, this B4 is the climax of the song.

EXAMPLE 11.5 Foster, "Oh! Susanna" mm. 9–16

Oh, Su - san - na! Oh, don't you cry for me, For I come from A - la -

ba - ma with my ban - jo on my knee.

ASSIGNMENT 11.1

Writing Keyboard Accompaniments

After you have harmonized a melody by choosing appropriate I, IV, and V chords, you can play the chords at the keyboard by arranging the notes to fit under one hand, as shown in Example 11.6. Learn these patterns in each hand separately: they are arranged to connect one note smoothly with the next.

KEY CONCEPT When you connect chords:

- aim primarily for smooth motion by step or skip; avoid leaps, except in the bass;
- if two consecutive chords share tones, keep the common tone in the same part;
- correctly resolve dissonant intervals and scale degrees with strong tendencies (like $\hat{7}$–$\hat{1}$).

Example 11.6 gives the basic phrase progression in parallel keys—D major and D minor (harmonic minor). The fingering pattern is the same for both, but in minor keys you lower $\hat{3}$ and $\hat{6}$ by a half step in the tonic and subdominant chords. When accompanying a song, these patterns would likely be played either in the right hand with the chord roots in the left (part b), or with the melody in the right hand and the chords in the left (part c).

EXAMPLE 11.6   Keyboard arrangements of I, IV, and V

(a) Finger numbering

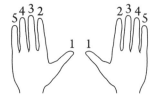

(b) Basic phrase (I–IV–V–I) with right-hand chords

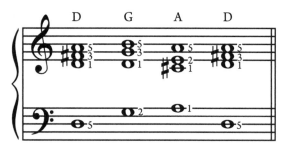
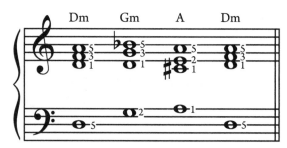

(c) Basic phrase (I–IV–V–I) with left-hand chords (melody in right hand)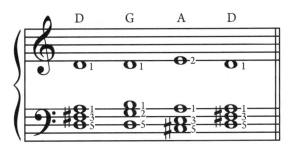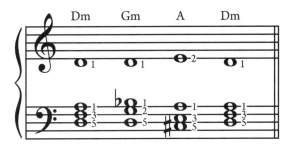

(d) In keyboard settings, avoid jumping between root-position chords
(in either hand)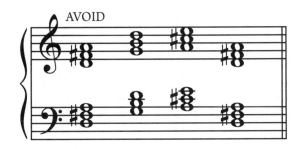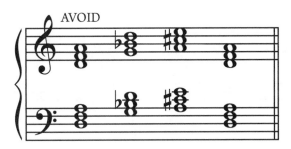

Parts (b) and (c) show the basic phrase progression (I–IV–V–I) with the chords connected correctly. Part (d) shows poor **chord connection**, which is avoided in keyboard settings because of its lack of smooth motion. If you wish, you may substitute a V^7 for the V chord; do this by replacing $\hat{2}$ (E, the fifth of the chord) with $\hat{4}$ (G, the seventh of the chord), as Example 11.7 shows.

EXAMPLE 11.7   Basic phrase progression with V^7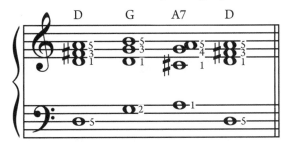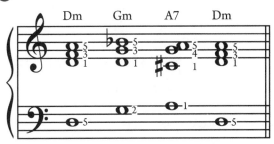

The opening portion of your melody may provide an opportunity to extend the tonic harmony with a IV chord. Example 11.8 illustrates a common way to connect I and IV.

EXAMPLE 11.8   Extending the tonic harmony with IV

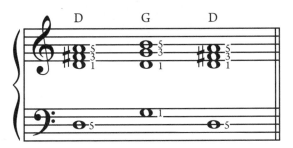 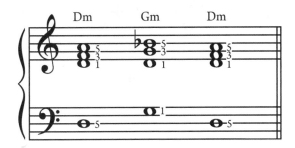

TRY IT #3

Using Example 11.6 as your model, write the chord connections specified below (for one hand, as the clef indicates).

(a) G

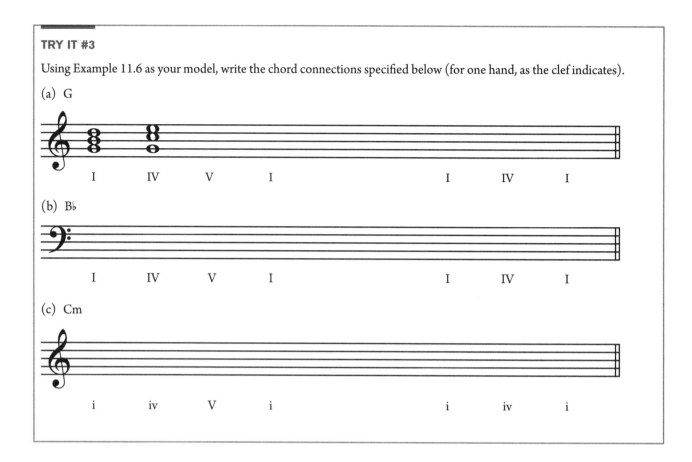

(b) B♭

(c) Cm

Another way to write keyboard accompaniments for songs is to take these basic progressions and play them in different keyboard styles. Example 11.9 shows four simple accompaniment patterns for the beginning of the familiar tune "Merrily We Roll Along," harmonized with only I and V chords. Part (a) is a chordal pattern with roots in the bass on the downbeat and chords in the right hand delayed to beat 2. Part (b) is a more rhythmic version, where the chords come on the & of each beat (the offbeat) and $\hat{5}$ is played in the bass on beat 2, similar to a Sousa march. For a chordal accompaniment of a triple-meter melody, you might use a waltz bass—one bass note on the downbeat and chords on beats 2 and 3 (see the Schubert Waltz in B Minor, anthology, p. 396).

EXAMPLE 11.9   "Merrily We Roll Along"

(a) With chords displaced to beat 2

(b) With Sousa-style accompaniment

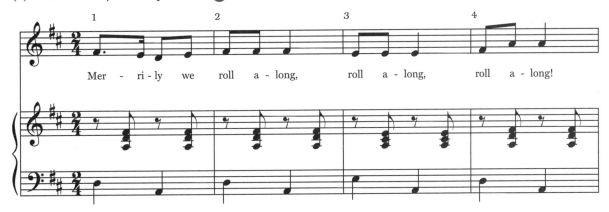

(c) With eighth-note arpeggiated accompaniment

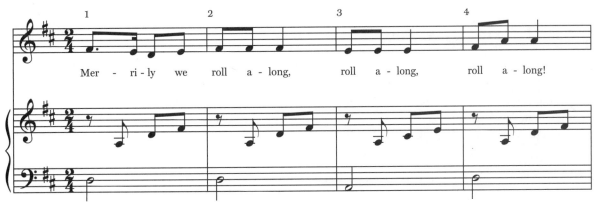

(d) With sixteenth-note arpeggiated accompaniment

Parts (c) and (d) show arpeggiated accompaniments, which are often used in lyrical settings. An **arpeggio** is the "spreading out" of chord tones by playing them one pitch at a time rather than together. In part (c) the chord is arpeggiated as even eighth notes and in (d) as sixteenths. Try each of these to see what different effects the accompaniment can have on the character of a melody.

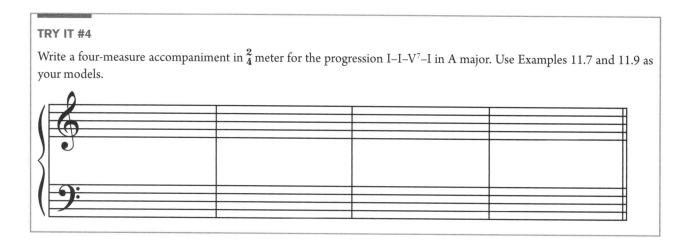

Write a four-measure accompaniment in $\frac{2}{4}$ meter for the progression I–I–V⁷–I in A major. Use Examples 11.7 and 11.9 as your models.

ASSIGNMENT 11.2

Form in Later Popular Music

After 1950, the terminology for labeling sections of songs began to change, as verse–refrain form became less popular. In its new usage, the term **verse** designates a musical section that appears in a song multiple times with the same music but a different text, while **chorus** refers to a section of music that is repeated with the same (or similar) text. Listen to the beginning of The Beatles' "Ticket to Ride"; the form is shown in Figure 11.5.

FIGURE 11.5   Form in Lennon and McCartney, "Ticket to Ride" ⬇

	Intro		4 measures
a	Verse	"I think I'm . . ."	8 measures
	Chorus	"She's got a . . ."	8 measures
a'	Verse	"She said . . ."	8 measures
	Chorus	"She's got a . . ."	8 measures
b	Bridge	"I don't know . . ."	9 measures
a	Verse	"I think I'm . . ."	8 measures
	Chorus	"She's got a . . ."	8 measures
	Outro		2 measures

After a brief instrumental introduction (an **intro**), the song begins with the verse followed by the chorus. The music for the verse then repeats, with different text, followed by the chorus. Before the final verse and chorus, there is a **bridge**, a term that now denotes music that contrasts with the verse and chorus and appears in the second half of the song to prepare for the last statement of the verse and/or chorus. The verse and chorus return after the bridge, making an **a a' b a** pattern. Finally, the song ends with a concluding **outro**—instrumental music to end the song. An outro may consist of a simple "repeat and fade" (common in the 1960s) or other concluding music.

This song also illustrates the use of a **hook**—a musical setting of a few words or a phrase, usually including the title, that is repeated and becomes the most "catchy" or memorable part of the song. For this song, the hook ("a ticket to ride") occurs in the chorus, as is typical, though a hook may appear in other positions in other songs.

In recent years, song forms have expanded beyond the basic sections considered so far. Vocal sections of a song may be broken up by instrumental passages, including an **instrumental break** (a section in the middle of a song played only by instruments, often based on the verse), a **link** (a short instrumental connector between sections), and a **rap break** (like an instrumental break but with spoken rhythmic text). Intros may be extended, with new ideas entering, and sections may be repeated multiple times. For example, the song "I Gotta Feeling" by The Black Eyed Peas begins with an extended introduction, followed by four repetitions of the chorus (performed over the intro music). Prior to the first rap break, the repetition builds momentum, preparing for the entry of the spoken text, which substitutes for a sung verse. The form of the opening of this song is shown in Figure 11.6.

FIGURE 11.6   Form in the opening of The Black Eyed Peas, "I Gotta Feeling" ⏷

Instrumental intro part 1		8 measures
Instrumental intro part 2		8 measures
Chorus 1	"I gotta feeling"	8 measures
Chorus 2	"A feeling . . ."	8 measures
Chorus 3	"A feeling woohoo"	8 measures
Chorus 4	"A feeling woohoo"	8 measures
Rap break (verse)	"Tonight's the night"	8 measures

Songs may also include short sections before and after the chorus: a section after a verse that prepares for the entrance of the chorus is called a **prechorus**, and in very recent songs, some songwriters include a **postchorus** after a chorus to prepare for the return of the verse. A prechorus, link, and outro are all illustrated Taylor Swift's "Love Story," as shown in Figure 11.7.

FIGURE 11.7   Form in Taylor Swift, "Love Story" ⏷

Instrumental intro		8 measures
Verse 1	"We were both . . ."	8 measures
Verse 2	"I see the lights . . ."	8 measures
Prechorus	"That you were . . ."	8 measures
Chorus	"Romeo take me . . ."	8 measures
Link		2 measures
Verse 3	"So I sneak out . . ."	8 measures
Prechorus	"Cause you were . . ."	8 measures
Chorus	"Romeo take me . . ."	8 measures
Chorus	"Romeo save me . . ."	8 measures
Instrumental interlude		8 measures
Bridge	"I got tired . . ."	8 measures
Chorus	"Romeo save me . . ."	8 measures
Chorus	"Marry me Juliet . . ."	8 measures
Outro		9 measures

ASSIGNMENT 11.3

Did You Know?

Meredith Willson (1902–1984) enjoyed a flourishing career in both the classical and popular worlds. He played flute in the New York Philharmonic under conductor Arturo Toscanini and also performed in the band led by John Philip Sousa. Willson worked on several popular radio shows in the 1930s–1950s, but achieved real fame in the late 1950s with his Broadway show *The Music Man*, for which he wrote the lyrics as well as the music. The cast album from this show won the very first Grammy ever presented, and the show won eight Tony awards, including best composer and lyricist. Fans of classic rock may know "Till There Was You" from the Beatles' hit recording of the early 1960s, with Paul McCartney on vocals. More recently, almost fifty years after its original composition, Rod Stewart recorded the song on his album "As Time Goes By" (2003).

Terms You Should Know

32-bar song form
arpeggio
antecedent phrase
bridge (2 meanings)
chord connection
chorus
climax
conjunct motion
consequent phrase
disjunct motion
form

hook
instrumental break
intro
leap
link
motive
outro
period
   contrasting
   parallel
postchorus

prechorus
quaternary song form
rap break
refrain
skip
verse (2 meanings)
verse–refrain form

Questions for Review

1. How many phrases make up a period? How may they be related melodically (at the beginning) and harmonically (at the cadences)?
2. How are the phrases of quaternary song form related? What are typical formal designs, in addition to **a a' b a''**?
3. What guidelines should you follow when connecting chords?
4. What are some ways that you can turn a chordal harmonization into a piano accompaniment?
5. What are some new formal sections used in recent popular songs?

Reading Review

Match the terms on the left with the best answer on the right.

_____ (1)   half cadence   (a) melodic presentation of a chord, one pitch at a time

_____ (2)   parallel period   (b) stepwise melodic motion

_____ (3)   chord connections   (c) music that is repeated with different text

_____ (4)   conjunct   (d) the **b** phrase in **a a b a** form

_____ (5)   disjunct   (e) consists of four phrases

_____ (6)   bridge   (f) typical cadence for the first phrase of a period

_____ (7)   arpeggio   (g) **a b** phrase design

_____ (8)   verse   (h) **a a'** phrase design

_____ (9)   contrasting period   (i) melodic motion characterized by skips and leaps

_____ (10) quaternary song form   (j) should aim for smooth motion, keeping common tones in the same part

Ⓢ Additional review and practice available at wwnorton.com/studyspace

Class Activities

A. Reading rhythms

Rhythm review: Each of the following rhythms incorporates familiar patterns. In addition, you will encounter a march conducted in two with syncopated rhythms and two ways of indicating repetition.

Rhythm 1

Hint: Remember to conduct in two, as indicated by the "cut time" signature.

Rhythm 2

When you reach the *D.C. al Coda* instruction, return to the beginning and perform until the ⊕ (coda sign), then skip to the ⊕ on the last line.

Rhythm 3

Read measures 1–4 (first ending, marked with a "1."), then repeat; this time skip from measure 3 to the second ending in measure 4 (marked with a "2.") and continue to the end.

B. Singing at sight

Divide each melody into two phrases and determine whether the period is parallel or contrasting. Write your answer in the blank and be prepared to explain it. Then practice the melodies as in previous chapters.

Melody 1 Tony Velona and Remo Capra, "O Bambino," mm. 1–8

Phrase structure: _____

Melody 2 "Home, Dearie, Home"

Phrase structure: _____

Oh,   Bos - ton's a   fine   town, with ships___ in   the   bay,   and

I   wish in my heart   it was there I was to - day,   I wish in my heart I was

far a - way from here,   sit - ting in my par - lor and talk - ing to my dear.

Melody 3 Alan Price, "The House of the Rising Sun," mm. 1–8

Phrase structure: _____

Very slow
mp

There is___   a house___ in New Or - leans, _____ they call___   the Ris - ing

Sun. _____   and it's been___ the ruin___ of man - y a poor boy, _____   and

God, _____   I   know _____   I'm   one. _____

C. At the keyboard

1. Play the basic phrase progression below at the keyboard with your right hand, and play the root of each chord with your left hand. Then play it again in the following keys: C major, F major, G major. If necessary, write it in the new key first and then play.

Basic phrase with dominant seventh

2. Play the progression again using accompanimental patterns: one note (the root) in your left hand and chords in your right hand. Be prepared to play any of the following patterns (refer to Example 11.9 for samples of each pattern).

- Play the root in your left hand on beat 1 and the chord in your right on beat 2
- Play the same pattern in triple meter with the chord repeated
- Arpeggiate the chords

Workbook ASSIGNMENT 11.1

1. Writing a parallel period

Write an eight-measure parallel period, following the guidelines in the chapter. After you write the first four measures, copy measures 1–2 as measures 5–6 to create a parallel structure. Use the treble-clef staff for the melody; a blank staff is provided in case you want to sketch triads or seventh chords beneath (this is optional). You may write for an instrument or think in terms of a vocal phrase; if the latter, set a text to your melody. Be prepared to perform your melody in class.

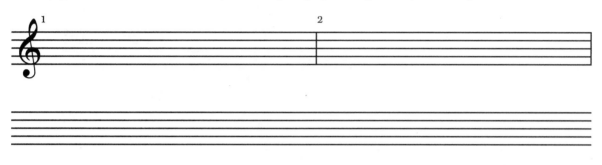

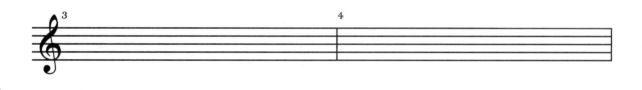

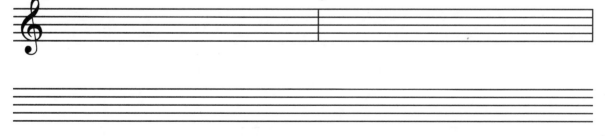

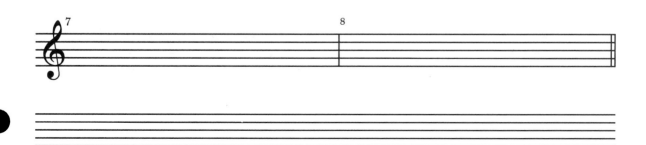

2. Writing a contrasting period

Write an eight-measure contrasting period. After you write the first four measures, set measures 5 and following with a different melodic contour and a different rhythmic pattern. Use the treble-clef staff for the melody; as before, a blank staff is provided in case you want to sketch triads or seventh chords beneath. You may write for an instrument or think in terms of a vocal phrase; if the latter, set a text to your melody. Be prepared to perform your melody in class.

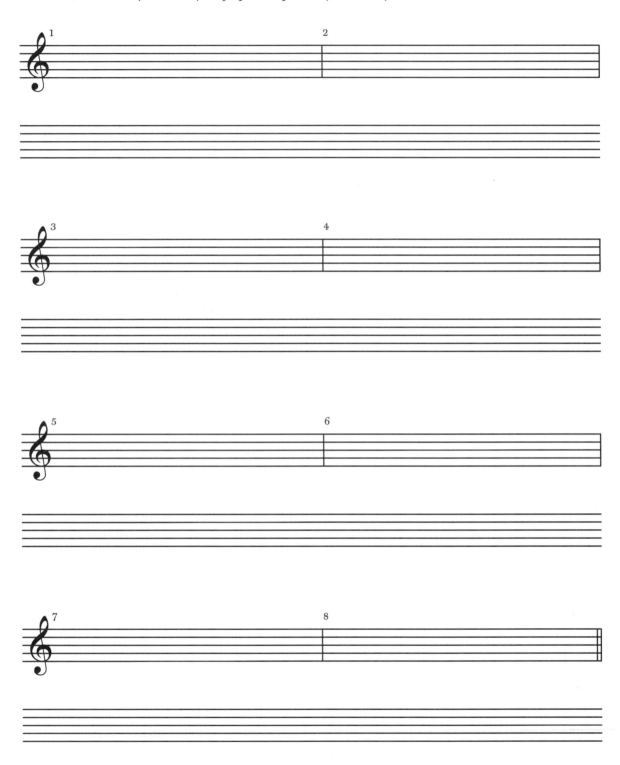

Workbook ASSIGNMENT 11.2

1. Writing chord progressions

Write the chord progressions below on the bass-clef staff. Include the key signature, and write each chord in whole notes. Commas and periods in the chord progressions indicate the end of a phrase; label the cadence at the end of each phrase (AC or HC).

a. A♭: A♭–A♭–E♭–E♭, A♭–A♭–E♭7–A♭.

b. F: F–C7–F–C7–C7, F–B♭–F–C7–F.

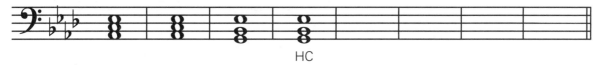

2. Writing a piano accompaniment from chord symbols

Write a piano chord in the bass clef for each chord symbol below. Circle and label any passing or neighbor tones in the melody, and identify any half or authentic cadence by writing HC or AC below the staff.

a. "Simple Gifts," mm. 1–9 🔊

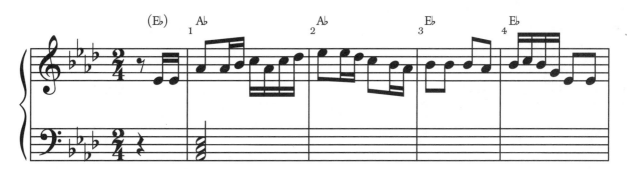

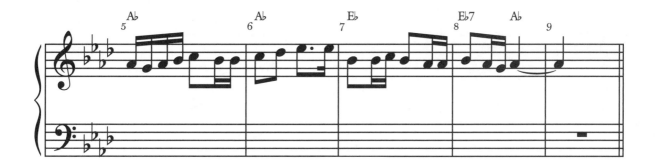

Text: 'Tis the gift to be simple 'tis the gift to be free
     'Tis the gift to come down where you ought to be
     And when we find ourselves in the place just right,
     'Twill be in the valley of love and delight.

b. "The Ash Grove"

c. On your own staff paper, write a full piano accompaniment for one of these melodies, a or b. Take the chords you wrote and compose a piano part that could accompany a singer. Notate with right- and left-hand parts, on a grand staff. Choose a chordal or arpeggiated texture, as described in the chapter. Add dynamic and tempo markings to make your accompaniment as musical as possible.

3. Analysis

Gather the notes in the left-hand part and notate them on the blank staff. Write the chord symbols for the pitches you have notated. Finally, label the circled pitches in the melody as passing (P) or neighbor (N) tones.

Mozart, Piano Sonata in C Major, K. 545, first movement, mm. 1–4

Workbook ASSIGNMENT 11.3

Analysis

1. Larson, "Seasons of Love," from *Rent* (anthology, p. 372) ⬇
The chord progression in measures 1–4 is the foundation for most of the song. Trace this four-measure harmonic pattern through the song, marking where it appears on your anthology score, then answer the following questions.

a. After measures 1–4, where does the progression next appear? _____

b. How many times does the progression appear before other harmonic progressions are introduced? _____

c. (1) What part of the song is accompanied by this four-measure progression?

(circle one)   Verse   Chorus

(2) What is the connection between the repeated four-measure progression and the lyrics?

d. (1) What part of the song begins when a new chord progression appears?

(circle one)   Verse   Chorus

(2) What words appear in the sections that don't feature the initial four-chord progression?

e. Complete the chart below, showing the location of the introduction, verse(s), and chorus(es). Include measure numbers for each section, and indicate the locations of authentic cadences. (Hints: Scan the chord symbols, looking for C7 to F (V⁷–I) at stopping points. The repeating chord progression does not include a cadence.)

mm. 1–4   mm. 5–20
Introduction

f. How is "love" set differently from the remainder of the text?

2. Green Day "21 Guns" ⬇

Listen to this song (either the original Green Day version, linked to on StudySpace, or the version from the Broadway musical *American Idiot*), then fill in the form chart. Include section names (intro, verse, chorus, bridge, instrumental break, outro), the start of the first line of text in each section, and the number of measures in each section (conduct in $\frac{4}{4}$ meter and count the measures). If there is a refrain at the end of a verse, indicate its text and location. For any instrumental breaks, write "no text" and indicate what section the break is based on (if it is identifiable).

Section Name	Start of Text	Number of Measures
Intro	no text	4
Verse	"Do you know . . ."	8

Workbook   AURAL SKILLS 11.1

Listen to an excerpt from an old popular song, and complete the following exercises. 🔊

1. Complete the rhythm of the melody in **C**.

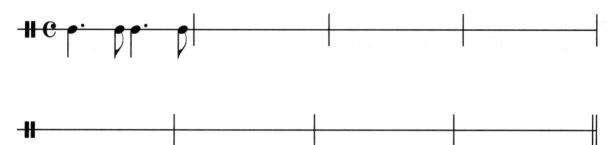

2. Write the melody with solfège syllables or scale-degree numbers, beginning with $\hat{1}$–$\hat{6}$–$\hat{7}$–$\hat{6}$–$\hat{1}$ (*do–la–ti–la–do*).

3. Beginning as shown, notate both the pitches and the rhythm of the melody on the staves below.

4. The first two melodic pitches create which interval?

(a) m3   (b) M3   (c) P4   (d) P5

5. The last two melodic pitches create which interval?

(a) P5   (b) m6   (c) M6   (d) P8

6. The excerpt is a single eight-measure phrase that starts with a two-measure motive. Which of the following statements best describes how the motive recurs in the melody?

(a) The opening motive's return is delayed until the cadence.

(b) The opening motive is repeated down a step, then restated with the original pitches.

(c) The opening motive is embellished with passing tones.

(d) The opening motive is embellished with neighbor tones.

7. The bass line moves in half notes. Beginning as shown, notate the pitches and rhythm of the bass. (Hint: You will need to use an accidental in measure 4.)

8. The first two bass pitches create which interval?

(a) P5   (b) m6   (c) M6   (d) P8

9. The excerpt concludes with which type of cadence?

(a) half   (c) imperfect authentic

(b) deceptive   (d) perfect authentic

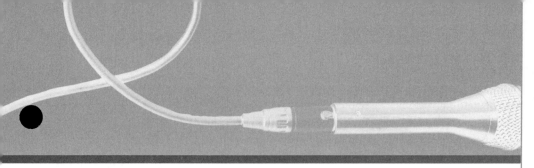

TOPICS:

- pentatonic scales
- the blues scale and the 12-bar blues
- seventh chords
- chord extensions and sus chords

MUSIC:

- Count Basie, "Splanky"
- George and Ira Gershwin, "'S Wonderful!" from *Funny Face*
- James Horner, Barry Mann, and Cynthia Weil, "Somewhere Out There," from *An American Tail*
- John Newton, "Amazing Grace"
- Joel Phillips, "Blues for Norton"
- "Wayfaring Stranger"

CHAPTER 12

Blues and Other Popular Styles

Pentatonic Scales

In addition to major and minor scales, folk, jazz, and popular musicians typically employ pentatonic and blues scales. For an example, look at the melody for "Amazing Grace," shown in Example 12.1. In this melody, there are only five scale degrees, $\hat{1}$, $\hat{2}$, $\hat{3}$, $\hat{5}$, and $\hat{6}$ in G major. This is a **major pentatonic** scale. Since $\hat{4}$ and $\hat{7}$ are missing, there is no $\hat{7}$–$\hat{1}$ or $\hat{4}$–$\hat{3}$ half-step motion. Melodies based on the major pentatonic scale typically are harmonized with chords from the major scale.

EXAMPLE 12.1   Newton, "Amazing Grace"

(a) Score

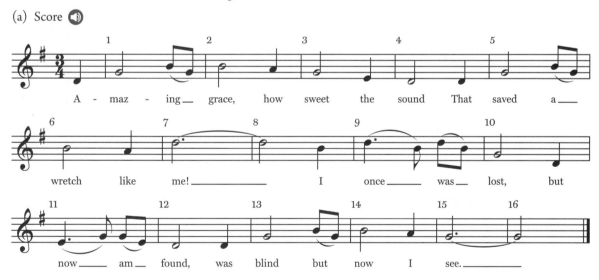

(b) G major pentatonic scale

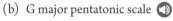

303

Listen to Example 12.2, "Wayfaring Stranger," another pentatonic melody. From the key signature, the sound of the melody, and the beginning and ending notes, you might guess that the tune is in D minor, but the melody includes only five notes of the D natural minor scale: $\hat{1}$, ♭$\hat{3}$, $\hat{4}$, $\hat{5}$, and ♭$\hat{7}$. This scale is known as the **minor pentatonic**. Melodies based on the minor pentatonic scale are often harmonized with chords from the natural minor scale. These are not the only possible pentatonic (five note) scales; other pentatonic scale types are heard in non-Western musics.

EXAMPLE 12.2   "Wayfaring Stranger"

(a) Score

I am a poor_____ way - far - ing stran - ger_____ a trav - 'ling

through_____ this world of woe;_____ yet there's no sick - ness, toil or

dan - ger_____ in that bright world to which I go._____

(b) D minor pentatonic scale

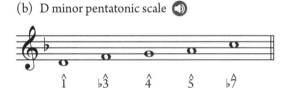

$\hat{1}$ ♭$\hat{3}$ $\hat{4}$ $\hat{5}$ ♭$\hat{7}$
do   me   fa   sol   te

Example 12.3 compares the major and minor pentatonic scales beginning on C: both share C and G ($\hat{1}$ and $\hat{5}$), and each has the quality of the third associated with its name, major or minor.

EXAMPLE 12.3   C pentatonic scales

(a) Major pentatonic

$\hat{1}$ $\hat{2}$ $\hat{3}$ $\hat{5}$ $\hat{6}$
do   re   mi   sol   la

(b) Minor pentatonic

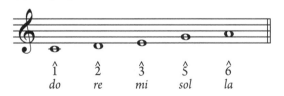

$\hat{1}$ ♭$\hat{3}$ $\hat{4}$ $\hat{5}$ ♭$\hat{7}$
do   me   fa   sol   te

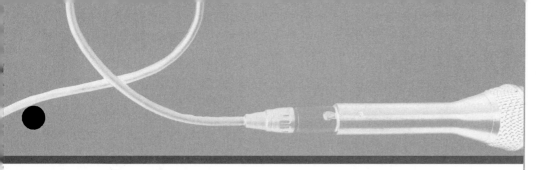

TOPICS:

- pentatonic scales
- the blues scale and the 12-bar blues
- seventh chords
- chord extensions and sus chords

MUSIC:

- Count Basie, "Splanky"
- George and Ira Gershwin, "'S Wonderful!" from *Funny Face*
- James Horner, Barry Mann, and Cynthia Weil, "Somewhere Out There," from *An American Tail*
- John Newton, "Amazing Grace"
- Joel Phillips, "Blues for Norton"
- "Wayfaring Stranger"

CHAPTER 12

Blues and Other Popular Styles

Pentatonic Scales

In addition to major and minor scales, folk, jazz, and popular musicians typically employ pentatonic and blues scales. For an example, look at the melody for "Amazing Grace," shown in Example 12.1. In this melody, there are only five scale degrees, $\hat{1}$, $\hat{2}$, $\hat{3}$, $\hat{5}$, and $\hat{6}$ in G major. This is a **major pentatonic** scale. Since $\hat{4}$ and $\hat{7}$ are missing, there is no $\hat{7}$–$\hat{1}$ or $\hat{4}$–$\hat{3}$ half-step motion. Melodies based on the major pentatonic scale typically are harmonized with chords from the major scale.

EXAMPLE 12.1   Newton, "Amazing Grace"

(a) Score 🔊

(b) G major pentatonic scale 🔊

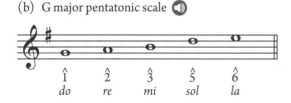

Listen to Example 12.2, "Wayfaring Stranger," another pentatonic melody. From the key signature, the sound of the melody, and the beginning and ending notes, you might guess that the tune is in D minor, but the melody includes only five notes of the D natural minor scale: $\hat{1}$, $\flat\hat{3}$, $\hat{4}$, $\hat{5}$, and $\flat\hat{7}$. This scale is known as the **minor pentatonic**. Melodies based on the minor pentatonic scale are often harmonized with chords from the natural minor scale. These are not the only possible pentatonic (five note) scales; other pentatonic scale types are heard in non-Western musics.

EXAMPLE 12.2   "Wayfaring Stranger"

(a) Score

(b) D minor pentatonic scale

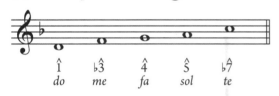

Example 12.3 compares the major and minor pentatonic scales beginning on C: both share C and G ($\hat{1}$ and $\hat{5}$), and each has the quality of the third associated with its name, major or minor.

EXAMPLE 12.3   C pentatonic scales

(a) Major pentatonic

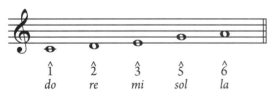

(b) Minor pentatonic

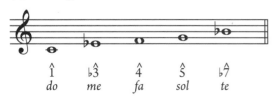

TRY IT #1

For each tonic pitch given, write the major pentatonic scale on the left and the minor pentatonic on the right. Think of the major and minor key signatures, and use the scale degrees shown in Example 12.3 to help you.

Major pentatonic: Minor pentatonic:

$\hat{1}, \hat{2}, \hat{3}, \hat{5},$ and $\hat{6}$ $\hat{1}, \flat\hat{3}, \hat{4}, \hat{5},$ and $\flat\hat{7}$

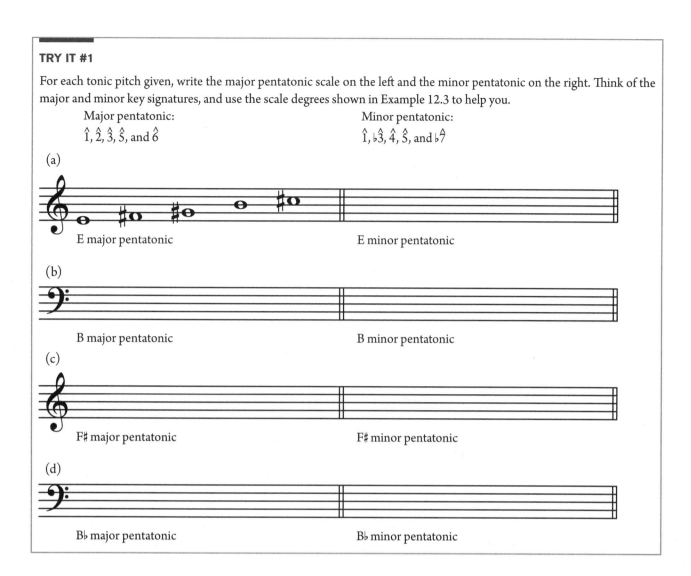

(a) E major pentatonic — E minor pentatonic

(b) B major pentatonic — B minor pentatonic

(c) F♯ major pentatonic — F♯ minor pentatonic

(d) B♭ major pentatonic — B♭ minor pentatonic

Like relative major and minor keys, there are major and minor pentatonic scales that share the same pitches, but have different tonic notes, as shown in Example 12.4. One easy way to remember the pattern of the pentatonic scales is to think of the black keys on a piano. Play the black keys from F♯ to F♯ (or G♭ to G♭) as shown in Example 12.4 to make a major pentatonic scale with F♯ as tonic. Then play the same collection of black keys from D♯ to D♯ (or E♭ to E♭) to make a minor pentatonic scale with D♯ as tonic.

EXAMPLE 12.4   Black-key notes as major and minor pentatonic scales

(a) Major pentatonic scale starting on F♯

$\hat{1}$ $\hat{2}$ $\hat{3}$ $\hat{5}$ $\hat{6}$
do *re* *mi* *sol* *la*

(b) Minor pentatonic scale starting on D♯

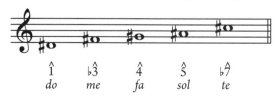

$\hat{1}$ $\flat\hat{3}$ $\hat{4}$ $\hat{5}$ $\flat\hat{7}$
do *me* *fa* *sol* *te*

The Blues Scale and the 12-Bar Blues

The blues, which grew out of African American musical practice, has become one of the most important influences on popular music in the world today. Listen to "Blues for Norton," written for this text by Joel Phillips (anthology, p. 399). It is scored for jazz **combo**, a small instrumental ensemble usually consisting of (at least) a solo instrument, keyboard, and drum set (snare drum, bass drum, and cymbals). The solo instruments in this combo are clarinet and alto saxophone. Usually, as here, the drummer's rhythms are improvised and not notated in the score.

Listen to the last few measures, while following the score in Example 12.5a. The key signature suggests that the work is in F major, but the melody features a repeated and prominent ♭$\hat{3}$ (A♭). The piano part includes both A♭ and A♮, and sometimes plays $\hat{3}$ (A♮) while the solo instrument plays ♭$\hat{3}$ (A♭), as in measures 23–24. In addition, the piano has both $\hat{7}$ and ♭$\hat{7}$ (E♮ and E♭). The lowered third and seventh scale degrees are two of the possible **blue notes** in this style, which help give the blues its distinctive sound. They both come from the **blues scale**, shown in part (b).

EXAMPLE 12.5   Phillips, "Blues for Norton," mm. 20–24

(a) Score

(b) Blues scale

> **KEY CONCEPT**   The blues scale shares most of its pitches with the minor pentatonic, with an added ♯$\hat{4}$/♭$\hat{5}$. A performance of a blues melody with accompaniment blurs the distinction between major and minor by including both $\hat{3}$ and ♭$\hat{3}$ and both $\hat{7}$ and ♭$\hat{7}$.

Example 12.6 shows the blues scale beginning on C; sing the scale to become familiar with its sound. The added "flatted fifth" (here, the F♯ or G♭) changes spelling with the direction of the melody: in performance, the player's intonation on this note may be slightly higher when ascending (F♯) and slightly lower when descending (G♭). The accidentals in the scale are the blue notes. When writing blues, use the major key signature of the tonic pitch and add accidentals as needed, as in "Blues for Norton."

EXAMPLE 12.6   Blues scale on C 🔊

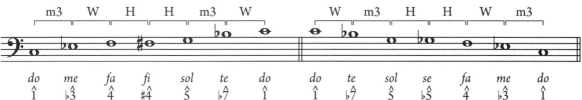

The anthology includes two scores for "Blues for Norton": one is a full score that shows what each instrumentalist plays on the recording (p. 384); more often, blues performers play from a **lead sheet** (p. 383), which gives the primary melody plus chord symbols. Instrumentalists improvise their parts from these musical cues. Follow the lead sheet as you listen to the recording. The piano part, not included in the lead sheet, is created by the pianist on the spot, following the chord symbols. Likewise, the bass player not only supplies the roots of the chords, but also adds considerable melodic and rhythmic interest to the performance with improvised stepwise motion and some arpeggiations of harmonies.

Example 12.7 gives the lead sheet for the first twelve bars of "Splanky." Listen while following the lead sheet. (The performance also includes a long piano introduction not shown here.) Compare the pitches of Example 12.7 with the blues scale shown in Example 12.6.

EXAMPLE 12.7   Count Basie, "Splanky," mm. 1–12 🔊

Basie's melody draws on the full blues scale on C except for B♭ (which, however, is present in the C7 chord, C–E–G–B♭). The F♯ ($\sharp\hat{4}$) in the ascending melody in measure 3 becomes a G♭ ($\flat\hat{5}$) in measure 4 when the melody descends. The notes E♮ and E♭ ($\hat{3}$ and $\flat\hat{3}$) are heard simultaneously, as is typical: the melody in measure 1 features the blue note E♭, while the C7 chord harmonizing it has E♮. Although the blues scale is based on the minor pentatonic scale, it is typically harmonized by chords from a major key. In "Splanky," the key signature provided is for C major, but the melody is based on the C minor pentatonic scale, necessitating many accidentals. This juxtaposition of major-key harmonies with the minor pentatonic scale in the solo parts accounts for much of the distinctive character of blues compositions.

Write blues scales that begin on the pitches given below, ascending and descending. Supply the appropriate major key signature, and add accidentals.

(a) Bb:

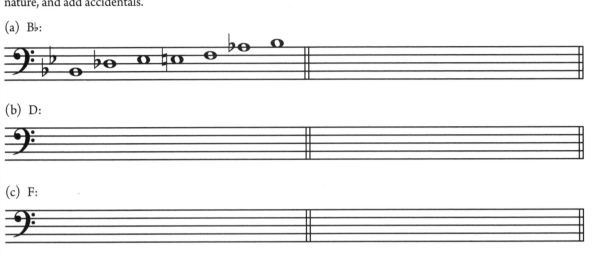

(b) D:

(c) F:

Another important aspect of blues style is its harmonic structure. Unlike a 32-bar song form, with four 8-measure phrases, the **12-bar blues** consists of a single harmonic progression or set of chord changes (called the **changes** by jazz musicians) that is repeated many times over the course of a performance. It is helpful to think of the progression as three 4-bar units, labeled (a), (b), and (c) in Figure 12.1. The progression begins with 4 measures of tonic harmony (a), followed by 2 measures of IV and 2 measures of I (b). The last 4 measures (c) feature the chords V–IV–I and end with a final tonic measure. This last measure may serve as a **turnaround**, with V or V⁷ instead of or after the tonic, leading back to the beginning (a) for another repetition of the chorus. Each harmony may be played as a triad or dominant seventh chord, as shown.

FIGURE 12.1 12-bar blues harmonic scheme

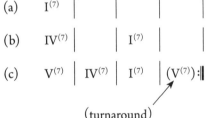

(turnaround)

In popular styles such as jazz and the blues, harmonic progressions and dissonance are treated differently from their counterparts in classical styles. First, the seventh chord is considered as stable as the triad. Seventh chords may appear on any degree of the scale and on nearly every change of chord. Second, while in classical music chordal sevenths are considered a dissonance that must resolve down by stepwise motion, in popular styles sevenths may be left unresolved for their color or dramatic effect. Third, the progression V–IV (or V⁷–IV⁷) is an integral part of the 12-bar blues (occurring at its final cadence) and is standard practice in rock, but it is rare in classical compositions and folk songs.

Example 12.8 shows the blues chord progression for "Splanky" in lead-sheet notation, without the melody. The four slashes in each measure mean that performers should improvise on each chord for four beats—the voicing and rhythm of the chord are up to the performer, in collaboration with the other members of the combo. The chords whose symbols are given in parentheses may be omitted.

EXAMPLE 12.8   Lead-sheet notation for 12-bar blues

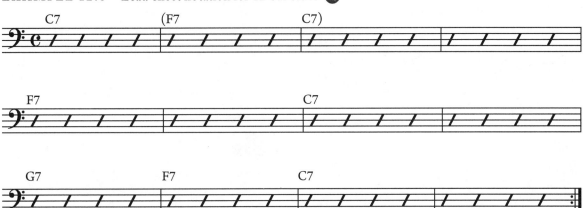

Listen again to "Splanky," following the chord changes; it may help to sing the chord roots along with the recording. Try out its progression at the keyboard (you can simply play the chord once per measure, or repeat it on each beat), then play through Basie's melody or create your own, drawing on the C blues scale from Example 12.6. In blues practice, players first perform the initial tune and progression (together called the **head**), then with each successive chorus, various performers improvise over the chord changes. The head usually returns at the end of the performance, and sometimes in the middle as well. The 12-bar blues progression was adopted by rock musicians in the 1950s and appears in songs of many styles after that time.

Seventh Chords

Seventh chords, pervasive in popular styles, may be built on every degree of the scale, resulting in many different types of sonorities.

> **KEY CONCEPT**   Seventh chords consist of four tones: a root, third, fifth, and seventh (see Chapter 9). A seventh chords is named for the quality of its triad plus the quality of its seventh.

Example 12.9 illustrates the five most common seventh-chord types, with an example of each built above middle C. A major-major seventh chord (MM7) is a major triad plus a M7; a minor-minor seventh chord (mm7) is a minor triad plus a m7. A MM7 is often called a **major seventh** for short, a mm7 is a **minor seventh**, and a major-minor seventh chord (Mm7) is a dominant seventh. A seventh chord built from a diminished triad and minor seventh (dm7) is typically called a **half-diminished seventh**, abbreviated ⌀7, and a chord built from a diminished triad and a diminished seventh (dd7) is a fully diminished seventh (or just a **diminished seventh**), abbreviated °7.

EXAMPLE 12.9   Seventh chords built above middle C

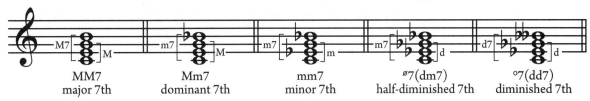

The quality of a seventh chord in a key depends on the scale degree of its root. The seventh chords built on each degree of the G major scale are given in Example 12.10, while Example 12.11 shows seventh chords built on the G minor scale. Since ♭$\hat{7}$ is typically raised in minor, the chords on $\hat{5}$ and $\hat{7}$ are written with an F♯; the chord on the leading tone in minor is therefore a diminished seventh, while the half-diminished seventh appears on $\hat{2}$. Together, these two examples list all the seventh chords commonly found in tonal music.

EXAMPLE 12.10   Seventh chords built above the G major scale 🔊

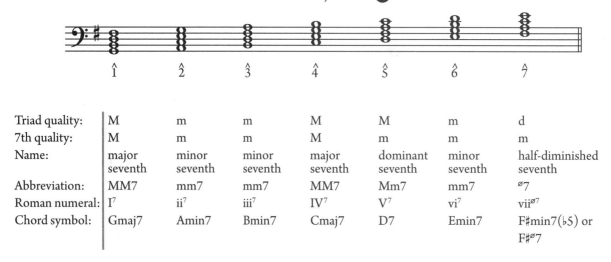

	$\hat{1}$	$\hat{2}$	$\hat{3}$	$\hat{4}$	$\hat{5}$	$\hat{6}$	$\hat{7}$
Triad quality:	M	m	m	M	M	m	d
7th quality:	M	m	m	M	m	m	m
Name:	major seventh	minor seventh	minor seventh	major seventh	dominant seventh	minor seventh	half-diminished seventh
Abbreviation:	MM7	mm7	mm7	MM7	Mm7	mm7	ø7
Roman numeral:	I⁷	ii⁷	iii⁷	IV⁷	V⁷	vi⁷	viiø⁷
Chord symbol:	Gmaj7	Amin7	Bmin7	Cmaj7	D7	Emin7	F♯min7(♭5) or F♯ø7

EXAMPLE 12.11   Seventh chords built above the G minor scale 🔊

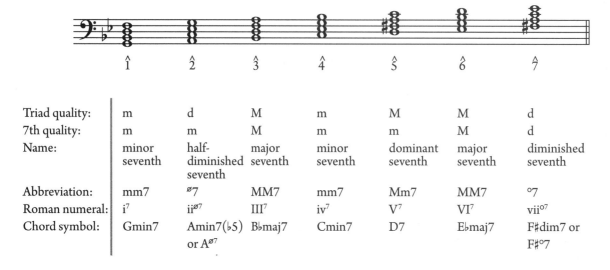

	$\hat{1}$	$\hat{2}$	$\hat{3}$	$\hat{4}$	$\hat{5}$	$\hat{6}$	$\hat{7}$
Triad quality:	m	d	M	m	M	M	d
7th quality:	m	m	M	m	m	M	d
Name:	minor seventh	half-diminished seventh	major seventh	minor seventh	dominant seventh	major seventh	diminished seventh
Abbreviation:	mm7	ø7	MM7	mm7	Mm7	MM7	°7
Roman numeral:	i⁷	iiø⁷	III⁷	iv⁷	V⁷	VI⁷	vii°⁷
Chord symbol:	Gmin7	Amin7(♭5) or Aø7	B♭maj7	Cmin7	D7	E♭maj7	F♯dim7 or F♯°7

The bottom rows of Examples 12.10 and 12.11 give the chord symbol for each seventh chord. Write augmented triads with the root plus an indication of the raised fifth, G(♯5), or with a small plus sign (G⁺). Diminished triads are indicated by Gdim or G°. Some lead sheets notate diminished triads as a minor chord with a lowered fifth: Gmin(♭5). Although seventh chords appear frequently in popular music, the labels used to designate them are not completely standardized. Alternate labels for seventh chords above C are listed in Figure 12.2.

FIGURE 12.2   Seventh-chord symbols

Seventh-chord type	Abbreviation	Chord symbol
Major	MM7	Cmaj7, CM7, Cma7, CΔ7
Dominant	Mm7	C7
Minor	mm7	Cmin7, Cmi7, Cm7, C–7
Half-diminished	ø7 or dm7	Cø7, Cmin7(♭5)
Diminished	°7 or dd7	C°7, Cdim7, Cd7

To spell a specific seventh chord above a given root, first spell the correct quality triad, then add the correct quality seventh. Example 12.12 illustrates the steps for writing a minor seventh chord above F:

(a) Spell a minor triad, F–A♭–C.

(b) Add the seventh (E) (a third above the fifth of the triad).

(c) Check the seventh's quality; if it is not correct, add an accidental. Since F to E is a major seventh, lower the E to E♭.

(d) Use this shortcut to check the quality of the seventh: invert the seventh to make a second. If the second is minor, the seventh is major; if the second is major, the seventh is minor.

EXAMPLE 12.12   Steps to spell a minor seventh chord

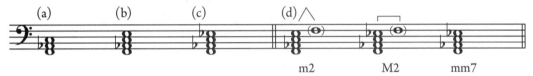

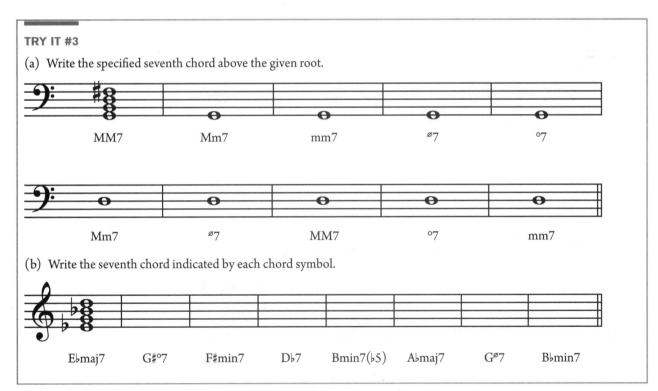

TRY IT #3

(a) Write the specified seventh chord above the given root.

(b) Write the seventh chord indicated by each chord symbol.

ASSIGNMENT 12.2, AURAL SKILLS 12.1

Chord Extensions and Sus Chords

Listen to "'S Wonderful!" while following the score in your anthology and focusing on the chord symbols above the staff. You will notice some new chords here. We conclude this chapter by exploring a few chord types that you may encounter in popular music, but these only scratch the surface of the harmonies available to composers today.

EXAMPLE 12.13   George and Ira Gershwin, "'S Wonderful!" mm. 29–36 🔊

The chords indicated in measure 29 begin with E♭, then change to E♭6, a chord with all the pitches of an E♭ major triad, plus a major sixth (C) above the root. Pitches added to triads or seventh chords are sometimes called **chord extensions**. This particular sonority is an **added-sixth chord**. There are other added-sixth chords in measures 33 and 35–36. The added sixth is generally a major sixth, whether the triad to which it is added is major or minor. Write the chord symbol with the name of its root (and quality) plus the label 6 or (add6). If you see C6 or Cadd6, write a C major triad plus a M6 (A); if you see Cm6 or Cmin(add6), write a C minor triad plus a M6.

Look at Example 12.14 for another type of chord extension: the **ninth chord**. In measure 22, the F9 chord consists of an F dominant seventh chord (F–A♮–C–E♭, the third and fifth appear at the end of the measure, and the D is an embellishing tone); the ninth is the G on the second beat. For MM7 or mm7 chords, the added ninth is usually a M9. In the case of the dominant seventh chord, it may be either a m9 or a M9 (as here). If you are writing in four voices and need to leave out one chord tone, omit the fifth. You may also find symbols for eleventh or thirteenth chords in some lead sheets. Simply add the eleventh (a P4) or thirteenth (a M6 or m6) above the bass to spell these chords.

EXAMPLE 12.14   George and Ira Gershwin, "'S Wonderful!" mm. 21–24

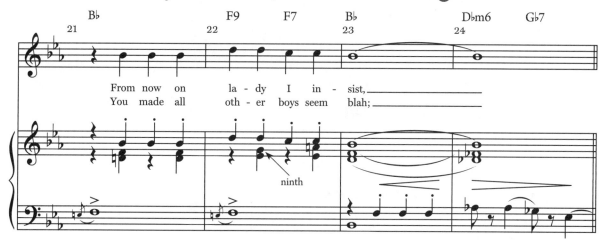

In addition to add6 and ninth chords, a third type of chord you may encounter in popular music is a **sus** (or **sus4**) **chord**; the chord might be labeled B♭sus or B♭sus4. In these chords, a fourth replaces the third in a triad: for example, Fsus is spelled F–B♭–C rather than F–A–C, making a dissonance that adds color to the harmony. (Sus chords are named for the suspension, an embellishment in classical style.) Example 12.15, from "Somewhere Out There," shows a sus chord in measure 2: the G7sus chord includes a C (fourth above G) retained throughout the measure.

EXAMPLE 12.15   Horner, Mann, and Weil, "Somewhere Out There," mm. 1–4

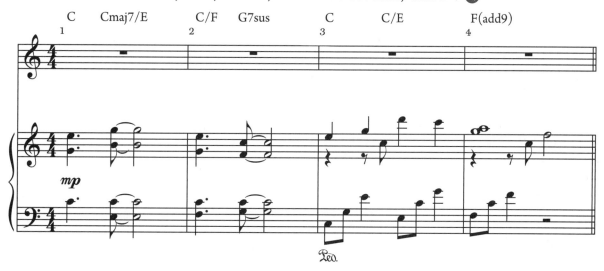

You can also use chord symbols to indicate inversions. Measures 1 and 3 of Example 12.15 illustrate how chord inversions are labeled: Cmaj7/E (m. 1) means to play a C major seventh chord in first inversion, with an E in the bass. Likewise, C/E (m. 3) means to play a C major triad with E in the bass. The C/F in measure 2 indicates there is a C triad over an F bass note—a passing tone in the bass part. You should now have a sufficient understanding of chord symbols to spell most chords you will find in a standard lead sheet.

Finally, as we near the end of this text, we challenge you to continue exploring music—by listening, playing, singing, and writing. Take some of the harmonies, forms, and styles introduced in the last two chapters and write some music of your own. Be curious, take more courses, and above all, experience music of many styles, periods, and regions. In the twenty-first century, the whole world of music is open to you. Explore and enjoy!

ASSIGNMENT 12.3, 12.4

Did You Know?

Early rock and roll owes much to the blues. Not only did rock musicians borrow the 12-bar blues progression and blue notes, in some cases they also reworked entire blues songs—either as "covers" (interpretations that acknowledged the original composers) or as "new" songs of their own. Rock-music scholars (and lawyers) have debated the question of when borrowed material becomes one's own and when it is protected by copyright law, but you may be interested to learn that some of Led Zepplin's most famous songs have blues roots. These include "Dazed and Confused" (compare with Jake Holmes's "I'm Confused"), "Whole Lotta Love" (compare with Willie Dixon's "You Need Love"), "Bring It on Home" (compare with a song with the same title by Willie Dixon), and the "Lemon Song" (compare with Howlin' Wolf/Chester Burnett's "The Killing Floor"). (For more on this question, see David Headlam's article "Does the Song Remain the Same?" in *Concert Music, Rock, and Jazz since 1945* (Rochester: University of Rochester Press, 1995), ed. Elizabeth West Marvin and Richard Hermann.)

Terms You Should Know

12-bar blues	diminished seventh chord	pentatonic scale
added-sixth chord	half-diminished seventh chord	major pentatonic
blue notes	head	minor pentatonic
blues scale	lead sheet	sus chord
changes	major seventh chord	turnaround
chord extensions	minor seventh chord	
combo	ninth chord	

Questions for Review

1. What distinguishes the major pentatonic from the minor pentatonic?
2. What distinguishes the minor pentatonic from the blues scale?
3. What is the standard harmonic progression for the 12-bar blues?
4. How is an extended blues piece structured (beyond the first 12 bars)?
5. Which seventh-chord types appear in jazz and popular styles?
6. How are seventh chords treated differently in popular styles and classical style?
7. Describe how seventh-chord qualities are represented in chord symbols.
8. What extensions may be added to triads and seventh chords in popular styles?
9. How are added-sixth and sus chords represented in chord symbols?
10. How are inversions specified in chord symbols?

Reading Review

Match the terms on the left with the best answer on the right.

_____ (1) sus4 chord

_____ (2) minor pentatonic

_____ (3) turnaround

_____ (4) combo

_____ (5) half-diminished seventh

_____ (6) added-sixth

_____ (7) diminished seventh

_____ (8) ninth chord

_____ (9) major pentatonic

_____ (10) lead sheet

_____ (11) blues scale

_____ (12) V–IV

(a) minor pentatonic plus $\sharp\hat{4}$ or $\flat\hat{5}$

(b) chord extension of a M6 above the root

(c) diminished triad plus diminished seventh

(d) diminished triad plus minor seventh

(e) _do–re–mi–sol–la_

(f) _do–me–fa–sol–te_

(g) progression common in blues and rock but not in classical music

(h) notation with melody and chord symbols

(i) chord extension of a third above the chordal seventh

(j) dominant chord at end of 12-bar blues to prepare for the next chorus

(k) chord with its third replaced by a fourth

(l) jazz instrumental performance group

ⓢ Additional review and practice available at wwnorton.com/studyspace

Class Activities

A. At the keyboard

1. Singing pentatonic scales

(a) "Will This Circle Be Unbroken" is based on the major pentatonic scale ($\hat{1}$–$\hat{2}$–$\hat{3}$–$\hat{5}$–$\hat{6}$; *do–re–mi–sol–la*). Play C–F, the dominant and tonic pitches, and sing the song with solfège syllables or scale-degree numbers.

"Will This Circle Be Unbroken," mm. 1–4

(b) Bartók's "Evening in Transylvania" is based on the minor pentatonic scale ($\hat{1}$–$\flat\hat{3}$–$\hat{4}$–$\hat{5}$–$\flat\hat{7}$; *do–me–fa–sol–te*). Play the first pitch of the melody, E, and sing the rest with solfège syllables or scale-degree numbers.

Béla Bartók, "Evening in Transylvania," from *Ten Easy Pieces*, mm. 21–29

2. Performing pentatonic scales

As you play each of the following exercises at the keyboard, sing up and down with solfège syllables, scale-degree numbers, and letter names.

(a) Major pentatonic

- Transpose (rewrite) "Will This Circle Be Unbroken" to G♭ major. Begin on D♭ and play only black keys.
- From each of the tonic pitches below, play a major scale. Perform the scale again, but omit $\hat{4}$ and $\hat{7}$ to create the major pentatonic scale.

(1) C   (5) E   (9) A♭

(2) D   (6) E♭   (10) G♭

(3) A   (7) F

(4) G   (8) B♭

(b) Minor pentatonic

- Transpose "Evening in Transylvania" so that it begins on E♭; play only on the black keys.
- From each of the tonic pitches below, play a natural minor scale. Perform the scale again, but omit $\hat{2}$ and ♭$\hat{6}$ to create the minor pentatonic scale.

(1) C
(2) D
(3) A
(4) G

(5) E
(6) E♭
(7) F
(8) B♭

(9) C♯
(10) F♯

3. Blues scales

To write a blues scale, treat its letter name (A♭, for example) as the tonic of a major key, and write the blues scale using that key signature (four flats). The blue notes—♭$\hat{3}$, ♯$\hat{4}$/♭$\hat{5}$, and ♭$\hat{7}$—will always require accidentals, no matter what the key signature.

| do | me | fa | fi | sol | te | do | do | te | sol | se | fa | me | do |
| $\hat{1}$ | ♭$\hat{3}$ | $\hat{4}$ | ♯$\hat{4}$ | $\hat{5}$ | ♭$\hat{7}$ | $\hat{1}$ | $\hat{1}$ | ♭$\hat{7}$ | $\hat{5}$ | ♭$\hat{5}$ | $\hat{4}$ | ♭$\hat{3}$ | $\hat{1}$ |

Now perform an ascending and descending blues scale from each note below. As you play, sing in a comfortable register with solfège syllables, scale-degree numbers, and letter names. Then notate each scale on your own music paper. Write the key signature of the major tonic, and notate the accidentals for each blue note.

(a) B♭
(b) E♭

(c) A
(d) G

(e) F
(f) D

(g) E
(h) F♯

4. Playing and spelling seventh chords

There are two ways to think about playing the five frequently used seventh chords: (a) the triad-plus-seventh strategy and (b) the triad-plus-third strategy. Each method is summarized.

(a) Triad-plus-seventh strategy:

Given a root and seventh-chord type, perform the appropriate triad, then add the correct type of seventh above its root.

Seventh chord	Triad quality	Plus this seventh
major (MM7)	major	M7
dominant (Mm7)	major	m7
minor (mm7)	minor	m7
half-diminished (ø7)	diminished	m7
diminished (°7)	diminished	d7

(b) Triad-plus-third strategy:

Given a root and seventh-chord type, perform the appropriate triad, then add the correct type of third above its fifth.

Seventh chord	Triad quality	Plus this third
major (MM7)	major	M3
dominant (Mm7)	major	m3
minor (mm7)	minor	m3
half-diminished (ø7)	diminished	M3
diminished (°7)	diminished	m3

Consider each pitch below to be the root of a seventh chord. Perform all five types of seventh chord from each root following either strategy. Play each at the keyboard root alone, then MM7, Mm7, mm7, ø7, and °7.

(1) D   (5) F   (9) E♭
(2) A   (6) C♯   (10) B♭
(3) F♯   (7) B   (11) C
(4) E   (8) G   (12) A♭

B. Singing at sight

Identify whether each melody uses the major or minor pentatonic scale.

Melody 1 "Riddle Song"   Scale type: _____

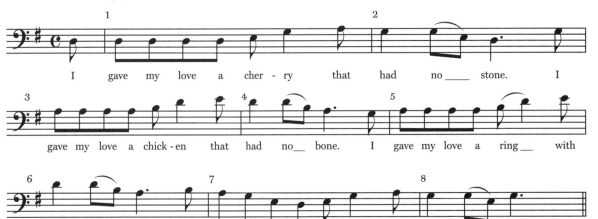

I gave my love a cher-ry that had no ___ stone. I

gave my love a chick-en that had no___ bone. I gave my love a ring ___ with

no end - ing. I gave my love a ba - by with no cry - ing.

Melody 2 George Gershwin, DuBose and Dorothy Heyward, and Ira Gershwin, "Summertime," from *Porgy and Bess*, mm. 16b–24a (adapted)   Scale type: _____

Your ___ dad-dy's rich _____ and your mam-ma's good look - in' ___

___ so hush lit-tle ba - by don't ___ you cry. _____

Melody 3 "Land of the Silver Birch" Scale type: _____

Land of the sil - ver birch, home of the beav - er,

where still the might - y moose wan - ders at will.

Blue lake and rock - y shore I will re - turn once more.

Boom did - dy boom boom boom did - dy boom boom boom did - dy boom boom boom!

C. Swung rhythms

For swing melodies 1–3:

- When there are chord symbols, play the chords at the keyboard. Initially, don't worry about rhythm or speed, just accuracy. When you can play the chords accurately, play them in rhythm, even if your tempo is slow.
- When you can play the chords in rhythm, sing along as you play. If necessary (especially for notes with accidentals), use the piano to help.
- These melodies may be sung with the eighth notes swung ♪♪ = ♪ ♪, and some feature syncopation.
- Swung rhythms, often used in jazz and blues, can be notated in simple quadruple meter with eighth notes beamed in groups of four: 4/4. Instead they are performed as if they were written in *compound* quadruple meter with accents on the *weak* parts of the beat: 12/8.
- With swung rhythms, listen for syncopations, accents, and melodic anticipations. (If it helps, rewrite in 12/8, as shown.)
- To practice swung rhythms, first, perform the example below "straight" (exactly as it is notated), then add "swing."

Swing Melody 1 Frank Perkins and Mitchell Parish, "Stars Fell on Alabama," mm. 1–8

Swing Melody 2 Harold Arlen, "Blues in the Night," mm. 1–12

Swing Melody 3 W. C. Handy, "Memphis Blues," mm. 1–12

Here, the swung rhythms are sixteenths, not eighths.

D. Call and response and improvisation

1. Hearing and writing blues riffs

Your teacher will play the harmonies of a 12-bar blues progression and perform a riff (a short melodic/rhythmic idea) in the first two measures. Memorize the riff, then perform it in measures 5–6 and 9–10 of the progression. There will be rests in measures 3–4, 7–8, and 11–12. Maintain the riff's pitch, rhythm, and tempo.

Options for performing your response

- Sing pitches only with solfège syllables, scale-degree numbers, or letter names
- Sing the rhythm only, on "la"
- Sing the pitches and rhythm
- Sing the root of each chord with solfège syllables, scale-degree numbers, or Roman numerals
- Conduct (or tap) with any of the above
- Play on the keyboard or another instrument

Options for writing your response

- Write solfège syllables, scale-degree numbers, or letter names
- Write note heads only on the staff
- Write the rhythm only
- Write both notes and rhythm on the staff
- Write chord symbols or Roman numerals

2. Improvisation

As a group, improvise based on the blues progression provided. While one or more class members play the chord progression, a soloist improvises (on voice, piano, or another instrument), choosing his or her pitches from the corresponding blues scale. Take turns swapping parts until each person has had the opportunity to improvise.

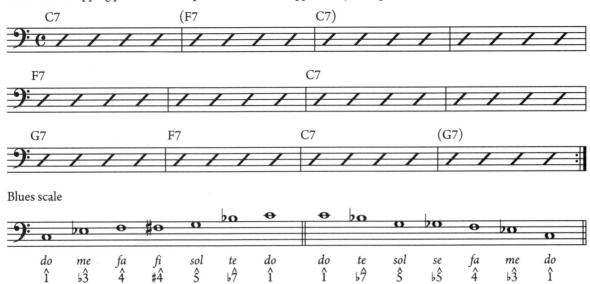

Blues scale

NAME _____

Workbook ASSIGNMENT 12.1

1. Pentatonic scales

a. Write the pentatonic scales requested below.

(1) F minor pentatonic

(2) Ab major pentatonic

(3) Bb major pentatonic

(4) G minor pentatonic

(5) Eb minor pentatonic

(6) C minor pentatonic

(7) D major pentatonic

(8) F# major pentatonic

b. Identify the pentatonic scale for each melody. Write the scale beneath the melody, and write the appropriate solfège syllables or scale-degree numbers beneath the scale; write the scale type in the blank.

(1) "My Paddle's Keen and Bright" 🔊

Practice the tune on solfège syllables or scale-degree numbers for performance in class as a round.

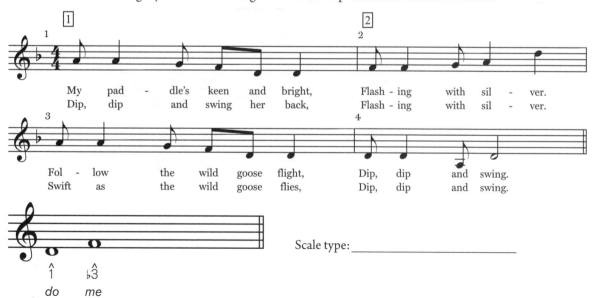

My pad - dle's keen and bright, Flash - ing with sil - ver.
Dip, dip and swing her back, Flash - ing with sil - ver.

Fol - low the wild goose flight, Dip, dip and swing.
Swift as the wild goose flies, Dip, dip and swing.

Scale type: _____

$\hat{1}$ $\flat\hat{3}$
do me

(2) Robert Lowry, "How Can I Keep from Singing?" mm. 1–8a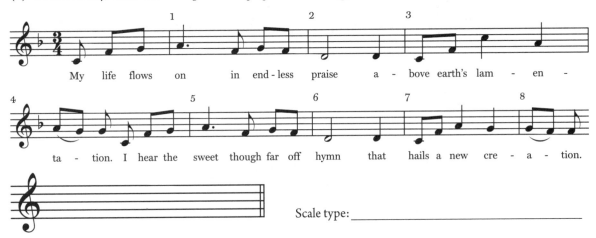

My life flows on in end-less praise a - bove earth's lam - en -

ta - tion. I hear the sweet though far off hymn that hails a new cre - a - tion.

Scale type: _____

2. Blues scales

Spell the blues scales that begin on the pitches given below. Write the appropriate key signature and accidentals (both ascending and descending).

a. Beginning on G:

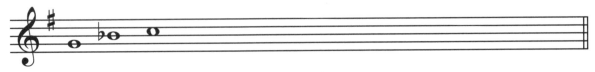

b. Beginning on B♭:

c. Beginning on D:

d. Beginning on E:

e. Beginning on F:

Workbook ASSIGNMENT 12.2

1. Spelling isolated seventh chords

Each pitch given below is the root of a seventh chord. Fill in the remaining chord members. Don't change the given pitch.

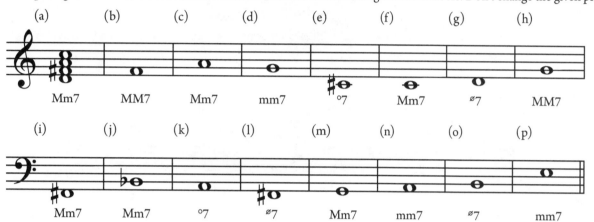

2. Writing blues progessions

Write the changes for 12-bar blues in both of the following keys. Write one chord symbol above each measure.

a. Bb

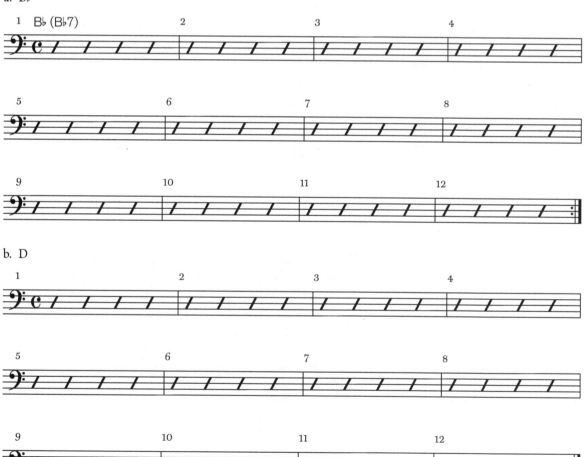

b. D

3. Analyzing a blues melody

a. The head (mm. 1–12) of "Splanky," shown below, is based on only a few short melodic ideas that are repeated and expanded. For example, the F–E♭–C of measure 2 could be considered an expansion of the opening E♭–C. Draw a circle around all the other fragments that are based on F–E♭–C.

b. Another basic idea is E♭–F–G♭ (F♯) in measure 1; draw a box around all the segments using those notes (some may descend rather than ascend, and boxes and circles may overlap). The longer melodic idea in measures 3–4 is based on these smaller segments.

c. Now look at the larger formal organization of the melody. There is a bracket over measures 1–4. Draw a bracket over each repetition of this four-measure melodic idea.

Basie, "Splanky," mm. 1–12

4. Writing a blues melody

Taking the melodies in "Splanky" and "Blues for Norton" as your models, write three melodic ideas on the staff lines below using a blues scale in the key of your choice. Next to each melodic idea, write at least one variant (for example, add, replace, or remove a note, or change the melodic direction). Then select two ideas (with their variants) and use them to make a 12-bar blues melody. Copy the melody on your own staff paper and be prepared to perform it in class.

Melodic idea 1:   Variants:

Melodic idea 2:   Variants:

Melodic idea 3:   Variants:

Workbook ASSIGNMENT 12.3

Writing a song

Your final project is to compose either a blues song (Assignment 12.3) or a popular song (Assignment 12.4) with lyrics. Use examples of these song types in your anthology as models. On your own staff paper, notate the song on a lead sheet that shows the melody, lyrics, and chord symbols. Read the instructions in their entirety (for both types of songs)—many guidelines are applicable to both styles. Prepare to perform your song, or arrange to have it performed, in class.

General guidelines

- Write a short introduction. This might consist of the last four measures of the song or a simple chord progression that establishes a mood.
- Include a "hook"—a recurring, memorable part of the music, the lyrics of which are often the song's title.
- Recall that many song lyrics are about love—trying to find love, being in love, losing a love.
- Employ text painting appropriate to your lyrics. For example, you might set the word "sun" or "moon" to the highest pitch in the phrase.
- Keep your melody and chord symbols simple; performers bring the music to life by embellishing the melodies and chords they find in lead sheets.
- Create a short coda, or tag. One possibility is to play the last four measures three times, making each repetition slower and more dramatic.

Blues song

Write a song with the following form:

| Introduction | a minimum of three statements of the twelve-bar blues progression, each with different lyrics | coda |

Creating the lyrics

Keep the language simple and direct, or even colloquial (for example, "You ain't nothin' but a hound dog," "My mama done tol' me," etc.). Each blues progression consists of three subphrases, each four measures long: measures 1–4 state an idea; measures 5–8 restate the idea in a varied form; measures 9–12 offer an outcome or a consequence.

You could think of blues lyrics as a kind of call and response, with a refrain.

Subphrase 1 (Call):	I	I	I	I
Subphrase 2 (Response):	IV	IV	I	I
Subphrase 3 (Conclusion):	V	IV	I	I (or V^7)

The lyrics to W. C. Handy's "St. Louis Blues" are a good example:

I hate to see that evening sun go down,	call
I hate to see that evening sun go down,	response
'Cause, my baby, he's gone left this town.	conclusion

Feelin' tomorrow like I feel today,	call
If I'm feelin' tomorrow like I feel today,	response
I'll pack my truck and make my get away.	conclusion

Creating the music

- Follow the blues progression shown, or transpose it to another key of your choice.
- Choose your melodic pitches from the blues scale below, or transpose it.
- Create a two-measure motive that you can vary.
- In measure 12, write a turnaround (the V chord).
- Model your song after Count Basie's "Splanky" (anthology, p. 338) or Phillips's "Blues for Norton" (p. 383).

Blues scale

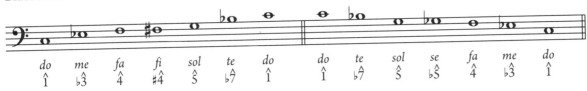

Work space

Workbook ASSIGNMENT 12.4

Writing a song

Your final project is to compose either a blues song (Assignment 12.3) or a popular song (Assignment 12.4) with lyrics. Use examples of these song types in your anthology as models. On your own staff paper, notate the song on a lead sheet that shows the melody, lyrics, and chord symbols. Read the instructions in their entirety (for both types of songs)—many guidelines are applicable to both styles. Prepare to perform your song, or arrange to have it performed, in class.

General guidelines

- Write a short introduction. This might consist of the last four measures of the song or a simple chord progression that establishes a mood.
- Include a "hook"—a recurring, memorable part of the music, the lyrics of which are often the song's title.
- Recall that many song lyrics are about love—trying to find love, being in love, losing a love.
- Employ text painting appropriate to your lyrics. For example, you might set the word "sun" or "moon" to the highest pitch in the phrase.
- Keep your melody and chord symbols simple; performers bring the music to life by embellishing the melodies and chords they find in lead sheets.
- Create a short coda, or tag. One possibility is to play the last four measures three times, making each repetition slower and more dramatic.

Popular song

Write a song with the following form:

| Introduction | **a a' b a'** or **a a' b a''** design, stated at least twice (with different lyrics) | coda |

Creating the lyrics

1. Writing your own

- One type of four-phrase song is the ballad, which tells a story. Let the **a** phrases narrate the story, and the bridge (**b**) encapsulate its emotional impact.
- Place rhymes at the ends of phrases, and within the phrase if you like.
- Think about incorporating other poetic devices, such as alliteration and double entendre.
- Try to let the rhythm of your melody approximate that of the spoken lyrics.

2. Setting a preexisting poem

- You may choose to set a poem if you find one that inspires you and fits the formal requirements of the song form. Spend some time considering both the form and meaning of the text. Look for
  - the accents, so you can place strong and weak syllables on strong and weak beats;
  - a parallel structure in the text that might suggest parallel melodic lines;
  - rhyming line endings that might suggest "musical rhymes" (similar motives);
  - repeated words or images that might be represented as musical ideas (text painting);
  - changes in the narration or imagery that would suggest musical change; and
  - a general sentiment or mood of the text that you would like to evoke through music.

Creating the music

- Write a motive that is memorable in its rhythm, contour, and pitches. Use this motive and variations of it throughout the song.
- Each phrase should end with a cadence: **a** (HC), **a'** (PAC), **b** (HC), **a'** or **a''** (PAC).
- The bridge, **b**, might be in a different key from **a**, be louder or more rhythmically active, feature a different accompaniment pattern, or sound in a higher register.

- Make each phrase four or eight measures long, so that the body of your song will be sixteen or thirty-two measures. Sixteen-measure songs we have studied include "Oh! Susanna" (**a a' b a'**), "Greensleeves" (**a a' b b'**), and "When Johnny Comes Marching Home" (**a a' b c**). Thirty-two measure songs include "Till There Was You" (**a a' b a'**), "'S Wonderful!" (refrain: **a a' b a''**), "Somewhere Out There" (**a a' b a''**; **b** and **a''** are extended beyond eight measures), and "My Funny Valentine" (**a a' b a''**; **a''** is extended).
- If you prefer, and with your teacher's permission, choose a different design, such as **a a' b b'**, **a b a b**, or **a a' b c**.
- If you want to create a simple keyboard accompaniment, use harmonic progressions and accompaniment patterns from Chapter 11 as models. Otherwise, you may simply notate melody, lyrics, and chord symbols.

Work space

NAME _____

Workbook   AURAL SKILLS 12.1

Listen again to an excerpt we studied before, and complete the following exercises. 🔊

1. Which is the meter signature of the excerpt?

(a) $\frac{2}{4}$ (b) $\frac{3}{4}$ (c) $\frac{9}{8}$ (d) $\frac{12}{8}$

2. Melodic pitches 1–2 create which interval?

(a) M2   (b) M3   (c) P4   (d) P5

3. Melodic pitches 3–5 outline a triad with which quality?

(a) major   (c) augmented

(b) minor   (d) diminished

4. Write the melody with solfège syllables or scale-degree numbers. Your answer should begin with $\hat{5}$–$\hat{7}$–$\hat{1}$ (*sol–ti–do*).

5. Write the bass line with solfège syllables or scale-degree numbers. Hint: It includes three chromatic pitches (with accidentals).

6. Notate the pitches and rhythm of the melody and bass line on the following staves. Begin the melody (which opens with a two-pitch anacrusis) on C4 and the bass line on F2. Include the meter signature, bar lines, key signature, and accidentals. Beam notes appropriately given your choice of meter.

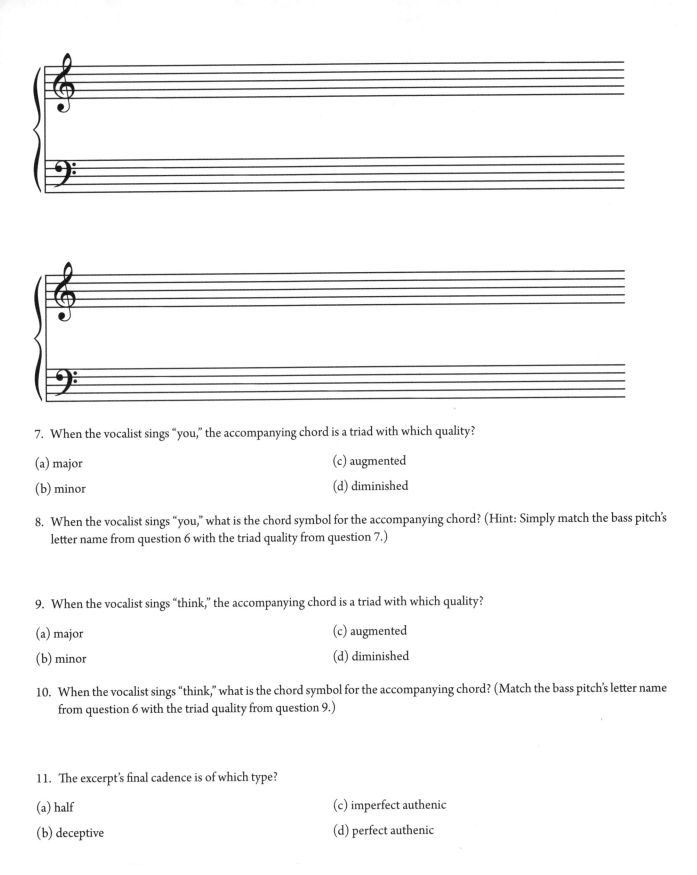

7. When the vocalist sings "you," the accompanying chord is a triad with which quality?

(a) major

(c) augmented

(b) minor

(d) diminished

8. When the vocalist sings "you," what is the chord symbol for the accompanying chord? (Hint: Simply match the bass pitch's letter name from question 6 with the triad quality from question 7.)

9. When the vocalist sings "think," the accompanying chord is a triad with which quality?

(a) major

(c) augmented

(b) minor

(d) diminished

10. When the vocalist sings "think," what is the chord symbol for the accompanying chord? (Match the bass pitch's letter name from question 6 with the triad quality from question 9.)

11. The excerpt's final cadence is of which type?

(a) half

(c) imperfect authenic

(b) deceptive

(d) perfect authenic

Anthology

Johann Sebastian Bach, Invention in D Minor   334

Béla Bartók, "Bulgarian Rhythm" (No. 115), from *Mikrokosmos*   336

Count Basie and Neil Hefti, "Splanky"   338

Ludwig van Beethoven, Piano Sonata in C Minor, Op. 13 (*Pathétique*), second
    movement, excerpt   339

John Barnes Chance, *Variations on a Korean Folk Song*, excerpt   341

Jeremiah Clarke, *Trumpet Voluntary* (*Prince of Denmark's March*), excerpt   345

Stephen Foster, "Oh! Susannah"   350

George and Ira Gershwin, "'S Wonderful!" from *Funny Face*   351

Patrick S. Gilmore, "When Johnny Comes Marching Home"   356

"Greensleeves," arr. John Duarte; arr. Norbert Kraft   357

Don Henley, Glenn Frey, and Randy Meisner, "Take It to the Limit"   358

"Home on the Range"   363

James Horner, Barry Mann, and Cynthia Weil, "Somewhere Out There,"
    from *An American Tail*   364

Scott Joplin, "Solace"   368

Jonathan Larson, "Seasons of Love," from *Rent*, excerpt   372

Wolfgang Amadeus Mozart, String Quartet in D Minor, K. 421,
    third movement   377

Mozart, *Variations on "Ah, vous dirai-je Maman,"* excerpts   379

"My Country, 'Tis of Thee" (America)   381

John Newton, "Amazing Grace"   382

Joel Phillips, "Blues for Norton" (lead sheet)   383

Phillips, "Blues for Norton" (full score)   384

William "Smokey" Robinson, Jr., "You've Really Got a Hold on Me"   387

Richard Rodgers and Lorenz Hart, "My Funny Valentine,"
    from *Babes in Arms*   392

Franz Schubert, Waltz in B Minor, Op. 18, No. 6   396

"Simple Gifts," traditional; arr. Aaron Copland (from *Appalachian Spring*)   397

Meredith Willson, "Till There Was You," from *The Music Man*   398

Johann Sebastian Bach (1685–1750)

Invention in D Minor

Around 1720, Bach composed a number of two-voice contrapuntal keyboard works, called inventions, for his ten-year-old son, Wilhelm Friedemann. Bach's inventions were intended to teach students how to play two simultaneous lines on the harpsichord and how to develop a musical idea in the course of a piece.

From *Johann Sebastian Bach: Keyboard Music*. New York: Dover Publications Inc.

Count Basie and Neil Hefti

"Splanky"

Count Basie was one of the most prominent figures in the Swing Era. He began as a piano player in New York, but moved to Kansas City in the late 1920s. In the 1930s he formed the Count Basie Orchestra, a big band that became well known through live radio broadcasts and a recording contract with Decca. His "One O'Clock Jump" was recognized by National Public Radio as one of the 100 most influential American musical works of the twentieth century. "Splanky" was composed and arranged for the Basie band by Neal Hefti, who won a Grammy for the tune. Hefti collaborated with Count Basie throughout the 1950s. Recorded performances of this piece typically begin with an introduction prior to the music shown here. The piece was originally composed in D♭, but the version here is transposed to C for ease of reading.

Ludwig van Beethoven (1770–1827)

Piano Sonata in C Minor, Op. 13 (*Pathétique*), second movement, excerpt

Beethoven composed the *Pathétique* Sonata in 1799, at age twenty-seven, during his first decade composing and performing in Vienna. The subtitle, *Pathétique*, which would have appealed to nineteenth-century audiences, means "with pathos." The work was dedicated to Prince Karl von Lichnowsky, who was a supporter and patron to both Mozart and Beethoven. In the recordings that accompany this text, this excerpt is performed on fortepiano, an early keyboard from Beethoven's era.

From *Ludwig van Beethoven: Complete Piano Sonatas, Volume 1*. New York: Dover Publications Inc.

John Barnes Chance (1932–1972)

Variations on a Korean Folk Song, excerpt

Chance's *Variations on a Korean Folk Song,* written in 1967, is based on the folk song "Arirang," which Chance first heard while in Korea with an army band. Like all of his compositions, this piece is for wind ensemble. This folk song is still well known in Korea and abroad (it appears, for example, in the 1990 Presbyterian hymnal with English text), and has often served as the theme for variation sets by other composers.

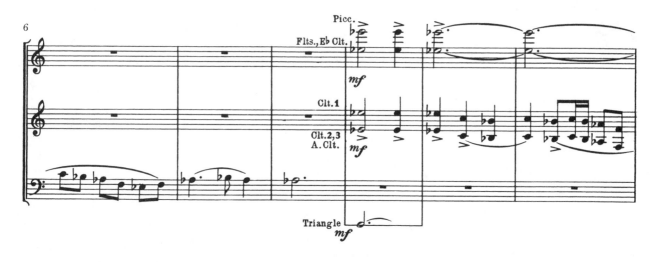

Jeremiah Clarke (1674–1707)

Trumpet Voluntary (Prince of Denmark's March), excerpt

The *Trumpet Voluntary* was likely originally written for solo harpsichord around 1700. It has become famous through the 1878 arrangement for trumpet and organ by Henry Wood. Wood mistakenly believed that the piece was by Henry Purcell, a misattribution that was not corrected until the 1940s.

Arranged by Sue Mitchell Wallace and John H. Head

Stephen Foster (1826–1864)

"Oh! Susanna"

Stephen Foster was a prolific songwriter of the mid-nineteenth century, whose songs, in addition to "Oh! Susanna," include "Old Folks at Home," "Beautiful Dreamer," "Jeanie with the Light Brown Hair," and "Camptown Races." Although some of his songs seem to glorify the slavery and plantations of the Old South, he was born in Pittsburgh and only visited the South once. Foster's early songs were written for minstrel shows—a popular form of entertainment in which singers and dancers impersonated African Americans by performing in blackface—yet he was friends with abolitionists and in later years wrote songs that attempted to portray black culture with sensitivity and dignity.

2. It rained all day the night I left
   The weather was so dry;
   The sun so hot I froze myself,
   Susanna, don't you cry.
   Chorus

3. I had a dream the other night,
   When everything was still.
   I thought I saw Susanna
   A-coming down the hill.
   Chorus

4. The buckwheat cake was in her mouth,
   The tear was in her eye,
   Says I, "I'm coming from the South."
   Susanna, don't you cry.
   Chorus

George and Ira Gershwin

"'S Wonderful!" from *Funny Face*

George and Ira Gershwin wrote "'S Wonderful!" in 1927 for the Broadway musical *Funny Face*. The musical starred Fred Astaire and was eventually made into a film. Though the film is radically different from the play, this song appears in both. The team wrote over two dozen Broadway and Hollywood shows, and in 1932 their "Of Thee I Sing" was awarded the Pulitzer Prize for drama.

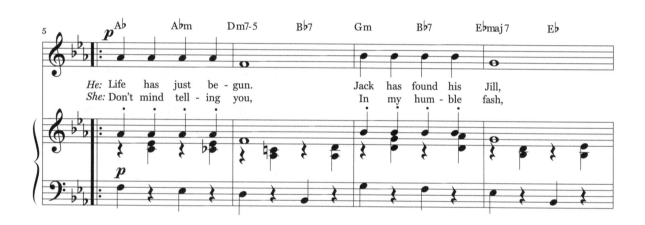

He: Life has just be - gun.   Jack has found his Jill,
She: Don't mind tell - ing you,   In my hum - ble fash,

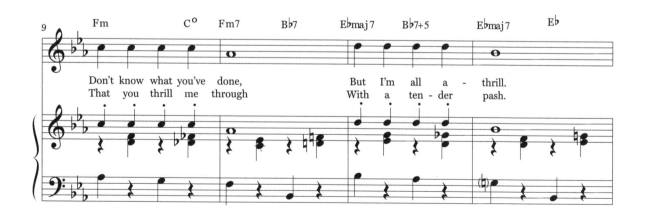

Don't know what you've done,   But I'm all a - thrill.
That you thrill me through   With a ten - der pash.

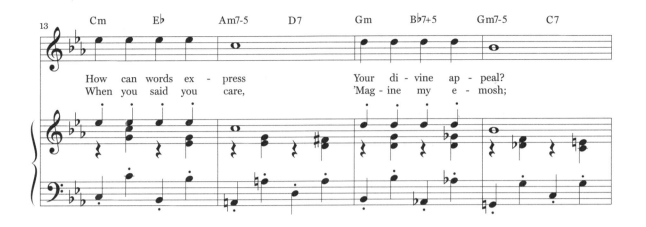

How can words ex - press Your di - vine ap - peal?
When you said you care, 'Mag - ine my e - mosh;

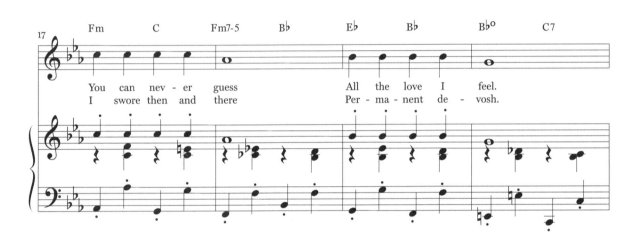

You can nev - er guess All the love I feel.
I swore then and there Per - ma - nent de - vosh.

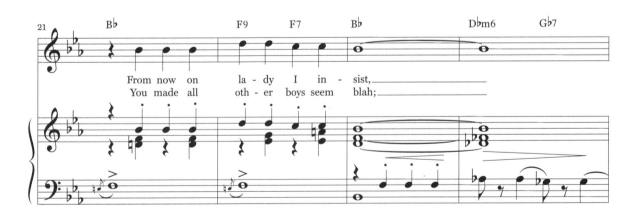

From now on la - dy I in - sist,____
You made all oth - er boys seem blah;____

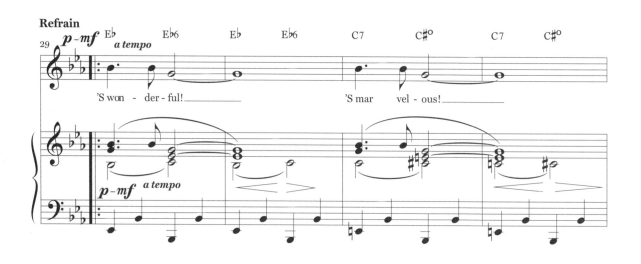

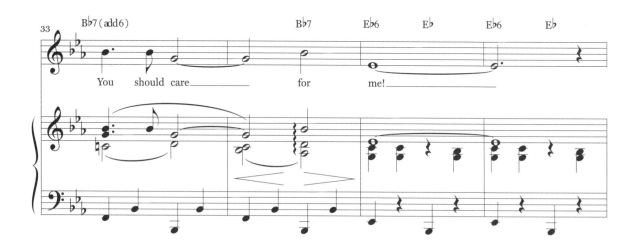

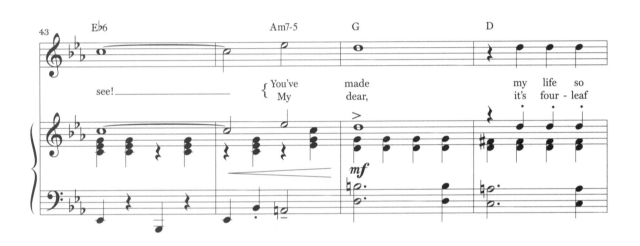

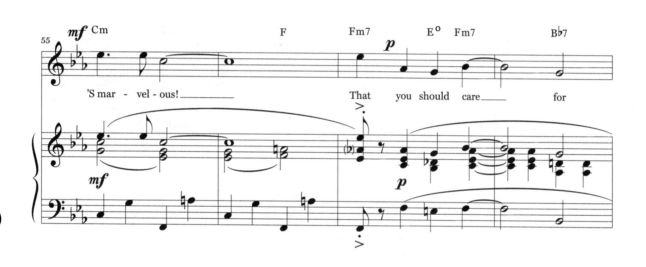

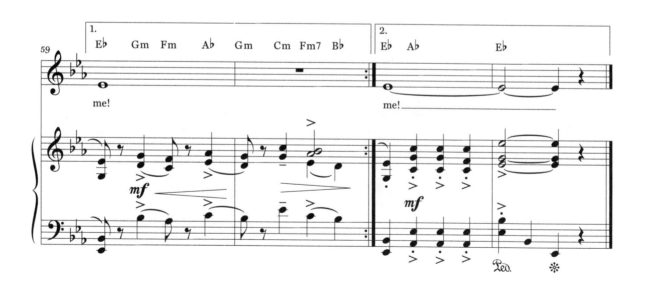

Patrick S. Gilmore (1829–1892)

"When Johnny Comes Marching Home"

Patrick Gilmore was born in Ireland in 1829 and immigrated to Boston in 1849, where he was a significant band leader. Gilmore wrote "When Johnny Comes Marching Home" during the Civil War, when his band served the Massachusetts 24th Regiment. Two of Gilmore's lasting contributions to American culture include the founding of the first Promenade Concert in America, the forerunner of the Boston Pops concerts, and the establishment of Gilmore's Concert Garden, which became Madison Square Garden.

1. When John-ny comes march-ing home a-gain, Hur - rah! ____ Hur - rah! ____ We'll
2. Get read - y for the Ju - bi - lee, Hur - rah! ____ Hur - rah! ____ We'll

give him a heart - y wel - come then, Hur - rah! ____ Hur - rah! ____ The
give ____ the he - ro three times three, Hur - rah! ____ Hur - rah! ____ The

men will cheer ____ the boys will shout, The lad - ies they ____ will
lau - rel wreath is read - y now To place up - on ____ his

all turn out, And we'll all feel gay When John-ny comes march-ing home. ____
loy - al brow, And we'll all feel gay When John-ny comes march-ing home. ____

"Greensleeves"

"Greensleeves" is a traditional English folk song; though its date of composition is unknown, it is first mentioned in print in 1580. The music originally accompanied a ballad about a woman, referred to as Lady Greensleeves, who discourteously rejects a suitor. The music has also been used to set numerous other texts, including the well-known Christmas carol "What Child Is This?" Excerpts from two arrangements for solo guitar are shown here.

Arranged by John Duarte

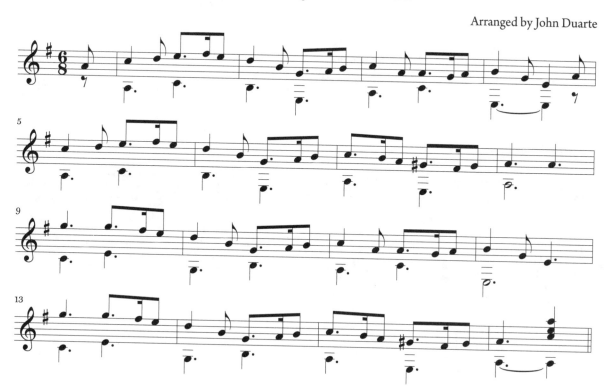

Arranged by Norbert Kraft

Don Henley, Glenn Frey, and Randy Meisner
"Take It to the Limit"

Don Henley, Glenn Frey, and Randy Meisner were members of the Eagles, one of the first bands to combine rock with country music in the early 1970s. "Take it to the Limit" is an ideal example of their style, since it was also recorded by country artists, such as Willie Nelson and Waylon Jennings. Frey and Henley (guitar and drums, respectively) first met while playing backup for singer Linda Ronstadt. After Randy Meisner (bass) and Bernie Leadon (guitar) joined, the Eagles recorded their first album in 1972. Their second album, *Desperado*, was a "concept album" about the American Old West. Other famous songs by the Eagles include "Take It Easy," "Best of My Love," "One of These Nights," and "Hotel California."

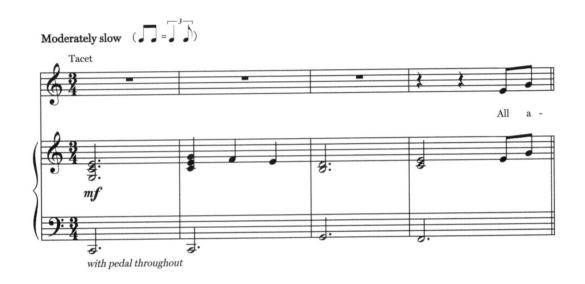

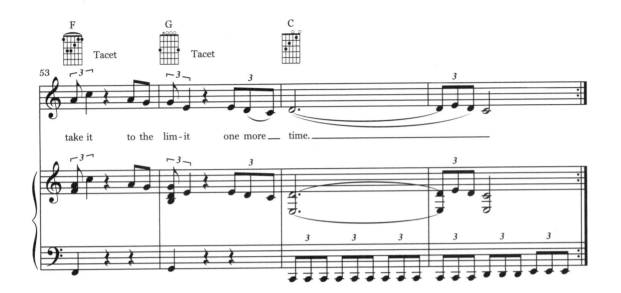

take it to the lim-it one more time.

"Home on the Range"

This song, from the 1870s, is the official state song of Kansas. Its lyrics have appeared in several forms by different authors; the original, by Brewster Higley ("The Western Home"), was published in 1873, but the most familiar lyrics today are those written by John A. Lomax in 1910. The melody was composed by Daniel E. Kelly, an amateur musician who played violin with a family band. The song has become a folk anthem of the American West and has appeared in many plays and movies, including "Where the Buffalo Roam" (performed by Neil Young, 1980) and "The Messenger" (performed by Willie Nelson, 2009).

2. How often at night when the heavens are bright
   With the lights from the glittering stars;
   Have I stood there amazed and asked as I gazed
   If their glory exceeds that of ours.
   Chorus

3. Oh, give me a land where the bright diamond sand
   Flows leisurely down the stream;
   Where the graceful, white swan goes gliding along,
   Like a maid in a heavenly dream.
   Chorus

James Horner, Barry Mann, and Cynthia Weil

"Somewhere Out There," from *An American Tail*

This song was featured in the 1986 Steven Spielberg–produced animated film *An American Tail*, a story of Russian immigrant mice and their adventures traveling to the United States, where they believe there are no cats. "Somewhere Out There" is sung by characters Fievel and Tanya Mousekewitz, who are separated and reunited during the movie. It was also recorded in a pop version that was played over the closing credits. This latter version, sung by Linda Ronstadt and James Ingram, became a hit single that eventually peaked at number two on the Billboard charts.

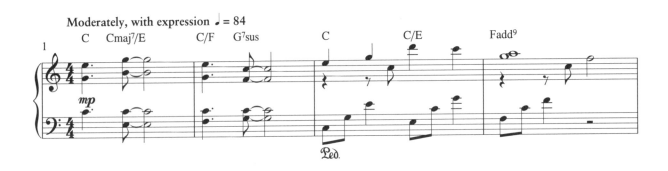

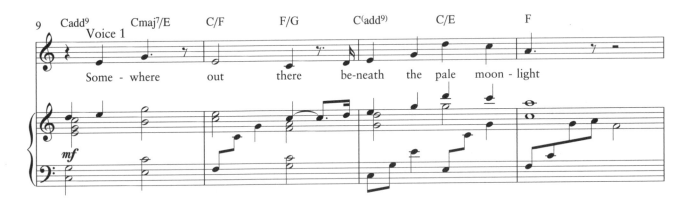

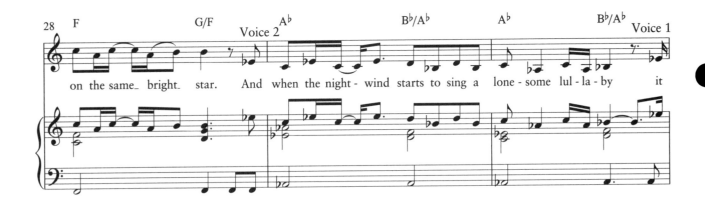

on the same_ bright_ star. And when the night - wind starts to sing a lone - some lul - la - by it

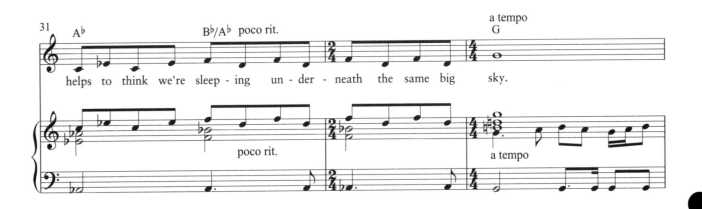

helps to think we're sleep - ing un - der - neath the same big sky.

Some - where out there if love can see us through,

then we'll be to-geth - er some - where out there, out where dreams come

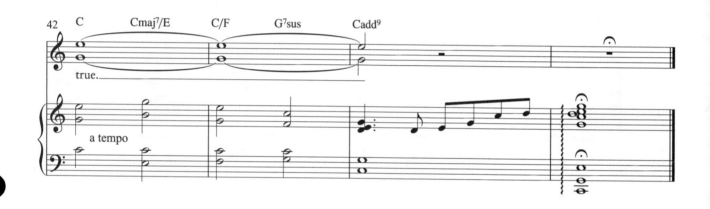

true.

Scott Joplin (1868–1917)

"Solace"

"Solace," published in 1909, is not a typical rag, though it does make use of the syncopation that characterizes ragtime. It is sometimes listed with the subtitle "A Mexican Serenade," and it bears some resemblance to the tango. Like other Joplin compositions, "Solace" was made famous by its inclusion in the 1973 film *The Sting,* starring Paul Newman and Robert Redford.

From *Scott Joplin: Complete Piano Rags.* New York: Dover Publications Inc.

Jonathan Larson (1960–1996)

"Seasons of Love," from *Rent*, excerpt

This song opens Act II of the rock opera *Rent*, written by Jonathan Larson and collaborators and based on the opera *La bohème* by Giacomo Puccini (which premiered a century earlier). Tragically, Larson died the night before his musical's off-Broadway opening in 1996. The show went on to a long and successful run on Broadway, winning a Tony Award and a Pulitzer Prize. It deals with poverty among artists in New York City's East Village, as well as the scourge of HIV/AIDS. The song's "five hundred twenty-five thousand six hundred minutes" is the number of minutes in a (non-leap) year. "Seasons of Love" was sung (with different lyrics) on Steve Carell's second-to-last episode playing Michael Scott on the television show *The Office*.

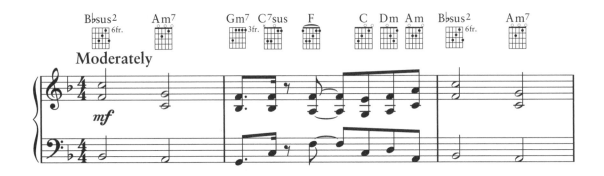

five hun-dred twen-ty-five thou-sand mo-ments so___ dear.___

Five hun-dred twen-ty-five thou-sand six hun-dred min - utes.

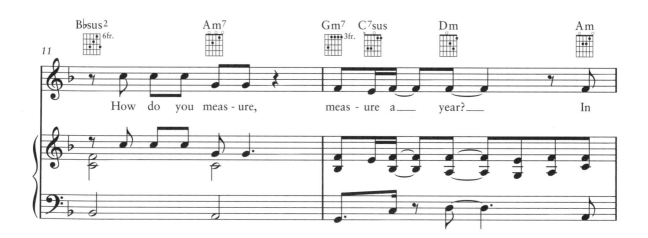

How do you meas-ure, meas-ure a___ year?___ In

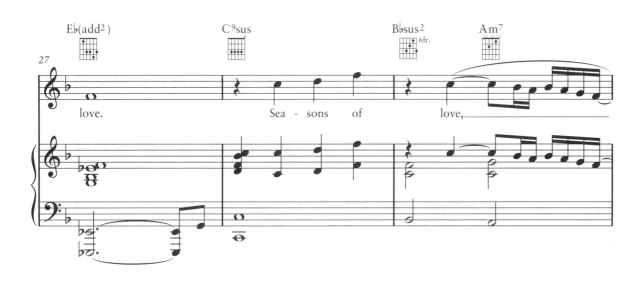

Wolfgang Amadeus Mozart (1756–1781)

String Quartet in D Minor, K. 421, third movement

This quartet, composed in 1783, is part of a set of six quartets that Mozart published together and dedicated to Haydn. During Mozart's lifetime, Haydn's quartets were widely admired; in his "Haydn Quartets," Mozart takes inspiration from the older composer.

From *Wolfgang Amadeus Mozart: Complete String Quartets*. New York: Dover Publications Inc.

Menuetto D.C.

Wolfgang Amadeus Mozart

*Variations on "Ah, vous dirai-je Maman," * excerpts

Mozart composed this theme and variations early in the 1780s. The theme is a French folk song, "Ah, vous dirai-je Maman," the same tune as "Twinkle, Twinkle, Little Star." Because this tune is so familiar, it makes this variation set an ideal vehicle for studying variation technique.

From *Mozart Masterpieces for Solo Piano.* New York: Dover Publications Inc.

"My Country, 'Tis of Thee" (America)

This tune, setting different texts, has been the national anthem of Britain, Germany, Denmark, and Prussia. In 1831, Samuel Francis Smith was given a score of the German version by American hymnist Lowell Mason, who asked for a translation. Instead, Smith was inspired to write new lyrics, which have become beloved as an American patriotic song.

1. My coun - try, 'tis of thee, Sweet land of lib - er - ty,
2. My na - tive coun - try, thee, Land of the no - ble free,

Of thee I sing; Land where my fa - thers died, Land of the
Thy name I love; I love thy rocks and rills, Thy woods and

pil - grims' pride, From ev - ery moun - tain - side Let free - dom ring.
tem - pled hills; My heart with rap - ture thrills Like that a - bove.

John Newton (1725–1807)

"Amazing Grace"

John Newton, composer of and collaborator on hundreds of Christian hymns, is most famous for his lyrics to "Amazing Grace." Newton's words have been sung to various melodies over the years, but in the early nineteenth century they were joined to the tune shown here, *New Britain*. Newton was an ordained minister of the Church of England for the last forty years of his life. He served in London and Olney, where he and collaborator William Cowper published *Olney Hymns*, which includes the text of "Amazing Grace," in 1779. Newton spent his younger years as the captain of an English slave ship and converted during a storm at sea. "Amazing Grace" is thought to be autobiographical; phrases like "a wretch like me" refer to his days as slave trader.

Through many dangers, toils, and snares,
I have already come;
'Twas grace has brought me safe thus far,
And grace will lead me home.

The Lord has promised good to me.
His word my hope secures;
He will my shield and portion be
As long as life endures.

Joel Phillips (b. 1958)

"Blues for Norton"
Lead Sheet

Joel Phillips, one of the authors of this text, composed "Blues for Norton" on June 6, 2006—6-6-06. Although Christians often view the number 666 negatively, Kabbalistic Jews see it as the number of creation and physical perfection of the world (according to Genesis, the world was created in six days). "Norton" has six letters, so Philips's music is based on a six-note riff stated in each of six phrases. Ideally the work would be performed by a sextet! The smaller notes in measures 13–22 show how a second solo instrument can interact with the first in a call-and-response texture.

Joel Phillips
"Blues for Norton"
Full score

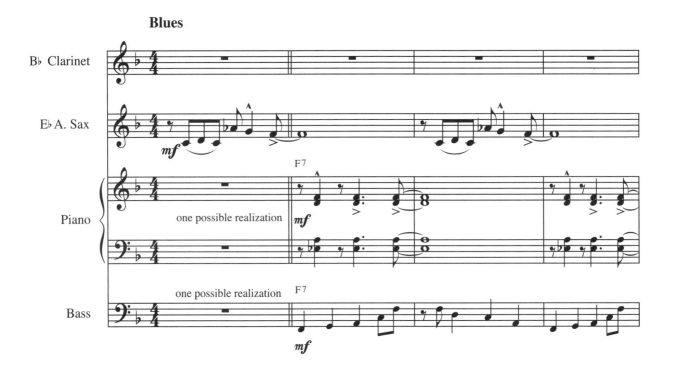

William "Smokey" Robinson, Jr. (b. 1940)

"You've Really Got a Hold on Me"

Smokey Robinson was born in Detroit in 1940 and founded the Miracles, one of the first Motown groups managed by Berry Gordy, Jr. "You've Really Got a Hold on Me" was recorded by the Miracles in 1962 and was one of their top songs. It was inducted into the rhythm and blues Hall of Fame in 1998. Other hits by the Miracles include "Shop Around," "I Second that Emotion," and "The Tears of a Clown." Many other artists have covered "You've Really Got a Hold on Me," including the Beatles, the Supremes, the Temptations, and more recently Cyndi Lauper, Rod Stewart, and Bobby McFerrin. The smaller notes (for example in mm. 13–18) indicate interaction between the soloist and back-up singers in a call-and-response texture.

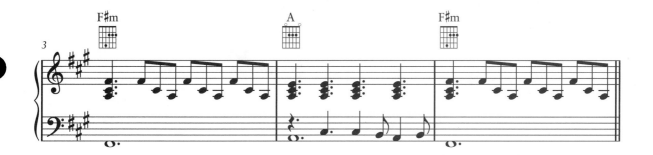

I don't___ like you,___ but I___ love you;
I don't___ want you,___ but I___ need you;
I wan - na leave you,___ don't wan - na stay here;

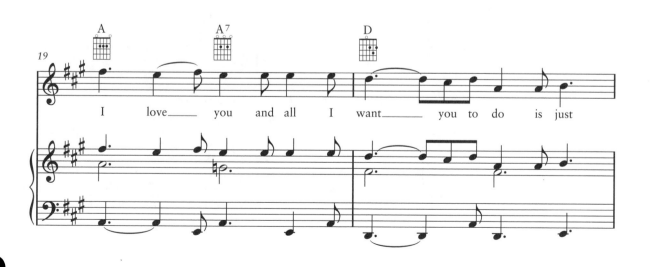

Richard Rodgers and Lorenz Hart

"My Funny Valentine," from *Babes in Arms*

Richard Rodgers (composer) and Lorenz Hart (lyricist) wrote over 500 songs together, primarily in the 1920s and 1930s. Among their most famous songs are "My Funny Valentine" (1937) and "Blue Moon" (1934), both of which have been recorded by countless artists. "My Funny Valentine" comes from the 1937 musical, *Babes in Arms*, which tells the story of young people putting on a show—a musical within a musical. Other famous songs from this show include "The Lady Is a Tramp" and "Johnny One Note." In 1939, the musical was made into a film starring Judy Garland and Mickey Rooney, and directed by Busby Berkeley.

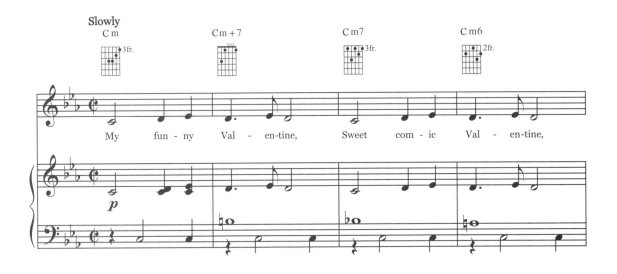

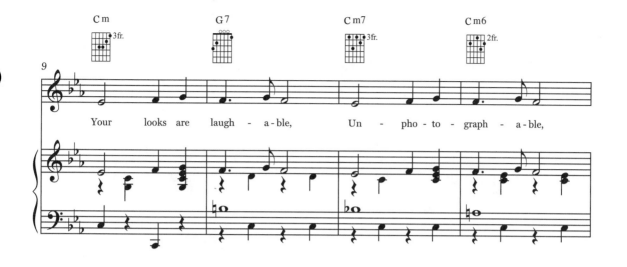

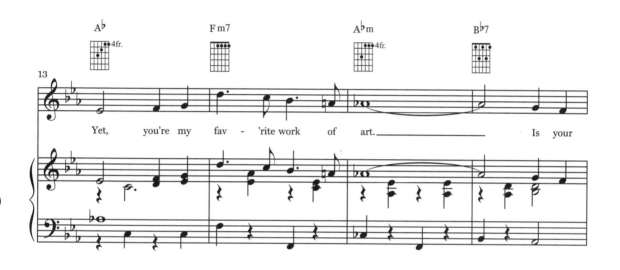

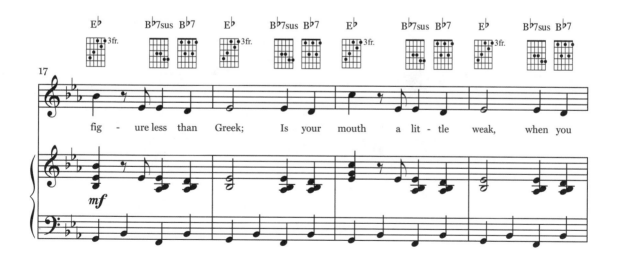

Each day is Val - en-tine's day. _____

Franz Schubert (1797–1828)

Waltz in B minor, Op. 18, No. 6

The waltz is a German dance in triple meter that enjoyed great popularity in the nineteenth century. This one belongs to a set of dance pieces Schubert composed in 1815. At parties, Schubert frequently improvised short piano waltzes, like this one, for dancing.

From *Franz Schubert: Dances for Solo Piano*. New York: Dover Publications Inc.

"Simple Gifts"

The tune "Simple Gifts" was written in 1848 by Elder Joseph Brackett, Jr., a member of the American Shaker religious order. While often considered a hymn, it was originally intended for dancing, as its lyrics suggest: "to turn, turn will be our delight, 'till by turning, turning we come round right." "Simple Gifts" has been arranged by many artists, including folk singer Judy Collins and composer Aaron Copland for the ballet *Appalachian Spring*, the source of one version that appears here. Even more recently, the tune was featured in a work titled "Air and Simple Gifts," composed by John Williams for the 2009 inauguration of President Barack Obama.

Original Version

Adapted from Aaron Copland, *Appalachian Spring*
(clarinet in B♭, sounds one step lower than written)

Meredith Willson (1902–1984)

"Till There Was You," from *The Music Man*

This song comes from Willson's musical *The Music Man*, which opened on Broadway in 1957.
In writing both the words and music, Willson drew on his Iowa childhood to tell the story of
a con man, Harold Hill, who arrives in the fictitious town of River City, Iowa, to start a band,
or so he claims (in reality he plans to swindle the town out of money for uniforms and instruments). He instead falls in love with the town's librarian, Marian, who sings this song. The song
was included in film versions of the musical in 1962 and 2003. The Beatles recorded a version
of it in 1963.

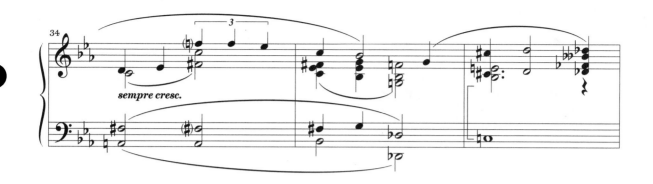

Appendix 1

Try It Answers

Chapter 1

TRY IT #1

(a) C   (b) E   (c) G   (d) E   (e) D   (f) C   (g) E   (h) D   (i) B   (j) E   (k) A
(l) E   (m) F   (n) B   (o) D

TRY IT #2

(a) (1) B   (2) C   (3) F   (4) G   (5) D   (6) A   (7) D   (8) F   (9) G   (10) E
(11) C   (12) E

(b)

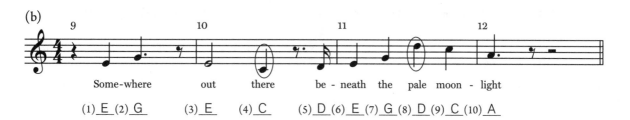

Some-where out there be - neath the pale moon - light

(1) E (2) G   (3) E   (4) C   (5) D (6) E (7) G (8) D (9) C (10) A

TRY IT #3

(a) (1) F   (2) G   (3) D   (4) B   (5) F   (6) A   (7) C   (8) G   (9) B   (10) E
(11) A   (12) C

(b)

(1) F   (2) G   (3) A   (4) C   (5) F (6) D   (7) C   (8) A

TRY IT #4

(a) (1) B3   (2) C6   (3) D4   (4) B5   (5) F3   (6) C4   (7) E6   (8) A5   (9) A3   (10) D6

(b) (1) G3   (2) A2   (3) D4   (4) E2   (5) F4   (6) E3   (7) C2   (8) B3   (9) F2   (10) C3

TRY IT #5

(a) (1) G3   (2) F3   (3) G1   (4) C2   (5) F1

Chapter 2

TRY IT #1

(a) (1) F♯　(2) C　　(3) B♭　　(4) F　　(5) C♯　　(6) C♭　　(7) G♯　　(8) D♯

(b)

　　　(1) D♯　　E♭　　(2) F♭　　E　　(3) C♯　　D♭　　(4) F♯　　G♭

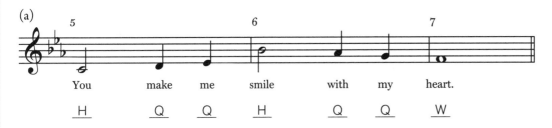

　　　(5) D♭　　C♯　　(6) G♭♭　　F　　(7) A⤫　　B　　(8) D♯　　E♭

TRY IT #2

(a) (1) G♯ or A♭　(2) C♯ or B♯　(3) B♭ or A♯　(4) F or E♯　(5) D♯ or E♭　(6) G♯　(7) B♭　(8) E　(9) D♯　(10) A♭

(b) (1) H　　(2) H　　(3) W　　(4) W　　(5) H　　(6) W　　(7) N　　(8) N　　(9) W　　(10) H
(11) H　　(12) H　　(13) W　　(14) H

(c) H, W, H, W, H

Chapter 3

TRY IT #1

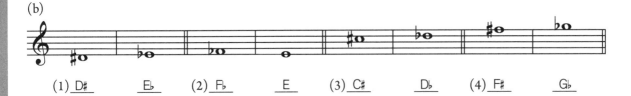

TRY IT #2

(a)

　　　You　　make　　me　　smile　　with　　my　　heart.
　　　H　　　Q　　　Q　　　H　　　Q　　　Q　　　W

(b)

　　some-one's　say-ing　a　prayer_____　　that we'll　find　one a - noth-er_____
　　Q　　Q　　E　E　　　S　　　　E　H　　Q　E　E　E　Q　E

TRY IT #3

Meter signature	Beats per measure	Beat unit	Beat division
$\frac{3}{8}$	3	♪	♬
$\frac{2}{2}$	2	𝅗𝅥	♩ ♩
$\frac{4}{8}$	4	♪	♬
$\frac{3}{2}$	3	𝅗𝅥	♩ ♩
$\frac{3}{4}$	3	♩	♫

TRY IT #4

(a)

(b)

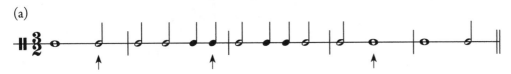

(c)

TRY IT #5

(a)

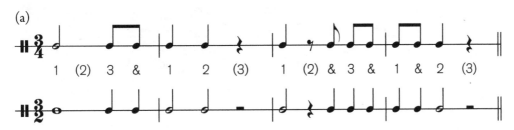

1　(2)　3　&　1　2　(3)　1　(2)　&　3　&　1　&　2　(3)

(b)

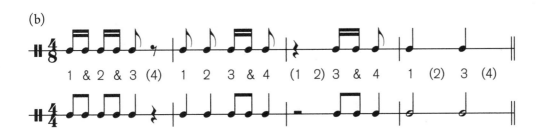

1　&　2　&　3　(4)　1　2　3　&　4　(1)　2）3　&　4　1　(2)　3　(4)

Chapter 4

TRY IT #1

(a)

1 (2) & 3 & (1) 2 3 a 1 & (2) & 3 1 (2) 3)

(b)

1 e & a (2) & 1 & (2) e & a 1 a 2 & (1) & 2 a 1 (2)

(c)

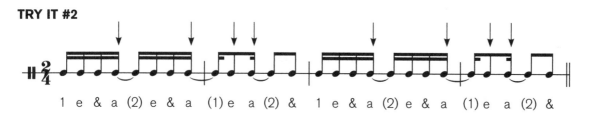

1 (2) (3) & 4 & 1 a (2) & 3 (4) 1 e & a 2 a 3 & (4) & 1 (2 3 4)

TRY IT #2

1 e & a (2) e & a (1) e a (2) & 1 e & a (2) e & a (1) e a (2) &

TRY IT #3

Some-where out __ there __ some-one's say-ing a prayer _____ that

we'll find one a - noth - er _____ in that big some - where out __ there.

Chapter 5

TRY IT #1

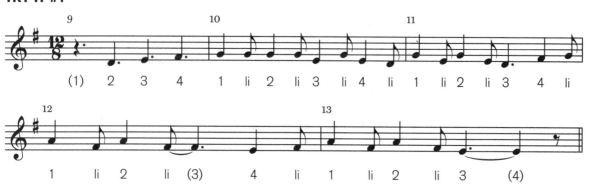

(1) 2 3 4 1 li 2 li 3 li 4 li 1 li 2 li 3 4 li

1 li 2 li (3) 4 li 1 li 2 li 3 (4)

TRY IT #2

(a)

(b)

(c)

(d)

Chapter 6

TRY IT #1

(a) (1)

(2)

(b) (1)

(2)

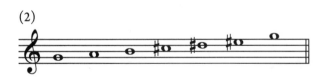

TRY IT #2

(a)　　　　　　　　　　　　　(b)

(c)　　　　　　　　　　　　　(d)

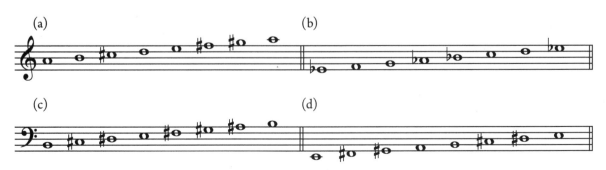

TRY IT #3

(a)

(b)

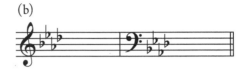

(c)

(d)

(e)

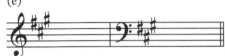

(f)

TRY IT #4

(a) B   (b) D♭   (c) A♭   (d) D   (e) A   (f) B♭   (g) F♯   (h) E   (i) G♭   (j) F

TRY IT #5

- Key signature suggests: A♭ major
- First six scale degrees: $\hat{5}$–$\hat{5}$–$\hat{1}$–$\hat{1}$–$\hat{2}$–$\hat{3}$
- Last six scale degrees: $\hat{1}$–$\hat{1}$–$\hat{2}$–$\hat{1}$–$\hat{7}$–$\hat{1}$
- Key of piece: A♭ major

Chapter 7

TRY IT #1

(a) F major   F natural minor

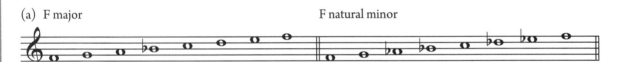

(b) B major   B natural minor

(c) A major   A natural minor

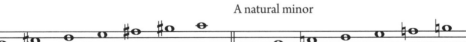

TRY IT #2

(a) C natural minor   C harmonic minor

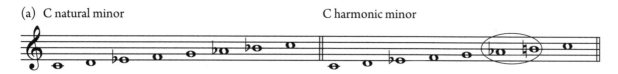

(b) F# natural minor   F# harmonic minor

(c) G natural minor   G harmonic minor

(d) C# natural minor   C# harmonic minor

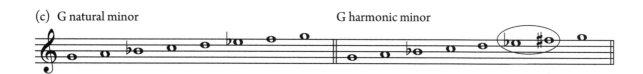

TRY IT #3

(a) B melodic minor

(b) F melodic minor

TRY IT #4

(a) C# minor	(b) F minor	(c) B minor	(d) C minor	(e) G# minor	(f) D minor
(g) G minor	(h) A minor	(i) Bb minor	(j) D# minor	(k) F# minor	(l) E minor

TRY IT #5

(a)

Relative major: A   F# harmonic minor scale

(b)

Relative major: G   E harmonic minor scale

(c)

Relative major: D   B melodic minor scale (ascending)

(d)

Relative major: D♭   B♭ melodic minor scale (ascending)

Chapter 8

TRY IT #1

(a) 3   (b) 7   (c) 8   (d) 2   (e) 5   (f) 3   (g) 7   (h) 4   (i) 3   (j) 6
(k) 7   (l) 2

TRY IT #2

(a) (1) P5   (2) M7   (3) M2   (4) P4   (5) M6   (6) PU   (7) M3   (8) m3   (9) P4   (10) m7
(11) m6   (12) M2   (13) P5   (14) PU

(b) (1)   (2)   (3)   (4)   (5)   (6)   (7)

(8)   (9)   (10)   (11)   (12)   (13)   (14)

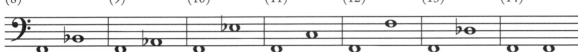

TRY IT #3

(a) m3   (b) m3   (c) M2   (d) P4   (e) M3   (f) P4   (g) M2   (h) P4   (i) P4   (j) m3
(k) m3   (l) m2   (m) M3   (n) P4   (o) M3   (p) m2   (q) m3   (r) P4   (s) M2   (t) P4

TRY IT #4

(a) (1) m3, M6 (2) m7, M2 (3) P5, P4 (4) P5, P4 (5) M6, m3 (6) M3, m6

(b) (1)   (2)   (3)   (4)   (5)   (6)   (7)   (8)   (9)   (10)

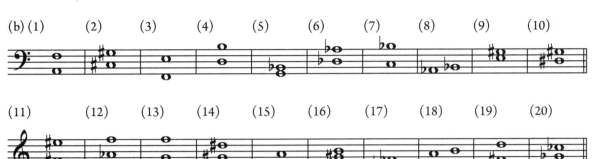

(11)   (12)   (13)   (14)   (15)   (16)   (17)   (18)   (19)   (20)

TRY IT #5

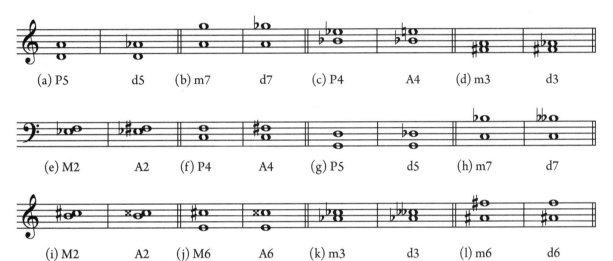

(a) P5   d5   (b) m7   d7   (c) P4   A4   (d) m3   d3

(e) M2   A2   (f) P4   A4   (g) P5   d5   (h) m7   d7

(i) M2   A2   (j) M6   A6   (k) m3   d3   (l) m6   d6

TRY IT #6

Compound: m10   m10   P11   P12
Simple: m3   m3   P4   P5

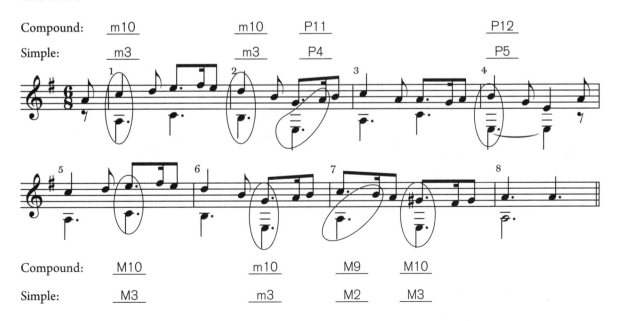

Compound: M10   m10   M9   M10
Simple: M3   m3   M2   M3

Chapter 9

TRY IT #1

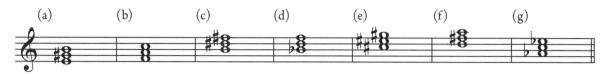

TRY IT #2

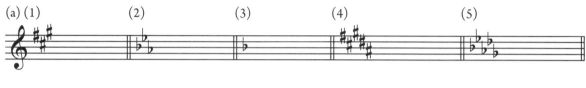

TRY IT #3

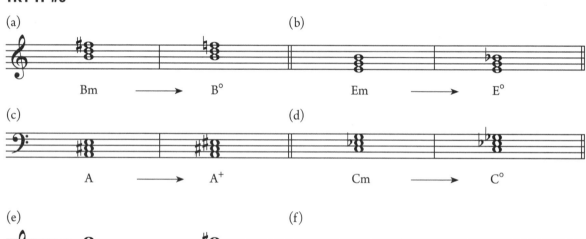

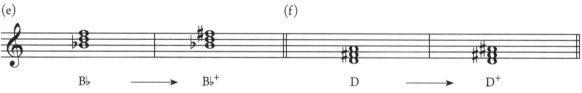

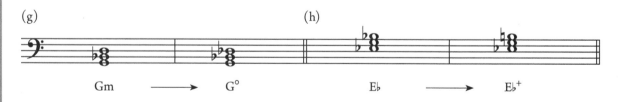

TRY IT #4

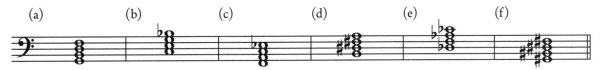

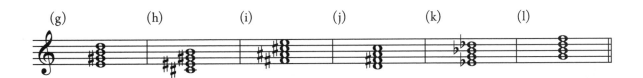

Chapter 10

TRY IT #1

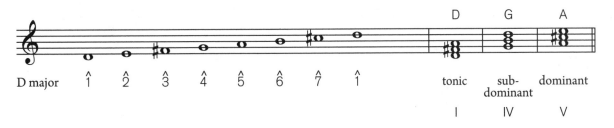

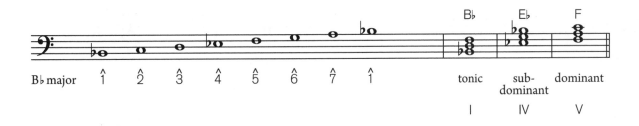

TRY IT #2

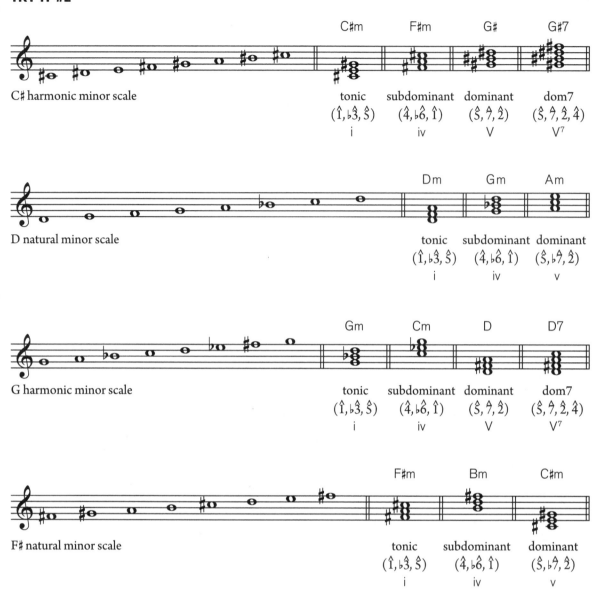

TRY IT #3

(a) Key: F, cadence: IAC   (b) Key: g, cadence: HC

Chapter 11

TRY IT #1

a a' b a'

TRY IT #2

a	**a'**	**b**	**a'**
mm. 29–36	mm. 37–44a	mm. 44b–52a	mm. 52b–60

TRY IT #3

(a) G

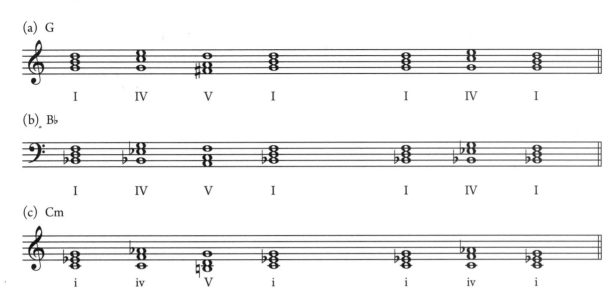

(b) Bb

(c) Cm

TRY IT #4

One possible answer:

Chapter 12

TRY IT #1

(a)

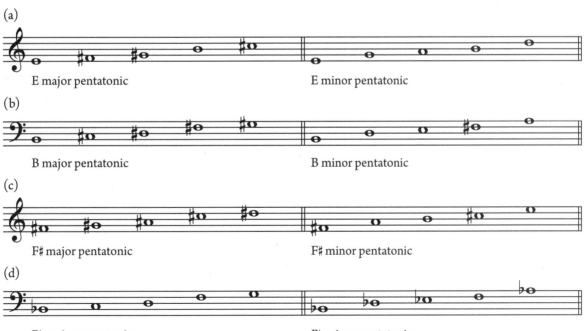

E major pentatonic   E minor pentatonic

(b)

B major pentatonic   B minor pentatonic

(c)

F♯ major pentatonic   F♯ minor pentatonic

(d)

B♭ major pentatonic   B♭ minor pentatonic

TRY IT #2

(a)

(b)

(c)

TRY IT #3

(a)

MM7   Mm7   mm7   ⌀7   °7

Mm7   ⌀7   MM7   °7   mm7

(b)

E♭maj7   G♯°7   F♯min7   D♭7   Bmin7(♭5)   A♭maj7   G⌀7   B♭min7

Appendix 2

Reading Review Answers

Chapter 1

(1) h	(2) c	(3) i	(4) f	(5) q	(6) g	(7) d	(8) a
(9) o	(10) p	(11) r	(12) j	(13) l	(14) n	(15) e	(16) m
(17) k	(18) b						

Chapter 2

(1) e	(2) b	(3) h	(4) c	(5) l	(6) g	(7) f	(8) a
(9) j	(10) i	(11) k	(12) d				

Chapter 3

(1) g	(2) i	(3) c	(4) e	(5) s	(6) j	(7) a	(8) k
(9) q	(10) m	(11) h	(12) n	(13) d	(14) f	(15) r	(16) p
(17) o	(18) b	(19) l					

Chapter 4

(1) c	(2) a	(3) b	(4) f	(5) h	(6) e	(7) i	(8) d
(9) g							

Chapter 5

(1) f	(2) j	(3) a	(4) i	(5) l	(6) k	(7) m	(8) n
(9) p	(10) e	(11) d	(12) g	(13) h	(14) o	(15) b	(16) c

Chapter 6

(1) d	(2) g	(3) i	(4) h	(5) l	(6) e	(7) o	(8) c
(9) f	(10) n	(11) m	(12) a	(13) j	(14) b	(15) k	

Chapter 7

(1) g	(2) a	(3) b	(4) j	(5) c	(6) h	(7) f	(8) e
(9) d	(10) i						

Chapter 8

(1) e (2) i (3) a (4) j (5) o (6) v (7) f
(8) w (9) h (10) k (11) c (12) m (13) t (14) b
(15) y (16) g (17) r (18) s (19) l (20) u (21) x
(22) p (23) q (24) n (25) d

Chapter 9

(1) l (2) g (3) i (4) d (5) b (6) o (7) r (8) t
(9) k (10) v (11) c (12) h (13) p (14) e (15) q (16) n
(17) f (18) m (19) a (20) j (21) s (22) u

Chapter 10

(1) e (2) d (3) k (4) c (5) i (6) n (7) m (8) f
(9) j (10) g (11) l (12) a (13) h (14) b

Chapter 11

(1) f (2) h (3) j (4) b (5) i (6) d (7) a (8) c
(9) g (10) e

Chapter 12

(1) k (2) f (3) j (4) l (5) d (6) b (7) c (8) i
(9) e (10) h (11) a (12) g

Appendix 3
Glossary

12-bar blues: See *blues progression.*
32-bar song form: See *quaternary song form.*

A

a a b a: See *quaternary song form.*

accent: Stress given to a note or some other musical element that brings it to the listener's attention. Accents can be created by playing louder or softer, using a different timbre or articulation, speeding up or slowing down, or slightly changing rhythmic durations.

accidental: A symbol that appears before a note to raise or lower its pitch chromatically, without changing its letter name. See also *sharp, flat, natural, double sharp,* and *double flat.*

accompaniment: Music played by keyboard, guitar, or other instruments providing harmonies to support a sung or played melody.

added-sixth chord: A root-position triad with an extra pitch a major sixth above the bass note.

Alberti bass: An accompaniment pattern popular in the time of Mozart, in which a three-part chord in the alto, tenor, and bass is arpeggiated with the pattern bass-alto-tenor-alto while the soprano part performs the melody.

alto: The second-highest voice in four-part (SATB) writing, notated in the treble clef, usually directly below the soprano; usually sung by women with lower voices.

alto clef: A C-clef positioned on a staff so that the middle line indicates middle C (C4).

anacrusis: A beat that precedes a downbeat, sometimes shown in an incomplete measure (the rest of the measure is notated at the end of the section). Also called an upbeat or pickup.

antecedent phrase: The first phrase of a period, ending with an inconclusive cadence (usually a half cadence).

arpeggio: A chord played one pitch at a time.

articulation: How a pitch is sounded, including various ways of bowing or plucking stringed instruments and tonguing wind and brass instruments.

ascending contour: A musical line that generally goes up, from lower pitches to higher ones.

asymmetrical meter: Meter with beat units of unequal duration. These irregular beat lengths are typically (though not always) created by five or seven beat divisions grouped into unequal lengths such as 2 + 3 or 2 + 3 + 2.

augmented interval: An interval one chromatic half step larger than a major or perfect interval.

augmented second: The distance between $\flat\hat{6}$ and $\hat{7}$ in the harmonic minor scale; equivalent to three half steps.

augmented triad: A triad that has major thirds between its root and third and between its third and fifth. The interval between its root and fifth is an augmented fifth.

authentic cadence: A conclusive cadence in which $V^{(7)}$ progresses to I.

B

bar: See *measure.*

bar line: A vertical line, extending from the top of the staff to the bottom, that indicates the end of a measure.

basic phrase: A phrase that consists of an opening tonic area (T), an optional predominant area (P), a dominant area (D), and tonic closure (T, a cadence on I).

bass: The lowest voice in four-part (SATB) writing, notated in the bass clef; usually sung by men with lower voices.

bass clef: Clef positioned on a staff to indicate F; its two dots surround the F3 line. (Also known as the F-clef.)

beam: A line that connects two or more note stems within a beat unit.

beat: The primary pulse in musical meter. Normally represents an even and regular division of musical time.

beat division: The secondary pulse in musical meter; beats may be divided into two parts (simple meter) or three parts (compound meter).

beat subdivision: A further division of the beat division into two parts; for example, for a quarter note in simple meter, the beat divides into two eighths and subdivides into four sixteenths.

beat unit: The duration assigned to the basic pulse.

blue note: One of three pitches (of the blues scale) that appear in jazz and popular music for expressive effect: $\flat\hat{3}, \sharp\hat{4}$ (or $\flat\hat{5}$), and $\flat\hat{7}$.

blues progression: A chord progression (normally twelve bars long) typical of the blues: four measures of I, two measures each of IV and I, one measure each of V, IV, and I, finishing with I (or V for a turnaround). All harmonies may be either triads or seventh chords.

blues scale: The minor pentatonic scale plus $\sharp\hat{4}/\flat\hat{5}$. Since the blues scale includes $\flat\hat{3}$ and $\flat\hat{7}$, it blurs the distinction between major and minor when it is used over a major-key blues progression.

bridge: (1) The contrasting **b** section in an **a a b a** 32-bar song form. (2) A section in a popular song that contrasts with the verse and chorus, and enters more than halfway through the song to prepare for their return.

C

C-clef: A moveable clef that identifies which line on a staff designates middle C (C4) by the point at which its two curved lines join together in the middle. Common C-clefs include the alto and tenor clefs.

cadence: The end of a phrase, where harmonic, melodic, and rhythmic features mark the close of a complete musical thought. See also *authentic cadence, half cadence, deceptive cadence, plagal cadence.*

change in mode: Transforming a melody or harmony from major to minor, or the reverse, by altering the quality of $\hat{3}$, $\hat{6}$, and $\hat{7}$.

changes: Jazz term for harmonic progressions; short for chord changes.

changing meter: Meter that changes from measure to measure.

chord: Pitches sounded at the same time. See also *triad, seventh chord.*

chord extension: Pitches added to triads or seventh chords (e.g., ninths, elevenths).

chord members: The pitches that make up a chord.

chromatic: Pitches from outside a diatonic (major or natural minor) scale. The chromatic collection consists of all twelve pitches within an octave.

chromatic half step: A semitone spelling that uses the same letter name for both pitches (e.g., D and D$\sharp$).

chromatic scale: A scale consisting of all twelve pitches within the octave; the distance between each note and the next is a half step.

circle of fifths: A circular diagram representing the relationship between keys; clockwise motion around the circle shifts a key up by a P5 and removes a flat or adds a sharp; counterclockwise motion shifts a key down by a P5 and removes a sharp or adds a flat.

clef: A symbol on the far left of a staff that shows which pitch (and octave) is represented by each line and space. See also *treble clef, bass clef, C-clef, alto clef, tenor clef.*

climax: The musical high point of a melody or piece.

combo: A small instrumental ensemble for playing jazz or popular music, usually consisting of (at least) a solo instrument, keyboard, and drum set.

compound duple: Meter with 2 beats in a measure, each beat divided into 3 (e.g., $\frac{6}{8}$ or $\frac{6}{4}$).

compound interval: An interval larger than an octave.

compound meter: Meter where the beat divides into threes and subdivides into sixes. The top number of compound meter signatures is 6, 9, or 12 (e.g., $\frac{9}{4}$ or $\frac{6}{8}$).

compound quadruple: Meter with 4 beats in a measure, each beat divided into 3 (e.g., $\frac{12}{8}$ or $\frac{12}{4}$).

compound triple: Meter with 3 beats in a measure, each beat divided into 3 (e.g., $\frac{9}{8}$ or $\frac{9}{4}$).

conclusive cadence: A relatively strong cadence that can end a section or piece.

conducting pattern: A specific pattern, one for each meter, that conductors outline by moving their arms in the air to help keep performers playing together in time.

conjunct motion: Melodic motion that is primarily by step, making a smooth line.

consequent phrase: The second phrase of a period, ending with a strong harmonic conclusion, usually an authentic cadence.

consonance: A relative term based on acoustic properties of sound and on the norms of compositional practice. A consonant interval—unison, third, fifth, sixth, or octave—is considered pleasing to hear. A fourth is considered a consonance when written melodically but a dissonance when written harmonically.

consonance, imperfect: The intervals of major and minor thirds and sixths.

consonance, perfect: The intervals of a unison, fourth, fifth, and octave.

contour: The shape of a melody; its motion up and down. Common contours include ascending, descending, arch, V-shape, and wave.

contrary motion: Two melodic lines or voices moving in opposite directions.

contrasting period: A period in which the two phrases do not share the same initial melodic material.

crescendo: An indication to increase the dynamic level.

D

deceptive cadence (DC): The cadence $V^{(7)}$–vi in major or $V^{(7)}$–VI in minor.

deceptive resolution: Motion from V^(7) to vi in major or V^(7) to VI in minor that does not end a phrase.

decrescendo: See *diminuendo*.

descending contour: A melodic line that generally goes down, from higher pitches to lower ones.

diatonic half step: A semitone spelling that uses different letter names for the two pitches (e.g., D and E♭).

diatonic scale: Scales made by rotating the step pattern W–W–H–W–W–W–H; the major and natural minor scales, and the modes (Dorian, Phrygian, Lydian, Mixolydian, and Locrian) are all diatonic scales.

diminished interval: An interval one half step smaller than a minor or perfect interval.

diminished seventh chord: A seventh chord consisting of a diminished triad with a diminished seventh above its root.

diminished triad: A triad that has minor thirds between its root and third and between its third and fifth. The interval between its root and fifth is a diminished fifth.

diminuendo: An indication to decrease the dynamic level; same as *decrescendo*.

disjunct motion: Melodic motion primarily by skip or leap that does not make a smooth line.

dissonance: A relative term based on acoustic properties of sound and on the norms of compositional practice. A dissonant interval—second, fourth (in common-practice harmony), tritone, seventh, or any augmented or diminished interval—is considered unpleasant or jarring to hear.

division: See *beat division*.

dominant: (1) Scale degree $\hat{5}$; (2) the triad built on $\hat{5}$.

dominant seventh chord: A seventh chord consisting of a major triad with a minor seventh above its root.

dot: Rhythmic notation that adds half of a note's own value to its duration (e.g., the duration of a dotted half note equals a half note plus a quarter note).

double flat: An accidental (♭♭) that lowers a pitch two half steps without changing its letter name.

double sharp: An accidental (×) that raises a pitch two half steps without changing its letter name.

doubling: (1) Reinforcing a melodic line by adding voices or instruments at the unison or octave. (2) A pitch of a triad or seventh chord that appears in two parts to make four parts in SATB writing.

downbeat: The first beat of a measure, which has the strongest accent or emphasis; named for the downward motion of the conductor's hand.

duple meter: Meter with two beats in each measure.

duplet: In compound meter, a division of the beat into two, instead of three, equal parts.

duration: The length of time represented by a note or rest.

dynamic level: The degree of loudness in performance. Extends from ***ppp*** (very soft) to ***fff*** (very loud).

E

eighth note: A stemmed black (filled) note head with one flag or beam (♪); equivalent to two sixteenth notes.

embellishing tone: Pitches that decorate or fill in between chord tones in a melodic line.

enharmonic: Different names for the same pitch (e.g., E♭ and D♯).

enharmonic equivalence: The idea that two or more possible names for a single pitch (e.g., C♯, D♭, B×) are musically the same.

extension: See *chord extension*.

F

fifth: Within a triad or seventh chord, the pitch located a fifth above the root.

figures: Arabic numerals used to represent chords as intervals above a bass note.

first inversion: A triad or seventh chord with its third in the bass.

flag: A short arc attached to the right side of a note stem, at the opposite end from the note head; each flag divides the duration of a note in half (e.g., a sixteenth note has two flags and is half of an eighth note, which has one flag).

flat: An accidental (♭) that lowers a pitch by one half step without changing its letter name.

form: A pattern of repeated, similar, and contrasting passages in a piece of music.

forte (*f*): A loud dynamic level. A louder dynamic level is ***ff*** (*fortissimo*); a softer dynamic level is ***mf*** (mezzo forte).

G

grand staff: Two staves, one in treble clef and one in bass clef, connected by a curly brace; typically used in piano music.

H

half cadence (HC): An inconclusive cadence on the dominant.

half-diminished seventh chord: A seventh chord consisting of a diminished triad with a minor seventh above its root.

half note: A stemmed white (hollow) notehead; its duration is equivalent to two quarter notes.

half rest: A silence represented by ▬ sitting on top of the third staff line; equal in duration to a half note.

half step: The distance between a pitch and the next closest pitch on the keyboard.

harmonic interval: The span between two pitches played simultaneously.

harmonic minor scale: See *minor scale*.

harmonic rhythm: The rate at which chords change (e.g., one chord per measure or one chord per beat).

head: In jazz or blues, the main musical idea played at the beginning of the piece; it recurs, alternating with sections of instrumental or vocal improvisation.

homophony: Texture in which all voices are vertically aligned to move together in the same (or nearly the same) rhythm.

I

imperfect authentic cadence (IAC): An authentic cadence weakened (1) by inverting V or (2) by the soprano ending on a scale degree other than $\hat{1}$.

inconclusive cadence: Ending that is used for the first phrase of a period or prior to the end of a section; any type of cadence other than a perfect authentic cadence.

interval: The distance between two pitches.

interval inversion: Transformation of an interval that results from displacing one pitch by an octave such that the interval size and quality change. When perfect intervals are inverted they remain perfect; major intervals become minor (and vice versa); augmented intervals become diminished (and vice versa). The size of an interval and its inversion sum to 9 (e.g., m2 becomes M7, P4 becomes P5, etc.).

interval quality: The difference between two intervals of the same size (e.g., third, fourth, fifth) that span a different number of semitones. Interval quality can be major, minor, perfect, diminished, or augmented.

intro: Music, usually instrumental, that introduces a popular song.

introduction: Music at the beginning of a piece that prepares for the entry of the main melody.

inverted chord: A chord with its third, fifth, or seventh (instead of the root) in the bass.

K

key: (1) Music in a major or minor key employs notes of the major or minor scale so that the first note is the primary scale degree around which all others relate hierarchically. Keys are named by the first scale degree and the type of scale used (e.g., G minor). (2) The levers on an instrument that can be depressed with a finger to make a pitch sound (e.g., piano keys).

key signature: A pattern of sharps or flats (or no sharps or flats) that appears immediately following the clef on a staff, showing which notes, in any octave, are to be sharped or flatted consistently throughout the piece. The key signature helps identify the key of the piece, but each signature is used for two keys—one major and one minor.

L

lead sheet: Performance score for jazz and popular music consisting of a melody and chord changes.

ledger line: Extra lines drawn through the stems and note heads to designate a musical pitch located above or below the staff.

letter name: The name for a particular pitch, A–G, that corresponds to its place on the staff or a musical instrument.

M

major interval: Seconds, thirds, sixths, and sevenths above $\hat{1}$ of a major scale.

major key: Music comprised of notes drawn from the major scale; the key is named by the first scale degree and type of scale (e.g., B major).

major pentachord: The first five notes of a major scale (e.g., C–D–E–F–G in C major).

major pentatonic: A five-note scale consisting of $\hat{1}$, $\hat{2}$, $\hat{3}$, $\hat{5}$, and $\hat{6}$ of a major scale.

major seventh chord: A major triad with a major seventh above its root.

major scale: A seven-note scale beginning *do* ($\hat{1}$)–*re* ($\hat{2}$)–*mi* ($\hat{3}$) with the pattern of whole and half steps W–W–H–W–W–W–H; it shares the same key signature as its relative minor.

major tetrachord: A series of four notes that form an ascending W–W–H pattern; building block of a major scale.

measure: A unit of grouped beats; beginning and ending with bar lines.

mediant: (1) Scale degree $\hat{3}$; (2) the triad built on $\hat{3}$.

melodic interval: The distance between two notes played one after another.

melodic minor scale: See *minor scale*.

melody: (1) A succession of pitches and rhythms in a single line; (2) the main musical idea, or "tune," in a piece of music.

melody and accompaniment: A musical texture with a melody in one part and accompanying chords in the other.

meter: The grouping and division of beats in regular, recurring patterns.

meter signature: A sign that appears at the beginning of a piece, after the clef and key signature: the upper number indicates the meter type and the lower number indicates which note gets the beat; also called a time signature.

metrical accent: An emphasis on a note resulting from its placement on a strong beat.

metronome: A mechanical device that clicks at an even rate, where the number of clicks per minute may be adjusted; used to establish a tempo for musicians to practice with a steady beat.

mezzo forte (*mf*), mezzo piano (*mp*): Medium dynamic levels between *piano* and *forte*; *mp* is louder than *p*, and *mf* is softer than *f*.

middle C: C4; the C located at the center of the piano keyboard.

minor interval: Thirds, sixths, and sevenths above $\hat{1}$ of a minor scale; seconds between $\hat{7}$ and $\hat{1}$ in a major, harmonic minor, or ascending melodic minor scale.

minor key: Music comprised of notes drawn from the minor scale; the key is named by the first scale degree and type of scale (e.g., B minor).

minor mode: Mode incorporating $\flat\hat{3}$, $\flat\hat{6}$, and $\flat\hat{7}$ (compared to the major mode), with a minor tonic triad.

minor pentachord: The first five notes of a minor scale (e.g., C–D–E♭–F–G in C minor).

minor pentatonic: A five-note scale consisting of $\hat{1}$, $\flat\hat{3}$, $\hat{4}$, $\hat{5}$, and $\flat\hat{7}$ of a minor scale.

minor scale: A seven-note scale beginning *do* ($\hat{1}$)–*re* ($\hat{2}$)–*me* ($\flat\hat{3}$) that occurs in three forms: natural, harmonic, and melodic minor. The natural minor scale is an ordered collection of pitches arranged according to the pattern of whole and half steps W–H–W–W–H–W–W; it shares the same key signature as its relative major. The harmonic minor scale has raised $\hat{7}$. The melodic minor has raised $\hat{6}$ and $\hat{7}$ ascending, but takes the natural minor form descending.

minor seventh chord: A minor triad with a minor seventh above its root.

modal scale degrees: The third, sixth, and seventh scale degrees, which are one half step lower in minor keys than in major.

modulation: A change of key, usually confirmed by a perfect authentic cadence.

monophony: A single unaccompanied line. May be performed by a single voice or instrument, or by a group playing in unison or octaves.

motive: The smallest recognizable musical idea. Motives may be characterized by their pitches, contour, and/or rhythm, but rarely include a cadence. Generally they are repeated (exactly or varied).

musical alphabet: The letters A, B, C, D, E, F, and G, which are used to name musical pitches.

N

natural: An accidental (♮) that cancels a sharp or flat.

natural minor scale: See *minor scale*.

neighbor tone: A melodic embellishment that decorates a pitch by moving a step above or below it, then returning to the original pitch.

ninth chord: A seventh chord with a ninth added above the bass.

note: The representation of a musical sound with a note head on the staff. The position of the note head indicates the pitch; whether the note head is black (filled) or white (hollow) and the presence of a stem, beam, or flag indicates the duration.

note head: A small oval used to notate a pitch on the staff. Hollow, or white, note heads normally represent a longer duration than black, or filled, note heads.

O

octave: (1) The distance of eight musical steps; the interval size 8. (2) The particular part of the musical range where a pitch sounds (e.g., C4, or middle C, is a C in a particular octave).

octave equivalence: The concept that pitches eight steps apart (sharing the same name) sound similar.

octave number: An Arabic number used with a pitch's letter name to indicate in which register that pitch sounds (e.g., C4 is the C in the fourth octave, or middle C)

offbeat: A weak beat or weak portion of a beat.

outro: In popular music, the concluding musical idea, after the last verse or chorus. May consist of a "repeat and fade" of music that has been heard before.

P

parallel keys: Major and minor keys sharing the same letter name, but with different pitches for $\hat{3}$, $\hat{6}$, and $\hat{7}$ (e.g., F major and F minor).

parallel major: The major key that has the same tonic as a given minor key (e.g., F minor's parallel major is F major). The parallel major raises the third, sixth, and seventh scale degrees of a minor key.

parallel minor: The minor key that has the tonic as a given major key (e.g., F major's parallel minor is F minor). The parallel minor lowers the third, sixth, and seventh scale degrees of a major key.

parallel motion: Two melodic lines or voices moving in the same direction by the same interval. Parallel fifths and octaves are not generally permitted in SATB writing, though parallel thirds and sixths are common.

parallel period: A period in which the two phrases begin with the same melodic material.

passing tone: A melodic embellishment that fills the space between chord members. Passing tones are approached and left by step in the same direction.

pentatonic scale: A five-note scale. See *major pentatonic* and *minor pentatonic*.

perfect authentic cadence (PAC): A strong conclusive cadence in which (1) root position $V^{(7)}$ progresses to root position I, and (2) the soprano moves from $\hat{2}$ or $\hat{7}$ to $\hat{1}$.

perfect interval: Unisons, fourths, fifths, and octaves above $\hat{1}$ in a major or minor scale.

period: A musical unit consisting of two phrases. The first phrase ends with an inconclusive cadence (usually a half cadence); the ending of the second answers it with a more conclusive cadence (usually a PAC).

phrase: A basic unit of musical thought, similar to a sentence in language. The typical phrase—like most sentences—has a beginning, a middle, and an end. A phrase must end with a cadence.

piano ($\boldsymbol{p}$): A soft dynamic level. A softer dynamic level is $\boldsymbol{pp}$ (*pianissimo*); a louder dynamic level is $\boldsymbol{mp}$ (*mezzo piano*).

pickup: See *anacrusis*.

pitch: A musical sound in a particular octave or register.

plagal cadence (PC): The cadence IV–I (iv–i in minor), sometimes called the "Amen cadence." Because the IV–I motion often follows a conclusive authentic cadence, some musicians view plagal cadences as an extension of the tonic harmony.

Q

quadruple meter: Meter with four beats in each measure.

quality: See *interval quality, triad quality*.

quarter note: A stemmed black (filled) note head ($\quarternote$); equivalent to two eighth notes.

quarter rest: A silence represented by $\quarterrest$; equal in duration to a quarter note.

quartet: A musical texture comprised of four voices or instruments.

quaternary song form: A song form consisting of four phrases, usually with an **a a b a** or **a b c b** design. Each phrase is generally eight bars long, though some folk songs may have four-measure phrases. In **a a b a** form, the first two phrases begin the same (they may be identical or differ at the cadence). They are followed by a contrasting section (the bridge) and then a return to the opening material.

R

raised submediant: Raised $\hat{6}$ in the melodic minor scale.

refrain: (1) The section of a song that recurs with the same music and text. (2) In verse-refrain form, the second section of the song, after the verse; generally in **a a b a** or quaternary song form.

register: The highness or lowness of a pitch or passage; the particular octave in which a pitch sounds.

relative keys: Major and minor keys that share the same key signature (e.g., C major and A minor).

relative major: The major key that shares the same key signature as a given minor key. The relative major has the same pitches as its relative minor but it begins on $\flat\hat{3}$ of the minor key.

relative minor: The minor key that shares the same key signature as a given major key. The relative minor has the same pitches as its relative major, but it begins on $\hat{6}$ of the major key.

resolve: To move the voices of an interval or triad from dissonance to consonance.

rest: A duration of silence.

rhythm: The durations of pitch and silence (notes and rests) used in a piece.

rhythm clef: Two short, thick, vertical lines at the beginning of a single-line staff; used to notate unpitched percussion parts.

rhythmic motive: A motive that maintains its rhythm, but changes its contour and intervals.

Roman numerals: A symbol used to represent the scale degree a chord is built on, as well as its quality.

root: The lowest pitch of a triad or seventh chord when the chord is spelled in thirds.

root position: A chord voiced with the root in the bass.

S

SATB: An abbreviation indicating the four voice ranges: soprano, alto, tenor, and bass. Also indicates a particular musical style or texture: hymn or chorale style.

scale-degree names: Names for the position of a note or triad in a scale; these include tonic, supertonic, mediant, subdominant, dominant, submediant, leading tone, and subtonic.

scale-degree numbers: Numbers for the position of a note or triad in a scale, written with a caret over a number (e.g., $\hat{1}$, $\hat{5}$).

scale step: The position of a note in a scale; identified by scale degree names or scale degree numbers (e.g., tonic, $\hat{1}$).

score: Notated music.

second inversion: A triad or seventh chord voiced with its fifth in the bass.

semitone: Half step.

seventh: An interval spanning seven letter names; as a dissonance, the seventh above the root of a chord normally resolves down.

seventh chord: A four-note chord with a third, fifth, and seventh above its root; a triad with a third added above its fifth.

sharp: An accidental ($\sharp$) that raises a pitch a half step without changing its letter name.

similar motion: Two melodic lines or voices moving in the same direction, but not by the same interval. This type of motion connects two harmonic intervals that are not the same size.

simple duple: Meter with two beats in a measure, each beat divided into two (e.g., $\frac{2}{4}$).

simple interval: An interval of an octave or smaller.

simple meter: Meter where the beat divides into twos and subdivides into fours. The top number of simple meter signatures is 2, 3, or 4 (e.g., $\frac{3}{4}$ or $\frac{4}{4}$).

simple quadruple: Meter with four beats in a measure, each beat divided into two (e.g., $\frac{4}{4}$).

simple triple: Meter with three beats in a measure, each beat divided into two (e.g., $\frac{3}{4}$ or $\frac{3}{8}$).

sixteenth note: A stemmed black (filled) notehead with two flags or beams ($\eighthnote$); two sixteenth notes equal an eighth note.

slur: An arc that connects two (or more) different pitches. Slurs affect performance articulation but not duration. In piano music, they tell the performer to play the slurred notes smoothly; in vocal music, the slurred notes are sung on one syllable or in one breath.

solfège, fixed-do: A singing system in which a particular syllable is associated with a particular pitch (*do* is always C, *re* is always D, etc.) no matter what the key.

solfège, moveable-do: A singing system in which a particular syllable is associated with a particular scale step (*do* is always $\hat{1}$, *re* always $\hat{2}$, etc.) no matter what the key.

soprano: The highest voice in four-part (SATB) writing, notated in treble clef; usually sung by women with higher voices.

staff: The five parallel lines on which music is written. Plural form is staves.

stem: A vertical line attached to a note head; it generally extends upward if the note is written below the middle line of the staff and downward if the note is written on or above the middle line.

subdivision: See *beat subdivision*.

subdominant: (1) Scale degree $\hat{4}$; (2) the triad built on $\hat{4}$.

submediant: (1) Scale degree $\hat{6}$; (2) the triad built on $\hat{6}$.

subtonic: (1) Scale degree $\flat\hat{7}$ of the natural minor scale, located a whole step below the tonic; (2) the triad build on $\flat\hat{7}$.

supertonic: (1) Scale degree $\hat{2}$; (2) the triad built on $\hat{2}$.

sus chord: In popular music, a chord with a fourth above the bass instead of a third. The fourth does not necessarily resolve to a third.

swung eighths: A performance practice where a rhythm notated with even eighth notes is performed unevenly, with more time allotted to the first eighth and less to the second in each pair.

symmetrical meter: Meter with beat units of equal duration.

syncopation: Rhythmic displacement of accents created by dots, ties, rests, dynamic markings, or accent marks.

T

tempo: How fast or slow music is played.

tempo marking: An indication, often in Italian, printed in a score to indicate how fast the music is to be played. Typical markings, from slow to fast, include *adagio, andante, allegro, presto*.

tendency tone: A chord member or scale degree whose dissonant relation to the surrounding tones requires a particular resolution (i.e., chordal sevenths must resolve down, and leading tones must resolve up).

tenor: The second-lowest voice in four-part (SATB) writing, notated in bass clef usually directly above the bass; usually sung by men with higher voices.

tenor clef: A C-clef positioned on a staff so that the fourth line from the bottom indicates middle C (C4).

tetrachord: A four-note segment of a scale with a particular pattern of whole and half steps.

text painting: Musical depiction of the words from, or the general meaning of, a song's text or title.

texture: The number of instruments playing (solo or ensemble), the number of different melodies sounding at once, and the relationship of those melodies to each other.

third: Within a triad or seventh chord, the pitch located a third above the root.

third inversion: A seventh chord with its seventh in the bass.

tie: A small arc connecting note heads of two (or more) identical pitches to indicate the durations are to be combined together, without rearticulating the pitch. Used to notate durations extending across a bar line and for durations that cannot be represented with dotted notes.

timbre: Describes the instrumentation or quality of a musical sound.

tonic: (1) Scale degree $\hat{1}$; (2) the triad built on $\hat{1}$.

transpose: To renotate a melody or harmony at a different pitch level or in a different key while maintaining the intervals between its elements.

transcription: (1) A rhythmic pattern rewritten in a different meter, where it sounds the same if it is played at the same tempo. (2) A piece written for one instrument or ensemble arranged to be played by another (e.g., an orchestra piece transcribed for band).

treble clef: Clef positioned on a staff to indicate G by means of the end of its curving line; it circles the line that represents G4. (Also known as the G-clef.)

triad: A three-note chord with a third and fifth above its starting point, or root.

triad and seventh chord positions: See *inverted chord*.

triad names: Names for triads based on the scale degrees of their roots; these include tonic, supertonic, mediant, subdominant, dominant, submediant, leading tone, and subtonic.

triad quality: A description of a triad according to the quality of its stacked thirds and outer fifth: major, minor, diminished, or augmented.

triple meter: Meter with three beats in each measure.

triplet: In simple meter, a division of the beat into three, instead of two, equal parts.

tritone: An interval made up of three whole tones or six semitones; an augmented fourth or diminished fifth. By some definitions, only an augmented fourth is a tritone, since only this spelling of the interval spans three whole steps.

turnaround: At the end of a blues progression, a V or V^7 chord to prepare for the repeat of the progression.

U

unison: The interval size 1, or the distance from a pitch to itself. Voices or instruments that are performing the same melody with the same rhythm in the same octave are said to be playing "in unison."

upbeat: The beat that precedes a downbeat; named for the upward lift of the conductor's hand. Also known as an anacrusis.

V

variation: Repetition of a passage with changes to any number of basic musical features including the melody, cadences, rhythms, key, mode, length, texture, timbre, character, and style.

verse: (1) A section of a song that returns with the same music but different text; (2) in popular song forms, the first section of verse-refrain form. In this form, the verse is usually not repeated.

verse-refrain: A song form associated with Tin Pan Alley; a verse that is not repeated sets the stage or tells the story and is followed by a refrain, which is normally in quaternary song form.

W

whole note: A stemless white (hollow) notehead (○); its duration is equivalent to two half notes.

whole rest: A silence represented by ▬ hanging below the fourth staff line; equal in duration to a whole note.

whole tone: An interval that spans two adjacent half steps.

whole tone scale: A scale with the pattern W–W–W–W–W; it has only whole steps between adjacent scale members.

Appendix 4

The Overtone Series

Every musical pitch played by an instrument, or sung by a voice, is a complex tone, consisting of a fundamental (lowest) pitch plus a series of overtones that sound faintly above it. Example A4.1 shows an overtone series above C2. Overtones (also called partials) are naturally occurring phenomena, created by the vibrations of strings, vocal chords, or columns of air. Partials are often numbered: the fundamental is the first partial, the octave above is the second partial, and so on. The partials shown with black note heads sound out of tune compared to a piano.

EXAMPLE A4.1 Overtone series with C2 Fundamental

The characteristic timbre—or color—of an instrument is created by the different strengths (or amplitudes) of overtones, resulting from the shape of the instrument's resonating space. For example, a flute has a strong fundamental, a somewhat weaker second partial, and very weak higher partials. An oboe has more sound from higher overtones than from lower overtones.

The interval between the first and second partials (the octave from C to C) may be represented by the ratio 2:1 (relating the frequencies of the two pitches). Throughout the series, each ratio between partial numbers represents the interval between the pitches, such as 3:2 (C–G, perfect fifth), 4:3 (G–C, perfect fourth), 5:4 (C–E, major third), and so on. The intervals with smaller numbers tend to correspond with acoustic consonances, and higher numbers (e.g., 16:15, minor second) with dissonances. These ratios also represent the divisions of a string (e.g., on violin, guitar, or cello) where a performer would place his or her fingers to create these intervals, as Figure A4.1 shows. If you play an open string, then divide it in half and play the string again, the second pitch is an octave above the first. For brass players, the overtones are open notes (played without depressing any valves or moving the slide on a trombone)— changing the air pressure and speed moves the sound between pitches in the overtone series.

FIGURE A4.1 Divisions of a string to produce P8, P5, and P4

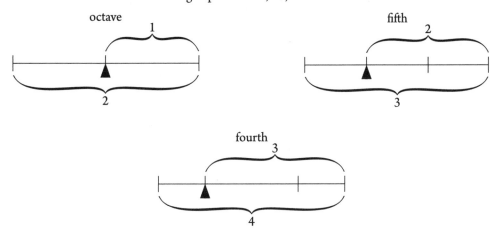

Appendix 5

The Diatonic Modes

Playing the seven white keys from C to C (with no sharps or flats) makes a C major scale, also known as the Ionian mode. Playing through the white keys starting on different notes (D to D, E to E, etc.) forms other diatonic modes, as shown in Example A5.1. There are six traditional diatonic modes (in order, from C): Ionian, Dorian, Phrygian, Lydian, Mixolydian, and Aeolian. (As a shortcut to learning the six mode names, think of a sentence that gives you the first letter of each mode, like "I don't particularly like magic acts.") A seventh mode, Locrian (part g), was identified in the late Renaissance but deemed unusable; it was not used in composing music until the twentieth century. The traditional diatonic modes are found in twentieth- and twenty-first-century jazz, popular, and folk music, as well as in art music.

EXAMPLE A5.1 The diatonic modes as rotations of the C major scale

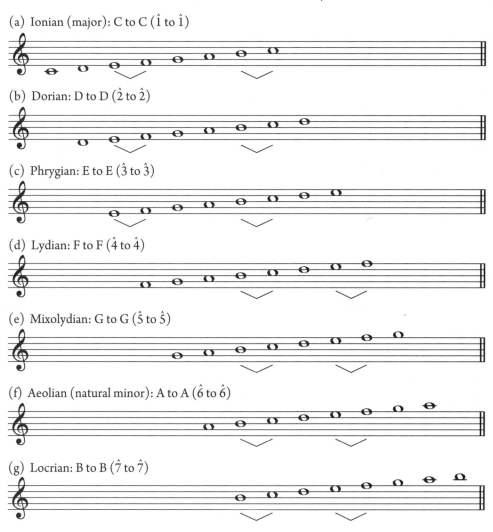

(a) Ionian (major): C to C ($\hat{1}$ to $\hat{1}$)

(b) Dorian: D to D ($\hat{2}$ to $\hat{2}$)

(c) Phrygian: E to E ($\hat{3}$ to $\hat{3}$)

(d) Lydian: F to F ($\hat{4}$ to $\hat{4}$)

(e) Mixolydian: G to G ($\hat{5}$ to $\hat{5}$)

(f) Aeolian (natural minor): A to A ($\hat{6}$ to $\hat{6}$)

(g) Locrian: B to B ($\hat{7}$ to $\hat{7}$)

One way to identify the mode of a piece is by the "relative" method: think of the major key associated with the work's key signature. A major (Ionian) melody typically rests on $\hat{1}$ of the major key as its most stable pitch, while a minor (Aeolian) melody rests on $\hat{6}$. If $\hat{2}$ of the major key seems to function as the most stable pitch, then the melody is in Dorian mode. Look at "Greensleeves" (Example A5.2). The sharp in the key signature suggests G major, but $\hat{2}$ of that key (A) is the most stable pitch and the melody ends on A: the melody is Dorian.

EXAMPLE A5.2 "Greensleeves," mm. 1–8

Because the major and minor scales are familiar, you may also hear the modes as alterations of these scales. The modes can be grouped into two families, according to whether the third scale degree comes from the major or minor pentachord. For each mode, one pitch is altered in comparison with the parallel major or minor scale. Example A5.3 summarizes this approach, with each mode beginning on C.

EXAMPLE A5.3 Modes (on C) grouped by families

(a) Based on major pentachord (with $\hat{3}$)

(b) Based on minor pentachord (with $\flat\hat{3}$)

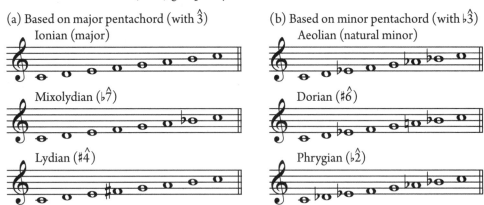

To write a mode beginning on any pitch, use either the relative or parallel method, as shown in Example A5.4. Both methods yield the same result; you can write the mode using one method and check it using the other.

To write a Dorian scale beginning on G:

A. Relative method (part a):

1. Write note heads on the staff from G to G.
2. Remember that Dorian begins on $\hat{2}$ of a major scale; G is $\hat{2}$ in F major.
3. F major has one flat, so add a flat to B.

B. Parallel method (part b):

1. Remember that Dorian sounds like natural minor with a raised sixth scale degree.
2. Write a G natural minor scale, with two flats (B♭ and E♭).
3. Raise ♭$\hat{6}$ by changing E♭ to E♮.

EXAMPLE A5.4 Relative and parallel methods of writing modes on any pitch

(a) Relative method:

1. and 2. Write pitches G to G, and think of the scale (F major) in which G is $\hat{2}$

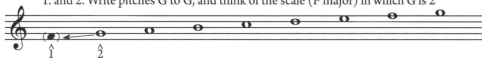

3. Add accidentals from key signature of F major.

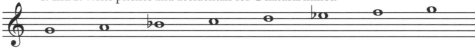

(b) Parallel method:

1. and 2. Write pitches and accidentals for G natural minor.

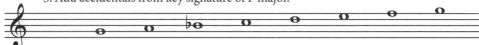

3. Raise $\flat\hat{6}$ to $\hat{6}$

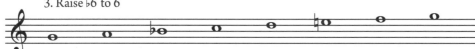

Appendix 6

The C-Clefs

Music reading starts with knowledge of the treble and bass clefs, but there are other clefs as well. Instruments with a middle range, like the viola, read clefs known as C-clefs. The C-clef may appear in different positions on the staff, where its distinctive shape identifies which line is middle C by the point at which the two curved lines join together.

The two C-clefs used most often today are the alto and tenor clefs (Example A6.1). When middle C is the third line, the clef is called an alto clef (part a, read by violists). When middle C is the fourth line, the clef is a tenor clef (part b, read by cellists, trombonists, and bassoonists). Some players regularly read more than one clef: for example, bassoonists, trombonists, and cellists read both bass and tenor clefs.

EXAMPLE A6.1 The alto and tenor clefs

(a) Alto clef

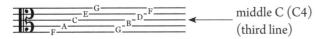

middle C (C4)
(third line)

(b) Tenor clef

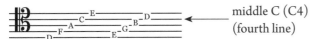

middle C (C4)
(fourth line)

A C-clef may sit on any line of the staff. Depending on its position, it may be called a soprano, mezzo-soprano, alto, tenor, or baritone clef. While the only C-clefs you will probably see in modern scores are the alto and tenor clefs (shaded in Example A6.2), you may come across the others in older scores. To read these clefs, practice counting the lines and spaces in thirds, as for the other clefs.

EXAMPLE A6.2 The C-clefs

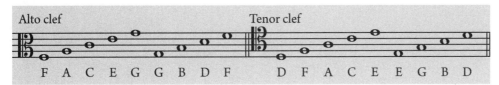

Appendix 7

Basic Guitar Chords

Guitar chords are often illustrated using fretboard diagrams—pictures showing where to place your fingers on the guitar to produce a particular chord. The six vertical lines on a diagram represent the six strings of the guitar, with the lowest sounding string on the left and the highest sounding on the right. The horizontal lines represent the frets (small raised bars that run perpendicular to the strings). In standard tuning, the open strings of a guitar produce E2, A2, D3, G3, B3, and E4, as shown in Figure A7.1. These pitches are customarily written an octave higher, in treble clef, as shown.

FIGURE A7.1 Open strings on the guitar

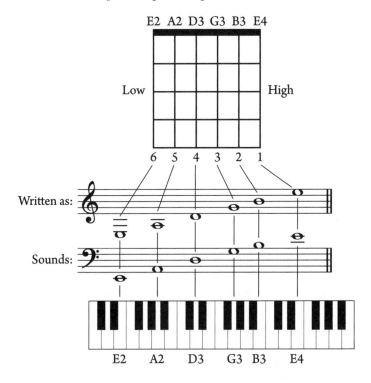

The placement of pitches on the guitar is shown in Figure A7.2. To read this diagram, look at the low string in the illustration. The open string sounds E2; if you place your finger in the space before the first fret, you produce F2, the next note is F♯2 or G♭2, the next G2, and so on. You can continue up this string to E3 on the twelveth fret (indicated by two diamonds, rather than one, as on the third, fifth, seventh, and ninth frets): fingering here sounds an octave above the open string. The diamonds shown in Figure A7.2 help performers quickly locate frets; they may vary in shape or in placement (the arrangement here is the most common). The bass guitar uses the same string arrangement as a standard guitar, but only has the four lowest strings, which are tuned to sound an octave below those on the six-string guitar (E1, A1, D2, G2).

FIGURE A7.2 Pitches on a guitar fretboard

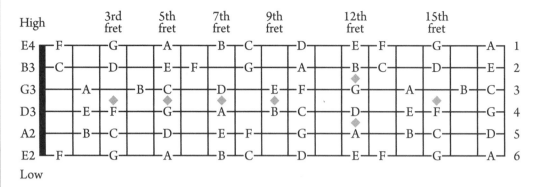

As an aid to performers, scores sometimes include fretboard diagrams, like the one shown in Figure A7.3, with chord symbols. A small o at the end of a string (shown at the top of the diagram) means that the string is played but not fingered; and an x in the same position means the string should not be played (it is not part of the chord). Black dots show you where to place your fingers on the fretboard. Each chord can be played in a variety of ways, but the basic chords shown are useful for beginners. Consult other resources (online or in the library) to build your repertoire of chords.

FIGURE A7.3 How to read a fretboard diagram

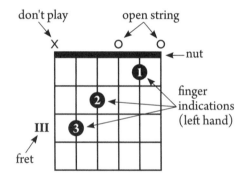

The guitar chords often taught first are E, A, D, G, and C (major, Figure A7.4a) and Em, Am, and Dm (minor, part c). The letters below each symbol show the pitches played by each string (a dash means that a string is not played). The choice of which finger to use for each note varies somewhat depending on the chords played before and after (and the performer's preference), but some basic fingerings are indicated by the finger numbers (1–4 from index finger to pinky) in this example. Some major chords are easily made into dominant sevenths by changing one note, as shown in part (b). Though transforming a major chord (part a) to minor (part c) only involves one pitch (and a motion of one fret), the fingerings change to make the notes easier to reach. Three other useful, but somewhat more challenging, chords are shown in part (d): F (index finger plays two strings), B7 (a little awkward at first), and Gm.

The chords in Figure A7.4 can be combined to play basic phrase progressions in the keys of A, D, G, or C major, and in A and D minor, as shown in Figure A7.5. You can also add ii and vi in C major (Dm and Am) and G major (Am and Em) and explore other combinations of these harmonies.

FIGURE A7.4 Basic guitar chords

(a) Major chords

 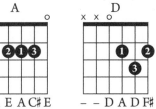  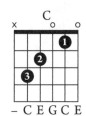

E   A   D   G   C

E B E G♯ B E   – A E A C♯ E   – – D A D F♯   G B D G B D   – C E G C E

(b) Dominant seventh chords

 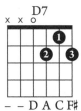 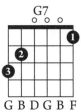

E7   A7   D7   G7

E B D G♯ B E   – A E G C♯ E   – – D A C F♯   G B D G B F

(c) Minor chords

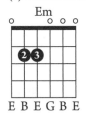 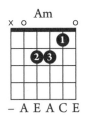 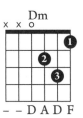

Em   Am   Dm

E B E G B E   – A E A C E   – – D A D F

(d) F major, B7, and G minor

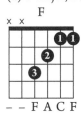 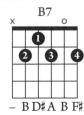 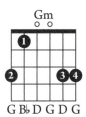

F   B7   Gm

– – F A C F   – B D♯ A B F♯   G B♭ D G D G

FIGURE A7.5 Progressions made from basic chords

	I	IV	V	V⁷
A major	A	D	E	E7
D major	D	G	A	A7
G major	G	C	D	D7
C major	C	F	G	G7

	i	iv	v	V	V⁷
A minor	Am	Dm	Em	E	E7
D minor	Dm	Gm	Am	A	A7

Appendix 8
Piano Fingerings for Selected Scales

In this book, class activities have used scale fingerings that are very easy for locating pitches at the keyboard. If you are interested in studying piano further (or if your teacher directs), here are standard fingerings for the major and natural minor scales, where the thumb is 1 and the pinky is 5. Either hand may play in any octave; scales are often learned one hand at a time, then practiced with the hands one octave apart.

EXAMPLE A8.1 Major scales

EXAMPLE A8.2 Minor scales

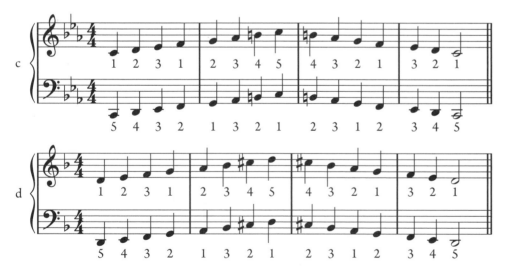

Appendix 9

Connecting Chords

General guidelines for connecting chords in SATB style (four-voice hymn style, with soprano, alto, tenor, and bass voices) follow. These basic principles may be adapted for keyboard and other styles. They are intended to create: (1) smooth connections between chords, by step or common tone; (2) independence of voices, minimizing motion in the same direction; and (3) the correct resolution of tendency tones, such as $\hat{7}$ and chordal sevenths.

EXAMPLE A9.1 Chord connections in authentic cadences

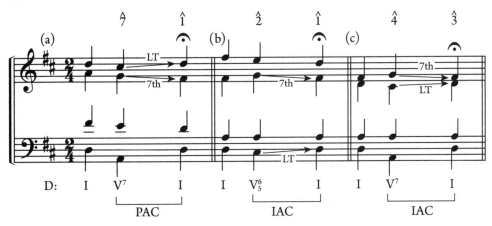

When you connect chords:

1. If the chords have a pitch or pitches in common (called **common tones**) in one of the three upper voices, try to keep these common tones in the same voice part. (In Example A9.1b and c, A3 appears in the tenor in all three chords.)
2. When there is not a common tone, move the upper voices by step if possible. (In Example A9.1, the soprano and alto always move by step.) The upper parts (soprano, alto, and tenor) are more likely to move step by step or common tone than the bass, which sometimes skips between chord roots.
3. Tendency tones, such as the leading tone ($\hat{7}$) and the sevenths of chords, must move by step as marked in the example:
    -   The leading tone moves up by step to $\hat{1}$.
    -   Chordal sevenths move down by step.
4. Let some pairs of voices (soprano and alto, soprano and bass, tenor and alto, etc.) move in opposite directions, if possible. This is called **contrary motion**. (In part a, the soprano and bass move up in the last two chords, while the alto and tenor move down. In part c, the soprano/alto and soprano/bass pairs move in contrary motion.)

5. When pairs of voices move in the same direction, check the type of interval between them and adjust if necessary:

- If the voices create two different intervals (called **similar motion**), the chord connection is acceptable.

- If the voices create two intervals of the same size (called **parallel motion**), check the interval type:

  □ If the intervals in parallel motion are both imperfect consonances (third to third or sixth to sixth), this is acceptable. This is shown in the soprano and alto in the last two chords of part (b), both sixths.

  □ If, however, the parallel intervals are both perfect consonances (P5 to P5, P8 to P8, or PU to PU), you will need to revise the chord connection. These are called **parallel fifths**, **parallel octaves**, and **parallel unisons**, which are generally not found in SATB style, though you may see them in popular music.

Music Credits

Photo Credits

Index of Musical Examples

"21 Guns" (Green Day), 300

"Ah, Belinda, I am prest," from *Dido and Aeneas* (Purcell), 172
"All Because of You" (Bono and U2), 268
"All Time High" (Barry and Rice), 28
"Alleluia" (Boyce), 262
"Alleluia" (Mozart), 199
"Amazing Grace" (Newton), 22, 47, 49, 52, 75, 303, 382
"American Pie" (McLean), 73
Anderson, Maxwell, "September Song," 134
Arlen, Harold
    "Blues in the Night," 320–21
    "We're Off to See the Wizard," from *The Wizard of Oz*, 107
"Ash Grove, The," 298
"Aus meines Herzens Grunde" (Bach), 201

Bach, Johann Sebastian
    "Aus meines Herzens Grunde," 201
    Invention in D minor, 150, 188–89, 334–35
    "Jesu, Priceless Treasure," 261
    Musette, BWV Anh. 126, 134
    "O Haupt voll blut und Wunden," 67
    "Wachet auf," 251
"Banana Boat Song," 199
Barry, John, "All Time High," 28
Bartók, Béla
    "Bulgarian Rhythm," 99–100, 115, 336–37
    "Change of Time," 116
    "Evening in Transylvania," 316
    "Fifth Chords," 116
    "From the Diary of a Fly," 116
    "In the Style of a Folk Song," 115
    "Syncopation," 101
    "Two-Part Study," 116
    "Unison," 116
Basie, "Splanky," 307, 308–9, 326, 338
Beethoven, Ludwig van
    Pathétique Sonata, 67, 69, 76, 339–40
    Sonatina in G, Romanze, 135
    String Quartet in F Major, Op. 18, No. 1, second movement, 111
"Better Times Are Coming" (Foster), 260–61
Black Eyed Peas, "I Gotta Feeling," 289
Bliss, Philip B., "Wonderful Words of Life," 107
"Blue Rondo à la Turk" (Brubeck), 100–101
"Blues for Norton" (Phillips), 5, 54, 208, 252, 306–7, 383–86

"Blues in the Night" (Arlen), 320–21
Bono
    "All Because of You," 268
    "Miracle Drug," 65
    "One Step Closer," 268
Boyce, William, "Alleluia," 262
Brubeck, Dave, "Blue Rondo à la Turk," 100–101
"Bulgarian Rhythm," from *Mikrokosmos* (Bartók), 99–100, 115, 336–37
"Butterfly, The," 111

"Can't Help Falling in Love," from *Blue Hawaii* (Weiss, Peretti, and Creatore), 81
Capra, Remo, "O Bambino," 293
Cerf, Christopher, "Dance Myself to Sleep," from *Sesame Street*, 94
Chance, John Barnes, *Variations on a Korean Folk Song*, 4–5, 42, 53, 341–44
"Change of Time" (Bartók), 116
Chartres, 253
"Circle of Life," from *The Lion King* (John and Rice), 7, 22
Clarke, Jeremiah, *Trumpet Voluntary (Prince of Denmark's March)*, 46, 50, 172, 177, 208, 345–49
"Clementine," 269
"Come, Follow Me," 135
Copland, Aaron, "Simple Gifts," from *Appalachian Spring*, 1, 397
Creatore, Luigi, "Can't Help Falling in Love," from *Blue Hawaii*, 81
Croce, Jim, "Time in a Bottle," 152
"Cruella de Vil" (Leven), 29

"Dance Myself to Sleep," from *Sesame Street* (Cerf and Stiles), 94
Darion, Joe, "The Impossible Dream," from *Man of La Mancha*, 110
"Dona nobis pacem," 262
"Down in the Valley," 230
"Drink to Me Only," 142

"Edelweiss" (Rodgers and Hammerstein), 267
Edwards, Clara, "Into the Night," 81
"Evening in Transylvania" (Bartók), 316

"Fifth Chords" (Bartók), 116
Foster, Stephen
    "Better Times Are Coming," 260–61
    "Oh! Susanna," 249–50, 282–83, 350

Frasier, theme from (Miller), 42
Frey, Glenn, "Take It to the Limit", 57, 74, 75, 245, 254, 358–62
"Frog in the Bog, The" (Loomis), 135
"From the Diary of a Fly" (Bartók), 116

Gershwin, George and Ira
    "'S Wonderful!" from *Funny Face*, 45–46, 172, 179–80, 281, 312, 313, 351–55
    "Summertime," from *Porgy and Bess*, 318
Gilmore, Patrick, "When Johnny Comes Marching Home," 91, 92, 149, 271, 356
"Go Down, Moses," 256–57
Green Day, "21 Guns," 300
"Greensleeves," 42, 91, 178, 192, 277–79, 357

Hammerstein, Oscar, II, "Edelweiss," 267
Handel, George Frideric, "Rejoice greatly," from *Messiah*, 112
Handy, W. C., "Memphis Blues," 320
"Hanukkah Song," 272
Harburg, E. Y., "We're Off to See the Wizard," from *The Wizard of Oz*, 107
Harline, Leigh, "Hi-Diddle-Dee-Dee," from *Pinocchio*, 109
Hart, Lorenz, "My Funny Valentine," 49, 75, 154–55, 267, 392–95
Haydn, Joseph, Seven German Dances, No. 6, 229
Hefti, Neil, "Splanky," 307, 308–9, 326, 338
Henley, Don, "Take It to the Limit," 57, 74, 75, 245, 254, 358–62
Hensel, Fanny Mendelssohn
    "Nachtwanderer," 93
    "Schwanenlied," 111
Heyward, DuBose and Dorothy, "Summertime," from *Porgy and Bess*, 318
"Hi-Diddle-Dee-Dee," from *Pinocchio* (Harline and Washington), 109
"Home, Dearie, Home," 294
"Home on the Range," 95, 96–97, 253–54, 255, 363
Horner, James
    "My Heart Will Go On," 61
    "Somewhere Out There," from *An American Tail*, 4, 18, 20, 49, 57, 61, 75, 86, 267, 313, 364–67
"House of the Rising Sun, The" (Price), 294
"How Can I Keep from Singing" (Lowry), 200, 267, 324

"I Gotta Feeling" (Black Eyed Peas), 289
"I Had a Little Nut Tree," 229
"Ich hab' im Traum geweinet," from *Dichterliebe* (Schumann), 114
"Imperial March," from *The Empire Strikes Back* (Williams), 42
"Impossible Dream, The," from *Man of La Mancha* (Darion and Leigh), 110
"In the Style of a Folk Song" (Bartók), 115
"Into the Night" (Edwards), 81

"Jesu, Priceless Treasure" (Bach), 261
Joel, Billy, "Piano Man," 22
John, Elton, "Circle of Life," from *The Lion King*, 7, 22
Joplin, Scott
　"Pine Apple Rag," 73
　"Solace," 10, 25, 27, 30, 67, 70, 71, 86, 87, 368–71

King, Carole, "You've Got a Friend," 86

"Land of the Silver Birch," 319
Larson, Jonathan, "Seasons of Love," from *Rent*, 48, 57, 61, 86, 87, 299, 372–76
Leigh, Mitch, "The Impossible Dream," from *Man of La Mancha*, 110
Lennon, John
　"Norwegian Wood," 93
　"Ticket to Ride," 288
Lerner, Alan Jay, "Wand'rin' Star," from *Paint Your Wagon*, 81
Leven, Mel, "Cruella de Vil," 29
"Lindenbaum, Der," from *Winterreise* (Schubert), 142
"Little Brown Jug," 269
Loewe, Frederick, "Wand'rin' Star," from *Paint Your Wagon*, 81
Loomis, Harvey Worthington, "The Frog in the Bog," 135
"Love Me Tender" (Presley), 65, 142
"Love Story" (Swift), 289
Lowry, Robert, "How Can I Keep from Singing," 200, 267, 324

Mann, Barry, "Somewhere Out There," from *An American Tail*, 4, 18, 20, 49, 57, 61, 75, 86, 267, 313, 364–67
"Masters in This Hall," 142
McCartney, Paul
　"Norwegian Wood," 93
　"Ticket to Ride," 288
McLean, Don, "American Pie," 73
Meisner, Randy, "Take It to the Limit," 57, 74, 75, 245, 254, 358–62
"Memphis Blues" (Handy), 320
"Merrily We Roll Along," 286
"Michael Finnigin," 57, 255–56
Miller, Bruce, *Frasier*, theme from, 42
"Miracle Drug" (Bono and U2), 65
Mission: Impossible, theme from (Schifrin), 10, 100

Mozart, Leopold, Burleske, 229
Mozart, Wolfgang Amadeus
　"Alleluia," 199
　Piano Sonata in C Major, K. 545, 201, 298
　String Quartet in D Minor, K. 421, third movement, 57, 158, 377–78
　"Sull' aria," from *The Marriage of Figaro*, 112
　Variations on "Ah, vous dirai-je Maman," 20, 50, 147–48, 152, 208, 379–80
　Variations on "Lison dormait," 59
"Music Alone Shall Live," 200
"My Country, 'Tis of Thee," 45–46, 213–14, 215, 216, 222, 223, 225, 251, 252, 381
"My Funny Valentine," from *Babes in Arms* (Rodgers and Hart), 49, 75, 154–55, 267, 392–95
"My Heart Will Go On" (Horner), 61
"My Paddle's Keen and Bright," 323

"Nachtwanderer" (Hensel), 93
Nelson, Willie, "On the Road Again," 28
Newton, John, "Amazing Grace," 22, 47, 49, 52, 75, 303, 382
"Norwegian Wood" (Lennon and McCartney), 93
"Nun danket," 236

"O Bambino" (Velona and Capra), 293
"O Haupt voll Blut und Wunden" (Bach), 67
"O magnum mysterium" (Victoria), 172
"Oh! Susanna," (Foster), 249–50, 282–83, 350
"Old Hundredth," 234
"On the Road Again," 28
"Once More My Soul," 164
"One Step Closer" (Bono and U2), 268

Pachelbel, Johann, Canon for Three Violins and Keyboard in D Major, 238
Parish, Mitchell, "Stars Fell on Alabama," 320
Peretti, Hugo, "Can't Help Falling in Love," from *Blue Hawaii*, 81
Perkins, Frank, "Stars Fell on Alabama," 320
Phillips, Joel, "Blues for Norton," 5, 54, 208, 252, 306–7, 383, 384–86
"Piano Man" (Joel), 22
"Pine Apple Rag" (Joplin), 73
Presley, Elvis, "Love Me Tender," 65, 142
Price, Alan, "The House of the Rising Sun," 294
Purcell, Henry, "Ah, Belinda, I am prest," from *Dido and Aeneas*, 172

"Rejoice greatly," from *Messiah* (Handel), 112
Rice, Tim
　"All Time High," 28
　"Circle of Life," from *The Lion King*, 7, 22
Richie, Lionel, "Three Times a Lady," 65
"Riddle Song," 318

Robinson, Smokey
　"You've Really Got a Hold on Me," 95, 98, 99, 101–2, 125, 128, 387–91
Rodgers, Richard
　"Edelweiss," 267
　"My Funny Valentine," 49, 75, 154–55, 267, 392–95
Root, George, "There's Music in the Air," 200

"'S Wonderful!" from *Funny Face* (the Gershwins), 45–46, 172, 179–80, 281, 312, 313, 351–55
St. George's Windsor, 253
"St. James Infirmary," 230
Schifrin, Lalo, theme from *Mission: Impossible*, 10, 100
Schubert, Franz
　"Der Lindenbaum," from *Winterreise*, 142
　Waltz in B Minor, 67, 72, 149–50, 247–49, 286, 396
Schumann, Robert, "Ich hab' im Traum geweinet," from *Dichterliebe*, 114
"Schwanenlied" (Hensel), 111
"Seasons of Love," from *Rent* (Larson), 48, 57, 61, 86, 87, 299, 372–76
"September Song" (Weill and Anderson), 134
"Shalom, Chaverim," 142
"Shenandoah," 199
"Silent Night," 92
"Simple Gifts," from *Appalachian Spring* (Copland), 1, 397
"Simple Gifts" (traditional), 128, 279, 297, 397
"Solace" (Joplin), 10, 25, 27, 30, 67, 70, 71, 86, 87, 368–71
"Somewhere Out There," from *An American Tail* (Horner, Mann, and Weil), 4, 18, 20, 49, 57, 61, 75, 86, 267, 364–67, 313
Sousa, John Philip, "The Stars and Stripes Forever," 42, 51, 87, 119, 270
"Splanky" (Basie and Hefti), 307, 308–9, 326, 338
"Stars and Stripes Forever, The" (Sousa), 42, 51, 87, 119, 270
"Stars Fell on Alabama" (Perkins and Parish), 320
Stiles, Norman, "Dance Myself to Sleep," from *Sesame Street*, 94
"Sull' aria," from *The Marriage of Figaro* (Mozart), 112
"Summertime," from *Porgy and Bess* (George Gershwin, DuBose and Dorothy Heyward, and Ira Gershwin), 318
Swift, Taylor, "Love Story," 289
"Syncopation" (Bartók), 101

"Take It to the Limit" (Henley, Frey, and Meisner), 57, 74, 75, 245, 254, 358–62

"There's Music in the Air" (Root), 200
"Three Times a Lady" (Richie), 65
"Ticket to Ride" (Lennon and McCartney), 288
"Till There Was You," from *The Music Man* (Willson), 50, 119, 206, 279–80, 398–402
"Time in a Bottle" (Croce), 152
"Twinkle, Twinkle, Little Star," 122
"Two-Part Study" (Bartók), 116

U2
    "All Because of You," 268
    "Miracle Drug," 65
    "One Step Closer," 268
"Unison" (Bartók), 116

Variations on a Korean Folk Song (Chance), 4–5, 42, 53, 341–44
Variations on "Ah, vous dirai-je Maman" (Mozart), 20, 50, 147–48, 152, 208, 379–80

Variations on "Lison dormait" (Mozart), 59
Velona, Tony, "O Bambino," 293
Victoria, Tomás Luis de, "O magnum mysterium," 172

"Wachet auf" (Bach), 251
"Wade in the Water," 271
"Wand'rin' Star," from *Paint Your Wagon* (Lerner and Loewe), 81
Washington, Ned, "Hi-Diddle-Dee-Dee," from *Pinocchio*, 109
"Wayfaring Stranger," 256–57, 304
Weil, Cynthia, "Somewhere Out There," from *An American Tail*, 4, 18, 20, 49, 57, 61, 75, 86, 267, 313, 364–67
Weill, Kurt, "September Song," 134
Weiss, George David, "Can't Help Falling in Love," from *Blue Hawaii*, 81
"We're Off to See the Wizard," from *The Wizard of Oz* (Arlen and Harburg), 107
"When I Fall in Love" (Young), 200

"When Johnny Comes Marching Home" (Gilmore), 91, 92, 149, 271, 356
"Whoopee Ti-Yi-Yo," 106
"Will This Circle Be Unbroken," 316
Williams, John, "Imperial March," from *The Empire Strikes Back*, 42
Willson, Meredith, "Till There Was You," from *The Music Man*, 50, 119, 206, 279–80, 398–402
Wonder, Stevie, "You Are the Sunshine of My Life," 18
"Wonderful Words of Life" (Bliss), 107

"Yankee Doodle," 270
"You Are the Sunshine of My Life," (Wonder), 18
Young, Victor, "When I Fall in Love," 200
"You've Got a Friend" (King), 86
"You've Really Got a Hold on Me" (Robinson), 95, 98, 99, 101–2, 125, 128, 387–91

Index of Terms and Concepts

12-bar blues, 308–9, 314
32-bar song form, 279–81

accelerando, 46
accents
    displaced, 72–74
    metrical, 46–47
accidentals, 25–30
    double flats, 27–29
    double sharps, 27–29
    flats, 25–27
    naturals, 25–27
    sharps, 25–27
adagio, 46
adagio cantabile, 76
added-sixth chords, 312, 313
alla breve, 51
allegretto, 46
allegro, 46
alto, 213
anacrusis, 49, 52
andante, 46
andantino, 46
antecedent phrase, 278
arpeggio, 287
arrangements, keyboard, 284–88
articulation, 72
asymmetrical meters, 99–101
augmented intervals, 188–91, 192
augmented second, 150
augmented triads, 217
authentic cadence, 250, 254

bars, 47
bar lines, 47
basic phrase, 250
    subdominant in, 253–54
bass, 213
bass clef, 4–5
    drawing a, 11
    ledger lines and, 7, 8–9
beams, 47
    in compound meters, 95
    notating, 47–48
    for rhythmic patterns, 71
beats
    strong, 46
    weak, 46
beat division, 51–53, 93
beat subdivisions, 69
    in compound meters, 94–95
    in simple meters, 69–71

beat unit, 49
    in compound meters, 91, 96
    in simple meters, 51
blue notes, 306
blues scale, 306–8
bridge (in 32-bar song form), 280
bridge (in later popular music), 288

cadences, 249
    authentic, 250, 254
    deceptive, 250–51
    half, 250
    imperfect authentic, 250
    perfect authentic, 250
    plagal, 250, 252
    types of, 250–53
Cage, John, 55
change in mode, 148
changes, 308
changing meters, 101–2
chords, 213. *See also* chord extensions; domi-
    nant seventh chords; first-inversion
    chords; root-position chords; second-
    inversion chords; seventh chords;
    third-inversion chords; triads
chord connection, 285
chord extensions, 312–13
chord members, 214, 222
    fifth, 214, 222
    root, 214, 222
    seventh, 214, 222
    third, 214, 222
chord progressions, 250
    basic phrase, 250
    keyboard arrangements of, 284–88
chorus, 288
chromatic half steps, 31, 120
chromatic scale, 120
circle of fifths, 129
    major key signatures and, 129
    minor key signatures and, 156–58
clave rhythm pattern, 72
clefs, 3–5
    bass, 4–5
    rhythm, 52–53
    treble, 3–4
climax, 282
combo, 306
common time, 50. *See also* quadruple meter
compound intervals, 191–92
compound meters, 91–99
    compound duple, 91–93, 96

compound quadruple, 93, 96
compound triple, 93, 96
meter signatures for, 92–94,
    96–97
subdivisions in, 94–95
syncopation in, 97–99
conducting patterns, 46
conjunct motion, 281
consequent phrase, 278
consonant intervals, 192–93
contour, 1
contrasting period, 278
cut time, 51, 72

deceptive cadence, 250–51
deceptive resolution, 251
diatonic, origin of term, 130
diatonic half steps, 31, 121
diatonic scales, 121
diminished intervals, 188–91, 192
diminished seventh chords, 309–11
diminished triads, 215, 217
disjunct motion, 281
dissonant intervals, 192–93
dominant, 122–23
dominant seventh chords, 222–24
    inversion of, 223–24
    in major keys, 246–47
    melody harmonization with, 245–49,
        256–57
    in minor keys, 247–49, 256–57
    spelling, 224
dominant triad, 216
    in major keys, 246–47
    melody harmonization with, 245–49, 254,
        256–57
    in minor keys, 247–49
dot, 50, 54
dotted notes, 50
dotted-quarter beat unit, 91
dotted rests, 54
double flats, 27–29
double sharps, 27–29
doubling (in chords), 214
doubly augmented intervals, 190
doubly diminished intervals, 190
downbeat, 46
duple meter, 45–46
    compound duple, 91–93
    simple duple, 45–46, 50
duplets, 97–99
dynamic levels, 47

eighth notes, 47
eighth rests, 54
embellishing tones, 255–56
    neighbor tones, 255
    passing tones, 255
enharmonic spellings, 26–27, 28, 29–30
    for augmented and diminished intervals, 190

F-clef. *See* bass clef
fifth (of chord), 214, 222
figures, 214
first-inversion chords, 214–15, 223–24
fixed *do* solfège, 122
flags, 47–48
flats, 25–27
flatted fifth, 307
form, 277
    32-bar song form, 279–81
    in later popular music, 288–89
    period, 278, 281–82
    quaternary song form, 278–79, 282
    verse-refrain form, 281
forte, 47
fortissimo, 47
Foster, Stephen, 258
four-phrase song form, 278–79

G-clef. *See* treble clef
Gershwin, George, 193
grand staff, 9–10
grave, 46
guitar tabs, 249–50

half cadence, 250
half-diminished seventh chords, 309–11
half notes, 47
half rests, 54
half steps, 26, 30–33
    chromatic, 31, 120
    diatonic, 31, 121
    hearing, 32–33
harmonic intervals, 178–79
harmonic minor, 149–51, 153
harmonic rhythm, 249
head, 309
homophonic texture, 213
hook, 288
hymn style, 213

imperfect authentic cadence, 250
improvisation, 75
instrumental break, 289
intervals, 30, 177–78
    compound, 191–92
    consonant, 192–93
    dissonant, 192–93
    enharmonically equivalent, 190
    half step, 26, 30–33
    harmonic, 178–79
    inversion of, 181–82, 186–87
    melodic, 178

simple, 191
sizes, 178
spelling methods for, 182–88
spelling triads by, 218, 221
unisons, 179
whole step, 27, 30–33
interval quality, 179–81
    augmented, 188–91, 192
    diminished, 188–91, 192
    doubly augmented, 190
    doubly diminished, 190
    major, 181–88, 192
    minor, 181–88, 192
    perfect, 180–88, 192
intro, 288
inverted chords, 214–15, 223–24
inverting intervals, 181–82

John, Elton, 12
Joplin, Scott, 33

key signatures, 125
    determining, 127–28
    identifying key from score, 158–59
    for major keys, 125–28
    for minor keys, 156–58
    spelling triads by, 218–19
keyboard, piano
    half and whole steps on, 31
    ledger lines and, 6–9
    naming white keys on, 3, 26
    with octave numbers, 6
keyboard arrangements, 284–88
    styles of, 286–87

larghetto, 46
largo, 46
lead sheets, 307, 309–13
leading tone, 123, 217, 218
leading-tone triad, 216
leaps, melodic, 281
ledger lines, 6–9
    drawing, 12
    landmarks for, 8
letter names, pitch, 2, 26–27
link, 289

major intervals, 181–88, 192
major keys, 121
    melody harmonization in, 246–47, 255–56
    seventh chords in, 310
    signatures for, 125–28
    triads in, 215–16
major pentatonic scale, 303, 305
major scales, 121, 153
    spelling intervals by, 182–84
    spelling triads by, 218, 220
    writing, 123–25
major seventh chords, 309
major tetrachord, 123–24
major triads, 214, 215, 217

measures, 47
mediant, 123
mediant triad, 216
melodic intervals, 178
melodic minor, 151–52, 153
melodies, writing, 281
melody and accompaniment texture, 248
melody harmonization
    with basic phrase model, 249–50, 253–54, 256–58
    embellishments, 255–56
    with triads and dominant seventh chords, 245–49
meter
    asymmetrical, 99–101
    changing, 101–2
    compound, 91–99
    duple, 45–46, 50
    quadruple, 45–46, 50
    simple, 45
    symmetrical, 99
    triple, 45–46
meter signatures, 49–51
    for compound meters, 92–94, 96–97
    for simple meters, 49–51
metrical accents, 46–47
metronome, 76
mezzo forte, 47
mezzo piano, 47
middle C, 3
minor intervals, 181–88, 192
minor keys, 148
    identifying from score, 158–59
    melody harmonization in, 247–49, 256–57
    parallel keys, 147–48
    seventh chords in, 310
    signatures for, 156–58
    triads in, 216–18
minor mode, 148
minor pentatonic scale, 304–5, 306, 307
minor scales, 148, 153
    harmonic minor, 149–51, 153
    melodic minor, 151–52, 153
    natural minor, 148–49, 153
minor seventh chords, 309
minor triads, 214, 215, 217
modal scale degrees, 148
moderato, 46
modulation, 155
motives, 282
movable *do* solfège, 122
Mozart, Wolfgang Amadeus, 159
Mozart family, 159
musical alphabet, 3
musical contour, 1

natural minor, 148–49, 153
    relative, 155
naturals, 25–27
neighbor tones, 255
ninth chords, 312, 313

notation guidelines
 beaming of rhythmic patterns, 71
 beams and flags, 47–48
 beams in compound meters, 95
 clefs, 11
 for duplets, 99
 ledger lines, 12
 note heads, 3
 notes and stems, 11
 unisons and seconds with stems, 179
notes, 1
 dotted, 50
 eighth, 47
 half, 47
 quarter, 47
 sixteenth, 48
 whole, 48
note heads, drawing, 3, 11

octave, 2, 180, 192
octave equivalence, 2
octave numbers, naming pitches with, 6, 7
outro, 288

parallel keys, 147–48
 parallel major, 148
 parallel minor, 148
parallel period, 278
passing tones, 255
pentatonic scales, 303–5
 major pentatonic, 303, 305
 minor pentatonic, 304–5, 306, 307
perfect authentic cadence, 250
perfect intervals, 180–88, 192
period, 278
 contrasting, 278
 parallel, 278
 writing, 281–82
phrases, 249
 antecedent, 278
 consequent, 278
 keyboard arrangements of, 284–88
 paired, 277–78
pianissimo, 47
piano (dynamic level), 47
piano keyboard
 half and whole steps on, 31
 ledger lines and, 6–9
 naming white keys on, 3, 26
pickup, 49, 52
pitch, 1
pitch notation, 1–9
 ledger lines for, 6–9
 letter names, 2, 26–27
 naming with octave numbers, 6
 staff, 3
 treble and bass clefs, 3–5
 writing pitches in score, 11–12
 writing pitches with accidentals, 29–30
plagal cadence, 250, 252
postchorus, 289
prechorus, 289

prestissimo, 46
presto, 46

quadruple meter, 45–46, 50
quality (of triads), 214
quarter notes, 47
quarter-note beat, rhythmic subdivisions
 of, 70
quarter rest, 54
quaternary song form, 278–79
 writing, 282

raised submediant, 153
rap break, 289
refrain, 281
register, 7
relative keys, 154–56
 relative major, 155, 156
 relative minor, 155–56
resolution, 192–93
rests, 53–55
 in compound meters, 95
 eighth, 54
 half, 54
 quarter, 54
 in simple meters, 53–55
 sixteenth, 54
 whole, 54
rhythm, 47
 counting in simple meters, 51–53
 counting in compound meters, 91
rhythm clef, 52–53
rhythmic notation, 47–49
 dots in, 50
rhythmic variations in performance, 75–76
ritardando, 46
Robinson, Smokey, 102
rock and roll, 314
Roman numerals, 216, 217
root (of chord), 214, 222
root-position chords, 214–15, 221, 223–24

SATB, 213
scales, 119–21. See also specific scale types
 blues, 306–8
 chromatic, 120
 comparing, 153
 diatonic, 121
 major, 121, 153
 minor, 148, 153
 pentatonic, 303–5
 whole-tone, 120–21
scale degrees, 121–23
 dominant, 122–23
 leading tone, 123
 mediant, 123
 in minor, 153
 modal, 148
 raised submediant, 153
 subdominant, 123
 submediant, 123
 subtonic, 153

supertonic, 123
 tonic, 121, 122
scale steps. See scale degrees
score, 1
 writing music in a, 11–12
second-inversion chords, 214–15,
 223–24
semitone. See half step
seventh (of chord), 214, 222
seventh chords, 309–11
 diminished, 309–11
 dominant, 222–24
 half-diminished, 309–11
 major, 309–11
 minor, 309–11
 spelling, 311
 symbols for, 311
seventh chord inversions, 223–24
 first inversion, 223–24
 root position, 223–24
 second inversion, 223–24
 third inversion, 223–24
sharps, 25–27
simple intervals, 191
simple meters, 45
 counting rhythms in, 51–53
 simple duple, 45–46, 50
 meter signatures for, 49–51
 simple quadruple, 45–46, 50
 simple triple, 45–46
 subdivisions in, 69–71
 syncopation in, 72–74
sixteenth notes, 48
sixteenth rest, 54
skips, melodic, 281
slurs, 72
solfège, 122
 fixed do, 122
 movable do, 122
soprano, 213
sound quality, 7
staff, 1
 grand staff, 9–10
 ledger lines and, 6–9
staff notation, 3
stems, 1
 drawing, 11
steps, melodic, 30–32. See also half steps;
  whole steps
strong beat, 46
subdominant, 123
subdominant triad, 216
 in basic phrase model, 253–54
 in major keys, 246–47
 melody harmonization with, 245–49,
  256–57
 in minor keys, 247–49
submediant, 123
submediant triad, 216
subtonic, 153
subtonic triad, 217
supertonic, 123

supertonic triad, 216
sus chords, 313
swung eighths, 75
symmetrical meters, 99
syncopation, 72–74
    in asymmetrical meters, 100
    in compound meters, 97–99
    in simple meters, 72–74

tacet, 55
tempo, 46
tempo markings, 46, 76
tendency tone, 123
tenor, 213
tetrachords, 123–24
    major, 123–24
texture, 213
    homophonic, 213
    melody and accompaniment, 248
third (of chord), 214, 222
third-inversion chords,
        223–24
ties, 71
timbre, 7
Tin Pan Alley, 193
tonic, 121, 122

tonic triad, 216
    in major keys, 246–47
    melody harmonization with, 245–49,
        256–57
    in minor keys, 247–49
transcription, 75
transposition, 122
treble clef, 3–4
    drawing a, 11
    ledger lines and, 6, 8–9
triads, 213–22
    in major keys, 215–16
    melody harmonization with,
        245–49
    in minor keys, 216–18
    names of, 216
    spelling, 218–22
triad inversions, 214–15
    first inversion, 214–15
    root position, 214–15, 221
    second inversion, 214–15
triad qualities, 214
    augmented, 217
    diminished, 215, 217
    major, 214, 215, 217
    in major keys, 215–16

    minor, 214, 215, 217
    in minor keys, 216–18
triple meter, 45–46
triplets, 74
tritone, 189
turnaround, 308

unison, 179
upbeat, 46, 49, 52

verse
    in 32-bar song form, 281
    in later popular music, 288
verse-refrain form, 281
vivace, 46

weak beat, 46
whole notes, 48
whole rests, 54
whole steps, 27, 30–33
    hearing, 32–33
whole tones. See whole steps
whole-tone scale, 120–21
Willson, Meredith, 290
writing music in a score, 11–12
writing pitches with accidentals, 29–30

Russia (formerly Soviet Union)

Ukraine

ngary

Turkey

Iran

Gaza

Israel
(Historic Region
of Palestine)

Afghanistan

Yemen

India

Bhutan

Burma

Thailand

China

Japan

Taiwan

Laos

Borneo

Republic
Congo

Zimbabwe

South Africa

Australia

New Zealand

Tonga

Enduring
VISIONS

Enduring VISIONS

WOMEN'S ARTISTIC HERITAGE AROUND THE WORLD

Abby Remer

Davis Publications, Inc.
Worcester, Massachusetts

Enduring Visions: Women's Artistic Heritage Around the World
Copyright © 2001 Abby Remer

Front Cover: (left to right) Taíno, *Duho*; Wounaan, *basket*; Kuna, *mola*; Ukranian, *pysanky*; Mbuti, *barkcloth*.
Back Cover: Polish, *animation*; Aboriginal, *hubcaps*.
Half-title page: Cakchiquel Maya, *Huipil*, c. 1970s. San Antonio Aquascalientes, Guatemala. Courtesy David Irving. Photo Al Vatter.
Frontispiece: (left) Oopik Pitsiulak (b. 1946), *Oopik Thinking*, 1990. Dark green stone, glass beads, and wool cord. 5 x 4½ x 2½"
    (12.7 x 11.5 x 6.4 cm). Courtesy the artist. (right) Wounaan, *Basket*, 1997. Courtesy and photograph Raul E. Cisneros.
Table of Contents: Yang Fong, *Baby Carrier*, detail, 1979. Courtesy Gayle Morrison Collection.

Publisher: Wyatt Wade
Editorial Director: Helen Ronan
Production Editor: Carol Harley
Manufacturing: Georgiana Rock
Copyeditor: Deborah Sosin
Design: Cyndy Patrick

Library of Congress Catalog Card Number: 00-109477
ISBN: 87192-524-9

Dedication
To the creative, imaginative, and courageous women of all cultures and time, for their vision, which extends far beyond what our eyes can see.

Acknowledgements
First and foremost, to Helen Ronan for her initial suggestion for this book and her steadfast support, feedback, and guidance. Second, to Carol Harley, for her eagle eye and deep dedication to bringing *Enduring Visions* to life. Many thanks as well to the devotees, curators, scholars, gallery directors, and collectors who reviewed the sections pertaining to their field of expertise. I have tried throughout to rigorously check my information to avoid any unintentional misrepresentation or inaccuracies. Finally, a warm thanks to Michael Remer, Biscuit, Pepper, Rilla, and Murray.

Donors to the Vision Fund

Amy Bachrach

David Brunetti

Jacqui Byrne

Daniel and Julie Cort

Tad Crawford

Leslie and Martin Darhansoff

Dr. Louise DeCosta

Leo H. Dworsky

Dr. Harold and Beryl Towbin Esecover

Tom J. Ferber

Dr. Carol Fineberg

Timmie Gallagher

Joy Horwich

Raymond Klausen and John S. Harrington

Ed Kleiman

Joyce Kleiman

Larry Levine and Herb Glaser

Susan Marks

Elaine McManus

Rita Mendelsohn

Dr. Jay Moses

Phyllis and Stan Newman

Katherine Wharton Rabinowitz

Jane Remer

Michael and Patricia Remer

Muriel Silberstein-Storfer

Bruce Solotoff

Corinne Smith

Bernice Steinbaum

Gerald and Geraldine Weinberger

Thanks to the Money for Women/Barbara Deming Memorial Fund, Inc. for their financial help and moral support.

Table of Contents

Preface   vi
Introduction   vii

1 Africa   2
Linking the Secular and Sacred Realm   2
Sacred Earth/Heavenly Connection: Women's Pottery in Nigeria   4
Cultural Declarations: Ndebele Women's Beadwork and Murals   10
Rejoicing in the Forest: Mbuti Barkcloth Painting   14
The Power of Cloth: Kuba *Kasai* Textiles, Rank, and Prestige   16
The Magic of Stone: Shona Female Carvers   18
Art as Necessity: Weya Women's *Sadza* Resist Fabric Painting   22

2 Arab World   26
Politics and Identity   26
Migrating Feasts for the Eyes: Middle Eastern Nomadic Art   28
Precious Jewel: The Jewish Yemeni Bride from Head to Hands   31
New Views/Ancient Roots: Contemporary Female Arab Artists   35

3 Asia   40
Abundant Diversity   40
Devotional Paintings on Earth and Paper:
    The Rural Art of Mithila Women   42
Heavenly Cloth: Rural Indian Wedding Embroideries   46
A Noble Pursuit: Female Traditional Chinese Painters   48
Nimble Fingers, Unfading Art: Chinese Women's *Hua Yang*   54
Flowers of Devotion: Japanese *Ikebana*   56
Imperative Ritual Cloth: *Puas* by Iban Women   58
Weaving for a Nation: Bhutan's Premier Art   60
Continuity Amid Adversity: Hmong *Pa ndau*   62

4 Caribbean   66
Intersecting Cultures   66
Seats of Power and Prestige: Taíno *Duhos*   68
Sacred Art and Inner Vision:
    Self-taught Female Painters of Haiti and Jamaica   70
Twist and Cross: *Mundillo* Lace of Borikén   76
Cross-cultural Odyssey: Transatlantic Fashion Design   80

5 Eastern Europe   82
Ever Old/Ever New   82
Eggs of Heaven: Ukrainian *Pysanky*   84
Rural Cuttings: Polish *Wycinanki*   87
The Silver Screen for Social Change:
    Female Soviet Filmmakers of the Twenties   89
Moving Visions: Eastern Bloc Women in Animation   94
"Now I Lay Me Down to Sleep": Hungarian Women's *Ágyvitel*   98

6 Latin America   100
Persistent Heritage   100
Andean "Gold": Ancient Fabric of Life   102
Linear Abundance: Designs and Healing in Amazon Shipibo Pottery   104
Molas: Fabric Mosaic Blouses   106
Spirit Weavers: Nature and Belief in Wounaan Baskets   110
Bold Truths in Cloth: Chilean *Arpilleras*—The Art of Social Protest   112
Art and Revolution: Nicaragua's Solentiname Painters   116

7 Oceania   120
Sustaining Ancestral Bonds   120
Nature's Bounty: Women's *Ngatu* in the Kingdom of Tonga   122
Blending Cultures/Reclaiming Heritage: Hawaiian Quilts   124
The Land as Catalyst and Metaphor: Aboriginal Women's Art   128
Power of the Past, Forging the Future: Female Maori Artists   132

8 United States and Canada   136
Binding Family and Community   136
Echoes of Home: Quilts of Enslaved African Women   138
Bridging the Atlantic: West African Roots in Gullah Women's Art   140
A World Apart: Spiritual Faith and Amish Quilts   144
Drawing as Witness: Miné Okubo, Citizen 13660   146
Keeping It Together: Female Mexican-American Folkways   148
Arctic Images: The Art of Cape Dorset Inuit Women   152

Summary   156
Notes   157
Pronunciation Guide   161
Bibliography   162
Index   164

Preface

◠◡◠   I've craved new vistas virtually my entire life. I fortunately found early on that the arts offer me joyous journeys to real and imagined territories.

As an arts and cultural education consultant, I work with objects, exhibitions, and concepts that are magical vehicles to other realms. Art opens doors to cultures; people; values; and ways of thinking, perceiving, and communicating that greatly enrich my life. And as a woman, I am especially fascinated by how females express their unique viewpoints.

Imagine my delight when Helen Ronan, my gifted editor at Davis Publications, and I were contemplating "what's next" after my last book, *Pioneering Spirits: The Lives and Times of Remarkable Women Artists in Western History*. In her quiet, inimitable way, Helen queried, "What about a companion text—something that covers female artists around the world from prehistory on, in the non-European tradition?"

My heart leaped, and I knew I was off on another multiyear sojourn. I've experienced some of the happiest hours of work while researching and writing *Enduring Visions: Women's Artistic Heritage Around the World*. The project has posed tremendous challenges as well, not the least of which has been deciding which art, media, and regions to pursue, and which, unfortunately due to space limitations, must be left out.

A number of factors helped determine the parameters for *Enduring Visions*. Plenty of books exist about contemporary female artists from many cultures but virtually none about their collective, historical endeavors. Most texts on indigenous historical work ignore the sex of the artist entirely and focus primarily, if not exclusively, on male domains. After investigating for a number of years, I was both surprised and pleased to find that whether working long ago or today, women around the world constantly have used art as a means of social, spiritual, political, and personal expression. Women's non-Western art forms often are stupendous in and of themselves, and simultaneously reveal the artists' powerful and integral role within their communities. Much of their art today maintains its ceremonial or utilitarian value.

Unearthing information on women's indigenous visual expressions has been a special adventure, and my discoveries ultimately defined the book's final contents. I spent countless hours searching libraries, following leads from bibliographies, footnotes, and photography captions. I contacted curators, historians, scholars, gallery owners, collectors, and artists. Random conversations with friends, colleagues, or family members, as well as information from newspaper or magazine articles sometimes led to blessed finds.

> Women's non-Western art forms . . . reveal the artists' powerful and integral role within their communities.

The Internet too was essential, providing links from one person or institution to the next, until I'd finally hit gold and feel rewarded for my perseverance. Sometimes I found numerous references on a particular art form, and in other instances barely any at all. The notes reflect some of the main sources of information, and the bibliography includes additional selected resources. Of course, I also had invaluable conversations with knowledgeable individuals who helped steer my course.

Introduction

Finally, I looked at the boxes of material I'd gathered and started to formulate the table of contents. Though dictated by the availability of information and images for reproduction, I tried hard to cover a broad range of geographic areas, media, and chronological periods within each chapter. I likewise intentionally included certain types of expressions that cross cultures and time, such as women's weaving, which has long been and remains a vital mode of female creativity around the globe.

Enduring Visions focuses primarily on women's indigenous expressions because so little is gathered and easily accessible on the subject. I occasionally do, however, include Western styles—when women's entry into this field is unusual, for example, with Soviet filmmakers of the 1920s; or relatively new, as with the Shona female carvers in Zimbabwe. In these instances, women typically bring to bear distinctly female perspectives on their art and also make visual links to their ancient heritage. And don't forget that the fine arts versus crafts division is a purely Western conceit.

Enduring Visions presents a distilled mosaic of women's art around the world. I've explored a greater number of endeavors in certain locales than others, because there are more distinctly female art forms and also more research about them. Ultimately though, *Enduring Visions* does not take an encyclopedic approach but rather bastes together, possibly for the first time, selections that illuminate women's immensely creative and imaginative undertakings.

Abby Remer, September 2000

⋒ ᴗ ⋒ Women across cultures and time have been artists, although limited from the beginning of history by the consuming tasks of housework, childcare, and, certainly, constraining social attitudes. Too many people think that females historically made only "functional" daily articles. In truth, there rarely has been such a clear-cut separation between sacred works and everyday utilitarian objects in indigenous societies. Women's ornamentation on tools, clothing, or the walls of their village homes transforms what the West considers "ordinary" items into art that carries profound meaning. Images can invoke the graces of one's gods, recall an ancient lineage, or denote inherited rights and privileges of an owner. The items themselves typically are alive with the spirit of the plant, clay, or bark that remains within the finished piece.

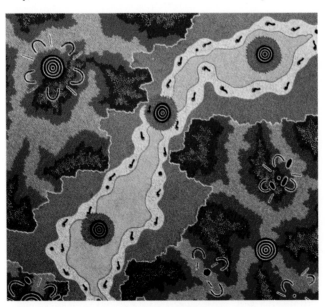

Fig. 1 How does Maureen Hudson Nampinjinpa offer a journey through time and space? Her painting is an aerial view of a long walkabout to sacred sites in Central Australia that are intimately linked to her ancestors. The "U"s are women Nampinjinpa meets, and the circles are campsites and waterholes she visits. Maureen Hudson Nampinjinpa (b. 1959), *Women's Dreaming*, 1997. Acrylic on canvas, 69" x 71" (175 x 180 cm). Courtesy Dreamtime Gallery.

Fig. 2 **Mbuti women translate both the sights and sounds of their forest surroundings into visual form. Motifs for stars, flying insects, and snakes run along the vertical column on the right.** Mbuti, Ituri Forest, Northeastern Congo, *Pongo* or *Murumba* (barkcloth), c. 1970s. Natural pigments on pounded bark, 14½ x 27¾" (37 x 70.5 cm). Collection of Andrés and Vanessa Moraga, Berkeley, CA. Photography B. Forrest.

Furthermore, females always have made art specifically for religious contexts. Historians, nonetheless, commonly study ritual items in stone, wood, and metal made by men; and taboos often routinely excluded females from these media. Yet on every continent, women's sacred art abounds.

Nigerian women, historically and today, fashion figurative ceremonial pottery that honors gods of fertility and abundance, while Indian mothers still embroider wedding tents with representations of deities who will bless their daughters' marriages with happiness and many children. Female Aborigines from Australia cover bark, canvas, and their bodies with designs related to their all-important and potent ancestors. The women's contact with the divine helps to ensure the well-being of their people. In every way, women's art around the world has been and remains integral to the social, political, economic, and also sacred core of their communities.

A sense of continuity and change infuses women's work, which typically calls upon exceedingly old artistic customs to help affirm individual identity. This ancient connection weds the past to the present—and provides a visual legacy for future generations. Nevertheless it is important to note that women's creative traditions have never been static. They live, breathe, and transform, influenced by forces both internally and externally, such as the influx of Western media or ideas.

The artists, however, rarely stress novelty—a significant criterion in the Western hierarchy. Quality is more frequently based on the person's skill rather than the Western European notion of uniqueness. For instance, Kuna women of Panama's Yala sea islands prize invisible needlework in their reverse appliqué blouses, Gullah females along the southeastern coast of the United States must deftly handle the fiber of their sweetgrass baskets, and Native Hawaiian women should emphasize stunning color contrasts when stitching quilts. Individuality might come across in the way Bhutanese female weavers arrange culturally established elements into fresh, innovative motifs, which admirers then reinterpret.

While women's art invariably has been imperative to the artist's culture, in recent decades these endeavors sometimes have become tremendous acts of courage—fighting repression and poverty. Mothers and grandmothers of the "disappeared" in Chile stitched arresting visual denouncements chronicling atrocities of General Augusto Pinochet's dictatorship. Self-taught Solentiname peasant painters in

Nicaragua aligned art making with their hope for a better future under Sandinista rule.

Many women have learned that their artwork will bring them a much-needed income to help provide for their families. In Weya, a small native reserve village in Zimbabwe, women invented a new resist dye fabric technique, similar to batik, using *sadza*, their dietary staple of cornmeal mush, to achieve personal and economic freedom, despite the anger this liberation ignited in their husbands.

Fearless females in every country today continue to use art as part of their historical roles as healers and cultural bearers. The women's ancestors must be proud and thankful that they carry on their heritage in both old and ever-new impressive ways. *Enduring Visions* offers a window into women's inspiring and eternally vital creativity, across the globe and through the centuries.

Fig. 3 **Robyn Kahukiwa painted the front of this traditional *whare* (house) built by Haeata, a Maori women's collective. The images speak to current social issues and Kahukiwa's ancient heritage. See pages 133–134 for more about this artwork.** Robyn Kahukiwa (b. 1940) (Ngati Porou, Te Aitanga-A-Hauiti, Ngati Hau), *Ko Hineteiwaiwa Te Whare*, 1984. Mixed media on board, approximately 9' (2.7 m) high. Collection Fletcher Challenge Corporation. Copyright, photograph, and permission courtesy the artist.

1 Africa

Linking the Secular and Sacred Realm

Is there a separation between art and life in traditional African culture? All works are indispensable components of daily existence, which itself is closely tied to the sacred realm. Although there is no singular African identity, Africans traditionally believe a living force or energy exists within not just people but all objects as well. Women's artistic efforts directly influence the social and, frequently, the spiritual fabric of their communities. Their endeavors, which come from the earth's natural riches, often are decorative and symbolic, and also communicate with the cosmos. Women transform the ordinary into the extraordinary—for instance, converting clay dug from the earth's surface into figurative pots that speak to and honor the gods. Moreover, women's art helps construct and maintain a culture's ideology. It is essential to farming, hunting, birth, initi-

1-1 Can you discern nature-based images adorning this compound wall? *Uli* (body painting) designs of the Igbo women of southeastern Nigeria strongly influence their mural motifs, which can relate to nature—sky, water, forest, or animals. These motifs can symbolize strength, power, and bravery. A senior wife, or skilled artist, typically oversees the painting, which is meant to beautify the home and assert both clan and individual identity. Igbo, *Uli Patterns*, 1987. Clay pigments on mud surface. Photography M. Courtney-Clarke.

1-2 How do Mbuti women reinforce their peoples' connection to the natural world?
They literally craft the forest into wearable art—painted barkcloth that itself reflects shadow-and-sunlight patterns through trees, insect trails, and nature spirits. Pongo or Murumba, *Mbuti Barkcloth,* Ituri Forest, Northeastern Congo. c. 1980s. Natural pigments on pounded inner bark, 28½ x 15½" (72 x 39 cm). Collection of Andrés and Vanessa Moraga, Berkeley, CA. Photography B. Forrest.

ation, marriage, death, and healing rituals that shape the way people interact with and perceive the world.[1]

In most traditional African societies, women and men maintain a distinct division of labor. In artistic production, women primarily work in soft materials while men use wood, ivory, and metal. Taboos help protect the distinct rights and privileges of male and female artistic domains. Occasionally, men and women participate in each other's media. Men weave the raffia cloth that Kuba women of the Democratic Republic of the Congo cover with velvety embroidered abstractions. Among the Bamana of Mali, women join men as blacksmiths, an almost exclusively male-dominated profession in Africa associated with access to supernatural powers.[2]

African women use their own materials, as well as symbols and designs, to express their view of the visible and unseen realms. As Margaret Courtney-Clarke, the renowned photographer of African women's work, states, "Their art, like all art, means to delight the eye, console the troubled mind, appease the highest authority, and educate children in the way of the world."[3]

Sacred Earth/Heavenly Connection: Women's Pottery in Nigeria

◉ ◡ ◉ Clay comes from Mother Earth and, since earliest times, African females have dominated pottery making. In working with the earth's flesh, they brush up against the spirits and ancestors residing there.[4] Women scoop out the soft material at sacred sites and then give birth to a fantastic array of vessels, echoing their roles as mothers.

Picture a woman in Nigeria around the eighth millennium BCE forming the oldest known ceramic remains.[5] She and her ancestors fashioned wares for cooking; dyeing cloth; smoking meats; frying foods; and storing ashes, charcoal, firewood, water, clothing, and provisions.[6]

But African women also molded crucial anthropomorphic and zoomorphic vessels related to the sacred realm. Many scholars have wrongly assumed that African men constructed these amazing items because males retained the privilege of carving sacred figurative forms in wood. The women's fascinating ceramics nevertheless demonstrate their strong participation in, and influence on, the spiritual life of their cultures. Women's pottery has long helped construct social and ritual meaning, often augmenting their responsibilities as priestesses, diviners, holy persons, and healers.[7]

Edo Women Potters: Creativity and Productivity

Within the Edo kingdom of Benin, Nigeria, female potters produce sacred items for Olokun cult shrines. The deity himself inspires the artist or priestess (known as an *omakhe*), directly through a dream, providing guidance and protection against accident and witchcraft during the creative process.[8] Both men and women sculpt life-size tableaux representing the undersea palace of the Bini god of the waters. Females, however, are responsible for the central shrine objects—fine figurative pots that initiates keep filled with water. (Fig. 1-3) How does the sculpted ware indicate the relationship

1-3 The pythons slithering around the sides of this evocative ware are messengers of the gods. The artist unified the entire piece with incised markings, some replicating women's scarification marks and others creating an eye-catching decorative design. Edo people, Benin. *Benin Figurative Pot for Olokun Shrine.* Ceramic, 13⅜ x 11¼ x 11¾" (34 x 28.5 x 30 cm). The British Museum. Collected 1948.

between Olokun and Edo women's essential role in the community's continuity? The ceramic "devotee" carries life inside her pregnant belly and milk within her swollen breasts, just as the vessel itself cradles fresh river water,[9] a liquid intimately tied to the river deity, Olokun, who is responsible for fertility.

Bini women particularly worship Olokun because of his association with childbirth. He provides offspring and, in Benin society, large families are a source of wealth and prestige.[10] Bini women typically maintain a domestic altar to Olokun. Parents install a small shrine at the birth of a daughter for her protection and well-being. The bride will move the shrine to her husband's home when she marries.[11]

According to Bini mythology, Olokun's father created the first human beings out of clay—the same material artists themselves use to mold pots and shrines.[12] Women's lives, therefore, parallel the divine as they bear children and form vessels, like the gods, with the earth's resources.

Yoruba Female Potters: Fertility and the Divine

Yoruba women of Nigeria similarly produce fertile female figures on wares that glorify King Erinle— the mighty sovereign of the seas and the underwater kingdom. (Fig. 1-4) Like Olokun for the Edo, King Erinle is responsible for the continuity and prosperity of Yoruba society. Every domestic altar to the god must have one of these ceramic, lidded vessels.[13] Devotees drop river stones inside the figure's bulging "belly," suggesting seeds of new life.[14] Initiates also fill the vessel every sixteen days with active water from the river or sea—the very essence of King Erinle himself.[15]

Female Edo potters complete each lid with a proud bust. The scarification on the figure's cheeks and forehead frequently resemble those of the pot's patron. These marks, which signify rank, maturity, and beauty, link the vessel to the donor. The hairstyle, along with the figure's flawless skin, portrays a young woman in her prime, healthy and ready for her reproductive role.[16] All the features help elongate the woman's head, which to the Yoruba is the essence of personality and spiritual protection derived from God.[17]

Labor of Love Pottery production is back-breaking labor. Women often walk miles for the best-quality clay. After intensive preparation and molding, the women endure tremendous heat when removing their vessels from firing. Artists finally load the wares on top of their heads and traipse off to local and regional markets.

1-4 Abatan was a prestigious senior member of the Erinle cult and a magnificent master potter. Her figure's braids, shoulders, breasts, forehead, cheeks, bridge of her nose, and scarification marks all swell slightly, breathing life into this vessel associated with fertility. Abatan, *Awo ota erinle ("Vessel for the stones of Erinle")*, 20th century. Ceramic with iron chain necklace, approx. 16" (40.6 cm). Nigeria, central Egbado Yoruba. Courtesy Robert Thompson.

Igbo Women Potters: Sustenance and Procreation

In southeast Nigeria, female Igbo potters also helped mediate between the supernatural and worldly arena for their people's longevity. They were both diviners and artists in the Ifijioku (Yam Spirit) cult. Adherents consecrated the pots during the October yam harvest and festival, placing the ware in a shallow hole, filled with water and surrounded by fresh yams.[18] The hardy vegetable physically sated empty stomachs, and, by extension, its precious sustenance brought new life into women's wombs. How did artists refer to family and procreation in their vessels? (Fig. 1-5) In the bountiful grouping, one wife is pregnant, another nurses, and a child sits before them.

Igbo women created exceptional wares for Ifijioku cult shrines until the early decades of the twentieth century. Their elaborately hand-

1-5 How does the Igbo artist indicate that the central man is one of rank? He is wealthy enough to have two wives who wear elaborate hairstyles and body decoration. Their fans, like the husband's top hat, bead necklace, sacrificial fowl, and ivory trumpet, further affirm his stature. Kwale, *Ibo Yam Spirit Figurative Shrine for Cult of Ifijioku.* Ceramic, 18½ x 14⅛ x 9⅞" (47 x 36 x 25 cm). The British Museum. Collected in 1880.

molded and incised pots, with multiple handles and spouts, were the community's finest examples, because, according to Igbo belief, people must only serve the gods and ancestors with the best.[19]

Female Dakakari Artists and the Eternal World

Nigerian women do not only create ceramics associated with reproduction. For instance, how might these animated creatures be linked to the afterworld? (Figs. 1-6, 1-7) Dakakari women of northwest Nigeria have formed both human and animal vessels, perhaps for centuries, as offerings to ancestral spirits. Their distinctive items crown low, cylindrical earthen grave mounds of important

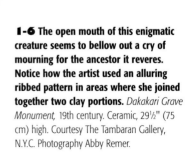

1-7 What does this accordion-necked being represent? Possibly it is a new-born goat, which stands as a perpetual "sacrifice" to the family's ancestors. *Dakakari Grave Monument,* 19th century. Ceramic, 25" (63.5 cm) high. Courtesy The Tambaran Gallery, N.Y.C. Photography Abby Remer.

1-6 The open mouth of this enigmatic creature seems to bellow out a cry of mourning for the ancestor it reveres. Notice how the artist used an alluring ribbed pattern in areas where she joined together two clay portions. *Dakakari Grave Monument,* 19th century. Ceramic, 29½" (75 cm) high. Courtesy The Tambaran Gallery, N.Y.C. Photography Abby Remer.

tribal men and women.

Only females from select family groups can sculpt these fascinating terracotta monuments. The artists carefully guard their skills, passing them down from mother to daughter, or to females in the extended family.[20]

The potters mold an impressive array of objects. Elephants are the largest and most expensive commissions, followed by antelopes, bush cows, buffalo, goats, and, occasionally, camels. Riders sitting on top of creatures similar to the one in Fig. 1-6 may represent chief warriors. In some areas, people consider single standing female and male beings to be servants for the deceased, who have "gone to live with God."[21]

Dakakari women also fashion pseudo vessels called "pots of the grave," which are permanently sealed and hold offerings of honey. They resemble regular ceramic ware or calabashes, and are used by the dead in the afterlife. People can buy these functional vessels for commemorative use at market, but must directly commission a female potter for the more superlative figurative works.

The Dakakari traditionally honor their ancestors each year to secure good fortune in a ceremony during which they "feed" the vessels a mixture of guinea corn flour and water.[22] Like the Chinese or ancient Egyptians, the Dakakari venerate the dead, hoping to influence their own future.

Longuda Female Potters: Health and Healing

Nigerian women also produce ceramics that affect people's spiritual and physical health. For the Longuda, pots can help cure the ill. Women from this tribe in the Gongola Valley of northeastern Nigeria are both healers and artists. They create appealing *kwandalha* wares used in the healing cult of the same name. (Fig. 1-8) Longuda women use the pots in divinatory rites to diagnose and cure disease. When a patient consults them, they first take soft clay and touch the person's head and abdomen, inducing the spirit to leave the body and enter the earthen material instead. Artists then fashion a vessel in human form and, when complete, circle it around the patient's head. The person will later fire the item at home and deposit it in a nearby shrine where the disease-causing spirit can be appeased.[23,24]

1-8 How did female artists transform these pots into unusual ware? Outstretched hands, expressive faces, and rough surface textures animate the healing vessels. *Longuda Healing Vessels (kwandalha)* from Dangir, Nigeria. Photograph (1981) and permission Marla C. Berns.

Nigerian Women's Prevalence in Ceramics

Ga'anada and Bena women, also from the Gongola Valley, likewise create some of their culture's ritual vessels that help maintain the survival and well-being of individual and group. Throughout Nigeria, in fact, female potters—like their foremothers—produce works for utilitarian purposes. They also make imperative, ritual ceramics bound to the gods who help keep life on its proper track.

Cultural Declarations: Ndebele Women's Beadwork and Murals

◐ ◡ ◐   How did countless decades of persecution give rise to Ndebele mural painting in South Africa? (Fig. 1-9) Although considered traditional, the art form first came into being as recently as the 1940s.

The wall paintings emerged out of adversity. The women's striking, geometric images visually declare the tribe's identity, which white invaders and the later apartheid government nearly destroyed after decades of conflict and dislocation. Ndebele women began to pour their creative energies onto the walls, as if crying out "we are still here" after they and their families were forced onto desolate farmland without adequate facilities.

An Old, Yet New, Art Form

The women's wall paintings are definitely modern, but are knitted to the past. In the mid-1800s, if not before, women used their fingers to create *kguphu*—engraved straight, squiggled, and curving parallel-line motifs in wet plaster walls of cow dung and mud. Some Ndebele believe that their ancestors demanded the creation of these spiritually potent designs, which would protect people's homes from evil spirits and ensure tribal continuity.[25]

Despite its antecedents, the women's boldly painted geometric compositions of the 1940s were actually very new. Ironically, outsiders flocked to see what they mistakenly perceived as an historically "traditional" Ndebele expression. People's interest was so keen that the government moved the entire village with the first murals to an area northwest of Pretoria. They marketed it as an authentic, "traditional" tourist village, dressing Ndebele men and women in ritual wear instead of their modern clothing.[26] The commercialization of this fictional community nonetheless brought the women much-needed money, as visitors paid to see their homes. The village also inspired Ndebele women living in other territories to develop their own painting styles.

The wall decorations are not sacred, but the designs do connect to the tribe's ritual structure. Women teach young girls the fine points of painting during their initiation.[27] Ndebele women also renew their images for significant celebrations and ceremonies, as for a boy's all-important passage into manhood.

Initially, murals were fairly simple geometric compositions, abstracting the domestic environment. Women soon began filling in the designs so that there was almost no distinction between image and background. More recently, the artists have appropriated symbols of domestic wealth, such as telephone poles, staircases, electric lights, and airplanes (see Fig. 1-9) into their motifs. Ironically, in many outlying villages, these items may actually be far beyond reach. Many women's employment as domestic help, hours away in white suburban homes, furnishes fodder for their dreams.

Artistic Criteria Ndebele women do not paint for acclaim. What sets off one's work from another is her style of decoration and choice of colors. People will call wall work or beaded garments "good," referring to their quality or the inventiveness of a design. Ndebele have no word for "beauty."

I-9 What image does Betty Mahlangu incorporate from the urban environment into her compound design? Her abstracted airplane nestles snuggly within the geometric designs. An Ndebele woman's wall painting can describe the world—or the one she wishes to see. *Ndebele home painted by Betty Mahlangu,* 1983. Photography M. Courtney-Clarke.

Ndebele Women's Beadwork: A Parallel Art Form

Urban-inspired imagery finds its way into the women's magnificent beadwork as well. (Fig. 1-10) Unlike the recent murals, however, the women indeed have beaded for centuries. Archaeological evidence indicates that beads infiltrated the area through trade with the East at least as early as the first few centuries CE. Ndebele women began working with beads that came from Czechoslovakia starting in the mid-nineteenth century, when European traders first brought them to present-day eastern Transvaal.[28]

During the 1880s, women created white beaded pieces with just a hint of delicate, colored abstraction. (Fig. 1-11) By the 1920s and 1930s, Ndebele artists introduced new designs symbolically relating to the

domestic environment, as they did in the later wall murals. Over time, these emblems have lost their original associations but remain an integral part of all female life.

Women welcome newborns to the tribe and ensure good fortune with an *umucu*, a single strand of beads. Young girls wear simply beaded, soft loin aprons strung around their waists. (See Fig. 1-10) After initiation, elaborate stiff beaded aprons symbolically guard their chastity. Suitors know that a young woman is

1-10 Letty Ngoma richly adorns both her walls and blanket. Women customize commercial blankets with original beadwork, working freehand without preliminary sketches, and adding spectacular strips throughout their marriage. In earlier days, females wore their blankets whenever they appeared in public.
Letty Ngoma, *Ngurara, ceremonial blanket,* 1983. Cloth and beads. Photography M. Courtney-Clarke.

ready for marriage when she dons decorated skirts that alluringly draw attention
to her hips and buttocks.

Naturally, beadwork also pervades
traditional marriage garments. Likewise,
after a woman's son completes his initiation his mother nobly wears a narrow
headband with two thin, head-to-ground
beaded strips. This *linga koba* ("long
tears") signifies her "loss of a son," as he
becomes an adult. The linga koba reflects
the mother's own mature status.[29]

Not every Ndebele girl currently learns
to bead. Families often hire specialists to
make ceremonial wear. Sadly, traditional
styles are becoming obsolete as young
patrons demand the now-fashionable broad
geometric "party designs," which lack the
refinement of the earliest examples and the
complexity of those their mothers wear. Still,
some women tuck away special pieces for
future generations. They use these hidden
treasures to communicate with the ancestors—
who they believe would not recognize nor
honor the more modern expressions.[30]

1-11 Does this minimal design recall European twentieth-century
abstraction? The fine beads and elegant red and blue design indicate that
this *tshgholo* is over 100 years old. Although considered a marriage apron,
Ndebele women actually don this five-paneled piece only after giving birth
to their first child. *Tshgholo, traditional ceremonial skirt,* c. 1900. Beads.
Photography M. Courtney-Clarke.

Buried Beads If women
have used beads for cen-
turies, then why don't examples prior to the nineteenth
century exist? Ndebele
women today pass on their
prized beaded work to
female relatives, but in earlier
times, their ornate wear was
buried with them, to be
worn by the deceased's new
incarnation.

Rejoicing in the Forest: Mbuti Barkcloth Painting

The forest is everything to the Mbuti. It is nurturance and a sacred sanctuary for this nomadic hunting-and-gathering tribe living for generations within the Ituri rain forest in northeastern Congo. The fractured geometry of the forest's leaves and branches permeate Mbuti art (Figs. 1-2, 1-12), allowing people to communicate with one another and the nature spirits.

Barkcloth painting is a communal effort, paralleling the tribe's egalitarian system. From an early age, young boys turn to the forest, learning to separate a tree's outer layer from its inner skin and skillfully make the fiber supple by scraping, pounding, and placing it in water or over fire. Women too search the forest, gathering roots, leaves, and fruits for dyes. They use twigs, twine, or sometimes their fingers as brushes, and sit with the cloth, often folded into sections, on their laps as they work. A woman might paint alone or another occasionally may take over her work, adding a separate "voice" to the piece. (See Fig. 1-12.) They complete the wearable paintings in a matter of hours.

1-12 Is each side of the cloth the same? Perhaps one or more women made this work, although it is not unusual for a single artist to change styles midstream. The designs are abstract, but some might relate to the Mbuti's environment, invoking insects, stars, and vines. Pongo or Murumba, *Mbuti Barkcloth*, Ituri Forest, Northeastern Congo, c. 1970s. Natural pigments on pounded inner bark, approx. 18 x 28" (46 x 71 cm). Collection of Andrés and Vanessa Moraga, Berkeley, CA. Photography B. Forrest.

Mothers swaddle their infants at birth in the forest's embrace, symbolically transforming them into *bamiki bandura*, "children of the forest"—born of a tree.[31] Adults also wear barkcloth garments daily and during tribal rituals: a boy's puberty ceremony, a girl's *ima* (initiation), weddings, and funerals.[32] Women wrap narrow rectangular items around themselves like a skirt, while men belt square cloths about their waists.

The forest pervades the designs as well. The women's improvised lines charge, like flights of fancy, across the soft surface at tremendous velocity. The filigree segments loosely evoke the stars, shifting shadows made by sunlight shining through leaves, and the snakes, insects, and creatures amongst the trees. (Fig. 1-13) Many images are abstract. The Mbuti treasure the complexity of a design over its resemblance to reality. Women intentionally incorporate voids and empty spaces within their compositions. (See Fig. 1-13.) Mbuti *yeyi* (polyphonic singing), at which women excel, includes these same breaks or quiet. Both the women's spontaneous art and music revere the ever-shifting movement and stillness, noise and silence, inherent in the sights and sounds of their natural surroundings.

An Ancient History In a text from 2000 BCE, ancient Egyptians called the Mbuti "pygmies," referring to their small physical stature, and praised their creative powers. The Mbuti today still daily express their exuberant joy of living through mime, music, storytelling, and women's painting on bark, faces, and bodies.

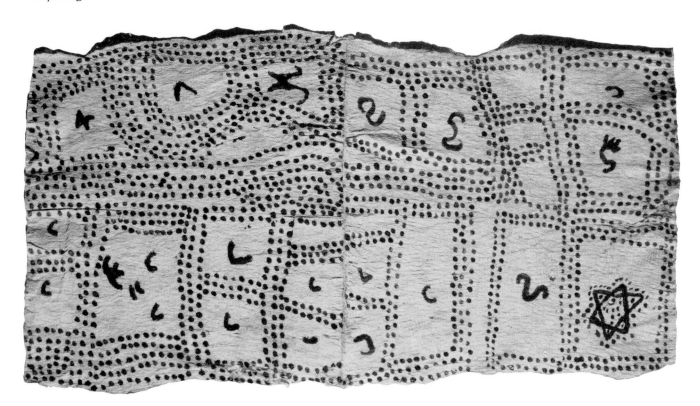

1-13 Do the artist's marks evoke birds, butterflies, snakes, celestial patterns, or ant trails? Mbuti women share motifs—painting themselves, children, and barkcloth—but their exact meaning remains elastic and elusive. Notice the interplay between the images and pregnant empty spaces. Pongo or Murumba, *Mbuti Barkcloth,* Ituri Forest, Northeastern Congo, c. 1970s. Natural pigments on pounded inner bark, approx. 29½ x 15½" (75 x 39 cm). Collection of Andrés and Vanessa Moraga, Berkeley, CA. Photography B. Forrest.

The Power of Cloth:
Kuba *Kasai* Textiles, Rank, and Prestige

How might a clever young girl catch the eye of a king? According to Kuba legend, Kashashi—just such an inventive young person—learned that the monarch was going to hold a dance where all the beautiful women of the kingdom would appear. Kashashi hid herself away in a hut, covering a skirt with the most spectacular embroidery. When she wore the skirt to the dance, the king was so enchant-ed that he married her. *Kasai* embroidery was born.[33]

For the Kuba, who today live in the Democratic Republic of the Congo (formerly Zaire), clothing does more than protect people from the elements. It is essential to the political, cultural, and religious fabric of society. Boys gather the fibers of the raffia palm and men weave it into cloth. Women dye the textiles with natural pigments. They then embroider it free-

hand, experimenting with patterns drawn from memory, creating superb velvety panels with dazzling stitched and cut-pile (plush) geometric motifs.[34] (Fig. 1-14) Women stitch every day, in between working the fields and caring for the home and family.[35] An exquisite plush piece may take many months or even years to complete.[36]

Kasai Embroidery Historically

Fine raffia cloth has ancient roots in Kuba culture. Traditionally, noble Kuba women embroidered cloth during their pregnancy. Beyond their intrinsic beauty,

these prestige items signaled the fact that a prosperous or royal husband could afford to have his several wives working on such luxury pieces, instead of toiling in the fields.[37]

In the nineteenth century, a young groom would weave a raffia skirt that his mother or sister would embroider, and then he would offer it to his prospective mother-in-law as part of the brideprice.[38]

In public ceremonies, Kuba men historically wore raffia skirts gathered about their hips, with the upper end folded over a belt and the lower edge hanging down below their knees. Women draped embellished skirts around their bodies.[39] The charcoal, ochre, creamy beige, and earthen brown patterns shimmered as wearers danced in the festivities.

Women's Embroidered Works Today

Kasai cloth currently remains most significant in the passing from this world to *ilueemy*, the land of the dead, where the deceased resides until her or his spirit returns to earth in a generation or so.[40] The Kuba prepare someone of high rank for this journey by burying the body in many layers of embroidered skirts. People would consider the dead to be nude without them.[41] The cloth affirms the person's status and wealth, which in turn helps the clan maintain esteem.

Although most Kuba today dress in modern garments, many use raffia textiles at funerals. Women embroider during long periods of mourning.[42] These engaging works that women decorate serve as strong connections to the afterlife and as emblems of ancestral ethnic identity amid a rapidly changing contemporary world.

1 - 14 Can you trace the geometric design on this raffia cloth without lifting your finger off the page? Children play a game of drawing this same *mbolo* motif in the sand. The never-ending pattern symbolizes the birth-life-death cycle and the harmony of all things. *Kasai Raffia Cloth,* The Democratic Republic of the Congo, c. 1970. Raffia, 50½ x 21½" (128 x 55 cm). Courtesy The Liberty Textile Collection.

The Magic of Stone: Shona Female Carvers

◠◡◠ Might a woman have carved these ancient, mysterious bird-capped columns from Great Zimbabwe in southeast Africa? (Fig. 1-15) Ancestors of the Shona—possibly females, although likely males, sculpted eight of these tremendous works for the eastern enclosure of the magnificent cultural capital, which thrived from around 800 CE to the 1400s.

The sex of the ancient artists remains a mystery. So does the reason that their carving tradition completely disappeared for hundreds of years once the Portuguese arrived in the early sixteenth century, followed by the British in the late 1880s. Women, however, were soon among the ranks of those sculptors who suddenly took chisel to stone once again, starting in the mid-twentieth century. (Fig. 1-16) This extraordinary sculpture renaissance seems to have begun in 1957, when the newly appointed director of the country's National Art Gallery, Frank McEwen, defied colonialists' expectations for a museum of western European work and instead sought out and

1-15 The bird-topped monoliths from the ancient civilization of Great Zimbabwe are sometimes called *Shiri ya Mwari*, or Bird of God, which perhaps served as ancestral links to heaven. People adopted the birds as their national emblem after their victory in the war of liberation in 1980. *Ancient Bird Capitals of Great Zimbabwe.* Photograph © Robert Holmes 1992.

nurtured indigenous expressions.[43]

McEwen, and then others, helped found small art communities and workshops. The artists experimented and assisted one another, but their creative process was, and remains, deeply rooted in the supernatural realm.

Shona Art and the Spirit World

Everything in the Shona world is controlled by powerful spirits. Sculptor Bernard Takawira explains, "With all those spirits around, magic is bound to creep into our sculpture."[44]

The ancestral spirits, *midzimu*, often come to the artists in dreams, inspiring people to translate their visions into stone.[45] *Midzimu* guide the artist at every step, from selecting the raw material to carving and polishing the finished product. The spirit's good will is particularly important during the firing stage, which is unique to Shona sculpture. Hours, even months of work, can suddenly end in an explosion of a million shards if the stone is heated too quickly. But the flames are necessary to expand the pores in the sculpture's surface, preparing it for layers of wax that will bring out the piece's alluring natural colors.[46]

Despite its ancestral connection, the artwork is neither sacred nor ceremonial. And unlike much other African art, they are not functional objects for daily living. The Shona carve pieces for themselves as aesthetic items to adorn homes and villages, although of late the sculptures are becoming popular in the international art market. Each composition, nonetheless, stems from Shona culture and spiritual legacy, thereby embodying the people's long-held values and beliefs.

1-16 **What connects this contemporary sculpture to the ancient capitals in Fig. 1-15? Locadia Ndandarika, the foremother of modern female Shona sculptors, retains a similar simplicity of form. She imbues her stone with a regal bearing that carries the title.** Locadia Ndandarika, *Pride of My People,* 1998. Serpentine, 23½ x 8½ x 10½" (57 x 22 x 27 cm). Spirits in Stone Galleries, Zimbabwe Sculpture, Inc. Photography Anthony Ponter, Zimbabwe Sculpture, Inc.

1-17 Agnes Nyanhongo began sculpting under her father's tutelage. She honors all African women through Runako, or "most beautiful woman," who has fulfilled her destiny as the spiritual cornerstone of the sacred family unit. Nyanhongo states, "I think it's important to use art to spread traditional stories. I want my sculpture to send messages to my children and grandchildren so they will never forget our culture." Agnes Nyanhongo, *Beautiful Woman*, c. mid-1990s. Serpentine, 10 x 7 x 7" (25 x 18 x 18 cm). Spirits in Stone Galleries, Zimbabwe Sculpture, Inc. Photography Anthony Ponter, Zimbabwe Sculpture, Inc.

Shona Women Sculptors

Female Shona artists infuse a uniquely female perspective into themes relating to the spirit world, mythology, family, and folklore. Many, particularly within the youngest generation, also tackle modern issues, such as women's rights and social concerns. Regardless of the subject, the women's works share a bold physical presence, often softened by the delicacy of alternating polished and rough surfaces. (Fig. 1-17) But it is the art's emotional content, the ability to immediately evoke feelings and the senses that makes the strongest impact. The Shona greatly honor emotions. For instance, they name children after feelings such as happiness, gratefulness, or thanks.[47]

There are thirty-five or more female sculptors today among the hundreds of male compatriots. Despite recent changes in Zimbabwean society (including the war of independence won in 1980, in which women fought alongside men), these women's voyage has not always been easy.

The earliest female to chisel is Locadia Ndandarika (see Fig. 1-16), whose first-generation artist-husband showed no respect for her work when she began in 1969. Ndandarika eventually divorced him, successfully sold her art, and raised the family alone. She insists, "Women must help each other to learn so they can become free."[48] Women do mentor one another, and Agnes Nyanhongo (see Fig. 1-17), acknowledged by many as one of Zimbabwe's finest sculptors, now even has several young male apprentices.[49]

The Lingering Mystery

The question still remains: Why, after centuries of rest, did Shona stone carving suddenly spring back to life in the late 1950s? Possibly anonymous carvers were working all along, as their ancestors had, but the white colonialists neither recognized nor recorded the creativity around them.

When Frank McEwen opened shop, Shona artists with absolutely no prior training intuitively gravitated to sculpture. They immediately started producing pieces of tremendous force that resonated with art from various cultures around the world. Until recently, however, Shona artists were geographically and politically isolated from outside sources. Perhaps the skills lay dormant for generations within their blood. Or maybe the ancestor spirits, who can see the past, present, and future, empowered the people's new endeavors.

Women today remain integral to Shona sculpture's evolution. They help to nurture it, like the babes they strap to their backs—shaping the living stone with their personal visions, voices, and experiences.

1-18 **What is the overriding emotion of Mavis Mabwe's work? The entwined embrace captures the Shona's esteem for love, which ideally extends from the sacred family unit to the greater love of all humanity. Similar to other female Shona sculptors, Mabwe expresses ideas of deep personal concern.** Mavis Mabwe, *Lover's Embrace*, c. mid-1990s. Spirits in Stone Galleries, Zimbabwe Sculpture, Inc. Photography Anthony Ponter, Zimbabwe Sculpture, Inc.

Art as Necessity: Weya Women's *Sadza Resist Fabric Painting*

I-19 How does the artist unite her composition? She arranges images of female village life into an interlocking mosaic of related colors. Each form connects with another and yet succinctly captures women's work of bearing food, cooking, making pottery, and childcare. *Weya painting,* between 1989–92. *Sadza* resist, 38½ x 54" (98 x 137 cm). Courtesy Luisella Garlick. Photography Laura Yates.

Poverty bore down upon them. Many men were unemployed or had abandoned their wives and children for urban jobs and the lure of city living. The Shona women of Weya, a small native reserve village in Zimbabwe, turned to art for survival.

Over a few short years, starting in 1988, Ilse Noy, a German from the Volunteer Service, helped the Shona develop various distinct creative endeavors. The women initially worked with appliqué, and then a courageous group took up brush and paints for the first time in their culture's history. A Weya artist recalls, "Painting was difficult. We had never done anything like that before—drawing everything. Using brushes."[50] In 1989, some women pursued embroidery and still others invented *sadza* fabric painting, in which they used cornmeal mush in a resist technique similar to batik. The artworks quickly sold in both national and international markets.

Female Weya Artists Today

Weya women continue to spend much time in their fields and gardens, working on art at other moments. Their special visions depict rural village life (Fig. 1-19), traditional lore, political and social problems, and the arena of medicine, spirits, and witchcraft. (Fig. 1-20)

Most artists pack their background space with figures,

I-20 A Weya woman explains, "The world of the spirits is close to the world of everyday life for us, the Shona. Some are benevolent, like the 'curing spirit' who brings information about where to find and how to use medicines. Some are revengeful and are dangerous. Some announce themselves as ancestors who bring their family members protection."[55] Baboons, snakes, lizards, and hippos are examples of the creatures the Shona associate with the spirit realm. *Weya painting.* Courtesy Luisella Garlick. Photography Laura Yates.

creatures, and border designs relating to nature. (Fig. 1-21) Unlike the few male painters, the women are unconcerned with naturalism. Instead, they focus on generating interesting combinations with symbols loosely tied to the observable world.

The women originally belonged to a cooperative. They donated part of their earnings to pay for raw materials and the marketing of their finished products. Some artists currently live in the city and sell directly to galleries and shops. Their ability to earn a living is vitally important. As one comments, "I pay school fees for the children and buy clothes for them because their father doesn't work. Now I am earning the money in the family. If I was not painting, the children would not be going to school."[51]

Breaking New Ground

Weya women speak repeatedly of their new freedom— not just economic, but also within their social roles. Taboos about what they may or may not say in public, and in front of men, no longer apply. After depicting anything and everything in their artwork, the women no longer avoid topics such as men's drunken escapades or sexual exploits. The women, however, have found that buyers are not interested in scenes describing black-white social

A Conflict of Values
A Weya woman explains, "In the workshop cooperative, women who step out of the ordinary attract too much attention. Europeans brought ideas of competition that were foreign to our community. They confuse many relationships."

relations nor images of Chimurenga (the war of liberation in which many women fought against apartheid and English colonial rule, before Rhodesia became Zimbabwe in 1980).[52] Female artists instead focus on images of daily life in all its permutations.

Shona women historically wove barkcloth blankets and baskets and fashioned ceramic ware. They had never painted scenes around them. At first many men were against the women's new undertaking, but the artists' impressive income soon changed most of their minds. Some men, though, still objected, threatened by their wives' financial independence. The women's earnings often far exceeded those of their husbands, fathers, and brothers.[53] The painters' prosperity occasionally caused friction among the women as well. Jealous neighbors who did not paint sometimes accused an accomplished artist of witchcraft, a serious accusation that the Shona use to guarantee that no one person becomes too powerful. Successful female artists often hide their talents. They continue to paint nonetheless—to express themselves and earn money to provide for their families.

Through this fresh art form, Weya women have gained a sense of equality with men. They also generate cultural pride as outsiders demonstrate interest in their world. Through art, "We show how we are living in the villages, our daily life. . . . Our children will know how we were living if the pictures are hanging in the galleries."[54]

1-21 Notice how the artist has sprinkled decorative motifs on the butterfly, the two creatures pounding maize, the one at the water pump, and over the flower petals. The alternating floral bands and the U-shaped frame further emphasize the picture's two-dimensionality. *Weya painting,* 1989–92. *Sadza* resist, 38 x 56" (96.5 x 142 cm). Courtesy Luisella Garlick. Photography Laura Yates.

2 Arab World

Politics and Identity

Conflict, rather than art, perhaps most readily leaps to mind when thinking about the Middle East. Battles, economic hardship, and political turmoil infiltrate daily life throughout the region, from Morocco to Iraq.

There is no one "Arab" culture. Diverse countries, ethnic groups, belief systems, sects, and cultural traits populate the area. Art by Arab women echoes this expansive medley, forging an identity amid a plethora of influences. But politics is never far from sight, specifically or indirectly touching each group's expressions.

Nomadic women sustain centuries-old weaving traditions that remain integral to their itinerant lifestyle. Modern incursions and local governments, however, threaten historical ways, affecting the quality and destination of the women's products. Their superb handwork frequently ends up in foreign homes instead of the artists' family compounds.

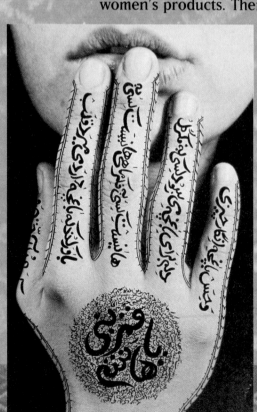

Politics too displaced the Jews of Yemen, who had inhabited the land since the third century CE. Increasingly few of the young women living in exile in Israel today practice the embroidery or ceremonial henna body painting of their ancestors. Traditions and rites transform or melt away as groups resettle on lands not originally their own.

Female Arab artists working in contemporary media actively participate in the international dialogue.

2-1 Is Shirin Neshat's gesture an act of intimacy or silencing? Her self-portrait explores both the mystique and allure popularly attributed to Arab women—while also probing Islam's strict limitations on women's personal freedom. Shirin Neshat, *Untitled (Hand over Mouth)*, 1996. Gelatin silver print and ink, 66 ½ x 48" (169 x 122 cm).

2-2 Laila Shawa critiques Arab society and, in particular, women's problematic position within it. Her highly sensuous decoration and color emphasize the culture's tendency to perceive Arab women as objects. The veils on the blind figures prevent them from tasting the tantalizing ice cream—an enticing Western commodity—which they hold within their grasp. Laila Shawa, *The Impossible Dream,* 1988. 102 x 76" (259 x 193 cm). Courtesy the artist.

At times their nonfigurative art contains few discernible visual links to the past—until we realize that Arabic geometric abstraction preceded twentieth-century European modernism by hundreds of years. A growing number of Arab women artists living at home and abroad are now addressing politics directly with narrative images, frequently examining the human cost of armed conflict. These women are breaking culturally defined roles that had previously limited them. Female Arab artists working in all media and traditions, then, are continuing to meet the ever-changing reality of their lives with engaging visual works.

Migrating Feasts for the Eyes: Middle Eastern Nomadic Art

◉◡◉ A woman sits outdoors weaving. Her carpets are her home, comfort, and security—an inseparable part of tribal life. Despite popular belief, nomadic existence is not one of surviving with just the barest necessities. She and her community require a substantial amount of material wealth to maintain their twice-yearly migrations. They have tents, ropes, bedding, cooking and herding tools; costly horses and camels for transportation; and livestock that provide meat, milk, leather, and the all-important wool for the women's weaving creations.[1]

Preparing for the trip to the summer pasture, the woman looks around. Virtually every object reflects her inventions. She has woven the tent doors, interior screens, wall decorations, and floor carvings as well as the many storage bags that contain household articles. When her family arrives at their next destination, she might stack carpets high for bedding or throw large ones over pillows to create instant "sofas." While they are traveling, the woman's weaving will adorn the animals, as saddlebags (Figs. 2-4, 2-5) and pannier blankets.

Unlike her sisters working in cottage industries or small-town and village workshops, the woman makes textiles for personal, functional use rather than sale to outsiders. She discards worn articles, replacing

2-3 How does the weaver carry our gaze across her fabric? She alternates the pastel-hued zigzags, which interlock so tightly that our eyes shift effortlessly from one component to the next. This Turkish woman's work probably served dual purposes, functioning as a divan pillow when not used for toting grain. Nomadic Tribe, Turkey, *Grain Sack*, c. 1970. 32 x 22" (81 x 56 cm). Courtesy The Liberty Corporation.

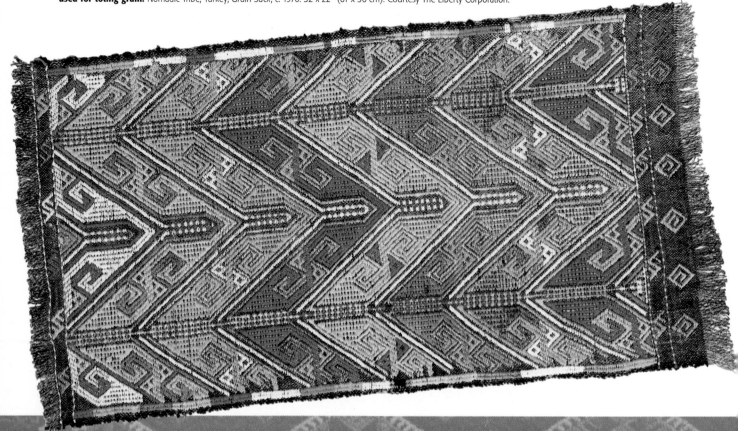

them with fresh items. Each piece, though, is a work of art—a sumptuous display of collective and personal visual inclinations. At an early age, the woman memorized a wide repertoire of small designs. Weaving freehand now, she quickly completes a small sack before a trip, mixing and matching patterns and colors for variation. Bold hues, empty space, proportion, and the wool's alluring texture, rather than complex compositions, infuse her piece with an authentic energy paralleling an ancient way of life.

2-4 How does the composition on this saddlebag compare to the one in Figure 2-5? Artists from the same tribe typically work with a defined set of patterns and color combinations that they apply to particular objects. The octagonal, stepped "gul" motif is the single most important Middle Eastern image. The word in Persian translates as "flower," and "roundel" in Turkish. Nomadic Tribes, Afghanistan, *Saddle Bag,* c. 1960. Wool on cotton foundation, 19 x 46" (48 x 117 cm). Courtesy The Liberty Corporation.

Turkmen Women's Textiles

Female Turkmen, primarily living in Turkemenistan, have always devoted great care to items that decorate the bridal tent and animals in a wedding procession. The bride's artistry might have helped win her future husband's heart, illustrating her ability to construct the goods and garments that will keep their family together. The young woman's appealing materials will greet the wedding guests and also important visitors throughout the couple's life. The family later will use the wife's weavings at home, on picnics, and at prayer, sitting on both traditional and sometimes sacred patterns.

Women's Art and Changes in Nomadic Life

Outsiders commonly romanticize nomadic existence—the seasonal migration on open plains and shared lifestyle. Images on the oldest surviving carpet from 400–300 BCE depicting horseback riders with saddlebags attest to its ancient roots. But tribal living has long been harsh. Over the centuries, strong centralized governments have forced independent tribespeople into permanent settlement areas or relocated them to strategic positions to act as buffers against neighboring enemies.

Nadir Shah in Persia, during the first half of the eighteenth century, forcibly relocated several tribes to the periphery of his land as human shields against invaders. In the last 100 years, collectivization, confiscation, expulsion, and even liquidation have taken a toll, exterminating not only a way of life but whole ethnic groups as well.[2]

The women's weavings mirror societal changes. Females now living in small villages primarily fashion textiles for sale rather than their own needs. Consequently, distinct ancestral motifs disappear as designs from various regions intermingle, and weavers abandon indigenous bag and pouch forms for those that might sell more quickly.[3] The women's work may remain aesthetically stunning, but the essence of who the artists are, their discrete identity, frequently no longer resides within the weft and warp of their threads. We must look to nomadic females who still produce objects for themselves to find examples that remain charged with ancient, cultural significance.

Sacred Threads

The Yuncu tribe of western Turkey consider their weavings to have sacred or magical properties and, hence, don't wish the pieces to leave the community.

2-5 An Afghani tribesperson would have laid this bag across a saddle so that each end hung down, leaving a pouch on either side. Nomadic women create an immense variety of articles to cover every need for itinerant life.
Nomadic Tribes, Afghanistan, *Saddle Bag*, c. 1960. Wool on cotton foundation, 19 x 46" (48 x 117 cm). Courtesy The Liberty Corporation.

Precious Jewel: The Jewish Yemeni Bride from Head to Hands

A young Yemeni Jewish bride sat in all her splendor (Fig. 2-6), but how did she arrive at this momentous day? For any young Yemeni Jewish woman before the mid-twentieth century, the weeks just before marriage would have been a dizzying whirl of activity, although, in fact, the seeds for this event began years before. As a small child, her mother carefully instructed the girl in the arts of embroidery and basket making—skills that would determine her economic worth when her father arranged a marriage around puberty. The more impressive her embroidery, the greater the *mohar* (bridewealth) her father could demand from his future in-laws.[4] Marriages represented the joining of two families and the investment of property—not affairs of the heart. Many young girls never saw the groom until the wedding festivities.

Yet there was plenty to occupy any Yemeni bride-to-be. The celebration began the previous week at the Sabbath of the Bride, when her family graciously hosted the bridegroom's relatives. The outstanding large meal, singing, and storytelling ushered in the *hinna* ceremony, marking the girl's separation from her natal home.[5]

2-6 The Jewish Yemeni bride wears all her finery. According to strict religious law, she covers her hair with a *gargush*. The hood carries gilt coins and filigree jewelry–the woman's private means that she could sell in times of need and replace when prosperity returned. *Yemeni Bridal Outfit,* San'a, 1930s. Gold brocade coat, undergarments of white dress and wide reddish dress, leggings with embroidered silver and red silk threads, pear-embroidered crown with fresh flowers. The Israel Museum, Jerusalem. Photography Yihyeh Haybi.

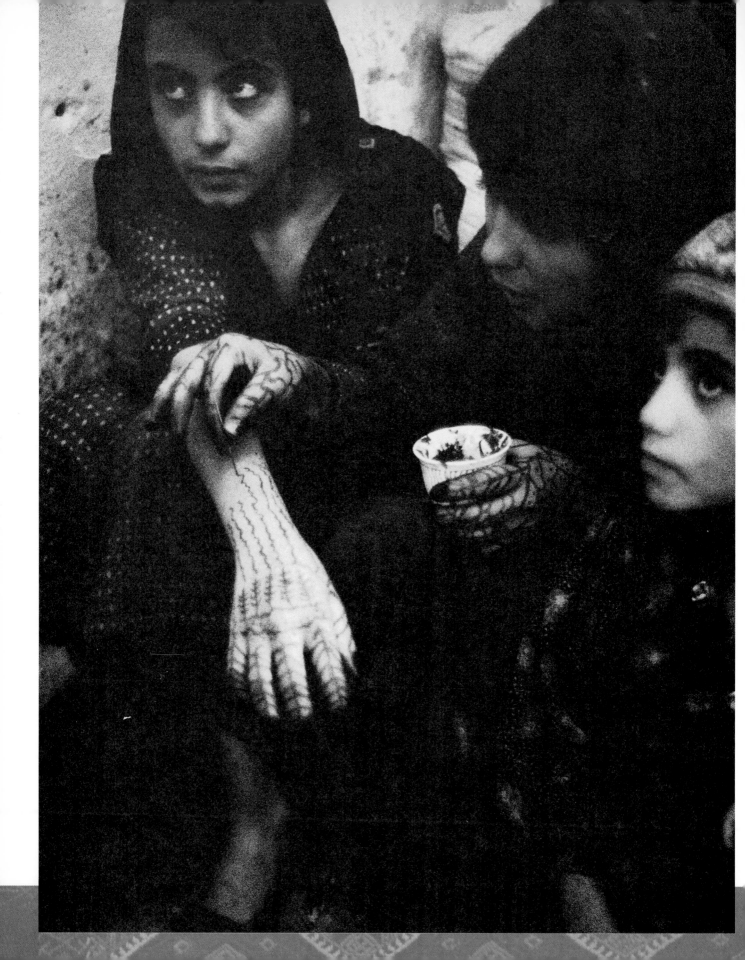

Hinna Celebration

Female relatives, as experienced wives and mothers, dramatized songs and stories, instructing the bride on her future role, particularly about the relationship with her mother-in-law, who would exercise authority over her married life. The girl also learned Jewish family purity rituals and other ancient customs. Jews lived in Yemen at least as early as the third century CE.[6] Their ceremonies and accompanying dress, with the women's unique embroidery, helped them sustain a distinctive identity within this small Muslim country in the southern part of the Saudi Arabian peninsula.[7]

Learning her future responsibilities was essential, but most exciting was the final evening before the wedding, when women came up, one at a time, to apply henna filigree to the bride's hands. (Fig. 2-7) The paste, made with crushed leaves of the henna plant, kept the bride's body cool, because she would be hot enveloped in her elaborate wedding attire. The henna also symbolized fertility, brought luck, and protected against the evil eye. Applying the potent substance was like a prayer for an everlasting and bountiful marriage.[8] The dark reddish-brown dye furthermore would offset the bride's many silver rings, pleasingly drawing attention to her slender hands, one of the few exposed areas of her body.

Bridal Garments

Why did the bride arrive on her wedding day so richly adorned that she could hardly move? (See Fig. 2-6.) The young woman literally wore her dowry, carrying it with her as she left the nest of her parents' home and entered her husband's family's household. Coins dangled from her gold brocade *gargush*, a hoodlike garment females wore from early childhood until menopause.[9] Jewish men, renowned as expert metalworkers, fashioned her many ornate silver beaded necklaces. Women too handled the precious material, mingling thin strands of gold and silver with colored thread in their singular Yemeni embroidery style.[10]

Jewish Women and Embroidery

The Bible notes that Jewish women and men both originally wielded needles,[11] although stitchery became a feminine skill as the centuries progressed. Isolated in their homes, women embroidered as a means of beautifying their interior sanctuaries, and the pieces they stitched for the synagogue extended their reach to the religious realm.[12]

2-7 Before a marriage ceremony, Jewish Yemeni women gather together to apply henna paste to the bride's hands. The dye symbolically is meant to bring luck and physically helps lower the woman's body temperature, helping to keep her cool beneath traditional wedding garments. *Yemeni Girls Applying Henna,* 1991. Photography and copyright Joan Roth.

Yemeni Jewish Embroidery

Yemeni Jews, however, only embroidered secular clothing. Yet a young girl's talents played a large part in determining her marriage prospects. Later, with a daughter at her side, a wife would embroider the leggings of women's trousers after finishing household chores.[13] Here, the bride's own leggings, richly sewn with silver and red silk threads, remained buried beneath two underdresses and an overlaying gold brocade coat. The *shareh*—a woman specializing in preparing brides—assembled the various parts of the outfit and jewelry together, borrowing from several families.[14] She also framed the bride's head with fresh fragrant flowers and gave her branches of rue, to ward off evil.[15]

Yemeni Jews in Israel

The Jews of Yemen lived in a hostile environment and, from 1881 on, waves immigrated to Palestine, whenever laws allowed. In 1949–50, nearly 50,000 left for Israel, seeking a better life. Their exodus left a gaping hole in Yemen's artistic life.[16]

Young Yemeni Jewish women in Israel today mostly have left behind the world their foremothers had known so long. Some do rent traditional wedding garments sewn by expert needleworkers but only wear them for the hinna ceremony, donning contemporary gowns for the marriage vows. Still, their clothes for the hinna ritual, lovingly embroidered and arranged by Yemeni Jewish women, help mark this special rite of passage, from daughter to wife—from youth to adulthood—when she will begin a family of her own, contributing to the longevity of an ancient heritage.

The Ancient Art of Henna Painting Women in India, Africa, and the Middle East have stained their bodies with crushed paste made from henna leaves for over 5,000 years. The plant originally came from Egypt. Women often apply henna for birthday, anniversary, and wedding celebrations, an act that is a meditation and spiritual practice.

New Views/Ancient Roots: Contemporary Female Arab Artists

What connects Samia Halaby's kinetic computer painting and Laila Shawa's arresting photograph? (Figs. 2-8, 2-9) Although both were created by women of the Arab world, there is no more a monolithic modern Arab art style than there is unity in contemporary Western art. Female Arab artists, in fact, participate in the same diverse international artistic dialogue as their sisters in other regions.

Arab women historically expressed themselves through embroidery, rug weaving, and decorative

2-8 Samia Halaby honors the "brass" of strong women of color in America who demand to be heard. Her modern work is part of a large international dialogue, and yet many centuries of Arabic abstract art simultaneously informs its interplay of flat, geometric shapes. Samia A. Halaby (b. 1936), *Brass Women*, 1996–97. Kinetic computer painting, ink-jet print, 4¾ x 6¼" (12 x 16 cm). Courtesy of the artist.

painting—traditions many sustain today. Western influence originated in 1798 with Napoleon's Egyptian campaign and the ensuing colonialist incursions of the nineteenth century, bringing European artists to record the "exotic" Oriental world. Arab artists in turn began to travel and train in Western fine-arts academic styles. By the 1930s, many female Arab artists had overcome strong societal hurdles.[17,18] Today they still must negotiate between the cultural demands of being good wives and mothers and pursuing independent artistic careers.[19]

Links to the Past
Samia Halaby

The question remains, is there a distinct "Arab-ness" to these women's expressions? Their contemporary media—photography, painting, and computer art—is global. Roots of the women's heritage, however, are subtly visible. For instance, Samia Halaby's tessellated images are gently informed by the pervasive geometric abstractions of her homeland. (Fig. 2-8) Background and foreground vie for space in her painting, like the tiny glass tiles of mosaics and inlaid marble found throughout the Arab world.

Abstraction was not born with twentieth-century European modernism but much earlier in medieval Arabic art.[20] Halaby's symbols and figures, embedded within a flat, two-dimensional surface, imply space and time, while lightly echoing the ancient geometric designs in Persian carpets, Asian drapery, and architectural inlaid marble. *Brass Women* nonetheless speaks of contemporary concerns. Halaby developed the series in response "to a discussion with a friend about the strong Black and Latino women we admired. It is an homage to Black American women who speak loudly in defense of their rights."[21] Halaby herself first experienced discrimination as a Palestinian who had to flee her homeland as a youngster, when the State of Israel was established in 1948. Nonetheless, Halaby's main artistic preoccupation always has been with the picture plane itself, which she maneuvers electronically.

Brass Women is a kinetic abstraction that the artist performs in collaboration with musicians. She manipulates the shapes, based on gestures of the human figure, at a computer keyboard. Each key is a "brushstroke," linked to color, images, or timing that affect the results on the monitor. "It is as though a brush were to be pre-loaded with ideas rather than paint."[22]

Laila Shawa

Evidence of the Arab world is more immediately discernible in Laila Shawa's art. (Figs. 2-2, 2-9) Her photographic-silkscreen series "The Walls of Gaza" (Fig. 2-9) is at once universal and specific, as is Halaby's theme. Shawa investigates the tensions of her birthplace in Gaza during the Intifada, which broke out in 1987. Various Palestinian political factions inscribed directives for strikes, memorials, and confrontations on neighborhood walls—one of the

2-9 Laila Shawa conveys the transition of her Gaza homeland from sleepy Palestinian seaside town to war zone. How does she heighten the emotional impact of her image? The Arabic writing on the wall speaks of the struggle for freedom, and Shawa's "targeted" youth indicates the long-term effects of conflict on children. Laila Shawa (b. 1940), *Target* from "The Walls of Gaza," 1992. Photograph, 59 x 37¾" (150 x 96 cm). Courtesy of the artist.

few means of mass communication available. Shawa caught the fleeting daily messages before the Israeli Defense Force quickly erased them. She heightens the poignancy of the walls as metaphoric battlegrounds by capturing images of youngsters before them. "I was forced to photograph children because they were all over the walls in the camps in Gaza. . . . Children are the future of any nation, if you target them physically or culturally, you have achieved control over

their future."[23] The round, red geometric filter emphasizes the point but also attempts to organize the turmoil of armed conflict. "The geometric shapes carry mathematical and immutable truths . . . and ultimately, they provide a sense of order that I hope will prevail in our chaotic, torn, and divided existence."[24] Shawa uses contemporary media to explore a political situation that tragically resonates with war-torn populations around the world.

Shirin Neshat

Shirin Neshat also looks at violence through the camera's lens, raising unnerving issues that mine cultural stereotypes and expectations of Iranian women. (Figs. 2-1, 2-10) Neshat dresses herself in the black *chador* (veil) that women in Iran, her native land, have worn since the 1970s revolution that transformed the country from the Shah's Westernized Persia into a strict, religious state.[25]

In Fig. 2-10, the nearly full-scale, silk-screened image is paradoxical, ambiguous. The figure is not the docile, mysterious "Oriental" female of romantic Western notions. The black *chador*, which honors the Islamic law concerning the body, acts as a backdrop for both her rose and gun. Beautiful and sensuous, the Iranian woman warrior is ready to fight and even die for her love of God.[26] Ardor, spirituality,

death, and terrorism confusingly coexist. This role is far from new, as a long line of Arab female fighters always have been considered equal to men in battle, although never in daily life.[28] Neshat conveys the complexity of Iranian women's identity through mainstream media, while her sinuous calligraphy instantly evokes a centuries-old tradition. The fluid ink is both visually and literally poetic. Neshat veils images of strong women with religious sensual writings by feminist Iranian poets.

Ultimately, Arab female artists, in their homeland and abroad, are as different as the many countries they inhabit. All, however, grapple with modern artistic materials, and often contemporary visual vocabulary, to declare and share their truths. These women's creative endeavors are based in the present but stand solidly on fertile historical ground.

2-10 Does Shirin Neshat's figure fulfill the romantic stereotype of seductive Eastern women? "The Women of Allah" series addresses the perplexing contradictions of Iranian women, where femininity, spirituality, martyrdom, and brutality can intermingle. Shirin Neshat (b. 1957), *Seeking Martyrdom* from "The Women of Allah," 1993–97. Black-and-white photograph with hand coloring, 5 x 3' (1.5 x .9 m). Courtesy Annina Nosei Gallery, New York.

3 Asia

Abundant Diversity

How do Asian women's artworks relate to the region's multitude of peoples, religions, dialects, and customs? Female expressions have long reflected and been essential to each culture—calling on ancient roots as their foundation.

For centuries, women's creations have protected loved ones in times of transition. Females in India's Mithila province paint deities and legendary heroes on the mud walls and floors of their huts for rites surrounding courtship, marriage, and procreation. Likewise, Indian Hindu mothers continue to embroider textiles with divine symbols that bless their daughters when they marry. For the Hmong, originally in Southeast Asia, women fashion distinct garments that mediate with the spirits when babies enter this world or the deceased leave it for the next. Within Borneo, Iban women historically wove powerful *puas* that were essential to guarding people from the "heat" emitted by a headhunter's prize wrapped within the cloth.

Asian women also have participated in age-old visual traditions primarily dominated by men. Hundreds of years ago, female Chinese artists first took pen to paper, looking to both nature and the gods for subject matter. A spiritual reverence for the land likewise remains evident in Japanese flower arranging, an endeavor that women began to infiltrate as early as the eighteenth century.

From the beginning, Asian women have practiced an important array of art forms that parallel the land's ancient cultural wealth. They continue to develop arresting and tremendously varied art from many different materials, mirroring and supporting the region's abundant cultural diversity and infusing daily life with great beauty.

3-1 Although painted in the 1970s, An Ho's work follows an elegant ink-on-silk tradition that has existed for centuries. Unlike Western art's emphasis on the unique and new, traditional Chinese painting is concerned with barely perceptible changes to ancient styles. Ho studied with a mentor for seventeen years, as her predecessors would have done in earlier generations. An Ho (b. 1927), *Prunus and Birds,* c. 1970s. Ink and color on silk, 11½ x 7½" (29.4 x 19.4 cm). Courtesy L. J. Wender Fine Chinese Art, New York City. Photography Steve Williams.

Devotional Paintings on Earth and Paper: The Rural Art of Mithila Women

A young woman walks slowly through a gathering of eligible men, tentatively holding a stunning artwork. She stops and presents the *kohbar* to her heart's choice. In rural matriarchal Mithila society, a girl (although often her parents) officially selects a husband. The young lady's *kohbar*—a drawing filled with complex imagery—is a visual marriage proposal demonstrating her mastery of an ancient romantic symbolism.[1] Abstract motifs and animals such as fish, tortoises, frogs, and crocodiles represent fertility.[2]

Like their foremothers, women of the Mithila province in northeast India do not just paint these "letters (or rather pictures) of intent." Their artworks also pervade weddings, one of the community's most significant occasions. Just days before the wedding, a bride draws a large *kohbar* on the earthen walls of her marriage chamber.[3] Blessed and protected by the deities depicted in the woman's composition, the couple will rest in this room for four days and nights before consummating their union, which they hope will be graced with children.[4]

Indian Mythic Roots of Creativity An Indian tradition traces Adi Saki as the original creator. She is the first woman and an artist, who spins the thread of creation—creating, conceiving, and destroying simultaneously.

3-2 In the Ramayana narrative, the divine royal couple, Rama and Sita, embody the ideals of perfect ruler and chaste wife, respectively. Mithila women have looked to Sita, who is born anew in every painting, as a role model. She devotedly follows Rama into exile for fourteen years, saying, "As shadow to substance, so wife to husband." *Rama and Sita in the Garden,* c. 1970. Watercolor ink on paper, 30 x 22" (76 x 56 cm). Courtesy Syracuse University Art Collection.

3-3 Hanuman, the general of the monkey army, is Rama's faithful servant. He ultimately finds Sita in a grove, held captive by the evil king Ravana who abducted her by trickery. Hanuman, in the upper left, communicates with Sita, implied by the dotted lines, reassuring her that Rama is on his way. *Hanuman with Sita in Ashoka Grove*, c. 1970. Watercolor ink on paper, 22 x 30" (56 x 76 cm). Courtesy Syracuse University Art Collection.

Mithila Women's Artistic Training

As youngsters, females learn the rich iconography that they will paint throughout their lives. The images interweave Sanskrit culture (Old Indic sacred literature), Tantric ritual (mystical practice that unites people with the cosmos), ancient folklore, and popular religion. In addition to references to procreation and the Hindu deities, women describe scenes from the classic Sanskrit narrative, the Ramayana, showing the life, loves, and wild adventures of India's heroes and gods. (Figs. 3-2, 3-3, 3-4)

Historically, artists brewed magical colors from plants at home. Today, some buy commercial pigments, available since the 1960s. Women outline their compositions in black with a twig, bamboo, or rice straw, and wrap cotton rags or stray strands from a sari around the thin stick to fill in the forms with brazen colors.[5] It may take a week or more to complete a large, detailed painting.[6]

Styles vary from village to village, but artists typically draw figures in profile—although the eyes stare straight ahead. (Fig. 3-4) These startling gazes, which communicate directly with the viewer, are the central point of power. Women, therefore, only paint the pupils once the rest of the image is complete.[7]

Beauty and Function of Mithila Women's Art

Why are the paintings so much more than decoration? The compositions have powerful spiritual associations. Artists visualize the gods while working in a yogic, meditative state.[8] The women's devotional pictures later serve as personal prayers that accompany

3-4 The great king Rama, an incarnation of Vishnu (from whom everything proceeds) rescues Sita with the aid of his brother Lakshmana and the general Hanuman. For Hindus, time is not linear, so the adventures and lives of the gods, written thousands of years ago, remain meaningful today. *Rama et al. Cross Ganges River,* c. 1970. Watercolor ink on paper, 22 x 30" (56 x 76 cm). Courtesy Syracuse University Art Collection.

meditation. If an artist is successful, the deity she portrays will inhabit her painting, transforming it from an illustration to a sacred object, embodying the deity's good will for the ceremony or ritual.[9]

The women are channels, and ancient themes and forms pass through them, educating successive generations about folklore, legends, and religion. Their work celebrates love and regeneration, commemorates rites of passage, and relates to seasonal religious festivities that implore the gods to help the community survive the region's scorching sun, prolonged monsoons, and other natural phenomena.

Mithila Women and the Arts Mithila women sustain community life through their traditional storytelling, dancing, singing, and artwork, all integral parts of the culture's festivals, ceremonies, processions, and rituals.

Fleeting Expressions

What happens to the artists' splendid paintings over time? They are ephemeral prayers. Women rejoice in making these works, but the pieces themselves are not meant to last. Soon after a wedding, damp mops wipe away the lower portion of the murals and the humid air flakes and peels the designs from the upper walls. During the festivities, adults give the fragile paper drawings to children as playthings, which they quickly crumple and shred beyond recognition. This is as it should be, for the art loses its transitory power once the related ceremony or ritual is complete.

The potent works parallel the people's beliefs, which stress that nothing should be held too tightly, because all is fleeting and will fade. Yet, every time a Mithila woman puts her hand to paper or the earth's surface, she upholds an ancient art that has flourished in the land for at least three thousand years.

Ancient Traditions— Contemporary Expressions Mithila women have painted the mud walls of their homes for about 3,000 years. The Indian government recently began to honor the art form by commissioning murals for urban hotels, public buildings, and railroad stations. Former Prime Minister Indira Gandhi also had Mithila women paint the walls of her residence.[10]

Heavenly Cloth: Rural Indian Wedding Embroideries

◠ ◡ ◠　Imagine staring straight up in a huge wedding tent at this large ceiling embroidery suspended above. (Fig. 3-5) A Hindu mother in a rural community painstakingly stitched every thread, making sure that guests could easily view the design from any angle. She poured love for her daughter into the cloth, which hovers like the heavens over the festivities.

Weddings are enormously important social occasions in India. For centuries, families have gone all out—even borrowing money or goods from relatives or friends—to welcome guests in a luxurious manner. The tent accommodates visitors, who might begin arriving anywhere from a day ahead to just before the ceremony. Beneath the mother's stitchery, people dance, earthy music fills the air, and a sumptuous feast sates the hungry.

The bride and groom often only meet for the first time in the middle of the revelry. Their parents arranged the marriage—more a merger between two families than alliances of affec-

3-5 In 1925, a mother in Rajasthan, a state in northwestern India, filled her large ceiling embroidery with sacred images designed to bless her daughter's wedding. Many images depict Hindu gods, who in this religion actually are aspects of a single ultimate godhead. Rajasthan, India, *Ceiling Embroidery*, c. 1925. 68 x 60" (173 x 152 cm). Courtesy The Liberty Corporation.

Child Marriages
Rajasthan traces the origin of child marriages to Muslim invasions more than 1,000 years ago. Families married off their daughters almost from birth to try to protect them from invaders who might rape or kidnap unwed Hindu girls. Some parents today continue the practice, despite its illegality, to ensure that they will not have to support single daughters in the future.

tion. The children had no say in the match and many girls are wed by fifteen years of age, some even before they are five years old.[II]

On the auspicious day, the young lady dresses in her finest garments to meet her future husband.

Her mother's exquisite needlework floats above them with images meant to bring the couple blessings from the gods.

A Mother's Hand

The artist stitched four symmetrically placed images of Ganesha (see Fig. 3-5), the elephant-headed god of wisdom, around the eternal circle. Hindus pray to Ganesha to remove all difficulties and, so, appropriately he sits watch over the marriage rites. Nandi, the divine bull of pleasures, brings promise of delight to the union. The pink lotus blossoms are the sacred flower of Buddhism and, along with the many plants, blooms, and peacocks, represent harmony with nature. The mother adds a four-armed, bent cross in the center—an ancient symbol representing the mystic unity of four pervading the Hindu religion.

As much as the elegant embroidery honors the bride, it also visually testifies to the mother's accomplishments—her technical skill as a housewife and emotional devotion as a parent.

Indian Cloth in a Changing Society

The bride's mother upholds a longtime rural tradition. Historically, textiles were an inseparable part of India's many tribal cultures. When colonial invaders assaulted these societies, however, they introduced the Western notion of craft and suddenly wrenched the women's essential enterprises from the core of their daily lives. They also removed art's cultural connotation and replaced it with commercial undertones.[12]

Traditional works soon began to fade as most women started mass producing textiles for sale rather than their own use. Today, some 25 million females across India work in tin-shed "craft" factories rather than at home creating unique heirlooms.[13]

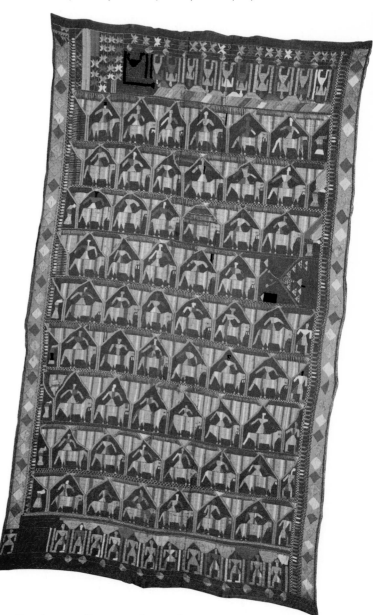

3-6 Indian mothers in Punjab begin embroidering a cloth with silk floss at their daughter's birth. The child will use the *phulkari* as part of her wedding apparel and for bedcovers when she begins her own family. Here, the rows of men on horseback and the diamond border create a rich, abstract decorative design that lends a tapestry effect to the fabric. Punjab, India, *Phulkari*, c. 1950. Silk floss on woven cloth, 93 x 58" (236 x 147 cm). Courtesy The Liberty Corporation.

Yet there still are mothers who carry on the ancient ways, making textiles that are both individual and communal expressions.

A Noble Pursuit: Female Traditional Chinese Painters

◎ ◡ ◎　How did Chinese women fare as artists in a culture that demanded foot binding, seclusion, and absolute obedience to men? Despite enormous obstacles, some women actually did achieve acclaim from the start. Female Chinese artists, in fact, had a better chance of becoming accomplished artists than their sisters in the West because of the unique socioeconomic framework in which Chinese painting developed.

The Evolution of Chinese Art

Ancient Chinese potters first carved picture motifs into Neolithic pots between 5000 BCE and 2000 BCE. The images evolved into written characters, which artists incised into bone and bronze, during the Shang dynasty (roughly the seventeenth through the eleventh century BCE). Calligraphers later applied their hand to silk during the Han dynasty (207 BCE–220 CE), and finally to paper in 105 CE when Cai Lun, an official in the emperor's court, is credited with inventing the material. The art of writing and painting in China remained inextricably linked to this new, inexpensive, and portable medium.

Artists typically were painters and poets. Critics judged them equally for their poetic abilities as for the quality of their calligraphic and painting brushstrokes. The artists' sublime ink markings expressed the essence of their character.[14]

For instance, in landscape painting, female painters, like males, became skilled at using various brushstrokes and different intensities of ink to produce fluid marks that captured nature's essence while simultaneously communicating the artist's character. (Fig. 3-7) Bamboo represented the qualities of uprightness, strength, and moral integrity, as well as the flexibility to bend with the prevailing winds of change. Artists also regularly penned elegant calligraphic poems within their compositions. These

3-7 How did Guan Daosheng evoke a sense of atmosphere in her long scroll? She offset the sharp, striking dark strokes with feathery brushwork. Other artists greatly admired her innovative method of depicting bamboo in the mist after a fresh rain. Guan Daosheng (1262–1319), *Bamboo Grove in Mist* (detail), 14th century. Handscroll, ink on paper, 6 x 44¼" (15 x 112.4 cm). Yale University Art Gallery, Gift of Mrs. William H. Moore for the Hobart and Edward Small Moore Memorial Collection.

3-8 The painter, poet, and celebrated courtesan Ma Shouzhen was famous for painting orchids and bamboo in the style of the earlier and most famous female artist, Kuan Tao-sheng. Courtesans frequently specialized in orchids because the bloom symbolized purity in seclusion, and Chinese men enjoyed thinking of these women as cloistered treasures. Ma Shouzhen (1548–1604), *Colored Fungus, Orchids, Bamboo, and Rocks* (detail), 1604. Hand scroll, ink and color on gold-flecked paper, 10½ x 90⅜" (26.5 x 229.5 cm). Indianapolis Museum of Art, photograph © 1988 Indianapolis Museum of Art.

marks, too, as well as the images they evoked, expressed something quintessential about the maker.[15]

Female Chinese Artists: Subject Matter

How could women excel in landscape painting (see Fig. 3-7) when they so rarely ventured outside their homes, whereas men traveled about with ease? Only in peacetime might a woman occasionally accompany a male relative to some official post, snatching glimpses of the countryside from a sedan chair or boat. Most often, though, females followed the traditional Chinese practice of emulating existing ancient paintings. Their artistic freedom came from their personal interpretation of an older precedent.

Female artists excelled in still lifes as well. (Fig. 3-8) It would be easy to assume that women artists created flower, plant, bird, and insect paintings because they

3-9 How did Miss Qiu heighten the ethereal quality of the Goddess of Mercy? People claimed she painted images of Guanyin with "compassionate countenances . . . as well as with a beauty and elegance rendering them mysteriously transcendent; one look and you knew they were from the brush of a woman."[16] Miss Qiu, *White-robed Guanyin*, mid-late 16th century. Collection National Palace Museum, Taipei, Taiwan, Republic of China.

could easily observe these subjects in their private gardens, or in light of the ancient Chinese tradition of associating females with various blossoms. Male painters, however, also specialized in this highly esteemed genre.[17]

Within these works, women's lines once again had to demonstrate their integrity, separate even from the images they portrayed. Flowers, butterflies, and the like were appropriate subjects for presentation paintings that educated Chinese women typically gave at birthday celebrations or other special occasions.

Elite Chinese women and men rarely painted figures. The imperial court usually employed professional artists for these commissions. When women did depict figures, they favored female subjects, such as the Bodhisattva Guanyin. (Fig. 3-9) People prayed to paintings of this Goddess of Mercy for special favors. She helped anyone, not just monks on their path to enlightenment. Creating portraits of Guanyin, furthermore, was itself an act of devotion.[18]

Female Invention
Women are linked from the start to Chinese art in a legend that attributes the origin of painting to Lei, the younger sister of the legendary emperor Shun (c. 2200 BCE).[19]

Women Artists in Chinese Society

The earliest records of female artists come from the T'ang dynasty (618–907 CE)[20] and a number made their mark in every era. What were these pioneers like? They came from various walks of life. Some belonged to well-educated, upper-class families. Others were connected by blood or marriage to scholar-officials. These men trained for official administrative positions in the government, yet devoted their passion to calligraphy, poetry, and painting.[21] Scholar-officials were well versed in classical literature and comported themselves within the confines of particular prescribed behavior. Women within this aristocratic class—often the wives, sisters, or daughters of artists—could safely pursue their creative endeavors because their work was sanctified as an admirable, lofty pastime.

Why would courtesans of the intelligentsia also become renowned artists? (See Fig. 3-8.) High-class courtesans were not merely sexual playthings but spent their lives entertaining sophisticated gentlemen. They pleased clients with refined accomplishments in music, singing, poetry, and art. Their talents made them well-rounded companions. Even though carnal favors

Art in Context Ma Shouzhen (see Fig. 3-8), one of the "Eight Famous Courtesans," was nicknamed "River Orchid" indicating her fame for rendering the traditional subject. Shouzhen held banquets and literary gatherings, and exemplified the talents that select higher-class courtesans cultivated in literature and the arts.

sometimes were required, their main occupation was to provide engaging intellectual stimulation. As diverting partners, courtesans could cultivate their minds and talents, unlike the majority of Chinese wives, who were denied anything more than a rudimentary education, because it was not considered appropriate for "respectable" females.

Chinese women hardly held enviable positions within society, and yet, compared to women in the West, their access to training was less difficult. European female artists found nearly insurmountable odds when knocking at the restricted doors of a master's studio or male-dominated guilds. In China, though, the scholarly pursuit of painting took place at home—in the library or private garden, thus allowing women to express their creativity without abandoning the domestic sphere.[22]

Artists of both sexes trained by studying antique scrolls and instruction manuals and spent endless hours practicing the marks they would need for calligraphy and painting. They did not develop a personal style until well into middle age.

Female Chinese artists nonetheless faced numerous challenges. Conservative men limited most women's access to literature, fearing it would distract them from their filial duties. Men demanded that women bind their feet and their minds, remain subordinate, and refrain from any participation in public life. As an oft-quoted popular saying reflects, "Only the untalented woman is virtuous."[23] Didactic texts required females to be obedient daughters, submissive wives, self-sacrificing mothers, and chaste widows.[24]

Despite commonly stifling situations, female Chinese artists throughout the centuries persevered, finding precious hours to express their passion. (Figs. 3-1, 3-10)

Female Artistic Mentors
Members of the imperial court pursued amateur painting and sometimes, talented gentry women came to teach the empress, princesses, and imperial concubines. Among the gentry, young girls usually studied with their mothers or other female relatives. Skilled courtesans likewise normally trained novices in their care.

3-10 The contemporary Chinese artist An Ho trained in the traditional, scholarly manner—studying with a master, reading the Chinese classics, practicing calligraphy, and imitating the most important paintings of the earlier T'ang and Song dynasties. She remains one of the few artists left with a strong foundation in earlier orthodox Chinese painting style. An Ho (b. 1927), *Ascending to the Mountain Pavilion,* 1996. Ink and color on silk, 22½ x 15¾" (57 x 40 cm). Courtesy L. J. Wender Fine Chinese Art, New York City. Photography Steve Williams.

Nimble Fingers, Unfading Art: Chinese Women's *Hua Yang*

How many hours did it take Sophie Yuan to cut the intricate red lines in *Young Scholar for the Future*? (Fig. 3-11) One slip of the knife or scissors would destroy at least a month of daily work. Artists can never paste torn pieces together again.

Yuan practices *hua yang*, one of China's most ancient art traditions, which women have dominated since early times. Yuan's picture has the same delicacy as fine charcoal drawing. But as we see in the small work, even her subtlest lines—such as the tiny feathers of the singing bird—are cut paper.

The History of Chinese Paper Cuts

Hua yang began in China during the early second century CE. The art initially had regal bearing; paper was a precious commodity only the very wealthy could afford. Emperors ordered palace artists to create spring scenes that inspired courtiers to pen splendid poems. Royal and noble women cut scenes in their leisure time, placing the emblems in their hair—a fashion trend that lasted more than 1,000 years.[25]

Hua yang became a folk art during the Northern and Southern dynasties (317–589 CE). Virtually all women learned paper cutting. The art also embodied the Chinese philosophy of tranquility, while cultivating patience and concentration—important attributes for proper young ladies.

Hua yang reached its zenith during the Sui (589–618 CE) and T'ang (618–907 CE) dynasties. Emblems symbolizing harmony, longevity, and good fortune entreated spirits and ancestors to bless people's homes during festivals, holidays, weddings, and birthdays. Chinese characters, figures, and animals deco-

3-11 Sophie Yuan creates different lines for every object. The birds, symbols of spring and new life, represent good wishes for the young scholar's future. Yuan uses a traditional Chinese painting subject but produces a distinctly personal and energetic interpretation. Sophie Yuan (b. 1948), *Young Scholar for the Future*, 1995. Red paper, 8¼ x 8¼" (21 x 21 cm). Courtesy of the artist.

3-12 Can you almost hear the firecrackers that would accompany this dragon dancing in a New Year's celebration? The powerful creature chases the circular "pearl," an emblem of good luck, straight across the picture plane. Sophie Yuan (b. 1948), *Dancing Dragon*, c. 1996–97. Red paper, 5¼ x 9" (13 x 23 cm). Courtesy of the artist.

rated doorways and, in remote provinces, sun and moonlight still shine through semitransparent cuttings pasted onto windows—adding color to bleak rooms, as they have for generations. Women also historically used cut designs to decorate presents, candy containers, and table services. They attached intricate trimmings to pillows, hats, walls, fans, and screens and fashioned paper stencils for clothing and shoe embroidery patterns.[26] Artists could choose simple designs or complex scenes inspired by mythology, legends (Fig. 3-12), opera, great Chinese heroes, and traditional landscape painting.

In the early years of the republic (after the overthrow of the Manchu dynasty in 1911), village women and country girls continued to snip paper images. More recent political upheavals have not entirely erased the tradition, although many females have less leisure time. Nonetheless, Chinese women at home and abroad sustain the ancient art today, converting simple single sheets of paper into lively, unique visions of ancient Chinese culture.

Chinese Dragons

Since ancient times, Chinese people have believed that dragons are associated with water, descending into the rivers and seas and then rising to live among the rain clouds. Thus, in spring, these magical creatures are said to bring rain and new life.

Flowers of Devotion: Japanese Ikebana

⊙◡⊙ What could be more feminine than an exquisite flower arrangement? (Fig. 3-13) Surprisingly, for many centuries, only men made these far from "still" still lifes. The art began in China during the sixth century. Buddhist adherents created beautiful displays as offerings to the Buddha. Flower arranging traveled to temples in Japan, where the art form remained as simple devotional tributes until the thirteenth century.

By the fifteenth century, nobles and courtiers practiced the art. They incorporated decorative displays in their palaces, filling hallways and niches with extraordinary blooms. Over the next hundred years or so, aristocratic men in their leisure time created large arrangements to impress visitors.

Simultaneously, the increasingly popular Japanese tea ceremony began to exert its own influence on the floral form. The tea ceremony unites discriminating individuals and refined objects. With this in mind, the tea masters rejected ostentatious flower compositions in favor of more discrete designs, which they placed in special alcoves.

Standing Tall Artists begin flat-dish *ikebana* with three flowers or branches: the "subject," which as the tallest symbolizes heaven; the "secondary," representing humans; and the shortest "object," which stands for the earth. After achieving a simple asymmetrical balance, the artists adds leaves, flowers, or branches to complete a design in which line is more important than color.

3-13 Elaine Jo is an executive master at the Ichiyo School of Ikebana. She has studied for many years to create *ikebana* that look deceptively simple. Notice how Jo developed an engaging relationship between the flowers and the surrounding space. Elaine Jo (b. 1930), *Pussy Willow, Aspidistras leaves, Gerbera,* 1988. Courtesy Elaine Jo, Ichiyo School of Ikebana. Photography Kenichi Ogoshi.

Japanese Women and *Ikebana*

Women gained a foothold in the art now referred to as *ikebana* by the eighteenth century. The smaller scale made it easier for them to handle the materials. Soon females dominated flower arranging, which became a requisite part of every young lady's cultured upbringing.

Many Japanese women currently fashion *ikebana*. Students flock to various schools, learning the classical traditions that stem from the sixteenth through eighteenth centuries, or investigating the freestyle forms that initially took root in the early twentieth century. (Fig. 3-14)

Despite women's presence, men head most of the approximately 3,000 schools. But there are honored female masters; women started the important Chiko and Priestess schools many years ago. It takes at least twelve years of serious work to become a master, including countless hours of study, running a school chapter or branch, continual demonstrations to groups, and helping students achieve their certification.

Ikebana is more than a rigorous pastime. It is a centuries-old endeavor that visually conveys the ancient Japanese reverence toward nature. Women have proudly excelled in this art for nearly 300 years, working with the earth's gifts to clearly express, not just imitate, the beauty and energy of life itself.

3-14 Elaine Jo excels in the freestyle form, which allows a broader interpretation than the classical tradition. Her work demonstrates the Ichiyo School's belief that flower arranging is most fulfilling when it reflects oneself. An artist's imagination and feelings are as essential to creative design as the materials. Elaine Jo (b. 1930), *Dried foxtail millet, Chinese bell-flower, Seedpot plant,* 1988. Courtesy Elaine Jo, Ichiyo School of Ikebana. Photography Kenichi Ogoshi.

Imperative Ritual Cloth: *Puas* by Iban Women

⊙ ☺ ⊙   "Men take heads, we women make cloth."[27] Iba, an Iban weaver from Borneo, the largest island of the Malaysian archipelago, refers to how men traditionally achieved status—through head-hunting—while women gained recognition by creating intricate textiles. Females historically welcomed hunters home with *puas*, blanket-sized ceremonial cloths that would hold the all-important trophy heads. (Fig. 3-15) The textile designs could contain the spiritual "heat" of the prizes and protect anyone who handled them from the curses of their former owner.[28]

Although headhunting declined in the mid-1800s and ceased in the 1920s, women today continue to weave powerful textile patterns. Their cloths are fundamental to Iban ceremonies. Many of the 500,000 to 550,000 Iban people living in northwestern Borneo are nominal Christians but still observe old customs.[29] In ritual contexts, women's *puas* protect, erect a barrier, or decorate a space.

For instance, the textiles permeate the momentous and prestigious Iban ritual festivity celebrating the mighty war god Singlang Burong. *Pua* cloths decorate the tribe's huge longhouses and adorn the men and women during ceremonial tasks. People place ritual offerings to the gods on splendid *puas* lying on the ground. *Puas* cover shrines and serve as awnings over sacrificial pigs, which are slaughtered at the culmination of the ceremony. Iban women also carry coconuts symbolizing trophy heads in the cloth, singing the praises of the warriors who captured them.[30]

Puas are critical to the tribe's well-being in other ways, touching people from birth to death. The Iban place newborns upon the woven fabric and carry them in the material to ritual river baths. *Puas* decorate longhouses at weddings. During rites for pregnant women, shamans rub patients down with the spectacular textiles. The Iban leave this world with *puas* as well, sheltered in the material, which also serve as grave goods.

Puas and the Spirit Realm

How does the cloth's ritual power affect the artistic process? The Iban consider weaving a dangerous procedure because of its strong spiritual association. They equate women's weaving to headhunting—both involve the possibility of injury or even death. Women are at great risk if they do not secure the support of helping spirits and powerful charms, especially when conducting the specific rites associated with dyeing the threads. Only a chosen few dare to carry out this rite, which earns them the equivalent prestige as the males who led headhunting parties.[31] In this egalitarian society, people

> **Pua Education** Mothers and grandmothers teach young girls to weave at about seventeen, when they are almost ready to marry. It takes even the most mature weavers many months to complete a single, complex *pua*.

attained distinction through deeds rather than inherited roles of leadership, and weaving remains women's primary access to status.

Long ago, Iban women learned the art of patterning cloth in their dreams.[32] They still receive visions today and their artistic innovation and consummate skill remain central to a culture that firmly relies on the social and ritual significance of the women's wondrous cloth.

3-15 Imagine this bold fabric sitting on the ground or hanging in a long-house during an important ceremony. Starting in the 1940s, many Iban weavers began to abandon traditional abstract patterns for more figurative compositions. The three male ancestral figures here confront us directly. The delicate linear crocodile motifs beneath their feet represent spirits who can be potentially harmful creatures if not correctly appeased. Iban Tribe, Borneo. *Male Figures,* c. 1970. Cotton, 76 x 43" (193 x 109 cm). Courtesy The Liberty Corporation.

Weaving for a Nation: Bhutan's Premier Art

How can a young Bhutanese woman attract a husband? A good match may hinge on her artistry and ingenuity with cloth. Prospective grooms will consider a woman's technical skill and creativity in dyeing, designing, and weaving exquisite textiles for personal adornment and royal or noble commissions. (Fig. 3-16) In Bhutan, where men produce all sacred art and much secular work as well, weaving is an exclusively female domain and women's primary means of individual creative expression.[33]

The tiny country is nestled in the Himalayas between India and Tibet, with a population of less than three-quarters of a million people. Despite Bhutan's tentative steps toward modernization, the nation steadfastly retains its cultural identity through women's textile traditions. Weavers are esteemed artists, honored for their talent and stunning mastery of color, composition, and pattern. Their fabric creations are enormously important, because cloth pervades every facet of daily life.

Cloth Criteria The social and commercial value of a woman's textile is based on her ability to create harmonious color combinations and invent new motifs, which admirers then reinterpret themselves. Regardless of individual accomplishments, Bhutanese women believe that weaving reinforces female reproductive abilities.

The Prevalence of Cloth

The Bhutanese use weavings for covers, containers, and garments, which convey an owner's social status. People also give gifts of cloth to mark special occasions, such as career promotions, weddings, and funerals. Textiles are crucial to the country's Buddhist rituals. Women weave rich materials that men embroider and sew into various items used in *dzongs* (fortress-monasteries) and temples. Throughout the country, weaving is wealth, prestige, capital, and a form of payment.[34]

Women's art also helps shape and affirm national identity. In 1989, the monarchy decreed the *kira*, a woman's wrapped garment (see Fig. 3-16) and men's *gho*, a modified Tibetan men's robe, the country's official attire to be worn in public.[35]

Bhutanese folk legends reveal that the women's art has ancient precedents and, in particular, the elite's relationship to cloth is quite old. For centuries, noble houses employed permanent weavers or purchased fabric from local women who worked at home.[36] Since the monarchy was established in 1907, queens have maintained personal weaving workshops with a special class of female weavers known as *thagthami*. Today, the queen still sets the newest trend with her latest *kira* designs.

Bhutanese Women's Weaving Today

While women initially made exquisite fabrics only for royal and noble patrons, now more than eighty percent of Bhutanese females earn money by weaving for the larger population. Some younger women, though, no longer learn to work on looms at home, as they devote increasing time to formal education and employment in Bhutan's growing urban businesses. Less expensive factory-produced fabrics that imitate Bhutanese patterns also flood the market. But even as Bhutan wrests itself from the West's romantic notion of an isolated Shangri-la, some female master weavers continue to produce intricate brocades and linear patterns that were virtually unknown to outsiders just two decades ago.

3-16 A weaver created this striking *kira* for royalty. She framed the central patterned area with two long red and orange bands, and wove each of the three vertical sections separately, making it nearly impossible to match the border ends precisely. The owner would have worn the ankle-length cloth over a blouse, wrapped around her body and pinned at her shoulders. Bhutan, *Wrap,* c. 1970. 32 x 50" (81 x 127 cm). Courtesy The Liberty Corporation.

Continuity Amid Adversity: Hmong Pa ndau

◠◡◠   As the Hmong New Year closes in, historically, Hmong women in Laos and neighboring Southeast Asian countries race against time. They must finish an entire set of costumes begun twelve months ago for every family member. No one can wear old flower cloth, or *pa ndau*, to the New Year's festival, which celebrates the harvest's end. Fresh attire honors the fortunes of the past year and heralds prosperity for the future.[37]

The intensely decorated textiles are part of courtship during the annual celebration. Marriageable Hmong men and women wear their finest dress, with eye-catching stitchery, gently swaying pleats, shimmering colors, and dangling coins that help attract a prospective mate. (Fig. 3-17) A young woman's bride price will be in direct proportion to how much and how well she has sewn before her engagement.[38]

Hmong Textile Traditions

The Hmong for centuries have worn distinctive needlework that distinguishes them from their neighbors, helping preserve a unique culture in remote mountain farming villages. Over hundreds of years, mothers have taught daughters the intricate embroidery, appliqué, reverse appliqué, and batik that defines each subgroup.

Girls learn technical skills and the meaning of their images, which allude to the natural and spiritual world. Many emblems are meant to protect the owner's soul. Hmong believe that everyone possesses a number of souls, which can be frightened or stolen away, possibly leading to illness or even death.

The soul is particularly vulnerable at the beginning

and end of human life. Grandmothers, therefore, sew *pa ndau* baby carriers (Figs. 3-18, 3-20) and clothing to disguise the child as a "flower," hiding the baby from evil forces.[39] Middle-aged women begin heavily embroidering garments for elders that protect them in the transition from this world to the next.[40] The layers of thick clothing warm the dead as they jour-

3-17 The woman on the left is wearing a Blue/Green Hmong outfit, while the young lady on the right dons White Hmong garments. Today, they sustain the tradition of wearing fine, freshly stitched clothing for the all-important New Year's festival. *Two Young Women.* Hmong New Year, December 1986, Fresno, California. Courtesy Gayle Morrison Collection.

ney in spirit back to China, the Hmong's initial homeland. The departed must wear the distinctive *pa ndau* designs so that ancestors in the spirit domain will recognize the person, and she or he can be reborn as a Hmong. Unclaimed souls will wander forever, potentially wreaking havoc on the living.[41]

Forces of Change

It is not just in the afterlife that the Hmong journey from one place to another. From the beginning, they have had to keep moving to maintain their liberty. Many believe that the Hmong first lived in central China, as early as 2300 BCE, but the dominant Chinese forced the people south over the centuries. By the mid-nineteenth century, some groups migrated farther south to the mountains of Laos, Burma (Myanmar), Vietnam, and Thailand.[42] As staunch allies of the United States government, the Hmong in Laos had to flee again in 1975 when the conquering Lao communists enacted horrific reprisals against them after United States troops withdrew from the Vietnam War.[43]

Over the next decade, the communist government slaughtered or starved to death roughly 50,000 Hmong[44] and interned countless others. Survivors fled to Thailand on foot through the jungle, taking only what they could carry, which, for a lucky few, included their best traditional clothing—threads of an ancient lineage. In poverty-ridden refugee camps, young girls joined mothers in sewing circles.[45] International relief organizations sold the women's indigenous art abroad. The

3-18 Mothers tote their children in a carrying cloth made of two panels. The larger piece goes around the baby's bottom and the smaller rectangle supports the child's back. A long sash strapped crosswise keeps the child close. Some Hmong mothers and grandmothers in America and Southeast Asia still use these carriers daily. *Blue/Green Hmong Baby Carrier.* Cloth, 13 x 21" (33 x 53 cm). Courtesy Gayle Morrison Collection.

3-19 Study the detail in the embroidered history and exodus story on this huge piece of cloth. The artist records her people's passage from China into Burma, Laos, and Thailand. The refugee internment camp and airplane about to leave the country complete the story in the foreground. *Hmong Story Cloth*, Ban Vinai refugee camp, Thailand, early 1990s. Cloth, 100 x 66" (254 x 168 cm). Courtesy Gayle Morrison Collection.

proceeds were often their only source of income.[46]

Almost 100,000 Hmong immigrated mostly to the United States, starting in 1975.[47] No longer farmers, women earned money by marketing their needlework. But now they had to tone down their resplendent palette to suit subdued American tastes. They fashioned wall hangings, bedspreads, pillow covers, pot holders, and the like in addition to their traditional wear.

Foreign influences galvanized new customs. In refugee camps, illustrated books, journals, school texts, and Bibles stimulated embroidered story cloths. (Fig. 3-19) The Hmong, who had no figurative art tradition, began chronicling their culture's ancient legends, traditional village life, and personal accounts of the brutal war experience and forced relocations. Their panels transformed the people's ancient oral storytelling tradition into visual form.[48]

Hmong women in Asia and abroad currently adapt their talents to changing times and environments, as they have throughout history. Their contemporary items incorporate the best of the old while embracing fresh influences, helping keep Hmong identity alive and evolving.

3-20 Yang Fong spent hours stitching this incredibly intricate work that both physically and symbolically protects the baby in its embrace. Yang Fong, *Baby Carrier,* detail, 1979. Courtesy Gayle Morrison Collection.

4 Caribbean

Intersecting Cultures

What forces have formed the many distinct Caribbean cultures? Diverse societies have long cross-pollinated in this sunny oasis. Vast numbers of indigenous people originally inhabited the area, carrying on ancient ways for centuries. Women often were imperative as religious, political, and family leaders, frequently holding esteemed positions, as important as men's, that kept the world in balance. The women's artistic statements, like those of native peoples elsewhere, were an intrinsic component of daily life, as well as a means of communicating with the supernatural realm.

Subsequent European invaders imposed patriarchal values on these thriving nations. They quickly dismantled women's importance, destroying or forever altering the core structure of people's lives.

Soon colonizers imported kidnapped Africans to work newly claimed lands, adding a new mix to the cultural climate. The captives' ancient heritage seeped into emerging traditions, which were a brew of many independent African

4-1 Taíno potters developed their own ceramic style, distinguished from that of their South American predecessors. Female descendants still practice these skills in distinctive red clay. *Alicia Cheverez at Work in Borikén* (Puerto Rico). Courtesy and property of Taino Tribal Council.

4-2 Does Elijah use a subdued palette? She often changes colors when instructed by her visions. Elijah's arresting banners, filled with biblical motifs, retain the same immediacy as the murals she first painted on the walls of her church. A Swiss evangelist friend eventually persuaded her also to put brush to canvas.[1] Elijah (b. 1952), *The Lion Who Conquered All*, 1997. Enamel on canvas, 36 x 42" (91 x107 cm). Courtesy Cavin-Morris, Inc.

beliefs and remaining Native American customs. Enslaved black women worked creatively, making cloth, religious items, and functional ware that resonated with ancestral power while also charting fresh artistic territory. Their endeavors provided an expressive outlet that helped people survive the unimaginable hardships of bondage.

Western European conventions simultaneously infiltrated the sacred arts and secular expressions that coalesced in the various islands over time. Today, although no longer constrained by slavery, art still sustains Caribbean women— providing economic relief and nourishing emotional and spiritual growth as they and their loved ones move toward the future.

Seats of Power and Prestige: Taíno *Duhos*

◉☻◉ Imagine stumbling on a forgotten treasure deep inside a Caribbean cave. (Fig. 4-3) You gently pull the impressive wooden structure from its den, wondering how many centuries the bench has remained hidden. A roaring curiosity sends you back to the island's earliest written records.

Accounts by Spanish explorers traveling with Christopher Columbus describe their initial contact with the Taíno, who populated islands known today as Cuba, the Bahamas, Borikén (Puerto Rico), Jamaica, and Hispaniola (Haiti and the Dominican Republic). *Caciques* (chiefs) ruled politically, socially, and economically complex communities that flourished from the thirteenth to the sixteenth centuries.[2] And ritual seats, or *duhos*, were one of the most potent symbols and agents of leadership.

What better way for temporal and spiritual rulers to honor allies, kin, or foreign dignitaries at lavish feasting ceremonies or ritual ball games than to perch them on such an elaborate stool?[3] *Cacique* Gaucanagarí welcomed Columbus with just this

"courtesy and veneration."[4] Not only male but also female chiefs, *cacias*, controlled these elite objects, which served as emblems of authority and helped secure alliances. Women occupied all positions in Taíno matrilineal society, where status, name, and property descended along the female line.[5] Both women and men carved the magnificent *duhos*, probably chiseling them with hard stone tools and polishing their surfaces with sand or porous rocks.[6]

Links to Another Realm

What are the incised designs on the *duho* shown in Fig. 4-3? Is the creature from this world? The grinning four-legged animal, with a partially humanlike head, represents a *zemi*—a Taíno god or deified ancestor. The figure supported the owner as she or he conferred with the divine during the *cohoba* ritual, during which chiefs and shamans inhaled a hallucinogenic vegetable of the same name.[7] Mortals and spirits temporarily joined in the ensuing trance, paralleling the meeting of the owner's actual body and the carved

4-3 What would it feel like to sit within this startling creature? Both women and men crafted the all-important *duhos*—ritual stools—out of wood, coral, or stone. Ecstatic visions during the *cohoba* ceremony possibly inspired the stylized spiral and curvilinear motif. *Duho*, 1200-1500 CE. Wood and manatee bone, 17¾ x 24½" (45 x 62 cm). Museo del Hombre Dominicano. Photography copyright Dirk Bakker 1996. Courtesy El Museo del Barrio, New York.

being on the *duho*. In this altered state, the Taíno's earthly representative invoked aid and protection from the other realm.

This seat, then, did not simply manifest social and political power but also was a vehicle to the supernatural arena and the community's well-being. No wonder people buried these poignant items with their owners or stowed them away in caves—far from Spanish hands, which either ransacked them for European collections or destroyed the carved beauties as signs of "heathen" idolatry. A few hundred surviving examples provide precious traces of the role art, artists, and also women played in maintaining the foundation of Taíno society, which colonizers virtually eradicated within just thirty years of contact.[8]

Sacred Art and Inner Vision: Self-taught Female Painters of Haiti and Jamaica

◉ ☻ ◉ How do works by Haitian and Jamaican female artists of African descent hold their people together? The women's ancestors were snatched from their African homes and forced into slavery, replacing the native Taíno population the Spanish already had missionized, enslaved, and finally decimated. Paintings by these women today embody a wide range of spiritual beliefs and practices that helped keep the captives alive, and now infuse descendants with hope and solace as they battle contemporary ills of poverty, and social and political adversity.

African Roots of Black Caribbean Art

The art of the African diaspora reaches back to the people's original countries, but the works are not simply transplanted expressions. Enslaved blacks disguised aspects of their heritage in order to elude the ever-watchful eye of white masters, who forbade any display of their African past. Captives assembled new pan-African religions, taking bits and pieces of their previous customs and freely borrowing from European Christianity and traditions of indigenous peoples on the islands. Visual expressions as well as sacred singing, dancing, music, and storytelling remained at the heart of these fresh fusions.

Haitian Vodou

Within Haiti, Vodou was vital to the country's black inhabitants. Vodou, the Creole spelling of a word from the Fon language, means "sacred energies or forces." This dynamic practice, a powerful social binder for the slave population, democratically combined elements of African Fon and Congo spiritual customs with Roman Catholicism, European mysticism, Freemasonry, and native Taíno influences.

Perhaps the majestic Ezili Dantó (Fig. 4-4) was instrumental in helping abducted Africans secure their freedom in Haiti centuries ago. She is one of the key spirits, or *Iwa*, in the Vodou religion. As a fierce, hard-working mother, Ezili Dantó fights ferociously to protect those seeking her aid.[9] in 1791, escaped slaves possibly beckoned her from the many hundreds of *Iwa* during a nighttime Vodou ceremony. This ceremony helped ignite a rebellion leading to the establishment of Haiti as the first free black Caribbean republic in 1804.

> **Women, Power, and Religion** Sexism remains strong in Haitian culture, yet women attain power and respect through participation in Vodou. They can enter all ranks of initiation and ceremonial roles, and *mambos* (priestesses) in particular are highly respected, addressed with honor as "Maman."

Haitian Female Artists
Francoise Eliassant

Despite approximately 200 years of liberty, Haitians currently face substantial poverty and social troubles. Vodou remains central to many people's lives, and its art, like that of Francoise Eliassant (see Fig. 4-4), is an essential ingredient to the practice. Paintings and

4-4 Ezili Dantó is one of seven manifestations of the goddess of love and is associated with the Christian Black Madonna. Her *kwish*, a clay vessel to hold water for libation, keeps the liquid cool despite the island's tropical heat. Francoise Eliassant (b. 1958), *Ezili Dantó*, 1994. Oil on canvas, 14 x 18" (35.5 x 46 cm). Courtesy of "The Electric Gallery" http://www.egallery.com.

adorned objects are living tools that can call and honor a specific *lwa*, who is attracted by beautiful and dynamic items. As part of a home altar or one in a Vodou temple, an artist's creation helps the *serviteur* (worshipper) communicate with the spirits, asking for guidance and assistance. A painting like Eliassant's becomes a static, aesthetic item only if sold on the tourist market and removed from its initial context. For the artist, the picture is a visual extension of Vodou—potent in and of itself.[10]

Eliassant never trained formally in art. She and other Haitian self-taught painters are part of a movement that gained international attention in the late 1940s. An American watercolorist, DeWitt Peters, journeyed to the country in 1943, on a wartime assignment to teach English. Appalled that there was no organized outlet for the island's many talented artists, Peters quickly helped establish the Art Center, which provided materials, exhibition space, and marketing.[11] The organization nurtured a large outpouring of self-expression in which artists tapped memories of Africa, slavery, liberation, Vodou culture, and everyday life.[12]

4-5 Louisianne Saint-Fleurant's riotous, electric brushwork creates an overall design that enhances the work's two-dimensionality. The *Marasa*—sacred twins—broadly symbolize the sacredness of all children. An *oungan* (priest) or *mambo* (priestess) invokes them at the beginning of each Vodou ceremony. Louisianne Saint-Fleurant (b. 1922), *Untitled*, n.d. Courtesy Pan American Art Gallery.

Louisianne Saint-Fleurant

There have been a continuous handful of women among the many male-dominated "schools" or styles of Haitian art. Born in 1922, Louisianne Saint-Fleurant (Fig. 4-5) is considered the *marraine* or godmother of the Saint-Soleil school.[13] Like other nonacademically-trained painters, Saint-Fleurant flattens her picture plane, presenting a spirit (possibly Ezili Dantó), surrounded by flora and fauna, and also the Marasa Vodou twins, who represent abundant life.

When the French intellectual and critic André Malraux visited Saint-Fleurant in the 1970s, he wrote about the pervasiveness of the island's religion: "In the final analysis, the painter paints because he or she is 'mounted' (possessed) and paints what the *Loa* (older word for *Iwa*) wants."[14]

Jamaican Women Painters
Elijah

Are female artists in nearby Jamaica likewise tied to the spiritual lifeblood of their communities? A sense of the sacred saturates their highly individualistic work.[15] The African-Christian Zion Revival religion defines the compositions of Pastor Geneva Mais Jarret, or Elijah. (Fig. 4-6) Born in 1952, she lives in one of Kingston's toughest ghettos, sheltering children who were orphaned by drug wars.[16] Elijah has constructed a spiritually charged, physical oasis by

4-6 Is Elijah's painting of this world? The artist's work is an intimate part of her religious services. The biblical motifs and visions have profound spiritual power and establish a personal discussion with the universe. Elijah (b. 1952), *The Wise Shepherd*, 1995. Enamel on canvas, 23 x 31" (58 x 79 cm). Courtesy Cavin-Morris, Inc.

painting her church walls, strung banners, and individual canvases with lions, visionary symbols, biblical figures, and her own dreams.[17] Elijah's art is an extension of her preaching, and the ecstatic colors and bold images immediately convey her passionate convictions.[18]

A sense of spirituality courses through the work of many Jamaican self-taught artists. The pieces also are linked by another connection—the African tradition of art's association with function. The art carries political, social, or religious messages to the community at large. Each supremely individual expression simultaneously becomes an integral aspect of cultural development and continuation.[19]

4-7 What figures dominate this composition? The police loom large, as they do in Evadney Cruickshank's everyday world. While their presence here might ensure order and safety, in other paintings Cruickshank depicts the policemen abusing their power within the community. Evadney Cruickshank (b. 1940), *First Police*, 1996. Oil on board, 16½ x 20½" (42 x 52 cm). Courtesy Cavin-Morris, Inc.

Evadney Cruickshank

As noted, for many Jamaicans, spirituality is an inseparable part of life, and African threads pervade the island's dominant religions, including Zion Revival, as well as *Kumina* and Rastafarianism. The visual work itself sustains ancient oral traditions, a crucial method of communication at the core of the African diaspora.[20]

While Elijah shares the "story" of her people's beliefs, Evadney Cruickshank records the less than idyllic "tales" of social, political, and economic realities that continue to rock her nation, even after its 1962 independence.[21] (Fig. 4-7) Underlying tensions between citizens and police in Cruickshank's unnerving painting capture the ever-present danger of violence and fear coursing through countryside towns. The danger comes not just from criminals, but confrontations with the police, who use their power both in beneficial and destructive ways.

Cruickshank's candid depictions of rural existence, however, remain tinged with a spiritual awareness. They remind us of people's inability to control the earthly realm and graphically relate how the spirits play games with us in daily life.[22]

But Cruickshank's works, and those of other female artists in Haiti and Jamaica, ultimately instill a sense of hope. Their spiritual content allows the artists to give back sacred energies to the earth and God, and also complements women's roles as priestesses and preachers.[23]

Women and Creative Time

Why are there far fewer female than male artists? Women in Jamaica and Haiti face challenging odds as family caretakers amid the economic and social hardships in their nations, leaving few hours for personal, artistic pursuit.[24] Nonetheless, the women's inventive, arresting creations are an ingenious mode of survival, and, in enduring centuries-old challenges, their art not only helps resist defeat but supports people's desire for spiritual, emotional, and economic liberation.

A Visual Legacy

Jamaica's fine-art scene took root in the late 1930s, but the country's cultural expressions had flourished well beforehand. In the past and today, ubiquitous wall paintings document everything from musicians to gang territories, banners define sacred spaces, and images abound in church murals and on ritual staffs.[25]

Twist and Cross: Mundillo Lace of Borikén

The clack of antique wooden bobbins fills the air. (Fig. 4-8) A woman sits with others on the patio in Borikén (Puerto Rico), a tropical Caribbean island, creating extraordinary lace garments for her newborn daughter. Mother, friends, and relatives welcome the child to this world in a wash of lace: gowns, booties, bonnets, shoulder cloth, and a receiving blanket. Lace articles will continue to mark significant moments in the girl's life: baptism, graduations, *quinceñera* (a girl's fifteenth birthday), and wedding.[26]

The women have mastered many forms of needlework but greatly prefer *mundillo* or bobbin lace, the island's signature tradition. They begin the process by mounting a paper pattern on a roller. The lacers then deftly twist and cross fine cotton thread wound around long, thin bobbins that hang from pins stuck in the pattern. (Fig. 4-9)

4-8 *Mundillo* originated in Europe and arrived in Borikén with the conquistadors. Lacemakers pass thread, attached to wooden spools called bobbins, around the pins stuck in the pattern mounted on the roller. Bobbin lace is softer and easier to drape than the finer needle lace, yet sturdy enough for everyday use. *Lacemaker in Moca, Puerto Rico,* 1998. Photograph by Bob Krist for the Puerto Rico Tourism Company.

Lace's Cross-cultural Migration

Priests and nuns who followed the Spanish conquistadors to the island in the sixteenth century introduced the art to young girls, because it was a traditional occupation of wives back home. Needlework embodied proper feminine virtues of patience, discipline, and industriousness. Lace did not originate in Spain, however; it has much older roots. Ancient Chinese, Egyptians, Persians, and Greeks made a kind of lace,[27] and the Greek poet Homer made references to net veils of woven gold.[28] Various types of embroidery related to lace existed throughout the ages in the Middle East, and by medieval times both bobbin and needle lace had migrated to Italy and the Low Countries,[29] eventually spreading throughout the continent over the centuries.

European Lace Lore
King Louis XIV of France wore bobbin lace, which was such the rage that wealthy females faced the rear when traveling in coaches so that no one could steal their lace-trimmed caps. After the revolution, lace was banned, but devious citizens secretly trimmed their underwear with lace. Others took dogs to Belgium, starved them, and covered their emaciated bodies with lace and a top layer of fur, smuggling the precious material back when re-crossing the border.

4-9 *Mundillo* refers to the name of the lace as well as the padded roller that turns the work. The word in Spanish literally means "little world." The roller is unique to Borikén, or Puerto Rico. In Spain, women use a pillow. *Mundillo.* Courtesy Lucy Betancourt.

Female Borikén Lacemakers

Why did Borikén prove to be such fertile ground for the European-based tradition? Native islanders had perfected looming and weaving, along with basket-making and pottery, long before the invaders arrived. Diego Alvarez Chanca, a doctor and companion to Columbus on his second voyage, was thoroughly impressed by the women's skill, stating, "They owe nothing to those of our country."[30] Quite the reverse was true. The Spanish quickly co-opted their abilities and nuns began teaching young native girls lace making to meet the needs of their own community—garments for statues in the Catholic churches, clothes for the altars, and vestments for religious officials.[31]

By 1880, both convents and public schools around the country instructed girls in needlework. When the founder of the Order of Notre Dame came to the island in 1915, he discovered the sumptuous wear made by the region's impoverished women. To help out, he further emphasized its study in the mission's school and established ties with tourist ships, which brought the ladies' goods to lace-starved foreign markets.

Females during these boon years exhibited their virtuosity with complex lace designs of landscapes, country homes, figures playing instruments, and even roasted pigs. They produced these images solely for tourists. Artists incorporated (as they do today) motifs from the surrounding lush flora and fauna into items for their own homes.[32]

The United States knocked at Borikén's doors for lace instead of Europe after World War I. This increased demand helped artists support their families, as husbands left Borikén to find employment on the mainland.[33]

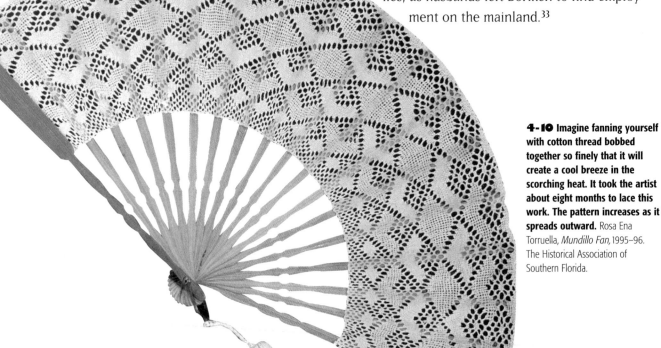

4-10 Imagine fanning yourself with cotton thread bobbed together so finely that it will create a cool breeze in the scorching heat. It took the artist about eight months to lace this work. The pattern increases as it spreads outward. Rosa Ena Torruella, *Mundillo Fan,* 1995–96. The Historical Association of Southern Florida.

4-11 What images did the lacemaker add to her sheer piece? Moving the bobbins one over another, she inserted a name, delicate flowers, and also animal motifs, which appear in each corner. *Lacemaker in Moca, Puerto Rico,* 1998. Photograph by Bob Krist for the Puerto Rico Tourism Company.

A woman on the patio today, making lace garments for her baby girl, recalls how her grandmother's early life had revolved around lace. By six years old she could create simple lace patterns and in the next year or so found herself working two or three hours before school, often returning to the task each evening, aided by candlelight, feet tucked inside a burlap sack to protect her from marauding mosquitoes.[34]

The art nearly died out during the 1950s, but the mother was one of the people who took up lace making again during its revival in the late 1960s and 1970s.[35] Unlike her grandmother, she does not need to lace to make ends meet. But the art is no less precious. It is an integral aspect of her cultural heritage, a physical expression with links to past centuries and a country across the ocean. The woman laces about four hours per day for as many months to create her daughter's new blanket. She includes many flowers, because the difficulty in making the oval petals will demonstrate to her child, and those in future generations, a tremendous love and dedication to both her craft and family.

Cross-cultural Odyssey: Transatlantic Fashion Design

⌒‿⌒ How did Millie Sequoia David successfully sell an entire leather and suede fashion line in the tropics of Jamaica? Island residents were drawn, despite the warm climate, to her distinctive attire—fantasies that allowed the wearers to feel wonderful.

Sequoia's childhood imaginings of luxury, while growing up in Grenada, became the wellspring of her work. "For the first seven years, I had a very active dream life. I continually pictured myself as an Egyptian princess, carried around in a litter." A sense of royalty pervades her clothing today, but it took time to develop this singular style.

Sequoia loved fashion as a youngster, poring over international magazines at the local library and imagining herself a model. Eventually Sequoia's father sent her inland to learn sewing, in an effort to subvert endless hours on the beach. Sequoia was startled to discover that she could execute designs inside her head.

She studied marketing, however, not design, at the Fashion Institute of Technology upon moving to New York City in 1973. She worked with *haute couture* (high fashion) at prestigious Manhattan department stores. For fun, Sequoia and friends created outrageous outfits that got them in the doors of exclusive night spots. When people kept inquiring where they could buy such clothes, Sequoia suddenly realized she could make money with her own designs.

African Inflections

Sequoia's first collection, with modern geometric black-and-white fabrics, sold well, but she truly began to find her "voice" after becoming intrigued by Brazilian music. The pounding drums and rhythmic dance inspired her to investigate African culture more seriously and incorporate its influences directly into her work. Shades of various African movement and sound remain visible in her fabric patterns and the actual lines of her clothing. (Fig. 4-12)

Sequoia moved to Jamaica in 1983, where, against strong odds, government ministers and housewives alike craved her suede and leather African-inspired apparel. Roots of the people's original homelands across the Atlantic swelled in the designs, as did a client's sense of self when wearing garments that let one imagine an ancient royal lineage.

Living in Atlanta now, Sequoia continues to produce exceptional wear, buying fabrics from traders who acquire textiles overseas. She feels her clothes are part of "an orchestrated effort by many African Americans to recapture what has been lost, what has been stolen, and what we have abandoned."

Sequoia, nonetheless, diligently defies easy classification. "I am African American because I've lived in America for over twenty years. I'm African Caribbean because I was born there. But mostly I'm African. As my ex-husband used to say, 'If an orange came from China, was planted and bore fruit, would you call it a Chinese-American orange?' It would remain an orange."

The Look of the Future

Sequoia embraces a fluid sense of identity that has begun to transform her designs into partnerships. "They are no longer just mine. I create something and people say, 'I'd like that with a slimmer waist, or a wider collar.' So it's really no longer my coat. The direction we need to go in, particularly as black artists, is toward collaboration." Interestingly, it is exactly this collaboration—between designer and client, maker and wearer—that creates the stunning fashions that allow people to feel so undeniably unique.

4-12 What might it feel like to don one of these African-inspired designs? Sequoia fashions clothes "that glorify the body and bring out the royalty in you." A sense of majesty informs all her work, stemming from childhood fantasies of living as an Egyptian princess. Millie Sequoia David (b. 1958), *Leather and Suede Outfits,* c. 1983. Courtesy of the artist, Ites International, Atlanta, GA.

5 Eastern Europe

Ever Old/Ever New

Women in Eastern Europe, the mysterious borderland between the West and Asia, straddle two artistic traditions. One is centuries old: the historical indigenous creations, or folk expressions, which have always been a part of the population's life. Cut-paper compositions, painted eggs, and heavenly embroidery are just some of the stuff of which dreams are made; they resonate with ancient spirituality. Throughout the generations, women use humble materials to create dazzling artwork that asserts and strengthens their cultural identity.

5-1 What part of this image immediately catches your eye? Polish animator Alina Maliszewska used a strong sense of design to create the fantasy of the film's title. Alina Maliszewska, *Przygoda w paski* (A Striped Adventure), 1960. Animation cel. Courtesy Marcin Glzycki.

Popular traditions continue today in many regions, sustained by females who pass skills down from mother to daughter, despite an often adverse political and social climate. The fracturing of old ways by communism, socialism, and related forms of leadership have made the survival of women's traditional art particularly remarkable.

It also is fortunate that the government-promoted "social realist"

5-2 Did Czech artist Anna Zemánková strive for strict botanical documentation? She once said of her images, "I am growing flowers that are not grown anywhere else." Zemánková turned to art in her sixties, typically completing a single piece in her kitchen between 4:00 a.m. and 7:00 a.m. Classical music transported her into a trance-like state in which she drew visionary, biomorphic forms without preplanning. Anna Zemánková (1908–86), *Trepetalky*, 1966. Oil pastel on paper, 34¾ x 24½" (88 x 62 cm). Courtesy Cavin-Morris, Inc.

style did not entirely saturate the fine-art arena. Radical, avant-garde modes emerged in painting, photography, filmmaking, animation, and the like, regardless of official opposition. The artists' desire to explore ever-new frontiers overcame official determination to mold art to the supposed needs of the masses.

Ironically, it was socialist and communist governments that altered the daily fabric of life for women in the East, opening the gates for them in an unprecedented manner both at home and in comparison to the West. Eastern European females entered all fields previously available only to men, including those in the arts. And like men, women made modern art that crossed national boundaries and yet maintained a distinctive regional flair. These extraordinary female pioneers set the stage for Eastern European women artists today who examine individual and universal concerns as their countries redefine themselves amid a constantly changing social order.

Eggs of Heaven: Ukrainian *Pysanky*

◠◡◠   When is an egg not simply food? When it's an ancient art form, harking back to 4000 BCE.[1] Most people associate decorated eggs with Easter, but, in fact, the custom dates to pagan times.

So what was the journey like for the humble egg from human sustenance to mighty spiritual symbol? Ukrainian folktales tell of people long ago worshiping the sun, the most powerful deity, which brought life to all things. Birds—the god's chosen creation, could come near the sacred sun, unlike people on earth. Ukrainians couldn't catch the feathered creatures, yet they were able to obtain their eggs, which became magical objects, a source of life.[2]

Christianity came to the Ukraine in 988 CE, but

5-3 Women say they "write" on their *pysansky*, a word that comes from the Ukrainian verb *pysaty*, "to write." For older artists, like Alexandra Romanenko, their eggs were not only Christian symbols but also represented hopes of a Ukraine free from Soviet rule. Alexandra Romanenko, *Pysanka (Ukrainian Easter Egg)*, 1982. Courtesy Southwest Folklore Center of the University of Arizona Library. Photography James S. Griffith.

5-4 Alexandra Romanenko's *pysanka* is ready for presentation to relatives or respected outsiders. The painted eggs have been an important national emblem to Ukrainians around the world, who kept the art alive during Soviet domination of their homeland. Alexandra Romanenko, *Pysanka (Ukrainian Easter Egg),* 1982. Courtesy Southwest Folklore Center of the University of Arizona Library. Photography James S. Griffith.

people incorporated existing *pysanka* customs into the new religion. They were far too vital to die out. Eggs became synonymous with Christ and the resurrection. Women initially created *pysanky* (the plural form of *pysanka*) for pagan spring rituals that herald-ed life's reemergence after each desolate, barren winter. Now the small painted works, miracles of birth, symbolized the astonishing rise of Christ from the dead, bearing new life and hope to the faithful.

Pysanky Today

Women today in Eastern Slovakia, Carpatho-Ruthenia, and America still cover their creations with complex designs that harbor some of their original pagan meanings. Triangles that initially signaled air, fire, and water currently represent the Holy Trinity.[3] Fish for pre-Christian Slavs were an important food source but have become images of Jesus; and the cross-hatched motif representing nets refers to Christ's promise to His disciples that they would become "fishers of men."[4]

To become adept at *pysanky*, women must learn a wide symbolic vocabulary consisting of approximately 200 patterns. Birds, flowers, trees, deer, wheat sheaves, and the like reveal something about their ancestors' beliefs. The artists weave the images into intricate compositions.

The process is slow and careful. A woman first covers any area she wants to remain shell white with wax, drawing with either a pin head or hollow writing instrument, called a *kistka*. The artist then plunges the *pysanka* into the lightest color dye, say yellow, and allows it to dry. She next applies wax over areas to stay yellow, protecting these regions as well during the next dye bath. The woman continues this batik-like method, progressing to darker colors. Her advance from light to

dark is not purely practical. Darker hues represent the heart and, hence, the dyeing order reflects the ultimate triumph of love and faith.[5] After the final bath, the artist holds her *pysanka* to a candle flame, gently melting the wax from its surface.

The sparkling pigments also communicate meaning: black for remembrance; white for purity; blue for health; yellow for spirituality; and red for love, victory, blood, or the resurrection.[6]

What do the women do with their jewels once complete? They take them to church on Easter Sunday for the priest to bless and then give them away as gifts.[7] They present older people with darker *pysanky* painted with rich designs, paralleling the full life they already have led. The eggs for younger folks contain more white—the blank pages of their life.[8]

Recipients place the cherished treasures on display at home, sometimes in large brandy snifters or their original offering baskets (Fig. 5-4). The egg dries up inside the painted cocoon, remaining there forever as part of this beautiful gift of life.

Hutsul *Pysanky* The Hutsuls—who live in the Carpathian mountains of western Ukraine—say that decorated eggs can save them from the evil serpent chained to a cliff. Every year the terrifying beast sends out his lackeys to check on the number of *pysanky* produced. If the women have made too few, the serpent's chains loosen and he can wander the earth, causing ruin. If the painters have been productive, the being's chains choke him close for another year, and the female artists have saved the day yet again.

5-5 Some traditional *pysanky* designs: the sun (life and growth), evergreens (eternal youth and health), hen (fertility), another sun or star motif, butterfly, wheat (good health and bountiful harvest), fish (Christianity), flower (love and good will), deer (good will, wealth), ram, and pussy willows. Illustration courtesy of Jo Miles Schuman.

Rural Cuttings: Polish *Wycinanki*

How did nineteenth-century Polish farm women decorate their newly whitewashed cottage walls for the upcoming Easter celebration? What could they do with the basic tools around them—huge sheep shears and colorful sheets of paper? (Fig. 5-6) Imagine the skill and patience it took to create such lacelike *wycinanki* with unwieldy scissors, especially cutting free-hand without any preliminary sketches.[9]

Young and old gathered, sharing in the pleasure of creating these two-dimensional silhouettes. Women in Poland and America today still create images relat-ed to the countryside, roosters, trees, flowers, stars, and religious symbols,[10] reflecting the art's rural ori-gin. Women begin each piece by cutting from the out-ermost edge of a doubled-over sheet, snipping away the background from the design.

Every region developed its own distinctive style over time. In Lowicz, artists often glue successively smaller, contrasting colored details over a black structural shape. (See Fig. 5-6.) Women cut a single, shiny sheet into lengthwise or circular compositions for Kurpie designs. The *wycinanki* in Lublin echo the

5-6 Barbara Glinski learned *wycinanki* from her mother in Poland. She practices in the United States, affirming the connection to her original home-land. Glinski adds extensive paper details to her perfectly symmetrical rooster and tree motif, a favorite Polish paper-work theme. Barbara Glinski, *Wycinanki (Polish Paper Cutting)*, 1983. Courtesy Southwest Folklore Center of the University of Arizona Library. Photography James S. Griffith.

women's elaborate embroidery. In fact, females across the country specialize in weaving and embroidery, as well as decorating men's carpentry and pottery with painted images.[11]

In some rural communities women still paste *wycinanki* to their farmhouse walls, or use them to decorate stables, barns, or even rocks and eggs. (Fig. 5-7) Many, however, now make examples to be framed. They might sell these items to outsiders in urban centers or people in other countries. This folk expression has become a serious undertaking—artists enter exhibitions and competitions that judge the work on its originality and craftsmanship.[12]

Yet, *wycinanki* is ultimately not a commercial or public venture. The women's colorful paper works brighten homes for special occasions or serve as vibrant visual memories that recall a family's heritage.

Paper Cuts Across the World
The paper arts began in China, spreading by the fourteenth century to Japan, and then the Middle East and Europe, via the Silk Road. One hundred years later, people around the world practiced the art, as seen in Mexican women's *papel picado*, Japanese *kirigami* or *mon kiri*, German *scherenschnitte*, and French silhouettes. Although the artists share a common medium, each paper cut reflects its maker's distinct origin, beliefs, and aesthetic inclinations.

5-7 Unlike Ukrainian women, who paint their Easter eggs (see Fig. 5-3 on page 84), Polish artists glue intricate cut-paper designs to their surfaces. The largest example in the basket is a duck egg. Barbara Glinski, *Polish Easter Eggs,* 1988. Courtesy Southwest Folklore Center of the University of Arizona Library. Photography James S. Griffith.

The Silver Screen for Social Change: Female Soviet Filmmakers of the Twenties

◑ ◡ ◐ What does the film image shown here seem to indicate about the role of Soviet women just ten years after the 1917 Russian revolution? (Fig. 5-8) What part did female Soviet directors have in shaping these images? The former Soviet Union, once the largest country in the world, was the first nation to legally declare women's equality to men. Law and reality, unfortunately, did not exactly correspond. Cinema images to the contrary, life both before and after the revolution was not easy for women.

5-8 Did Ol'ga Preobrazhenskaya's film romanticize rural life in the new social order? Female peasants at the time did not actually play frivolously on swings but rather drove tractors, worked the farm, and endlessly tended the home. Ol'ga Preobrazhenskaya, *Babi Ryazanskye (Peasant Women of Ryazan)*, 1927. Black-and-white still.

Soviet Women

Lenin (chair of Soviet government, 1917-22) championed women's rights, calling for females to move from the private domestic domain to the public workplace. The state was to provide household services such as collective childcare, laundries, and the like, but never fulfilled its promise. Women still are caught in the "double burden" of working full time in two spheres.[13]

Neither female nor male directors exposed this bind in the early years. In fact, they rarely addressed the "woman question" at all; the fundamental division for commentary was between the classes—the bourgeoisie and the proletariat.

Early Russian Filmmaking

The cinema burst onto the scene just as the old tsarist rule was disintegrating. Its rapid development charts the changes in the country, women's lives, and their representation on screen.

The first moving picture, made by the French Lumière brothers, was shown in Russia in 1896 as part of the festivities surrounding the coronation of Tsar Nicholas II.[14] Critics who later viewed it at music halls across the nation immediately cited its powerful possibilities. The old royal regime ignored this potential, but the Bolsheviks immediately co-opted the nascent art for their own purposes. The tantalizing modern technology could reach the workers and peasants, eighty percent of whom were illiterate, "educating" them about their place and responsibilities in the fledgling socialist regime.[15] The Bolsheviks nationalized the film industry, clearly signaling its intended use by placing cinema under the control of the Commissariat for Enlightenment in 1919.[16]

Initial Female Soviet Filmmakers
Esfir' Shub

Before the revolution, audiences had devoured theatrical costume dramas produced by both Russian filmmakers and foreign directors. The current gov-

5-9 Esfir' Shub purchased old footage of the royal family from American firms for *The Fall of the Romanov Dynasty*, and re-edited the material into what she termed an "idealized montage." Two reasons underlined her technique. At the time, unused stock was scarce, and also foreign material had a "bourgeois" tinge, which Shub could reassemble into a proletariat statement. Esfir' Shub (1894–1950), *Padeniye Dinasti Romanovikh (The Fall of the Romanov Dynasty)*, 1927. Black-and-white still.

ernment now demanded realism, not fiction, to be cinema's hallmark. Lenin preferred documentary newsreels, devoid of distracting stories that might open the public's eyes to "reality."[17] The public, meanwhile, would have none of it, and instead flocked to view the celluloid antics of Charlie Chaplin and Buster Keaton[18] imported from the capitalist West.

One of the most significant directors to try to wean audiences off foreign films was female. Esfir' Shub pioneered a cinema technique—the "compilation" or montage method, in which she literally recut existing footage and wrote accompanying text to produce a totally new film.[19] Her renowned first endeavor, *The Fall of the Romanov Dynasty*, became the epitome of experimental Soviet cinema. (Fig. 5-9) She brilliantly juxtaposed documentary material recording the harsh life of the peasants prior to the revolution with opulent shots of the tsarist court, thus creating penetrating political material.[20] In one instance, a caption reading "sweat" appeared on screen between images of the poor working the land and royalty dancing merrily away on Nicholas II's yacht.[21] Although herself an influential female director, Shub did not address women's position specifically during the 1920s. That effort would have to wait until the next decade.

Did filmmakers, in fact, honestly reflect fresh gender roles for the "new Soviet woman"? Male avant-garde directors generally portrayed females within old gender stereotypes—madonna, prostitute, victim, or evil temptress—frequently ignoring their actual jobs as nurses, teachers, factory workers, and advocates for social change. Female film characters usually served as symbols—good ones for the proletariat and bad for the bourgeoisie.

How did these on-screen images correspond to women's true existence? Soviet women indeed entered careers previously open only to men, becoming pilots, parachutists, construction laborers, and so on. But many were ghettoized in poorer-paying careers associated with female labor: the service industries, clothing, and health care.[22]

Furthermore, regardless of strides in the public sector, it was clear both on and off screen that every woman's primary responsibility was to birth baby citizens for the state.[23]

Other Early Female Directors Lilya Brik in the 1920s, and Vera Stroeva, Yuliya Solntseva, and Margarita Baraskaya in the next decade were the foremothers of generations of female directors, script writers, film editors, camera operators, and critics, who still grow in number despite ongoing male prejudice.

5-10 Ol'ga
**Preobrazhenskaya contrasts
the new Soviet woman with
the "victim" peasant of the
past in her landmark movie,
one of the first to address
female roles. Even though she
includes a strong-willed
daughter, representing
options open to women after
the revolution, her cinemato-
graphic approach recalled
earlier drama films.** Ol'ga
Preobrazhenskaya, *Peasant
Women of Ryazan,* 1927. Black-
and-white still.

Ol'ga Preobrazhenskaya

The director Ol'ga Preobrazhenskaya straddled both the domestic and public realm. She made films for and about youngsters during the 1920s, thereby working within a feminine tradition of child rearing.[24]

Preobrazhenskaya began her career as an actress and started directing before the revolution in 1916, becoming the country's first female filmmaker. Preobrazhenskaya's debut film for adults, *Peasant Women of Ryazan*, (Figs. 5-8, 5-10) contrasted the old and new Soviet woman. An impoverished "victim" peasant bride, Anna (see Fig. 5-10), is a carryover from the prerevolutionary melodramatic film days. She marries into a patriarchal household and is raped by her father-in-law while her husband is away. Anna bears his child but is rejected by her returning spouse, and so drowns herself in the river. Vasilisa, Anna's sister-in-law, however, is a model of female courage, leaving her family to live with a lover and, appropriately, founds a home for orphaned children.[25] Preobrazhenskaya was the first female director to examine the new Soviet woman, yet she did so within the confines of old-school narrative style.

Female Reflection on the Soviet Screen

It was Esfir' Shub who planned to use the vanguard method to explore issues of women's equality within the new government. Her 1933 script for *Women* included actual people, not actresses, as heroines: a female leader of a village council, others constructing the Metro, and a black woman who moves to the Soviet Union to participate in the opportunities of the new society. Shub also addressed serious social problems, such as prostitution and homelessness of orphaned children.[26]

Why didn't this look at women's brave new life ever make it to the screen? After Stalin took power in 1929, the experimental cinema that Shub had helped form came under suspicion. The new "socialist realist" movies had to steer clear of "art" and concentrate solely on "educating workers in the spirit of communism."[27] The screen was a tool of the political party and Shub's script did not conform to the mandate for simple plots and heroes. She kept directing into the 1940s, but never regained her previous acclaim. The films under Stalin had to wholly reflect an idealized political, not social, "reality."[28]

Why didn't early female directors delve more deeply into the "woman question" during the 1920s? After the revolution, "equality" meant laboring just like men. Maleness remained the standard too, as having a "man's brain" was considered a compliment. The atmosphere was not conducive to exploring distinctly female themes.[29]

Even today, many post-Soviet Russian women have little in common with contemporary Western feminists, who initially rallied against female bonds to home. They crave less, not more, time for careers so they can enjoy their families. The home is seen as a sanctuary, an ideal that began during the Communist era. Only here could Soviet women be individuals, not anonymous members of the masses.[30] Nonetheless, early female directors, although few in number, did help shape cinema's development. And their depiction of women, both in what they did and did not address, mirrors the shifting sands of the period's prevailing ideologies.

Moving Visions: Eastern Bloc Women in Animation

◉‿◉ Beautifully rendered still images flicker in the dark, moving effortlessly across the screen. What role have women played in this alluring blend of art, magic, and technology?

In the eastern bloc countries, females contributed to animation from its blossoming just after the turn of the century. Unlike fast-paced, antic American Walt Disney-type cartoons, Eastern and Central

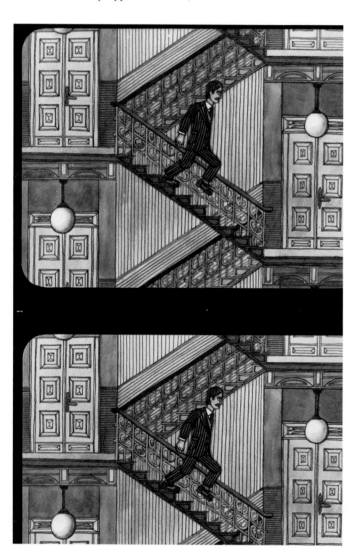

European counterparts more closely reflected avant-garde painting trends, emphasizing abstraction and formal visual qualities over the storyline. (Fig. 5-11) The tales themselves often were somewhat somber and contained an underlying lesson, unlike the lighter fare found in the United States.

Why were women fundamental to animation? Females entered all areas of the workforce in unprecedented numbers throughout the eastern bloc, as communism and socialist governments dramatically altered the structure of everyday life during the early twentieth century. From the onset, therefore, women stood alongside men as animators, directors, inkers, colorists, production managers, camera operators, and script writers.[31]

Eastern European Female Trailblazers

Starting in the 1920s, the Russian Brumberg sisters, Valentina and Zinaida, like their male peers, relied on their nation's wealth of fables and traditional puppet theater for inspiration.[32] German art student Lotte Reiniger created one of the earliest animated feature films in 1926, using only cut-out silhouettes, moved frame by frame under the camera, over a flat wooden board.[33]

5-11 Polish animators often emphasize abstract and graphic elements. Notice the abundant linear designs that play off the sole figure. Can you detect the slight variation from one cel to the next that suggests the man's descent? Zofia Oldak's film is about a man who works so hard the whole week that he no longer enjoys nature. Zofia Oldak, *Natura (Nature)*, 1977. Animation cel. Courtesy Marcin Gizycki.

Franciszka Themerson, together with her husband, inaugurated experimental animation in Poland, making seven fascinating abstract films between 1930 and 1945. However, Themerson and other accomplished women, including Zofia Oldak (see Fig. 5-11) followed by Alina Maliszewska (Fig. 5-12) and Katarzyna Latallo (Fig. 5-14), never received the same recognition as men, especially abroad, partially because of the male-oriented promotional policies of the state-run film agency.[34]

But women in these socialist countries didn't yearn for separate female recognition and, from the beginning, were active in every aspect of the industry, as particularly evident in the Czech Republic. One pioneer after the Second World War was Hermina Tyrlova, who masterfully animated various soft materials and fabric.[35] Tyrlova was a splendid puppeteer, carrying on an ancient tradition.[36]

Just how old is the art of puppet-making? A 25,000-year-old puppet made of mammoth ivory, one of the oldest surviving examples, was found in the Moravian region of the country.[37] Puppetry often still profoundly influences the Czech Republic's style of animated movement and design, making characters seem like dolls as compared with the American tendency to present the figures as real and alive.[38]

5-12 In these cels, a man sits on a stool, followed by a man who sits on his knees, followed by another, and so forth. When the stool finally breaks, the first man sits on the knees of the last figure. Alina Maliszewska's philosophical joke is a metaphor for human solidarity, a Polish specialty in the 1960s and 1970s. Alina Maliszewska, *Na Jednym Stolku (On One Stool)*, 1972. Animation cel. Courtesy Marcin Gizycki.

5-13 Czech animation is always rich, and unlike many Western cartoons, intends to bring something of value to children, not simply offer thrilling distractions. The evocative brushwork in *Nils and the Wild Geese* exemplifies the high artistic quality of the country's animation artists. *Nils and the Wild Geese,* 1996–97. Designer, Jitka Walterová; director, LibuSe CihaRová. Courtesy Gene Deitch and Zdenka Deitchova.

Present Perspective

Zdenka Deitchova, a female executive producer, reflects back today over her over fifty-three years at the Czech Bratri v Triku animation studio. "There were women in every job, director, animation, background painting, film editing, camera, etc. ... There was no difference between men and women there, except in one department. Most of the inking and painting of the animation cels was done by women. I suppose this was because females are more patient."[39] Deitchova, who has worked in virtually all animation positions, insists, "Communism was a far greater restriction than male domination. But we were luckier than most because making children's films (Fig. 5-13) was considered 'innocent,' and the communists did not bother us as much as in some professions, such as journalism and other writing." Women, like men, shared concerns "about getting enough money, having the right conditions for work, and so on. We all have the same problems!"[40] Referring to the studio's symbol, Bratri v Triku

(Brothers in Trick), Deitchova explains that women never took offense at the term "brothers." This might be due to a linguistic element: In Czech, "sister" indicates a hospital nurse, a holdover from the time when the profession was filled with Catholic nuns. So "Sisters in Trick," (trick coming from the term "trickfilm" or stop-motion animation) would have inaccurately indicated that they were nurses in film.[41]

Deitchova insists that there was no sexual discrimination in the Prague studio, and directors assigned jobs according to people's talents. She epitomizes the feelings of many other females from former Soviet bloc countries: "I have to say that I am very irritated by all the fuss Americans make about 'Women's Lib.' I have never needed that! I am liberated all by myself, and my women colleagues here feel the same way! I am accepted as a professional, and that is what I wanted."[42]

As talented and skilled individuals, Eastern and Central European females in animation have helped sustain a wondrous art that remains integral to their country's cultural heritage amid the shifting, tempestuous political climate of the last century.

Love and Art Behind the Iron Curtain Hundreds of American films and cartoons, including episodes of *Tom and Jerry*, *Popeye*, and *Krazy Kat*, were animated in Communist Czechoslovakia during the height of the cold war. The American stories were directed by Gene Deitch, who agreed to go behind the iron curtain for a few days to work with the country's reservoir of talent. Some forty years later, Deitch happily remains in his adoptive homeland with his wife, Zdenka Deitchova. When he first arrived at the Bratri v Triku studios, he suggested renaming it "Brothers and Sisters in Trick" because of the large number of female employees.

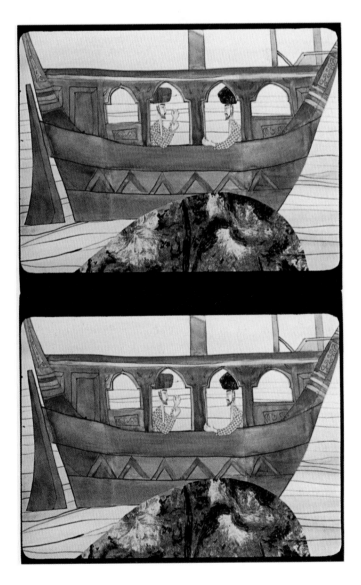

5-14 Where does this story occur? Katarzyna Latallo animates "The Adventures of Sindbad" from *The One Thousand and One Nights*. Sindbad's seven voyages were based on the experiences of merchants from ancient Iraq, trading with the East. Latallo captures the tale's mixture of past and present, memory and imagination, in her graphic, monochromatic style that differs greatly from her American counterparts. Katarzyna Latallo, *Przygody Sindbada Zeglarza (Adventures of Sindbad)*, 1969.

"Now I Lay Me Down to Sleep": Hungarian Women's Ágyvitel

⌒‿⌒ Could anyone ever have squeezed into this *ágyvitel*—a copiously pillowed bed? (Fig. 5-15) There is certainly no room to comfortably settle down. But the ornamental ensemble, an essential component of traditional nineteenth-century Hungarian peasant homes, was never meant to support a good night's rest.

In fact, unlike its ordinary, private counterpart, this furniture had a very public function. Mother and daughter worked for years to produce the sumptuous bedding, which they proudly displayed at home in the *parádés szoba* ("best room") once the young child reached a marriageable age.[43] The family hoped that the girl's fine workmanship would attract an eligible bachelor.

The splendid bedding then served the couple, visually declaring their match to the entire village, when young people carried the *ágyvitel* through the streets, dancing and singing ribald verses.[44] After the procession, half-serious, half-joking negotiations took place with the future in-laws before the ornamented furniture entered the bridegroom's abode.[45]

Bedding in the New Home

The bedding's transition from one house to another represented the newlywed's secular covenant, paralleled by their union at church.[46] Symbolically, it also carried wishes for a happy and fruitful coupling.

Women poured great love and energy into their fabric creations. They "dressed" the bed in different

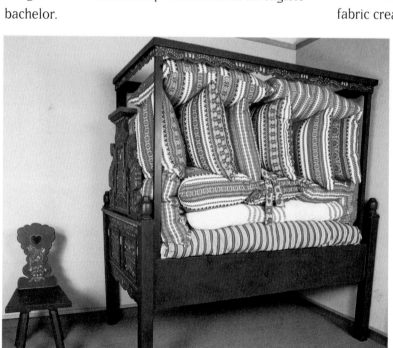

clothes, just as they would themselves, to suit various occasions. Sheets, pillowcases, and counterpanes (bedspreads) changed with the seasons. Women fashioned special pieces to mark life's most crucial moments. Following childbirth, only the most intimate family and friends would witness the specially covered bed, and also the baby's head gently resting on the small top pillow temporarily placed in the cradle.[47]

5-15 Would people sleep in this overstuffed bed? In Hungarian peasant homes, no one ever slept in these ceremonial furnishings, exhibited in the "best room." Richly decorated *ágyvitel* (bedding) symbolically reflected the passing seasons, a child's birth, and, eventually, a family member's death. *Ornamental Bed.* Courtesy American Hungarian Foundation. Photography Mark Rocha, Mark 1 Productions.

5-16 Imagine the time it must have taken to create all the extraordinary cloth that traveled with a bride to her new home. Village women and young girls, dressed in their own elaborately stitched garments, helped the bride make this important transition. *Hungarian Women Packing the Bride's Dowry Before the Wedding.* Early 20th century. Mingei International Museum.

At death, the larger community once again viewed the bed furnishings, which generously padded the bier. After the funeral, women returned the textiles to the bed, using the mourning bedclothes for a year or longer.

Hungarian Women's Needlework

In many Hungarian villages, people defined their relationship to another by stating that they visited someone for a funeral or wedding.[48] These events were a frame of reference, reinforcing human connections. And women's handiwork deepened the ties. In Tura, for instance, a bride would embroider several dozen handkerchiefs for new relatives before her wedding. The stitching's color or design indicated the nature of the relationship. She only used blue yarn for an in-law's gift, for example.[49] In the southern Danube region, women provided "mourning handkerchiefs" to the bereaved's family at funerals, once again bonding the group together during a demanding time.

Hungarian women's masterful work, full of color and dazzling motifs, pervaded the special rituals that defined village existence, and complemented the complex social structure in which they and their families lived.

6 Latin America

Persistent Heritage

Despite pervasive *machismo*, or male orientation, in the Latin American region, spanning from Mexico through the tip of South America, females have been and continue to be strong matriarchal presences. While men outwardly seem to dominate society, women's art—from historical weaving and pottery to recent oil paintings—remains a constant and sustaining factor that helps preserve their heritage and communities.

The ancient vitality of female creations is seen, for instance, in the pre-Columbian origins of Shipibo ceramics. Potters on the shore of the Ucayali River in Peru continue their ancestral tradition, fashioning intricately patterned anthropomorphic vessels that link art, medicine, and the sacred sphere—thereby supporting the health and healing of the tribe.

Across Latin America, women's art has been particularly essential in times of trouble. Solentiname peasant painters of Nicaragua used their brushes to help fight both emotional and financial poverty during the Somoza regime (1937–79). Chilean *arpilleristas* stitched cloth tapestries full of anguish and rage over family members who "disappeared" during General Pinochet's brutal dictatorship (1973–90).

6-1 What might you carry in a bag like this? Both women and men of the Ngobe-Bugle, who live in the western province of Panama, transport their belongings (sometimes even babies) in these resilient string bags or *chakaras* along steep mountain trails. The women also weave larger versions for ceremonial occasions. Ngobe-Bugle, *Chakara*, 1990s. Palm fiber, bark, and commercial goods. Courtesy and photograph copyright Merran Gray 1997.

6-2 Older Mayan women in Guatemala still recount to young girls how long ago, the god Xmucane assigned every village a weaver's saint who would pass on the secrets of the community's seven sacred designs. The women's exquisite clothing immediately reveals the weaver's region, village, language, sex, marital status, socioeconomic level, family affiliation, aesthetic tastes, and technical proficiency. Ixil women from Nebaj wrap their hair in woven cloth that gracefully frames their faces. *Ixil Maya Women, Nebaj.* El Quiche, Guatemala. Courtesy David Irving. Photograph Paul Harbaugh.

The works speak of the artists' courage to express themselves despite potential danger. They denote the strength the women derive from joining in collective creative efforts regardless of the obstacles.

A sense of purpose also infuses women's older and diverse textile traditions. For centuries, artists have created works that can communicate a person's sex, age, affiliation, and status. Cloth's unique motifs, whether in the form of weavings from one of the many Mayan peoples in Guatemala or the Kuna's reverse appliqué fabric blouse panels from Panama, uphold a distinct heritage and identity. This sense of self and means of preserving culture, achieved through the women's expressions, has been crucial as foreign forces continue their long-standing encroachment on indigenous rights and ways. When all else is lost, wearing women's stunning textiles can help protect both body and soul.

Women's commitment to their art and communities remains steadfast throughout the enormous diversity of Latin American cultures. And their persistence against all odds—whether fading traditions, outside interference, or political oppression—underlies each poignant and arresting expression.

Andean "Gold": Ancient Fabric of Life

ᴖᴗᴖ Settling debts in ancient Peru was no easy matter. People had no coins or bills. Instead, they used textiles as a form of exchange to pay tributes and taxes, and also for religious offerings.

Ancient Andean women fashioned exquisite fabrics for the elite and less elaborate cloth for commoners. Their textiles touched every important rite of passage and social occasion. Distinctive costumes were an indispensable part of people's identity, reflecting their religious, social, and economic status. By 2500 BCE, Peruvian artists had developed techniques to produce practically every known type of fabric.[1]

Women used cotton and alpaca fibers, tropical bird feathers, and even bat fur and human hair, which had religious significance.[2] When Spanish colonialists later brought sheep to the land, women also began to weave with wool and, by the end of the nineteenth century, switched from using natural dyes to commercial European imports.

Outstanding Visual Communicators

Ancient Peruvians had no writing system, but the women's woven motifs "spoke" a visual language. Mythological creatures were

6-3 Can you distinguish the two central figures? The weaver depicted two deities and surrounding stylized animal forms. The unusual tapestry probably served as a small altar decoration. Paramonga, Peru, *Altar Decoration*, c. 700 CE. 7½ x 13" (19 x 33 cm). Courtesy The Liberty Corporation.

associated with the sacred world. (Fig. 6-3) Rulers and commoners alike wore garments both during this life and in their transition to the next. People wrapped the deceased in layers of woven cloth as a supreme offering to these sacred ancestors. The gorgeous textiles helped them stay in the good graces of the dead, who they believed were close to the gods and demons and, therefore, mediators between this realm and the beyond.[3]

Throughout the centuries, people regarded the art with the utmost esteem. Women primarily were the master weavers and work baskets full of spindles, balls of cotton, and wool yarn or thread have been discovered in their grave sites. It was an all-consuming task, and females even spun while walking.[4]

Women wove garments for themselves, families, local leaders, and deities. Inca women, in a temple to the sun in Cuzco, for instance, produced the finest textiles, which were distributed as gifts to military and local leaders, or used as offerings. Some were even burnt in ritual fires or thrown into rivers to honor the great deity.

Archaeologists have found 4,000-year-old fabric in Peru.[5] Surviving examples testify to women's long history of artistic virtuosity. Andean females nurture the tradition today, weaving distinctive garments for themselves (Fig. 6-4) despite the trend toward Western clothes and increasing production for export.

6-4 Ancient Peruvians had no written language. But women wove emblems inspired by nature, mythology, and religion. Their magnificent modern textiles retain elements of earlier times. What creatures in this women's mantle can you detect amid the veritable menagerie of real and imaginary forms? Quechua Indian, Cuzco, Peru, *Lliclla*, mid-20th century. Handspun wool, 40 x 32" (102 x 81 cm). Courtesy David Irving, Ethnographica. Photography Al Vatter.

Linear Abundance: Designs and Healing in Amazon Shipibo Pottery

"Everything is covered with designs." So says a Shipibo song. Imagine patterns, like those on the anthropomorphic vessel (Fig. 6-5), covering every conceivable surface in a village along the Ucayali River in east Peru. These linear, geometric motifs originally embraced virtually all structures: house posts and beams, thatched roofs, square mosquito tents, boats, paddles, kitchen utensils, and hunting tools. Women wove, embroidered, beaded, and painted meandering patterns on textiles, their bodies, beadwork, and, of course, an impressive array of ceramic ware.[6]

Female Shipibo Potters

Today, as in earlier times, not every woman is a master potter. An outstanding artist treats and cherishes the clay as she would a lover. She also remains forever tied to her vessel. The Shipibo destroy a woman's works after she dies, ritually throwing the pieces into the lake or river. Although expert potters practice constantly, they must also have *shina*, a Shipibo term implying imagination and alertness. Patterns fill an artist's dreams and waking thoughts. Her images are a vital bond to the sacred realm. The people closely link art, medicine, and their belief system. Historically, when treating a patient, shamans would enter a trance and then fill either bark paper or wooden boards with designs. A woman would then paint pottery with these images, which the spirits had conveyed.[7]

Ceramic Motifs Today

After nearly 300 years of missionization, few of even the oldest females alive remember the specific meaning and origins of their spiritually based motifs. What remains important is the artist's handling of paint. Her vessel is merely an empty canvas to fill with an inexhaustible variety

Women's Work Shipibo artists make their pot walls thin. But the clay from the river bank remains remarkably sturdy, sometimes even a bit elastic, because of the women's expert construction and firing techniques. Most wives have their own pottery hut, located at the edge of the family compound toward the river or forest, where they can work peacefully, separate from the commotion of daily activities.

of evenly spaced, continuous geometric designs. Every piece is unique. The women believe that because there is no exact repetition in a person's life, the same should hold true for ceramics. Their inter-weaving decorations change from pot to pot, just as the waters in the rainy season constantly alter the course of surrounding rivers, streams, and tributaries.

An increasing number of Shipibo women currently are replacing their vessels with plastic, enamel, and aluminum substitutes, or making ceramics to earn welcome tourist dollars.[8] There are still girls, howev-er, who learn by their grandmother's side. These young women preserve the spiritual and therapeutic designs that their ancestors have created for over 1,200 years.

6-5 How many decorated fields did the woman produce on this vessel, which held *chicha* (a liquor made from maize) for festive occasions? The artist drew the dark black formlines on each of the distinct horizontal bands. A pupil, possibly a granddaughter, might have added the interior marks, but only a master would have painted the fine filler work seen on the figure's face. Shipibo, *Joni Chomo*, c. 1940s. Ceramic, approx. 30" (76 cm) high. Courtesy Craft Caravan, Inc. Photography Abby Remer.

Molas: Fabric Mosaic Blouses

◠ ‿ ◠   *Yer dailege!* Beautiful! This is the phrase the Kuna from Panama's Yala sea islands apply to objects that delight them—perhaps splendid flowers from nature or a woman's expertly constructed *mola*. *Mola* is the Kuna word for clothing, dress, or blouse, although people often mistakenly use it to refer to just the appliquéd panel.

Imagine the weeks of work a Kuna woman put into the octopus design. (Fig. 6-6) She began learning the complicated reverse and regular appliqué techniques at her mother's knee. She likely tried simple sewing at barely three or four years old. By about five, the child might have cut fabric pieces for other women to use in their *molas*. At seven or eight, she could sew a small portion of her mother's work. The girl later learned to master the challenging reverse appliqué method of carefully cutting through the top layers of cloth and tucking and stitching them under to reveal brilliant, jewel-like fabrics below. (Fig. 6-7) She also learned how to embroider the final intricate details such as eyelashes, hair, letters, or feathers.

Mola Designs

The women's hieroglyphic textiles reflect the harmony in which they live with the gods, animals, fauna, and flora of their tropical environment. Nature pervades their multicolored motifs. Kuna myth and lore

6-6 How did the artist vary her sea-creature design? Examine the arrangement and colors of the triangles in each corner. The maker did not leave a speck of undecorated space. Her straight and curved cuts and tucks reveal a blaze of hues beneath. Many women wear *molas* like these every day but particularly delight in showing off new ones at fiestas, parades, or ceremonies. Carti Suitupo Chapter Cooperative, *Octopus Mola* (back view), 1997. Cotton reverse appliqué. Carti Suitupo Island, San Blas Islands, Kuna Yala Region. Courtesy Raul E. Cisneros.

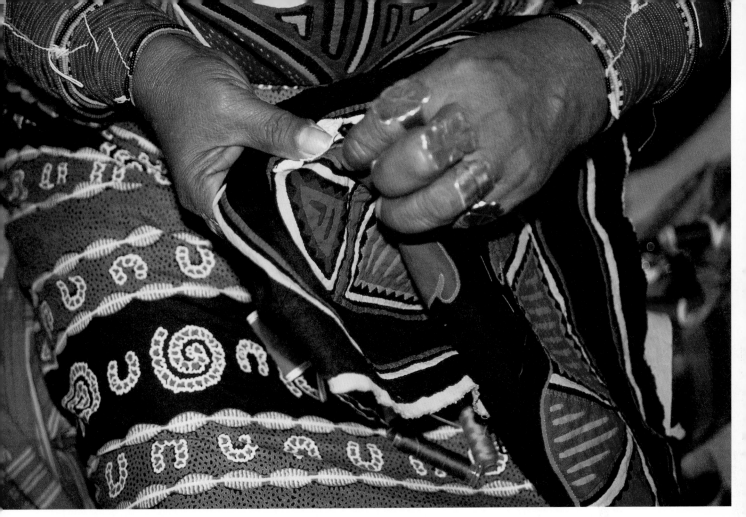

6-7 Notice how this woman stitches a turned-under section of cloth, revealing the bright color below the black fabric. In addition to a *mola*, she is wearing a wrap skirt called a *saburet* and bands of Czechoslovak beads, around her arms. Carti Suitupo Chapter Cooperative, *Kuna Woman Sewing,* 1997. Carti Suitupo Island, San Blas Islands, Kuna Yala Region. Courtesy Raul E. Cisneros. Photography Raul E. Cisneros.

are also evident, as in the octopus—a Kuna devil symbol. Women likewise portray everyday life—people tending the fire or hunting—and complex ceremonies, such as a wedding, curing rite, or girl's *inna* (puberty feast). Bible themes are visual remnants of life with the Christian missionaries who came in the wake of Spanish invaders, pirates, adventurers, sea captains, and traders.[9]

Although the Kuna have remained relatively isolated and their culture intact, foreign influence has made inroads. Even though acculturation is not always beneficial, *molas* may never have evolved without outside contact. Nineteenth-century trading ships introduced the women to new materials—cotton cloth, thread, scissors, needles. The 1914 opening of the Panama Canal also had an impact. Kuna men left their island homes to work in the American military bases, and with their earnings brought inexpensive, mass-produced goods back to their families. Women borrowed images from these magazines, cereal boxes, record-album covers, and the like. They transformed commercial pictures that caught their fancy into splendid, fabric mosaic abstractions, often unaware of or intentionally casting aside their original associations. What mattered was whether the composition made a good design—one that impressed their friends. Women knew they were successful when others interpreted the patterns themselves, removing the images even further from their initial sources.

After World War II, doctors, explorers, and, later, Peace Corps volunteers, tourists, and entrepreneurs started visiting the region more frequently. The women's depictions of airplanes, political posters, as well as American sporting events, such as boxing (Fig. 6-8) and baseball, illustrate the people's increasing interaction with the non-Kuna community.

Kuna women have used imported materials, and sometimes imagery, to invent an entirely unique expression. *Molas*, however, were not without precedent. The repeated geometric designs on early examples resemble patterns women have applied to their bodies since pre-Columbian times.[10]

Enhancing Natural Gifts
Imu, the mythological grandmother or midwife, bestows *kurgin*, natural talent or abilities, on the Kuna. Women further enrich their *mola*-making skills by bathing their hands in water that holds leaves laced with geometric designs, or burning the foliage and passing their hands through the potent smoke.

Expert Needlecraft

Artists judge *molas* by a large number of criteria, requiring even spacing of forms, tiny stitches, intense color contrasts, and complex compositions that include slight subtleties designed to break the design's symmetry. The Kuna prize compositional innovation, but a woman's work must retain its quality and, most importantly, capture the very essence of the subject.

Practice is key in honing sewing skills, but the Kuna believe someone's ability to make truly beautiful *molas* is attributed to *kurgin*, natural intelligence, aptitude, or talent. Imu, the Kuna's mythological grandmother, distributes *kurgin* to all people in varying degrees and it can apply to any skill (for example, hunting or eloquent speaking) in addition to *mola* making.[11]

Cultural Identity

The Kuna have kept their culture alive despite centuries of foreign interference: first the Spanish conquistadors; then Colombian rulers; and finally the Panamanian government, which in the early 1900s banned traditional dress. It is not surprising then that the Kuna, who gained autonomy for the San Blas Reservation in 1925, developed a singular costume to declare and help preserve their individual ethnic identity. Not even their closest neighbors today share the distinctive *mola* tradition, which differentiates the Kuna from the outside world.

6-8 Did the artist leave any empty space? She filled the background, foreground, and even the boxers and surrounding audience members with delicate, multicolored designs. This fine *mola* contains variety, symmetry, and difficult stitching. Kuna Yala, *Boxers,* 1970s. Cotton reverse appliqué. Panama. Private collection.

Spirit Weavers:
Nature and Belief in Wounaan Baskets

How do Wounaan baskets relate to their surroundings? (Fig. 6-9) The tribe lives in the Darién rain forest of southeastern Panama, and women rely solely on the tropical environment to create their vibrant expressions. They collect palms from the *chunga* tree and other plants, painstakingly removing the spines to free the strips for weaving. The artists also find dye sources in the forest: leaves, roots, bark, and fruit provide a rich palette of hues.

Wounaan oral tradition, tales, chants, and songs teach the young always to live in harmony with the natural world. All is connected, just as the vines of

the forest intertwine. The women seek unity with the land as they weave organic materials into exquisite baskets.

Nature dwells both physically and spiritually in the women's art. Women incorporate the energy of the forest's creatures—toucans, spiders, parrots (Fig. 6-11), grasshoppers, butterflies, and trees—into their wares. Mesmerizing geometric patterns correspond to their body painting, which scholars have traced back to pre-Columbian pottery and rock drawing.[12]

Women employ many different types of baskets for domestic and personal purposes. Large ones tote

6-9 Wounaan women weave decorative baskets with many spectacular colors, completely derived from natural dyes. The vessels vary from a few inches to more than a foot high. Do you notice anything special about the bottom of these examples? An artist usually begins with a central design that serves as her trademark. *Wounaan Baskets,* 1997. Courtesy Raul E. Cisneros. Photography Raul E. Cisneros.

small animals or fish; others relate to agriculture, which is the mainstay of the people's lives. Women weave birdcages, fish traps, chicken nests, backpacks, and also ceremonial crowns.

For the Wounaan, life remains fairly unchanged from a century ago; many live much as their ancestors did before the Europeans arrived. The Panamanian government and foreign companies, however, are invading their land— logging, building roads, and slashing and burning the forest for farms and cattle ranches. Amidst this decimation, Wounaan women find it increasingly difficult to locate the organic plants for their spirit weavings, which keep their people at one with nature.

6-11 Women fashion baskets from *chunga* leaves, which Wounaan spiritual healers also use to adorn ceremonial flutes and staffs used in therapeutic rites. For the Wounaan, the organic material contains evil spirits. *Wounaan Basket,* 1997. Courtesy Raul E. Cisneros. Photography Raul E. Cisneros.

6-10 You almost can hear the Darién rainforest come alive in this woman's work. Was she inspired by the feathers of the rainforest's breathtakingly beautiful birds or the leaves, branches, and flowers around her? *Wounaan Basket,* 1997. Courtesy Raul E. Cisneros. Photography Raul E. Cisneros.

Bold Truths in Cloth: Chilean Arpilleras—The Art of Social Protest

○◡○ Bits of thread and scraps of fabric represented the only hope for countless Chilean women who lost children, husbands, fathers, and brothers to the brutal Pinochet military dictatorship. (Fig. 6-12) Although the authoritarian regime ended in 1990, most of these women still have never located their loved ones—family who simply vanished. Even worse, the bodies of the "disappeared" who have been found in recently unearthed mass graves confirm that they suffered harrowing deaths.

How did Chilean women survive nearly unspeakable daily horrors? Many literally pieced their shattered lives together through art. They used the female sewing tradition to make appliqué images of pain, love, and protest called *arpilleras*, which gave voice to their anger and sorrow—despite the dangers of doing so during the repressive regime.

Invention from Necessity

The women's art was born out of a group effort and communal support. Many *arpilleristas* initially met one another while making futile inquiries at morgues, cemeteries, prisons, detention centers, and police headquarters early in the nightmare years that began in 1973, when General Augusto Pinochet led a military coup against President Allende's government.[13] The

6-12 The artist's brother, Newton Morales, disappeared in 1974. Once during their search, Violeta Morales and her sister-in-law found a guard who reported that Newton was nicknamed "Tough Guy" because he took beatings so well. When the women pleaded to see him, another police officer emerged and told them, "Newton Morales has never been here." He pointed a gun at her sister-in-law's baby and said he would shoot if they did not leave. Violeta Morales (b. 1934), *No to Torture (Movement Against Torture Sebastian Acevedo Organization)*, 1980. Courtesy Margorie Agosín. Photography Emma Sepulveda.

Catholic Church formed the Vicariate of Solidarity, the only Chilean organization that publicly denounced the junta's atrocities.[14]

In 1974, a group of grief-and-poverty-stricken women gathered in the Vicariate's inner patio. When a church official gave them leftover cloth, the women began their first tapestries.[15] With needle and thread, these brave *arpilleristas* started to pour out their suffering, denounce the military's abhorrent acts, and produce valuable artworks whose sale would rescue their families from dire poverty; they were now heads of households since their men had "disappeared."

Making an *arpillera* was a daring act. The autocratic regime killed people for less. But in the country's *machismo* atmosphere, officials tended to focus on men, who were generally considered more dangerous to the government's authority. Yet females were victims too—arrested, raped, tortured, and murdered. The *arpilleristas* were undeterred. They remained the nation's conscience throughout the reign of terror. The women stitched their stories in fabric and also staged moving public protests, such as chaining themselves to the fences of the supreme court building or Pinochet's house, fearlessly demanding human rights.

The authorities tried to forbid the *arpilleristas* their artistic expression, raiding the women's homes, issuing threats, and confiscating shipments. But the Church and sympathetic individuals smuggled the graphic textiles out of the country, introducing the

6-13 Even exhausted sleep did not always bring relief. A woman dreams of her missing son as protesters raise their arms screaming, "Where are they? Where are they?" The bright-yellow, three-dimensional curtains offer a small glimmer of hope and offset the picture of the missing man on the dresser top. Irma Muller, *Woman Dreaming,* 1990. Courtesy Marjorie Agosín. Photography Emma Sepulveda.

harsh realities of Chilean life to the outside world through art.

The Power of Cloth

Arpilleras are political denouncements of inexpressible crimes—crimes that the dictatorship denied had occurred. When the women went looking for their loved ones, officials told them their sons had fled the country, a husband had left them for another woman, or the person simply did not exist.[16] The fabric panels, often with three-dimensional figures and real items, such as toothpicks for police clubs and tiny slips of paper demanding food and justice, maintain a loving dialogue with the disappeared.

6-14 The workshops were havens where the *arpilleristas* could find support, and, for the first time, become involved in their country's politics. Men at home, often unemployed, sometimes resented their wives' new roles. One woman relates, "It was hard. . . . The men wouldn't let us go out. I was clouted a few times. I was given black eyes. But I had to earn something so that we could eat. Later, I began to enjoy the work because I learned new things." Unknown, *Arpillera Workshop*, n.d. Courtesy Marjorie Agosín. Photography Emma Sepulveda.

The artists pictured what was impossible to put into words. While the cloths chronicle actual horrors, they also contain small rays of hope, the only thing that sustained the women. One artist, María Eugenia, explains, "The *arpilleras* were a beautiful kind of therapy for me. . . . To relieve my anguish I made my *arpilleras*."[17] (Fig. 6-14)

The workshops the Vicariate established in the shantytowns became the families the women had lost—those who had disappeared as well as the relatives who were now too scared to associate with them. Anita, an *arpillerista*, stated, "Here in the workshop we tell jokes, we laugh, we cry and we console one another."

The *arpilleristas*' bold political actions planted the seeds for the mass social protest that blossomed in the 1980s and eventually led to the dictatorship's end in 1990 (even though Pinochet remained commander-in-chief until 1998 and declared himself senator for life).[18] Subsequent governments, sadly, have never acknowledged the women's fundamental role in helping to restore democracy, nor have they helped locate information about the thousands of missing persons.[19]

As Chile surges forward, urgently wishing to put its painful past behind, the widows of the nation are left with unanswered questions after twenty or more years of searching. A small group of the original artists, many of whom are well into their seventies and eighties, continue to create tapestries of hope and protest. Their art keeps the spirit of resistance alive and remains a poignant testament to and tangible memory of those who are gone, demonstrating that their deaths were not in vain.

6-15 Courageous women hold a banner in front of the church, demanding to know where their loved ones or "disappeared" have been taken. The work's bright sun and foliage almost allow us to forget the enormous danger of protesting in public during Pinochet's military regime. Unknown, *Donde Estan Los Detenidos Desaparecidos? (Where are the disappeared detainees?)*, n.d. Courtesy Marjorie Agosín. Photography Emma Sepulveda.

Art and Revolution: Nicaragua's Solentiname Painters

◠ ◡ ◠ The breathtaking beauty of Solentiname fortunately outweighed the miserable poverty of the 1,000 or so *campesinos* who barely eked out a living in the thirty-eight-island archipelago in Lake Nicaragua. The love of God, art, and their land helped sustain the community. By learning to paint their surroundings (Fig. 6-16), people recognized, as the artist Olivia Silva Guevara put it, "To see everything as part of a holy life, the life of God, and of the nature created by God for people."[20] A strong sense of spiritual, ecological, and political commitment infuses Solentiname painting, which has grown

6-16 Hilda Vogl Garciá grew up among peasants because her father, a German immigrant, was an agronomist and farm manager. These people daily supplied her family with food when they were starving after Somoza imprisoned her father and other Germans in Nicaragua during World War II, hoping to trade them to America in exchange for military aid. Hilda Vogel García, *Untitled,* 1988. Approx. 16 x 24" (41 x 61 cm). Photograph and permission courtesy John Brentlinger.

6-17 Is Rosa Pineda's nighttime scene illuminated by unseen moon rays—or the internal, religious light of the community? The luminous, jewel-like quality of Pineda's painting, and those of her sister (Fig. 6-18), is typical of Solentiname art. Her "mirrored" creatures breathe, flutter, and squawk, creating an overall abstract pattern from pristine colors and precise brushwork. Rosa Pineda, *Espejo (Mirror)*, 1992. Approx. 12 x 20" (30 x 51 cm). Photograph and permission courtesy John Brentlinger.

organically out of the people's unique history.[21]

The journey from remote peasant outpost to an internationally known, self-sufficient artistic community began in the mid-1960s. A forty-year-old poet and priest, Ernesto Cardenal, built a small spiritual center in Solentiname, where the poor, as elsewhere in the country, suffered under Anastasio Somoza's regime.

Cardenal's biggest contribution was through art. One day a man brought him water in a gourd he had decorated with pictures, explaining that he and his wife loved to paint. Cardenal brought the couple materials, and they created simple but pleasing drawings. Soon, many men, but even more women, began producing pictures, which Cardenal sold first in Managua and later abroad.[22]

Solentiname Painting

What attracted audiences to Solentiname work? There is a direct honesty about the peasant paintings, which describe the land and people, such as those by the sisters Rosa and Elena Pineda, part of the first generation. (Figs. 6-17, 6-18)

None of the painters had formal training in Western perspective, three-dimensional modeling, anatomy, or composition. The artists taught one another, lending support and criticism. First and foremost, the pictures had to come from direct experience. They should not look like photographs, yet, as Elena Pineda states, "We paint the beauty of the world. But we paint it realistically, so that people will know what it is."[23] (See Fig. 6-18.)

The artists never shied away from political messages, portraying Somoza's National Guard torturing Christ or a woman giving birth without a doctor. Although the compositions always had to be appealing, the women strove to change people's basic perceptions through art, thus helping bring about the revolution.

The path to freedom was not easy. During the civil war, Somoza bombed Solentiname for aligning with the Sandinistas, the left-wing Nicaraguan political group that tried to organize peasant support. Many who were not jailed or killed fled to Costa Rica, finally returning to paint and rebuild their beloved community after the Sandinistas prevailed in July 1979.[24]

Life improved for Solentiname painters in the 1980s. Cardenal, who became Minister of Culture, helped organize exhibitions around the world.

Galleries opened in Nicaragua, many run by women, who continued to outnumber male painters.

Shifting Sands

What happened when the Sandinistas lost power in 1990? The new authorities abolished the Ministry of Culture and even destroyed murals that the Solentiname painters had contributed to parks and buildings in Managua.[25] The artists survive though, despite setbacks to the revolution they helped foster. The women's paintings remain filled with the same authentic optimism that supported their community during the hardships of the earlier Somoza regime. Their canvases sell before the paint is barely dry. The demand is great and the women need money for food, clothing, education, and community improvement.

Art continues to transform the lives of people in Solentiname, especially the lives of women. Their love of nature, of God, and dedication to a better future helps them, as Olivia Silva remarks, "begin to take pleasure in everything."[26]

A Female Majority Women dominated the initial group of Solentiname artists. Painters included Rosa, Elena, and Blanca Pineda, as well as Rosita Arano, Julia Chavarriá, Elba Jimenez, Mariana Ortega, Mariana Silva, and the many females of the Guevara family.

6-18 Elena Pineda's daylight sky silhouettes her central tree, which spirals up toward the heavens, reminding us of the people's commitment to nature and spirituality. Pineda is president and founder of the Union of Painters and Artisans of Solentiname and runs a gallery in two locations in Managua. Elena Pineda, *Arbol de Mango en Solentiname (Mango Tree in Solentiname)*, 1995. Approx. 16 x 24" (41 x 61 cm). Photograph and permission courtesy John Brentlinger.

7 Oceania

Sustaining Ancestral Bonds

Have you ever sat around the kitchen table, swapping stories of earlier times; flipped through photo albums; or served holiday meals that your great-grandparents once ate? These are ways that we keep family history alive. Across Oceania, women from diverse origins use art to create a direct line from their predecessors to today.

Ancestral affiliations historically determined one's place in Oceanic society, and garments immediately broadcast this information. Women's early *tapa* cloths in New Zealand, and later elaborate fur and feather-adorned cloaks, protected against the elements. More importantly, the works denoted rank, age, sex, marital status, and clan affiliation. Ancestors formed who you were—and what you wore imparted this information to others.

Women throughout the South Pacific incorporated Western materials into their textiles when white missionaries, sailors, traders, and settlers invaded their societies. But they did not blindly absorb foreign art forms. Women in each culture developed their own unique styles and inclinations. In quilting, for instance, Native Hawaiian women employed Western techniques to create indigenous expres-

7-1 Maori women reigned supreme in weaving and experimented with new patterns and materials in their cloaks during the nineteenth century. What European element is evident on this dress cloak? A woman fashioned European wool, acquired through trade, into hanging tassels or tags that would swing gently, enhancing the wearer's movements. Each garment had its own *mauri*, or lifeforce, and people honored spectacular cloaks with individual names. Maori, *Korowai (Dress cloak with ornamental tags and tiny pompoms)*, late 19th century. Courtesy Robyn Kahukiwa.

7-2 Are the women painting realistic or abstract images? Each motif relates to their ancestral sites and stories around them.
Tandanya, *Aboriginal Women Painting Dreamtime Imagery*. Australian Tourist Commission.

sions, fabrics that carried ancient ancestral images and meaning. And like their garments of old, people revered the now potent quilted works, using them in time-honored social and ceremonial customs that distinguished them from their Western counterparts.

A sense of one's forebears saturates Australian Aboriginal women's weaving, pottery, painting, and carving. Virtually all their traditional work has for centuries related to the artists' sacred sites, still inhabited by the ancestors' spirit and power.

Maori women as well as others throughout the region also keep ancestral spirits alive through contemporary media. Female artists in each country participate in the international fine-arts dialogue. Their paintings and sculptures frequently speak of modern concerns, investigating how to articulate and retain a sense of identity and lineage in mainstream society. Many intrepid women address centuries of political and economic discrimination through their art, forging a stronger future by calling upon the strength of their people's past.

Nature's Bounty: Women's *Ngatu* in the Kingdom of Tonga

◠ ◡ ◠ Tongan *ngatu* (barkcloth) production has been a strenuous endeavor for centuries. Even today, a group of women, who live on one of the eastern chain of the kingdom's raised coral islands in the South Pacific, will sit in pairs opposite each other, rhythmically pounding the fiber over an upturned canoe. Like their foremothers, they had earlier tended the paper mulberry trees, brought to the region by their predecessors from Southeast Asia.[1] After stripping, soaking, and pounding the inner bark, the group next beats or pastes the individual pieces together to create a larger textile. The artists finally rub natural pigments into the cloth, laid over design tablets, or stamp abstract and naturalistic motifs onto its surface. (Fig. 7-3) Historically, someone might have slept on the fabric to flatten it, gingerly placing the textile under a mat for several nights.

The women's creations in the past could reach up to 100 meters in length, and some *ngatu* measured a mile long.[2] During events for royal or other important families, parallel lines of women walked forward, holding the artwork between them to present to an honored guest.

Women's *Ngatu* in Pacific Society

In various regions of the Pacific, *tapa*—the general term for Polynesian and Melanesian barkcloth—connected people to the sacred realm. People paraded barkcloth spirit masks through the village, wrapped carved deities in the fabric, or sometimes made images of their gods from the prized material. The women's exquisite goods retain their importance today as gifts and exchanges at traditional ceremonies, especially births, weddings, and funerals. The women in the northern and southern islands of Tonga also produce a significant amount of *ngatu* for trade with Tongans living on nearby islands and abroad, as well as for American Samoans, who rely on the barkcloth for their traditional ceremonial exchanges.[3]

Men and women in Tonga now primarily buy Western-style clothes, but brides and grooms or dancers frequently still don special *ngatu*.[4] The cloth's designs visually signal clan allegiance, convey spiritual significance, and immediately identify its source. Some motifs are ancient, tracing back into Indonesia, while others are more recent innovations.[5]

Yet even as the modern, industrial world makes inroads into the daily culture, Tongan women keep alive creative practices that their ancestors practiced for thousands of years.[6]

What's in a Name?

People apply the word *tapa* to barkcloth worldwide. The term derives from the Samoan word *tapa*, which refers to the undecorated border of the barkcloth sheet.[7]

The Woman in the Moon

A Polynesian legend recounts how the god Tangaroa punished the goddess Hina for the racket she made pounding *tapa*. After several warnings, he eventually had her killed. Hina's spirit ascended to the moon, where she remains for all to see, forever beating white *tapa*, and serving as the patroness of arts and crafts.

7-3 Each area in the South Pacific had its own barkcloth style. The one here, divided by broad lines, is typical of Tonga. The art of fashioning bark fiber into cloth stretched from Africa (see Figs. 1-12, 1-13 on pages 14-15) to South America but achieved its greatest refinement in this region. Tonga, South Pacific, *Ngatu*, c. 1960. Mulberry tree bark, 57 x 66" (145 x 168 cm). Courtesy The Liberty Corporation.

Blending Cultures/Reclaiming Heritage: Hawaiian Quilts

What did four royal Hawaiian women in 1820 make of the New England Protestant missionaries who wished to teach them Western quilting? The women had never sewn calico piecework, but they and their foremothers had long worked in groups when making *tapa* (pounded barkcloth). (See Fig. 7-3.) This Western-style "sewing circle" was nothing new to them.[8]

Quilting caught on with the Native populace, not just royalty, but immediately carried connotations far

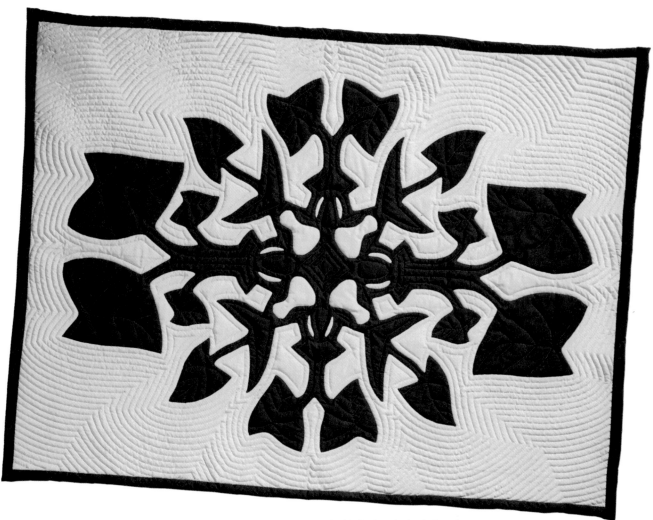

7-4 This crib quilt is called *Loʻi Kalo (Taro Pond)*. Polynesian voyagers brought this food to the land. The tuber was so important that no one was permitted to argue once it was served at a meal. The taro *(karo)* design also signifies King Kamehameha I, who unified the Hawaiian Islands and was a great taro farmer early in life. Alana Nohealani Dean (b. 1968), *Loʻi Kalo (Taro Pond)*, keiki (baby) quilt. Cotton and polyester fabric, 45 x 60" (114 x 152 cm). Courtesy Alana Nohealani Dean, Aloha Quilts. Photography Camera Hawaii.

7-5 Notice how the artist cut the border as part of the image in certain motifs. Hawaiian quilt patterns always are made in one piece to indicate an unbroken spirit. Colors such as red and yellow maintain their royal associations from earlier textile traditions. Alana Nohealani Dean (b. 1968), *Boat Ride to Lanai* turquoise on dark blue, *Awapuhi Melemele (Yellow Ginger)* yellow on dark blue, *Traditional Ulu (Breadfruit)* forest green on red, *Kukui Nut (Candle Nut)* black on yellow, *Laua'e (Fragrant Fern)* forest green on lime green. Cotton and polyester fabric, 22 x 22" (56 x 56 cm). Courtesy Alana Nohealani Dean, Aloha Quilts. Photography Camera Hawaii.

beyond the female household chore the missionaries introduced. Making quilts became pivotal to Hawaiian life in a rapidly changing world. The women's creations were a source of cultural pride as foreign domination obliterated indigenous gods, language, and religion.[9]

From Old to New

Hawaiian artists did not blindly accept the imported artistic technique. Women initially transferred *tapa* motifs to the new medium. When they did borrow Western quilt images, the artists reinterpreted the designs according to their own lives. Females imbued the compositions with meanings that expressed and reflected their ancestors' talents and beliefs, documenting the beauty of their land, heritage, and legends in textile form.[10] Westerners, for instance, had no equivalent design of a taro plant, which was a Hawaiian staple and represented family. (See Fig. 7-4.) Furthermore, flower motifs often reflect Hawaiian identity and frequently relate to legends.

Each Hawaiian family previously had its own design, marks of their *kupuna*, or ancestors that visually delineated their lineage. Now every family instead created a unique quilt emblem, which they carefully guarded and passed on to future generations. An ethical code guaranteed that no one would ever replicate another's pattern. To copy or wear someone else's crest was stealing and brought death because one would have taken part of the artist's spirit.

Hawaiian Women's Appliqué Quilts

Missionaries originally taught patchwork-style quilting, which required cutting pieces of fabric into small geometric shapes and then stitching them artfully together. By about the mid-1800s, however, Hawaiian women began to produce more appliqué works, whereby they cut their own designs out of cloth and then sewed them to a fabric background. The Hawaiian seamstresses could not see the point of cutting up the huge precious bolts of cloth steadily streaming in from the numerous traders and whalers on their way to or from the Orient.[11] Hawaiian appliqué, with its distinct echo or contour quilting (see Fig. 7-4), so eclipsed the earlier patchwork style that it quickly became the ubiquitous "traditional" Hawaiian quilt. Hawaiian legend attributes appliqué's

invention to the story of a young girl tracing the shadow of a tree's leaves onto fabric, and then sewing the textile onto a larger textile backing.[12]

In Hawaiian appliqué, a woman folds a single-colored sheet into eighths, and then draws her design or cuts it free-hand to create a quadriaxially symmetrical composition. (Fig. 7-5) Her image usually has personal meaning, and she might give the design a poetic name to refer to a special event or feeling.[13] The motif must stand out, accentuated by highly contrasting color choices. Her needlework, most importantly, has to be minute and evenly spaced, especially in the rippling contours that follow the image or define its details.

Sustaining Ancient Traditions in a Modern World

Hawaiian quilts quickly took on the spiritual and social function of the earlier *tapa* cloth. People still give these prestigious quilts to prominent individuals, draping the fabric over the person's shoulders as in days of old.[14] The quilts are imperative too as presents. They swathe a newborn babe at birth, couples during a wedding, and the dead at a funeral.[15]

Although the women's quilts can rest on beds to decorate homes during special occasions, people never sleep or even sit on them. Everyone respects and honors the quilt and the artist's spirit that resides within it.[16]

Earlier Tools European traders, whalers, and subsequent missionaries introduced needles, scissors, and cotton thread to the Hawaiian Islands. For centuries, however, native women had sewn and mended their barkcloth with natural materials and bone needles.

7-6 Compare this Cook Island 1940s textile to the Hawaiian quilts to see the migration of quilting techniques. Women in this neighboring land call their work *tivaevae manu*—which translates approximately as "true quilting." They cut cloth folded into fourths or eighths and then sew the silhouette image onto a solid background. Unlike their Hawaiian counterparts, though, there is no contour or echo quilting. Unknown, *Kiss-Me-Quick,* early 1940s. Tivaevae Manu. Courtesy Jasmine Underhill. Photograph Neil Penman.

Hawaiian quilts are tangible symbols of affection and esteem. Creating them is a labor of love as well, because it can take an artist some years of back-breaking work to complete a large textile. The women's fabrics continue to preserve and perpetuate Hawaiian cultural traditions that have been threatened by outside forces. They help cultivate a sense of self—an individual identity as Hawaiians live in mainstream society. Where *tapa* once existed, quilts now reign. In festivals and rites, museums and hotels, on postcards and T-shirts, the stitched designs express the essence of Hawaiian heritage, both the past and the ever-evolving present.

The Land as Catalyst and Metaphor: Aboriginal Women's Art*

⋒ ⋓ ⋒ Art helps bind Australian Aboriginal and Torres Strait Islanders to the land. Women use the earth's treasured resources in their body decoration, paintings, carvings, and weavings—traditions reaching back thousands of years.

This profound kinship to the earth is far more than physical. The people's very essence is tied to their surroundings and stories of its formation. The Dreamings, or stories, tell of creator ancestors whose epic travels across the land formed its rocks, trees, rivers, mountains, plants, and animals. The spirits of these forebears continue to inhabit the natural environment today. When Aboriginal women visually represent their stories, the objects themselves carry the spirits' power and help sustain life for each generation.[17]

Aboriginal Women's Work in Wood

Northern Territory

Women throughout the continent transform the earth's wood into elegant items that tangibly bridge the supernatural and human realms. In Maningrida, Northern Territory, females as well as males carve and paint spirit poles that are integral to sacred rituals. (Fig. 7-7) The people of this area believed the "mimi spirits" were the first humans, who created the laws and artifacts. Elders still recount legends of these beings to teach the young appropriate behavior that governs people's relationship to the land and one another. The tales and corresponding visual works map out ancient morals that continue to resonate.

Central Desert

Females in the Central Desert also have long used wood to create portable items that carry references to specific sites. The women often cover *coolamon*

7-7 Women carve and paint evocative "mimi spirit poles," which sit upright in the ground during ceremonies that honor these first human forms. Images of mimis appear on Australian rock art dating back over 40,000 years. Maningrida, Northern Territory, *Mimi Spirit Carving*, c. 1996. Wood. Courtesy Dreamtime Gallery.

*Indigenous Australians, please note that this section includes the names of deceased people and images of their work.

7-8 Women in the Western Desert cover wares with intricate patterns, symbolizing geographical features of the land, seasons, animals, and vegetation as well as events of the creation time. The people's songs are similarly like oral road maps of their stories. Warmun, Kimberely, *Hand Painted Coolamon (Gathering Bowls) and Music Sticks*, 1998. Mulga wood. Courtesy Dreamtime Gallery.

(large oblong gathering dishes) (Fig. 7-8) and other carrying bowls with complex patterning.

Where are the land's features in the *coolamon's* abstract design? (See Fig. 7-8.) Far from pure decoration, the rich symbolism is rife with multiple connotations. For example, concentric circles could denote important locales—a waterhole, life source, campground, or fireplace. The large white "U"s, on the other hand, might represent seated figures. These

readings, however, suggest the topmost layer of potential meaning for the symbols. In fact, only the most learned initiates of a clan can fully comprehend the onion-skin layers of sacred significance. The women likewise cover their music sticks (see Fig. 7-8) with abstract "landscapes" in dotted patterns, which visually recall the rhythms they beat out in related ceremonies.

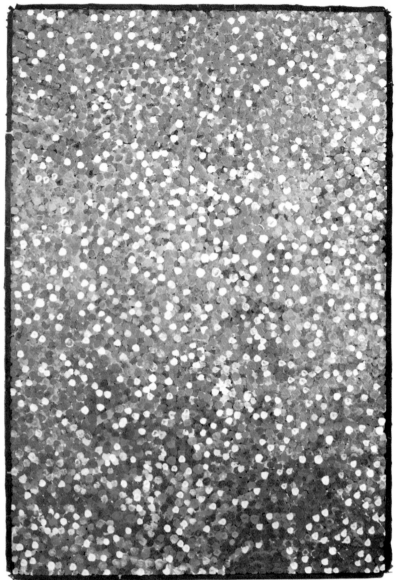

The Land and Aboriginal Women's Art
Emily Kame Kngwarreye

The advent of modern media has not diverted Aboriginal female artists from their connection to the land. How is this evident in the work of Emily Kame Kngwarreye—whose full name should not be spoken out loud, following Aboriginal custom for the deceased?[18] (Fig. 7-9) Like other artists of Utopia, a community in the Central Desert, Kngwarreye presents an aerial perspective of her sacred site, burying its distinctive features beneath a shimmering swath of brushstrokes.

Born about 1910 at Alhalkere, Utopia station, Kngwarreye lived a traditional lifestyle in the outback on a cattle station, first coming into contact with white people at about age nine. Until her death in 1996, she was a leading woman in ceremonial and ritual knowledge. Kngwarreye practiced sand and body painting before experimenting with mainstream art materials in her late sixties. She and colleagues began with batik in a workshop-type setting in the late 1970s but soon experimented in additional media, using contemporary materials to keep their ancestral stories alive.[19]

7-9 Emily Kame Kngwarreye created a journey in paint over her ancestral sites. The evocative rhythms of her large-scale canvas parallel the heat and energy of the accompanying ceremonies, which she described as "looking after country." Kngwarreye explained about her work, "This is my country, this is me." Emily Kame Kngwarreye (approx. 1910–96), *Women's Dreaming*, 1991. Acrylic on canvas, 72 x 48" (183 x 122 cm). Courtesy Austral Gallery-Australian Contemporary Art, St. Louis, MO.

Nontraditional Media

When Aboriginal and mainstream worlds collide, artists have found they can use urban debris as unconventional supports for work that actually reveres the land. Starting in the 1990s, Aboriginal women joined men in ridding the bush of abandoned, broken-down cars, literally transforming these symbols of dispossession and degradation[20] into positive artistic statements. Women painted car hubcaps (Fig. 7-10), doors, and trunks with visions of their ancestral domain. The reflective, metallic surfaces enhance the earthly resonance of this spare-part art.

Maintaining Ancient Links

Virtually all indigenous Australians historically produced items representing and symbolizing their world and beliefs. Weavings, dances, sand drawings, and handmade instruments were not considered "art," or separate from daily life.

In the past 200 years, colonizers have caused drastic changes in Aboriginal societies, denying the country's original inhabitants their land and rights—and introducing the alien concept of "artist" in the Western European sense. Aboriginal women in both cities and outlying areas have gained international renown in the contemporary art scene. Although some use mainstream materials in modern styles, much of their work still reinforces the relationship between the visible and unseen world, so that the land and its original creators will continue to support future generations.

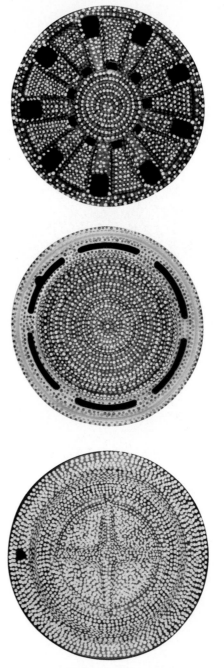

7-10 The artists effortlessly merge ancient designs with contemporary circular hubcaps. Kathline Petyarre (born approx. 1940) (top and bottom) and Gloria Petyarre (born approx. 1945) (middle), *Painted Hubcaps,* 1993. Acrylic on hubcaps, 14" (36.5 cm) diam. Courtesy Austral Gallery-Australian Contemporary Art, St. Louis, MO.

Power of the Past, Forging the Future: Female Maori Artists

ᘓᗉᘓ We feel like our ancestors are with us all the time.

—*artist Robyn Kahukiwa*

What was life originally like for Maori women, and how did their creative expressions help nourish the lifeblood of their communities? The first Maori sailed from Polynesia to Aotearoa (New Zealand) just over 1,000 years ago. When white missionaries and settlers arrived in 1814, they began imposing English patriarchal law, Christianity, and Western mores on the many different Maori nations, forever damaging the equality that had existed between the sexes. In the

7-11 Robyn Kahukiwa's royal relative, Hinematioro, lived in the first half of the eighteenth century. She led war parties of men into battle and accomplished many other legendary deeds. The *karearea*, New Zealand falcon, is Hinematioro's guardian, a spiritual link between the earth and sky who brings messages to the gods. Robyn Kahukiwa (b. 1940) (Ngati Porou, Te Aitanga-A-Hauiti, Ngati Hau), *Hinematioro,* 1988. Oil on loose canvas. Collection Kahukiwa family.

7-12 The spiraling spirit, birdlike creatures loop in and out of the historical and modern images. Robyn Kahukiwa infuses her painting with sacred colors: red, the color of mother earth, and blue, the hue of father sky. Robyn Kahukiwa (b. 1940) (Ngati Porou, Te Aitanga-A-Hauiti, Ngati Hau), *Tihei Mauriora (This Is My Life, My Breath*, or *I Am Here)*, Detail from *Ko Hineteiwaiwa Te Whare*, 1984. Mixed media on board, 78¾ x 39½" (200 x 100 cm). Collection Fletcher Challenge Corporation. Copyright, photograph, and permission courtesy of the artist.

Maori worldview, everything is interconnected and females were essential to the whole. They ensured the continuity of lineage—a crucial element of Maori culture—and served as mediums, seers, and even chiefs, influencing the military, social, political, and spiritual realms.[21]

Female Maori Art: Contemporary Materials, Ancient Connections

Robyn Kahukiwa

Genealogy and bonds to the past saturate all traditional Maori life. "We acknowledge our dead, our ancestors who sparkle as stars in the night sky," reads the beginning of a Maori creation narrative.[22] As contemporary Maori artist Robyn Kahukiwa explains, "Genealogy is the backbone of our society and it goes back to the gods."[23] Maori people do not worship their ancestors but always refer to them because they are the source of everything. (Fig. 7-11)

Maori women today, especially artists, call upon the strength of their ancient heritage to revitalize Maori identity after decades of patriarchal colonization and appalling governmental injustices. Yet Kahukiwa, like other women, looks to both the old and new to celebrate the *mana* (personal prestige, spiritual essence) of her people.[24]

Notice the potent carved ancestral female figure echoed by the modern woman in her enormous wall-sized work, *Tihei Mauriora*. (Figs. 3, 7-12, 7-13) This pair shouts out the welcoming chant of the title, a Maori proverb meaning, "This is my life, my breath." The "breath" metaphorically extends from the deject-

7-13 In *Taniwha Wounded But Not Dead*, the arching lizard-type being is guardian of a river, sea, or mountain. For Kahukiwa, it symbolizes Maori people, "who are wounded by colonization, but are not extinct." Robyn Kahukiwa (b. 1940) (Ngati Porou, Te Aitanga-A-Hauiti, Ngati Hau), *Taniwha Wounded But Not Dead*, Detail from *Ko Hineteiwaiwa Te Whare*, 1984. Mixed media on board, approx. 9' (2.7 m) high. Collection Fletcher Challenge Corporation. Copyright, photograph, and permission courtesy the artist.

ed Maori man on the far right, who faintly grasps the colonizer's flag, to the mixed-blood toddler bravely staring us in the eye. The blond child, representing generations of cross-cultural contact, is tied by lineage to Maori people and gods. For Kahukiwa, all children of pure or mixed descent must learn to cherish their ethnic history, which expands—or "breathes"—into the future.

Kura Te Waru Rewiri

The painter Kura Te Waru Rewiri also is intensely aware of her genealogy, stating, "I would never venture into a work without first identifying my tribal links."[25] Te Waru Rewiri borrows a figure from Ngati Whatua, one of her tribal areas, for *Te Ripeka (The Crucifix)*. (Fig. 7-14) But she hangs the creature on a huge Christian cross. Did the invader's religion crucify Maori art and culture? Is the spirit a sacrificial lamb? Or does the image represent the adaptability of Maori people to accommodate Christian values while still

Maori Women and Conflict Resolution Women could initiate peace negotiations between warring factions, and their marriages to opponents cemented social, economic, and political ties among groups. Men typically went to war, but women sometimes fought as well, particularly when defending children and the elderly if enemies attacked a settlement while the men were away.

maintaining Maori bonds? Te Waru Rewiri remarks, "Colonization of my people has tainted our memories of who we were." Her art makes no final judgment, but ultimately won't let us ignore the influence of colonization.

Ongoing Cultural Bearers

Many contemporary female Maori artists, like their foremothers, are the resilient guardians of their living cultural heritage—one that is steeped in history but also is in a continuous natural state of flux. These women cull from modern Western and ancient tribal traditions, generating vibrant, innovative expressions. They tackle fresh subjects, ideas, and materials in ways that their ancestors never dreamt of but could only admire. And as leaders and females, they are overturning two centuries of imposed patriarchal limitations on their power and significance.

7-14 Kura Te Waru Rewiri explains that her painting is about "the concept of the superimposition of Christian values over our traditional beliefs." But she never presents pat answers and her art explores the possibility for a positive coexistence. Kura Te Waru Rewiri (b. 1950) (Ngati Kahu, Ngati Raukawa), *Te Ripeka (The Crucifix)*, 1985. Acrylic on board, 47¼ x 31½" (120 x 80 cm). Collection of Waikato Museum and Art Gallery. Copyright, photograph, and permission courtesy of the artist.

8 United States & Canada

Binding Family and Community

North America pulses with unique traditions, styles, and cultures—and women's artistic output reflects this variety. Women's endeavors also have long served as the thread that helps lace together families and communities. Their work maintains cultural identity and reflects distinct and often challenging experiences.

Centuries before European invaders arrived, Native women stitched clothing, bags, and accessories—both daily and ceremonial items that identified as well as protected. The artists' work today, however, remains a vital means of visually declaring each group's distinct heritage. Native women in recent times also have probed Western artistic media. With modern means, many of them continue to address issues of tribal identity.

8-1 Bessie Harvey collaborated with God and nature: "You see a face in any piece of wood, and it's just askin' for help, help to come out… God creates the roots and stumps and shapes them by the insects…designin' my pieces." Born in Georgia, Harvey married at fourteen and had eleven children. Pursuing art eased the pressures of raising a family. Harvey's inspired figures relate to "Old Africa," which she conceived as a paradise where all black people once lived in harmony.[1] Bessie Harvey (1928–94), *Untitled*, 1989. Paint, found objects, wood, 52 x 23 x 22" (132 x 58.4 x 56 cm). Courtesy Cavin-Morris Gallery.

8-2 Spirituality suffused Nellie Mae Rowe's life and art. "Drawing is the only thing I think is good for the Lord. When I wake up in glory, I want to hear, 'Well done, Nellie, well done.'" Rowe began making art at an early age in rural Georgia. During her sixties, she filled her home—nicknamed "the playhouse"—with drawings, sculptures, and painted Vodou-like dolls made entirely from chewing gum. Nellie Mae Rowe (1900–82), *Untitled*, c. 1980. Wax crayon and pencil on paper. Courtesy Ricco/Maresca.

Enslaved African women dedicated precious personal hours to quilting—expressions that kept loved ones warm and covered, while visually linking the artist and her family to their origins across the ocean. Gullah women, as well as other African-American females, continue to nurture similar artistic customs with their quilt and basket making, supporting ancestral ways that have survived centuries of adversity.

Other women have visually expressed their experiences of oppression. During World War II, the American government forced some 110,000 people of Japanese descent into guarded, fenced camps. Some captives turned to art to document the atrocities. Their searing images record events that often were too painful to decribe in words.

Immigrants also have relied on art to address feelings of displacement and preserve part of the past in a new land. Mexican-American women, for instance, practice many arts—from impressive culinary creations to delicate paper formations—tilling the soil of their ancient roots.

Women across America and Canada practice every artistic form, whether new or old, secular or sacred. Their expressions foster pride—in themselves, and their people's history.

Echoes of Home:
Quilts by Enslaved African Women

◉ ◡ ◉   Boisterous dancing, singing, gossiping, and courtship games whirled about the women as they stitched quilts in small groups. Spirited quilting parties were rare moments of joy for enslaved Africans in America, stripped of their ancestral language, gods, and customs. Women, as the backbone of the community, organized these jubilant events.[2]

At first, male captives must have been surprised when slave owners assigned women textile tasks in America. These tasks were a male domain back home. But plantation masters divided slave labor according to Western terms, and females became the mistresses of the art, if not of their own lives.

Enslaved African women in the main house worked for, and sometimes with, the owner's wife, creating quilts that essentially were indistinguishable from Anglo-made counterparts.[3]

But enslaved women managed to insert memories of their assorted western and central African civilizations into their own stitched covers.[4]

Sometimes the pieces featured bold colors and strong geometric shapes, which recalled cloth's function a continent away where a design immediately had to declare a person's tribal affiliation so one could quickly discern friend from foe while hunting or in battle. Enslaved women might create asymmetrical compositions (Fig. 8-3) and unexpected breaks in pattern, which was common to African weaving and reflected the belief that these diversions confused and slowed evil spirits who could travel only in straight lines.[5] (Also see "Bridging the Atlantic: West African Roots in Gullah Women's Art," page 140.)

> **Stitching Toward Freedom**
> Enslaved African women sometimes earned money performing extra sewing for their masters, neighboring plantation owners, or townspeople. Elizabeth Keckly bought her freedom and later become a dressmaker in Washington, D.C., eventually working for Mary Todd Lincoln.

8-3 Is the design on this slave-made quilt perfectly symmetrical, as was the case on most Anglo bedcovers? The two potted plants on either side are oriented in different directions, adding complexity to the minimally colored composition. *Slave-made Appliqué Quilt with Flower Pots,* c. 1860. Cotton. Collection of Old Capitol Museum of Mississippi History.

Enslaved women filled their covers with emblems, narratives, and Bible scenes, confessing emotions, thoughts, and concerns. Their textiles sometimes held the path to freedom, with stitched escape routes, star maps, or motifs that signaled a safe haven along the Underground Railroad.[6] Women sewed these hidden messages into quilts, which then could be left out in plain view.

Quilting parties under-scored the community's pen-chant for working together. A manager arranged for elder-ly slaves who no longer tilled the fields to prepare the quilt tops before a cele-bration. During the festivi-ties, women normally sewed in teams of four around each quilt.[7] Less elaborate round-robin quiltings also were communal efforts, when women went from cabin to cabin on different nights to help one another produce enough covers for their families.[8]

8-4 Bedroom suite carved by slaves, and hanging quilts sewn by enslaved black women. Brought to Buxton, Canada, by Reverend King. Buxton Historic Site and Museum. Photography Shannon Prince.

Little Remaining Evidence
Enslaved African women rarely appear in historical records, primarily because their work, especially that accomplished in their "spare" time, was of little economic concern to male slaveholders. Even their immense efforts of sewing, weaving, and quilting for the entire plantation was "women's work," and, hence, of no interest to the men. Wear and tear, fire, theft, and sale, as well as the anonymity of the artists, have left scant documentation or physical evidence despite the women's tremendous outpouring.

Men at both the large and small affairs threaded needles, held the light, kept the fire going, served as dancing partners, and, sometimes, escorts.[9] But their role was minimal. Women reigned supreme, providing for the physical needs of loved ones while nourishing textile customs with traces of their African heritage.

Bridging the Atlantic: West African Roots in Gullah Women's Art

◖◡◖ How do these coiled baskets touch two continents and cross the centuries? (Fig. 8-5) Gullah women today fashion the distinctive wares as their forebears, descendants of West African captives, had during the 335 years of slavery. In fact, American slavery began in 1526 on the Sea Islands, stretching along the southern coast from Florida to the Carolinas, rather than in Jamestown in 1619 as most people believe.

Gullah Basketry and African Roots

Gullah women's basketwork reverberates through the generations, with echoes from the artists' original West African homelands. Their coiling methods, for instance, resemble those used in Senegambia, the Congo, and Angola, as well as Mali and Sierra Leone.[10]

During American plantation days, Gullah women constructed baskets for fanning rice, harvesting nuts, winnowing grains, and carrying and storing goods. The vessels were essential to the agricultural way of life. Enslaved women also fashioned flower or sewing baskets for the plantation mistress and tiny models that served as toys for youngsters.[11]

Gullah language and traditions, like the women's baskets, contain aspects from the divergent West African societies of the original captives, along with American influences. The new culture enabled the enslaved people to retain ties to their ancestral her-

8-5 Every summer and fall for generations, Gullah women harvest their own basket materials, a time-consuming, back-breaking task required even before the weaving preparation begins. *Gullah Basket Weavers Rena Singleton* (left) *and Assistant Nellie Singleton* (right), *Outside Their Home on St. Helena Island, Beaufort, South Carolina.* Sweetgrass, rush, palmetto fronds, and pine needles. Courtesy Delphine Fawundu/ADAMA images.

itages and also forge a distinct identity in a foreign land. Gullah basket making, oral history, and the like remained intact even after invading Union troops landed on Hilton Head Island in 1861, scattering plantation owners from their land.[12]

Following the Civil War, freedwomen and men formed their own self sufficient Sea Island communities, but basket making began to wane. Later, in the 1930s, Works Project Administration employees encouraged female elders in the community to revive the practice, suggesting that they sell their articles for supplementary income along Route 17—newly paved and streaming with tourists. These women's descendants still dot the highway (see Fig. 8-5), sitting by their stands with other artists, sharing stories while they work.[13] Nonetheless, weavers always take their endeavors seriously, severely criticizing flimsy, hurriedly built ware. Sea grass, palmetto, and pine straw needles fade over time and loosen in a poorly woven piece.[14]

8-6 Vera and Ethel Manigault practice Gullah sweetgrass basketry, an art their forebears brought to the Sea Islands from Africa over 300 years ago. Gullah women make functional pieces for fanning, rice and pea husk, and toting laundry, as well as those they sell to tourists for holding household items or display. Vera and Ethel Manigault, *Sweetgrass Baskets*, late 1990s. Sweetgrass, palmetto leaves, long pine needles, and bull rush. Courtesy Vera Manigault, Mt. Pleasant, SC.

Women, Men, and Gullah Baskets Gullah mothers, aunts, grandmothers, and older sisters teach girls sweetgrass basket making as soon as they can hold and manipulate the material. Boys practice too, until about age ten, when it becomes "women's work" and they move on to other duties. Interestingly, men used to teach boys the sweetgrass basket art, but it has become a female domain over the years.[19]

Tourists buy woven mats, bead trays, purses, hats, and wastebaskets as folk art, but Gullah women also continue to weave certain vessels for themselves, carrying on the ways of their predecessors.[15]

Gullah Women's Quilts

The women also create quilts, which like the coiled ware express a continuation and transformation of African traditions in the United States. Initially, enslaved seamstresses produced European-style articles for the "big house" but inflected their own items with African chords. Gullah "strip quilts," in which women stitched small strips together to form longer ones united into a final top layer, recall Ashanti Kente cloth. In Africa, weavers formed long strips of the Kente cloth on belt looms, eventually sewing them into a larger sheet. Their kelly green, red, and sapphire blue tones resonate in Sea Island fabrics, as do darker hues of items made by the Ewe people of West Africa.[16]

8-7 What distinguishes this patchwork quilt from ones made by the Amish (see Figs. 8-9, 8-10)? Traces of the Gullah women's African heritage are seen in the tied knots, which had ritual and symbolic significance in many African societies. Carolee Holmes Brown, *Gullah patchwork quilt* (detail). Photograph and permission Marquetta L. Goodwine.

The knots on Gullah examples (Fig. 8-7) also have African links. In various societies, as among the Igbo, tying knots in string or vines was performed in rituals to communicate with one's ancestors, invoking their guidance and protection.[17]

The analogies continue. The Fon of Benin (formerly Dahomey) appliquéd figures to symbolize people and events relating to their lineage, history, and family code. Gullah family members similarly can identify the origins of each tiny patch of cloth, whether from special garments, daily wear, drapes, or household scraps, converting the quilt into a visual, patchworked chronicle of the family's former times.[18] (Also see "Echoes of Home: Quilts of Enslaved African Women," page 138.)

Pressures of Change

The women's basket work has lately become more challenging. Tourists overrun their once-secluded islands. Commercialization, mining developments, and resorts have destroyed many Gullah communities. Pollution and private ownership inhibits the availability of the artists' sacred resources.

Nonetheless, the women, through their basket and quilt making, and also sea work and storytelling, battle intrepidly to keep Gullah culture very much alive, ensuring its continuity.

Artists of the Sea Gullah women also are expert artists of the sea (Fig. 8-8), participating alongside men in casting nets, anchoring them strongly between their teeth while flinging the webbed fiber out over the water. They bog for oysters, dig clams, set crab traps, and go shrimp riding, separating out the crustaceans by size and tossing too-small specimens back into the water. Of course, their toil has just begun, because they also clean, prepare, and finally present the sumptuous catch that nourishes their families.

8-8 Carolee Holmes Brown "shuckin' oysters" on St. Helena Island, South Carolina. Photograph and permission Marquetta L. Goodwine.

A World Apart:
Spiritual Faith and Amish Quilts

◠◡◠ Twelve women sit around a wooden frame, fingers flying as they stitch a simple geometric quilt in startling colors. Little girls hold needles and thread for their moms and teenage sisters, who begin early to stitch quilts from colored material and bits of old clothing for their future families.

There is no light from the local electric company, nor modern appliances within the sparsely furnished home. People use a horse and buggy instead of cars. The women dress in solid, mostly subdued hues, yet there is sincere joy in their talk about recent births and marriages. They swap advice on child rearing, home remedies, garden hints, and household tips. Without televisions, videotapes, computers, radios, or telephones, visiting on this quilting day, or "frolic," provides entertainment and nurturance, as the women experience the strong support of their friends.

Is this nineteenth-century America? Well, it was, but scenes like this continue today largely unchanged for the Amish, whose tight-knit communities populate Pennsylvania, Ohio, Indiana, Illinois, Missouri, Iowa, Nebraska, and beyond.[20] The Amish shun the entrapments of modern society. Their entire existence—how the Amish live, work, socialize, and worship—reflects their faith in God, consistent with Jesus' teachings in the Bible's New Testament. The Amish abide by strict codes established more than 400 years ago in Europe, before adherents came to the New World in 1728. Stringent rules, based on the Scriptures, separate members from outside influences.

8-9 Where is the "Sunshine and Shadow" mentioned in the name of this quilt design? The tiny squares create an expanding series of diamonds that flow from dark to light. Amish farm life too is allied with the eternal renewal of nature's seasons. The "English," as the Amish call outsiders, sometimes use this same sort of pattern, but the wider borders seen here are distinctly Amish. Unknown Amish quilter, *Sunshine and Shadow,* c. 1940. Wools, 80 x 80" (203 x 203 cm). Lancaster County, PA. Private Collection. Photograph courtesy The Quilt Complex. Photography Sharon Risedorph.

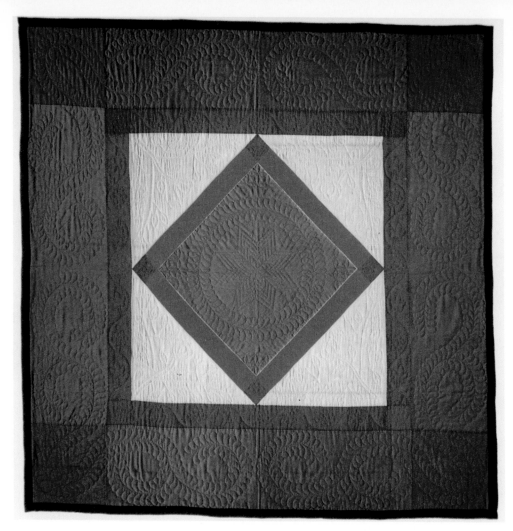

8-10 Quilts are intertwined with Amish life and belief. An Amish hymn states: "This is the light of the heights, This is my Jesus Christ, The rock, on whom I stand. Who is the diamond." The quilter solidly embraces her diamond, one of the oldest Amish patterns, with other simple shapes. The half-hidden stitchwork of various floral motifs and central bursting star create a subtle, complex surface despite the composition's overall simplicity. Unknown Amish quilter, *Diamond,* c. 1920–30. Wools, 77 x 77" (195 x 195 cm). Lancaster County, PA. Private Collection. Photograph courtesy The Quilt Complex. Photography Sharon Risedorph.

Amish women infuse their quilts with the same profound sense of spiritual reverence that fills their existence. Simple patterns parallel a fairly constrained lifestyle. Sewn squares, triangles, and diamonds abstractly echo the shapes artists see in the straight-lined fields, fencing, and architecture about their farms. The only complexity is the women's fine, nearly invisible decorative stitching, which often fills each abstract section with a different linear motif. (See sewn floral details in Fig. 8-10.)

But where in Amish life are the brilliant contrasts of color that the women use so gloriously in their bed, cradle, and couch covers? God provides the earth's bounty, and the women's splendid colors reverberate with the hues of their gardens, harvests, and flowerbeds.

Color abounds in the women's quilts and nature. The passion of their breathtaking hues animates the restrained designs, thus embodying the people's deep religious convictions that sustain them as they live near—but not like—their neighbors.

Drawing as Witness: Miné Okubo, Citizen 13660

◐◡◑ This was not Nazi Germany, yet Miné Okubo became imprisoned within her own land. No words, only images, could accurately convey her experience as one of 110,000 people of Japanese ancestry who were wrenched from their homes in Oregon, Washington, California, and southern Arizona, and shipped to "relocation" camps. President Franklin D. Roosevelt signed the order in February 1942, amid rampant fear of a Japanese invasion during World War II.[21] Okubo, an art student from the University of California, turned to her art profession for solace.

In Tanforan Assembly Center, a converted racetrack in San Bruno, California, Okubo kept a visual journal of ink-and-rice-paper drawings to depict her miserable surroundings (Figs. 8-11, 8-12); photographs and cameras were illegal. She wanted to document the "crazy things constantly happening in the camp, with close to ten thousand people confined in an area of a mile square."[22] Her pictures record armed guards keeping constant watch; evacuees standing in line for hours awaiting meager meals; and uninhabitable, overcrowded barracks, many made from dilapidated animal stables.

Okubo remembers, "Tanforan was awful. My brother and I didn't have proper clothing or equipment—just a whisk broom to sweep out all the manure and dust in our stable. . . . You could hear all the people crying, the people grinding their teeth; you could hear everything."[23]

The government shipped Okubo to a permanent camp in Topaz, Utah, in November 1942, where the desert climate shocked many who could not acclimate to the swings in temperature, from a soaring 106°F in summer to as low as −30°F in winter.[24] (Fig. 8-13) Okubo drew it all, people struggling

8-11 Miné Okubo recorded how evacuees had to help install the fence posts and watchtowers that imprisoned them. Years later, she reflects, "I express the content of reality—that which is universal and timeless... I'm an individual who wants to contribute to the betterment of this world." Miné Okubo (b. 1912), from *Citizen 13660*, 1944–46. Courtesy of the artist.

8-12 People wore *getas*, traditional wooden clogs, sometimes building them a foot high to avoid the mud during the morning and evening rush to the washrooms. Miné Okubo (b. 1912), from *Citizen 13660*, 1944–46. Courtesy of the artist.

to survive the devastating sewage smells, contaminated water, and invading insects. Men and women toiled away, helping to erect the fences and watchtowers that would corral them. (See Fig. 8-11.)

Art once again gave Okubo direction after her release from the camp. She moved to New York City in 1944, when *Fortune* magazine requested she illustrate the April issue on Japan. Okubo remained there, on the opposite coast from her original home. Time has mellowed Okubo's and other prisoners' recollections of the harsh ordeal. But her art-

work, first published in book form one year after the war's end, remains a vivid testament. Okubo recalls, "I had the opportunity to study the human race from cradle to grave, and to see what happens to people when reduced to one status and condition."[25]

8-13 Blinding dirt, along with a former Boy Scout band, greeted Miné Okubo and others when they arrived at the Central Utah Relocation Project. "When we finally battled our way into the safety of the building we looked as if we had fallen into a flour barrel." Miné Okubo (b. 1912), from *Citizen 13660*, 1944–46. Courtesy of the artist.

Keeping It Together: Female Mexican-American Folkways

What connects cut-paper flowers and paper-wrapped eggs, birthday cakes, and Catholic home altars or Virgin of Guadalupe shrines? Mexican-American women make all these items, which help unite a people and their culture. The women and their artwork are the glue that "keeps it all together,"[26] creating stability and continuity within the family and community, and reinforcing links to the supernatural world.

Mexican-American Women's Domestic Art

Mexican-American culture is complex. Spanish-Catholic and pre-contact native customs fuse with Western mainstream conventions. Mexican-American female art traditions reflect this broad diversity, starting at home—the heart of the family. Many women construct large *nacimientos* (nativity scenes),

8-14 Innumerable details—lace curtain, foliage, wildlife, as well as the yarn that falls across Mary's Bible, or wood shavings at Joseph's feet—fill this small portion of Aurelia Araneta's intricate *nacimiento* (nativity scene). Aurelia Araneta, *The Holy Family At Home*, 1996. University of Arizona Museum of Art. Photography Jim Griffith.

complex three-dimensional illustrations of biblical and other images. (Fig. 8-14) Mexican markets, full of miniature fruits and vegetables, and women grinding corn on stone *metates* are favorites, along with manger and birth motifs. Artists take great pride in the colors and details of their labor-intensive structures, which convey fervent religious devotion and tie their family's abode to the spiritual realm.

A young girl's *quinceaña* can be one of the most momentous events for Mexican-American families. This elaborate fifteenth-birthday celebration, typically including a Mass and formal dance, honors the child's entry into womanhood. If a mother doesn't retreat into the kitchen for days to produce the enormously elaborate, tiered birthday cake, she will hire another to do so. (Fig. 8-15) The baker completes the edible sculpture with swirls of delicious white-on-white texture resembling lace and wire flowers covered with alluring frosting.

Food, an often ignored folk expression, literally and symbolically nourishes a sense of ethnic identity. One item, the egg, particularly extends Mexican-American women's influence beyond the confines of the home.

8-15 Guadalupe Rubio creates magnificent cakes, which resemble Italian versions, for *quinceaña* and marriage celebrations. She made this exact arrangement twenty-five years earlier for her brother's wedding. Guadalupe Rubio, *Quinceaña cake*, 1996. University of Arizona Museum of Art. Photography Jim Griffith.

(Fig. 8-16) In an earlier era, young couples joyfully broke *cascarónes* over each other's heads. In fact, the Spanish word for "eggshell," *cascarón*, is related to the verb *cascar*, meaning "to break or shatter." The burst shells let loose sprays of confetti, candies, or even perfume or ashes.

Some believe this courtship ritual derives from the wish to bestow blessings on the happy recipient.[27] The custom was first prevalent at Carnival, that period of feasting and partying just before the deprivations of Lent.[28] Even 150 years ago, Mexican women made their wares at market during the holiday. Like today, revelers could buy simple examples, or fancy *cascarónes* encased in paper wreaths or disguised as tiny figures.

Children, however, rather than young adults, now smash one another with *cascarónes* at the many outdoor fairs, festivals, religious feasts, and church bazaars that define the community's annual cycle.[29] The women's paper-and-egg creations integrate the young into the intergenerational festivities.[30]

8-16 In southern Arizona, women sometimes place eggshells in long paper cones, fringed with paper ribbons, tinsel, and feathers that blow in the wind or trail through the air as people swipe them down upon unsuspecting companions. *Cascarónes*, 1990. Courtesy Folklore Center of the University of Arizona Library. Photography Jim Griffith.

Mexican-American Women's Art and the Spirit World

Women's paper arts are essential to another communal event: *el Día de los Muertos* (the Day of the Dead), a combination of Catholic and pre-Hispanic observances. This both merry and serious fiesta on November 2nd overflows with humorous and sacred sentiments. At cemeteries, people sell food and drink, and children make merry. The women's paper floral *coronas*, or wreaths, (Fig. 8-17) establish communication between the mundane and supernatural realms. Loved ones gather about the altars and graves of their dead, cleaning the site and replacing last year's paper garlands with fresh ones.[31]

The Mexican passion for flowers stems back to ancient times, when people considered blooms and the goddesses and gods as one. Actual specimens were the preserve of emperors, priests, and nobility, strewn at their feet and treated as jewels.[32]

Females today on both sides of the border construct paper flowers for both secular and sacred purposes. Some in Mexico learn in sweatshops, churning out blossoms en masse. Others, including many women in Arizona, consider themselves professionals, mistresses of an art in which they can proudly create up to nineteen or more individual species of flowers in various stages of unfolding.[33] The women's floral creations hark back to Mexican roots, while also providing physical continuity to the present and future. Their artistry is tightly bound to female roles of mothers and wives—the caregivers, nurturers, and providers within their families and communities. As both women and artists, they help forge the underlying structure of their culture, which continues to evolve.

Ancient Paper Art Traditions

Mexican women have worked with fine colored tissue paper since pre-Columbian times, when annual treasure galleons brought this versatile material from the Orient en route to Spain. Even earlier, native Mexicans made paper from tree bark or maguey plants.

8-17 Mexican-American women's paper flowers link the living and dead. On graves, shrines, and altars they communicate between the mundane and supernatural world. Josefina Lizárraga learned flower-making skills as a girl in her native state of Nayarit, Mexico. Today she owns a successful florist shop in Tucson, Arizona, while sometimes creating paper flowers and arrangements to ensure that the art is not lost. Josefina Lizárraga, *Corona (paper flower wreath)*, 1992. Courtesy Folklore Center of the University of Arizona Library. Photography Jim Griffith.

8-20 Does this sculpture resemble a Western European seascape? Kenojuak Ashevak looks to the invisible Inuit supernatural realm to express her vision of the untamed water. "I am not trying to show what anything looks like in the material world." Kenojuak Ashevak (b. 1927), *Sea Spirit with Seal*, 1965. 8 x 11½ x 7¾" (20.8 x 29.2 x 19.8 cm). Permission of the artist. Photography Inuit Art Centre.

Ancient Roots, Modern Visions

How does another of the early sculptors, Qaunak Mikkigak, bridge both contemporary and older customs in her work? (Fig. 8-19) Born in an igloo in 1932, Qaunak grew up helping her mother fetch water, prepare seal blubber for lamp oil, and chew caribou hides to soften them before sewing—typical tasks for Inuit girls. Although bone relief was supposedly a man's art, both her mother and father were talented carvers. Qaunak registers glimpses of the past in her own creamy tusk. Multicolored dogs tug a sled, with two hunters chasing after a mighty, white polar bear. This immense animal stands on the bird's back like a totem image. Qaunak seamlessly unites the older artistic carving tradition with the modern, abstracted stone form below.

Qaunak literally depicts an Arctic scene in the tusk, but other women, including Kenojuak Ashevak, follow the Inuit tendency to depict the spirits that inhabit the earth's resources rather than describing the visible landscape. (Fig. 8-20) Born in 1937, Kenojuak intimately knows the lure and power of the sea. She drove dog teams when stalking seals as a teenager,[39] and to this day insists, "What I enjoy very much is going fishing... Listening to the wild birds while fishing is just beautiful."[40]

Kenojuak's seal and sea spirit are one. The mammal rides the being's back as if it were a gently rolling wave. She eloquently shows how, for the Inuit, spirits reside in all things, including the land, sea, ice, animals, and forces of nature.

The women's art often reflects how essential the community, especially the family, is to surviving in such a challenging environment. Oopik Pitsiulak's sculpture (Fig. 8-21) calls on her own experiences as a

and antlers—learned printmaking and sculpture. These latter items earned far more money than the women's stitching, despite the longer hours it took women to fashion their fabric pieces.

The women, spurred by the need to make money to support their families and a desire to explore the new media themselves, soon ventured forth into printing and the "masculine" art of stone carving. They immediately found their own authentic artistic voice in the modern methods. Pitseolak explains, "I became an artist to earn money, but I think I am a real artist... It takes much thinking [to be an artist], and I think it is hard to think. It is hard like housework."[38]

Overcoming entrenched divisions of labor, the women began to pour out visions that captured, in both medium and content, the tenuous dance between tradition and modern, mystical and rational that flows through their life as they adapt and adjust to changing times.

mother, demonstrating the supremacy of the matrilineal bond. Tall and proud, Oopik strides forward, literally and symbolically becoming her children's foundation. The sculpture's adornment harks back to Oopik's grandmother, who taught her how to bead. Oopik, born in 1946, celebrates the strength of all traditional Inuit women, their artistry and responsibilities, in her imaginative self-portrait.

During the early 1990s, Oopik attended an Inuit women's organization meeting, which brought her an astonishing new perspective. "I started to see how women think; how they have an artistic way of forming things, like carvings, sewing, any female art. That's when I started to realize: that women have real important roles...We can do a lot. Women are very capable... It made me realize that women are good; that women are strong."[41]

This strength is the very basis of the women's creativity, helping them make and also chronicle their journey from the land to settlements, and from historical living patterns to modern life. They use art as an opportunity to share with us, and their own future generations, the intersection of Inuit culture and those of lands beyond.

8-21 Oopik Pitsiulak feels that her art is about "making my thoughts a reality." She greatly admired her grandmother. "She was a real woman... Because I learned beading from my grandmother, I am working at it today." Oopik Pitsiulak (b. 1946), *Oopik Going for Water*, 1990. Green stone, glass beads, wool fabric, wool cord, seal hide, tanned leather, 25 x 7½ x 10" (63.5 x 19 x 25.5 cm). Permission of the artist. Photography Inuit Art Centre.

Summary

Many Worlds—Common Bonds

What links women's kaleidoscopic artistic efforts? Women's nonwestern art, across cultures and throughout time, embraces social attitudes, customs, values, and beliefs. Their endeavors intersect the functional, aesthetic, secular, and sacred realms. The work's very essence both mirrors and formulates the world around them.

Women have always made art that reflects the profound, ongoing transitions in their cultures. But female "traditional" work has never been static, frozen under glass. "Artways" and "folkways" invariably have evolved in response to outside influences and internal forces. What will happen, though, to the unique nature of women's indigenous expressions in the future, as modern communication and advancing technology threaten authentic cultural diversity? Will massive globalization, growing interdependence, and increasing industrialization eliminate singular characteristics? Or will women, as they have before, respond with ever-more imaginative solutions that affirm personal and group identity?

If history is any indication, women will continue to passionately create art that illuminates, strengthens, extends, and enriches their societies. Their distinct visions of the world invariably will touch those around them, while also maintaining a critical dialogue between past and future generations.

About the Author

Abby Remer has written extensively about art and culture, including her two previous books *Pioneering Spirits: The Lives and Times of Remarkable Women Artists in Western History* and *Discovering Native American Art.* She works with organizations nationwide as an arts and cultural education consultant, developing innovative materials and programs.

Along with her degree in art history from Oberlin College and a Masters in Museum Education from Bank Street College of Education, Ms. Remer spent her early career working in the education departments of numerous New York City museums. Currently, in addition to other consulting projects, she teaches graduate courses at New York University.

Notes

Chapter 1

1 Marla C. Berns, "Art, History, and Gender: Women and Clay in West Africa," in *The African Archaeological Review*, 11 (1993): 141.

2 Lisa Aronson, "Women in the Arts," in *African Women South of the Sahara*, eds. Margaret Jean Hay and Sharon Sticher (New York: Longman Publishing, 1995), p. 123.

3 Margaret Courtney-Clarke, *African Canvas: The Art of West African Women* (New York: Rizzoli, 1990), p. 17.

4 Aronson, p. 132.

5 Jacqueline Chanda, *African Arts and Cultures* (Worcester, MA: Davis Publications, Inc., 1993), p. 102.
Note: For early eras, the letters BCE, meaning "before common era," and CE, for "common era," have been used in place of the traditional BC ("before Christ") and AD ("anno Domini" or "in the year of our Lord").

6 Aronson, "Women in the Arts," pp. 130–131.

7 Nigel Barley, *Smashing Pots: Works of Clay from Africa* (Washington, D.C.: Smithsonian Institution Press, 1994), p. 63.

8 Paula Ben-Amos, "Artistic Creativity in Benin Kingdom," *African Arts Magazine* 19, no. 3 (May 1986): 60–61.

9 Barley, *Smashing Pots*, p. 81.

10 Paula Ben-Amos, *The Art of Benin* (Washington D.C.: Smithsonian Institution Press, 1995), p. 68.

11 Barley, *Smashing Pots*, p. 81.

12 Ben-Amos, "Artistic Creativity," p. 60.

13 Robert Thompson, "Abatan: A Master Potter of the Egbado Yoruba," in *Tradition and Creativity in Tribal Art* (Los Angeles: University of California Press, 1969), p. 131.

14 Ibid. p. 140.

15 Robert Thompson, *Black Gods and Kings: Yoruba Art at UCLA* (Bloomington: Indiana University Press, 1976), p. chapter 9/2.

16 Thompson, "Abatan," pp. 150–151.

17 Thompson, *Black Gods and Kings*, p. chapter 9/1.

18 Herbert Cole and Chike C. Aniakor, *Igbo Art: Community and Cosmos* (Los Angeles: University of California, 1984), p. 80.

19 Ibid. pp. 79–80.

20 Allen Bassing, "Grave Sculptures of the Dakakari," in *The Visual Arts: Plastic and Graphic* (New York: Mouton Publishers, 1979), p. 297.

21 Allen Bassing, "Grave Monuments of the Dakakari," *African Arts Magazine* 6, no. 4 (1973): 39.

22 Ibid. p. 36.

23 Barley, *Smashing Pots*, p. 91.

24 Marla Berns, "Containing Power: Ceramics and Ritual Practice in Northeastern Nigeria" (unpublished, forthcoming).

25 Ivor Powell, *Ndebele: A People & Their Art* (New York & London: Cross River Press, 1995), pp. 48–49.

26 Ibid. p. 52.

27 Margaret Courtney-Clarke, *Ndebele: The Art of an African Tribe* (New York: Rizzoli, 1986), p. 31.

28 Ibid. pp. 108–109, 121.

29 Ibid. pp. 126–135.

30 Ibid. p. 126.

31 Vanessa Drake Moraga, "An Eternity of Forest: Paintings by Mbuti Women," brochure, Diggs Art Gallery, Winston-Salem State University, Feb. 5–April 1, 1999.

32 Vanessa Drake Moraga, "An Eternity of Forest: Paintings by Mbuti Women," on the UC Berkeley Art Museum web site (www.bampfa.berkeley.edu/exhibits/mbuti/brochure.html).

33 Monni Adams, "Kuba Embroidered Cloth," *African Arts* 12, no. 1 (1979): 33.

34 Correspondence with Vanessa Moraga, independent curator and scholar, August 4, 1999.

35 Patricia Darish, "Dressing for the Next Life: Raffia Textile Production and Use Among the Kuba of Zaire," in *Cloth and the Human Experience*, eds., Annette B. Weiner and Jane Schneider (Washington, DC: Smithsonian Institution Press, 1989), p. 124.

36 Adams, "Kuba Embroidered Cloth," p. 35.

37 Ibid.

38 Darish, "Dressing for the Next Life," p. 128.

39 Adams, "Kuba Embroidered Cloth," p. 30.

40 Darish, "Dressing for the Next Life," p. 135.

41 Ibid.

42 Correspondence with Vanessa Moraga, August 13, 1999.

43 Betty LaDuke, *Africa: Women's Art, Women's Lives* (Trenton, NJ: Africa World Press, Inc., 1997), p. 87.

44 Anthony and Laura Ponter, *Spirits in Stone: The New Face of African Art* (Glen Ellen, CA: UKAMA Press, 1997), p. 31.

45 Ibid. p. 158.

46 Ibid. p. 152.

47 Ibid. p. 91.

48 Ibid. p. 170.

49 Ibid. p. 171.

50 Ilse Noy, *The Art of the Weya Women* (Harare, Zimbabwe: Baobab Books, 1992), p. 28. (Note: all quotes are anonymous in order to protect the women's confidences.)

51 Ibid. p. 44.

52 LaDuke, *Africa: Women's Art, Women's Lives*, p. 145.

53 Noy, *The Art of the Weya Women*, p. 44.

54 Ibid. p. 71.

55 As recorded by Luisella Garlick. (Note: all quotes are anonymous in order to protect the women's confidences.)

Chapter 2

1 Jon Thompson, *Oriental Carpets: From the Tents, Cottages and Workshops of Asia* (New York: Penguin Group, 1993), p. 79.

2 Ibid. p. 77.

3 Ibid. p. 97.

4 Lisa Gilad, *Ginger and Salt: Yemeni Jewish Women in an Israeli Town* (San Francisco: Westview Press, 1989), p. 18.

5 Ibid. p. 18.

6 Ester Muchawsky-Schnapper, *The Jews of Yemen: Highlights of the Israel Museum Collection* (Jerusalem: The Israel Museum, 1994), p. 16.

7 Muchawsky-Schnapper, *The Jews of Yemen*, p. 20.

8 Matty Jankowski, "Traditional and Contemporary Mehandi Henna Painting" (New York: Circle Arts Inc., 1982).

9 Muchawsky-Schnapper, *The Jews of Yemen*, p. 66.

10 Ita Aber, *The Art of Judaic Needlework: Traditional and Contemporary Designs* (New York: Charles Scribner's Sons, 1979), p. 13.

11 Ibid. pp. 2–3.

12 Ibid. p. 10.

13 Gilad, *Ginger and Salt*, p. 17.

14 Muchawsky-Schnapper, *The Jews of Yemen*, p. 60.

15 Ibid.

16 Ibid. p. 19.

17 Helen Khal, *The Woman Artist in Lebanon* (Beirut: Institute for Women's Studies in the Arab World, 1987), p. 25.

18 Hind Al-Soufi Assaf, "Historical Overview," *Al-Raida Magazine* 13, no. 73 (Spring 1996): 12–13.

19 Ibid. p. 11.

20 Samia A. Halaby, "Contemporary Arab Women Artists," October 14, 1993, unpublished article.

21 Correspondence with the artist, October 23, 1998.

22 Correspondence with the artist, October 23, 1998.

23 Correspondence with the artist, June 30, 1998.

24 Laila Shawa, *Laila Shawa and Wijdan* (London: The October Gallery, 1994).

25 Martha Schwendener, "Shirin Neshat" in *The New Art Examiner*, December 1995.

26 Octavio Zaya, "Shirin Neshat: Armed and Dangerous" in *aRUDE*, Spring 1996, p. 55.

27 Schwendener, "Shirin Neshat."

Chapter 3

1 Yves Véquaud, *The Women Painters of Mithila* (New York: Thames and Hudson, 1977), p. 17.

2 Pupul Jayakar, *The Earth Mother: Legends, Goddesses, and Ritual Arts of India* (New York: Harper & Row, 1990), p. 112.

3 Véquaud, *The Women Painters of Mithila*, p. 17.

4 Ibid. p. 18.

5 Jayakar, *The Earth Mother*, p. 107.

6 Betty LaDuke, "Traditional Women Artists in Borneo, Indonesia, and India" in *Women's Art Journal* 2, no. 1 (Spring/Summer 1981): 19.

7 Jayakar, *The Earth Mother*, pp. 107–108.

8 Véquaud, *The Women Painters of Mithila*, pp. 25–26.

9 Ibid. p. 21.

10 Ibid. p. 31.

11 John F. Burns, "Though Illegal, Child Marriage is Popular in Part of India" in *New York Times*, May 11, 1998, p. A8.

12 Dr. Jyotindra Jain, "Art and Artisans: Tribal and Folk Art in India" in *The Necessity of Craft: Development and Women's Craft Practices in the Asian-Pacific Region*, ed. Lorna Kaino (Nedllands, Western Australia: University of Western Australia Press, 1995), p. 29.

13 Ibid. p. 28.

14 Lorri Hagman, "Ladies of the Jade Studio: Women Artists of China" in *Women Artists: Recognition and Reappraisal from the Early Middle Ages to the Twentieth Century*, eds. Karen Pertersen & J. J. Wilson (New York: Harper & Row, 1976), p. 148.

15 Ibid. p. 148.

16 Marsha S. Weidner, *Views from the Jade Terrace: Chinese Women Artists, 1300–1912* (Indianapolis: Indianapolis Museum of Art, 1988), p. 17.

17 Ibid. pp. 24–25.

18 Ibid. p. 23.

19 Ibid. p. 17.

20 Ibid. p. 18.

21 Ibid. p. 13.

22 Ellen Johnston Laing, "Women Painters in Traditional China," in *Flowering in the Shadows: Women in the History of Chinese and Japanese Painting*, ed. Marsha Weidner (Honolulu: University of Hawaii Press, 1990), p. 84.

23 Hagman, "Ladies of the Jade Studio," p. 154.

24 Weidner, *Views from the Jade Terrace*, p. 16.

25 Nancy Zeng Berliner, *Chinese Folk Art: The Small Skills of Carving Insects* (NY: New York Graphic Society, 1986), p. 100.

26 Ibid. p. 109.

27 Traude Gavin, *The Women's Warpath: Iban Ritual Fabrics from Borneo* (Los Angeles: UCLA Fowler Museum of Cultural History, 1996), p. 13.

28 Ibid. p. 26.

29 Ibid. p. 15.

30 Ibid. pp. 23–24.

31 Ibid. p. 27.

32 Ibid. p. 19.

33 Diana K. Myers and Susan S. Bean, eds., *From the Land of the Thunder Dragon: Textile Arts of Bhutan* (Salem, MA: Peabody Essex Museum, 1994), p. 85.

34 Ibid. pp. 16–17.

35 Ibid. p. 17.

36 Ibid. p. 87.

37 Joanne Cubbs, *Hmong Art: Tradition and Change* (Sheboygan, Wisconsin: John Michael Kohler Arts Center, 1986), p. 21.

38 *Flower Cloth of the Hmong* (Denver: Denver Art Museum, 1985), p. 5.

39 Ibid. p. 23.

40 Ibid.

41 Ibid.

42 Ibid.

43 Cubbs, *Hmong Art: Tradition and Change*, pp. 6–7.

44 Correspondence with Gayle L. Morrison, Hmong Oral History Project, April 28, 1998.

45 *Flower Cloth of the Hmong*, p. 7.

46 Cubbs, *Hmong Art: Tradition and Change*, p. 27.

47 Correspondence with Gayle L. Morrison, Hmong Oral History Project, April 28, 1998.

48 *Flower Cloth of the Hmong*, p. 9.

Chapter 4

1 Randall Morris, *Redemption Songs: The Self-Taught Artists of Jamaica* (Winston-Salem State University: Diggs Gallery, 1997), p. 48.

2 Joanna M. Ostapkowicz, "To Be Seated with 'Great Courtesy and Veneration': Contextual Aspects of the Taíno Duho" in *Taíno Pre-Columbian Art and Culture from the Caribbean*, eds. Fatima Bercht, Estrellita Brodsky, John Alan Farmer, Dicey Taylor (NY: The Monacelli Press, 1998), p. 44.

3 Ibid. p. 64.

4 Ibid. pp. 63–64.

5 Ibid. p. 21.

6 *The Art Heritage of Puerto Rico: Pre-Columbian to the Present* (New York: El Museo del Barrio, 1973), p. 27.

7 Ostapkowicz, "To Be Seated with 'Great Courtesy and Veneration,'" p. 64.

8 Holland Cotter, "Out of the Caribbean Past, The Art of a Lost People," *New York Times*, Sunday, November 23, 1997, p. 47.

9 Holland Cotter, "Dazzling and Devout Voodoo Energy," *New York Times*, Friday, October 9, 1998, p. 36.

10 Conversation with Quincy St. George at the exhibition "Sacred Arts of Haitian Vodou." American Museum of Natural History, October 24, 1998.

11 Seldon Rodman, *The Miracle of Haitian Art* (Garden City, NY: Doubleday and Company, Inc., 1974), p. 23.

12 Marie-José Nadal Gardère, *La Peinture Haitienne: Haitian Arts* (Paris: Nathan Publications, 1986), p. 22.

13 Ibid. p. 93

14 Ibid.

15 Morris, *Redemption Songs*, p. 8.

16 Conversation with Shari Cavin, Co-director Cavin-Morris Gallery, July 10, 1997.

17 Morris, *Redemption Songs*, p. 48.

18 Ibid.

19 Ibid. p. 23.

20 Ibid. p. 16.

21 Ibid. p. 15.

22 Ibid.

23 Ibid. p. 46.

24 Ibid. p. 14.

25 Ibid. p. 24–25.

26 "Artisans and Old Lace" in *Travel Holiday Magazine*: 50.

27 David E. Schwab, *The Story of Lace and Embroidery* (New York: Fairchild Publications, Inc., 1951), n.p.

28 Mary Eirwen Jones, *The Romance of Lace* (London: Spring Books, n.d.), p. 15.

29 Gabrielle Pond, *An Introduction to Lace* (New York: Scribner's Sons, 1973), p. 13.

30 Annie Santiago de Curet and April Kingsley, "Puerto Rican Lacemaking: A Persistent Tradition" in *Borinquen Lacers Inc.* 6 (March 1995): 4.

31 Ibid.

32 Ibid.

33 Ibid.

34 Ibid. p. 5.

35 Ibid.

Chapter 5

1 Sofika Zielyk, "The Ukrainian Easter Egg," 1995, web site: http://news.std.com/sabre/UFP-WWW_Etc/Culture/Pysanka.html.

2 Ibid.

3 Ibid.

4 James S. Giffith, "Pysanky" in "Southern Arizona Folk Arts," web site: http://dizzy.library.arizona.edu/images/folkarts/pysanky.html.

5 Ibid.

6 "Polish Folk Art," web site: http://copland.udel.
   edu/~ivanitch/index.htm.

7 Ibid.

8 Zielyk, "The Ukrainian Easter Egg."

9 Jo Miles Schuman, *Art From Many Hands*
   (Worcester, MA: Davis Publications, Inc., 1981),
   p. 68.

10 Ibid. p. 66.

11 Ibid. pp. 66–67.

12 Ibid. p. 67.

13 Lynne Attwood, *Red Women on the Silver Screen:
   Soviet Women and Cinema from the Beginning to
   the End of the Communist Era* (London: Pandora
   Press, 1993), p. 12.

14 Ibid. p. 17.

15 Ibid. p. 10.

16 Ibid. p. 26.

17 Ibid. p. 32.

18 Ibid. p. 31.

19 Ibid. p. 143.

20 Ibid. p. 34.

21 Ibid. p. 33.

22 Ibid. p. 54.

23 Ibid. p. 47.

24 Ibid. p. 142.

25 Ibid. p. 50.

26 Ibid. p. 145.

27 Ibid. p. 54.

28 Ibid. p. 125.

29 Ibid. p. 144.

30 Ibid. p. 12.

31 Interview with Zdenka Deitchova, September 1,
   1998.

32 John Halas, *Masters of Animation* (Topsfield, MA:
   Salem House Publishers, 1987), p. 24.

33 Ibid. p. 32.

34 Marcin Gizycki, "Splendid Artists: Central and
   Eastern European Women Animators" (web site
   http://www.awn.com/mag/issue1.2/articles1.2/
   gizycki.html).

35 Halas, *Masters of Animation*, p. 48.

36 Gizycki, "Splendid Artists."

37 Interview with Alexander Marshack, June 21, 1999.

38 Jen Nessel, "Made in Prague, Bound for the U.S.,"
   New York Times, Sunday, August 9, 1998, p. 23.

39 Interview with Zdenka Deitchova, September 1,
   1998.

40 Interview with Zdenka Deitchova, September 1,
   1998.

41 Correspondence with Gene Deitch, August 18,
   1998.

42 Interview with Zdenka Deitchova, September 1,
   1998.

43 Tamás Hofer and Edit Fél, *Hungarian Folk Art*
   (New York: Oxford University Press, 1979), p. 13.

44 Ibid. pp. 13–14.

45 Ibid. p. 13.

46 Ibid. p. 14.

47 Ibid. p. 14.

48 Ibid. p. 16.

49 Ibid. p. 16.

Chapter 6

1 B. J. Casselman, *Crafts from Around the World*
   (Creative Home Library, 1975), p. 132.

2 Ferdinand Anton, *Ancient Peruvian Textiles*
   (London: Thames and Hudson, 1984), p. 14.

3 Ibid. p. 15.

4 Hugo Munsterberg, *A History of Women Artists*
   (New York: Clarkson N. Potter, 1975), p. 9.

5 Anton, *Ancient Peruvian Textiles*, p. 8.

6 Angelika Gebhart-Sayer, *The Cosmos Encoiled:
   Indian Art of the Peruvian Amazon* (New York:
   Center for Inter-American Relations, 1984), p. 4.

7 Ibid. p. 7.

8 Ibid. p. 6.

9 Ann Parker and Avon Neal, *Molas: Folk Art of the
   Cuna Indians* (Barre, MA: Barre Publishing, 1977),
   p. 132.

10 Ibid. p. 57.

11 Mari Lyn Salvador, *Yer Dailge: Kuna Women's Art*
   (Albuquerque: University of New Mexico, 1978),
   p. 22.

12 G.R. Stuart and W. Warner, "Spirit Weavers,"
   Native Peoples, August/September/October
   1996, p. 75.

13 Marjorie Agosín, *Scraps of Cloth: Chilean Arpilleras* (Trenton, NJ: The Red Sea Press, 1987), p. 1.

14 Marjorie Agosín, *Tapestries of Hope, Threads of
   Love: The Arpillera Movement in Chile, 1974–1994*
   (Albuquerque: University of New Mexico Press,
   1996), p. 9.

15 Ibid. p. 12.

16 Ibid. p. 16.

17 Ibid. p. 18.

18 Isabel Allende, "Pinochet without Hatred," *New
   York Times,* January 17, 1999, p. 27.

19 Agosín, *Tapestries of Hope*, p. 33.

20 John Brentlinger, "The Ideal and The Real:
   Campesino Painters of Solentiname, Nicaragua."
   Unpublished essay.

21 Ibid.

22 Betty LaDuke, *Compañeras: Women, Art, & Social
   Change in Latin America* (San Francisco: City
   Lights Books, 1985), p. 17.

23 John Brentlinger, *The Best of What We Are:
   Reflections on the Nicaraguan Revolution*
   (Amherst: University of Massachusetts Press,
   1995), p. 344.

24 Ibid. p. 338.

25 Ibid. p. 339.

26 Ibid.

Chapter 7

1 Roger Neich and Mick Pendergrast, *Traditional
   Tapa Textiles of the Pacific* (London: Thames and
   Hudson, 1997), p. 9.

2 Ibid. p. 45.

3 Correspondence with Wendy Arbeit, author of
   Tapa in Tonga (Hawaii: University of Hawaii Press).
   June 22, 1999.

4 Wendy Arbeit, *Tapa in Tonga* (Honolulu:
   University of Hawaii Press, 1995), pp. 44–45.

5 Ibid. p. 15.

6 Ibid. p. 9.

7 Prendergrast, *Traditional Tapa Textiles of the
   Pacific*, p. 9.

8 Joyce D. Hammond, *Tifaifai and Quilts of
   Polynesia* (Honolulu: University of Hawaii Press,
   1986), p. 30.

9 Poakalani and John Serrao, *The Hawaiian Quilt: A
   Spiritual Experience* (Honolulu: Mutual Publishing,
   1997), p. 9.

10 Hammond, *Tifaifai and Quilts of Polynesia*, p. 38.

11 Correspondence with Alana Nohealani Dean,
   Aloha Quilts, July 8, 1997.

12 Hammond, *Tifaifai and Quilts of Polynesia*, p. 43.

13 Ibid. p. 20.

14 Ibid. p. 55.

15 Ibid. p. 58.

16 Poakalani, "Hawaiian Quilting Page: Traditions and
   Superstitions of Hawaiian Quilting," web site,
   1996.

17 Avril Quaill, *Marking Our Times: Selected Works
   of Art from the Aboriginal and Torres Strait
   Islander Collection at the National Gallery of
   Australia* (Canberra: National Gallery of Australia,
   1996), p. 6.

18 Following the custom of the Aboriginal people, the
   full name of an artist who passes on should not be
   spoken out of respect for the deceased and the
   family.

   Emily Kame Kngwarreye passed away in 1996, in
   her eighties. The substitutes, Kwementyai (meaning "no name") and/or the artist's skin (clan)
   name, are used instead.

19 Vivien Johnson, *Aboriginal Artists of the Western
   Desert: A Biographic Dictionary* (New South
   Wales: Craftsman House, 1994), pp. 13–14.

20 Correspondence with Dr. Simon Pockley,
   independent scholar, Melbourne, Australia.
   February 28, 1999.

21 Annie Mikaere, "Maori Women: Caught in the
   Contradiction of a Colonised Reality," Taumauri.
   Waikato Law Review 2 (1994): 128.

22 John Maori Royal, *New Zealand Today: Maori
   Viewpoints*, exhibition catalog, Firehouse Art
   Gallery, Nassau Community College, 1997, p. 1.

23 Interview with Robyn Kahukiwa, September 16, 1997.

24 *Robyn Kahukiwa Works from 1985–1995* (Wellington, New Zealand: Bowen Galleries, 1995), p. 6.

25 Interview with Kura Te Waru Rewiri, September 8, 1997.

Chapter 8

1 Shari Cavin Morris, "Bessie Harvey: The Spirit of Wood," *The Clarion* 12, no. 2/3 (1987): 44–49.

2 Gladys-Marie Fry, *Stitched from the Soul: Slave Quilts from the Ante-Bellum South* (New York: Dutton Studio Books, 1990), p. 69.

3 Ibid. p. 15.

4 "African American Quilts," web site http:// xroads.virginia.edu/-UG97/quilt/atrads.html.

5 Ibid.

6 Ibid.

7 Fry, *Stitched from the Soul*, p. 71.

8 Ibid. p. 74.

9 Ibid. p. 80.

10 Dale Rosengarten, "Spirits of Our Ancestors: Basket Traditions in the Carolinas" in *The Crucible of Carolina: Essays in the Development of Gullah Language and Culture*, ed. Michael Montgomery (Athens, GA: University of Georgia Press, 1994), p. 133.

11 Ibid. p. 131.

12 Marquetta L. Goodwine, web site African Kultural Arts newworkx(AKANx): http://users.aol.com/ queenmut/Afrikan_Network.html.

13 Rosengarten, "Spirits of Our Ancestors," p. 131.

14 Ibid. p. 132.

15 Ibid.

16 Ibid. pp. 135–136.

17 Jacqueline L. Tobin and Raymond G. Dobard, *Hidden in Plain View: A Secret Story of Quilts and the Underground Railroad* (New York: Doubleday, 1999), p. 76.

18 Rosengarten, "Spirits of Our Ancestors," p. 136.

19 As per letter Marquetta L. Goodwine, June 8, 1998.

20 Phyllis Haders, *Sunshine and Shadow: The Amish and Their Quilts* (Clinton, NJ: The Main Street Press, 1976), p. 7.

21 Miné Okubo, *Citizen 13660* (Seattle, WA: University of Washington Press, 1983), pp. 12–16.

22 Deborah Gesensway and Mindy Roseman, *Beyond Words: Images from America's Concentration Camps* (Ithaca: Cornell University Press, 1987), p. ix.

23 Ibid. p. 68.

24 Okubo, *Citizen 13660*, p. 183.

25 Ibid. p. ix.

26 As per telephone interview with James S. Griffith, June 24, 1997.

27 James S. Griffith, *A Shared Space: Folklife in the Arizona-Sonora Borderlands* (Logan: Utah State University Press, 1995), p. 161.

28 Ibid. p. 56.

29 Ibid. p. 58.

30 As per telephone interview with James S. Griffith, June 24, 1997.

31 Griffith, *A Shared Space*, p. 21.

32 Marian Harvey, *Mexican Crafts and Craftspeople* (Philadelphia: The Art Alliance Press, 1987), p. 19.

33 As per telephone interview with James S. Griffith, June 24, 1997.

34 Odette Leroux, Marion E. Jackson, and Minnie Aodla Freeman, eds., *Inuit Women Artists: Voices from Cape Dorset* (Vancouver: Douglas & McIntyre, 1994), p. 47.

35 Ibid. p. 44.

36 Ibid. p. 47.

37 Ibid. p. 15.

38 Jean M. Humez, "Pictures in the Life of Eskimo Artist Pitseolak," *Women's Art Journal* 2, no. 2 (Fall 1981/Winter 1982): 35.

39 Leroux, *Inuit Women Artists*, p. 97.

40 Ibid. p. 98.

41 Ibid. p. 195.

An Ho (b. 1927), *Guihua and Bird*, detail, 1996. Ink and color on silk, 12 x 13" (30 x 33 cm). Courtesy L. J. Wender Fine Chinese Art, New York, NY. Photography Steve Williams.

Pronunication Guide

Note: The pronunciations of artists' names may be found in the index.

Chapter 1

bamiki bandura (bah me key baan do rah)
Edo (Eh doh)
Ifijioku (If ee gee o ku)
Igbo (e gBow)
ilueemy (e lu eh me)
Kasai (kah sigh)
kghuphu (go pooh)
Kuba (koo bah)
kwandalha (kwand allah)
linga koba (linga koh bah)
Longuda (Long oo dah)
mbolo (m bow low)
Mbuti (m BOO tee)
Midzimu (midzee moo)
Ndebele (N deh BELL lay)
omakhe (O mah kay)
sadza (sad zah)
Shiri ya Mwari (She re yah Mwah ree)
Shona (Show nah)
tshgholo (she go low)
uli (ou LEE)
umucu (u moo koo)
yeyi (yeh yee)
Yoruba (YOUR u bah)

Chapter 2

chador (shah door)
gargush (gar gush)
hinna (HE nah)
mohar (MOH har)

Chapter 3

Bodhisattva (Bow dee saat vah)
dzongs (dzongs)
gho (go)
Guanyin (GWAH yin)
Hmong (mung)
hua yang (HWAH yahng)
ikebana (ee kay bana)
kira (kheer rah)
Kohbar (ko bar)
Kuan Tao-sheng (Gwan Dow Shung)
Mithila (MIT teh lah)
pa ndau (pon dow)
phulkari (pull car ee)
pua (pooh ah)
T'ang (tahng)
thagthami (tagh tah me)

Chapter 4

Boriken (BOOR e ken)
cacias (kah see ahs)
caciques (kah see kes)
cohoba (ko ho bah)
duhos (dew hos)
Iwa (lou ah)
Kumina (Kou mee nah)
kwish (kweesh)
mambo (mam bow)
Marasa (mar a sah)
marraine (mahr rain)
mundillo (mun dee yo)
oungan (who gan)
quinceñara (keen sen nyah rah)
Rastafarianism (Rasta far e an ism)
serviteur (sehr vee tuhr)
Taíno (TAH ee no)
zemi (zeh me)

Chapter 5

ágyvitel (adyah vee tell)
Bratri v Triku (BRAHT-trzhee vtrickoo)
kirigami (kee rhee ga mee)
kistka (keest kah)
Kurpie (Koor pearh)
Lowicz (Wow veach)
Lublin (Lub lyn)
mon kiri (mun kee rhee)
papel picado (pah pell pea kah do)
parádes szoba (pah rah desh sew bah)
pysanka (PEH sahn kah)
pysanky (PEH sahn keh)
scherenschnitte (SHARE en schnit ta)
wycinanki (vi chee NON-key)

Chapter 6

Allende (A yen day)
arpilleras (AR pea yehr as)
arpilleristas (R pea yher e stahs)
chakaras (SHAH kar ahs)
chicha (chee chah)
chunga (chung gah)
campesinos (kahm peh seen ohs)
Cuzco (Kooz ko)
Imu (e moo)
inna (en nah)
Ixchel (E shell)
Ixil (Esheel)
kurgin (kurr gin)
machismo (mah cheez mow)
mola (moh lah)

Chapter 7

Nahuatl (nah wha tel)
Nebaj (Nay bahh)
Ngobe-Bugle (No bay Boohg lay)
Pineda (Peen eh dah)
Pinochet (Pea no shay)
saburet (SAH bur ay)
shina (she nah)
Shipibo (Ship pea bow)
Solentiname (Sole en tehh naam eh)
Somoza (Soam o zah)
Ucayali River (Oo kah YAH lee)
Vicariate (Ve car e ah tay)
Wounaan (Woo oo nah ahn)
Xmucane (Sh mu cahn a)

Chapter 7

Aborigine (AB uh rij uh nee)
Alhalkere (Ahl kare ri)
Aotearoa (aa oo tea ror a)
coolamon (ku la mun)
Hina (he nah)
Hinematioro (Hin ee ma ti ooro)
kalo (kah low)
Kamehameha (Kah may hah may hah)
kupuna (ku pooh nah)
Maningrida (Man in gree da)
Maori (Mao ree)
Ngatu (Ngaa too)
Ngati whatua (Ngaa ti fa too a)
Tangaroa (tahn ga row ah)
Taniwha (Tun e fa)
tapa (tah pah)
tivaevae manu (tee vy vy mah nu)
whare (fa ree)

Chapter 8

Benin (Beh NEEN)
el Dia de los Muertos (L dee ah day lohs mwehr
  tohs)
cascarónes (kas kar own s)
coronas (kore own ahs)
Ewe (eh veh)
Fon (Fon)
getas (geh tahs)
Gullah (Gull ah)
Kente (Ken tay)
metates (may tah tace)
nacimientos (nah see me n tos)
nayarit (nay are eet)
quinceaña (keen say ahn nyah)
titirtugait (tit ear too gate)

Bibliography

Africa

Aronson, Lisa. "Women in the Arts." In *African Women South of the Sahara*. eds. Margaret Jean Hay and Sharon Stichter. New York: Longman, 1984.

Barley, Nigel. *Smashing Pots: Works of Clay from Africa*. Washington, DC: Smithsonian Institution Press, 1994.

Cole, Herbert and Chike C. Aniakor. *Igbo Art: Community and Cosmos*. Los Angeles: University of California, 1984.

Courtney-Clarke, Margaret. *Ndebele: The Art of an African Tribe*. New York, Rizzoli, 1986.

———. *African Canvas: The Art of West African Women*. New York: Rizzoli, 1990.

Darish, Patricia. "Dressing for the Next Life: Raffia Textile Production and Use Among the Kuba of Zaire." In *Cloth and the Human Experience*. eds. Annette B. Weiner and Jane Schneider. Washington, DC: Smithsonian Institution Press, 1989.

Erhinyodavwe, Benson Agro. *The Life and Works of Princess (Mrs.) Elizabeth Aghayemwence Olowu*. Matriculation Number 8300119, Faculty of Creative Arts, University of Benin, Nigeria, July 1987.

LaDuke, Betty. *Africa: Through the Eyes of Women Artists*. Trenton, NJ: Africa World Press, Inc., 1991.

———. *Africa: Women's Art, Women's Lives*. Africa Lawrenceville, NJ: World Press, 1997.

Meurant, George and Robert Farris Thompson. *Mbuti Design: Paintings by Pygmy Women of the Ituri Forest*. New York: Thames and Hudson, Inc., 1995.

Noy, Ilse. *The Art of the Weya Women*. Harare, Zimbabwe: Baobab Books, 1992.

Ponter, Anthony and Laura. *Spirits in Stone: The New Face of African Art*. Glen Ellen, CA: UKAMA Press, 1997.

Powell, Ivor. *Ndebele: A People & Their Art*. New York & London: Cross River Press, 1995.

Arab World

Gilad, Lisa. *Ginger and Salt: Yemeni Jewish Women in an Israeli Town*. San Francisco: Westview Press, 1989.

Khal, Helen. *The Woman Artist in Lebanon*. Beirut, Lebanon: Institute for Women's Studies in the Arab World, 1987.

Muchawsky-Schnapper, Ester. *The Jews of Yemen: Highlights of the Israel Museum Collection*. Jerusalem: The Israel Museum, 1994.

Nashashibi, Salwa. *Forces of Change: Artists of the Arab World*. Lafayette, California: International Council for Women in the Arts; Washington, DC: National Museum of Women in the Arts, 1994.

Thompson, Jon. *Oriental Carpets: From the Tents, Cottages and Workshops of Asia*. New York: Penguin Group, 1993.

Asia

An Intelligent Rebellion: Women Artists of Pakistan. Curated by Salima Hashmi and Nima Poovoya-Smith. Bradford: Cartwright Hall; Wakefield, England: Cherry Print Limited, 1994.

Berliner, Nancy Zeng. *Chinese Folk Art: The Small Skills of Carving Insects*. New York: New York Graphic Society, 1986.

Cubbs, Joanne. *Hmong Art: Tradition and Change*. Sheboygan, Wisconsin: John Michael Kohler Arts Center, 1986.

Dysart, Dinah and Hannah Fink. *Asian Women Artists*. Australia: Craftsman House, 1996.

Fister, Patricia, with guest essay by Fumiko Y. Yamamoto. *Japanese Women Artists 1600–1900*. New York: Harper & Row, 1988.

Gavin, Traude. *The Women's Warpath: Iban Ritual Fabrics from Borneo*. Los Angeles: UCLA Fowler Museum of Cultural History, 1996.

Jayakar, Pupul. *The Earth Mother: Legends, Goddesses, and Ritual Arts of India*. New York: Harper and Row, 1990.

Kaino, Lorna, ed. *The Necessity of Craft: Development and Women's Craft Practices in the Asian-Pacific Region*. Nedlands: University of Western Australia Press, 1995.

Myers, Diana K. and Susan S. Bean, eds. *From the Land of the Thunder Dragon: Textile Arts of Bhutan*. Salem, MA: Peabody Essex Museum, 1994.

Weidner, Marsha S. *Views from Jade Terrace: Chinese Women Artists 1300–1912*. Indianapolis: Indianapolis Museum of Art; New York: Rizzoli, 1988.

Weidner, Marsha S. *Flowering In the Shadows: Women in the History of Chinese and Japanese Painting*. Honolulu: University of Hawaii Press, 1990.

Caribbean

Gardère, Marie-José Nadal. *La Peinture Haitienne: Haitian Arts*. Paris: Nathan Publications, 1986.

Growing Beyond: Women Artists of Puerto Rico. Curator Susana Torrevella Leval. Washington, DC: Museum of Modern Art of Latin America, Organization of American States, 1988.

Jones, Mary Eirwen. *The Romance of Lace*. London: Spring Books.

Morris, Randall. *Redemption Songs: The Self-Taught Artists of Jamaica*. Winston-Salem State University: Diggs Gallery, 1997.

Ostapkowicz, Joanna M. "To Be Seated with 'Great Courtesy and Veneration': Contextual Aspects of the Taíno Duho." In *Taíno Pre-Columbian Art and Culture from the Caribbean*, eds. Fatima Bercht, Estrellita Brodsky, John Alan Farmer, Dicey Taylor. New York: The Monacelli Press, 1998.

Pond, Gabrielle. *An Introduction to Lace*. New York: Scribner's Sons, 1973.

Eastern Europe

Attwood, Lynne. *Red Women on the Silver Screen: Soviet Women and Cinema from the Beginning to the End of the Communist Era*. London: Pandora Press, 1993.

Hofer, Tamás and Edit Fél. *Hungarian Folk Art*. New York: Oxford University Press, 1979.

Latin America

Agosín, Marjorie. *Scraps of Life: Chilean Arpilleras*. Trenton, NJ: The Red Sea Press, 1987.

———. *Tapestries of Hope, Threads of Love: The Arpillera Movement in Chile, 1974–1994*. Albuquerque: University of New Mexico Press, 1996.

Anton, Ferdinand. *Ancient Peruvian Textiles*. London: Thames and Hudson, 1984.

Brentlinger, John. *The Best of What We Are: Reflections on the Nicaraguan Revolution*. Amherst: University of Massachusetts Press, 1995.

Harvey, Marian. *Mexican Crafts and Craftspeople*. Philadelphia: The Art Alliance Press, 1987.

LaDuke, Betty. *Companeras: Women, Art, & Social Change in Latin America*. San Francisco, CA: City Lights Books, 1985.

LaDuke, Betty. *Latin American Women Artists 1915–1995*. Milwaukee: Milwaukee Art Museum, 1995.

Oceania

Aboriginal Women's Exhibition. New South Wales: Art Gallery of New South Wales, 1991.

Hammond, Joyce D. *Tifaifai and Quilts of Polynesia*. Honolulu: University of Hawaii Press, 1986.

Keeler, Chris, ed. *Women's Work: Aboriginal Women's Artefacts in the Museum of Victoria*. Introduction: exhibition catalog. Melbourne: Museum of Victoria, 1992.

Johnson, Vivien. *Aboriginal Artists of the Western Desert: A Biographic Dictionary*. New South Wales, Craftsman House, 1994.

Neich, Roger and Mick Pendergrast. *Traditional Tapa Textiles of the Pacific*. London: Thames and Hudson, 1997.

Quaill, Avril. *Marking Our Times: Selected Works of Art from the Aboriginal and Torres Strait Islander Collection at the National Gallery of Australia*. Canberra: National Gallery of Australia, 1996.

Teilhet, Jehanne. "The Role of Women Artists in Polynesia and Melanesia." In *Art and Artists of*

Oceania. eds. Sidney M. Mead and Bernie Kernot. Mill Valley, CA: The Dumore Press Ethnographic Arts, 1983.

Weiner, Annette B. "Why Cloth? Wealth, Gender, and Power in Oceania." In *Cloth and Human Experience*. Washington, DC: Smithsonian Institution Press, 1991.

United States and Canada

Ferrero, Pat, Elaine Silber, and Julie Hedges. *Hearts and Hands: The Influence of Women and Quilts on American Society*. San Francisco: Quilt Digest Press, 1987.

Fry, Gladys-Marie. *Stitched From the Soul: Slave Quilts from the Ante-Bellum South*. New York: Dutton Studio Books, 1990.

Gesensway, Deborah and Mindy Roseman. *Beyond Words: Images from America's Concentration Camps*. Ithaca: Cornell University Press, 1987.

Griffith, James S. *A Shared Space: Folklife in the Arizona-Sonora Borderlands*. Logan: Utah State University Press, 1995.

Leroux, Odette, Marion E. Jackson and Minnie Aodla Freeman, eds. *Inuit Women Artists: Voices from Cape Dorset*. Vancouver: Douglas & McIntyre, 1994.

Miné Okubo: An American Experience. Oakland, CA: Oakland Art Museum, 1972.

Okubo, Miné. *Citizen 13660 Drawings and Text by Mine Okubo*. Seattle: University of Washington Press, 1983.

Rosengarten, Dale. "Spirits of Our Ancestors: Basket Traditions in the Carolinas." In *The Crucible of Carolina: Essays in the Development of Gullah Language and Culture*. ed. Michael Montgomery. Athens, GA: University of Georgia Press, 1994.

Tobin, Jacqueline L. and Raymond G. Dobard, Ph.D. *Hidden in Plain View: The Secret Story of Quilts and the Underground Railroad*. New York: Doubleday, 1999.

General

Casselman, B. J. *Crafts from Around the World*. Creative Home Library, 1975.

Elinot, Gilian, et al., eds. *Women and Craft*. London: Virago Press, 1987.

LaDuke, Betty. *Women Artists: Multicultural Visions*. Trenton, NJ: Red Sea Press, Inc., 1992.

Remer, Abby. *Discovering Native American Art*. Worcester, MA: Davis Publications, Inc., 1997.

Schuman, Jo Miles. *Art From Many Hands*. Worcester, MA: Davis Publications, Inc., 1981.

Weiner, Annette B. and Jane Schneider, eds. *Cloth and Human Experience*. Washington, DC: Smithsonian Institution Press, 1989.

Articles, Brochures, and Papers

Adams, Monni. "Kuba Embroidered Cloth." *African Arts* 12, no. 1 (1979): 24–39.

Assaf, Hind Al–Soufi. "Historical Overview." *Al-Raida Magazine* 13, no. 73 (Spring 1996): 12–23.

Bassing, Allen. "Grave Monuments of the Dakakari." *African Arts Magazine* 6, no. 4 (1973): 36–39.

Ben-Amos, Paula. "Artistic Creativity in Benin Kingdom." *African Arts Magazine* 19, no. 3 (May 1986): 60–63; 83.

Berns, Marla, C. "Ceramic Arts in Africa." *African Arts* 22, no. 2 (Feb. 1989): 32–36; 101–102.

———. "Art, History, and Gender: Women and Clay in West Africa." *The African Archaeological Review* 11 (1993): 129–148.

———. "Containing Power: Ceramics and Ritual Practice in Northeastern Nigeria." (unpublished, forthcoming).

Brett-Smith, Sarah. "The Doyle Collection of African Art." *Record of The Art Museum Princeton University* 42, no. 2 (1983): 9–34.

Frank, Barbara E. "More Than Wives and Mothers: The Artistry of Mande Potters," *African Arts* 27, no. 4 (Autumn 1994): 26–37.

Glaze, Anita J. "Woman Power and Art in a Senufo Village," *African Arts* 8, no. 3 (Spring 1975): 24–29; 69–68; 90–91.

Goldman, Shifra. "Latin Visions and Revisions." *Art in America*, May 1988, pp. 138–47.

Humez, Jean M. "Pictures in the Life of Eskimo Artist Pitseolak." *Women's Art Journal* 2, no. 2 (Fall 1981/Winter 1982): 30–36.

Imperato, Pascal James and Marli Shamir. "Bokolanfini, Mud Cloth Painting of the Bambara of Mali," *African Arts* 3, no. 4 (Summer 1970): 32–41; 80.

Moraga, Vanessa Drake. "An Eternity of Forest: Paintings By Mbuti Women." Winston-Salem State University: Diggs Art Gallery, February 5– April 1, 1999.

Smith, Fred. "Male and Female Artistry in Africa." *African Arts* 19, no. 3 (May 1986): 28–29.

Warner W., and G.R. Stuart, "Spirit Weavers." *Native Peoples*, August/September/October 1996: 73–76.

Willis, Liz. "Uli Painting and the Igbo World View." *African Arts Magazine* 23, no. 1 (May 1986): 62–67; 104.

Multi-Media Resources

The Hands of the Potter. 26 min., color, 1991. Videotape revealing the magic of the Sundi potter Helene Tangui, from the lower Zaire River region of the People's Republic of Congo, as she forms moist clay into perfect pots. Available for loan from the National Museum of African Art, at 950 Independence Avenue, SW in Washington, DC Education Department (202) 357-4600 ext. 221. (http://www.si.edu/organiza/museums/africart/educ/eduvideo.htm)

Threads of Survival. 25 mins, video. Hmong life told by master weaver Nhu Fang Yand and her daughter-in-law. L & S Video Inc., 45 Stornowaye, Chappaqua, NY 10514. Phone 914/238-9366 or 212/841-0216; Fax 914/238–6324; email: VideoPaint@aol.com

Who'd A Thought It. 30 mins., video. A chronicle of the rich tradition of African-American quiltmakers from slavery to contemporary times. (The Anacostia Museum and Center for African American History and Culture; 1901 Fort Place, SE, Washington, DC 20020, 202-287-2061.)

Related Web Sites

"African American Quilts." http://xroads.virginia.edu/-UG97/quilt/atrads.html

"An Eternity of Forest: Paintings by Mbuti Women." http://www.bampfa.berkeley.edu/exhibits/mbuti/brochure.html

"Gullah/Geechee Sea Island Information." http://users.aol.com/queenmut/GullGeeCo.html

"Carpatho-Rusyn Pysanky—Color and Beauty at Eastertime." http://www.carpatho-rusyn.org/customs/gcupisan.htm

"Eggs with Flair (pysanky)." http://www.geocities.com/Heartland/Meadows/1889/

"Hawaiian Quilting Page: Traditions and Supersititions of Hawaiian Quilting," http://www.poakalani.com/quilt/culture.html

"History of Ukranian Eggs." http://www.fullfeed.com/-wrldcrft/kitseggs/history.html

"La Cadena Que No Se Corta/The Unbroken Chain: The Traditional Arts of Tucson's Mexican-American Community." http://dizzy.library.arizona.edu/images/cadena/cadena.html

"Madhubani Paintings: The Women Painters of Mithila." http://www.khazana.com/folk/mithila.html

"Splendid Artists: Central and Eastern European Women Animators." http://www.awn.com/mag/issue1.2/articles1.2/gizycki.html

"Southern Arizona Folk Arts." http://dizzy.library.arizona.edu/images/folkarts/

"The Art of Being Kuna." http://www.conexus.si.edu/kuna/eng/intro/index.htm

"World Wide Quilting Page." http://quilt.com/mainquiltingpage.html

Index

A

Aborigines, Australian, viii, 121, 128–131
abstraction
  and Arabic art, 27, 36
Afghanistan, 30
Africa, 2–25
African-Americans, 137–143
African influence
  on Black Caribbean art, 70
  on Gullah art, 141–142
Africans
  in the Caribbean, 66, 70
  enslaved in America, 137–143
ágyvitel, 98–99
Akan, 8
Amazon, 104–105
American Samoa, 122
Amish quilts, 144–145
animation
  in Eastern Europe, 94–97
  Polish, 82
Anyi, 8
Aotearoa (New Zealand), 132–135
appliqué
  of Chile, 112–115
  of Hmong, 62–65
  quilts of African-Americans, 138
  quilts of Hawaii, 126–127
  of Weya, 22
Arabic art, 26–39
Araneta, Aurelia, 148
Arano, Rosita, 118
Arizona, 149–150
arpilleras, 100, 112–115
Ashanti Kente cloth, 141
Ashevak, Kenojuak (Ash-a-vak, Kan-oo-jhu-ak), 154

Ashoona, Pitseolak (Ah-sho-na, Pit-see-o-lack), 152–154
Asia, 40–65
Australia, viii, 121, 128–131

B

Baffin Island, 152–155
Bahamas, 68
Bamana, 3
Baraskaya (Bara-ska-ya), Margarita, 91
barkcloth
  of Hawaii, 124–127
  of Mbuti, viii, 3, 14–15
  of pre-Columbian Mexico, 151
  of Shona, 25
  of the South Pacific, 122–123
baskets
  Gullah, 140–141, 143
  of Panama, 110–111
  of Shona, 25
  of Yemeni Jews, 31
batik, 62–65, 130
beadwork, 12–13
bedding, ornamental, 98–99
Benin, 4–5, 142
Bhutan, ix, 60–61
bobbin lace, 76–79
body painting
  of Australia, 130
  of Igbo, 2
  of Panama, 110
  of Yemeni Jews, 26, 32–34
bone relief, 154
Borikén (Puerto Rico), 66, 68, 76–79
Borneo, 40, 58–59
Bratri v Triku animation studio, 96–97

Brik, Lilya (Brick, Li-lee-ya), 91
Brown, Carolee Holmes, 143
Brumberg, Valentina, 94
Brumberg, Zinaida (Zee-nah-ee-dah), 94
Buddhism, 56, 60–61
Burma (Myanmar), 63

C

cakes, Mexican-American, 148, 149
California, 146
calligraphy, 48
Canada, 136–145, 152–155
Cape Dorset Inuit, 152–155
Cardenal, Ernesto, 117
Caribbean, 66–81
Carpatho-Ruthenia, 86
carpets, 28–30
carving
  of New Zealand, 133–134
  stone, 18–21
  wood, 68–69
cascarónes, 149–150
Central Desert of Australia, 130
ceramics. *See* pottery
chakaras, 100
Chavarriá, Julia, 118
Cheverez, Alicia, 66
Chile, ix, 100, 112–115
China, 40, 41, 48–55
Christian symbols
  on pysanky, 84–86
cinema, 89–92, 91
cloth. *See* fabric
clothing
  of barkcloth, 15
  beaded, 12–13
  design, 80–81

of Kuba, 16–17
of Panama, 106–109
of Peru, 103
of Yemeni Jews, 33–34
Congo, viii, 3, 14–15
Cook Island, 127
coolamon, 128–129
coronas, 151
Courtney-Clarke, Margaret, 3
crocheting, 36
Cruickshank, Evadney (Crook-shank, Ee-vad-knee), 74–75
Cuba, 68
cut-paper. *See* paper cutting
Czech Republic, 95–97
    artist, 83

D

Dakakari, 7–8
Dantó, Ezili, 70–71
Danube region, 99
Daosheng, Guan (Dow-shung, Gwahn), 48
Darién, Panama, 110–111
David, Millie Sequoia, 80–81
Dean, Alana Nohealani, 124, 125
Deitch, Gene, 96–97
Dietchova, Zdenka (Dye-tch-aw-vah, Zdenk-ah), 96–97
drawings, Japanese-American, 146–147
duhos, 68–69
dye, 16, 110

E

Eastern Europe, 82–99
Eastern Slovakia, 86
echo quilting, 126–127
Edo, 4
eggs
    painted, 82, 84–86

paper-decorated, 88
paper-wrapped, 148, 150
Eliassant, Francoise (El-ay-sahn, Frahn-swaz), 70–72
Elijah (Jarret, Pastor Geneva Mais), 67, 73–75
embroidery
    Arabic, 36
    of Eastern Europe, 82
    of Hmong, 62–65
    of Hungary, 99
    Indian wedding, 46–47
    of Kuba, 16–17
    of Panama, 106–109
    of Yemeni Jews, 31, 33, 34
Eugenia, María, 115

F

fabric
    of Bhutan, 60–61
    of Borneo, 58–59
    of Chile, 100, 112–115
    of Hawaii, 120–121, 124–127
    Kasai, 16–17
    of Latin America, 100–103
    of Panama, 106–109
    of Shona, 22–25
    See also clothing, textiles
fashion design, 80–81
filmmakers, Soviet, 89–93
flower arranging, 40, 56–57
Fong, Yang, 65
food, 148–150
France, 88
funerary cloth, 103
funerary pottery, 7–8

G

Garciá, Hilda Vogl, 116
gargush, 31
garments. *See* clothing

Gaza, 36, 37
Germany, 88
Ghana, 8
gho, 60
Glinski, Barbara, 87, 88
Great Zimbabwe, 18–21
Grenada, 80
Guanyin, 50–51
Guatemala, 101
Guevara (Gwear-vah-rah), Olivia Silva, 116
Gullah, ix, 137, 140–141, 143

H

Haeata, ix
Haiti, 70–73, 75
Halaby, Samia, 35–36
Harvey, Bessie, 136
Hawaii, ix, 120–121, 124–127
henna body painting, 26, 32–34
Himalayas, 60–61
Hindu, 43, 46–47
hinna ceremony, 31–33
Hispaniola, 68
Hmong, 40, 62–65
Ho, An, 41, 52–53, 160
Houston, James, 153
hua yang, 54–55
hubcaps, painted, 131
Hungary, 98–99
Hutsuls, 86

I

Iban weaving, 40, 58–59
Ichiyo School of Ikebana, 56–57
Igbo, 2, 6–8
ikebana, 40, 56–57
Inca, 103
India, 40, 42–47
Inuit, 152–155
Iran, 38–39

Israel, 26, 34
Ituri Forest, 14–15
Ivory Coast, 8
Ixil Maya, 101

J

Jamaica, 67, 70, 73–75
Japan, 40, 56–57, 88
Japanese-Americans, 137, 146–147
Japanese tea ceremony, 56–57
Jarret, Geneva Mais (Zhah-ray, Zhe-nay-vah May) (Elijah), 67, 73–75
Jewish Yemeni, 26, 31–34
Jimenez, Elba, 118
Jo, Elaine, 56–57

K

Kahukiwa (Kah-who-key-wah), Robyn, ix, 132–134
Kasai textiles, 16–17
Keckly, Elizabeth, 138
kira, 60
kirigami, 88
Kngwarreye (Ung-warh-ay), Emily Kame, 130
kohbar, 42
Krinjabo, 8
Kuba, 3, 16–17
Kuna, viii, 101, 106–109
Kurpie, 87
Kwale, 6

L

lace, 76–79
landscape painting, 49–50
Laos, 62–65
Latallo, Katarzyna (La-tah-lo, Kahta-rzhee-na), 95
Latin America, 100–119
Lizárraga (Lee-zharr-ah-gah), Josefina, 151

Longuda, 8, 9
Lowicz, 87
Lublin, 87–88

M

Mabwe (Mah-bway), Mavis, 21
McEwen, Frank, 18–19, 21
Mahlangu, Betty, 11
Malaysia, 58–59
Mali, 3
Maliszewska, Alina (Mahlee-shev-skah, Ahl-eenah), 82, 95
Malraux, André, 73
Manchu dynasty, 55
Manigault, Ethel, 141
Manigault, Vera, 141
Maningrida, Australia, 128
Maori, ix, 120, 132–135
marriage
    and pottery skills, 8
    bedding for, 98–99
    embroidery for, 46, 62
    garments for, 13, 31, 34
    Olokun shrine pots, 5
Maya, 101
Mbuti, viii, 3, 14–15
Melanesian barkcloth, 122
Mexican-Americans, 137, 148–151
Mexico, 88
Middle East, 26–39
Mikkigak, Qaunak (Micky-gak, Kwan-I-ak), 153, 154
mimi spirit poles, 128
Mithila, 40, 42–45
molas, 106–109
mon kiri, 88
Morales, Violeta, 112
Muller, Irma, 113
mundillo lace, 76–79
murals
    of India, 42
    of Mithila, 45

of Nicaragua, 118
of South Africa, 10–11

N

nacimientos, 148–149
Nampinjinpa (Na-pa-gin-pa), Maureen Hudson, vii
Ndandarika (Ndahn-dah-ree-kah), Locadia, 19, 20
Ndebele, 10–13
Nebaj, Guatemala, 101
Neshat, Shirin, 26, 38–39
New Zealand (Aotearoa), 120, 132–135
ngatu, 122–123
Ngobe-Bugle, 100
Ngoma, Letty, 12
Nicaragua, ix, 100, 116–119
Nigeria, 4–9
North America, 136–145
Northern Territory, Australia, 128
Noy, Ilse, 22
Nunavut, 153
Nyanhongo (Nyan-hongo), Agnes, 20

O

Oceania, 120–125
Okubo, Miné, 146–147
Oldak, Zofia (Awl-dahk, Zhaw-fia), 95
Olokun shrine pots, 5
Ortega, Mariana, 118

P

painted car hubcaps, 131
painted eggs, 82, 84–86
painting
    of Australia, 121, 128, 130–131
    of China, 41, 48–53, 160
    of Haiti, 70–73
    Inuit, 153
    of Jamaica, 67, 73–75
    Maori, 133–135
    of Mithila, 42–45

of New Zealand (Aotearoa), 132, 133
of Nicaragua, 100, 116–119
of Shona, 22–25
wall, 10–11
Palestine, 34, 36–37
Panama, viii, 101, 106–111
pa ndau, 62–65
papel picado, 88
paper cutting
of China, 54–55
of Eastern Europe, 82
Mexican-American, 88, 148, 151
of Poland, 87–88
paper flowers, 151
patchwork quilts, 141–145
Peasant Women of Ryazan, 89,
92–93
Pennsylvania, 144–145
Persia, 30
Peru, 100, 102–103
Peters, DeWitt, 72
Petyarre, Kathline, 131
photography, 35–39
phulkari, 47
Pineda, Blanca, 118
Pineda, Elena, 118–119
Pineda, Rosa, 117, 118
Pitsiulak, Oopik (Pit-see-o-lack,
Oo-pick), 154–155
Poland, 87–88, 95
Polynesian barkcloth, 122–123
Pongo or Murumba, viii, 3, 14–15
pottery
and basket weaving, 110
of China, 48
of Nigeria, 4–9
of Peru, 100, 104–105
of Taíno, 66
Prague, 97
Preobrazhenskaya (Praya-obrah-
jhen-ska-ya), Ol'ga, 89, 92–93

printing
Inuit, 153
pua, 58–59
Puerto Rico. *See* Borikén
Punjab, 47
puppetry, 95
pysanky, 84–86

Q
Qiu (Cheo), Miss, 50
Quechua Indians, 103
quilts
of African-Americans, 138–139
Amish, 144–145
Gullah, 141–143
of Hawaii, 124–127
quinceaña cake, 149

R
raffia, 16–17
Rajasthan, 46
Ramayana, 42–44
Reiniger, Lotte (Rine-igger, Lawty), 94
religion, viii
and African roots, 70
and Jamaican painters, 73–75
reverse appliqué
and Hmong, 62–65
of Panama, 101, 106–109
Romanenko, Alexandra, 84–85
Rowe, Nellie Mae, 137
Russia, 89–92

S
sadza fabric painting, 22–25
Saint-Fleurant, Louisianne (San
Flur-ahn, Lu-ee-zee-anne), 72–73
Saint-Soleil school of Haitian art, 73
San Blas, Panama, 106, 108
sand painting, 130–131
Sanskrit culture, 43

Sanwi, 8
scherenschnitte, 88
sculpture
Inuit, 153–155
of African-Americans, 136
of Shona, 18–21
Sequoia (Millie Sequoia David),
80–81
Shawa, Laila, 27, 35–37
Shipibo, 100, 104–105
Shona, 18–25
Shouzhen, Ma (Show-jen, Mah), 49
Shub, Esfir' (Shoeb, S-feer), 90–93
silhouettes, 88
silkscreen, 36–37
Silva, Mariana, 118
Silva, Olivia, 118
Singleton, Nellie, 140
Singleton, Rena, 140
social realist style, 82–83
Solentiname, Nicaragua, 100, 116–119
Solntseva (Soln-stz-eva), Yuliya, 91
South Africa, 10–13
South Carolina, 140–141
Southeast Asia, 40, 62–65
South Pacific, 120–125
Soviet cinema, 89–93
spirituality, 2
and Aboriginal art, 128
and African pottery, 4–9
Amish, 145
and Haitian painting, 70–73
and Iban puas, 58
and Mithila painting, 44
and Shona art, 19
and Taíno duhos, 68
and Ukrainian pysanky, 84
and weaving, 58–59
Wounaan basket weavers, 110
still life painting, 50–51

stone carving
    Inuit, 153–154
    Shona, 18–21
    Taíno, 68–69
storytelling, 64
strip quilts, 141–143
Stroeva (Stro-yah-va), Vera, 91
Sui dynasty, 54–55
sweetgrass basketry, 140–141

T

Taíno, 66, 68–70
Takawira, Bernard, 19
T'ang dynasty, 51, 52, 54–55
Tao-sheng, Kuan, 49
tapa
    and Hawaii, 124–127
    in New Zealand, 120
    of Tonga, 122–123
tapestries
    of Chile, 112–115
    of Peru, 102–103
tea ceremony, 56–57
Te Waru Rewiri, Kura (Tee Wah-ru
    Ree-were-ray, Korr-rah), 134–135
textiles
    of African-Americans, 138–139
    of Bhutan, 60–61
    of Borneo, 58–59
    of Chile, 112–115
    of Hawaii, 124–127
    of Hmong, 62–65
    and India, 46–47
    of Kuba, 16–17
    of Latin America, 100–101
    of Middle Eastern nomads, 28–30
    of Panama, 106–109
    of Turkemenistan, 29
Thailand, 63, 64
Themerson, Franciszka (Temm-
    ersohn, Frahn-sis-ha), 95
tivaevae manu, 127

Tonga, 122–123
Torres Strait Islanders, 128
Torruella, Rosa Ena, 78
tshgholo, 13
Tura, Hungary, 99
Turkemenistan, 29
Turkey, 28, 30
Tyrlova (Teer-law-vah), Hermina, 95

U-V

Ucayali River, 104–105
Ukraine, 84–86
uli, 2
United States, 136–141
Utah, 146–147

Vietnam, 63
Vodou, 70, 72

W-Z

wall painting, 10–11
Walterová, Jitka, 96
weaving
    of Afghanistan, 29
    of African-Americans, 138
    of Bhutan, 60–61
    of Borneo, 58–59
    of Kuba, 16–17
    of Maori, 120
    of Maya, 101
    of Middle Eastern nomads, 28–30
    of Ngobe-Bugle, 100
    of New Zealand, 120
    of Persia, 30
    of Peru, 102–103
    Turkmen, 29
weddings
    bedding for, 98
    clothing for, 31, 33–34
    and India, 42, 46–47
West Africa, 140–141
Weya, 22–25

whare, ix
wood carving, 68–69
Wounaan, 110–111
wycinanki, 87–88

Yala, Panama, 106–109
Yemeni Jews, 26, 31–34
Yoruba, 5
Yuan (You en), Sophie, 54–55
Yuncu, 30

Zemánková, Anna, 83
Zimbabwe, ix, 18–25